Complete Physical Education Plans for Grades 5 to 12

Second Edition

Isobel Kleinman

Human Kinetics

Library of Congress Cataloging-in-Publication Data

Kleinman, Isobel, 1946-
   Complete physical education plans for grades 5 to 12 / Isobel Kleinman. — 2nd ed.
    p. cm.
  ISBN-13: 978-0-7360-7123-9 (soft cover)
  ISBN-10: 0-7360-7123-7 (soft cover)
  1. Physical eduction and training—Study and teaching (Secondary) 2. Physical education and training—Study and teaching (Elementary) 3. Lesson planning. I. Title
  GV362.K54 2009
  613.7'1—dc22

                       2008026577

ISBN-10: 0-7360-7123-7
ISBN-13: 978-0-7360-7123-9

The Web addresses cited in this text were current as of September 23, 2008, unless otherwise noted.

Acquisitions Editor: Scott Wikgren; **Developmental Editor:** Ragen E. Sanner; **Assistant Editor:** Anne Rumery; **Copyeditor:** Alisha Jeddeloh; **Proofreader:** Pamela Johnson; **Permission Manager:** Dalene Reeder; **Graphic Designer:** Nancy Rasmus; **Graphic Artist:** Kathleen Boudreau-Fuoss; **Cover Designer:** Bob Reuther; **Photographer (cover and interior):** © Human Kinetics, unless otherwise noted; **Photo Asset Manager:** Laura Fitch; **Photo Production Manager:** Jason Allen; **Art Manager:** Kelly Hendren; **Associate Art Manager:** Alan L. Wilborn; **Illustrator:** Tim Brummett; **Printer:** McNaughton & Gunn

Printed in the United States of America   10 9 8 7 6 5 4 3

The paper in this book is certified under a sustainable forestry program.

Human Kinetics
Web site: www.HumanKinetics.com

United States: Human Kinetics
P.O. Box 5076, Champaign, IL 61825-5076
800-747-4457
e-mail: humank@hkusa.com

Canada: Human Kinetics
475 Devonshire Road Unit 100, Windsor, ON N8Y 2L5
800-465-7301 (in Canada only)
e-mail: info@hkcanada.com

Europe: Human Kinetics
107 Bradford Road, Stanningley, Leeds LS28 6AT, United Kingdom
+44 (0) 113 255 5665
e-mail: hk@hkeurope.com

Australia: Human Kinetics
57A Price Avenue, Lower Mitcham, South Australia 5062
08 8372 0999
e-mail: info@hkaustralia.com

New Zealand: Human Kinetics
P.O. Box 80, Torrens Park, South Australia 5062
0800 222 062
e-mail: info@hknewzealand.com

                                      E4891

Contents

PART I   Introduction

PART II   Fitness Units

PART III   Creative Movement and Dance Units

PART IV   Team Sports Units

PART V Individual and Dual Activity Units

Lesson Finder

»continued

»continued

»continued

»continued

»continued

»continued

»continued

»continued

»continued

»continued

»continued

»continued

About the Second Edition

Physical educators I have met have told me that they love *Complete Physical Education Plans for Grades 7-12* and that it is the only book they use. That has delighted me. It has also left me feeling guilty to learn that it is the only professional resource they use. The first edition was never intended to be more than a guide for producing a fabulous program that integrated all that was important for developing a successful physical education program. It wasn't intended to replace the specialty books that explain skills and strategies.

Once I learned that my book was the sole tool of so many educators around the world, I decided to make the second edition a more complete resource. *Complete Physical Education Plans for Grades 5 to 12, Second Edition* keeps the elements that people love about the first edition while adding more. The second edition widens the grade and age range to include students from 5th through 12th grade. All the introductory lessons in the beginner units introduce basic skills in such a graduated way with such clear movement patterns that they are perfect for using with 5th and 6th grade children. The second edition also includes three new chapters: an introductory unit on field hockey, an introductory unit on lacrosse, and a unique educational gymnastics chapter with three units that guide movement exploration in such a way that the unit can be used to teach gymnastics or creative dance equally well.

Most importantly, when a new skill is introduced, lessons include instructions on the body mechanics and how to teach it to anyone learning the movement for the first time. Teachers jumping directly to the intermediate and advanced units should check for the lessons that introduce a skill and how to do it. Most fundamental skills are fully described in the beginner units.

To make life even easier for the teacher and the student, a CD-ROM is included that enables full-page printouts of study sheets, extension projects, student portfolio checklists, unit quizzes (with answer keys), tournament charts, fitness charts, and some sport score sheets. There is also a lesson finder that lists the chapters and lessons with their corresponding handouts for quick reference. Additionally, the entire book is on the CD-ROM so that teachers may print out lessons, full units, tests, or whatever they need and not have to carry the book around.

With this book, I no longer feel guilty. Teachers will be able to teach skills correctly even if they have no other book on their shelf. Everything teachers need to teach is in one place, so even if they are unfamiliar with the skills, basic rules, or strategies, it is all in the lesson for them and their students to learn in an integrated fashion and in a progression that will keep the students active, learning, successful, and excited about coming into the gym.

PART I

Introduction

Using Units and Lesson Plans

Speakers do not arrive at the podium without an outline, and drivers don't start a road trip without knowing the route to their destination. By the same token, teachers should never start something new without knowing what they want to cover in the unit and how much of that unit is going to be taught and how on a given day.

Units and Lesson Plans

Lesson plans are as vital to quality education as road maps are to travelers who want to reach their destination without wasting precious vacation time. Similar to road maps, lesson plans allow you to choose a direct route. They focus on what is important so that students can be effectively active in the limited class time.

Plans simply cannot account for all variables, nor can they always be followed as prescribed. In 31 years of teaching secondary physical education, I have yet to plan a unit or even a lesson that did not require some adjustment. I suspect that the same will be true for you. Sometimes I was lucky and had time to plan the changes, but most often the changes came about because of a last-minute situation requiring me to think on my feet.

Fully aware of this need to make changes, as well as the national call for accountability in education, I packaged *Complete Physical Education Plans for Grades 5 to 12* as a comprehensive guide to quality physical education that includes forms, worksheets, and other items that you can print as needed. But it is you who must gauge the readiness of your students and the speed with which they learn, and it is you who must make adjustments based on the differences between classes. It is you who must quickly adapt when rain forces your class indoors to a smaller teaching area than originally planned. It is you who must think on your feet when the school schedule changes and class time is shortened. It is you who adapts to a myriad of factors in order to teach quality lessons. Therefore, it is for you that I have included a CD-ROM and so much detail in lessons that introduce a skill, rule, or strategic concept for the first time.

Keeping in mind the many possible variables that can disrupt the best plans, *Complete Physical Education Plans for Grades 5 to 12* provides full learning units with lessons that include the mechanics of each skill in the framework. Lessons lead the user through highly developed skills progressions that begin during warm-ups and integrate relevant cognitive concepts and rules while students are physically active. Lessons comply with the National Association for Sport and Physical Education (NASPE) national standards (see the following chapter to see how).

DETOURS ON A TEACHER'S MAP

Veteran physical educators know the many things that happen to cause a change in the best of lesson plans. For instance, here are some scenarios:

- *The weather just won't cooperate.* Physical educators must consider the weather and be ready to adjust plans as necessary. Lessons written for large outdoor spaces must be modified when it rains or is too cold and teachers are forced indoors. The methods for teaching in large outdoor spaces are not practical for smaller ones.

- *They cut my class time.* Class time is reduced even further when schools shorten classes to accommodate open school night, assembly programs, in-school field trips, fire drills, and pep rallies.

- *My principal asked me to drop physical education for a few days and teach the state-mandated bus drill and AIDS lecture.* You had planned to end the unit on the 10th lesson—then your administrator tells you to drop physical education to do something else for a few days. Now you'll have to figure out how to finish up the unit and also change the intervening lessons.

- *I planned a test, but only 10 kids showed up.* Your class suddenly shrinks, but not before you planned to introduce something new, run a tournament, or have a quiz. You're all ready, but only half the class shows up. The other half is on a field trip.

- *I got to the gym and couldn't use it.* You arrive to meet your class and find you have no place to work because the custodian has decided to change the light bulbs in the middle of the gym floor during your class. Or the grounds crew has decided to mark the field for an interscholastic game. Or a group took over the gym for a blood drive or to decorate for the junior prom. Whatever the reason, the space you had planned for is not available.

- *My eighth-period class is three lessons behind.* Your classes at the same grade level are like night and day. In one period they are highly mature and skilled; another class later in the day is difficult to keep on task and has much weaker skills.

No lesson plan can cover all these contingencies. All you can do is plan the ideal lesson and then be ready to switch gears.

Education thrives when a teacher's individuality and creativity flourish in the classroom. Lessons reflect a general plan, not a style. There is no way to write a detailed plan without knowing certain information, such as the specific class size, length of class, facilities available, materials at hand, experience of students, and climate you teach in. The lessons in *Complete Physical Education Plans for Grades 5 to 12* are terrific teaching tools. They give a clear starting point, address issues left unsaid by previous books, encourage the use of every last minute of class, and draw that map to quality physical education that everyone hopes to follow.

The freedom to use your own style, pace lessons to your classes' advantage, use drills you like, disregard ones that you don't, and end up with a written product in no time is made possible by the book and CD-ROM combination. Customizing and storing lessons become easy. You can pull up lessons on the screen, print, and electronically file them for later use. Even quizzes, fitness tests, handouts, letters to parents, checklists, tournament charts, skills rubrics, fitness charts, and tables are on the CD-ROM. Since the chapters are modular and the units written by experience level, their format allows you to choose the units and lessons that are right for your situation. If you have students who have never participated in an activity before, you can take the beginner unit and use it. If they have had some experience, you can pick up the next level in the chapter and use that. Any of the units can be easily inserted into your existing curriculum or used as building blocks for developing a new curriculum.

Meeting National Standards

Although the units and lessons in this book were created to be flexible, they have clear direction—to meet the national physical education standards developed by the NASPE. Chapter 2 outlines those standards and shows how units, lessons, and assessment tools are designed for compliance. If you would like a copy of *Appropriate Practices for High School Physical Education,* the document is available from NASPE.

Chapter Format

Each chapter has a learning experience outline describing what the units in the chapter cover. In addition, each chapter provides several handouts: a student portfolio checklist, a study sheet, and an extension project that you can use to enhance your students' learning experience and record keeping. Each experience level in each chapter has its own unit of lessons that provide an easy template from which to work. And, with the exception of the fitness testing chapter (chapter 4), each unit concludes with a skills rubric and short quiz appropriate for that level.

The following is an overview of the chapter format:

Chapter overview
- Study sheet
- Extension project
- Student portfolio checklist
- Learning experience outline

Beginner unit
- Beginner lessons
- Beginner rubric
- Beginner quiz
- Beginner quiz answer key

Intermediate unit (if included)
- Intermediate lessons
- Intermediate rubric
- Intermediate quiz
- Intermediate quiz answer key

Advanced unit (if included)
- Advanced lessons
- Advanced rubric
- Advanced quiz
- Advanced quiz answer key

Some lessons may have other handouts in addition to the ones listed here. Those handouts appear with the corresponding lesson.

Chapter Overview

The chapter overview gives a quick picture of what you will find in each chapter. It appears in outline form but does not show the breakdown for each unit.

Handouts

Each chapter includes handouts that can be copied from the book or printed from the CD-ROM and shared with parents and students. The study sheet contains fun facts about the activity and its history, as well as an explanation of skills, positioning on the court, strategies, and rules. This information can be used to pique students' interest or simply to enrich their general knowledge.

The student extension project asks students to think about the benefits of the unit, relevant health and fitness information, and how they can participate in the activity outside of school. The handout is designed for students and parents so they can understand the value of the activity. It is also designed to encourage students to identify people with whom they will be able to play so that they can continue participating in the activity outside of class.

Student Portfolio Checklist

A student portfolio checklist lists what has been planned for the duration of the unit. Students can check off what they learned and keep a cumulative record. The checklist identifies broad categories of skills, rules, activity responsibilities, and strategies and groups them in no particular sequence. For instance, the badminton checklist does not mention playing the game until the end of the list, though games can and should be played well before students have learned all the skills, rules, and strategies listed. The checklist is not a teacher's tool; it is the student's personal record of the learning experience.

Learning Experience Outline

This outline addresses the administrative considerations necessary for the unit. It includes an outline of the skills, rules, and strategies planned in the lessons from the beginner to advanced levels. It lists materials needed and spells out how to modify the gym, fields, or outdoor facilities in order to conduct the unit successfully. It addresses safety concerns, and it also provides tips for student inclusion and other special considerations. Finally, it outlines assessment strategies and lists resources to help teachers understand the skills and get ideas for additional drills.

Lessons by Experience Level

Lessons are progressive and grouped by experience level. They should be followed in sequence if the progression is to be meaningful. You need not cover all new material in one grade. However, if you decide to divide the lessons of a unit and continue them in subsequent years, it is best to limit the number of introductory skills planned in the earlier lessons and instead get on with the game after students are fairly successful with three fundamental skills. The reason for this will be explained in the discussions of game play and tournaments later in this chapter.

The scope of each unit varies. Somewhat consistent with my experience in the northeastern United States, where gym space is at a premium and winter brings us indoors much of the year, the units are planned around those limitations. Activities that can accommodate everyone and that afford the highest level of participation in small spaces, such as volleyball, dance, and fitness training, are given the most attention and are the longest units.

Some activities reappear every year (e.g., volleyball, fitness, football, basketball, dance), and others do not (e.g., golf, badminton, pickleball, tennis). Some chapters have one unit (beginner), others have two units (beginner and intermediate levels), and others have units for all three experience levels. The activities that reoccur from level to level provide fresh content and build on past experience, so students will not be doing the same old thing every year.

The following provides an overview of the lesson plan.

- **Facilities**—Describes the way the facilities need to be arranged.
- **Materials**—Spells out what equipment and supplies are needed.
- **Performance goals**—These are the general and specific activity goals of the lesson.

The constant aim of each lesson is developing and maintaining physical fitness, so I have written lessons that increase the knowledge component without compromising the activity component. Information is to be shared and reviewed during warm-ups, motivational discussions, demonstrations of new skills, teachable moments, and cool-downs. A lot more information can be learned in bite-size quantities presented at appropriate times rather than all at once.

- **Cognitive goals**—These knowledge goals of the unit can include concepts, facts, or understandings that enrich the learning experience and encourage critical thinking. They can involve specifics of the sport, such as rules and strategies, or scientific principles that influence success. They can even deal with psychosocial factors such as being responsible citizens, being realistic about oneself and one's teammates, taking initiative, and assuming leadership roles. For the sake of convenience, sometimes the sequence of the lesson allows you to read all the material that you should share with the class in one place. If bringing the class together for the full information requires using more than a few minutes at a time, cut it down! Explanations should be given in small, relevant bites, so if the whole message is long, use whatever time your kids need to catch their breath to complete the explanation. Keeping cognitive goals in mind will also help you to recognize teachable moments. These are wonderful opportunities to enhance student understanding, but stopping class to share what happened should be kept to a minimum. Use the teachable moment to coach individual students. If the issue is important for the class to learn, share it during the cool-down or save the insight for discussion during the review or introductory remarks in the next lesson.

- **Lesson safety**—An ounce of prevention is worth a pound of cure in physical education. This section provides information to help prevent accidents before they happen. It also highlights factors that might compromise the kind of emotional environment you want to maintain in class. I draw attention to possible presenting issues of poor interaction between students so no emotional wounds are inflicted and left to fester. You are alerted to be vigilant and to follow through with the offender and follow up with the offended.

- **Motivation**—Introduces ideas that help students see the relevance of a lesson and encourage their best efforts. Successfully used, this information widens students' perspective and stimulates their excitement. Remarks may come from resources that include current events, sport records, cultural diversity, school news, scientific principles, class standings, or personal stories. I include stories of my own in the lessons and encourage you to replace them with some of yours. The personal touch is always more successful with students.

  Let me give an example of how motivation can change everything, as it did for me when introducing the dance unit to a class filled with 8th-grade boys who did not want to dance, no way, no how. One day, when class time was reduced and it was useless to gear up for activity, I showed dance excerpts of the movie *White Nights,* hoping that it would be good preparation for the dance unit. As I saw how dazzled the students were when Barishnykov did 10 pirouettes and then challenged his tap-dancing security supervisor to do the same, I replayed the scene and then asked them how many pirouettes they could do. From that moment on, it was much easier to teach dance. The boys began to see dance as an athletic, challenging activity worthy of their attention.

- **Warm-ups**—These serve two purposes: to increase the heart rate so the blood flows and prepares the soft tissue for activity and to begin the learning process. This section not only suggests that you do mimetic exercises during warm-ups, it gives a breakdown of how to introduce each movement pattern that students need to learn for the sport, explains how that pattern should be performed, encourages them to repeat it a number of times, and begins the movement memory process so that new skills are learned and reinforced during the warm-up. This is the basis for mimetics, a concept that will be discussed shortly (see page 10).

- **Lesson sequence**—Lists a successful progression for teaching new skills and introducing cognitive concepts so that the class keeps moving. The sequence incorporates awareness of rules, strategies, laws of motion, and socialization in small bits that are not only relevant to the action of the day but easy for students to learn without creating too much downtime. If covering the small bits of information turns into long-winded discussions, break up the explanation into two or three meaningful parts, send the students back to their activity with enough repetition that they need a break, call them back in for a rest, and complete the explanation.

* **Review and stretching**—Many questions arise at the end of each lesson. Exploring them fully could take the whole class, so you must pick and choose from what is there or find your own material to use for review. The review uses the Socratic method of learning, asking questions that emphasize important aspects of the lesson and making students think. It also provides a snapshot of how well the class understood the lesson.

* **Assessment**—Some lessons include an assessment section. Assessment plays a vital part in the educational process by providing the information you need to refine daily lessons, give direction to subsequent lessons, and evaluate student accomplishment.

* **Teacher homework**—Some lessons include a section that includes information that will help you to prepare for the following lesson.

Teachers must learn what their students need before they can meet those needs with good lesson planning, which requires observation and sensitivity. In addition, teachers must be able to ascertain if goals are actually reached so they can decide what to do next to help students succeed. Such decision making is most necessary during early lessons. If basic fundamentals are not acquired and the class moves on, students who have not learned those fundamentals will become frustrated and stop trying. If modest goals are not within the grasp of most students (90%) in the class, it is ill-advised to move on to more complex tasks. Teachers must do more than watch their students; they also must have the skills to assess what they see. Good observation and evaluation skills will provide insight for setting realistic class goals and for understanding when students need individualization.

Assessment also provides a basis for grading. Some teachers like to get a head start, teaching a skill and then grading it a few days later. However, learning paces differ, so I recommend delaying performance assessment until the end of the unit. Students who experience initial difficulty in picking up skills can become extraordinary with a little patience. Wonderful success stories come from students who have been given more time to get comfortable with the skills they are learning. This reasoning does not preclude the decision to give a daily grade for outstanding effort or achievement, but it does explain why tests are at the end of each unit level.

Other Handouts

A study sheet and an extension project that can be done at home or during a study session are available on the CD-ROM for duplication. According to NASPE, appropriate homework consists of learning experiences outside of class that reinforce skills and knowledge acquired within. I am not an advocate of assigning homework, but these handouts are useful for reinforcing what students learned and exploring what they can do on their own. How you have students use the study sheets and extension projects is completely up to you.

Performance Rubrics

Skills rubrics can be found for each experience level at the end of the unit. Each rubric identifies the learning progression of the most important skills at each level. The rubrics will help identify progressive accomplishments, crediting students with progress that will eventually help them reach skill mastery. The rubrics have been written so they can be used for self-assessment, peer assessment, or teacher assessment.

Written Quizzes

Short quizzes have been included for each activity at each experience level. In my first attempts at test writing and grading, the diagram and essays made it impossible for anyone but me to grade my quizzes. Imagine grading one test at a time when you have a stack of 400 and need to have grades in the next day! The quizzes in this book thus test a sample of the knowledge that should have been acquired, take no longer than 10 minutes to complete, and can be graded by scanner or students. Their brevity is intentional—as a teacher of the only subject requiring physical activity, I believe that nonactivity time should be kept to a minimum.

Certain problems are inherent in giving written tests in the gym. First, students forget they are taking a test and come with no pen or pencil. If they do remember to bring their writing implements, they frequently put them down when the games are about to get under way and then lose them. Second, some students have special needs that require individualized planning for testing them. In New York, individual educational plans (IEPs) contain information on the testing situation that works best for a specific student. Students might need extended time, a reader, a writer, or a computer. It is best to decide with them or their special education teacher how to meet their needs. If it is impossible to coordinate all student needs with that of classroom management, you might let students with special needs take the test with everyone else but deliver it to their resource room teacher for completion. Be aware that students frequently do not admit to needing such service, especially in front of peers, so it is up to you to follow through. If you know they have special needs or if you see that their quiz is incomplete, suggest that they take the extra time to finish. You must also have a plan for the students who cannot complete the test in the time allotted. You might want to give them an opportunity to finish while everyone is playing or have them turn it in at the end of the day or during their study hall.

Unique Aspects of *Complete Physical Education Plans for Grades 5 to 12*

Complete Physical Education Plans for Grades 5 to 12 does not include specific methodologies, but it does have teaching biases that make it unique. Each is a product of my educational philosophy and many years of experience teaching adolescent boys and girls.

Because of my belief in the Greek ideal of a balanced body and mind, because I believe a physical educator's primary goal is helping students learn to be active, and because I am concerned with the health of our young people, I emphasize almost constant class activity from the time students enter the class to the time they leave. And, since action without thought does not recommend itself to me, lessons integrate thinking and skill while emphasizing movement. As discussed earlier, this kind of teaching is done by imparting information in small bits so that the motion does not stop for more than a few minutes at a time. In this way, lessons are weighted toward action rather than talking and students have a chance to assimilate meaning in relevant bits. In writing this book, I have incorporated a teaching style that is consistent with my desire for lots of activity. First, practice time is an important aspect of my classes and plans. Second, mimetics, the strongest part of the warm-up, initiate learning without taking undue time to stop the class and demonstrate.

Practice Time

During practice time, the materials are out and the teacher is on the gym floor while students are dressing so students who dress more quickly can practice or play short games with friends before the formal start of class. Having materials out encourages most students to hurry, and the sitting and waiting factor common to so many physical education classes is eliminated.

A combination of constant class activity and lessons that integrate thinking and skill will help students to remain engaged in the physical education learning process.

Many teachers fear such a free atmosphere. They believe that discipline problems will increase and that they will be unable to control their class. However, allowing practice time not only motivates students to dress quickly and take advantage of the time to play, it is a particularly productive educational time. Students are more relaxed when practicing with friends in informal settings. They can learn and improve without being intimidated by thoughts of where they rank in comparison to others. They also have easier access to personal attention from their teacher. If everyone else is busy playing with their friends, the people you are helping do not feel as if they are drawing negative attention to themselves; their classmates are too involved with their own activity to notice.

It generally takes little encouragement to get students running in, taking materials, and practicing. Students come on the floor, ready to practice with their materials of the day, whether it be volleyballs, shuttlecocks, or soccer balls. And in dance, just leave music for the Limbo Rock on and see how fast the students slide in the door and begin their warm-up.

In 31 years of teaching, I have found that if sufficient equipment is available for everyone, both time and materials are used meaningfully during practice time. Rarely have I encountered discipline problems. Some students may fool around inappropriately, but by correcting their behavior immediately and giving them a chance to do the right thing, you can help them become cognizant of their actions and how they affect others. With a patient but firm hand, even the most difficult student appreciates the latitude of practice time and learns to be a responsible class member.

Mimetics

The idea for *mimetics* came about some years ago, when I was frustrated with the brevity of class time and motivated to get the most out of every learning opportunity. Students were having a tough time developing a correct bump pass in volleyball. Drills that had been successful in other classes simply did not work with them. They needed something more fundamental, so I started teaching movement patterns before the game, before giving out materials, before I even knew what to call it. And that is how I started using mimetics.

The purpose of mimetics is to mimic real motion. In our framework, it is the rehearsal of game skills outside the usual game context and in the absence of a ball. By practicing mimetics, students can develop the proper kinesthetic feel of complex movements easily and without performance pressure. If their introduction to a complex movement is a step-by-step approach outside the context of a game or drill, the whole movement pattern can be accomplished and repeated on cue without frustration. Because the repetition is so easy, it helps turn complex movement patterns into natural movement that flows. Mimetics can be used in many aspects of learning acquisition, and I use them to teach correct movement patterns for many skills.

Mimetics play a large role in the lesson plans. Skills such as the football throw, chest pass, overhead throw, layup shot, bump pass, set, spike, block, rebounding, tennis serve, or any action that requires timing and coordination can be rehearsed without the ball. Mimetics allow movement patterns to become a routine action for learners, who can then feel more comfortable transferring that movement from a simple exercise to moving drills where they have to coordinate with the ball. Practicing mimetics with proper footwork helps students anticipate game situations and react more quickly, especially if their teacher leads them while suggesting game scenarios.

The drills are a little like miming. A mime uses movement to tell a story without ever saying a word. In mimetics, students mime game-playing skills, without words and without the ball. Mimetics can begin and fortify the learning process while increasing blood flow and warming up muscles. Since their incorporation in my class routine, students have had real performance gains in half the time it used to take. The best product is their success and seeing the pleasure they get from being able to do something they did not think they could do. All told, the results have motivated the use of mimetics whenever possible. What follows is an example of how I would use mimetics in a basketball lesson where the performance goal is rebounding and my intention is to teach students without spending too much time sitting and talking.

First, I do not explain the purpose of my instructions; I simply ask the students to follow me while I guide the activity, giving them movement and voice cues that keep them moving as I continue to increase the complexity of what they are doing. As they finish one movement, I introduce the next.

1. "Jump as high as you can. Let's do it together, with me. Ready, jump." (Repeat 2-5 times.)

2. "Jump, but this time make your hands reach as high as possible when you're in the air." (Repeat 2-5 times.)

3. "While you're up there, make sure the palms of your hands face each other. Now, jump." (Repeat 2-5 times.)

4. "This time stretch those arms as high as you can. Imagine them grabbing a ball out of the air." (Repeat 2-5 times.)

5. "Land with spread feet so they take up lots of space." (Repeat 2-5 times.)

6. "Bring your arms down with the imaginary ball in your hands." (Repeat 2-5 times.)

7. "Come down from your jump with spread feet and elbows out." (Repeat 2-5 times.)

8. "Who can tell me what we are practicing?" (Remember, I didn't tell them what we were doing when I started the warm-up.) Students are now warmed up and taken directly into the motivation aspect of the lesson.

The next time class meets, all that needs to be said is, "Let's do 10 jumps to rebound." The students can follow you or a student leader. When students are ready for more complexity, you can ask them to "move in to rebound." With verbal cues, you can guide them a few steps forward, telling them to take steps to get to that imaginary spot in front of the rim and inside the basketball key. (Have them pick a spot on the ground a few feet in front of them as their imaginary spot.) They can be instructed to run to the spot, jump straight up, and then look at the spot they jumped from. Ask, "Did you land in the same place you took off from?" Expect to hear, "No." Try again and ask. Then ask them to try running to the spot, jumping and coming straight down so that they land where they left the ground. Again, ask to see if they landed on the same place they took off from. This exercise provides feedback about the body's momentum. When it is done, you not only warmed up the class but taught a new skill, enhanced basketball technique and knowledge, taught biofeedback, introduced a lesson in avoiding loose-ball fouls when rebounding, and taught everything without specific explanation, which will follow during the motivation or procedural part of the lesson.

Of course, this example is not meant to represent a full warm-up. Warm-ups should include other mimetics; for instance, mimetics that contribute to success in basketball skills such as pivoting, shooting, stopping, guarding, and turning to shoot. Warm-ups should also target exercises for the abdominal muscles. Stretching should be done after the heart rate has been raised. If you want your lesson to be time efficient, have students stretch during the cool-down while you review the lesson, rather than during the warm-up.

How to Drill for Skill Acquisition

For the most part, lessons introduce one new thing at a time and allow students to feel comfortable before moving on. Sometimes exceptions occur, though. In order to keep interest up, muscle fatigue down, and the learning curve rising, several fundamental skills can be combined and practiced in early lessons. For instance, if kicking is the objective, it must include stopping. The receiving partners need to stop the ball so they can kick it back. If the lesson is throwing, not only must catching be included, but because it is unwise to repeat the same motion during an entire class, base running might be added without taking up a lot of time to reorganize the class. By 5th grade, many students have had experience throwing, catching, dribbling, and kicking, and thus combining several fundamental skills in a first lesson is not the leap of faith it might appear. However, the idea of focusing on one skill or concept during each lesson is the guiding force behind all lessons.

Drills are crucial. It never seemed much of an art to me until I had a student teacher who was given complete responsibility for teaching one 8th-grade class. One day she was set to teach basketball dribbling. She wrote a complete lesson plan and, prepared and confident, she set out to teach it. She took attendance, led the warm-ups, explained the lesson, and lined the students up for the drill. The students were motivated. They listened and were 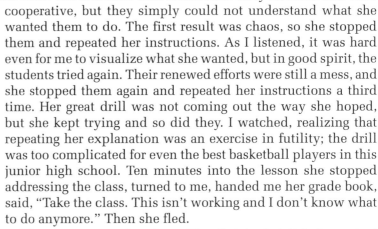 cooperative, but they simply could not understand what she wanted them to do. The first result was chaos, so she stopped them and repeated her instructions. As I listened, it was hard even for me to visualize what she wanted, but in good spirit, the students tried again. Their renewed efforts were still a mess, and she stopped them again and repeated her instructions a third time. Her great drill was not coming out the way she hoped, but she kept trying and so did they. I watched, realizing that repeating her explanation was an exercise in futility; the drill was too complicated for even the best basketball players in this junior high school. Ten minutes into the lesson she stopped addressing the class, turned to me, handed me her grade book, said, "Take the class. This isn't working and I don't know what to do anymore." Then she fled.

There are two points here. The first is that it is important to think on your feet. It is not always possible to gauge how a group will respond to your plan, and you must be ready to make changes. Second, when it comes to setting up drills, keep it simple. Students do not need to be dazzled with complex drills. They just want to learn, practice, and feel successful. It is incumbent on teachers to plan so that practice is safe, provides lots of repetition, allows easy access to feedback, maintains interest, is relevant to the students, and does not take a lot of time to set up.

The organizational formations suggested in these lessons are intentionally uncomplicated. They are designed to allow students to practice safely, have the most repetition possible in the shortest amount of time, and refine their skills, all while giving you a clear view of the entire group. As students progress, formations should change. Simple variations can facilitate goal

Teaching skills gradually allows students to hone their skills and abilities in preparation for successful game play.

changes, refine targets, and make practice more sophisticated while not overwhelming students with information. For instance, when you first teach the soccer dribble, it is best to give students their own ball and an uninterrupted area in which to dribble. As they get more competent, you might want to give them a breathing spell by having several people share a ball in a simple relay. You might have them run alongside one another and pass on a diagonal. You could use a person as an obstacle or receiver. You might ask that they pass to a target or a person waiting for the ball when they are halfway to the original goal. In each case, you are incrementally adding to their use of the dribble by combining it with other skills and formations.

Keeping the Environment Educational and Enjoyable

Competition can be painful if the only one who feels like a winner is the person or team with the best score. Keeping that in mind, competition is still encouraged in each sport unit in this book. The goal is not to eliminate losers until all but the best players remain; it is to encourage maximum participation against a variety of opponents in an equal field where everyone is included and has a job to do for the team.

Competition has too many benefits for teachers to avoid it because of its possible negative effects. It is a great motivator and, in the right environment, it is a useful educational tool. It encourages improvement, leads to greater physical effort, and makes games more exciting, each of which is a worthy outcome. To ensure that the competitive experience is healthy, teachers have to assume responsibility for setting meaningful goals, creating a competitive learning environment, providing students with an even field in which to play, and teaching them to feel like winners whatever the score happens to be.

Let me share an experience I had when I began teaching high school classes after having taught junior high classes for 18 years. I had come to the high school unconsciously programmed to believe that older was better and that the students would not need as much skills work or encouragement as they did when they were in junior high. Boy, was I surprised—what I believed was not even close to the reality. During the basketball unit, many high school students hung their heads during games, avoided the ball, seemed afraid to make a mistake, and looked as if they were intimidated by their lack of skill compared with the prowess of their highly skilled classmates. How did I react? I tried convincing them that they should shoot when they were open and reasonably near the backboard. I told them that the worst-case scenario was that they would miss and their teammates would try to rebound and put the ball back up again. It took almost the whole basketball unit to convince those students to try. When they finally did, they got so much pleasure from their efforts that I felt sad they had missed out on the fun for so much of the unit. There had to be a better way.

I did not discover a better method, though, until we were fortunate enough to have both sides of the gym and the use of all eight backboards so I could break up my rather large class into eight small groups. In the early lessons, I let them group as they wished, so they grouped with their friends. The practice groups were not of equal ability, but we were just drilling. We began by combining the performance goals of two earlier lessons, dribbling and shooting, so I assigned each group to dribble across the gym to shoot at an assigned basket before dribbling back. After everyone had a few turns, students were told to stay at the basket once they got there, keep shooting until their shot dropped in, and then dribble back to their line. After a few turns more, I changed the instruction, telling them if they shot and missed, they should dribble to another basket and shoot again. If the shot did not drop in, they should go to the next basket and shoot again, continuing on to different baskets until they sank a shot before dribbling back. The class did this several minutes. One by one, everyone saw the ball drop in.

Then I suggested keeping score and finding out which group could accumulate the most points. We did the simple drill first—dribble down, shoot until it goes in, and dribble back. From the time I said "Go" until they heard "Stop," they scored 2 points each time a member of their group dribbled to the basket, sank a shot, and dribbled back. The instant opinion was that the practice group with the best athletes in the class would outscore everyone else by far. Interestingly, though, when 3 minutes were up, a group with less skilled students scored one basket more than the team everyone thought would win. Were they excited?

You bet. All of the students were able to score and make a contribution to the group of friends they were playing with.

Variety being the spice of life, I mixed it up a little. I asked that they only take one shot and then come back whether they made it or not. Sometimes I told them to stay until it dropped in. Sometimes I asked them to dribble to the zone where they practiced their outside shot, shoot from there, and come back immediately if it scored, but if not, get the rebound and try a layup shot. If that dropped in, they scored 2 points for the group. No matter the rules, the objective of scoring and the success in doing it proved that everyone could score. Meanwhile, the drills enhanced their self-confidence and awareness that they all were capable of shooting and scoring when no one was interfering with their view of the basket.

My classes did not have a reluctant shooter thereafter and the tenor changed. Games and tournaments were no longer dependent on heroes but on whole teams. All the students felt free to shoot and were convinced they could make both an offensive and a defensive contribution because they knew they could score. Once they were part of a team effort, cooperation was high and they met the goals I set for them. In such an atmosphere, no matter who had the best score, everyone won.

Considering Facilities

You must consider the facilities that are available when planning your units and lessons. If facilities are inadequate, several questions need to be addressed before major decisions are made.

Should I Go Ahead With the Activity?

Many instructors bend over backward to teach an activity they love, never thinking of appropriate substitutions. But you would not teach swimming without access to a pool, so why include activities that do not allow full participation? For instance, I once had several classes of 50 students, three tennis courts, and no nearby wall to work with. The equipment situation was fine, but we had no space. Students would not have enough activity, enough experience with the materials, or enough time to master even basic skills. In this atmosphere, introducing tennis would be a lesson in frustration. Could I teach students tennis with so many students waiting to play? I decided to wait until I could come up with a good plan for teaching tennis that kept the whole class active.

Can I Keep the Students Active During Most of the Class Time?

If the answer to the question is no, perhaps you should not teach the activity. Curriculum decisions should not be automatic. If teaching a traditional activity does not make sense, start a new tradition.

What Can I Do to Enhance Participation When Facilities Aren't Optimal?

Here are some ideas when dealing with facilities that are less than optimal:

- Create additional learning stations. Divide the class into smaller groups and give each an assignment that lets the group stay active with limited materials and limited space.
- Modify the games to increase participation.
    - Change the number of players on a side.
    - Shorten the length of the game.
    - Rotate players between games and practice stations.

Let's say you want to teach tennis. You have three courts and have to accommodate 20 students. How can you modify your lesson so everyone is fully engaged?

- Dedicate one court to drilling skills with a teacher, highly skilled student, or ball machine and plan a systematic rotation from the drill court to two doubles courts.
- Divide regulation courts into minicourts, changing the focus from practice and games on full courts to practice and games for small-court control.
- Have 12 students play doubles on the three regulation courts and have the remaining 8 students work at stations outside the courts. Send them to work on the control or volley drills taught at the beginning of the unit, have them practice serving through a hanging hoop or a target on a wall, or have them practice hitting against a wall. Systematically rotate students onto the courts so everyone gets equal playing time.

What do you do if you have 30 students and just three courts?

- Stick to skills, assign 10 students to each of the three courts, and have a student leader, teacher, or ball machine feed balls to each line.
- Divide the class into three equally able groups and assign two groups to neighboring fields to play a team sport they have already learned while the other group has tennis lessons (assuming appropriate supervision is possible). Rotate the groups so everyone has the same number of tennis lessons before the unit ends.

If you have 50 students and three courts, it might not be worth it to teach tennis.

The United States Tennis Association (USTA) and the International Tennis Federation have excellent resources. The USTA produces publications designed to help teachers deal with conditions that are less than ideal.

Game Play

Competition is not inherently good or evil, and neither is game play. Equipping students to enjoy competitive sport has value. As students move toward graduation, goals change from acquiring skills to emphasizing their use outside of school. In sport, that usually means game play and competition. Competitive sports are great outlets for keeping active, meeting new people, and experiencing fulfillment while getting exercise. Competitive sports are a popular leisure activity, or there would not be so many sport leagues across the nation. And if Club Med did not include small-group lessons, activities, and games, it might not be such a popular vacation spot for young adults and families.

If approached and supervised appropriately, game play can bring out the best in people. I have watched the most disengaged students rush to get to class and start practicing just so they can play better in their games. I cannot even take the credit. It belongs to their friends and teammates who want their team to do its best and inspire them to make the effort. For instance, one girl who was initially reticent became motivated to learn how to do her part for her basketball team. After playing hard for her team for what must have been the first time in her teenage life, she came back to the locker room sweaty and happy and said, "Gee, Miss Kleinman, I never knew sweating could be so much fun." Isn't that what it is all about?

It is realistic to assume that if students leave us without enjoying what we teach, without enjoying activities that are vigorous and emotionally gratifying, and without enjoying the social environment we provide, they run the risk of becoming just what we hope they won't be—sedentary adults. Physical education has the responsibility for preparing students for a lifetime of healthy activity. To meet that responsibility, the skills we want students to master should also be fun. That is why lessons in this book not only emphasize gaining and mastering skills but using those skills in context as soon as possible in modified contests, real games, and class tournaments. Before competition starts to dominate the lesson, rules and regulations are taught and students develop a team identity so they can learn to work together, find a supporting role on the team, and gain added incentive to work as part of a group. Once they are on a team that needs them—and every team member is needed if game play is taught correctly—they become active participants every day. The end product is designed to meet physical educators' ultimate goals for students—enhancing their fitness, piquing their interest, encouraging their effort, generating good class relationships, and finishing the unit with good feelings.

Lifetime Activities Are More Than Just Sports

Sport enthusiasts will love having units that prepare them for playing in adult leagues, tournaments, and pickup games. Some students will enjoy playing for its own sake and others will love moving just for the fun of it. Whatever the motivating factor, *Complete Physical Education Plans for Grades 5 to 12* includes a variety of competitive and noncompetitive activities to accommodate all interests. Among the noncompetitive units are dance, educational gymnastics, conditioning and weight training, and self-testing activities.

Students who experience the entire package will be physically educated. They will be aware of the need to stay active, mindful of how good it feels to move, and confident enough in their learning skills to keep searching for that special activity that turns them on, such as cycling, scuba diving, climbing, skiing, and kayaking, to name a few. The 18 units in this book do not cover all activities, but they cover enough to guarantee a well-rounded approach, with experiences in many types of sport and lifetime activities, a rich fitness unit that varies each year, and a total program approach that educates the whole person, body and mind. English courses cannot cover all literature, and neither can physical education cover all activities. Our job is to set a tone for participation. An educated person doesn't know it all, but knows how and why to learn more. This book gives teachers the tools to create physically educated people with a love of being active.

It is important to teach students activities that they can use throughout their lives.

Planning Successful Tournaments

As students get older, it becomes more important to work as a team, solve problems together, use the skills they feel comfortable with, and challenge them to do even better than before. In elementary school, children are satisfied testing their skills in short games without any thought beyond winning a point. But from 8th grade on, the desire of many kids to test themselves grows, providing teachers with a wonderful opportunity to use that self-motivation to encourage continued development. For that reason, the sport units include class tournaments once the group has shown an ability to move the ball fairly well.

Creating successful tournaments doesn't happen by chance—it requires good planning and supervision. Here are some of the keys to creating and running successful tournaments.

Making Teams

If you have two to six teams in a class, make sure each is equally skilled. To do this, you must know your class and each student's skill level. After accounting for the important factors in a particular sport, such as height, speed, throwing accuracy, jumping ability, and previous experience, create teams that are as equal as possible. This gives every team an even chance to win.

Here are some things to think about when forming teams:

- If you want students to work together, make new friends, and learn to respect individual differences, it is best to split up cliques.

- On occasion, some players may attempt to dominate the game. Such players may try to control the ball and avoid the rest of their teammates. I have gotten around this problem in several constructive ways.

  - In basketball, I had students play their first practice games without allowing the dribble—the ball had to be passed to move it. Players started looking for the open person because they were forced to by the rules.

  - In volleyball, rather than allowing teammates to run in the way of someone else and smack the ball over the net, I gave rewards to those who could hit a bump pass that went to the center of their own side of the court. I also made a big deal out of good sets that were sent to the dominant net player. Needless to say, that encouraged the net player to be there to receive the ball instead of running all over the court to steal someone else's shot.

  - In football, when all else failed, I coached the other team, forcing the quarterback to eventually come around. The quarterback could not stand the constant interceptions that came with having the receivers double- and triple-teamed, which happened when opponents anticipated the likely receiver. Pretty soon, the quarterback was looking for an open receiver. At that point, no receivers were ignored and teams learned to play together.

  - When the competitive field is large, as in individual and dual sports (a class of 24 would have 12 doubles teams or 24 singles teams), class tournaments can be done in separate divisions, each with a different skill level. By making divisions, games can be played within the same skill level, which makes the tournament more fun for everyone.

I encourage teams to pick their own captains and cocaptains, but sometimes they need guidance if you want the leadership role to rotate to different people during the course of the year. You can accomplish this by simply asking them to choose someone who was never a captain before, or you can tell them who the captain is and allow them to choose a cocaptain. You might accomplish variety by simply having them choose people of opposite genders. Whatever you decide, you must supervise the teamwork to make sure that the natural leaders do not interfere with the chosen captains in a negative way.

These kinds of decisions are completely dependent on the nature of the class. The only constant in good tournament planning is the expectation that students use a good work ethic and that the competition does not leave anyone feeling intimidated.

Don't Stop Teaching

While tournaments are going on, don't stop teaching. Tournaments provide a great opportunity for observing how well students are applying skills in an authentic situation.

- As you observe, use teachable moments, offering advice, corrections, and positive reinforcement. Take advantage of the fact that some students learn more out of necessity when forced to use skills in a game context than during drills.

- Make sure everyone plays by the same rules and code of ethics.
- Get to all groups to compliment individuals on their accomplishments.
- Cheer for accomplishments that most students don't recognize, such as cheering for what seemed an unsuccessful effort to come up with the ball, and explain why (because it forced an opponent's error and secured the ball for the team after all). Compliment assists, broken-up plays, or when students have the right idea but execution was just a shade off.
- Encourage leadership, an understanding of the dynamics of the game, teamwork, and initiative.
- Encourage anticipation so teammates are backed up, not overrun.
- Teach students to be realistic. You want them to appreciate progress and real effort.
- Set up progressive goals that students can measure up to despite scores.

Success

It is important to create an atmosphere in which all students feel successful. Unfortunately, unless you are a magician, you cannot create success; that requires the student's effort. If students refuse to make an effort, teachers have to find a way to get them involved. Finding the right words and doing the right thing to get the disinterested student moving is almost an art. Resistant students need to trust you and the environment before they will risk trying something they might fail at. Most will be won over if the class atmosphere is consistently active, emotionally reinforcing, socially healthy, and appreciative of individual growth. In those few cases where nothing seems to work, you might remind students of the benefits of hard play. Maybe they need to realize that the benefits have nothing to do with winning or losing a game and more to do with looking good and feeling fit. Remind them of the calories they will burn and the cardiorespiratory benefits they will gain by playing hard. And, use yourself as a model. Ask them to play with you. Practice with them. Team up with them on the court.

In a culture that emphasizes winning, students must learn that participation is far more important than the final outcome. The old saying, "It's not whether you win or lose, it's how you play the game that counts," is a good start. Praising efforts that have no relationship to the score is one way of modeling this attitude. Recognizing good sportsmanship, excellent hustle, fabulous team play, improved skills, and so on can get students thinking more about values and less about the win. Focusing on these values enables everyone to be a winner.

Playing the Game

Having skill is vital to success, learning it is an important part of the process, and achieving it develops confidence and motivation, but having skill without using it in a game is virtually worthless. Some researchers advocate that students play the game before learning the skills in the belief that it is best to understand the context in which skills are used before learning how to do them properly. I began my career teaching girls only, but it took working with boys to learn how meaningful that theory is.

Experience has led me to believe there are real gender differences in learning styles. Boys tend to want to play first. They really don't think about needing to learn how, but once they play the game and realize how difficult it can be, they stop fighting efforts to teach them how to do it better. Girls often want to know what and how to do something before doing it. They tend to be more patient about learning skills and repeating them than boys are. The prospect of the game does not excite them until they feel they know how to play it.

To further illustrate the point of skills versus games, I'd like to share a story. I was at a new position in a school where I watched my colleagues teach several 8th-grade football lessons. Each day the kids got out on the field, lined up, and practiced a passing or defensive drill. Whenever I watched, they were drilling. I never once saw them play a game. When it was my turn to take the field and I brought my classes out, I noted that even the average 9th- and 10th-graders had a pretty impressive success rate during the passing drills. Both genders were accurate when throwing to a person on the run if they were up to 10 yards (9 meters) away. They could run square-out, square-in, hook, and even post patterns. What is more, they could hang on to the ball when they caught it.

They looked ready for a game, so the belts and flags came out for flag football. To my surprise, they needed to learn how to use them. After they learned how to use the belt and flags and kickoff rules were explained, the class was sent out to play. They sauntered to their field, obviously in no rush. After 5 minutes, half the groups were on the field, ready for their game; the rest had to be rounded up and cajoled. Finally, the game began. The quarterback made a good throw. The receiver caught it, ran a few steps, and threw it to someone else, who caught it and ran a few more steps. Then she too threw it to someone else. In shock, I stopped the action to correct it. When I did, I learned that these students, who had 2 or 3 years of football lessons, had only learned to throw and catch in all that time. They never were taught the game. That explained everything—their lack of enthusiasm, their sauntering to the field, their inability to use belts and flags, and their lack of the foggiest idea what to do with their skills in a game.

As a teacher, don't just focus on correction. Instead, give praise for efforts and recognition for a job well done so that everyone has the opportunity to feel like a winner.

Playing the game without the skills can be frustrating; however, learning skills without ever playing the game is also frustrating. I liken it to learning to read words but never getting the opportunity to read them in a sentence, an article, or a book. No one could approve of that type of reading. Why approve of it in sport?

Suggestions for Curriculum Development

Teaching a sport in season is so much easier. Students trying out for the school team, watching friends play, seeing a game live or on TV, and reading about it in the papers already have their interest raised. In addition, you can share examples of rules and strategies by citing something that happened in a game that has everyone talking. For instance, when teaching the importance of protecting the ball and how to do it legally, the appeal of the lesson is heightened when it takes place after a big game is won or lost because someone had the ball stolen at a crucial point in the game. If you tie the story to what you are teaching, students can relate to what you are saying.

Unfortunately, it is not always possible to take advantage of sport seasons. Many regions have only 2 or 3 months in the fall and spring when the weather is reliable enough to play outdoors. Most of the year is spent indoors in crowded facilities. If your school is like mine, the gym is used all year and is not only crowded but in constant demand. Given the limitations of facilities, the size of your staff, and the size of your classes, it can be a challenge to provide a program that includes individual sports. In my teaching situation, it only worked when we tiptoed around each other and were willing to compromise.

Knowing how varied each teaching situation is and realizing that swimming, track and field, adventure-based programming, and table tennis are not part of this text, I cannot prescribe an entire curriculum as if it is the best one possible—but I can assert that the one here is wonderful. Given a school year similar to ours with 38 weeks of class and classes on alternate days, or about 60 lessons lasting 45 minutes each, the following curriculum has a fine selection of activities and provides a useful example of arranging units.

Fifth Grade

Teach and then make games using the most basic skills.

- Soccer—8 lessons
- Folk dance—8 lessons
- Volleyball—8 lessons
- Educational gymnastics—8 lessons
- Fitness (aerobic activities)—4 lessons
- Basketball—8 lessons
- Track and field (not included in this book)—4 lessons
- Modified softball—4 lessons on fielding skills and concepts

Sixth Grade

Continue to focus on skills acquisition and the basic rules related to the skills. Then use the skills so that practice becomes a game by using relays or timed contests to see how many times, how far, or how fast they can do the skills. Plan a lesson at the end of the unit to integrate the skills into a real (but modified) game.

- Soccer—8 lessons
- Folk dance—8 lessons
- Volleyball—8 lessons
- Educational gymnastics—8 lessons
- Wrestling—4 lessons
- Fitness (aerobic activities)—6 lessons
- Basketball—10 lessons
- Modified softball (punchball and kick ball for fielding skills and concepts)—8 lessons

Seventh Grade

Use long units and emphasize fundamental skills and team cooperation.

- Adapt to locker room, including opening a lock and dressing in public—1 day
- Begin with fitness testing for a fitness index baseline—2 or 3 days
- Soccer—6 weeks
- Football throwing and catching skills—1 week
- Volleyball—6 weeks
- Aerobic dance (physical fitness)—4 weeks
- Basketball—5 weeks
- Educational gymnastics or wrestling—5 weeks
- Fitness reassessment—2 or 3 days
- Track and field—2 weeks
- Softball skills and modified game using fielding concepts—remainder of classes
- Locker cleanup and completion of student portfolios or cumulative records—1 day

Eighth Grade

Expect more consistency in fundamental skills, begin encouraging strategic control, and seek more team involvement.

- Football—6 weeks
- Soccer—2 weeks
- Dance or educational gymnastics—3 weeks
- Volleyball—6 weeks
- Aerobic dance (physical fitness)—4 weeks
- Fitness testing—1 week
- Basketball—5 weeks
- Pickleball or paddleball—5 weeks
- Softball—6 weeks

Ninth Grade

Increase the skills vocabulary, promote strategies when repeating activities, and introduce more individual and dual activities.

- Badminton—4 weeks
- Football—4 weeks
- Field hockey or lacrosse—6 weeks
- Dance (folk, square, country, and creative)—3 weeks
- Volleyball—6 weeks
- Weight training (physical fitness)—4 weeks
- Basketball—5 weeks
- Fitness testing—2 days
- Tennis or pickleball—4 weeks
- Softball—2 weeks

Tenth Grade

Expect greater control of the skills learned in 9th grade, more strategy, and more teamwork, and introduce more individual activities.

- Racket sport (tennis preferably)—4 weeks
- Football—3 weeks
- Field hockey, lacrosse, or soccer—3 weeks
- Dance (square, novelty, and folk)—3 weeks
- Volleyball—6 weeks
- Fitness—5 weeks
- Basketball—5 weeks
- Fitness testing—1 week
- Badminton, pickleball, or paddleball—4 weeks
- Softball—4 weeks

Eleventh Grade

Provide new athletic opportunities and leisure activities, and promote the development of social skills, leadership, group strategy, and athletic advantage.

- Team handball—4 weeks

- Golf—5 weeks
- Football or soccer—3 weeks
- Social dance—4 weeks
- Volleyball—6 weeks
- Physical fitness (choice of circuit training in weight room or aerobic training)—4 weeks
- Basketball—4 weeks
- Handball or paddleball—4 weeks
- Softball, lacrosse, or field hockey—4 weeks

Twelfth Grade

Provide more choice, some new team sports, and more lifetime activities.

- Team handball, field hockey, or tennis—4 weeks
- Football—2 weeks
- Lacrosse or soccer—2 weeks
- Badminton, handball, or pickleball—4 weeks
- Volleyball—7 weeks
- Social dancing (ballroom, country and western, and Cajun)—4 weeks
- Basketball—4 weeks
- Golf, wrestling, or educational gymnastics—6 weeks
- Softball, cross country, ultimate Frisbee, or lacrosse—4 weeks

Summary

Use these chapters as your road map to a wonderful physical education program with the knowledge that they have been developed by someone who is experienced and has tons of stories to tell that led her to these approaches, but who is not perfect and could certainly not make the perfect plan for every situation. You will have to think on your feet. I hope this book will help you do so with clarity once you are out there in front of your students.

Meeting National Standards for Physical Education

The NASPE national content standards for physical education are consensus statements that suggest elements that physical education professionals should incorporate in a quality physical education program. The standards provide direction toward an approach that will educate students so they graduate with the skills, knowledge, and motivation to engage in a lifetime of physical activity and healthy lifestyle practices. (A full list of the standards and a description of each are available on the NASPE Web site at www.aahperd.org/Naspe.) The standards assert that a quality physical education program does not focus on physical skill alone but rather provides a broad, balanced learning experience that also helps students develop their cognitive, social, and emotional skills. What follows is a discussion of how *Complete Physical Education Plans for Grades 5 to 12* meets the national standards for appropriate practices designated by NASPE.

Fully in line with the tenets of the national standards, the lessons in *Complete Physical Education Plans for Grades 5 to 12* are well balanced. They not only introduce motor skills and leave plenty of opportunity to allow refinement of those skills, they also promote a level of participation that will improve physical fitness while cognitive, social, and emotional understandings are achieved. A quick overview of the lesson plan shows how these important tenets are met.

- Each lesson contains performance goals and cognitive goals.
- The warm-up section calls for practice time and warm-ups that teach as well as warm up students, ensuring a high level of participation from the onset. It also promotes the skills acquisition and fitness goals of the national standards.
- Social and emotional skills are nurtured, particularly during planning of team activities.
    - All teams are created equal.
    - Class instruction and individual coaching hints during game play teach students how to work together.
    - As the level of play increases, lessons shift from a focus on skills acquisition to a focus on socialization, responsibility, initiative, cooperative learning, and ethics.

- Lessons give students time for practice to improve without pressure.
- The section on lesson safety highlights negative physical and psychological hazards that might crop up at particular points in a unit. It suggests how to guard against the negatives and how to deal with those that cannot be prevented outright.

To satisfy another tenet of the national standards, *Complete Physical Education Plans for Grades 5 to 12* offers a broad range of activities in 18 diversified units. Its table of contents is not the definitive list of activities that a physical education class should offer, however; a curriculum can vary due to regional differences and still meet NASPE recommendations. For example, handball is a popular game in my area and an excellent lifetime activity. It is also inexpensive, requires only one other person to play, can be played against almost any wall that has a concrete foreground, is so physical that fitness benefits abound, and is a great social outlet. Though handball is an excellent addition to my physical education program, I know that what is popular in New York City at the beginning of 21st century might not be as well received in other areas or during other times. The West Coast might favor in-line skating, mountainous areas downhill skiing, the Midwest cross-country skiing, and so on. It is impossible for this book to cover every activity that might interest students. Ultimately, my job and yours is to provide students with a solid foundation of skills, knowledge, and motivation that can apply across many activities so students are willing and able to seek a lifetime of activity and feel confident that when they are ready to learn something new, they will have the ability to learn it.

A major goal of the NASPE national standards is that programs use a variety of approaches to promote fitness, develop fitness knowledge, and increase emotional and social skills. To meet this goal, lessons in *Complete Physical Education Plans for Grades 5 to 12* are designed to maximize activity while encouraging students to think. This process occurs in a variety of ways. Sometimes the skills are taught outright. Sometimes, they are developed in response to a task (game situation). But always, activities begin at the bell and give students plenty of opportunity to practice and refine their skills. Concepts are woven into each demonstration, drill, and competition so that students understand what they are doing and why. Critical thinking, elicited throughout the lesson, helps students learn skills, improve their game plan, and answer leading questions at the end of the lesson during the review. Concepts integrated throughout each lesson can be assessed during a Socratic review or with the short written quizzes that follow each unit. Though beginner lessons emphasize skills more than subsequent lessons do, they include concepts and guidelines for teaching appropriate social and emotional behavior. Students have to learn to adjust to classroom work ethics, teacher-designated teams, responsibilities during tournaments, winning or losing, and all that goes into planning a team game strategy. Units have clear and realistic performance goals. Performance rubrics have been included at the end of each level and are suitable for self-assessment, peer assessment, or teacher assessment. General performance rubrics for activities not included in this book are provided in appendix B.

The following sections discuss the national standards and indicate how the lessons in this book fall into the proper practices category.

Refinement of Skills

Refinement of skills is a major goal that cannot take place in one lesson. In this book, meeting that goal begins by teaching the body mechanics of a skill during warm-ups. Mimetics, which was explained in chapter 1, is a great way to offer large-group practice that enables students to practice moving without the pressure of attending to anything other than the proper motion. In addition, lessons provide other practice opportunities that use the newly learned and practiced movement patterns in combination with materials. Practice opportunities are continually modified to increase speed, distance, and accuracy before combining new skills with those already learned. The rationale, practicality, and real-game purpose of a skill are identified early on. When possible, the skill is practiced as it would be used in a game. First, practice takes place without an opposing defense blocking the way (e.g., dribble to a goal and shoot, or set to a player who spikes). Then, after several days of practice and getting comfortable with the skill needed for offense, defenders are added to the equation. At this point, students are ready for the whole game.

Physical Fitness

The plans in this book organize physical activities to not only increase awareness and fitness but also fun, which is a prerequisite for any good physical education program. Fun is the best motivator—if students learn that participating is fun, they will be more likely to seek a lifetime of physical activity. However, enjoyment will not occur until students have real success

Give students the opportunity to practice and refine their skills so they are ready for the main event.

and feel as if they are somewhat in control. To achieve this, students need sport-specific skills, strength, and stamina. Admittedly, for many students the process of learning is not fun, so they are resistant. The lessons in this book account for that problem—the fun factor is not elusive and the pain factor is eliminated by the fitness factor.

In addition, each lesson aims to improve or maintain fitness. The goal of fitness is integral. *Complete Physical Education Plans for Grades 5 to 12* includes two fitness tests, one health based (Fitnessgram) and the other sports based (New York State Physical Fitness Screening Test). Each has norms and suggests a cumulative record so students can measure their improvement. In addition, the book includes two major fitness chapters, each unit focusing on fitness acquisition, health knowledge, and health safety. Fitness activities vary from level to level, as do the skills, safety concerns, and concepts that students will be learning. Lessons promote continual feedback using heart rate monitors, recovery rates, charting of daily circuit training progress, and biofeedback. With biofeedback, when new muscle groups are called into action, some students are left stiff and sore. Their body is telling them something, and they learn to listen. They learn to recognize their progress when their endurance and muscle strength improve. It does not take long before they appreciate that they are able to complete routines or keep up in games without feeling wiped out. This kind of feedback is not the principle of no pain, no gain. Students do not need to suffer pain to gain basic fitness benefits. Biofeedback can teach students the discomfort that occurs when one is not fit, but discomfort is different than pain.

Several batteries of activities indicate fitness levels and are included in the fitness testing chapter. This chapter explains how to most efficiently give the Fitnessgram and the New York State (NYS) Physical Fitness Screening Test, both of which make extensive use of standardized norms that can be exploited as teaching tools that give students another way of assessing themselves. Although relative fitness might not be fitness at all and statistical norms might not be a fitness indicator, the national standards encourage a variety of methods to give students feedback on their fitness levels. These two methods differ in that the Fitnessgram declares whether performance meets a healthy standard and the NYS fitness test uses statistics to show how students excel or fall below the average. In either case, norms help give students some sense of their success.

Using the scaled scores from the NYS fitness test can teach students to understand statistics, helping them to understand what the mean, median, and mode are and to appreciate that the largest segment of the population is considered to be average. NYS norms provide comparative analysis so students can measure themselves against a large population (the same-grade students in New York state) instead of just their classmates. They can compare their raw scores with those of other students of the same age, sex, and grade level to find out where they rank in the performance test. NYS fitness lessons test sport-related fitness and explain the bell curve, standard deviation, scaled scores, and percentile rank. Everything needed for a complete explanation is provided, including fitness forms, a bell curve with scaled scores, and charts broken down by age group, grade level, and sex.

Over the years I have seen how students react once they understand their percentile ranks. Their interest and reaction leads me to believe that this is important information for them. Knowing where they place among peers is not a turnoff. Instead, it motivates them to do their best. It's difficult to get students to work harder when they think that the best person in their class is the greatest and that everyone else is doing just fine. Norms give students a broader population with which to compare themselves. If the population represented by the charts performed better than them, then a teacher's prodding and pushing is more meaningful and students will react more favorably to future lessons.

Cognitive Goals

Cognitive goals are written into the lesson plans. Take, for example, the dribble. Along with learning how to dribble, students learn the reasons for it, the rules surrounding it, and the choices dribblers have. They learn some of the strategy, such as the reasons for not looking at the ball. They learn the physical laws affecting the return of the ball from the floor and the feel of equal and opposite reactions. They may even begin to understand more about

Use outside information to spark interest and encourage students to change their perceptions about activities they might not have considered before.

angles, because in the dribble, the lack of an angle will allow them to stay in one place while they bounce the ball. The addition of a small angle will let them move forward, and too much of an angle will make them lose control of the ball.

Cognitive understanding is enhanced by tying outside events and people in the news to the lesson. Sometimes outside information sparks interest and encourages participation, getting beyond the attitudinal and emotional barriers that kids sometimes set up to prevent learning. The motivation section suggests sharing information relevant to the lesson to get beyond students' resistance. For instance, when I introduced the dance unit the first years I taught coed classes, the boys were extremely resistant. Thank goodness for Lynn Swann. At the time he was a famous wide receiver who attributed his miraculous midair receptions and ability to land on his feet to ballet training. After I told his story, the guys who knew about his strength and courage on the football field took the information about dance quite differently. Their shock was enough to get them to back down from their opposition and I was able to move on with the plan for the day. When they had a similar reaction to tennis, feeling it was a sissy sport, information about the prize money that the top tennis players make changed their attitude in a nanosecond.

Perceptions and attitudes change if students can relate to the information you give them. Although I have included examples in the motivational section of many lessons, this information will get old, and teachers will have to change their heroes to meet the times and their region. Lynn Swann's story had a great impact on the students who saw him play every Sunday, but these days, most students have no idea who he is. His story won't have the same impact on students who have never heard of him.

Positive Social Behavior

The NASPE national standards call for the development of positive social behavior. Once again, *Complete Physical Education Plans for Grades 5 to 12* meets the challenge. Ethics, leadership, and citizenship are incorporated into lesson planning. Essential aspects of positive social behavior are included throughout the lesson plans, such as teamwork, personal responsibility, and appreciation of individual differences. Some units are social in nature (dance), and other units have phases wherein social activities are encouraged. Behavioral skills are an important aspect of each unit, though they are not assessed until training and maturity have had a chance to take effect. Behavior standards are part of the assessment system in the intermediate and advanced performance rubrics. The shaping of positive social behavior is left primarily to teachable moments.

Behavioral teachable moments vary in cause and action. If an activity is preferred or dominated by one sex, at some point in the unit poor behavior might need to be addressed. This is particularly true of immature groups. Let me share a situation that occurred in a coed 8th-grade flag football class. I made up teams so they were equal. Many of the boys, whose vision of football excellence was running 40-yard (37-meter) post patterns on every play, were downcast when they looked around and saw only one or two males on their team. Some refused to play. Others acted like male chauvinists and the six-on-six flag football game looked more like three on three. The guys took the ball, were the quarterbacks, and only threw to other guys on their team. Nothing I said changed their attitude, but soon the teachable moment took over. First, I set about teaching students how to plan, making use of the skills they had and working around their weaknesses. Understanding their strengths and weaknesses went hand in hand with encouraging defensive matchups that made sense (equal height, speed, or knowledge). This stifled some of the poor behavior, but not all.

Where the dominating male remained adamant about constructing plays that used only boys, I pointed out girls who were open. Still the quarterback would not throw them the ball. Instead, he risked interception after interception going for boys who were tightly covered, believing that somehow they would come up with the ball. The girls were frustrated, and I was frustrated. But, knowing it was best to let the game teach the lesson, I encouraged the other team to send their defense after the guy they knew would get the ball, double- and sometimes triple-teaming him. Eventually, I made my point and the quarterback finally abandoned his habit of ignoring the girls. When it worked out, and it always did, a girl received the ball and ran it in for a winning touchdown. The chauvinism disappeared completely and with it the antisocial behavior.

Bad language and negative attitudes are harmful to a healthy learning environment and should not be tolerated. Students need to learn to behave properly but will not do so if allowed to continue their behavior without correction. A technique that has worked for me involves temporarily removing the student from the activity, explaining that such behavior hurts feelings, and asking that the student apologize after recognizing that the class and teacher were hurt. With an apology to the class, the offending student can immediately reenter the game. Most often students learn to apologize. It takes a few minutes of cooling down before it happens, but once it does, with the exception of students with serious emotional problems, there is rarely a reoccurrence. Students with severe emotional problems may need the kind of intervention you are not able to provide. Do not feel embarrassed to use the support personnel in your building to get advice or have a place to send the student when all else fails. Meanwhile, the point is made and the situation is resolved quickly without anyone feeling victimized.

Complete Physical Education Plans for Grades 5 to 12 addresses the necessity of manipulating the environment so there is a place for everyone and the learning atmosphere is healthy. It reminds teachers of their homework—creating equal teams. It is expected that teachers will not let students talk their way off teams and will encourage students to make new friends. Lessons encourage a realistic acceptance of individual differences, discuss ways to identify strengths and weaknesses, and explain how to use them appropriately. In the final analysis, it is the teacher who maintains an atmosphere that promotes working together, accepting each other's limitations, living by the same rules, and eliminating egregious behavior.

Variety

The national standards call for variety, and *Complete Physical Education Plans for Grades 5 to 12* does much to comply. There are 18 activity chapters—2 on fitness and fitness testing; 6 on individual and dual lifetime sports; 1 on dance (teaching about rhythm, multicultural, and social activities); 1 on educational gymnastics; and 8 on team sports. There are 484 lessons, each teaching something new, whether it's a skill, idea, strategy, principle, or formation. Sports and activities repeated year after year (volleyball, basketball, fitness, dance) are not repetitious. Every lesson contains something new, expects better performance, increases knowledge, and raises the level of play.

- Sport activities are taught in a way students can enjoy. The emphasis is on how skills can be used in real play. Every lesson is designed for action. Relevant knowledge is imparted in short segments so it does not detract from the activity and can be easily assimilated.

- The fitness chapter presents three levels with three approaches, giving students who want a direct approach to fitness the options and knowledge about alternative ways to go about it.

- Dance is a chapter in itself. Numerous folk, square, country, social, and ballroom dances are suggested in three units so as to ease learning and produce different experiences. Variety ensures that some aspect of each lesson will appeal to different tastes and will be fun to do. Dance skills have an immeasurable lifetime social benefit. Dance skills are tapped during the aerobic fitness units in the lower levels and may also be the option chosen by juniors and seniors when developing their personal fitness program.

- Educational gymnastics uses a movement educational approach for using space, the body, and large equipment to find creative ways to move. Students who are not sport oriented will love the freedom to explore in this guided approach to movement. What is more, the chapter lends itself to dance choreography simply by eliminating lessons that incorporate equipment.

Instruction

The NASPE national standards call for instructional practices that lead to the following:

- Success: In *Complete Physical Education Plans for Grades 5 to 12,* activities are designed to increase basic skills incrementally so that within a lesson or two, students experience 100% success.

- Learning time: Time is adapted to class needs. Goals are realistic. Although most students will meet the goals by the end of each lesson, this text abandons the idea of moving ahead until 90% of the class is successful. The included CD-ROM enhances the teacher's ability to make such adjustments.

- Learning environment: Lesson plans give tips about how to deal with the frustrations that come up during the learning process and successful strategies for avoiding them. They identify activities in a clear progression so intermediate goals are apparent to everyone. Teachers and students can honestly cheer for accomplishments that might have seemed trivial to the uneducated eye.

- Feedback: A social environment like physical education is never absent of feedback, although sometimes it can be the wrong kind. Teacher feedback is necessary to undo the harm of demeaning and disrespectful comments from classmates and can be a wonderful teaching and motivational tool. This requires constant feedback, a sense of the mood of each student (those who are attacked are frequently unwilling to come forward and ask for help), and a willingness to involve oneself in the social drama of the group setting.

  A teacher's opinion is important. Teachers should be ready to compliment students on all kinds of intermediate successes because students frequently do not recognize the value of their actions, especially when their performance did not result in a score or the win they wanted. Games frequently have an unrecognized hero or two, and it is up to teachers to recognize the unrecognized. Their words are inspiring and a great learning tool if done in a meaningful way on a regular basis. I remember a well-respected physical education teacher asking an untenured teacher whether he was being observed that day because she heard the untenured teacher make so many positive comments during class. It turned out, he was. Positive feedback should not wait for a teacher's day of observation. It should be ongoing.

  Unfortunately, positive reinforcement becomes meaningless if it is inaccurate. I worked with someone who was so positive he could make anyone feel better. He never tired of trying. One day he asked someone to demonstrate her bump pass and then, though it was totally out of control, he told the student and the class that it was great. Feedback stops serving a good purpose when it is too general or untrue. It undermines the credibility of the person giving it and does not teach students how to improve. Teachers can be truthful and still say nice things about a poor performance, but they must be selective. In this case, there were positive details he could have addressed. The student had the courage to demonstrate in front of her peers. She reacted to the ball well, got under it, had her arms prepared properly, and had her knees bent. Those aspects were excellent and worthy of mentioning. But it was clear to the demonstrator and the class that something had gone wrong, because the ball sailed wildly out of control. It was up to the teacher to point out why. In this case, her follow-through was incorrect and the ball went flying behind her. Teachers who want kids to feel good about themselves can do so by highlighting the positive aspects of their performance before going on to explore ways to improve. Students appreciate honesty.

  Feedback should not be dependent on the teacher; other forms should be available, too. Feedback should be available from self-testing situations, scores and statistics, and classmates.

- Inclusion: The national standards call for instructional practices that provide for all students, regardless of their ability, gender, race, or ethnicity. In *Complete Physical Education Plans for Grades 5 to 12,* every student is involved, including those with medical problems or other disabilities. General teaching tips are given in each chapter's learning experience outline. They suggest ways to include students who cannot take part in the normal class activity. If teachers need more detail, it is suggested that they explore publications for adapted physical education.

- Practice: Practice makes perfect, and the lessons in this book provide many opportunities for more practice. A short practice time is set aside at the beginning of lessons so that students can practice individually and teachers can work with those who are having difficulties without taking up class time or making learning problems obvious to classmates. Warm-ups that include mimetics provide daily practice of correct movement patterns. Drills are uncomplicated and allow a lot of repetition. Every effort is made to provide enough practice that students become proficient within their age and experience level.

- Group formation: Groups are arranged in a variety of ways. During practice, students are organized by attendance rows or some other nondiscriminatory arrangement. Occasionally

It is important to provide a learning environment for all students, regardless of their ability, gender, race, or ethnicity.

students assemble with friends. Tournament teams are always prearranged by the teacher.

• Teaching styles: These styles vary according to the goals of the lesson. Sometimes groups are addressed as a whole and perform in unison, and other times the problem to be solved is given to everyone but developed individually. Sometimes lessons are specific to need and student. For example, an 8th-grade football captain complained that his team dropped his passes and that no one could hold on to the ball. He was frustrated because he used the pass exclusively and his team could never score without catching his passes. I used an individual discourse to redirect his thinking. On the way to the football field, I asked him a number of questions. Did the team practice throwing and catching before the game started? They did. Could they catch during practice? Yes, they never had problems at close ranges. What other ways could he advance the ball? He could run it, but never tried.

By answering leading questions, he realized he could control the ball with short passes or the run, get a few yards each play, use the clock, and avoid incompletes and interceptions by just going for the down markers and taking all three plays to get there. He got so excited that it did not matter that his team had lost all the previous games and could never win the tournament. When we got to the field, he ran off to start the game and try his new strategy. He was beaming on the return. You can imagine how excited his team members were when they used their strengths, avoided their weaknesses, and came up winners.

• Learning styles: To reach everyone and provide for all learning styles, lessons include demonstrations, coaching and sound cues, blackboard diagrams and charts, kinesthetic feedback, biofeedback, repetition, and technology when possible.

• Warm-ups: Warm-ups are planned and varied. They use time in a guided, safe, focused, and productive way.

Assessment

Assessment plays an important role in the national standards. *Complete Physical Education Plans for Grades 5 to 12* meets the assessment requirements in several ways.

- Assessment is ongoing. Daily observation helps teachers decide the best approach for subsequent lessons and appropriate ways to divide the class in teams and tournaments.

- Specific skills and behavioral goals are listed in a skills rubric at the conclusion of each unit for each skill level, as is a short quiz.

- Physical fitness testing allows students to compare previous performance to new performance as well as to others of the same age, sex, and grade level. It also allows students to measure themselves against a health standard.

- Classroom atmosphere during assessment is normal because it is reality based. It occurs during activity, when students do what they do and are not concerned about being graded.

- Self-assessment comes in many forms: student portfolio checklists, biofeedback (checking heart rates and output), recognition of one's performance among peers, measures against statistical norms, and objective assessment based on performance rubrics and quizzes.

- Outside assignments can lead to learning enrichment and parent feedback. The fitness unit asks students to inventory their family lifestyles and encourages sharing information at home.

- Interpretation to the public is provided through a letter to parents explaining and identifying the reason for fitness and the fitness ranking of their child, as well as via a sheet for every unit that explains the value of the activity and its benefit. The Fitnessgram reports provide a detailed analysis of students' activities and the health standard, and they individualize conclusions and suggestions based on the student's test results.

- Class attire is a school policy and is not addressed in this text with the exception of the dance and golf units, when students are asked to wear street clothes and sneakers since social dancing and golfing are usually done in street clothes and not in a special uniform.

Summary

In short, I have more than explained how *Complete Physical Education Plans for Grades 5 to 12* has met and exceeded the NASPE standards. You can follow the plans in each unit with secure confidence that you are doing the right thing, meeting national standards, raising the level of your students, and providing a healthy learning environment in which they can function well.

PART II

Fitness Units

Physical Fitness

Chapter Overview

1. Each lesson focuses on one key health-related fitness concept and includes at least 20 minutes of physical activity, a warm-up, and a cool-down. To explain the relevance of health-related fitness and how students can improve their fitness, the discussion includes the following:

   - The short- and long-term benefits of fitness (looking and feeling better, being able to do more, having better health and a longer life, avoiding major diseases, having a better quality of life)
   - How different activities have a different intensity and how intensity affects the burning of calories
   - How cardiorespiratory health improves through regular activity and why it is important to good health
   - Basic concepts in understanding the cardiorespiratory system and its functions:
     - Resting pulse and how to measure it
     - Finding one's maximum heart rate
     - Finding a beginner's target heart rate
     - Finding the target heart rate of someone who is regularly active
     - Why working in the target zone improves cardiorespiratory fitness
     - The significance of a recovery pulse
     - How long it takes for a healthy heart to return to rest after vigorous activity
   - The definition of fitness as it relates to good health
     - The role of flexibility and how to safely improve it
     - The role of muscular strength and how to safely improve it
     - Benefits of abdominal strength
   - How aerobic and anaerobic activity differ

»continued

»continued

- The role of endurance and appropriate methods for developing endurance
- The roles of warm-ups before and cool-downs after vigorous activity and appropriate methods for warming up and cooling down
- Body composition (muscle bulk versus body fat) and its relationship to good health
- Safety concerns during workouts
- Types of activities that most enhance cardiorespiratory fitness

2. Students develop a personal fitness program that includes activities to address muscular strength and endurance, aerobic fitness, flexibility, and body composition.

3. To enable students to keep track of all they have learned about fitness over the years, have a resource to check for facts they may have forgotten, and focus their thinking on where and how they can continue to participate in fitness activities, three student handouts have been included: a study sheet, extension project, and student portfolio checklist.

Physical Fitness Study Sheet

Fun Facts

- George W. Bush was the first president since John F. Kennedy to encourage the nation to follow his lead and become fit. He ran 4 to 6 miles (6.5-9.5 kilometers) daily until knee problems caused him to switch his aerobic workout to off-road biking.

- Roughly 80% of female executives spent their youth in sneakers and continue to be active. They credit being active in sports for the skills and discipline that helped make them successful in the boardroom.

- A pound (.5 kilogram) of muscle burns 50 extra calories a day. A 200-pound (91-kilogram) bodybuilder with 6% body fat burns more calories watching TV than a 160-pound (73-kilogram) woman with 30% body fat sitting next to him.

- Bursts of 10 minutes of exercise scattered throughout the day clear away artery-clogging fat better than a single 30-minute workout.

- Tennis champions Ivan Lendl and Martina Navratilova were the first tennis professionals to improve their on-court abilities with workouts off the court.

- Properly stretching the hamstrings helps prevent sciatic pain in the back.

History

The ability of humans to survive has been dependent on fitness for thousands of years. Our ancestors' survival depended on their energy and strength to hunt, kill, and bring back prey. From 2,500 to 200 BC, the teachings of Confucius encouraged regular activity to benefit health, and kung fu is the outgrowth of that belief. Striving to balance the spirit, body, and mind, the practice of yoga developed in India. Fitness was important in Persia in the Middle East because of the power it gave to armies. The ancient Greeks idealized physical perfection, believing that a healthy body was necessary to harbor a sound mind. Athens, the home of democracy, is also the home of the fitness ideal.

As societal roles became more specialized, with masses of people able to survive without using physical skill, the need for special attention to exercise simply to maintain physical fitness became more acute. Today, the pursuit of physical fitness is not only a growing personal goal but a major industry.

Important Terms

- interval training—Repeating intervals of high-intensity work are followed by intervals of rest or low activity.
- resistance training—Strengthening exercises work against an opposite weight or force.
- aerobic—Exercising with air (breath) promotes cardiorespiratory endurance.
- anaerobic—Intense activity (over 85% target heart rate) burns fuel without oxygen, producing lactic acid.
- resting pulse—The number of times the heart beats per minute when the body is at rest is your resting pulse.
- maximum pulse—The theoretical maximum heart beats per minute is 220 minus your age.
- target heart rate—The zone you should work in depending on your experience level and your goal to improve cardiorespiratory fitness is 65% to 85% of your maximum heart rate
- recovery pulse—The length of time it takes for your heart to return to a resting pulse after maximum exertion is your recovery pulse.

Physical Fitness Extension Project

Name _____ Date _____

Teacher _____ Class _____

What materials do you need to work out on your own?

Is there a fitness program at school? Who is the adviser?

Is there an after-school fitness program? Who is in charge?

Where can you work out outside of school?

Do you have friends who would join you? List their names.

What are the health benefits of participating in a fitness program?

Physical Fitness Student Portfolio Checklist

Name _____ Date _____

Teacher _____ Class _____

_____ Knows the components of personal fitness.

_____ Understands the importance of maintaining cardiorespiratory fitness.

_____ Understands the importance of maintaining flexibility.

_____ Understands the difference between strength and endurance.

_____ Understands how to measure physical endurance.

_____ Knows how to measure body composition and how to change it.

_____ Understands how body weight is affected by physical activity.

_____ Understands that fitness is related to personal health and happiness.

_____ Knows their personal fitness levels meet established health standards.

_____ Has followed a school plan to reach or sustain a healthy fitness standard.

_____ Has knowledge of safety factors involved in physical improvement programs.

_____ Is aware of the impact of activity on fitness, weight, appearance, and stress.

_____ Is developing interests and skills in lifetime activities.

_____ Has developed a lifetime plan to maintain and improve physical fitness.

From Isobel Kleinman, 2009, *Complete Physical Education Plans for Grades 5 to 12, Second Edition* (Champaign, IL: Human Kinetics).

Physical Fitness Learning Experience Outline

Contents and Procedure

1. Lessons focus on a key health-related concept as students warm up, have 20 minutes of robust activity, and stretch and cool down.

2. During extensive fitness activity, students gain insight into why physical fitness is important and how to improve theirs. These are the concepts taught:

    a. History of concern about physical fitness

    b. Relationship of fitness to health

    c. Health fitness standards and measures

    d. Cardiorespiratory response to different exercise levels

    e. Basic concepts of the cardiorespiratory system:

    - Resting pulse: what it is and how to measure it

    - Maximum pulse rate: how to determine it

    - What target pulse rate will improve cardiorespiratory fitness

    - Significance of recovery pulse

    f. What it means to work in a target heart rate zone

   g. Areas one must attend to in order to be considered fit
- Need for and method of maintaining or improving flexibility
- Need for and method of maintaining or improving muscular strength
  - Importance of abdominal strength
- Length of time it takes for a healthy heart to return to a resting pulse after vigorous activity

   h. How aerobic exercise differs from anaerobic exercise

   i. How to develop endurance

   j. Reasons for and proper methods of warming up and cooling down

   k. Muscle bulk verses body-fat composition

   l. Safety concerns (hydration, clothing, injury, healing, warming up, stretching)

   m. Understanding of the activities that most improve physical fitness

This chapter is not complete until students develop a personal program of fitness including weight resistance, aerobic training, or a combination of both.

Teaching Tips

All lessons in this book intend to enhance physical fitness, but this chapter is different—it specifically focuses on physical fitness. At the end of each unit in this chapter, students should understand why they should maintain their fitness and how they can do a variety of activities that will help them stay fit. Students will learn to consider activities for their health value as well as for enjoyment, and they will learn how to measure their progress as they partake in the activities.

The fitness chapter uses an interdisciplinary approach. As scientific and health concepts are explored during the students' workout, the gym becomes an unofficial physiology lab. Aerobic activity is the vehicle for cardiorespiratory fitness. Dance is the perfect aerobic fitness partner since it requires sustained activity that can be slow, moderate, or vigorous. While dancing to gain fitness, students learn

- social customs of different cultures,
- how to interact in a social forum,
- the relationship of weights to the laws of physics,
- the physiological principles behind resistance training,
- the relevance of strength, and
- how to relate health concepts to one's own functioning.

Students work harder if what they are asked to do is both fun and challenging and if their teacher is a role model. Exercise videos are a poor substitute for an active teacher in a large-group setting. Too often, the teacher sits to the side, turns on the TV, and expects students to enthusiastically imitate what they cannot hear or see well. Teachers don't always realize that only the students in front can hear the music and see the nuances on the screen. Television sound simply cannot be amplified sufficiently to be heard in a gym. Nothing compares to having a live role model who can respond to class difficulties with a smile, encouragement, and enthusiasm while demonstrating and leading the class through their self-consciousness. If you feel there is no choice but to use the TV, place the best students in front so the rest of the class can imitate them. Amplify the sound so everyone can hear the music. Music carries most students because they are inspired by the beat. If they can't hear it, many will lose interest and simply stop.

If you choreograph your own routine (being creative takes time, but it is worth it), build the routine by patching together dances you've created with dances you've already taught. When creating a dance pattern, match it to a tune that is popular with the students and has the correct energy level. With the students' help, choreograph two to four 16-beat passages. Teach one passage at a time and then combine them. Put on the music and have the students dance it through until the end of the music. (Note: Students work hard if they love the music and can learn the patterns quickly.) Once students know enough patterns that doing one after another will take the entire class time, put the music together so it will run through from warm-up to cool-down.

Here are some typical folk, square, and novelty dances with different energy levels (see chapter 5 for details) and some music suggestions:

- For warm-up or cool-down—Saturday Night Fever Walk, Stepping Out, Pata Pata, Virginia Reel, Bingo, Misirlou, or Oh Johnny Oh

- For moderate activity—Seljancica Kola, Mayim, Hot Lips, To Ting, Vé David, Teton Mountain Stomp, or any square dance that has everyone moving at once

- For high energy—Salty Dog Rag, Jessie Polka, Nebesko Kolo, Sevila Se Bela Loza, Hora, or Sicilian tarantella

- Great 5-minute songs for exercising the abdominal muscles—"Man in the Mirror" by Michael Jackson or "Nikita" by Elton John

- For stretching and cool-down—"Imagine" by John Lennon

Here are some more tips for teaching physical fitness:

- Choosing the right music is vital. It is the driving force for many students who would generally avoid sweating in other arenas. Make sure songs have an energetic, inspiring rhythm and that the words have a message you want students to hear.

- Students have varying cardiorespiratory responses to the same activity. Overweight or inactive students may find easy activities taxing and their heart rates may exceed the level at which they should be working. Do not draw attention to those students. Simply teach the class what to do to keep going even when they need to reduce the energy level. (To reduce the heart rate, limit the range of movement away from gravity and the number of body parts moving.) This reduces the stress placed on the heart. For example, students can stay on the ground when the others jump, do three reps instead of four, or use less arm motion.

- Although you should suggest that discomfort during exercise is not always negative and that improvement may not feel good in the beginning, be careful not to push students too hard. Teach them about heart rate, target zones, and workout goals.

- Make it clear that students should progress at their own rate and learn when they're working either above or below their target zone.

- Avoid weight training for young students. Their age, developing growth plates, and emotional immaturity make weight training more of a risk than a benefit, particularly if the school is equipped with machines built for adult frames. I highly recommend that grades 5 through 8 follow the aerobic program within these pages, the fundamentals of which can be safely used with any age group. NASPE approves of modified weight training programs using resistance bands, medicine balls, and light free weights, but I believe that these activities are better used when students are older and follow instructions better.

- After a book is published, rules, skills, and strategies may change. Check Internet sites listed in suggested resources to keep up with the changes.

Facilities

- The space must be clean. Students will be on the floor during part of the class.
- The weight room should be a designated area. Equipment should be checked for safety. Students who are so small that the major pieces of equipment cannot be adjusted to their bodies should not be allowed to use that equipment.

Materials

- Lifestyle Fitness Index form
- Pens or pencils
- Stopwatch
- Blackboard or marker board
- Personal charts on which students can mark classroom work on a daily basis
- Music player with an amplifier capable of projecting sound over the noise of the students as they work out
- Music for the entire routine (two slow songs for warm-up and cool-down, two moderate songs for abdominal work and for beginning the cool-down, two high-energy songs to move the heart rate to the highest target zone, and one slow and sustained song for stretching)
- Light free weights, resistance bands, or medicine balls (recommendations appear within lessons)
- Heart rate monitor
- Skinfold calipers
- Weight scale

Unit Timeline

There are three units in this chapter. Each includes the following:

- 5 or 6 lessons to introduce the cognitive approach in segments while students work out, with a minimum of 20 minutes of physical activity
- 6 or 7 lessons that dedicate 95% of the time to physical activity
- 1 or 2 lessons for the teacher to assess students' physical and cognitive accomplishments and for a culminating activity

Recommendations

- Beginners (5th-8th grades) concentrate on an aerobic program.
- Intermediate students (9th-10th grades) learn a weight program.
- Advanced students (11th-12th grades) participate in a guided independent study program. Students will make many of their own choices and design their own program based on a teacher-guided master plan.

Assessment

1. Review the students' daily work chart in a circuit or weight training program.
2. Check that students enrolled in the aerobic program will be able to
   - move continuously without pausing for rest,
   - have a 5-minute choreographed warm-up,
   - perform 20 minutes of activity in the target heart rate zone,
   - have a 5-minute cool-down, and
   - attain mastery.

Suggested Resources

About.com. 2008. Stretching exercises. http://physicaltherapy.about.com/od/flexibilityexercises.

Fitness Magazine and K. Andes. 1999. *The complete book of fitness: Mind, body, spirit.* New York: Three Rivers Press.

Mayo Clinic. http://mayoclinic.com/health/HealthyLivingIndex/HealthyLivingIndex.

Power, S.K., and S.L. Dodd. 1996. *The essentials of total fitness: Exercise, nutrition, and wellness.* Boston: Allyn and Bacon.

Strand, B.N., and M.J. Scantling. 1996. *Fitness education: Teaching concept-based fitness in schools.* Scottsdale, AZ: Gorsuch Scarisbrick.

Universal Fitness Tester. 1999. Aerobic fitness information. www.aerobictest.com/fitnessInfo.htm.

Supplemental Assignments

Study sheets, student portfolio checklists, and extension project sheets have been provided for convenience. They will help students remember what they were taught and focus on the importance of continuing to be active in the future.

Warm-Up and Stretching

Facilities

Clean, clear area large enough for class to be able to safely move in

Materials

- Music player with good amplification
- Selected music such as "Saturday Night Fever," or video or DVD of aerobic routine
- Lifestyle Fitness Index for every student to take home

Performance Goals

Students will do the following:

- Perform a rhythmic, low-impact, aerobic warm-up.
- Note that their heart rate is strong and rapid after a high-energy activity.
- Properly stretch all muscle groups.

Cognitive Goals

Students will learn the following:

- How health is associated with fitness
- A short history of the current health crisis
- That aerobic activity does not take one's breath away
- An aerobic warm-up (low impact, mild activity)
- Why flexibility is important and how to maintain it through stretching

Lesson Safety

A clean floor is necessary to reduce the possibility of infection when students lie down.

Motivation

Explain that there are many ways to warm up. A proper warm-up elevates the heart rate and warms major muscle groups, but it does not require speed or an extreme range of motion. By pacing activity to music, they can exercise without losing their breath, which will help them build their endurance and cardiorespiratory fitness. Mention that they will be learning and reviewing several ways to move to music that are fun and vigorous and that will make up a routine that can be done aerobically.

Warm-Up

With music on as students enter, begin either dancing (if you chose a song they know a footwork pattern for) or jogging to the music. Choose something enjoyable for its beat, length (3-5 minutes), popularity, and message.

Lesson Sequence

1. Demonstrate and teach the warm-up you chose for the routine. Choose a dance such as the Saturday Night Fever Walk (see chapter 5 for instructions) for its length (5 minutes) and the fun it will provide. If you're not dancing, assign an activity that lasts 5 minutes (jogging to a lengthy song) to warm up the large muscle groups.

2. After students learn the warm-up dance and dance it through, discuss the following:

   a. In the U.S. health crisis of the 1960s, young men dying of heart attacks brought the fitness movement under the leadership of John F. Kennedy.

   b. The current health situation in the United States includes a population that is dangerously overweight and inactive.

   c. Fitness, health, and the pursuit of happiness are interrelated—the heart, bones, cancer, stress, aging, attitude, and social life are affected by exercise.

3. Ask students to feel their heart beating by pressing either on the right side of their neck or on their wrist under the thumb (see figure 3.1). Jog, jump, or hop for 1 minute. Find the pulse again and ask about the difference. Tell them that you will explain more in the next class.

4. Teach how to properly stretch the quadriceps (see figure 3.2), hamstrings (see figure 3.3), gastrocnemius muscles (see figure 3.4), lower back (see figure 3.5), groin (see figure 3.6), shoulders (see figure 3.7), and neck (see figure 3.8).

   a. Count static stretches lasting 16 seconds each.

   b. Let students know that for stretching to be most effecive, they should

   - have warm muscles;
   - hold the position, reaching farther only as they loosen up; and
   - try holding the position for a minute, as recommended by physical therapists.

Figure 3.1 Finding your pulse.

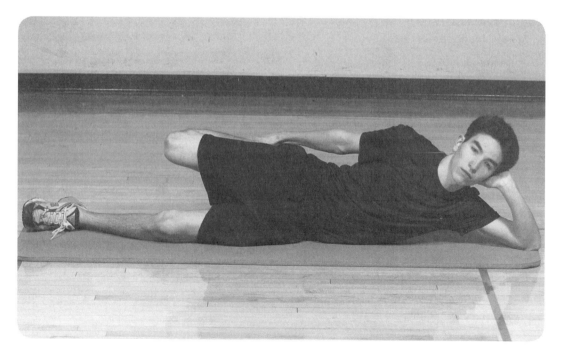

Figure 3.2 Quad stretch.

44

Figure 3.3
Hamstring stretch.

Figure 3.4 Gastroc-
nemius stretch.

Figure 3.5 Lower
back stretch.

Figure 3.6 Groin stretch.

Figure 3.7 Shoulder stretches.

a   *b*

Figure 3.8 Neck stretches.

a   *b*   *c*

Review

Ask if anyone thinks it is possible to be healthy but not fit. Explain that they have started a unit that will lead to dramatic improvement of their cardiorespiratory fitness. Fitness has several variables, and they just finished a lesson that should have piqued their interest about their heart and dealt with one aspect of fitness—their need to increase and maintain flexibility through stretching.

Homework

Ask students to take home the Lifestyle Fitness Index, read it, complete it with their family, and bring it back.

Lifestyle Fitness Index

Name _____ Date _____

Teacher _____ Class _____

This is a written test similar to the one devised at the request of the American Institute for Cancer Research and distributed in their 1997 summer issue.

_____ 1. Which best describes your activity level during the last 3 to 6 months?

   a. I participate in physical activity for a minimum of 20 minutes at least two to three times a week, such as brisk walking, jogging, swimming, cycling, weightlifting, and sports such as tennis, basketball, or handball.

   b. I participate in modest physical activity at least two to three times a week, such as golf, horseback riding, calisthenics, table tennis, bowling, or yard work.

   c. I do not regularly participate in recreational activities, sports, or other types of physical activity.

_____ 2. I make an attempt to increase my daily activity

   a. always (almost every day)

   b. occasionally (two to three times a week)

   c. seldom or never

_____ 3. I move at a relatively brisk pace (fast enough to tax my breathing, but not so fast I can't talk) without having to stop

   a. for 30 minutes

   b. for 10 to 20 minutes

   c. for 5 minutes or less

_____ 4. When I walk up a flight of stairs,

   a. I feel fine—it doesn't bother me

   b. I feel a little out of breath

   c. I feel very winded and tired

_____ 5. When I get up from a comfortable position,

   a. I have no problem

   b. I have to maneuver a little to get up

   c. I find it difficult to get up

_____ 6. If I have to carry two armloads of things and have to go the length of a football field to get to where I am going,

   a. without too much difficulty, I would make the effort to get there without help

   b. if I get there, my arms would be hurting and I would be out of breath

   c. no way would I bother—I would have someone come and get me in the car

_____ 7. I stretch my muscles or do yoga for at least 15 minutes

   a. regularly (3-6 times a week)

   b. about twice a week

   c. never

_____ 8. My back tightens up

   a. never

   b. during the day

   c. when I wake up

»continued

From Isobel Kleinman, 2009, *Complete Physical Education Plans for Grades 5 to 12, Second Edition* (Champaign, IL: Human Kinetics).

»continued

_____ 9. I would be able to balance on my strong leg

    a. 15 or more seconds

    b. more than 5 seconds but less than 15

    c. less than 5 seconds

_____ 10. Overall, I feel good about how much activity I do and how I eat

    a. almost all the time

    b. sometimes

    c. never

Scoring

Give yourself 3 points for each *a* answer, 2 points for each *b,* and 1 point for each *c.*

25 to 30 points: Congratulations, you're probably taking good care of yourself.

16 to 24 points: Not bad, but review your exercise program; increase intensity, duration, and flexibility.

Fewer than 15 points: This is a wake-up call. Accumulate 30 minutes of moderate exercise over the course of a day, every day. This will help shed weight, reduce stress, and reduce risk of certain types of cancers, heart disease, and other chronic illnesses.

From Isobel Kleinman, 2009, *Complete Physical Education Plans for Grades 5 to 12, Second Edition* (Champaign, IL: Human Kinetics). Reprinted, by permission, from the American Institute for Cancer Research, 1997, *American Institute for Cancer Research newsletter* (Washington, DC: American Institute for Cancer Research).

Learning About Heart Rate While Exercising at Varying Energy Levels

Facilities

Clean, clear area large enough for class to be able to safely move in

Materials

- Music player with good amplification
- Selected music such as "Saturday Night Fever," or video or DVD of aerobic routine
- Music for the abdominal and thigh routine
- Song with moderate to high energy

Performance Goals

Students will do the following:

- Move as they enter the room and finish the lesson by stretching.
- Measure their resting heart rate and their heart rate after a high-impact activity.
- Learn a high-energy activity, either a folk or a novelty dance that includes running, hopping, and a bit of jumping (if using a video, take an energetic section, break it down, teach it in parts, and have the class perform the high-energy section).
- Learn an abdominal-upper leg routine.

Cognitive Goals

Students will learn the following:

- The importance of flexibility (enables us to move through a full range of motion and prevents joint and muscle injury)
- That the heart is a muscle that works even when resting
- Two new aerobic activities

Lesson Safety

A clean floor is necessary to reduce the possibility of infection when students lie down.

Motivation

Music should be the driving force. Music that the students like to move to should be on as they enter the room, and students should start their warm-up to it as they enter. When the class has gathered, stop the music and ask them to lie down to rest because today they will learn more about how their heart works when they rest and when they work.

Lesson Sequence

1. Have students lie on the floor, explaining that they have to rest a few minutes in order to learn what their resting pulse is.

    a. Explain that the heart rate represents the number of times the heart beats in a minute. If they are wearing a heart rate monitor, they will get varied and immediate readings that show how hard the heart is working. To get a resting heart rate, they have to stop any activity, even standing, so they know how low their heart rate can get.

    b. Explain that the heart works even when it doesn't seem to (involuntary muscle).

    c. Teach how to find the pulse (use the index and middle finger to push on the wrist just below the thumb or push into the right side of neck, as in figure 3.1).

    d. Teach students that the throbbing they feel is a beat of the heart. Have them count it for 30 seconds. Multiply by 2 to get the resting heart rate.

2. Begin the warm-up routine taught in lesson 1.

3. Teach a routine that includes walking, running, jumping, or skipping. Teach in parts and in rhythm. Play the music through when each part is learned. Choose something that has no more than three parts and is self-repeating. For example, if you're using folk dance, try Sevila Se Bela Loza or the hora. If you want to use more modern music, try this rigorous 5-minute routine to Michael Jackson's "Beat It"—going counterclockwise, take 8 running steps forward, take 8 running steps backward with arms pumping in opposition, do 4 step-hops using same-side hand to touch the lifted heel, do 4 jumps so that legs straddle on first count and arms slap thighs, and then legs come together on second count and arms are lifted overhead. Repeat until the end of this almost 5-minute song.

4. Teach a routine for strengthening abdominal muscles and hip abductors. Try this routine to Elton John's "Nikita" or Bruce Springsteen's "My Hometown"—do 8 sit-ups with bent knees, roll to the right side and do 8 leg lifts with the left leg, and roll left to do 8 leg lifts with the right leg. Repeat until the end of the 5-minute song.

5. Conclude by doing stretches learned in lesson 1 as a routine to music, making sure each stretch is held 16 beats. Choose music that is slow and meaningful. Try John Lennon's "Imagine" or Michael Jackson's "Man in the Mirror."

Review

Ask the following:

- What activity helps the body avoid ripping its muscles and dislocating its joints? Discuss the importance and value of maintaining flexibility.

- Is the heart is an involuntary muscle or a voluntary one? Does it work when you rest?

- Can you remember your resting pulse? Did it get higher or lower when the body started moving? Anyone want to guess what it might be in the middle of moving to "Beat It"?

Physical Fitness
BEGINNER (GRADES 5-8)
LESSON 3

Increasing the Work Level and Measuring the Heart's Response

Facilities

Clean, clear area large enough for class to be able to safely move in

Materials

- Music player with good amplification
- Selected music such as "Saturday Night Fever," or video or DVD of aerobic routine
- Music for abdominal and thigh routine
- Music for a moderate- to high-energy routine
- Music for a high-energy routine such as Jessie Polka or Seljancica Kola, or a peppy, energetic tune such as Elton John's "Tell Me What the Papers Say"
- Heart rate monitors, if available

Performance Goals

Students will do the following:

- Raise their heart rate as they exert more effort.
- Perform a vigorous activity that can be sustained.

Cognitive Goals

Students will learn the following:

- The importance of the cardiorespiratory system to fitness
- How to find their theoretical maximum heart rate (220 beats – age = each person's maximum heart rate)
- What the saying "If you don't use it, you lose it" means in fitness

This book includes the standard formula of 220 minus age to calculate maximum heart rate, though a more precise formula is now available. Since the old formula is easy to remember, fairly accurate, and easier to use, we include it; however, if you want a precise calculation, go to www.fitnessforlife.org/HighSchool/teacher/TeachersInformation.cfm#formula.

Lesson Safety

A clean floor is necessary to reduce the possibility of infection when students lie down.

Motivation

Ask what they can expect from their hearts if they work longer, faster, and harder.

Lesson Sequence

1. Start with the designated warm-up.
2. Discuss how adding speed and more moving parts increases the demands on the heart. Use heart rate monitors if possible, noting how the heart rate increases with exercise.
3. Introduce a vigorous activity with jumps, runs, and arm movements. For example, try the Jessie Polka or a movement pattern to popular music with jumping, running, and arm swings. Or, use this routine to Elton John's "Tell Me What the Papers Say"—4 jogs in place with bent arms pumping, 4 twists in place, repeat the 4 jogs and 4 twists, 8 step-kicks in place starting with right step, left kick. Run 8 steps into the circle with arms circling forward, 8 steps back out with arms circling back. Step to right and bend for 4 windmills, touching right arm to left leg first. In place, bring elbows forward and back 4 times.
   - Teach the activity in segments.
   - Combine parts and sustain the activity until the music is over.
   - Have someone who performs well be the role model.
4. Get a reading of the heart rate and discuss the difference between resting rate and what it is now.
5. Do an abdominal routine. (If there's time, listen to "Beat It" or something similar.)
6. Conclude with the stretching routine.

Review

Ask the following:

- How can you make activity more demanding?
- When activity is too vigorous, how can you make it less demanding?
- What can you expect your heart to do when the activity is more vigorous?

Doing a Five-Part Routine While Learning About Maximum Heart Rate

Facilities

Clean, clear area large enough for class to be able to safely move in

Materials

- Heart rate monitors, if available
- Watch with second hand
- Music player with good amplification
- Selected music such as "Saturday Night Fever," or video or DVD of aerobic routine
- Music for abdominal and thigh routine
- Music for a moderate- to high-energy routine
- Music for a high-energy routine such as the Jessie Polka, or Seljancica Kola, or Elton John's "Tell Me What the Papers Say"

Performance Goals

Students will do the following:

- Measure their heart rate after it speeds up.
- Increase their aerobic routine to include a warm-up, moderate activity, vigorous activity, abdominal strength work, and stretching.
- Take a pulse reading after the warm-up and the most vigorous part of routine.

Cognitive Goals

Students will observe the following:

- How the cardiorespiratory system is affected by activity
- What happens to their pulse rate when doing different activities
- How high their heart rate goes after the most rigorous part of the routine

Lesson Safety

A clean floor is necessary to reduce the possibility of infection when students lie down.

Motivation

Music will be the motivating factor.

Lesson Sequence

1. Have soothing music playing as students enter. Ask them to lie down and relax, and then after a few minutes have them find their pulse. A heart rate monitor is effective here.
2. Perform the warm-up, telling students that they will need to take a pulse reading as soon as it is over. (If they have to count, signal when to start and stop, timing 30 seconds.)
3. Continue the routine, giving the same instructions at the end of the vigorous activity.
4. Begin the abdominal routine. Take a pulse reading afterward.
5. Perform the cool-down stretching routine. Take a pulse reading when it is over.

Review

Ask the following:

- What happened to the heart rate as the work got harder? What happened when it got easier?

- Do muscles get stronger or weaker with use?
- Is the heart a muscle that will benefit from more use?

Teacher Homework

Prepare and hang a chart of target heart rate zones (see lesson 5) relative to age.

Checking Heart Rates While Doing Moderate and Energetic Dances

Facilities

Clean, clear area large enough for class to be able to safely move in

Materials

- Chart of target heart rate zones plus Target Heart Rate Zones handout
- Heart rate monitors, if available
- Watch with second hand
- Music player with good amplification
- Selected music such as "Saturday Night Fever," or video or DVD of aerobic routine
- Music for abdominal and thigh routine
- Music for a moderate- to high-energy routine
- Music for a high-energy routine such as the Jessie Polka or Seljancica Kolo, or a peppy, energetic tune such as Elton John's "Tell Me What the Papers Say"

Performance Goals

Students will do the following:

- Perform the aerobic routine.
- Work in their target heart rate zone for at least 15 minutes.

Cognitive Goals

Students will learn the following:

- Components of working aerobically in one's target zone
    - Time
    - Heart rate
    - Oxygen use
- Updated recommendations for cardiorespiratory fitness (as of 2007, 1 hour of accumulated daily moderate exercise and 20 to 30 minutes of accumulated exercise at 60% to 85% of maximum heart rate)
- What is meant by *target heart rate*
- Their target heart rate zone
- Why people's zones differ and what it takes to reach them

Lesson Safety

A clean floor is necessary to reduce the possibility of infection when students lie down.

Motivation

Music and the fun of moving to it is the driving motivational force, so have the music for the warm-up on as students enter and have them participate as taught.

Lesson Sequence

1. After the warm-up and one vigorous song, check heart rates at the most vigorous point and ask students to remember them.
2. Finish teaching or introducing the last parts of the routine. Try adding Sevila Se Bela Loza to the routine. (See beginner dance unit in chapter 5 for instructions.)
3. Perform a moderate cool-down activity. Try Pata Pata. (See the beginner dance unit for instructions.)
4. Perform the stretching routine.

Review

Ask the following:

- Is your heart rate too high—are you losing breath? Can you reduce your effect doing the same activity?
- Is your heart rate too low? How can you increase your effort doing the same activity?

Teacher Homework

If the entire contents of the routine have been learned, record the songs so they run continuously. Start with the warm-up and then continue with a high-energy song, the song for abdominal workout, a more energetic song, a high-energy song, and a moderate song. End with the tune used for stretching. Here's a sample lineup: Saturday Night Fever Walk; "Beat It," "Nikita" or "My Hometown"; Sevila Se Bela Loza; "Tell Me What the Papers Say"; Pata Pata; "Imagine."

Target Heart Rate Zones

Name _____ Date _____

Teacher _____ Class _____

Age	Target heart rate zone (60%-85%)	Predicted maximum heart rate
9	126-180	211
10	126-178	210
11	125-177	209
12	124-177	208
13	124-176	207
14	124-175	206
15	123-174	205
16	122-173	204
17	122-172	203
18	121-171	202
19	121-171	201
20	120-170	200
30	114-162	190
40	108-153	180
50	102-145	170
60	96-136	160
70	90-123	150

Your actual values (determined from a graded exercise test) _____

Target heart rate: _____

Maximum heart rate: _____

From Isobel Kleinman, 2009, *Complete Physical Education Plans for Grades 5 to 12, Second Edition* (Champaign, IL: Human Kinetics).

Full Routine

Facilities

Clean, clear area large enough for class to be able to safely move in

Materials

- Music recorded in this sequence: warm-up, high energy, abdominal workout, moderate energy, high energy, moderate energy, cool-down dance (if time), and stretching
- Heart rate monitors, if available
- Watch with second hand
- Music player with good amplification

Performance Goals

Students will do the following:

- Perform in their target heart rate zone for a minimum of 15 minutes.
- Complete at least 30 minutes of activity without pause.

Cognitive Goal

Students will learn the minimal recommendation for achieving and maintaining cardiorespiratory fitness.

Lesson Safety

A clean floor is necessary to reduce the possibility of infection when students lie down. Remind students that if they are experiencing more than the usual discomfort, they should reduce their energy level and alert you.

Motivation

Music will be the motivation. Play it through the entire class.

Lesson Sequence

Music of already learned activities will provide the lesson sequence.

Review

Discuss the following:

- Is the routine getting easier for you to complete?
- Perhaps we are accomplishing our goal—fitness!

Evaluating Performance

Facilities

Clean, clear area large enough for class to be able to safely move in

Materials

- Recorded music for the aerobic dance routine
- Skills rubric for beginner's aerobic dance

Performance Goals

Students will do the following:

- Perform the beginner aerobic dance routine.
- Measure their recovery rate.

Cognitive Goals

Students will learn the following:

- How to assess cardiorespiratory fitness
- What the recovery rate is and how to measure theirs

Lesson Safety

A clean floor is necessary to reduce the possibility of infection when students lie down.

Motivation

After a few weeks of doing the routine, students know if it is getting easier to complete and can safely guess that if it is easier, they are also getting fitter. The time has come to learn how to measure the variables and get an objective measure of fitness. One way is to read the reactions of the body. The students watched how their heart met the challenge of working hard. Now, they will measure the speed at which it recovers from hard work. At the end of the routine, take notice of how long it takes for the heart rate to slow and return to resting once the activity stops. It is believed that the faster the heart rate returns to resting, the fitter you are.

Lesson Sequence

1. Do the entire beginner aerobic dance routine from start to finish.
2. Note the recovery pulse at the end of the first, second, third, fourth, and fifth minutes of stretching.

Review and Stretching

Stretching requires effort too, so students shouldn't expect that stretching will bring the heart to a true resting pulse rate. Ask the following:

- Whose heart rate decreased to 120 beats per minute at the end of the stretching routine?
- Whose got down to 100 beats per minute at the end of 5 minutes?
- That is great! The health standard after activity is completed is 120 beats after 5 minutes and 100 after 10 minutes. Lower than that is even better.
- Who has learned enough to share with their parents to help them to stay healthy?

Assessment

Assessment can be based on some or all of the performance standards in the beginner fitness rubric, the written quiz that follows, or the ability to meet predetermined goals measured by a fitness test.

The beginner physical fitness unit, which consists of aerobic dance, is recommended for grades 5 through 8, particularly since it is believed that resistance training should be avoided until most of the students' growing is complete. Specific dances have been suggested for the first year of the unit. It is hoped that when students take additional aerobic-fitness units, several changes take place.

1. Begin by assessing and charting the following (use the skills rubric as a guide):
   a. Resting heart rate, maximum heart rate, and average heart rate
   b. Flexibility
   c. Abdominal muscle strength
2. Introduce new dances and music so students become fitter and learn something new.
3. Finish by taking comparative measures of the following, as taken in the beginning: resting, average, and maximum heart rate; flexibility; and abdominal strength.

Beginner Physical Fitness Skills Rubric

Name _____ Date _____

Teacher _____ Class _____

	0	1	2	3	4	5
Flexibility Sit and reach	Must bend the knees to reach the knees with hand	Can reach knees	Can reach calves	Can reach ankle	Can grab sole of foot	Can touch nose to knees
Aerobic fitness Mile (1.5-kilometer) walk/run	Cannot complete	Takes full class	13-16 min	11-12:59 min	10-10:59 min	Less than 10 min
Abdominal strength 1 min sit-up test	Fewer than 9	10-19	20-24	25-29	30-39	40+
Upper-body strength Push-ups or pull-ups	Girls: 0-2 Boys: 0-3	Girls: 3-4 Boys: 4-6	Girls: 5-6 Boys: 7-9	Girls: 7-9 Boys: 10	Girls: 10 Boys: 11-13	Girls: 11+ Boys: 14+
Agility Sidestepping over lines 4 feet (1 meter) apart in 10 seconds (NYS fitness test)	Girls: 0-6 Boys: 0-8	Girls: 7-8 Boys: 9-12	Girls: 9-10 Boys: 13-15	Girls: 11-14 Boys: 16-18	Girls: 14-17 Boys: 19-20	Girls: 18+ Boys: 21+
Speed Shuttle run (NYS fitness test)	Girls: 29+ s Boys: 27+ s	Girls: 27.1-28.9 s Boys: 25.5-26.9 s	Girls: 25-27 s Boys: 23-25.4 s	Girls: 23.5-24.9 s Boys: 22-22.9 s	Girls: 22-23.4 s Boys: 20-21.9 s	Girls: 22 s or less Boys: 20 s or less
Balance Standing on one leg	0-2 s	3-4 s	5-8 s	9-12 s	13-18 s	19+ s

From Isobel Kleinman, 2009, *Complete Physical Education Plans for Grades 5 to 12, Second Edition* (Champaign, IL: Human Kinetics).

Beginner Physical Fitness Quiz

Name _____ Date _____

Teacher _____ Class _____

True or False

Read each statement carefully. If the statement is true, write a *T* in the column to the left. If the statement is false, write an *F*. If using a grid sheet, blacken in the appropriate column for each question, making sure to use the correctly numbered line for each question and its answer.

_____ 1. If you do more activity and eat the same amount, you are likely to lose weight.

_____ 2. If you need to catch your breath during an aerobic workout, you should slow down.

_____ 3. Shortened muscles and a reduced range of motion are the typical result of strengthening muscles without stretching them.

_____ 4. The best way to stretch is to bounce to the position you want to reach.

_____ 5. Football is an excellent aerobic activity.

_____ 6. The cardiorespiratory system is the body's engine.

_____ 7. The recommended minimum activity to achieve and maintain cardiorespiratory fitness requires that the heart rate be raised to 220 beats per minute.

_____ 8. Endurance means that you tire easily.

_____ 9. Physical strength and endurance are not important since our society is so wealthy that we can avoid doing physical things.

_____ 10. A good, quick way to reduce stress is to move your body so that you raise your heart rate.

Extra Credit

In the column on the left, put an *A* for activities that can be done aerobically and an *N* for activities that are anaerobic in nature.

_____ 1. Swimming

_____ 2. Weightlifting

_____ 3. Bicycling

_____ 4. Soccer

_____ 5. Tennis

From Isobel Kleinman, 2009, *Complete Physical Education Plans for Grades 5 to 12, Second Edition* (Champaign, IL: Human Kinetics).

Beginner Physical Fitness Answer Key

True or False

1. T—Use more calories than taken in.
2. T—Cannot participate for 20 minutes if you cannot breathe.
3. T—Strengthening exercises teach muscles to contract, thereby shortening them.
4. F—Static stretches are recommended to avoid injury.
5. F—Aerobic activity requires continuous motion with breath, and football is not continuous.
6. T—The heart, arteries, and veins are the engine for supplying the body with its energy needs.
7. F—The estimated maximum heart rate is 220 beats per minute, a rate that declines as one gets older.
8. F—Endurance is the ability to continue; tiring prevents endurance.
9. F—Physical activities are necessary to maintain health.
10. T—Raising your heart rate means you are doing activity, and physical activity reduces stress.

Extra Credit

1. A
2. N
3. A
4. N
5. N

From Isobel Kleinman, 2009, *Complete Physical Education Plans for Grades 5 to 12, Second Edition* (Champaign, IL: Human Kinetics).

Introduction to Weight Training: Upper Body

Facilities

- Clean, clear area large enough for class to be able to safely move in as everyone jogs, imitates exercises, and stretches at the same time
- Weight machines such as Universal or Nautilus that are certified as safe

Materials

- Music system with good amplification
- Selected music for the aerobic warm-up and stretching
- Weight machines with pins, free weights, resistance bands, or medicine balls

Performance Goals

Students will do the following:

- Take their resting pulse.
- Begin working on a circuit training program using the weight room, including the following:
  - Warm-up
  - Upper-body strength
  - Stretching

Cognitive Goals

Students will learn the following:

- A short history of fitness and its relevance to them, their families, and others
  - How lack of exercise leads to poor fitness
  - How personal health is enhanced by fitness
  - Current research on the effects of fitness
- How to reflect on personal fitness strengths and weakness
- What circuit training is and how it improves fitness
- What every good circuit should include
  - Warm-up
  - Specific exercises for improving strength
  - Specific exercises for improving flexibility
  - Specific exercises for improving agility
- What machines are used for aerobics (rowing machine, bike, treadmill, stair stepper)
- Exercises dedicated to strengthening the upper body

Lesson Safety

Most weight rooms have large machines for each exercise, but certainly not enough for everyone to do what is demonstrated at the same time. Rather than have everyone watch an activity and lose the opportunity to practice the proper body mechanics of each exercise, have all students do a set of exercise by imitating the motion of the person demonstrating. This keeps students active, safe, involved, and learning the right movement patterns during crucial introductory lessons. In addition, the following are needed for lesson safety:

- Enough space to allow the entire class to move safely
- Clean floor
- Equipment certified for safety

- Monitoring of students
  - Use of safe weights (This is a fitness program, not a bodybuilding program or challenge to see who lifts the most. Approaches and safety precautions differ for each.)
  - Proper breathing
  - Going through the entire range of motion
  - Avoiding machines that do not adjust to their size
  - No throwing free weights
  - No overloading bar
  - No using free bars without spotting

Motivation

In introducing this unit, explain that most people go to the gym to work out with weights so they can accelerate their fitness gains. Some people train to get stronger and increase muscle bulk. Others simply want more muscle definition that sculpts the body. Depending on how much weight is used and how many repetitions are performed, students can train for either goal or both. Explain that all the exercises can be done without weight but would require many more repetitions to get the same benefit. For these early days, explain that you want everyone to focus on the mechanics because you want them to get the benefits without risking the injuries. Emphasize that improperly using weights can accelerate injuries, too.

Warm-Up

The warm-up should be rhythmic and use large muscle groups. It should last 3 to 5 minutes and can be a jog to music, a dance already choreographed, or use of the aerobic equipment available (e.g., bikes, stair climbers, treadmills, and rowing machines).

Lesson Sequence

1. Give a short explanation of the following:
   a. National health crisis of the 1960s and of current times
   b. How fitness and health are interrelated, including the impact of exercise on the heart, bones, cancer, stress, aging, attitude, and social life
   c. Working a circuit for total-body fitness
   d. Ingredients of fitness
      - Cardiorespiratory endurance
      - Muscle strength
      - Muscle endurance
      - Flexibility (range of motion around a joint)
      - Body composition (bone and muscle mass compared with body fat)
2. Introduce exercise for the deltoids using the specific machine or free weight.
   a. Have a student demonstrate, making sure to emphasize proper alignment.
   b. Have students do a set (8-12 reps) as a group, with or without weight, making sure their motion is correct and that they are breathing properly.
3. Follow the same procedure for the biceps, triceps, latissimus dorsi, pectoral, and neck muscles.
   a. Use the appropriate machine, demonstrating how to set the proper seat alignment and find a weight that allows them to do 10 repetitions of the exercise.
   b. Have students mimic the proper exercise without weights.
   c. Remind everyone to breath properly.
4. End with a stretching routine (same one used in the aerobic program; see lesson 1 of the beginner unit).

Review and Stretching

As students stretch, remind them that all exercise can be done without weight, but that by adding some, they can accomplish the same thing in fewer repetitions. Have them imagine the number of reps they'd have to do and the time it would take to duplicate the effort of doing 10 contractions at a machine set at 40 pounds (18 kilograms). Weights make for time-efficient workouts and quicker muscle development.

Weight Training: Lower Body

Facilities

- Clean, clear area large enough for class to be able to safely move in as everyone jogs, imitates exercises, and stretches at the same time
- Weight machines such as Universal or Nautilus that are certified as safe

Materials

- Music system with good amplification
- Selected music for the aerobic warm-up and stretching
- Weight machines with pins
- Free weights, resistance bands, or medicine balls

Performance Goals

Students will do the following:

- Perform a warm-up.
- Complete their introduction to exercising the upper-body muscle groups.
- Perform exercises for the legs.
- Cool down while stretching.

Cognitive Goals

Students will learn the following:

- Dangers of using supplements to enhance performance
- Value of warming up (preventing injuries)
- Value of stretching (improving flexibility to prevent injuries)
- Exercises for the hamstrings, quadriceps, and gastrocnemius muscles
- Anterior cruciate ligament (ACL) injury prevention when strengthening the hamstrings
- Exercises for the ankle and hip joints

Lesson Safety

The following are required for lesson safety:

- Enough space to allow the entire class to move safely
- Clean floor to reduce the possibility of infection when students lie down
- Equipment certified for safety
- Monitoring of students
  - Use of safe weights
  - Proper breathing
  - Going through the entire range of motion
  - Avoiding machines that do not adjust to their size

- No throwing free weights
- No overloading bar
- No using free bars without spotting

Motivation

Explain that lots of athletes like power because they feel that it generates better performance and so they go to the gym to bulk up. This brings to mind Mark McGwire and Sammy Sosa, who exceeded home-run records beyond what anyone thought possible by doing strenuous weight training, but also using so-called natural supplements. In 2007, Mark McGwire lost the opportunity to get into the National Baseball Hall of Fame because of his use of supplements. This is an issue you should spend time talking about because some students have reached the age where they want to bulk up. Ask if the topic of natural supplements has come up in health class. Do any of them use natural supplements? Tell the class that you will discuss this and the dangers associated with these supplements later, but for now you want to teach them how to exercise their lower body.

Warm-Up

As students enter the room, they should begin the warm-up. Choose music that lasts 5 minutes and have them jog or dance to the music; use the rowing machine, bike, stair climber, and treadmill; or perform any combination of these, as long as students are all moving to each beat of the music.

Lesson Sequence

1. Introduce the upper-body muscle groups not previously taught and practiced.
   a. Have a student demonstrate how to align the machine correctly and how the exercise is performed on the machine.
   b. Have students all do the exercise with or without the weight.
   c. Make sure everyone breathes properly during the exercise.
2. Demonstrate the leg curl and proper alignment for the hamstrings.
   a. Explain the necessity of the hamstrings having at least 75% the strength of the quadriceps in order to avoid hyperextension and a possible tearing of crucial knee ligaments. Developing the quadriceps for power and ignoring the hamstrings endangers the knee. If hamstrings do not have 75% the strength of the quadriceps, the quadriceps can cause the knee to hyperextend, which will rip the ACL ligament that stabilizes the knee.
   b. Have students duplicate the exercise even if not at a machine.
   c. Show all the machines for the leg curl.
3. Demonstrate extension and proper alignment for the quadriceps.
   a. Have students duplicate the exercise even if not at a machine.
   b. Point out machines for upper quadriceps and lower quadriceps.
4. Repeat process for the gastrocnemius muscles and for ankle flexors.

Review and Stretching

As students stretch, lower the music to discuss the following:
- Supplements have widespread use, and use has changed over time.
  - Historic dangers of supplements
  - Monetary enticement to get more power
- Warming up and stretching are important.
  - Warmth makes muscles elastic; without elasticity, they can tear.
  - Stretching reminds muscles to return to their longest state.
  - Strengthening muscles also shortens them.
  - Rigorous training programs inadvertently promote shrinkage of muscles.
- The more advanced or older an athlete, the more important warm-ups and stretching are.
- Ask if anyone remembers why it is important to do leg curls when working to strengthen the quadriceps.

Circuit Training

Facilities

- Clean, clear area large enough for class to be able to safely move in as everyone jogs, imitates exercises, and stretches at the same time
- Weight machines such as Universal or Nautilus that are certified as safe

Materials

- Music system with good amplification
- Selected music for the aerobic warm-up and stretching
- Weight machines with pins
- Free weights, resistance bands, or medicine balls

Performance Goals

Students will do the following:

- Warm up.
- Perform new exercises for the lower body.
- Use proper alignment and breathing during each exercise.
- Perform exercises for the abdominal muscles, back, and neck.
- Cool down while stretching.

Cognitive Goals

Students will learn the following:

- Why it is important to strengthen the abdominal muscles
  - The back is structurally vulnerable.
  - Abdominal muscles neutralize the structural weakness of standing upright.
- How to perform remaining exercises for lower-body muscle groups
- How to identify and safely use machines for the abdominal and back muscles
- Different sets of exercises are needed to work the upper body, lower body, and torso
- A safe routine for working with weights

Lesson Safety

The following are required for lesson safety:

- Enough space to allow the entire class to move safely
- Clean floor
- Equipment certified for safety
- Disciplined environment where students are monitored to make sure they follow rules and guidelines established in earlier lessons

Motivation

After this lesson, students will have been introduced to every machine for every muscle group and can begin working out with a partner of choice at their own pace.

Warm-Up

Students will begin their warm-up to music as they enter the room.

Lesson Sequence

1. Complete whatever exercises have not already been introduced for the lower body, using the procedure indicated in previous lessons.

2. Discuss the following:
    a. General body alignment and why the back is prone to difficulties
    b. Why abdominal muscles are so important to strengthen
    c. The machine or exercise that students are to use daily for strengthening the abdominal muscles
    d. How to perform the exercise (with or without weight resistance)
3. Discuss the importance and methods of working the body safely.
    a. Develop opposite muscle groups equally.
    b. If there isn't enough time to do it all in one class, alternate upper-body, lower-body, and torso exercises.
4. Allow students to begin working out with partners for the remaining time.
5. Conclude each lesson with stretching.

Review and Stretching

As students stretch, ask the following:

- Why is so much attention given to developing abdominal muscles?
- Is it necessary to have a special machine or setup to develop the abdominal muscles?

Physical Fitness
INTERMEDIATE (GRADES 9-10)
LESSON 4

Breathing Technique

Facilities

- Clean, clear area large enough for class to be able to safely move in as everyone jogs, imitates exercises, and stretches at the same time
- Weight machines such as Universal or Nautilus that are certified as safe

Materials

- Music system with good amplification
- Selected music for the aerobic warm-up and stretching
- Weight machines with pins
- Free weights, resistance bands, or medicine balls

Performance Goals

Students will do the following:

- Pick a partner to work with.
- Follow the established routine at their own pace.

Cognitive Goals

Students will understand the following:

- Importance of breathing
    - Working with weights can be aerobic.
    - Weights alone will not enhance cardiorespiratory fitness.
    - Blowing the air out of the lungs on the thrust is important.
    - Counting out loud helps guarantee that you breathe; holding your breath is dangerous.

- How endurance improves by gradual increases in the following:
  - Length of time
  - Frequency of exercise
  - Intensity of exercise
- The best schedule for weight training

Lesson Safety

The following are required for lesson safety:

- Enough space to allow the entire class to move safely
- Clean floor
- Equipment certified for safety
- Disciplined environment where students are monitored to make sure they follow rules and guidelines established in earlier lessons

Motivation

After so many days of explanation, everyone is probably ready to begin marking their progress. Tell them to use as much of the equipment as they have time for and to ask whatever questions they have. Promise to move around to check that their equipment is set up properly, that their breathing is correct, and that they are moving through the whole range of motion instead of just part of it. If they can't do a full range of motion on one try, they must greatly reduce the weight they are using. Suggest a starting weight for upper-body exercises and a slightly greater weight for lower-body exercises.

Warm-Up

Warm up as usual—either use an aerobic dance routine that the class learned and liked in earlier grades, or play a song that is popular, 5 minutes long, and energetic and allow students to use the bikes, row machines, stair climbers, and treadmills until they are all occupied, with the rest of the kids jogging in place until the music is over.

Lesson Sequence

1. Discuss breathing:
   - How aerobic breathing allows people to improve cardiorespiratory fitness
   - Limitations of the weight-training approach compared with endurance
   - Importance of good breathing technique while lifting weights
2. Discuss the meaning of endurance and that to improve it they need to increase
   - length of time (minutes, hours, weeks, months of working out),
   - frequency of exercise (days per week), and
   - intensity of exercise (more weight, speed, repetition).
3. Explain that the best schedule for weight training is a one-day-on, one-day-off approach, with the off day dedicated to aerobic fitness.
4. Allow students to pair up so that while one is on a machine, the other can check alignment, put the pin in at the proper weight, and encourage the partner to complete the set of 10 reps before switching.
5. While the students work, remind them to do one set, use a full range of motion, breathe properly, and use weights that do not make them reach muscle burnout before 10 reps.

Review and Stretching

As students stretch, inventory what they accomplished in the class.

- Who exercised the abdominal muscles?
- Who did as many sets for the lower body as for the upper body?
- Who completed a set of 10 repetitions without having to change the weight?

Charting the Workout

Facilities

- Clean, clear area large enough for class to be able to safely move in as everyone jogs, imitates exercises, and stretches at the same time
- Weight machines such as Universal or Nautilus that are certified as safe

Materials

- Music system with good amplification
- Selected music for the following:
  - Aerobic warm-up
  - Stretching
  - Energetic popular background music
- Pens or pencils
- Weight-Room Workout Chart for each student
- Weight machines with pins
- Free weights, resistance bands, or medicine balls

Performance Goals

Students will do the following:

- Complete a circuit in the weight room.
- Record the weight used and number of reps for each exercise done.
- Perform exercises safely.

Cognitive Goals

Students will learn the following:

- What muscle burnout is
- How muscles are strengthened by repetition and resistance
- How muscle fatigue disables the muscle
- How strength increases by increasing the following:
  - Length of workouts
  - Frequency
  - Intensity
- How to use their personal weight-room workout chart
- How to work efficiently with a partner

Lesson Safety

The following are required for lesson safety:

- Enough space to allow the entire class to move safely
- Clean floor
- Equipment certified for safety
- Disciplined environment where students are monitored to make sure they follow rules and guidelines established in earlier lessons

Motivation

Today and each day from now on, students will pick up their workout chart. The chart not only will show them the progress they make, but remind them where they should start and if it is time to increase the weights they are using. Students should make an entry on everything they work at, including the length of the cardiorespiratory warm-up, the number of abdominal reps, and stretches. They should be sure not to overlook the entries about the amount of weight used and the number of repetitions. If they use weights that are so easy they did not reach muscle burnout by the 10th rep, they shouldn't do another set but rather make a notation to add more weight the next time. Entries should be placed under the date they were done.

Warm-Up

Begin the usual warm-up as soon as students enter the room.

Lesson Sequence

1. Before distributing the charts, have students do one set of curl-ups.
2. Discuss the following:
   - Strength, its meaning, and how to improve it
     - Length of practice
     - Frequency of practice
     - Intensity of practice
   - Muscle burnout
   - Advantageous work with partners by having partners
     - check alignment,
     - check proper weight and move the pin as needed,
     - record weight and number of reps accomplished, and
     - encourage the student to not give up before finishing the set.
2. Distribute charts and pens or pencils.
3. Allow class to proceed with the workout using the chart in the Weight-Room Workout Chart (page 70).
4. Be ready to answer questions, which might include the following:
   - How do I move the seat?
   - Where are the pins?
   - Which exercise machine do we use for the rowing?
5. Remind students to move through the full range of motion on each rep.
6. Have students complete their charts and return the pens, pencils, and charts.

Review and Stretching

As students stretch, ask if they have any questions. Discuss why the required exercises allow only one set.

Workout and Discussion of Enhancers

Facilities

- Clean, clear area large enough for class to be able to safely move in as everyone jogs, imitates exercises, and stretches at the same time
- Weight machines such as Universal or Nautilus that are certified as safe

Weight-Room Workout Chart

Name _____ Date _____

Teacher _____ Class _____

Date													
Duration of warm-up													
Number of abdominal reps													
Stretching													

Do 1 set of each. Record the weight used in the proper column.

Bench presses													
Shoulder presses													
Lat pull-downs													
Forearm curls													
Leg extensions													
Leg curls													

Optional exercises if time remains. Enter on date done.

Squats													
Toe raises													
Hip and back extensions													
Dips													
Chin-ups													
Lat raises													
Triceps press-downs													
Decline presses													
Arm crosses													

From Isobel Kleinman, 2009, *Complete Physical Education Plans for Grades 5 to12, Second Edition* (Champaign, IL: Human Kinetics).

Materials

- Music system with good amplification
- Selected music for the following:
  - Aerobic warm-up
  - Stretching
  - Energetic popular background music
- Pens or pencils
- Weight-Room Workout Chart for each student
- Weight machines with pins
- Free weights, resistance bands, or medicine balls

Performance Goal

Students will work in pairs as they complete the circuit and record their work.

Cognitive Goals

Students will learn the following:

- How goals define workout styles and results
  - Workouts to increase strength will increase muscle bulk.
  - Workouts for fitness use all muscles and achieve firmness.
- How to train safely
  - Prevention (clothes, water, breathing, correct equipment use)
  - Recovery (muscle fatigue, muscle injury, joint injury, dehydration)
  - Miracle enhancers for success

Lesson Safety

The following are required for lesson safety:

- Enough space to allow the entire class to move safely
- Clean floor
- Equipment certified for safety
- Disciplined environment where students are monitored to make sure they follow rules and guidelines established in earlier lessons

Motivation

Discuss training approaches for strength and bulk versus for total fitness. Explain that fitness is impossible if training is not safe. The first step in preventing injury is making sure that the body mechanics are sound and don't magnify potential injury. On the list of important safety aspects to cover are proper clothing, hydration, and breathing. Earlier lessons focused on body mechanics and breathing. People who are sick, fatigued, dehydrated, or injured need to recover.

Warm-Up

Do the established routine.

Lesson Sequence

1. Distribute charts and pens and pencils.
2. After discussing the motivation material, students should proceed with their own workout.
3. With 5 minutes left, complete the stretching routine and review.
4. Have students complete their charts and return the pens, pencils, and charts.

Review and Stretching

As students stretch, discuss what motivates users of steroids, creatine, or other substances for bodybuilding. Explore if your students are using any. Ask if they know how to build strength without changing their body chemistry. Ask if they know why so much fuss is made about making sure that athletes are no longer using steroids and why many organizations test their athletes for drugs regularly.

Physical Fitness
INTERMEDIATE (GRADES 9-10)
LESSONS
7-12

Complete Workout

Facilities

- Clean, clear area large enough for class to be able to safely move in as everyone jogs, imitates exercises, and stretches at the same time
- Weight machines such as Universal or Nautilus that are certified as safe

Materials

- Music system with good amplification
- Selected music for the following:
    - Aerobic warm-up
    - Stretching
    - Energetic popular background music
- Pens or pencils
- Weight-Room Workout Chart for each student
- Weight machines with pins
- Free weights, resistance bands, or medicine balls

Performance Goals

Students will do the following:
- Work in pairs following an established weight-room routine:
    1. Cardiorespiratory warm-up of 5 minutes
    2. Abdominal workout
    3. Alternate full sets for the upper and lower body, three sets for upper body and three sets for lower body
    4. Stretching routine
- Follow established safety procedures.
    - Wear proper clothing.
    - Take in water as needed.
    - Work at weight levels to induce muscle burnout in 10 reps.
- Monitor progress on weight-room charts.

Cognitive Goal

Students will learn about the dangers of using drug and natural-substance enhancers.

Lesson Safety

The following are required for lesson safety:

- Enough space to allow the entire class to move safely
- Clean floor
- Equipment certified for safety
- Disciplined environment where students are monitored to make sure they follow rules and guidelines established in earlier lessons

Motivation

Good music, individual charts, and the notion of sculpting their bodies and becoming fitter will encourage students to use their time wisely in the weight room.

Warm-Up

Perform the routine established for this unit.

Lesson Sequence

1. Begin aerobic warm-up upon entering. Distribute charts and pencils during the warm-up.
2. Follow the warm-up with at least one abdominal exercise.
3. As students work in pairs to complete their circuit, coach the following:
   - Proper breathing
   - Full range of motion
   - Correct alignment while lifting
   - Monitoring, cheering, and recording for one's partner
   - Using class time wisely
4. Have students complete their charts and return the pens, pencils, and charts.

Review and Stretching

While students stretch, address the issue of chemical enhancers. Discuss the positives before discussing the negatives, and be honest about your concerns. After the ban on steroids, the use of natural substances such as creatine grew. Sport figures have had great results with no observable life-threatening alterations, but the long-term effects are unknown. The unknown is scary—explain how steroids were the wonder drug for athletic performance in the late 1960s and early 1970s and how horrifying they became. Discuss how fen-phen, a natural substance, was used to help dieting in the 1980s until strokes and heart attacks threatened users. The results look good, but the impact 5 to 10 years down the line can be awful. Teach students to be skeptical.

At some point, indicate whether a weight-room workout is anaerobic or aerobic and discuss what makes it one or the other.

Assessment

Review the charts submitted by each student. Grades can be based on

- the ability to complete that which is required, increasing the weight over time, increasing the number of additional sets and muscle-group exercises, and quality of stretching and warm-up effort;
- the intermediate fitness rubric; or
- a physical fitness test and placement on statistical norms (see chapter 4) and the intermediate fitness quiz.

Intermediate Physical Fitness Skills Rubric

Name _____ Date _____

Teacher _____ Class _____

	0	1	2	3	4	5
Flexibility Sit and reach	Must bend knees to reach knees	Can reach knees	Can reach shins	Can reach ankle	Can grab sole of foot	Can touch nose to knees
Aerobic fitness Mile (1.5-kilo-meter) walk/run	Girls: 15+ min Boys: 12+ min	Girls: 14:01-15 min Boys: 11:01-12 min	Girls: 12-14 min Boys: 10:16-11 min	Girls: 11-11:59 min Boys: 8:46-10:15 min	Girls: 10-10:59 min Boys: 8:15-8:45 min	Girls: 9:59 min or under Boys: 8:14 min or under
Abdominal strength 1 min sit-up test	Fewer than 15	16-21	22-26	27-34	35-40	41+
Upper-body strength Push-ups or pull-ups	Girls: 2 or fewer Boys: 4 or fewer	Girls: 3-4 Boys: 5-6	Girls: 5-6 Boys: 7-8	Girls: 7-9 Boys: 9-13	Girls: 10-11 Boys: 14-16	Girls: 12+ Boys: 17+
Agility Sidestepping over lines 4 feet (1 meter) apart in 10 seconds (NYS fitness test)	Fewer than 8	9-12	13-15	16-18	19-20	21+
Speed Shuttle run (NYS fitness test)	Girls: 29+ s Boys: 27+ s	Girls: 27.1-28.9 s Boys: 25.5-26.9 s	Girls: 25-27 s Boys: 23.0-25.4 s	Girls: 23.5-24.9 s Boys: 22.0-22.9 s	Girls: 22.0-23.4 s Boys: 20.0-21.9 s	Girls: Less than 22 s Boys: Less than 20 s

From Isobel Kleinman, 2009, *Complete Physical Education Plans for Grades 5 to12, Second Edition* (Champaign, IL: Human Kinetics).

Intermediate Physical Fitness Quiz

Name _____   Date _____

Teacher _____   Class _____

True or False

Read each statement carefully. If the statement is true, write a *T* in the column to the left. If the statement is false, write an *F*. If using a grid sheet, blacken in the appropriate column for each question, making sure to use the correctly numbered line for each question and its answer.

_____ 1. Increasing the weight used will increase the heart rate.

_____ 2. Reduced flexibility reduces the risk of injury.

_____ 3. A 16-year-old who works at a heart rate of 100 beats per minute will not significantly improve cardiorespiratory fitness.

_____ 4. Tennis, volleyball, and basketball are good aerobic activities.

_____ 5. For cardiorespiratory improvement, activity should be ongoing for 20 to 35 minutes.

_____ 6. A set is a minimum of 8 to a maximum of 12 repetitions.

_____ 7. Muscle burnout is a symptom of muscle fatigue.

_____ 8. Good activity done incorrectly is still beneficial.

_____ 9. In order to increase the effectiveness of stretching, it is best to warm up muscles first.

_____ 10. One can be physically fit without being fast.

Extra Credit

Match the columns (1 point each).

_____ 1. pulse   a. movement through whole range of motion

_____ 2. flexibility   b. how to increase heart rate

_____ 3. anaerobic activity   c. 75% of maximum heart rate

_____ 4. target zone   d. evidence of a contracting heart muscle

_____ 5. faster and higher   e. running sprints

Intermediate Physical Fitness Answer Key

True or False

1. T—More effort raises the heart rate.
2. F—Loss of flexibility can cause muscle tears, ligament ruptures, and so on.
3. T—The minimum recommended rate is 151 beats per minute ($220 - 16 = 204 \times 75\%$ = 151 beats per minute).
4. F—Aerobics require continuous movement with breath, and these are not continuous.
5. T—These are the 1997 minimum recommendations.
6. T—A set is the number of times one lifts the same weight without stopping.
7. T—It's the feeling you get when the muscle cannot lift a weight again without rest.
8. F—Performing an exercise incorrectly leads to injury.
9. T—Warm muscles stretch farther than cold muscles.
10. T—Speed is not a function of fitness.

Extra Credit

1. d
2. a
3. e
4. c
5. b

Revisiting Fitness

Facilities

Clean, clear area large enough for class to be able to safely move in

Materials

- Music system with good amplification
- Selected music for an aerobic warm-up and stretching

Performance Goals

Students will do the following:

- Take their resting pulse at the conclusion of discussion.
- Do a 20-minute uninterrupted exercise routine that they have learned before:
    1. Warm-up—3 minutes
    2. Moderate activity—3 minutes
    3. Vigorous activity—8 minutes
    4. Moderate activity—3 minutes
    5. Stretching—3 minutes
- Take their pulse before stretching and after stretching.

Cognitive Goals

Students will learn the following:

- The importance of fitness and its value to a healthy life
- Their current health profile
- Relevant research
- The difference between a resting pulse and working pulse

Lesson Safety

Screen the class area to determine that the floor is clean and the equipment is certified for safety.

Motivation

Explain that as juniors and seniors, these are the last years that high school can influence their lifestyle choices. Explain how you would feel so much better if they left you knowing a healthy approach to exercise and fitness that they will enjoy as independent adults. Tell them that few people will go out of their way to do that which they do not like, even if they know it is good for them, so their mission this year is to create an individual fitness plan that they like doing. Review what they have learned and where the students fit in a fitness and health profile.

Warm-Up

The warm-up should involve rhythmic use of all large muscle groups.

Lesson Sequence

1. Ask the class to sit and come to resting pulse. Review fitness concepts.
    - Components of fitness are flexibility, muscle strength, muscle endurance, cardiorespiratory endurance, and body composition.
    - To maintain cardiorespiratory fitness, they should exercise for 20 to 40 minutes at 65% to 85% of their maximum heart rate every day.
    - Stretching is most effective if done when muscles are already warm.
    - If you don't use it, you lose it.
2. Take resting pulse.

3. Begin an activity routine that will go uninterrupted for 20 minutes and includes a warm-up, moderate movement, vigorous movement, moderate movement, and stretching, in that order. Use previously learned aerobic routines, aerobic DVDs that can be easily imitated, or a circuit with activity that does not stop.
4. Take pulse before stretching. While students stretch, explain that though they feel at rest, stretching does require work.
5. Take pulse after stretching. Note the number of beats that it has come down. Take a reading every minute until heart rate has effectively returned to a resting pulse.

Review

Explain that fitness used to be measured by how much work was done, how hard the heart worked to do it, and how quickly the heart recovered when the work was over. The information yielded an index that was said to predict cardiorespiratory fitness. Now machines are available that measure air intake and volume to predict aerobic fitness. In short, every few years someone comes up with another fitness measure. The field seems ever changing while norms become more elusive. What we know for sure is that physical fitness is important to physical and mental health, enjoyment of life, and the ability to avoid certain diseases. Explain that after years of partaking in fitness units, they should be aware of their strengths and weaknesses and know exactly what areas they need to focus on to get or stay fit. Everyone needs a plan to keep fit so that they can complete 20 to 40 minutes of moderately vigorous activity every day.

Physical Fitness
ADVANCED (GRADES 11-12)
LESSON 2

Fitness Potential of Various Activities

Facilities
- Clean, clear area large enough for class to be able to safely move in as everyone jogs, imitates exercises, and stretches at the same time
- Weight machines such as Universal or Nautilus that are certified as safe

Materials
- Music and DVD or video of student choice
- Recreational equipment that can be safely accommodated in the room, such as table tennis, jump rope, pool table, basketballs, volleyballs, handballs, badminton, and so on
- Heart rate monitors (at least one for each activity area)

Performance Goals
Students will do the following:
- Choose a recreational, aerobic, or weight-training activity.
- Analyze if the exercise of choice yielded the cardiorespiratory levels aimed for.

Cognitive Goals
Students will learn the following:
- Necessity of cardiorespiratory fitness
- How to develop cardiorespiratory fitness
  - Elevate heart rate continuously for 20 minutes.
  - Cannot be continuous if they have to stop to catch their breath.
- Their target heart rate zone
  - How it varies by age
  - How to find it ($220 - $ age $\times 75\%$)
- If their physical work of choice yields performance in target heart rate zone

Lesson Safety

The following are required for lesson safety:

- Enough space to allow the entire class to move safely
- Clean floor
- Equipment certified for safety
- Disciplined environment where students are monitored to make sure they follow rules and guidelines established in earlier lessons

Motivation

Explain that during this lesson, students can choose among several activities. Tell them what is available. (You might have to restrict choice to accommodate location and safety.) Explain that throughout the class, you will ask them to take a heart rate reading. As they do, they should keep moving because stopping to count will lower their heart rate. This is difficult without heart rate monitors, so review how to take their pulse if no monitors are available. Announce that it will be interesting to see if the activities they like to do can get their heart rate into a target zone capable of maintaining or improving cardiorespiratory fitness.

Warm-Up

For this lesson, students will be left to warm-up as they wish.

Lesson Sequence

1. Proceed with activities of choice, noting whether anyone remembered to warm-up.
2. Observe if students maintained their activity level throughout the class.
3. Fifteen minutes into the activity, ask students to find their pulse and take a reading or begin to count on your signal. Encourage them not to stop activity while they do so.
4. Allow the students to resume their activity.

Review

Share the following:

- Information you observed about their warm-up, work ethic, and stretching
- What students learned about heart rate stimulated by activities of their choice
  - Did it approach a sustainable target zone?
  - Did it require rest, which would cause heart rate fluctuation?
  - Did the highs and lows average into the target zone?

Teacher Homework

Fill out one of the student charts you will be distributing next lesson, using the routine you intend to lead the class through. Enlarge it on the blackboard or on a projector so they can see it and know how it was filled out.

Burning Calories

Facilities

- Clean, clear area large enough for class to be able to safely move in as everyone jogs, imitates exercises, and stretches at the same time
- Weight machines such as Universal or Nautilus that are certified as safe

Materials

- Equipment for a teacher-directed activity that gradually increases physical effort. You may use aerobic routines that students learned in the beginning unit or have them begin by walking, then jogging, then running, then running at top speed.
- Handouts that help to set up a personal workout program:
    - Weight-Room Workout Chart
    - General Physical Activities Defined by Levels of Intensity
    - Aerobic Dance Choreography Worksheet

Performance Goal

Students will burn some calories.

Cognitive Goals

Students will learn the following:

- How to correlate value of activity with that of weight control
- Calorie-burning values of some popular activities
- How to increase the burning power of each activity
- That the value is in completing the program, not working so hard that they have to stop to rest

Lesson Safety

Be vigilant that the high-energy section does not exceed the maximum target heart rate.

Motivation

After experimenting in the last class, this time activities will be teacher-chosen with the same goal in mind: getting and maintaining fitness. Tell the class to try to remember the physical effort required of them because after this lesson, they will be taking on the project of constructing a workout program of their own that they will use for the remainder of the unit.

Warm-Up

Do a rhythmic routine using large muscle groups.

Lesson Sequence

1. Discuss the value of food and the implications of consuming more than we can burn.
    a. Where we get energy
    b. How activity burns food intake
    c. How caloric burn is related to intensity
    d. Which activities yield most burn at a moderate intensity
    e. How weight can be affected by the amount of activity performed
    f. How to get a feel for the effort and burn of each activity
2. Announce and lead a classic warm-up, telling students that they will need a warm-up in the program they construct.
3. Announce and lead a moderate activity, reminding students that they will need a moderate activity in the program they construct. To save time, choose a moderately energetic dance from previous aerobic routines or from your dance unit (e.g., a square dance or Seljancica Kola).
4. Announce the target zone you'd like the class to get to, and lead the class in an activity with increased intensity. Make sure they understand that this section of the routine should last 10 minutes, but that you are abbreviating it for today so they can begin working on their routines. Again, to save learning time and to concentrate on the activity, choose a dance from a prior unit that uses high energy (e.g., Salty Dog Rag or Nebesko Kolo).

5. Announce that it is time to scale down the intensity and lead the class in a more moderate activity, such as a dance from a previous unit (e.g., Pata Pata, Saturday Night Fever Walk).

6. Have students conclude by following you as they cool down and stretch.

Review

Assign committees, giving each responsibility for choreographing part of the class aerobic dance routine. Distribute worksheets that will help organize their efforts (see Aerobic Dance Choreography Worksheet). Display the one you filled out so the whole class can see it. Explain that the form should serve as a guideline. Students will have class time to work on their routine, but some home planning will be necessary, such as getting the music and bringing it in. Entertain questions, and make sure students know that you are available if they need more answers. Explain that whatever they choose and however they choreograph it, they will teach it to their classmates and come to the front of the class to lead it each time their music comes on so everyone can follow them.

General Physical Activities Defined by Level of Intensity

The chart on page 82 is one of many. An Internet search will yield others that show how to calculate calorie burn by body weight, duration of exercise, and even heart rate achieved during the activity. Some of the best when we went to press can be found at www.rmafitness.com/calorie_chart.html and http://heart.kumu.org/calories.html.

Building a Fitness Routine

Facilities

Clean, clear area large enough for class to be able to safely move in

Materials

- Equipment for a teacher-directed activity that gradually increases physical effort
- Handouts that help to set up a personal workout program:
  - Weight-Room Workout Chart
  - General Physical Activities Defined by Levels of Intensity
  - Aerobic Dance Choreography Worksheet
- Music player for each group
- If using video, a recorder to record movements the students chose
- Pen or pencil for each group

Performance Goals

Students will do the following:

- Work on developing a routine.
- Burn calories.
- Use exercise to reduce stress.

Cognitive Goals

Students will learn the following:

- What stress is
- How to relieve muscle tension

Lesson Safety

Be vigilant that the high-energy section does not exceed the maximum target heart rate.

General Physical Activities Defined by Level of Intensity

Moderate Activity*	Vigorous Activity*
Comparison factors	
• Moderate activity is the average energy expenditure for a man 30 to 50 years old, or a woman 20 to 40 years old with a weight of about 154 lb (70 Kg).** • Requires 3.5 to 7 calories per minute. • An hour of moderate exercise uses 210-540 calories.	• Vigorous activity is the average energy expenditure for a man 30 to 50 years old, or a woman 20 to 40 years old with a weight of about 154 lb (70 Kg).** • Requires more than 7 calories per minute. • An hour of vigorous activity uses 540 calories.
Activities	
Walking—to class, shopping, pleasure at 3 to 4.5 miles per hour	Race walking—5 miles per hour or faster
In-line skating (leisurely pace)	Fast-paced in-line skating
Golf (if wheeling or carrying clubs)	Jogging, running
Using crutches	Wheeling a wheelchair
Hiking	Mountain, rock, or brisk uphill climbing
Biking at 7 to 9 miles per hour on level terrain	Biking at 10 miles per hour or higher, or uphill
Stationary biking with moderate effort	Stationary biking with more tension and speed
Water aerobics	Water jogging
Aerobic dancing	Aerobic dancing—high impact
Light calisthenics, yoga	Faster-paced exercises
Occupations requiring lifting, using power tools, extended period of moving	Competitive boxing, wrestling, sparring
Dancing—easy-paced ballroom, line, modern, ballet, and so on	Dancing—folk, square, clogging, professional ballroom at vigorous (faster) pace
Tennis, doubles	Tennis, singles or wheelchair tennis
Table tennis, badminton, target archery	Handball, racquetball, squash
Frisbee, curling, juggling	Cross country skiing, downhill ski racing
Softball, competitive volleyball	Competitive sports, beach volleyball
Shooting baskets	Basketball games
Swimming recreationally, diving, surfing	Swimming laps, water polo, scuba diving
Shoveling light snow	Shoveling snow—10 pounds or more per minute
Carrying a child 25 pounds or less up stairs	Carrying young children and groceries
Housework or general home construction	Hand sawing
Pushing a lawn mower	Pushing furniture, carrying 25 pounds up stairs, carrying 50 pounds down stairs
Twirling, playing musical instruments while moving	Playing with the kids
Kayaking or canoeing less than 4 miles per hour	Kayaking or canoeing more than 4 miles per hour
Fishing, hunting, horseback riding at a leisurely pace	Horseback riding—galloping, trotting, jumping
Playground activities	Rope jumping, skipping, jumping jacks
Gardening—raking, digging, hoeing, planting	Heavy-lifting garden work (10 pounds or more)

*Equal effort requires more energy from older people.

**Sitting quietly uses 1.2 calories per minute for a person weighing 154 pounds (or 70 kg).

Center for Disease Control, 2008, http://www.cdc.gov/nccdphp/dnpa/physical/pdf/PA_Intensity_table_2_1.pdf.

From Isobel Kleinman, 2009, *Complete Physical Education Plans for Grades 5 to12, Second Edition* (Champaign, IL: Human Kinetics).

Aerobic Dance Choreography Worksheet

Name _____ Date _____

Teacher _____ Class _____

Students in group	Responsibility (see list below)
1.	
2.	
3.	
4.	
5.	
6.	

Responsibilities

Provide the music, create choreography, teach the group, teach the class, demonstrate, and take notes for the group.

	Notes
Music selection and title	
Duration of the song	
Length of the introduction	
Beats per measure	
Goal of the routine (see list below)	

Goals

Warm up, target specific muscle groups, get heart rate in fat-burning zone, intermittently raise heart rate to maximum by requiring spurt of high energy, maintain continuous motion within targeted zone, cool down, and stretch.

	Notes
Energy level	
Target heart rate for this routine	
Group formation	
Direction of movement	

»continued

From Isobel Kleinman, 2009, *Complete Physical Education Plans for Grades 5 to12, Second Edition* (Champaign, IL: Human Kinetics).

»continued

Choreography

Choose direction of movement; whether the routine is done solo, in pairs, or in a group formation; what the footwork will be; the frequency of each type of step; and what the arms, hips, and shoulders do.

	First four measures	Second four measures	Third four measures	Final four measures
Direction of movement				
Solo, pairs, or group formation				
Footwork (describe steps and list frequency of steps)				
Body movement (describe steps and list frequency of steps)				
Arm movement (describe steps and list frequency of steps)				

From Isobel Kleinman, 2009, *Complete Physical Education Plans for Grades 5 to12, Second Edition* (Champaign, IL: Human Kinetics).

Motivation

Today, each group will create a routine with a specific goal. When the choreography is complete, the group that created it will teach, perform, and lead it whenever their music comes on in the routine. As in the past, once they know all the group routines, the music will be recorded together so the class has a continuous music program for the workout.

Warm-Up

Groups warm up by planning and practicing their routines for presentation.

Lesson Sequence

1. Let groups find their own space to develop their routine based on the assignment given at the end of the last class. If some forgot their music, let them choreograph the movement, and perhaps they can borrow a tune from the physical education library. Assign the following to groups:

   - Warm-up routine
   - Two moderate 3-minute routines
   - Three vigorous 3-minute routines (heart rate in target zone)
   - Abdominal and low back routine
   - Stretching routine for all large muscle groups

2. Give the class 20 minutes. Then ask if a group is ready to begin presenting and have them present, teach, and lead the class as everyone does the routine.

3. Continue to present other routines if there is time.

Review

Discuss stress, what causes it, its negative indicators, and how to rid oneself of it. Stress is a build-up of tension that often leads to feeling tired and worn down even when you haven't done anything to make you feel that way. Stress can be caused by many things, such as feeling like you're losing control, anger, frustrations, or pent-up energy. Some negative indicators of stress are feeling like you can't accomplish anything, like you can't focus, like you want to explode, or like you are too tired to do anything. Massive activity is a good way to relieve yourself of stress.

Completing Student-Designed Fitness Routine

Facilities

Clean, clear area large enough for class to be able to safely move in

Materials

- Music players for each group
- Handouts that help to set up a personal workout program:
  - Weight-Room Workout Chart
  - General Physical Activities Defined by Levels of Intensity
  - Aerobic Dance Choreography Worksheet
- If using video, a recorder to record movements the students chose
- Pen or pencil for each group

Performance Goal

Students will complete their routines and present them to the rest of the class.

Cognitive Goal

Students will assume responsibility for one aspect of the class road to aerobic fitness.

Lesson Safety

Be vigilant that the high-energy section does not exceed the maximum target heart rate.

Motivation

Tell students that they have 5 minutes to finish what they started in the previous class. In that time, they should practice so they can demonstrate and teach as a group. Each person in the group must know the routine well because when the music comes on for their routine, they will be expected to come to the front of the room and lead the class. In 10 minutes or so, they will begin making presentations to the class, thus setting up the class aerobic routine. You are aiming for fitness and joy, so keep the tone light and enthusiastic, and if possible, be a good sport and participate as a student in the class.

Warm-Up

Student practice and choreography serves as the warm-up.

Lesson Sequence

1. Groups have 5 minutes to practice and write the movement sequence.
2. Hold the group presentations in the following order:
    a. Warm-up routine
    b. Moderate activity of 3 minutes
    c. Second moderate activity of 3 minutes
    d. Vigorous activity of 3 minutes (should raise the heart rate to the target zone)
    e. Second vigorous activity of about 3 minutes
    f. Third vigorous activity of 3 minutes
    g. Abdominal and low back routine
    h. Stretching routine for all large muscle groups

Review

Ask to keep and record the music that was presented so you can make a master recording. If people haven't left their music, remind them to bring it to the next class.

Teacher Homework

Make sure the student music is recorded in proper sequence so the class can perform each routine in the order called for and the music can run without interruption.

Physical Fitness
ADVANCED (GRADES 11-12)
LESSONS
6-12

Student-Designed Workout

Facilities

Clean, clear area large enough for class to be able to safely move in

Materials

- Music player with good amplification
- Music for class routines
- Equipment needed for the routines (e.g., steps, light free weights)

Performance Goals

Students will do the following:

- Be active the full class time.
- Come to the front of the class to lead their group routine.

Cognitive Goal

Students will assume partial responsibility for everyone's fitness and fun.

Lesson Safety

Be vigilant that the high-energy section does not exceed the maximum target heart rate.

Motivation

Sharing the responsibility for teaching, demonstrating, and leading will be motivating.

Lesson Sequence

The music goes on. Groups lead their part of the routine by coming to the front of the room while their music is playing and leading the sequence they created. They return to the group formation when others come up to lead.

Review

Ask the following:

- What does the saying, "No pain, no gain," mean?
- Do you really have to be in pain to have a gain?

Assessment

- Retake the Lifestyle Fitness Index (page 48) and see how it has changed.
- Skills assessment can be based on a variety of performance standards:
  - Performance rubric
  - Improvement in physical fitness
  - Effort in assuming responsibility and being self-directed
- Knowledge will be assessed with the advanced physical fitness quiz.

Advanced Physical Fitness Skills Rubric

Name _____ Date _____

Teacher _____ Class _____

	1	2	3	4	5
Design of fitness program	Includes a 5-minute warm-up.	Includes 3-5 minutes working middle body (abs, low back, thighs).	• Includes 10-15 minutes working in heart rate of 120-130 bpm. • Circuit includes upper- and lower-body exercise.	• Includes 15 minutes at a heart rate of 140-155 bpm. • Circuit includes 15 minutes of high-energy aerobic exercise.	Includes 4-5 minutes to stretch and cool down.
Work output	Completes warm-up.	Performs all exercises for middle body.	Maintains heart rate at 120-130 bpm for 75% of the class.	Gets heart rate to 155 bpm or higher for 15% of the class.	Completes stretches with proper body mechanics.
Fitness level	Has improved fitness level.	Fitness level is in the 33rd percentile.	Fitness level is in the 50th-75th percentile.	Fitness level is in the 84th percentile.	Fitness level is in the 93rd-99th percentile.

From Isobel Kleinman, 2009, *Complete Physical Education Plans for Grades 5 to12, Second Edition* (Champaign, IL: Human Kinetics).

Advanced Physical Fitness Quiz

Name _____ Date _____

Teacher _____ Class _____

True or False

Read each statement carefully. If the statement is true, write a *T* in the column to the left. If the statement is false, write an *F*. If using a grid sheet, blacken in the appropriate column for each question, making sure to use the correctly numbered line for each question and its answer.

_____ 1. The heart of a 120-pound (54.5-kilogram) girl carrying 50 pounds (22.5 kilograms) in her backpack has to work less than a person weighing 170 pounds (77 kilograms).

_____ 2. Strengthening exercises shorten muscles and reduce their range of motion.

_____ 3. Stationary jogging at 80 steps per minute burns more calories than walking.

_____ 4. Dancing is a great way to burn calories and increase fitness.

_____ 5. Thirty minutes of daily exercise at 50% of maximum heart rate is the recommended level of activity to improve cardiorespiratory fitness.

_____ 6. The purpose of working in your target zone is to maintain activity that challenges the cardiorespiratory system without making you lose your breath.

_____ 7. Muscle burnout is a symptom of muscle injury.

_____ 8. Weightlifting, biking, basketball, tennis, and dancing burn nearly the same calories.

_____ 9. It is best to warm muscles up before stretching them.

_____ 10. Six 10-minute intervals of aerobic, strength, or stretching activity throughout the day will keep you fit.

_____ 11. There is bound to be some discomfort when working to raise your fitness level.

_____ 12. Improper alignment when lifting weights can cause serious muscular damage.

_____ 13. As people get fit or age, their resting pulse gets lower.

_____ 14. If the activity you are doing is fun, you cannot be working hard enough to improve your cardiorespiratory system.

_____ 15. Doing a day on and a day off of resistance training by alternating it with cardiorespiratory training is the best way to stay healthy and fit.

Extra Credit

Match the columns (1 point each).

_____ 1. Recovery rate   a. 60% of the maximum

_____ 2. Inactive person's target heart rate   b. Increases heart rate

_____ 3. Active person's target heart rate   c. 80 jogging steps in place

_____ 4. Highest caloric usage   d. Time to return to a resting pulse

_____ 5. Adding weight   e. 75% of the maximum

From Isobel Kleinman, 2009, *Complete Physical Education Plans for Grades 5 to 12, Second Edition* (Champaign, IL: Human Kinetics).

Advanced Physical Fitness Answer Key

True or False

1. F—They both need to move 170 pounds (77 kilograms); therefore, assume the same effort.
2. T—That is why stretching is important, particularly at the end of exercise.
3. T—Jogging has a higher intensity level than walking and therefore burns more calories.
4. T—While there are all levels of exertion, dance burns calories and, since it is aerobic, it is a wonderful way to improve cardiorespiratory fitness.
5. F—The range one should work in daily for cardiorespiratory fitness is 70% to 85%, though working at 50% is better than doing nothing.
6. T—By not losing your breath, you can continue your activity and build your endurance.
7. F—Burnout is the result of muscle fatigue, when the muscle cannot work until it rests.
8. T—Each burns just under .5 calories per minute.
9. T—Warm muscles stretch farther than cold muscles.
10. T—Accumulated activity counts, and such an interval workout can maintain fitness.
11. T—Not everyone finds sweating, muscle fatigue, and being physically tired comfortable.
12. T— It is important to learn the correct way to use weights and to set all machines correctly when you use them.
13. T—The heart becomes more efficient.
14. F—Finding something to do that is fun and elevates your heart rate to the target zone is not only possible, but encouraged!
15. T—Muscle fatigue and boredom can be avoided by alternating activity types.

Extra Credit

1. d
2. a
3. e
4. c
5. b

Fitness Testing

Chapter Overview

1. Teach students what is being measured and why. Two fitness assessments yield two types of data. The Fitnessgram is a health-related, criteria-based fitness test. The New York State (NYS) Physical Fitness Screening Test is a skills-related test with comparative norms for each age, gender, and grade level from grades 7 through 12.

   - The Fitnessgram includes $\dot{V}O_2$max for aerobic endurance, push-ups for upper-body strength, abdominal curls, hamstring and shoulder stretches for flexibility, trunk lift for trunk extension, body mass index (BMI), and skinfold measurements.

   - The NYS fitness test measures agility, abdominal strength, speed and agility, and cardiorespiratory endurance and can be completed in two lessons.

     - For agility (NYS), a 10-second test measures the ability to change direction (skills-related fitness).

     - For abdominal strength (both Fitnessgram and NYS), a test measures the strength necessary to prevent back problems and improve posture (health-related fitness).

     - Speed and agility (NYS shuttle run) are essential skills for sport (skills-related fitness).

     - For endurance, the mile (1.5-kilometer) test (NYS) or Progressive Aerobic Cardiovascular Endurance Run (PACER) (Fitnessgram) reflects a healthy heart (skills- and health-related fitness).

     - Tests provide either comparative data (NYS) or criteria data (Fitnessgram) for the best performance on a given day.

2. Teach the general benefits of measuring fitness.

   - Yields an opportunity to measure self-improvement over time.

   - Enables students to compare their performance against others of the same age, gender, and grade level.

   - Provides alerts and possible motivation when scores fall into the 16th percentile or lower.

»continued

»continued

- Gives students the opportunity to take responsibility for following testing and scoring rules.
- Offers students a connection to statistical concepts based on their activity (NYS) or against health criteria.

3. Teach statistical concepts such as what a scaled score is, what the percentile rank is, what a normal bell curve is, how rankings are devised, and where students fit on the normal bell curve when compared with others of their own age, gender, and grade.

4. Lead students in computing and recording their fitness-level index.

Fitness Testing Study Sheet

Fun Facts

Why test for fitness? Fitness is an important indicator of a healthy life, and it can be lost or gained with a change of lifestyle. It is important to know whether we are fit so that if we are not, we can work on it, and if we are already fit, we can maintain it.

Is it important to be the best in the class to be fit? When taking the Fitnessgram, you will find out whether you are in the healthy zone in a variety of areas. It is not important to have the longest reach, the fastest times, or the least body fat. It is only important that what you have and what you do falls into the healthy zone.

Why learn about a normal bell curve? Scientists and mathematicians have looked at many measures and learned that if they take them all, stack them up so they are organized into highs and lows, and connect all the stacks with dots, they get a bell curve where 1% of the scores are at the top, 1% are at the bottom, and all the others fall equally distant from the middle score. When that happens and all the scores are equally distributed on a curve, there is a normal distribution of all the possibilities. From that phenomenon springs the notion that if the scores reflect normal possibilities, then when we talk about fitness, the average range or above must be fit. However, if we did a statistical analysis of current fitness scores, the curve would be lopsided toward the bottom of the range. When this happens, we do not have a normal curve and what is average may not be fit. That is why performance on the NYS fitness test, which was statistically analyzed many years ago, gives us something to compare our performance to. It reflects a normal distribution of performance when a relatively fit generation handed in their scores across the state of New York.

Is there a difference between skill-related activities and fitness-related activities? Yes, there is—it is not necessary to do the most or be the fastest or reach the farthest. It is only necessary that what we do and how we let our body grow does not hinder our health or lifestyle.

Why is an achievement level 4 or a score in the 34th percentile acceptable in fitness when it is failing in other subjects? Teachers would love if everyone learned everything they taught and could score 100% when tested. However, when assigning values to performance scores, there is no such thing as a score of 100. If people have performed in the top 1% and thus have done better than 99% of the scores submitted, they have performed in the 99th percentile. Similarly, if scores fall in the low average range, they will be in a perfectly acceptable range of performance and in the 34th percentile. Though they did better than only 34 percent of their peers, that performance was perfectly all right!

Why would I want to compare myself with someone my age who may have been tested years ago? Curiosity would be my motivation, especially when my teachers and parents claim that their generation did better. Even today's sport heroes would love to be able to see how they would do against the athletes they grew up wanting to be like. All they can compete against is their record because their heroes can no longer perform at the level they did when they won their accolades.

Why do we use music when getting scores for the Fitnessgram? The best possible score is not important; being in the healthy zone of performance is. That is why some tests are done to music. It provides the same beat for everyone. No one will be going faster or slower, though some people might have to stop. The goal is to learn if you perform in a healthy range or not and how and where to improve in order to get or maintain health-related fitness.

How is it possible that my friends look so much bigger than me, but I weigh more? Fat composition and body weight are not necessarily the same. Muscle weighs far more than fat. The BMI will figure out how much of the body is fat.

»continued

»continued

How is it possible that my friend is thinner than I am and eats more? Many variables make us burn our caloric intake differently. Among them is how much activity we do. If we burn what we eat, we do not gain weight. If we don't, the body stores what we don't burn and we get bigger. For now, we must remember that muscle requires more nourishment and burns more calories than fat does. This is important to know because a high level of body fat is a risk factor for heart disease, stroke, high blood pressure, and high cholesterol.

What does sitting and reaching have to do with fitness? As important as having abdominal muscles strong enough to take the pressure off the spine is having flexibility that limits the risk of pulling a muscle in the low back. In youth, it is rare to suffer an aching back or sciatic pain because the damage is not done—yet. The curve of the human spine puts an extraordinary burden on the back. To help keep the spine in line, we strengthen both the abdominal and back muscles, but stretching helps keep them in line, too. Joint flexibility is crucial to avoiding serious injury. Repetitious activities strengthen muscles but make them shorter. Muscles need to be stretched to maintain range of motion because short or imbalanced muscles influence movement and have the potential to cause injury.

From Isobel Kleinman, 2009, *Complete Physical Education Plans for Grades 5 to 12, Second Edition* (Champaign, IL: Human Kinetics).

Fitness Testing Extension Project

Name _____ Date _____

Teacher _____ Class _____

List the areas of fitness in which you do well.

What can you do to keep it up?

Which areas of fitness do you need to work on?

What activities can you do to improve your weak areas?

List the names of friends who would be willing to work out with you.

Where can you work out outside of school?

From Isobel Kleinman, 2009, *Complete Physical Education Plans for Grades 5 to 12, Second Edition* (Champaign, IL: Human Kinetics).

Fitness Testing Student Portfolio Checklist

Name _____   Date _____

Teacher _____   Class _____

_____ Understands why it is important to score in the healthy fitness zone (HFZ).

_____ Has completed the mile and knows if aerobic capacity is in the HFZ.

_____ Has completed the curl abdominal strength test and knows if results are in the HFZ.

_____ Has completed the push-up strength test and knows if results are in the HFZ.

_____ Has taken two skinfold measures and knows own fat composition.

_____ Has taken two flexibility measures and knows if results are in the HFZ.

_____ Has completed 10-second agility test.

_____ Has completed sit-up strength test for 1 minute.

_____ Has completed the speed dash by running around cones separated 45 feet (14 meters) three times.

_____ Understands what fitness-level scores mean.

_____ Knows own fitness-level score for agility.

_____ Knows own fitness-level score for the abdominal strength test.

_____ Knows own fitness-level score for the speed dash test.

_____ Knows own fitness-level score for the mile (1.5-kilometer) walk–run.

_____ Knows if performance is in the statistical range considered average fitness, below average, or above average.

_____ Performs at least in the average fitness range.

_____ Is improving in performance on the fitness test, though not yet in average range.

_____ Is using best effort when being tested.

_____ Is self-motivated to pursue fitness on own.

From Isobel Kleinman, 2009, *Complete Physical Education Plans for Grades 5 to 12, Second Edition* (Champaign, IL: Human Kinetics).

Health-Based Fitnessgram

The Fitnessgram is a health-related fitness measure that uses technology to communicate results and their meaning to parents and students so that they know if the student is functioning in a healthy fitness zone.

The best possible score is irrelevant in this test. Subtests are done in cadence, sometimes to music, with a goal of simply assessing whether students perform in a healthy range and to provide information on how students can improve or maintain their health-related fitness. Testing technique and procedure are unique despite similarities to other tests measuring the same thing. When testing for abdominal strength and endurance, students are asked to stay in cadence with music, which leads them in doing 20 curl-ups per minute. Several subtests require learned expertise of the test administrator to measure, such as skinfold measurements. The data must be put in the computer to produce a report. Several subtests also require special equipment (skinfold calipers, curl-up strips, sit-and-reach boxes, measuring stick for trunk lifts). However, much of the equipment can be easily and inexpensively made. Given the number of subtests, the length of each, and the process of scoring and collecting data, I would not recommend giving this test as a self-contained unit. Some testing can and should be done alone, such as strength assessment. Others should be done in conjunction with other class activities to keep everyone active, such as skinfold measurements. Use the following lessons as a guideline.

Fitnessgram Learning Experience Outline

Contents and Procedure

1. Discuss the differences between health-based and skill-based fitness tests.
2. Teach what is being measured and why.
   a. Agility—ability to change direction
   b. Curls—abdominal strength
   c. Speed with change of direction
   d. Mile (1.5-kilometer) walk–run—aerobic endurance
   e. $\dot{V}O_2$max—aerobic endurance
   f. Push-ups—upper-body strength
   g. Shoulder stretch—flexibility
   h. Trunk lift—trunk extension, flexibility
   i. BMI—body fat
   j. Skinfold measurement—skinfold thicknesses of triceps and calf for calculating body fat
3. Teach that tests should represent a personal best on a given day.
4. Identify the benefits of measuring fitness.
   a. It provides an opportunity to measure self-improvement.
   b. It allows comparison of raw data with developed norms so students can compare themselves with a larger population of healthier, more active people (the post-Vietnam-War generation) of the same gender, age, and grade.
   c. Students performing in the 16th percentile or below should be encouraged to work toward an average- or above-range percentile rank.
   d. Students will be responsible for following test and scoring rules.
   e. Students will learn to understand statistical concepts that are part of feedback.
5. Teach the meaning of statistics and the significance of scaled scores showing rank.
6. Compute final scores that compare students with others of their own age, sex, and grade.

Teaching Tips

- Some tests have learned elements. For accurate student scoring, a review of procedure and scoring methods is essential, as is a practice run for first-time users.

Most students have more trouble scoring accurately than taking the test. Some will come up with variations that need immediate correction. Others do not focus and either forget to write down raw scores or simply make up something rather than leave it blank. Frequently the results are obvious—made-up scores often make no sense.

- Supply pencils and pens.
- Fill out forms before testing.
- Testing should take limited time from your program.
- Test results should be communicated as soon as possible
- The rationale for measuring fitness should be communicated not just during the testing phase of the program but on an ongoing basis so students understand how fitness is relevant in their lives and how to get and maintain it.

Facilities

A large, clean area where multiple activities can take place at one time.

Suggested Resources

AAHPERD. 2000. *Physical Best Instructor Video.* VHS. Champaign, IL: Human Kinetics.

American Fitness. www.americanfitness.net.

Brockport Fitness Test (working on a new edition).

Fitnessgram/Activitygram. 2008. www.fitnessgram.net.

Heyward, V.H. 1997. *Advanced fitness assessment and exercise prescription.* 4th ed. Champaign, IL: Human Kinetics.

Meredith, M.D., and G.J. Welk, eds. 2007. *Fitnessgram/Activitygram test administration manual.* 4th ed. Champaign, IL: Human Kinetics.

www.presidentschallenge.org/

Fitness Testing
FITNESSGRAM—BEGINNER, INTERMEDIATE, AND ADVANCED
LESSON 1

Cardiorespiratory Endurance: The Mile

Facilities

Quarter-mile (.4-kilometer) track free of obstructions

Materials

- Personal Fitness Record for Fitnessgram (see page 100)
- Pens or pencils for half of the class
- Stopwatch
- Enough markers to provide a marker to runners as they complete each lap for a total of three markers per person (e.g., cotton swabs, ice-cream sticks, tongue depressors, straws)
- Chart of the range of scores for the mile that indicate the healthy zone (see appendix C for all fitness testing charts)

Performance Goals

Students will do the following:

- Complete four laps (1 mile [1.5 kilometers]) around the track before the end of class.
- Obtain their raw score for a mile and enter it on their personal fitness form.

Cognitive Goals

Students will learn the following:

- How long a mile (1.5 kilometers) is and the time required to complete it
- What is being measured by completing the test (endurance)
- Strategies for completing the test
- That tests reflect the best they can do that day
- Whether their performance falls in the healthy range

Lesson Safety

Be alert to any health problems, including falls, wheezing, fainting, and seizures.

Motivation

Tell students that doing the mile (1.5-kilometer) walk–run is a test of endurance even when they pace themselves. This test should not resemble strolling in the mall. Once the scores (timed in minutes and seconds) are entered in the computer, students will get an index of their aerobic fitness. Explain that the average walking pace is 3 miles (5 kilometers) per hour, or 20 minutes per mile, but they should try to extend themselves and do their best so that their scores reflect more than a walk down the street.

Lesson Sequence

1. Remind students that any run longer than a dash requires pacing. If they cannot sustain the pace they start with, it is perfectly all right to slow down, but they should keep moving forward so they complete the distance during class time. Explain that inside of the track is the shortest distance and when possible, runners should stay on the inside. Encourage them to try for a shorter time than the last time they took the test.

2. Explain that you will give them a marker when they finish a lap, and once they complete the fourth lap and hold up the three markers so the timer can see the three markers, they will get their time.

3. After the laps are complete, have students record their raw scores on their fitness form and have an assistant collect the forms.

Review and Stretching

As students stretch, discuss the following:

- Is this your first time completing a mile? Congratulations!
- Announce what scores fell in the healthy zone for their age, grade, and sex.
- Congratulate the boy and girl with the best time.
- Ask who had a better time than last time (a better fitness rating).
- When dismissing class, suggest that they will feel better after a shower and a good night's rest.

Body Composition: Skinfold Testing

This is the most difficult test to administer and can create many risks for teachers. If the teacher does the measuring, as suggested by the developers of the program, it prevents her from actively supervising a working class. The test itself may embarrass students, putting the teacher in an awkward position. It also takes a lot of time to do correctly. It would be best to have the school nurse take the measurements during student screening exams. In lieu of that, teach students to take the measurements. If they are not receptive to having a buddy in class help them, consider involving the health office or having an aide supervise the class while you take individual students aside to take the measurements while the class is engaged in a safe activity. The value in not foregoing the skinfold measure is the high correlation between body fat and health risk. Teaching students to

Personal Fitness Record for Fitnessgram

Name _____ School _____

Age _____ Height _____ Weight _____ Grade _____

	Date _____		Date _____	
	Score	**HFZ**	**Score**	**HFZ**
Aerobic capacity				
Skinfold measurements				
Triceps				
Calves				
Total				
Curl-up				
Trunk lift				
Upper-body strength				
Flexibility				
Hamstrings				
Shoulders				

Note: HFZ indicates you have performed in the healthy fitness zone.

I understand that my fitness record is personal. I do not have to share my results. My fitness record is important because it allows me to check my fitness level. If it is low, I will need to do more activity. If it is acceptable, I will need to continue my current activity level. I know that I can ask my teacher for ideas for improving my fitness level.

_____ (Student's signature)

From Isobel Kleinman, 2009, *Complete Physical Education Plans for Grades 5 to 12, Second Edition* (Champaign, IL: Human Kinetics). Reprinted, by permission, from The Cooper Institute, 2006, *FITNESSGRAM/ ACTIVITYGRAM test administration manual*, 4th ed. (Champaign, IL: Human Kinetics), 100.

understand risk factors and to be vigilant about body fat may encourage them to do what it takes to reach or maintain a healthy level of body fat. (Page 35 of the *FITNESSGRAM/ACTIVITYGRAM Test Administration Manual, Fourth Edition,* offers excellent information on this topic.)

Facilities

Private space in the weight-room or aerobic dance room, enhanced by standing up some mats and taking measurements behind them

Materials

- Personal Fitness Record for Fitnessgram
- Pens or pencils (one per caliper)
- Calipers—One for every two students would be ideal
- Music for an aerobic dance routine or energetic music to work to as background music
- Chart showing body composition standards for the health zone (available in the *FITNESS-GRAM/ACTIVITYGRAM Test Administration Manual, Fourth Edition.*)

Performance Goals

Students will do the following:

- Perform their normal class fitness routine.
- Get scores for body fat from the calf and the back of the upper arm.
- Check to see if their scores fall in the healthy zone.

Cognitive Goals

Students will learn the following:

- Fat composition and body weight are not necessarily the same.
- Muscle weighs far more than fat and since it does, the BMI gives a better idea of the healthy zone than weight does.
- Devices such as portable bioelectric impedance analyzers might make taking the BMI easier.
- Muscle requires more nourishment than fat and thus burns more calories than fat.
- High levels of body fat put students at risk for heart disease, stroke, high blood pressure, and high cholesterol in adulthood.
- It is possible to reduce fat levels with exercise.
- Calibrating skin folds is not easy and cannot be done by oneself.

Lesson Safety

Once students are safely engaged in their weight-room or aerobic dance routines, begin working in small groups. If your students are able to measure each other, have the group size relate to twice the number of calipers available. If not, work with 2-4 students at a time.

Motivation

Announce that while students are doing their workout, you will ask them to pair off and one pair at a time come to the side so that each student can learn to do the skinfold measure and get their measurements. Let them know that you will take the measurements if they would prefer. At the end of the class, when everyone has been measured, you will explain why the measure was important to take, why you want them to know how to take it, and what their measure is.

Lesson Sequence

1. Demonstrate what students can expect. As the teacher, being the guinea pig takes pressure off your students, but it might also embarrass the person who is taking the measurement. It is your call. Premarking each site will help. You can ask everyone to eyeball each midpoint.

   a. Ask students to look at the middle of the back of your upper arm. Have someone pinch your skin and measure the fold it makes just above the midpoint (see figure 4.1).

   b. Put your foot on a raised surface so that the knee is at a 90° angle.

   c. Pinch the skin on the inside of the calf at its widest girth and measure that fold (see figure 4.2).

2. Ask students to find a buddy to partner with. Have the class begin working on their normal routine, whether it is conditioning, aerobic dance, or whatever activity they can safely do without your undivided attention. Once they are at work, have students come in pairs or small groups (depending on how many calipers you have) and supervise them as they take measurements for each other.

   a. Record the measurement.

   b. Check scores against the body composition fitness chart of the healthy zone.

Review and Stretching

As students stretch, explain the following:

- The measurements they took will be entered in the computer and converted by the computer into an index of body-fat composition. That index will indicate whether they need to change their body-fat composition in order to avoid the many health risks that are associated with high levels of body fat.
- The risks are dramatic but usually don't appear until they get a little older. The risks are so serious that they can shorten their life span, and they include the following: high blood pressure, high cholesterol, heart disease, and stroke. It is far better to take control of such factors, set up good health patterns, get used to them, and make them part of their

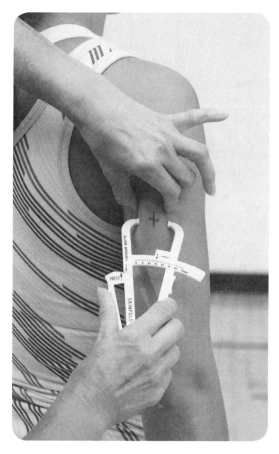

Figure 4.1 Calibrating the upper-arm skinfold.

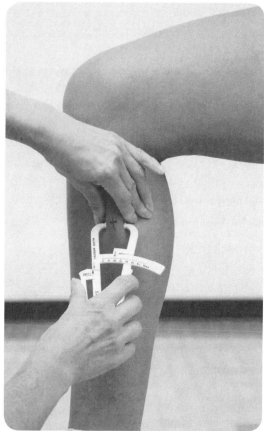

Figure 4.2 Calibrating the calf skinfold.

routine now than to go through the trauma of doing so once the health risks start affecting their lives.

- Explain that they can start avoiding such risks not just by watching their diet but also by doing more exercise.

Fitness Testing
FITNESSGRAM—BEGINNER, INTERMEDIATE, AND ADVANCED
LESSON 3

Muscular Strength, Flexibility, and Endurance

This measure determines the functional health of the musculoskeletal system. Muscular injuries often result from muscular imbalance, particularly at joints, as well as from loss of flexibility. When one side of an oppositional muscle group becomes much stronger and more developed than the other, hyperextension can result. Such is the case when an ACL ruptures in the knee. Weak hamstrings cannot counteract the stronger quadriceps, and when the difference gets too great for the weaker hamstrings to contain, the knee can hyperextend and rupture the ACL ligament. Equally important to note is that when one attempts to become stronger, muscles become thicker and shorter. To keep the full range of motion and prevent muscles from tearing, they must be stretched to their full length when they are warm. This is often best done after activity. Flexibility is the ability to stretch a muscle to its full length.

Facilities

Clean area where students can comfortably lie down

Materials

- Personal Fitness Record for Fitnessgram
- A pen or pencil for every two students
- Audio CD and sound system to play the music
- Mats with a 4.5-inch (11-centimeter) strip used for testing curls (consider taping the mats so you can give this test to half the class at once and not have to buy a special strip)
- 15-inch (38-centimeter) ruler for every two students
- One coin for every two students
- Chart showing the healthy zone for the curl-up, trunk lift, and push-up for the appropriate age group, grade, and sex

Performance Goals

Students will measure the following:

- Abdominal, upper-arm, and back strength
- Flexibility of the low back and shoulders

Cognitive Goals

Students will learn the following:

- Strong abdominal muscles help take pressure off the spine.
- Ignoring flexibility while developing strength puts students at a risk of injury.
- They should develop antagonist muscle groups equally to prevent injury.

Lesson Safety

Avoid possible infection due to contact with dirty surfaces.

Motivation

Explain that today's lesson will take several measurements in the strength, endurance, and flexibility categories. By the end of the lesson, everyone will understand the need for strong abdominal muscles and a constant effort to maintain flexibility while working to gain strength and endurance.

Lesson Sequence

1. Demonstrate a proper curl-up (see figure 4.3), showing how the hands slide from the nearest side of the testing strip to just over the far edge as you come up. Show how your head must touch the ground. (Testing form suggests that a piece of paper is left under the head and that the curl is not counted until the head returns to the paper and crinkles it.) The back should be on the mat with arms at the sides and the palms of the hands on the

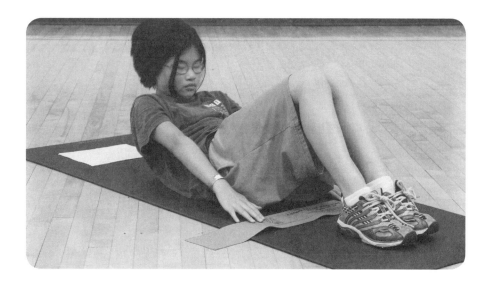

Figure 4.3 Testing abdominal strength with curl-ups.

103

mat, fingers touching the near side of the strip. Legs should be comfortably separated and bent at the knee at about a 140° angle with the feet as far out as possible and flat on the mat. Have students pair up and give them the following instructions.

- Stay on cadence (from music or your cadence call).
- Do one curl every 3 seconds.
- Continue to a maximum of 75 curls or a second error in form.
- Scorers should warn the students when they see a first form break but continue counting curls. At the second form break, stop counting and record the score on the partner's form.

2. Teach the trunk lift and demonstrate (see figure 4.4). Lying on the stomach with hands under thighs, lift the upper body off the mat while maintaining eye contact with the marker (coin) on the mat. Once up, hold the position long enough for the partner to measure the distance off the floor. Return to the ground slowly.

- Lifting up more than 12 inches (30 centimeters) is ill-advised.
- Use a flexible ruler to measure the distance between the floor and chin.
- Record the score in inches (or centimeters).
- The back muscles are the antagonist muscles for the abdomen and important for keeping the back in proper alignment.

3. Demonstrate and explain 90° push-ups. Show the push-up to extended arms and how the body should come down until elbows bend at a 90° angle to the floor (see figure 4.5).

- Explain that the push-up is done to cadence (one push-up every 3 seconds).

Figure 4.4 Measuring the trunk lift.

Figure 4.5 Down phase of a push-up.

- Have scorers concentrate on form, recording a total score as soon as the partner stops or has a second form break (back is not straight, arms do not extend, elbows do not come to 90° angle).

4. Gather students and read the range of scores that meet the healthy zone standard.

Review and Stretching

As students stretch, explain the following:

- Most of the students don't suffer from aching backs or sciatic pain because they haven't done as much damage as adults have to their skeleton. The human spine has a variety of curves that allow us to balance but also place an extraordinary burden on the muscles of the back and abdomen to keep them in line. Strengthening those muscles helps the back, but stretching them helps also. Anyone know why?

- Tell them that you ran out of time today, but that since flexibility in the lower back is so important to their structural health, you will be measuring it in the days to come.

FITNESSGRAM—BEGINNER, INTERMEDIATE, AND ADVANCED
LESSON 4

Flexibility

Maintaining joint flexibility is crucial to overall ability to function while avoiding serious injury. Young children usually have adequate flexibility, but older students who are doing conditioning and repetitive sport activities can find their strengthening muscles getting shorter and shorter. The Fitnessgram supplies data for two measures of flexibility: the back-saver sit and reach and the shoulder stretch. Shortened hamstrings or imbalanced hamstring flexibility will influence movement of the pelvis. This measure has no correlation to flexibility of the lower back. Similarly, students who do a lot of throwing and upper-arm conditioning often shorten their shoulder flexibility, which makes them lose range of motion and eventually may be responsible for serious injury to the shoulder joint. To maintain the full range of motion of joints and prevent their ligaments from tearing, joints must be stretched to their full range. This is often best done after activity, when the connective tissue is warm.

Facilities

Clean area where students can comfortably sit down

Materials

- Personal Fitness Record for Fitnessgram
- A pen or pencil for every two students
- Sturdy box that is 12 inches (30 centimeters) high with a measuring scale on its top and a 9-inch (23-centimeter) overhang over the side of the box where the foot rests so that the zero end of the measuring scale is nearest the student (see figure 4.6)
- Chart of the flexibility standard for operating in the healthy zone

Performance Goals

Students will measure the following:

- Right leg and left leg sit and reach
- Ability of the fingers to meet each other in a shoulder stretch

Cognitive Goals

Students will learn the following:

- Both their legs should have the same flexibility.
- If their fingers cannot touch behind their back, they will need to do more shoulder stretching.
- Maintaining joint flexibility is a matter of effort.

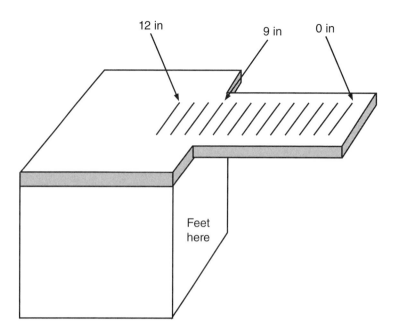

Figure 4.6 Back-saver sit-and-reach box.

Lesson Safety

Make certain that the majority of the class is engaged in an activity that does not need constant supervision because you will be overseeing two different activities at a time.

Motivation

As everyone works (I suggest this testing take place during a normal class when students are in the fitness unit), the class will be measuring the last items on the Fitnessgram. Allow students to measure in pairs and record their own scores. Students will take turns measuring their hamstring flexibility at the back-saver sit-and-reach box and then check to see whether they can reach both arms behind their back and get their fingertips to touch.

Lesson Sequence

1. Demonstrate the back-saver sit and reach (see figure 4.7). Sit with one leg extended so that the foot is against the side of the box and the measured overhang (or ruler) is above the leg. Keep one leg straight and the other bent so the knee is near the chest and the sole of the foot is on the floor. Reach forward with both hands evenly while keeping the head

Figure 4.7 Measuring the sit and reach.

106

up and back straight. Do this four times. Have a partner record the distance to the nearest half inch (centimeter) reached by the fingertips. Then switch legs and repeat.

    a. Ask students to take and record the measurements for both legs.

    b. Show that the measurement might differ between their right and left legs.

2. Explain the shoulder stretch and demonstrate. Reach the right arm over the shoulder and the left arm under the shoulder, trying to make them meet between the shoulder blades. Do they? Do the same with the left arm reaching over the shoulder and the right one reaching beneath. Do they meet? This is scored as a *yes* or *no*.

3. Start the class activity. Have pairs of students take and record their measurements for the back-saver sit and reach and the shoulder stretch.

    a.   Record scores.

    b.   Check whether scores fall into the healthy zone.

Review and Stretching

As students stretch, explain the following:

- Why it is important to be equally flexible on both sides
- How tightness can lead to back and hip problems
- How flexibility is lost
- How to regain a flexible joint by stretching daily

NYS Skills-Based Fitness Test

Although the Fitnessgram is the gold standard for health-related fitness tests, there is no skills-related fitness test that compares to the NYS fitness test and the normative information it provides. The norms for the NYS fitness test, which were developed in the 1970s, predate the obesity crisis and reflect the performance of a large population that was fitter than we have today. One may conclude that if today's students perform in the average or above-average achievement level on this skills-related test, they are relatively fit.

NYS Fitness Test Learning Experience Outline

Contents and Procedure

The NYS skills-based fitness test has four components—agility, speed and agility, abdominal strength, and endurance—with norms by gender for grades 7 through 12, ages 11 through 17. If students are alert and cooperative, they can complete it and learn their achievement level in two 40-minute classes.

Do the first three segments indoors in one day once students learn how to score the tests.

1. Half the class performs the 10-second agility test while their partners stand aside to score and record. They switch and the test is run again.

2. Half the class does 1 minute of half sit-ups while their partners make sure their knees are bent and their feet flat on the floor while partners hold their ankles, count the complete sit-ups, and record their total. They switch and the test is repeated.

3. A row of cones are set on a line 10 feet (3 meters) apart. This is the starting and finishing line. An equal number of cones are set 45 feet (14 meters) away opposite each starting cone; these mark the lane students must run in and around. Students wait in line well behind the starting line. One student comes alongside the right of the each cone, behind the starting line. On your signal, each student at each cone runs down to and around the far cone, doing three laps. The scorers listen for their runners' time as they return for the third lap. The timer starts yelling out the time—18, 19, 20, 21, 22, and so on—as the runners begin to come back to the finish line on their third lap.

4. Have all students start and complete the mile (1.5-kilometer) walk–run in one class. To do this accurately, use a marker system to keep track of completed laps. It is not unusual for students to cross the track or credit themselves for more laps than they have done. To avoid this, hand students a marker such as a straw or a tongue depressor (the nurse will probably accommodate you if you ask nicely) after each lap. When they complete four laps and can return three straws, give them a time. If your students are as creative as mine, they will anticipate this and start taking straws from the cafeteria. It is helpful to alternate what is used as a lap marker. If you anticipate continued problems, you might color or stamp an image on the sticks.

5. Provide all students with their achievement-level scores.

6. Explain the meaning of the statistics being used:
   - Normal frequency distribution
   - Normal bell curve
   - Percentile rank
   - Scaled scores (see appendix C for raw score conversion tables)

Teaching Tips
- Identify students who have difficulty following instructions and pair them with a helper.
- Do a reality check for scores that appear unreasonably high or low.

Facilities
Measure and pre-mark the testing area for the agility test and the placement of the cones for the shuttle run. Make three long parallel lines that are 4 feet (1 meter) apart from each other for the agility test. Make the lines long enough to accommodate at least 25% of the students at one time. Leave markers 45 feet (14 meters) apart to indicate where the cones for the shuttle run should be placed.

Materials
- NYS Physical Fitness Scorecards for each student; fall and spring sides available for entries
- A pen or pencil for every two students
- Stopwatch
- Blackboard, marker board, or other visual aid
- Enlargement of the statistical norms for each age group and grade level so it is visible from 20 feet (6 meters) away so that students can locate their scaled scores at the conclusion of the test and enter the ranked scores on their fitness cards
- Copies of the NYS norms for each grade level

Testing Timeline
Seventh Grade
- Day 1: Teach, demonstrate, and practice scoring of the first three subtests.
- Day 2: Test and record scores for agility, strength, and speed.
- Day 3: Test and record the mile (1.5-kilometer) walk–run.
- Day 4: Find achievement-level scores, explain their significance, complete the fitness card, and find the total level of fitness.

Eighth Through 12th Grades
- Day 1: Review agility, sit-up, and dash tests and scoring as they come up. Test and record scores. Provide immediate feedback via the achievement-level scores if possible.

- Day 2: Give and complete the mile (1.5-kilometer) walk–run, record scores, and locate achievement-level score.
- Day 3: Only if this cannot be completed earlier, complete physical fitness cards, reminding students of the meaning of achievement-level scores. Have students calculate their total fitness level. Then begin a new unit.

Assessment

All students should be held accountable for completing all fitness test items before the conclusion of the class in which it is given. The school should report fitness test scores to parents. Students whose achievement level falls below the 39th percentile should be taught to be concerned about their improvement. This can be done with

- a general discussion about the relevance of being average,
- a private discussion with the student, and
- a letter sent home suggesting your concerns and addressing lifestyle changes that might improve the student's health and performance.

Fitness Testing
NYS FITNESS TEST—BEGINNER
LESSON 1

Procedure and Scoring

Lesson 1 is for first-year students only. It is not recommended for classes that have already taken the fitness test once. For grade levels with experience, skip to the next lesson.

Facilities

1. Place tape along the length of the gym a minimum of 14 feet (4 meters) from the long wall.
2. Put down two more lines 4 feet (1 meter) from either side of the first line so that there are three lines that run the length of the gym and are 4 feet (1 meter) apart.
3. For the shuttle run, place a permanent marker (use tape or a painted mark somewhere on the floor or adjacent wall so you don't have to remeasure where you would place the cones for the shuttle run later on) 45 feet (14 meters) from the starting line of the agility test so the agility line can be used as the starting line for the shuttle run. If the mark is made on a wall, it will be a lasting reminder of where to place cones for the 45-foot (14-meter) shuttle-running lanes.
   - Make certain running lanes for the shuttle run are 10 feet (3 meters) apart.
   - Make certain that the finish line is 14 feet (4 meters) from a wall.

Materials

- NYS Physical Fitness Scorecards for each student
- Pens or pencils for half the class
- Stopwatch
- Minimum of 12 cones

Performance Goals

Students will do the following:

- Follow instructions as given.
- Score accurately and within the rules.
- Complete headings on their scorecards.

Cognitive Goals

Students will learn the following:

- Reasons for being tested
- What the test is measuring
- How to follow group instructions, including the rules and procedure of each subtest

Lesson Safety

Lanes and running areas must be set up so there is adequate space between them and students are not in danger of running into the walls or running into each other.

Motivation

Explain that students will be learning to take a quick measure of several skill and strength items that allow them to compare themselves not just to kids in this class or even this school but to kids in New York State who took this test in the 1960s and 1970s. It will be interesting to see how today's students match up. It will also be cool to keep a record and see how they change from year to year.

To be comparable, everyone must do exactly the same test under the same conditions as the original students; otherwise the scores will tell us nothing. That is why in this lesson everyone will have to learn how to do the test right. That concept is what scientists use to conduct studies—they eliminate the variables so they can draw conclusions that go beyond their laboratory. This test, too, will draw conclusions that go beyond what they anticipate from themselves and their friends at school.

Warm-Up

1. Jog around the work space for 1 to 2 minutes.
2. Stretch the quadriceps, hamstrings, gastrocnemius, and back muscles.

Lesson Sequence

1. Distribute scorecards and pencils and have students fill out headings.
2. Explain that the class will learn three of the four subtests today.
3. Collect the cards.
4. Demonstrate the agility test and teach how it is scored. Beginning position straddles the center line. On the *go* signal, the student sidesteps so one foot passes over the outer line on the right (or left), immediately sliding back to cross the center line and pass the left line with one foot. The student continues sliding left and right for 10 seconds while the scorer counts each line a foot passes over.
5. Have students count each line as the demonstrator's foot passes over it. Count out loud and in unison during a slow demonstration. Then do it for 10 seconds at a quicker pace with the class counting out loud.
6. Allow half the students to try the sidestepping test, scoring for themselves first and then scoring for a friend. As scorers, they should stand off to the side.
7. Demonstrate a proper sit-up (elbows crossed over chest, rise to touch the elbows to the knees with the ankles held by a partner).
8. Allow a limited time to try sit-ups with partner counting.
9. Demonstrate the shuttle run (see figure 4.8). (Set up several lanes so multiple students can run at once.) Runners start from behind and to the right side of a cone. On the *go* signal, they run to the cone they face, run around it, and run back. They complete three laps around the cones, running the final half lap at top speed because they no longer have to run around it. Have the timer call out the time on the stopwatch once the first person turns around the far cone on the last lap back to the starting line, counting 19, 20, 1 (no time to say "21"), 2, 3, 4, 5, and so on.
10. Have a trial run.

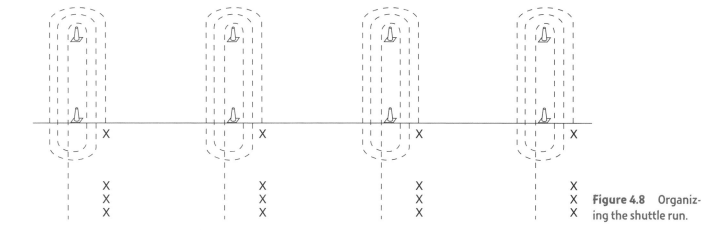

Figure 4.8 Organizing the shuttle run.

Review and Stretching

As students stretch, discuss the following:

- When counting the sidestepping test, do you count each time the person goes right and then left, or do you count each line his foot passes over?
- Should you count the sit-up when your partner comes up or goes down?
- How will you know what the runner's score is when so many people are running the shuttle run at the same time?
- It is important to sleep well, have a good breakfast, and remember their change of clothes because for any skills test, their performance should be their best work.

Assessment

Observe the ability of the class to respond to instruction.

New York State (NYS) Physical Fitness Scorecard

Name _____ Date _____

	Raw scores (actual score from the test)	Achievement-level score (based on NYS norms for age or grade)	Percentile rank (comparative score of same age group across NYS)
Agility Sidestepping test			
Strength 1 min sit-up test			
Speed Shuttle run			
Endurance Mile (1.5-kilometer) walk–run			
Total fitness level scores Rankings			

From Isobel Kleinman, 2009, *Complete Physical Education Plans for Grades 5 to 12, Second Edition* (Champaign, IL: Human Kinetics).

Reprinted, by permission, from New York State Education Department.

Testing Agility, Shuttle Run, and Abdominal Strength

This is the second lesson of NYS fitness testing for beginners and the first lesson of NYS fitness testing for intermediate and advanced students.

Facilities

Gym space taped and measured for the agility test and the shuttle run before the class arrives, with 12 cones placed to one side

Materials

- NYS Physical Fitness Scorecards (headings already filled out)
- Pens or pencils for half the class
- Stopwatch
- Minimum of 12 cones
- Charts showing percentile rank for each raw score of the age group and gender

Performance Goals

Students will record raw scores of the following:

- 10-second agility test
- 1-minute sit-up test
- Shuttle run

Cognitive Goal

Students will learn their personal best for the three tests.

Lesson Safety

Do not allow students to perform with anything in their hands. Have waiting students sit well behind the starting line of the shuttle run.

Motivation

Ask everyone to follow instructions efficiently and tell them if they do so, not only can they get done with the 2 minutes and 10 seconds of activity, but they will be able to find out if they rank in the average, above-average, or below-average categories compared with students of the 1960s and 1970s. Ask them to do their best.

Warm-Up

Jog around the work space for 1 to 2 minutes or do a line dance.

Lesson Sequence

1. Distribute fitness cards and pencils.
2. Begin the agility test after answering questions and reminding scorers to count each line that their partner's foot passes over. Remind students that the scoring is hard because their partner will be passing the line quickly and that they should count all lines, including the center line, but only the lines that the foot passes. Remind students taking the test to make sure their foot passes the outside line.
   a. Performer straddles the line and slides in either direction on *go.*
   b. Partner counts lines passed and records the score when *stop* is heard.
   c. The entire class can do the test in two shifts, at which time you should check for clear mistakes, incorrect scoring, and unrealistic numbers. Run a third trial for corrections only.

3. Begin the strength test for sit-ups.

   a. Half the class lines up facing the same direction.

   b. Emphasize the rules: Students must curl to sitting up, arms must be folded in front of the chest, elbows must touch the thighs coming up, and midback must touch the ground going down.

      Remind scorers to be accurate. Emphasize that if students are tired, it is all right to slow down; they should try to do as many as possible.

   c. Give the *go* signal and 1 minute later the *stop* signal. Be verbally encouraging as the minute goes by, telling students how much time is left and asking them to do another and another and another sit-up.

   d. Have the partners mark the sit-up score in the proper raw-score box. Do this in two shifts.

4. Begin the shuttle run.

   a. Line up students in equal lines behind each running lane.

   b. Remind students that they must be behind the cone until the *go* signal, that they have to do three laps around the sets of cones, and that when they turn around the far cone on the final lap, they should run to the finish line at their top speed.

   c. Remind scorers to give scores to the closest half-second once the runner passes the last cone. Also remind everyone that the scorers will only know the score if they can hear it being called out. If they get too excited and start cheering (which they always do), no one will hear the times.

   d. Run the first person at each station at the same time, making sure that scorers record the score as soon as the run is finished (scorers sometimes forget).

5. If time allows, give students the achievement-level scores and have them record them in the achievement-level column.

6. Collect the cards and pens or pencils.

Review and Stretching

1. As students stretch, comment that doing one's best, even for a short time, is tiring. Congratulate students whose scores reflect their best.

2. Help students get mentally prepared for next class. They are going to do four laps around the track—the mile (1.5-kilometer) walk–run. So, remind them to sleep well, have a good breakfast, and remember a change of clothing.

Assessment

Collect and check that fitness cards are filled out with raw scores for tests 1 through 3.

NYS FITNESS TEST—BEGINNER, INTERMEDIATE, AND ADVANCED

Testing Endurance: Mile Walk–Run

This is the third lesson of NYS fitness test for beginners and the second lesson for intermediate and advanced levels.

Facilities

Quarter-mile (.4-kilometer) track free of obstructions

Materials

- Partially complete NYS Physical Fitness Scorecards
- Pens or pencils for half the class
- Stopwatch

- Enough markers to provide 3 to each runner at a time (e.g., cotton swabs, ice-cream sticks, tongue depressors, straws)

Performance Goals

Students will do the following:

- Complete four laps around the track before the end of class.
- Convert the raw score for the test to achievement-level scores.

Cognitive Goals

Students will learn the following:

- How long a mile is and time required to complete it
- What the test is measuring (endurance)
- Strategies for completing the test
- That tests reflect the best one can do that day

Lesson Safety

Be alert to any health problems, including falls, wheezing, fainting, and seizures.

Motivation

This performance item is a real test of endurance if students don't do it as if they are strolling in their favorite store. As soon as they are done, they will convert the raw scores to achievement-level scores so they can compare themselves with classmates, friends in other classes, friends in other schools, and students of the same age and sex who took this test many years ago. It tests aerobic endurance if students get past the pleasure principle and try their best even though they're tired. Most people walk 3 miles (5 kilometers) per hour, or 20 minutes a mile, but in this class, they shouldn't. This test is supposed to measure their best output, not a casual walk, and they should do their best, which means running, jogging, or walking when they can't run or jog.

Lesson Sequence

1. Explain to students that you will give them a marker the minute they finish a lap and that once they complete the fourth lap and have three unbroken markers in hand, they will get their time.
2. Remind students that any run longer than a dash requires pacing. If they cannot sustain the pace they start with, it is perfectly all right to slow down, but they should keep moving forward so that they complete the distance during class time. Explain that the inside of the track is the shortest distance and when possible, runners should stay on the inside. Also encourage them to test their self-improvement by trying for less time than the last time they took the test.
3. After the test is complete, have students record their raw scores on their fitness card, and if time remains, learn their achievement level and record it. This can be done by having an assistant (an unprepared student, a medically excused student, or the first runner who ran ahead of the class) to read the norms for everyone.
4. Collect the fitness cards.

Review and Stretching

As students stretch, discuss the following:

- Is this your first time completing a mile? Congratulations!
- Announce what scores fell in the healthy zone for their age, grade, and sex.
- Congratulate the boy and girl with the best time.
- Did you do better than last time, when you were younger?
- When dismissing class, suggest that they will feel better after a shower and a good night's rest.

Assessment

Compare the collected statistics and previous performances.

Fitness Testing Feedback

This is the fourth lesson of NYS fitness testing for beginners and the third lesson for intermediate and advanced levels.

Facilities

Quiet space in which to communicate and a flat, firm, clean floor on which to sit and write

Materials

- NYS Physical Fitness Scorecards
- Pens or pencils for half the class
- Blackboard and chalk or marker board and markers
- Statistical norms chart for each age group and grade level for the mile (1.5-kilometer) walk–run that is visible from 20 feet (6 meters) away

Performance Goals

Students will do the following:

- Complete their physical fitness cards:
  - Each raw score will be converted to an achievement-level score.
  - Achievement-level scores will be tallied.
  - Total achievement-level scores will be converted to a fitness-level score and percentile rank.
- Begin their next unit when the paperwork is done.

Cognitive Goals

Students will learn the following:

- What a comparative score is
- What a percentile rank is
- What a scaled score is
- Where they stand when compared with others of the same sex, grade, and age
- How to draw conclusions about fitness, achievement, and personal results

Motivation

Now that raw scores have been entered, it's time to see where students stand. Ask if anyone has taken this test before and if so, can they tell whether their raw scores improved? Did they do more sit-ups this year than last, have a better mile time, do more side steps, or run the shuttle faster? Did their better score reflect their age and experience, or did they go up a notch in their peer group? Today they are going to learn that achievement-level scores will explain a lot.

Warm-Up

Do a long warm-up since the majority of this lesson will be academic. You might choose something in preparation for their next unit.

Lesson Sequence

1. Draw a normal distribution curve on the blackboard, including standard deviations, mean, range of scaled scores on the baseline, and percentile rank.
2. Explain the normal distribution curve, the meaning of average range in terms of the scaled (fitness-level) scores, and how they can find out their own fitness-level scores by reading the posted charts (see figure 4.9).
3. Explain what a percentile rank means and how to find theirs.

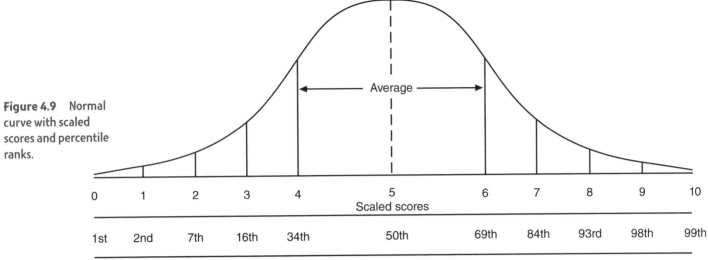

Figure 4.9 Normal curve with scaled scores and percentile ranks.

4. Return fitness cards, distribute pens or pencils, and have students enter their achievement-level scores.

5. Point out that some students do better on some test items (practice effect, natural speed) than others, but now it is time to look at the whole picture.

6. Teach students to calculate the total level of fitness.

7. When all entries on the cards are complete, collect them.

8. Seek out students who could only reach the 16th percentile to privately discuss the findings and make suggestions for future growth.

Review and Stretching

Discuss the significance of where the students stand now and where they should stand in terms of their physical fitness. Ask them to share this information with their parents.

Assessment

Compare student raw scores with statistics available from New York State. See appendix B for the NYS physical fitness norm conversion tables for appropriate grade levels.

Students whose fitness levels do not approach the average range should be encouraged to improve their effort in class and be more active at home. Enlisting the help of the students' parents is advised. A sample letter to parents can be found on page 117.

Sample Letter to Parents

School letterhead

Address

Town, state, and zip code

Parent's name

Parent's address

Parent's town, state, and zip code

Date

Dear _____,

We have just completed a physical fitness program designed to promote health, fitness, and an understanding of the importance of an active lifestyle. In concluding our unit, students took a New York State skills-based physical fitness test and measured their performance against scores of others of the same grade, age, and sex that were gathered and statistically analyzed by New York State. Our comparisons have left some concerns. After a concerted effort to improve everyone's physical fitness, _____ was not able to perform in the average range for the appropriate level.

_____ achieved a total percentile score of _____, meaning that _____ % of the students the same age, grade, and gender outperformed _____. While this score is not necessarily reflective of _____'s health, it did compare performance in agility, abdominal strength, speed, and endurance to many in a rather large sample. I am writing at this time to ask you to help us improve _____'s chances for a long and healthy life.

Would you help by stressing a lifestyle that sets aside more time and interest in large-muscle activities? Activities of an aerobic nature are especially helpful. Walking, jogging, dancing, kickboxing, bike riding, swimming, and other activities that raise heart rate and can be sustained continuously for 20 minutes are wonderful for cardiorespiratory improvement and fitness. Aerobic effort as well as stretching and strengthening activities will help elevate _____'s quality of life now and in the future.

Since none of us can trade in our bodies for a new one when we feel they let us down or we are tired of them, it is prudent to teach our young people how to take care of theirs now. Thank you for your time and effort.

Please feel free to contact me. I can be reached at _____ (school phone number and hours accessible).

Sincerely,

_____

PART III

Creative Movement and Dance Units

Dance

Chapter Overview

1. Teach the background of dance for motivation.
   - Value of dance historically and currently as a social outlet, an aerobic exercise, and an art
   - How local popularity of various dances has led to dance clubs for country-western, ballroom, swing, disco, and Latin dancing
   - How cultures have their own dances such as the mambo and tango

2. Teach terminology and how to match locomotion to words.
   - Basic locomotion—step, run, skip, slide, gallop
   - Basic dance formations—line, circle, square, file, longways, or contra
   - Basic dance positions—two hands joined and facing, promenade, varsouvienne, open social dance, closed social dance
   - Basic square-dance calls—circle, promenade, swing, do-si-do, allemande, grand right and left, star
   - Basic dance steps—two-step, polka, waltz, Schottische, mazurka

3. Focus on following directions:
   - Following calls
   - Following a line of direction
   - Synchronizing with large groups

4. Teach the importance of music and rhythm.
   - Staying on the beat
   - Picking up the rhythm of specific songs
   - Identifying folk dances

5. Assign partnering responsibilities (leading, following, going home, counterbalancing).

6. Stress etiquette and courtesy.

7. Encourage creative exploration.
   - Creating dance routines to favorite music
   - Creating a modern dance sequence
   - Taking movement sequence and playing with size, speed, and flow

Dance Study Sheet

History and Value

Dance has evolved over thousands of years from a form that might once have been ceremonial to one that is social or artistic. Cultural differences, the music of the time, the clothing people wear, and the social mores of the day all influence the type of dance that evolves and the place that dance has in a culture. As in painting, music, and literature, dance reflects the values of the time when it was created.

Imagine hip-hop danced to Baroque music by dancers in corsets and hoop dresses. Impossible! Imagine ballet performed by dancers in clogs and a chador. Impossible! Imagine men and women dancing in a close embrace when they are from cultures that frown on men and women associating together unless they are married. Impossible!

Common Square-Dance Terms

circle or promenade—Walk around the circumference of the square in a counterclockwise direction.

home—Side of the square where the men started at the beginning of the dance.

head couples—Couples with their backs to the music (couples 1 and 3).

side couples—Couples 2 and 4.

partners—Dancers to the men's right and the ladies' left.

corners—Dancers to the men's left and the ladies' right.

allemande—Forearm swing.

swing—Partners hold on to each other (in a variety of positions) while circling.

star—With hands in the center of the square or circle, everyone walks around its circumference.

grand right and left—Partners face each other (men counterclockwise, ladies clockwise), extend right hands to each other, walk by each other, extend left hands to the next person they see, walk by, and continue to extend opposite arms to the people they meet until they meet up with their partner again.

shuffle—A light walk.

do-si-do—With arms crossed at chest, walk forward, pass right shoulders, and back out to place.

clockwise (CW)—Move to the left when facing the center of the circle.

counterclockwise (CCW)—Move to the right when facing the center of the circle.

Common Dance Rules

- Women follow the lead of the men.
- When dancing in a formation, the follower is to the right of the leading partner.
- In partner-changing dances, the promenade is with the new partner.
- If dancers are without a partner after a partner change, they should go to the middle of the circle to find a new one (dance lost-and-found).

Folk Dances

Circle dances—Bingo, La Raspa, Greensleeves, Jessie Polka, Mayim, To Ting, Teton Mountain Stomp, Salty Dog Rag, Road to the Isles, Sicilian Tarantella, Hora, Doudlebska Polka, Vé David, Hot Lips, and Oh Johnny Oh

Line dances—Sevila Se Bela Loza, Seljancica Kola, Misirlou, Nebesko Kolo, and Achy Breaky Heart

»continued

»continued

Individual dances—Pata Pata, Saturday Night Fever Walk, Limbo Rock, and Stepping Out

Longways sets—Virginia Reel

Square dances—Red River Valley, Texas Star, Split the Ring and Around Just One, Arkansas Traveler, Bend It Tight, and Four in the Middle

Partner dances—Texas Two-Step and Cajun Two-Step

Ballroom dances—waltz, mambo, and cha-cha

Dance Extension Project

Name _____ Date _____

Teacher _____ Class _____

What equipment do you need to go dancing when not in school?

Name four places where you can dance when not in school.

Do you have friends who would go dancing with you? List their names.

Name five health and social benefits of participating in a dance program.

Name three activities you can do in your community that involve dance.

From Isobel Kleinman, 2009, *Complete Physical Education Plans for Grades 5 to 12, Second Edition* (Champaign, IL: Human Kinetics).

Dance Student Portfolio Checklist

Name _____ Date _____

Teacher _____ Class _____

_____ Able to move on beat and stay in rhythm.

_____ Has the energy to complete the Hora and Salty Dog Rag.

_____ Can perform basic locomotion—step, run, hop, jump, skip, slide, and gallop.

_____ Has learned basic dance steps—Schottische, two-step, polka, and waltz.

_____ Has learned simple circle dances—Mayim, Hora.

_____ Has learned line dances—Sevila Se Bela Loza, Nebesko Kolo.

_____ Can dance independently—Pata Pata, Limbo Rock, Achy Breaky Heart.

_____ Can dance in formation with partners—Greensleeves, To Ting, Vé David.

_____ Has learned to move in different directions while in formation.

_____ Has learned couples dance positions—skater's, varsouvienne, closed social.

_____ Can dance with a partner in social dance position—mambo, waltz.

_____ Can respond to basic square-dance calls—circle, promenade, swing.

_____ Can do partner-changing dances—Bingo, Texas Star, Oh Johnny Oh.

_____ Has learned to use counterweight to turn—buzz turn, pivot turn.

_____ Has learned the grand right and left.

_____ Appreciates the cultural diversity and history of dance.

_____ Has internalized proper social etiquette.

_____ Can perform up to six dances in one class.

_____ Is building social and ballroom skills—mambo, cha-cha, regional two-step.

Dance Learning Experience Outline

Contents and Procedure

1. Teach background for motivation.
   a. Dance as a natural aerobic activity
   b. Value of dance historically and in the present as a social outlet, an aerobic exercise, and an art
   c. How local popularity led to dance clubs for country-western, ballroom, swing, disco, and Latin dance
   d. How cultures have their own dances (samba, tango, cha-cha)

2. Teach terminology so students can match the proper locomotion to its term.

    a. Basic locomotion—step, run, skip, slide, gallop

    b. Basic dance formations—line (single, double, independent, differing direction), circle (facing in or out, moving counterclockwise or clockwise, single or double), square, file, longways or contra formation

    c. Basic dance positions—challenge, two hands joined and facing, promenade, varsouvienne, open social dance, closed social dance

    d. Basic square dance calls—circle, promenade, swing, do-si-do, allemande, grand right and left, star

    e. Basic dance steps—two step, polka, waltz, Schottische, mazurka

3. Focus on following instructions and direction.

    a. Following calls, as in square dance

    b. Following line of direction as in turn to right, follow line, and so on

    c. Following instructions in order to synchronize with large groups

4. Teach the importance of music and rhythm.

    a. Equate staying on beat to aspects of sport (not rushing shots, playing in one's own rhythm).

    b. Help students pick up the rhythm of specific songs.

    c. Encourage them to identify folk dances by the music being played.

    d. Equate staying in rhythm with a healthy, sustainable activity.

5. Teach partnering—how to lead, importance of following, going home, counterbalancing weight in spins and turns, and using the correct foot.

6. Teach and expect proper etiquette and courtesy.

7. Encourage creative exploration once fundamentals have been taught.

    a. Create dance routine to favorite music.

    b. Create modern dance sequence.

    c. Take movement sequence and play with size, speed, and flow.

Special Message to Teachers With No Dance Experience

The outline in front of you might look daunting. The range of dances per experience level might seem impossible, but covering this unit is definitely worth it. Regardless of your qualifications, at least 50% of your students will find your effort endearing, if not wonderful, especially if you have the confidence to tell them that you care enough to try but are not quite sure about the dance you are teaching. If you have no colleagues who can help, in almost every class there will be a couple of students who are willing to help you figure out how to fit the written instructions to music and help you get through the first few lessons. Most classes will go along with the experiment in good humor. So, go ahead with this program. Sure, it takes some tackling, but it will be easier and more rewarding if you elicit the help of your best dancing students to work through it.

Teaching Tips

•   It is probably best to acknowledge that many of your students will have had little or no exposure to dance and that many males in class will be resistant to learning dance even though when they grow older, the ability to dance will be a great icebreaker and allow them to meet lots of people. Remind them that although some young men might fear that dancing will make them seem less manly, men from many cultures have strong male participation. For example, men in Latin America and in Europe have prominent roles in social and performance dance; those men are respected and admired just as much as professional athletes are.

- Use explanations of cultures and the history of dance to motivate and teach diversity. Explore the development of the tango. Talk about how widespread dance is in community social halls in countries such as Argentina and Brazil. Discuss how dance marks cultural ceremonies, such as how Native Americans used a prayer dance for rain. Explain how for societies in which boys and girls were separated, dance was a way to flirt and show off their talents. Use films such as *Saturday Night Fever, Fame, Flashdance, White Nights, Shall We Dance, Dirty Dancing, Mad Hot Ballroom,* and *Strictly Ballroom* to motivate students and to find male role models. Stress once again that guys who dance are in great demand at any place where dancing occurs.

- These lessons provide a lot of variety, concentrating on accurate renditions of each dance. They use different songs and formations and have different cultural influences. Variety is the spice of life—so much diversity is fun, having fun wears down the reticent, and over time most students will get it right.

- Teach dances that have been introduced in countries other than the United States and include background about the dance, its purpose, and if and how it is used today.

- Introduce several new things a day while reviewing the dance activities learned before.

- The unit is planned to reach the skill level and experience of the group without treating students as if they are babies.

- Regardless of their likes and dislikes, students should be courteous and cooperative.

- Students with disabilities or temporary medical concerns should walk through all instructions if possible. Many activities will be suitable for them unless their condition prevents basic locomotion.

- Students will not necessarily be changing clothing during this unit. Dance is typically done in street clothes or dress clothes. Although there is a good chance they will be sweating as a result of their dancing, consider not having them change clothing for this unit. Students will welcome the opportunity to wear street clothes and you will welcome the fact you have 10 minutes more with them before they have to leave. It is suggested that you instruct them to wear clothing that will not be ruined by sweating and that they come to class with sneakers or special dance shoes so the dance floor will not be ruined.

- The dance unit is the most taxing instructional unit on a teacher's voice. And if the teacher is constantly dancing to model the dances for the students, it is the hardest on the body as well. Imagine dancing with every class, giving dance cues while the music is playing, and constantly cuing the kids until almost everyone has learned the dance for themselves. That is what I used to do, but as I got older I learned that actively participating in five dance classes a day was too wearing on my body and vocal cords. So, I looked for students who learned quickly, danced correctly, were on beat, and were not thrown off by those who weren't and had them become models for students who were not quite able to remember the dances. This has served several purposes well—it's good for my voice, body, and knees, and it's great for the students doing the modeling.

- Frequently, the best dancers are the ones who do not shine during the sport units. Being singled out as the ones that the whole class should look to, helping the teacher, and being in front of the room with all eyes on them boosts their self-esteem and generates such feelings of trust and camaraderie that once the unit ends and class is back to doing other activities, the dance standouts try harder, do better, and are happier than before.

Facilities

- A clean, well-ventilated room large enough so each student can move freely and small enough that the acoustics do not get lost is required. A room with a mirrored wall is preferable. It gives students in the back many more angles to move to so they can see your demonstrations. It also facilitates feedback, allowing you to see behind your back so you know where your directions are falling short and how and when students are having difficulty keeping up.

- A slick, clean floor is also needed. One that gives is preferable. Dancing on concrete or something similar is hard on the knees.

Materials

Assemble a music library of songs for the following dances.

- Beginner unit: Grand March, Bingo, Pata Pata, Savila Se Bela Loza, Hora, Saturday Night Fever, Virginia Reel, La Raspa, Greensleeves, Jessie Polka, Seljancica Kola, and Red River Valley
- Intermediate unit: Mayim, Limbo Rock, Misirlou, mambo music from *Dirty Dancing* or other, Achy Breaky Heart, Nebesko Kolo, Sicilian Tarantella, Texas Star, Stepping Out, To Ting, Teton Mountain Stomp, Salty Dog Rag, and Oh Johnny, Oh
- Advanced unit: Doudlebska Polka, Vé David, Hot Lips, country and Cajun dance music for the two-step, ballroom dance music specifically for the cha-cha, and music for square dances such as Arkansas Traveler, Gents Star Right, Promenade the Ring, Split the Ring and Around Just One, Bend It Tight, and Four in the Middle

In addition, this unit requires the following:

- Music player that amplifies without distortion
- Detachable speakers that can be moved in front of the microphone
- Voiceover microphone feature on the amplifier
- Wireless microphone or microphone with a long lead
- Specific dance instructions—Instructions to dances cited in this text are included. Most folk dance music includes inserts with instructions. Seek out a copy of *Dance Awhile*.

Unit Timeline

This chapter includes three units, one for each level, that offer 10 or 11 lessons each.

Assessment

A performance rubric and a written quiz can be found at the end of each unit.

Suggested Resources

Folk Dance Music. 2008. http://folkdancemusic.net/.

Kraus, R. 1950. *Square dances of today: How to teach and how to call them.* New York: Ronald Press.

Kraus, R. 1964. *Folk dance.* New York: Macmillan.

Pittman, A.M., M.S. Waller, and C.L. Dark. 2008. *Dance awhile: Handbook of folk, square, contra, and social dance.* 10th ed. Needham Heights, MA: Allyn & Bacon.

In addition, record inserts and record jackets usually include instructions.

Supplemental Assignments

Three student handouts have been provided for convenience. The student portfolio checklist will enable students to keep track of what they have learned about dance over the years. The study sheet will provide a resource to check for facts they may have forgotten. And the extension project will get them thinking about where, how, and with whom they might participate in dance outside of school.

Walk, Run, Schottische

Facilities

Ventilated room with a floor that gives and enough space for students to move freely

Materials

- Music for the Grand March, Pata Pata, and Sevila Se Bela Loza
- Sound system that can project music clearly throughout the dance space

Performance Goals

Students will do the following:

- Walk to a beat.
- Identify right from left.

Cognitive Goals

Students will learn the following:

- How to identify rhythm
- That marching always starts on the left foot
- That different countries use different rhythms
- How to follow in line

Lesson Safety

When dancing line dances, students who lead must learn to take their lines to open spaces in the room and move so that they are not racing and dragging the line behind them. They should be discouraged from trying to crash, running through other lines, and racing ahead of the music.

Motivation

Explain that the students will be learning how cultures around the world played and socialized in earlier times. They will hear different music, and they will have to imagine how styles and costumes were different and influenced how people could dance. They will learn that dance also was influenced by how socially conservative a culture was when the dances were developed. Explain that eventually, they will learn dances from countries such as England, Scotland, Mexico, the Caribbean, Israel, and Serbia and get an idea of how dance developed in the United States.

Explain that since people normally wear traditional dress when they dance, students will wear their regular clothes during this unit.

Warm-Up

A gradual, metered introduction to movements of the day will serve the purpose of a gross motor warm-up for this day and for the remainder of the dance unit. Since the dances do not start at top speed or ask for extreme movement, dancing itself is a good warm-up.

Lesson Sequence

1. March in place (Grand March)—no music, just cadence.
   a. Have everyone begin with the left foot and stay on called cadence.
   b. Ask them to chorus your cadence: "Left, left, left-right-left."
   c. Teach the following:
      - About face—Step L, pivot half-turn, step out on R foot.
      - Right turn—Step L, pivot quarter-turn R, step out on R foot.
      - Left turn—Step R, pivot quarter-turn L, step out on L foot.
      - Two-step halt—After signal, the next left–right ends the cadence.

>   d. In line, have students march, varying instructions (forward, right turn, about face, forward, left turn) until you say "Halt."
>
>   • Begin with no music.
>   • Try with music and instructions.
>
> 2. Teach Pata Pata (South Africa), teaching each set of four counts without music, then adding it together with the music. Once you have taught all of Pata Pata, add the music, calling instructions for the first four repetitions.
>
> 3. Teach Sevila Se Bela Loza (see figure 5.1). Be sure to introduce the country of origin, Serbia, and a little history of the dance and country.

Pata Pata

- 1-4—Touch R toe to right, step R back to place, touch L toe left, step L back to place. Add music and repeat a few times.

- 5-8—Lift hands so palms are forward, elbows are at the side, the toes move out, and the heels remain touching (5). Bring hands down to side and move heels out (6). Bring hands up and close heels (7). Bring hands down and close toes, cueing "Toes, heels, heels, toes" (8). Put music on and repeat the first eight counts a few times.

- 1-4—Bring R knee up, twisting toward L elbow, crossing midline of body (1). Touch R foot to ground to right side (2) and repeat (3 and 4), cueing "Right knee, down, Right knee, down."

- 5-8—Kick L foot forward (5). Step down in place (6). Quarter-turn R, stepping on R foot (7), then stepping L in place (8).

Sevila Se Bela Loza

Teach how this line dance follows the leader and retraces its steps (see figure 5.1). Teach both parts, put on music, and dance through, leading a line and calling instructions.

Part 1

Have students listen as the music changes and walk through part 1.

- 1-20—In line, begin on R foot and take 19 small running steps to the right. On the 20th step, step L, hop, and turn L.

- 1-20—Take 19 small running steps to the left. On 20th step, step L and turn to face forward.

Figure 5.1 Dancing Sevila Se Bela Loza.

Part 2

Introduce the Schottische (three steps and a hop). Starting on R foot, step R (1), bring L to R (2), step R (3) and hop (4), cuing "Step, together, step, and hop," then with L foot do another Schottische step (step, step together, step, hop). Have students do several Schottische steps to the right, several forward, and several to the left, repeating until they understand what a Schottische step is.

- 1-24—6 Schottische steps facing slightly right, starting to the right on the R foot (beats 1-4), then on L to left (5-8). Repeat three times in all, turning the body slightly each time the direction changes.

Review

Explain that in some cultures, boys and girls had to stay away from each other, but when they formed their lines in the dance, the boys' lines showed their interest by pursuing and flirting with the girls' lines.

Ask the following:

- Did any of the dances remind you of the military?

- Which seemed as if it were done a hundred years ago?

- Which encouraged a little hip action?

- Where do you think that one (Pata Pata) might have come from?

Assessment

Your observation skills should help you decide how quickly to move forward. If students follow your instructions, they will get a lot more from learning a variety of dances than waiting until they learn perfectly what you taught. However, if they are hopelessly lost, delay moving on.

Student Homework

Explain why students will not be changing to exercise clothes for the unit and that they will probably be sweating, so they should come to school in clothing that will not be ruined. Encourage them to lock their valuables and come to class in sneakers or dance shoes.

Dance
BEGINNER
LESSON 2

Line Dance, Circle With Partners

Facilities

Ventilated room with enough space for students to move freely and a floor that gives

Materials

- Sound system that can project music throughout the dance space
- Music for the Grand March, Pata Pata, Sevila Se Bela Loza, Seljancica Kola, La Raspa, and Hora

Performance Goals

Students will do the following:

- Use the Schottische in new ways.
- Dance a circle dance with and without partners and a line dance.
- Learn three new dances: La Raspa, Seljancica Kola, and the Hora.
- Identify popular folk dances of Mexico, Israel, and the former Yugoslavia.

Cognitive Goals

Students will learn the following:

- That the Schottische is a basic dance step consisting of three steps and a hop
- That when they all join hands, they make a circle

Lesson Safety

Remind students that line leaders have a responsibility to not move faster than the music or take such big steps that their line can't keep up. They should also turn their line so they don't head into walls or other lines.

Motivation

The first basic dance step the class learned, the Schottische, is used in dance more often than most other steps. Lots of hundred-year-old dances use a Schottische. The Schottische is simple—it is the three steps and a hop that the class learned for Sevila Se Bela Loza in the last lesson.

Lesson Sequence

1. Play music for Pata Pata as the class enters. Review it and dance it through.
2. Review the Schottische and Sevila Se Bela Loza. Dance it through.
3. Teach the line dance—Seljancica Kola.
4. Teach the Mexican partner dance—La Raspa.
5. Teach an Israeli circle dance, the Hora.
6. If time remains, review what was learned before. Ask for student requests.

Seljancica Kola

Begin with some history of the former Yugoslavia, including its merging and dividing. Then teach the steps, at first with no music, then dance through with music and instructions.

- 1-16—Take 4 side Schottische steps while facing the front wall, starting to the right on the R foot (1), cross L in back of R (2), step right on R (3), hop R (4), repeat pattern to the left, then right, then left.
- 1-8—Do 4 step-touches sideways (R, L, R, L), cueing R (1) touch L (2), L (3) touch R (4), R (5) touch L (6), L (7) touch R (8).
- 1-16—Face and move right, hop on R (1) and run L (2), R (3) L (4) R (5) L (6) R (7), pivot left on L (8), reversing the direction. Repeat, beginning on R in opposite direction. At count 8, hop and turn on L to face center.

La Raspa

Explain that it's a Mexican novelty dance based on a popular Mexican folk tune and teach the bleking step, at first with no music. Add music and dance through, calling out instructions over music.

- 1-8—Change of feet in place, using uneven rhythm, hop R, touch L heel forward (1-2). Leap on L, bringing it back to its place, touch R heel forward (3-4). Then four faster leaping heel touches: leap R touch L (5), leap L touch R (6), leap R touch L (7), leap L touch R (8). Repeat so students are comfortable with the bleking step.
- 1-32—Partners—In a circle, boys with backs to center, do 4 bleking steps starting on L foot, with couples holding hands so that when they thrust their R heel forward, they move their L arm forward and when they thrust their L heel forward, they move their R arm forward. Hook R elbows, holding L arm high, and skip around each other 8 steps, clapping on the last step. Reverse elbows and repeat. (Circle a total of 4 times.)

The Hora

Introduce the Hora as the national dance of Israel, a dance symbolic of strength and vigor done in an unbroken circle to music that increases in tempo. Walk them through the steps, then put music on and dance the dance through with them.

- 1-end—Step L (1), cross R behind L (2), step L (3), hop L while swinging R foot forward (4), step R, hop R while swinging L foot forward, continuing this pattern in a clockwise direction until the music ends.

Review

Ask the following:

- Which dance made you tired? Can you image doing it in a hot climate?
- What is the Schottische step?

Partnering and Mixers

Facilities

Ventilated room with enough space for students to move freely and a floor that gives

Materials

- Sound system that can project the music throughout the dance space
- Music for the Grand March, Pata Pata, Sevila Se Bela Loza, Seljancica Kola, La Raspa, and Hora, plus Bingo and Greensleeves

Performance Goals

Students will do the following:

- Learn the grand right and left.
- Learn two new dances: Bingo and Greensleeves.

Cognitive Goals

Students will learn the following:

- What a mixer is
- Appropriate behavior when dancing with different partners
- What a grand right and left is
- That there are partner folk dances
- That they are doing dances from the United States and England

Lesson Safety

Remind students that line leaders have a responsibility to not move faster than the music or take such big steps that their line can't keep up. They should also turn their line so they don't head into walls or other lines.

Motivation

Dance can be entertaining to watch. It is also a social activity. Sometimes it is so social, it allows everyone in a room to dance with each other. Today's first dance requires partners, but it does not require students to be married off to one another. On the contrary, this dance requires them to change partners. Remind students to listen to instructions and follow the best they can.

Warm-Up

Play music for Pata Pata as students assemble and invite students to join you on the dance floor. When everyone is there, review Pata Pata (if necessary) and dance it through. Then let them choose another dance they liked in previous classes to warm up to before teaching anything new. This routine will not only be the warm-up, but also part of the motivation. Getting students to instantly start the class by doing something they like is motivating.

Lesson Sequence

1. Have everyone partner off. There are lots of ways to partner students off. For instance, you can have an inside circle of boys and an outside circle of girls moving in opposite directions to music. When the music stops, their partner is whomever they are facing.

2. Teach the grand right and left: Partners face each other (girls travel CW or to the left, boys travel CCW or to the right), extend their R hand to each other and walk by them, passing R shoulders. Looking ahead, (girls CW, boys CCW), boys extend their L hand to the next girl, girls extend their L hand to the next boy, and they pass by L shoulders. They continue alternating R, L, R, L. Let them do this until they have chained around the whole circle and returned to their partner.

3. Teach the American mixer, Bingo. After the song is over, explain that they just learned the grand right and left and have them try it until they return to their partner. Then repeat the dance.

4. Teach the English country dance, Greensleeves.

5. If time permits review what they learned before. Entertain requests.

Bingo

- 1-8—In a double circle with partners side by side, walk CCW around the circle, singing, "There was a farmer who had a dog / And Bingo was his name-o."

- 1-16—The circle continues to move CCW while students join hands to form a single circle, girls moving to their partner's right, with everyone singing, "B-I-N-G-O / B-I-N-G-O / B-I-N-G-O / And Bingo was his name-o."

  - Partners face each other and clasp R hands as they sing "B."

  - They pass each other, going to the next with their L hand, singing "I,"

  - R hand to the next on "N," and

  - L hand to the next on "G."

  - On "O," they swing their new partner and then start from the beginning with their new partner.

Greensleeves

1. Have students get in formation with two couples facing CCW in a double circle with partners side by side, girls on the right, inside hands joined.

2. Identify couple 1 and couple 2.

3. Walk students through parts 1 and 2.

Part 1

- 1-16—Walk forward 16 steps.

- 1-16—Each set forms a star with R hands (couple 1 turn to join their R hands in the middle with the R hands of couple 2) and walk CW 8 steps around. Turn, form a star with L hands and walk 8 steps CCW, finishing with each couple facing CCW direction.

Part 2

Use two couples to demonstrate part 2.

- 1-4—Couple 2 join inside hands, make an arch, and walk forward 4 steps, while couple 1 join hands and back up under the arch 4 steps.

- 5-8—Couple 1 now form the arch and walk forward 4 steps while couple 2 back up under the arch 4 steps.

- This is repeated until couples are back in original formation in the circle.

Review

Tell students that the grand right and left is a square-dance call.

Dance
BEGINNER
LESSON 4

Polka

Facilities

Ventilated room with enough space for students to move freely and a floor that gives

Materials

- Sound system that can project music clearly throughout the dance space
- Music for the Grand March, Pata Pata, Sevila Se Bela Loza, Seljancica Kola, La Raspa, Hora, Bingo, Greensleeves, and polka music

Performance Goals

Students will do the following:

- Review the grand right and left.
- Learn the polka.
- Review all previous dances.

Cognitive Goals

Students will learn the following about the polka:

- It's another basic dance step.
- Basic steps go in any directions.
- It's a hop, step, step, step.
- The rhythm is ah (the hop), quick, quick, quick.
- The step begins on alternating feet.

Lesson Safety

At this point students should know that line leaders have a responsibility to not move faster than the music or take such big steps that their line can't keep up. They should also turn their line so they don't head into walls or other lines.

Motivation

Choose a dance the students can do without needing the whole class and put the music on so students can join you dancing as they enter the gym. When they are all assembled, bring them together to congratulate them on moving along so quickly. Explain that you understand that some students feel that they don't know what to do without having someone to follow. In truth, the class dashed through nine different dances and perhaps it is time to slow down and enjoy what everyone learned. Ask what the class would like to start with.

Lesson Sequence

1. Review the dance that the class wanted to start with, put on the music, and dance.
2. Review the grand right and left. Follow up with Bingo.
3. Teach the polka.
4. Finish class with student requests. Review requests by walking through the instructions if the dance has not been done twice or if you think the students need the review. If not, just put on the music and let them dance, cueing if necessary.

Polka

Have students do the polka to polka music by themselves, traveling CCW around the gym until they are comfortable with the footwork.

- 1-4—Hop R (1), step L (2), close R to L (3), step L (4)
- 5-8—Hop L (5), step R (6), close L to R (7), step R (8).

Review

Ask the following:

- Why is Bingo called a *mixer?*
- Do you have to memorize the steps to Bingo, or does the music give you clues? What clues?
- Can anyone explain the grand right and left?

Grand Right and Left

Facilities

Ventilated room with enough space for students to move freely and a floor that gives

Materials

- Sound system that can project music clearly throughout the dance space
- Music for the Grand March, Pata Pata, Sevila Se Bela Loza, Seljancica Kola, La Raspa, Hora, Bingo, Greensleeves, Jessie Polka, and Red River Valley, plus polka music
- Pinnies (excellent for cutting the confusion when there are not an equal number of girls and boys; they help students remember who should be inside, where their corner is, and who turns for the grand right and left)

Performance Goals

Students will do the following:

- Partner for square dance.
- Perform the grand right and left as part of a square dance.
- Use the polka step in a traditional folk dance, the Jessie Polka.
- Review and improve performance of dances previously learned.

Cognitive Goals

Students will learn the following:

- Vocabulary for square dance
    - Head and side couples
    - Promenade home
    - Swing
- Rules for square dance
    - Gents keep their partner to their right.
    - Gents bring their partner home.
    - Line of direction is CCW.
    - Sets of square dance calls always end in a promenade home.

Lesson Safety

Safety concerns in this lesson may change from physical safety to emotional safety. When partnering is involved, make sure that no student is left in an awkward position. Use a system where students don't choose partners. You can start by having the girls and guys form separate circles facing each other and march them around. When the music stops, that is their partner. If partnering is not a problem, then let students pick their own. It is not unusual these days to have girls partner with girls and boys partner with boys. Don't make an issue of it. Finally, be available to dance with the person who is without a partner.

Motivation

Have the music on as students enter the gym. Choose something they enjoy and of course, dance with them, because they will start dancing. Once they are all assembled, announce that this lesson they are going to learn some old favorites.

Lesson Sequence

1. Dance one request before teaching something new.
2. Teach the Jessie Polka.
3. Introduce square dancing.

- Squares have 4 walls.
- Couple 1 face away from the music and couple 3 face couple 1.
- Head couples are 1 and 3.
- Side couples are 2 and 4.
- Gentlemen always go to their home position in the square.
- Line of direction is CCW.
- Gentlemen (or leaders) have their partner on their right and their corner on their left.
- Leaders must put their partner on the right and bring them home.
- Dancers must listen to the calls and perform them immediately after hearing them.

4. Teach Red River Valley using the calls given in the instructions. (There are several versions; this is the easiest.)
5. If time allows, ask for student requests and review dances that have not already been done twice. Ask if those that have been done twice need to be reviewed.

Jessie Polka

1. Have students form groups of two or more with arms around each other's waist.
2. Teach part 1 (the heelie part), going CCW.
   - 1-2—L heel forward (1) and then step it in place (2).
   - 3-4—R toe in back (3) and then step it in place (4).
   - 5—R heel in front and then in place (5).
   - 6—L heel to left, then cross it over right, keeping weight on right (6)
3. Teach part 2.
   - 1-8—Take four polka steps in line of direction.
4. Walk through the whole dance a few times, and then put on the music.
5. After a few minutes, have students get in groups of 3 to 6, arms around each other's waist. As they dance, they should lean backward together (see figure 5.2) when they put their heels forward and lean forward when they put their toes back. The groups should follow the line of direction, CCW, performing in unison.

Figure 5.2 Dancing the Jessie Polka.

137

Red River Valley

Before you start to call the steps, teach how to regroup after a mistake wipes out the square. To regroup, they listen for the call to promenade, follow it, and try to follow each call thereafter. Put music on and allow them to make their own mistakes.

- First couple lead down the valley (couple 1 goes to couple 2).
- You circle to the left and to the right (only couple 1 and 2).
- Then you swing the girl in the valley (lady of couple 2).
- And you swing that Red River gal (couples 1 and 2).
- Then they lead right on down the valley (couple 3).
- And you circle to the left and to the right.
- Then you swing that girl in the valley.
- Then you swing that Red River gal.
- Then you lead on down the valley (couple 4).
- And you circle to the left and to the right.
- Then you swing the gal in the valley.
- Then you swing your own Red River gal.
- (Break; the visiting couple should now be home.)
- Do an allemande left on your corner.
- And a grand right and left halfway round.
- Then you promenade home with your darling.
- Promenade that Red River gal.

Review

Square dance was danced for hundreds of years and has a rule that requires the men to take their partners home.

- Does that say anything about the nature of the American male's role?
- Does it say something about the homestead and how important it was?

Cast-Off and Reel

Facilities

Ventilated room with enough space for students to move freely and a floor that gives

Materials

- Sound system that can project music clearly throughout the dance space
- Music for the Grand March, Pata Pata, Sevila Se Bela Loza, Seljancica Kola, La Raspa, Hora, Bingo, Greensleeves, Jessie Polka, Red River Valley, and Virginia Reel, plus polka music
- Pinnies

Performance Goals

Students will do the following:

- Dance the Virginia Reel.
- Improve performance of dances previously learned.

Cognitive Goals

Students will increase their dance vocabulary:

- Cast-off
- Reel
- Sashay
- Longways position (contra dance)
- Column left and column right

Lesson Safety

Make sure the emotional climate is healthy, particularly when it comes to partnering. Be available to dance with the person who is without a partner.

Motivation

Leave some music on for one of the dances the students have learned as the class enters. Once they assemble, explain that they have learned 10 dances. After they tackle a new one, a traditional American dance some might know—the Virginia Reel—they can enjoy the others they already learned.

Lesson Sequence

1. Teach the Virginia Reel.
2. Walk through the sashay, reel, and column march with the new head couple.
3. Put the music on and call out instructions as the class does the dance. If possible, use the song "Turkey in the Straw" and call the dance yourself.
4. Entertain student requests. Throw in a dance they haven't asked for in a while. Review it first.

Virginia Reel

Walk students through part 1 of the Virginia Reel. Four to eight couples should be in longways position, with couples facing each other. Then teach part 2, demonstrating first and then have the head couple of each set walk through it. Finally, teach part 3, the cast-off.

Part 1

- 1-4—Walk in 3 steps, acknowledge partner, walk back to place 4 steps.
- 5-8—Repeat, forward and back.
- 1-8—Join R hands with partner, circle right, and return to place in 8 steps.
- 1-8—Join L hands with partner, circle left, and return to place in 8 steps.
- 1-8—Join both hands with partner, circle CW, and return to place in 8 steps.
- 1-8—Partners do-si-do (pass R shoulders and back up into place) in 8 steps.

Part 2

- 1-16—Head couple join hands and sashay (slide) 7 1/2 steps down the center of the column, and then slide 8 steps to get back to original position.
- 1-until they are done—The head couple reel down the set. (The head couple hook R elbows and turn 1 1/2 times around. They go to the person in the opposite line, hook L elbows, and swing the opposite boy or girl. The head couple return to each other in the center for a right elbow swing and then on to the next person opposite for a left elbow swing. They continue, alternating swinging each other and swinging people in the opposite line until they have swung everyone in the opposite line and reached the foot of the set. They then join hands and sashay home.)

Part 3

To do the cast-off:

- Everyone turns to face the head of the set.
- The first boy leads his line to the left and toward the foot (the back) of the set, while the first girl leads her line to the right and back.

- The couple meet at the foot of the set, join both hands, make an arch, and let everyone march under their arch.
- The rest of the line moves forward until the column is reestablished with a new head couple.
- The first couple is now the last couple.

Review

Ask the following:

- What is another way of telling you to slide down the set?
- Can you describe a reel? Does the guy get to dance with all the girls in the set?
- Should the girl be to the right or left of the guy?

Review and Dance

Facilities

Ventilated room with enough space for students to move freely and a floor that gives

Materials

- Sound system that can project music clearly throughout the dance space
- Music for the Grand March, Pata Pata, Sevila Se Bela Loza, Seljancica Kola, La Raspa, Hora, Bingo, Greensleeves, Jessie Polka, Red River Valley, and Virginia Reel, plus polka music
- Pinnies
- Beginner skills rubric

Performance and Cognitive Goals

Students will review and improve performance of dances previously learned.

Lesson Safety

Make sure the emotional climate is healthy, particularly when it comes to partnering. Be available to dance with the person who is without a partner.

Motivation

Tell students that they have learned 11 dances. Today they're going to see how many they can do before the class ends. Who has a favorite they want to start with?

Lesson Sequence

Ask for student requests. Put on a dance they haven't asked for in a while.

Review

Ask the following:

- Can anyone name a dance where no one holds hands?
- How about a circle dance with the circle joined?
- What is it called when the four couples in a square join hands?
- What is it called when dancers join hands in the middle?
- Which dance gets its dancers to look like a spoke on a wheel?

Assessment

Let students know that they will have a short quiz, so if they have questions, they should ask. Post the beginner skills rubric and let the class know it is there in case they are curious about how they are being graded.

All Dancing

Facilities

Ventilated room with enough space for students to move freely and a floor that gives

Materials

- Sound system that can project music clearly throughout the dance space
- Music for the Grand March, Pata Pata, Sevila Se Bela Loza, Seljancica Kola, La Raspa, Hora, Bingo, Greensleeves, and polka, plus the Jessie Polka, Red River Valley, Virginia Reel, and Saturday Night Fever Walk
- Pinnies

Performance Goals

Students will do the following:

- Identify dances by their music.
- Review and improve their performance.

Cognitive Goal

Students will decide whether to add another dance to their repertoire.

Lesson Safety

Make sure the emotional climate is healthy, particularly when it comes to partnering. Be available to dance with the person who is without a partner.

Motivation

Have music from *Saturday Night Fever* on as they enter. When assembled, ask if they would like to learn the dance that John Travolta made famous in the movie, *Saturday Night Fever*—it's the Saturday Night Fever Walk.

Lesson Sequence

1. Teach Saturday Night Fever Walk, and teach it in parts. Students face the front wall.
2. The remainder of the class should be student choice.

Saturday Night Fever Walk

Anticipate that they will have trouble once the dance pattern turns left and they cannot see you any longer. Walk through it with a few turns, then put the music on and let them do it through, giving movement cues as they dance.

Part 1

Have students walk through part 1 a few times to music.

- 1-8—Walk back 3 steps, R (1), L (2), R (3), then touch L (4). Walk forward 3 steps, L, R, L, then touch R.
- 1-8—Turn right 3 steps, R (1), L (2), R (3), then touch L (4). Turn left 3 steps, L, R, L, then touch R.

Part 2

Have students walk through part 2 to the music.

- 1-4—Do 2 kick ball changes on R—kick R (1), put R down (and) step L (2), cueing "Kick right, ball, change, kick left, ball, change." Repeat 3-and-4.
- 5-8—Twist R (5), L (6), R (7), L (8).
- 1-8—Point R arm and leg to R (1), then cross R arm to L knee and R leg behind L heel (2). Repeat for a total of four times.

- 1-4—Roll hands 2 beats. Click heels 2 beats.
- 5-8—Point R foot forward (5), back (6), and to the side (7) and bring it in with knee up as you pivot left (8).

Review

Invite questions.

Dancing and Assessment

Materials

- Sound system that can project music clearly throughout the dance space
- Music for the Grand March, Pata Pata, Sevila Se Bela Loza, Seljancica Kola, La Raspa, Hora, Bingo, Greensleeves, and polka, plus the Jessie Polka, Red River Valley, Virginia Reel, and Saturday Night Fever Walk
- Pinnies

Performance Goals

Students will do the following:

- Identify dances by their music.
- Review and improve their performance.

Cognitive Goal

Students will decide whether to add a Scottish dance to their repertoire.

Lesson Safety

Make sure the emotional climate is healthy, particularly when it comes to partnering. Be available to dance with the person who is without a partner.

Motivation

Play the Saturday Night Fever Walk music as students enter.

Lesson Sequence

1. Review Saturday Night Fever Walk and dance it through.
2. Allow students to choose dances.
3. After a few of their selections, choose a dance they forgot about.
4. If giving a quiz, do it in lesson 10. It should take only 10 minutes.

Review

If giving a quiz, announce that it is coming up and review all items they should know.

- How do they know who is the head couple?
- How can they tell if they are going CCW?
- What is the definition of polka and a Schottische?
- What is the difference between a line and a circle?
- How can they explain a grand right and left?
- When one marches, what foot do they start on?
- Which dances had no partners? Which traditional dances avoided having girls and boys dance together?

Beginner Dance Skills Rubric

Name _____ Date _____

Teacher _____ Class _____

	0	1	2	3	4	5
Directions	No effort.	• Faces correct direction. • Moves in line of direction. • Changes line of direction only after seeing others do it.	• Knows left from right. • Will join group formation. • Gets into lines, circles, or longways position on verbal command. • Goes to the dance lost-and-found if without a partner.	• Anticipates direction changes. • Joins hands if requested. • Can do-si-do, elbow swing, and promenade home. • Follows square dance calls after they are made.	• Changes direction at appropriate times. • Courteous to partner. • Sashays, casts off, and reels. • Positions self properly in partner dancing.	• Knows all dances repeated more than three times. • Can lead others. • Recognizes dance by music. • Does the grand right and left without confusion.
Footwork	No effort.	• Steps, hops, runs, slides, and jumps on cue. • Knows left from right.	• Leaps, skips, and gallops on cue. • Goes left or right on cue. • Counts steps.	• Knows Schottische. • Can perform basic steps in any direction. • Counts steps so direction changes are on time. • Corrects self by following other dancers.	• Can combine footwork patterns without pause. • Knows the polka step. • Begins direction change on correct foot. • Steps flow into one another.	• Is role model. • Does dances correctly. • Can perform properly without needing a visual cue.
Rhythm	No effort.	• Can clap or stomp beat.	• Identifies tempo changes and can clap to them. • Able to walk, run, jump, hop, and slide on beat.	• Can do basic dance steps on beat. • Identifies musical phrases. • Can stay in sync with other dancers doing same pattern.	• All footwork is on beat. • Counts steps. • Follows square dance calls on cue.	• Able to keep rhythm without musical accompaniment. • Able to use other body parts rhythmically. • Stays on beat when others cannot.

From Isobel Kleinman, 2009, *Complete Physical Education Plans for Grades 5 to 12, Second Edition* (Champaign, IL: Human Kinetics).

Beginner Dance Quiz

Name _____ Date _____

Teacher _____ Class _____

True or False

Read each statement carefully. If the statement is true, write a *T* in the column to the left. If the statement is false, write an *F*. If using a grid sheet, blacken in the appropriate column for each question, making sure to use the correctly numbered line for each question and its answer.

_____ 1. Marching begins with the left foot.

_____ 2. The grand right and left begins by facing your partner, joining right hands, walking forward until passing right shoulders, and extending your free hand to the next person.

_____ 3. One polka is done to four beats of music.

_____ 4. Each polka step begins with the same foot.

_____ 5. In its time, Sevila Se Bela Loza was probably as popular as the popular dances danced at school dances today.

_____ 6. John Travolta had great acting success by dancing the Virginia Reel.

_____ 7. Traditional Serbian dances were done in lines.

_____ 8. A Schottische is a basic dance step whose proper execution requires four steps and a hop.

_____ 9. An Israeli circle dance requiring high energy is the hora.

_____ 10. *Promenade home* instructs gents to walk "home" with whomever they were dancing with when the instruction was given.

 From Isobel Kleinman, 2009, *Complete Physical Education Plans for Grades 5 to 12, Second Edition* (Champaign, IL: Human Kinetics).

Beginner Dance Quiz Answer Key

True or False

1. T
2. T
3. T
4. F—Each polka step begins on the alternating foot.
5. T
6. F—He danced the Saturday Night Fever Walk to disco music in the film, *Saturday Night Fever*. "Turkey in the Straw," the music used to dance the Virginia Reel, is hundreds of years old.
7. T
8. F—A Schottische is three steps and a hop, not four steps and a hop.
9. T
10. T

From Isobel Kleinman, 2009, *Complete Physical Education Plans for Grades 5 to 12, Second Edition* (Champaign, IL: Human Kinetics).

Mayim, Oh Johnny Oh, and Limbo Rock

Facilities

Ventilated room with enough space for students to move freely and a floor that gives

Materials

- Sound system that can project music clearly throughout the dance space
- Music for dances introduced in the beginner unit (Grand March, Bingo, Pata Pata, Sevila Se Bela Loza, Hora, Saturday Night Fever Walk, Virginia Reel, La Raspa, Greensleeves, Jessie Polka, Seljancica Kola, Red River Valley), plus music for new dances—Mayim, Limbo Rock, and Oh Johnny Oh
- Pinnies

Performance Goals

Students will do the following:

- Choose dances they remember and review and repeat them.
- Learn three new dances.
    - Cuban mambo
    - Mayim (Israeli rain dance)
    - Oh Johnny Oh (American dance)

Cognitive Goals

Students will learn the following:

- Grapevine step
- Rhythm for the mambo (quick, quick, slow)

Lesson Safety

Make sure the emotional climate is healthy, particularly when it comes to partnering. If partnering is not happening in a gracious way, line up the boys as they come in. Do the same with the girls and put on a line dance. When it's time to teach something new that requires a partner, have them face each other. Go through the instructions and have the couples walk through it with you. Then have the girls move one to the left so everyone has a new partner (girl on the very left has to run back to the boy on the right). Hopefully, finding a partner will not be an ordeal, but if it is, switch partners throughout the dances. Finally, be available to dance with the person who is without a partner.

Motivation

As students enter, play their favorite song from the beginner unit and encourage them to join you on the dance floor. After it plays through, remind them that usually people dance in street clothes and that is why the students don't have to dress in exercise clothes for the unit. Since they will probably sweat, they should remove their jackets and sweaters. To protect the floor, you might ask them to wear sneakers or dance shoes. Since they are not changing, you will expect them in class promptly. Encourage them to put their belongings to the side or in their lockers before you arrive.

Ask them to bear with you for a little while and do their best to get over any apprehensions because after getting started, they will come to love this unit if they don't already.

Lesson Sequence

1. Begin with student requests to set a positive tone and get the class moving quickly. Review a few measures for everyone since the dance has not been done in a year. After making sure most students are comfortable with the steps, put the music on.

2. Introduce Mayim, an Israeli dance that gives thanks to water.

3. Explain the following.
   - What a mixer is—It's a dance with partner changes.
   - Where your partner is in a single circle—Girls are to the right of their partner.
   - Where your corner is in a single circle—The adjacent person who is not your partner, or on boys' left and girls' right.
   - Why there is a dance lost-and-found and how to find it—During mixers, if someone is off, someone else down the line can wind up with no partner.
   - What to do if you are standing alone on the promenade—Go to the dance lost-and-found at the center of the circle and get a new partner.
   - The "I have no partner" rule—Get a partner during the promenade and join the promenade before the set starts again.

4. Teach Oh Johnny Oh as an American circle dance mixer.

5. Teach Limbo Rock, a modern novelty dance with Latin influence.

6. If time remains, entertain requests from last year.

Mayim

Join hands in a circle and walk through part 1 and part 2. Put on music, giving cues as they complete the dance.

Part 1

- 1-16—Take 4 Circassia steps to the left (cross and step R in front of L, turn slightly left (1), step L (2), cross R in back of L (3), take a springy step left (4). Repeat this combination step four times, cueing, "Cross, side, cross, side, cross."
- 1-16—Take 4 running steps toward the center, arriving with arms and head facing upward, singing "Mayim, mayim, mayim, mayim." Take 4 running steps back, finishing with arms extended straight and downward. Repeat, cueing, "Run in 2, 3, 4, run back, 2, 3, 4."
- Put music on and let students dance to the first 32 beats.

Part 2

- 1-4—Circle left (CW) with 4 running steps starting on R foot, finish facing center of the circle, cueing, "Run left, 2, 3, 4."
- 5-8—Hop on R foot, touch L toe in front and then to side (1-and); hop R touch L in front and then to the side (2-and). Repeat 2 times, cuing, "Hop right-and, 2-and, 3-and, 4-and."
- 1-16—Leap onto L foot, touch R foot across L and clap (1); touch R to side and swing arms to side (2); hop L, touch R across to R side, and clap hands (3); swing arms out to the sides (4). Repeat 4 times, cueing "Leap left-and, 2-and, 3-and, 4-and. . ."

Oh Johnny Oh

Couples (girls to the right of their partners) form a single circle moving CW. These are the calls:
- Oh, you all join hands and circle the ring (circle moves CW).
- Stop where you are, give your honey a swing (gents swing partners).
- Now swing that girl behind you (gents swing corner girl).
- Go back home and swing your own (gents swing partners).
- Allemande left with your corner (left-hand swing the corner).
- Do-sa 'round your own (do-si-do your partner).
- Now you all run away with your corner maid, singing "Oh, Johnny, oh, Johnny, oh" (promenade the corner, who now becomes the new partner).

After a walk-through to explain the calls, put on the music and allow whatever happens to happen.

Limbo Rock

Students face the front of the room. Walk through each part first without and then adding music as students grow more comfortable with the steps. Listen to musical phrasing and cue as the class moves.

Part 1

- 1-8—Do 4 rock steps (quick shift of weight with small steps). Take a 1/4 turn to right on R and begin rock step—step forward on L, rock back on R, step back on L, rock forward on R, step forward on L, rock back on R, step back on L, turn. Facing left on L, do rock step starting with R stepping forward, rock back on L, step back on R, rock forward on L, rock forward on R, step back on L, step back on R. Cue a quick count of "1, 2, 3, 4, 5, 6, 7, turn."
- 1-8—Facing left wall, repeat, starting with R stepping forward, back, back, forward, forward, back, back, and turn, cueing a quick count of "1, 2, 3, 4, 5, 7, turn."
- 1-16—Repeat the rock step facing right, then left. End the turn facing the front wall.

Part 2

- 1-8—Take 7 small, quick steps to the right: L foot begins with a crossover step in front of R. R steps to the side, L crosses in front of R, R steps to side. This continues for 7 beats, cross, side, cross, side, cross, side, cross. On count 8, hold to change direction.
- 1-8—Take 7 small, quick steps to the left: R foot initiates the cross-steps, and the previous sequence is repeated in reverse.

Part 3

- 1-8—4 mambo steps. L foot forward (quick), weight moves back over R (quick), L foot comes back together (slow) in one mambo step. R foot forward (quick), L back (quick), R together (slow) in second samba step.
- 1-8—Do 2 more mambo steps. Cue "Left, back, together, right, back, together."

Review

Ask the following:

- Which dance used the hips a lot?
- Which gave thanks for rain?
- Which made some of you get lost?
- If the rhythm is slow, quick, slow, what Latin dance are you doing?

Assessment

Observe if students are keeping up with the pace to determine if the lesson is going too fast or too slow and adjust accordingly. Consider whether to introduce so many new dances in one lesson. Do not let lack of perfection be the deciding factor. Variety is important in the beginning because you want students to catch the spirit and fun of dancing before worrying about being absolutely correct immediately.

Dance
INTERMEDIATE
LESSON 2

Mambo and Misirlou

Facilities

Ventilated room with enough space for students to move freely and a floor that gives

Materials

- Sound system that can project music clearly throughout the dance space
- Music for dances introduced previously (Grand March, Bingo, Pata Pata, Sevila Se Bela Loza, Hora, Saturday Night Fever Walk, Virginia Reel, La Raspa, Greensleeves, Jessie Polka,

Seljancica Kola, Red River Valley, Mayim, Limbo Rock, and Oh Johnny Oh) plus music for new dances—Misirlou and mambo music from *Dirty Dancing*

- Pinnies

Performance Goals

Students will do the following:

- Review and repeat Limbo Rock, Mayim, and Oh Johnny Oh.
- Learn a Greek-inspired dance that is used today, the Misirlou.

Cognitive Goals

Students will learn the following:

- A two-step is quick, quick, slow.
- A mambo step is quick, quick, slow.
- The difference between the two is the involvement of hips and arms.

Lesson Safety

Make sure the emotional climate is healthy, particularly when it comes to partnering. Be available to dance with the person who is without a partner.

Motivation

Have music for Limbo Rock playing as students enter the room and encourage them to join you as you dance to it. Then ask if anyone has gone to any weddings, bar mitzvahs, or confirmations lately and heard any traditional folk music playing. At most parties, a band leader trying to get everyone up and moving always uses traditional dances. Last year they learned the Hora, which is frequently performed at functions whether the group is Jewish or not. The Hora is a traditional dance that is still popular, and so is the Misirlou, which is based on a Greek traditional dance.

Lesson Sequence

1. Begin with a request from the floor. Do a quick review and dance the request through.
2. Introduce the basic two-step before showing how it is used in the Misirlou.
   a. Have students walk quick, quick, slow; quick, quick, slow; quick, quick, slow.
   b. Students form a large circle and then have the leader drop the hand of the person to his or her right so that the circle is broken, hands joined at shoulder height with elbows bent, leader on the right.

Misirlou

With no music, walk through parts 1 and 2 in rhythm. Then combine parts 1 and 2 and dance to music, giving instructional cues.

Part 1

- 1-5—Step with R foot to right (1) and pause (2). Point L in front of R (3) and pause (4). Swing L behind R heel and step on L (5).
- 6-8—Step R to side (6), step L in front of R (7), pivot on the ball of L to face slightly left (8).

Part 2

- 1-4—On R foot facing CW, one two-step forward—step forward on R (1), bring L to R (2), step forward on R (3), and balance on R (4).
- 5-8—One two-step back and balance on L—step back L (5), bring R to L (6), step L (7), and balance (8). Finish facing center.

Mambo

1. As Patrick Swayze did in *Dirty Dancing*, move the class around the gym using the basic mambo learned in Limbo Rock to move in different directions.
   a. Using small steps, keeping in rhythm, and dancing alone, have students change the direction of their footwork. Instead of forward, back, together as in Limbo Rock, go

forward, forward, in place two times; back, back, in place two times; turn, turn, in place; or combinations.

2. Do a quick review of Mayim and dance it.

3. Do a quick review of Oh Johnny Oh and dance it.

4. If there's time, take requests for dances learned previously.

Review

Ask the following:

- Which dance was American?
- Which had the most traditional music?
- Who can put into words a mambo step?
- How does the mambo step differ from the two-step?
- Does the two-step have only two steps? Put the dance pattern for the two-step in words.

Road to the Isles and Achy Breaky Heart

Facilities

Ventilated room with enough space for students to move freely and a floor that gives

Materials

- Sound system that can project music clearly throughout the dance space
- Music for dances learned previously (Grand March, Bingo, Pata Pata, Sevila Se Bela Loza, Hora, Saturday Night Fever Walk, Virginia Reel, La Raspa, Greensleeves, Jessie Polka, Seljancica Kola, Red River Valley, Mayim, Limbo Rock, Misirlou, mambo music, Oh Johnny Oh) plus music for new dances—Road to the Isles and Achy Breaky Heart

Performance Goal

Students will review and repeat some dances learned this year.

Cognitive Goals

Students will learn the following:

- The difference between basic dance steps (timing)
- What the Schottische is (three steps and a hop, evenly timed)
- How to get into varsouvienne dance position

Lesson Safety

Make sure the emotional climate is healthy, particularly when it comes to partnering. Be available to dance with the person who is without a partner.

Motivation

Put on some mambo music and encourage entering students to join you as you dance through it. When you are done, tell them that because they already know the Schottische step, you can take them on a quick trip to what sounds Scottish but is really American via a dance called Road to the Isles before doing a dance that Texans really love, Achy Breaky Heart.

Lesson Sequence

1. Teach varsouvienne dance position (see figure 5.3) and begin teaching Road to the Isles.

2. Teach Achy Breaky Heart, a country-western line dance.

3. Review Misirlou and dance it.

4. If time remains, fill student requests.

Road to the Isles

The dance is done in a circle with couples facing CCW in varsouvienne dance position. To teach it more easily, consider having all students face you at the front wall until they learn the pattern and how to turn. Teach the parts, then add music and have students dance while you call out instructions.

Figure 5.3 Varsouvienne dance position.

Part 1

- 1-4—Point L toe diagonally forward, then take 3 steps R beginning with the L foot crossing behind the R.
- 5-8—Point R toe diagonally forward, then take 3 steps to the left beginning with the R foot crossing behind L.
- 1-4—Point L toe forward, then point it back.

Part 2

The next part is easy, though some couples have trouble with the turn, so walk through the instructions and be prepared to stop and help them turn while remaining in varsouvienne dance position.

- 1-4—Schottische forward (3 steps and a hop) starting on L foot.
- 5-8—Schottische forward again (starting on R foot). On the hop and without dropping hands, half-turn R so the couples face the reverse direction.
- 1-4—Schottische forward on L, half-turning L on the hop, ending in original line of direction.
- 5-8—Take 3 steps in place (R, L, R, pause).

Achy Breaky Heart

- 1-4—Grapevine right—Step R to the right, cross L behind R, step R to the right, touch L toe to R.
- 5-8—Grapevine left—Step L to the left, cross R behind L, step L to the left, touch R toe to L, and hold (cross R in back).
- 1-8—L knee lift and bend, R knee lift and bend, L knee lift and bend, put down and hold.
- 1-8—Point R toe back, middle, forward, pivot 3/4 turn L, step R.
- 1-8—Step back L, step back R, lift L knee, 1/4 turn L, step close with L.
- 1-4—Take 4 steps backward, R, L, R, L.
- 5-8—Rock forward on R and back on L, forward R and back L.
- 1-4—R slide step, kick L, L slide step, kick R with 1/4 turn R.
- 5-8—Grapevine to right and hold.

Review

Ask the following:

- Which dance sounded Scottish?
- Which had music you have heard before?

Pas de Basques

Facilities

Ventilated room with enough space for students to move freely and a floor that gives

Materials

- Sound system that can project music clearly throughout the dance space
- Music for dances learned previously (Grand March, Bingo, Pata Pata, Sevila Se Bela Loza, Hora, Saturday Night Fever Walk, Virginia Reel, La Raspa, Greensleeves, Jessie Polka, Seljancica Kola, Red River Valley, Mayim, Limbo Rock, Misirlou, mambo music, Road to the Isles, Achy Breaky Heart, and Oh Johnny Oh) plus music for new dances—Nebesko Kolo and Sicilian Tarantella.
- Tambourines (optional)

Performance Goals

Students will do the following:

- Learn and dance Nebesko Kolo and Sicilian Tarantella.
- Review recent dances and dance them.
- Choose their favorites.

Cognitive Goals

Students will learn the following:

- Elevation added to the two-step makes it a pas de basques.
- Countries of origin often disappear from the map.

Lesson Safety

Make sure the emotional climate is healthy, particularly when it comes to partnering. Be available to dance with the person who is without a partner.

Motivation

Put on music for Achy Breaky Heart and encourage entering students to join you as you dance it through. You might want to follow up with a quick review of Achy Breaky Heart and dance it through again. Then explain that you are using dance steps as a building block that helps make learning new dances easier. The two-step can be done in many kinds of dances, from traditional dances over a hundred years old to modern social forms such as ballroom and country-western. Today's dance, Nebesko Kolo, is a fast line dance that adapts the two-step rhythm into a pas de bas. Nebesko Kolo is a line dance from Vojvodina. If anyone in class wants extra credit, they can research what country Vojvodina is in (Serbia).

Lesson Sequence

1. Introduce the pas de basque, a two-step with elevation.
2. Teach Nebesko Kolo (a line dance with joined hands).
3. Teach the Sicilian Tarantella as a flirtatious Italian dance.
4. If there's time, fill dance requests.

Pas de Basques

- 1-4—Slight leap R (1), step L in front of R (and), step R (2) (quick, quick, slow), then reverse second pas de basque, cueing, "Leap L together, L leap R together R."
- 5-8—Build pace, having students hop R, step L together, R , and then hop L, step R together, L repeatedly until they are comfortable doing the pas de basque.

Nebesko Kolo

Teach the parts separately. Then add together with music, reminding students when to turn.

Part I
- 1-16—Stamp and moving R on R foot, do four running two-steps. Turn L on last step.
- 1-16—Moving L, begin on R, take four running two-steps, and finish by facing center.

Part 2
- 1-4—Touch R foot forward (1) and back (2), and forward (3) and back (4).
- 5-20—Do 4 pas de basques, starting R.
- On the "and" of count 20—Stamp R without taking weight.

Sicilian Tarantella

The Sicilian Tarantella is a dance done to 6/8 musical timing. Mention similarities with square dance and Greensleeves (formation, do-si-do, and stars). This dance is done in sets of two couples, partners face each other, with boys side by side, girls side by side, and couple 1 nearest the music (with their backs to the wall). Teach the parts then dance with music while you call instructions.

Part 1
- 1-2—Step L and clap (1), hop on L while swinging R foot across (2).
- 3-4—Repeat in reverse, step R and clap (3), hop R, swing L foot across (4).
- 5-6—Two running steps in place.
- 1-4—Starting on L, circle in place (1, 2, 3, 4),
- 5-6—Men snap fingers, women shake tambourines or clap in place for two beats (5, 6).
- 1-48—Repeat above until the section has been done 4 times in total.

Part 2
- 1-4—Take 4 runs forward toward partner, L (1), R (2), L (3), R (4), dancers beginning to bend low.
- 5-6—Women shake tambourines, men snap fingers in place for two beats (5, 6).
- 1-4—Take 4 runs away, L (1), R (2), L (3), R (4), straightening up.
- 5-6—Women shake tambourines, men snap fingers in place for two beats (5, 6).
- 1-48—Repeat (4 times total).

Part 3
- 1-6—Head male does R elbow swing with opposite female (two steps to meet, four steps to swing).
- 1-6—Head female does R elbow swing with opposite male (two steps to meet, four steps to swing).
- 1-6—Head male does L elbow swing with opposite female (two steps to meet, four steps to swing).
- 1-6—Head female does L elbow swing with opposite male (two steps to meet, four steps to swing).

Part 4
- 1-6—Head male do-si-dos opposite female, passing R shoulders, without folding arms, but snapping fingers as they pass.
- 1-6—Head female do-si-dos the opposite male, passing R shoulders.
- 1-6—Head male do-si-dos opposite female, passing L shoulder.
- 1-6—Head female do-si-dos opposite male, passing L shoulders.
- 1-6—Dancers turn R, put hands on hips, L shoulders to center, and take 8 skips CCW in circle.
- 1-6—Dancers turn L, R shoulders to center, and skip CW 8 skips.

- 1-6—Dancers form a left-hand star and take 8 skips.
- 1-6—Dancers form a right-hand star and take 8 skips.

Review

Ask the following:

- Which dance was Italian?
- Which had music you have heard before?
- What is the difference between a pas de basque and a two-step rhythm? Does the pas de basque remind you of Irish dancing?
- Is *pas de basque* a French or English word? Can anyone translate?

Dance
INTERMEDIATE
LESSON 5

Texas Star and Stepping Out

Facilities

Ventilated room with enough space for students to move freely and a floor that gives

Materials

- Sound system that can project music clearly throughout the dance space
- Music for dances learned previously (Grand March, Bingo, Pata Pata, Sevila Se Bela Loza, Hora, Saturday Night Fever Walk, Virginia Reel, La Raspa, Greensleeves, Jessie Polka, Seljancica Kola, Red River Valley, Mayim, Oh Johnny Oh, Limbo Rock, Misirlou, mambo music, Road to the Isles, Achy Breaky Heart, Nebesko Kolo, and Sicilian Tarantella) plus music for new dances—Texas Star and Stepping Out
- Pinnies

Performance Goals

Students will do the following:

- Review and repeat dances learned this year.
- Learn a 1940s American soft-shoe novelty dance, Stepping Out.
- Learn some basic tap dance steps.
- Use the star in a square dance, Texas Star.

Cognitive Goals

Students will learn the following:

- What a star means in country and square dance
- That the brush step is a tap dance step

Lesson Safety

Make sure the emotional climate is healthy, particularly when it comes to partnering. Be available to dance with the person who is without a partner.

Motivation

Have music for either Limbo Rock or Achy Breaky Heart playing as the students arrive and invite them to join you. Dance it through and then announce that you will teach two American dances that are very different. One comes from a hoedown and the other from our jazz and tap dance heritage.

Lesson Sequence

1. Teach the Texas Star, an American square dance. Since the instructions are called, all you have to do is walk the students through some of the calls so they know what they mean. Teach them to listen and follow the call immediately after it is said. You might have to remind students what to do if the square messes up.

2. Before breaking up the square, review and perform Red River Valley.

3. Teach Stepping Out.

4. If time allows, entertain requests.

Texas Star

- Ladies to the center and back to the bar.
- Gents to the center for a right-hand star.
- Right hand crosses.
- Back with the left and don't get lost.
- Meet your pretty girl, pass her by.
- Hook the next gal on the fly.
- Star promenade (see figure 5.4).
- The gents swing out, the ladies swing in.
- Form that Texas Star again with the ladies in.
- Break that star and everyone swing.
- Promenade home with the new little thing.

Figure 5.4 Left-hand star promenade.

Stepping Out

Stepping Out starts on the L foot, everyone facing the same line of direction. Teach the parts of the dance separately then combine with music.

When the dance is done at first, there is full orchestration. When it is repeated, it is done to the sound of drum snares. When it begins the third time, there is silence until part 3 begins, at which point suddenly there is full orchestration again. Students love it because it is a challenge to dance in rhythm in silence and begin the third part when the music comes on.

Part 1

- 1-8—Step L (1), R brushes forward (2), R brushes across L (3), R brushes back to the right (4), R steps to the side (5), L cross-steps behind (6), R steps to side (7), L steps behind (8).
- 1-8—Step R (1), L brushes forward (2), L brushes across R (3), and L brushes back to the left (4), L steps to the side (5), R steps across behind (6), L steps to side (7), R crosses behind (8).
- 1-12—Circle L, R, L, R, step L; R brushes forward, across, and behind; then step R, L, R in place and hold.
- 1-28—Repeat all.

Part 2

- 1-4—Walk forward L (1), R (2), L (3), R (4), snapping fingers.
- 5-8—L makes circular brushing motion to the left (5), then begins 3 steps in place, L (6), R (7), L (8).
- 1-4—Walk back R, L, R, L, snapping fingers.
- 5-8—R brushes in a circular motion on the right side, then begins 3 steps in place, R, L, R.

Part 3

Repeat the first 28 counts of Part 1 once. It ends after the first circle and the stamps in place.

Review

Ask the following:

- Which dance seems older, Texas Star or Stepping Out?
- Which had music you would expect to hear when people are in jeans and boots?
- What do you think makes it difficult to move without music?

To Ting and Waltz

Facilities

Ventilated room with enough space for students to move freely and a floor that gives

Materials

- Sound system that can project music clearly throughout the dance space
- Music of dances learned previously (Grand March, Bingo, Pata Pata, Sevila Se Bela Loza, Hora, Saturday Night Fever Walk, Virginia Reel, La Raspa, Greensleeves, Jessie Polka, Seljancica Kola, Red River Valley, Mayim, Oh Johnny Oh, Limbo Rock, Misirlou, mambo music, Road to the Isles, Achy Breaky Heart, Nebesko Kolo, Sicilian Tarantella, Texas Star, and Stepping Out) plus music for new dance—To Ting

Performance Goals

Students will do the following:

- Dance at least five dances already learned.
- Learn a new dance, To Ting.

Cognitive Goals

Students will learn the following:

- The waltz and how to move to 3/4 timing
- Pivot turns
- A Danish dance that changes rhythm from 3/4 to 2/4 timing, To Ting

Lesson Safety

Make sure the emotional climate is healthy, particularly when it comes to partnering. Be available to dance with the person who is without a partner.

Motivation

Have music for Road to the Isles playing and ask students to join you as you dance to it. Entertain another request and dance it through before announcing that to date, they have learned three basic dance steps—the polka, Schottische, and two-step—and that this lesson will teach a fourth, the waltz, a dance done to 3/4 timing. As a basic step, the waltz can be done alone, in any direction, with a partner, and formally or informally. If they've seen ballroom dancing, they know that the waltz can look quite elegant, yet the waltz is also a popular Cajun dance that is not formal at all. To Ting, a folk dance from Denmark, is sophisticated musically. Some of it is to 2/4 time, and some of it is to 3/4 time and requires a waltz. The change in tempos and moods is rare and fun.

Lesson Sequence

1. Introduce the waltz and practice in open dance position.
2. Introduce closed dance position (see figure 5.5) and have students waltz in closed dance position. Boys start on L foot going forward, girls start on R foot going back.
3. Teach To Ting, walking through each part and then putting on music and walking through the part again.
4. The remainder of the lesson is left to student requests.

Waltz

- 1-3—In even rhythm, step forward L (1), to side on R (2), to close with L (3).
- 4-6—Step R (4), L (5), R (6).

To Ting

Teach To Ting, walking through each part and then putting on music and walking through the part again. Partners stand side by side in a double circle, arms of joined hands bent at the elbow with free hands on hips.

Figure 5.5 Closed dance position.

Part 1

Part 1 is done in 3/4 timing.

- 1-12—Moving forward and using the outside foot (boys L, girls R), take a waltz step turning away from partner, then another waltz step turning toward partner. Repeat.
- 1-12—In closed dance position, turn CW using 4 waltz steps while continuing the line of direction.
- 1-24—Repeat all 8 measures.

Part 2

Part 2 is done in 2/4 timing.

- 1-8—In conversation position (drop joined hands in closed dance position and stand side by side), take 4 steps forward, get into shoulder-waist position (boy's arm on girl's waist and girl's arm on boy's shoulders) and take a 4-step pivot turn.
- 1-8—Repeat.

Review

Ask the following:

- The waltz differs from other dances because of its timing. What is it?
- When dancing with a partner in closed dance position, when the leader goes forward what should the partner do?
- Is a turn easier if your weight leans away from the center of the couple or toward the center?

Dance
INTERMEDIATE
LESSON 7

Teton Mountain Stomp

Facilities

Ventilated room with enough space for students to move freely and a floor that gives

Materials

- Sound system that can project music clearly throughout the dance space

- Music for previously learned dances (Grand March, Bingo, Pata Pata, Sevila Se Bela Loza, Hora, Saturday Night Fever Walk, Virginia Reel, La Raspa, Greensleeves, Jessie Polka, Seljancica Kola, Red River Valley, Mayim, Oh Johnny Oh, Limbo Rock, Misirlou, mambo music, Nebesko Kolo, Sicilian Tarantella, Road to the Isles, Achy Breaky Heart, Texas Star, Stepping Out, and To Ting) plus music for new dance—Teton Mountain Stomp

Performance Goals

Students will do the following:

- Dance the Teton Mountain Stomp, an American folk dance.
- Improve performance of dances previously learned.

Cognitive Goals

Students will learn the following:

- How to use the laws of centrifugal force to improve their pivot turn
- The interaction allowing couples to move together in closed position

Lesson Safety

Make sure the emotional climate is healthy, particularly when it comes to partnering. Be available to dance with the person who is without a partner.

Motivation

Have music for Achy Breaky Heart playing as students enter and invite them to join you as you dance to it. Then announce that the class will concentrate on American dances for the day. Ask if they can name the American dances they've learned this year (Oh Johnny Oh, Achy Breaky Heart, Texas Star, Stepping Out). Ask if they can name the dances they learned last year (Bingo, Saturday Night Fever Walk, Virginia Reel, Red River Valley).

Lesson Sequence

1. Begin with several requests from the floor that are American only.
2. Teach Teton Mountain Stomp.
3. Fill dance requests for American dances.

Teton Mountain Stomp

Teton Mountain Stomp is danced in closed dance position with joined hands toward center of the circle, men face CCW. Before you teach the parts, review dancers lost-and-found and the pivot turn.

Part 1

- 1-4—With inside foot (boys L, girls R), step to center (1), step to close (2), step to center (3), step to close (4).
- 5-8—With outside foot, step out, step to close, step out, step to close.
- 1-4—With inside foot, step L (1), stomp R (2), step R (3), stomp L (4).

Part 2

- 1-4—In closed dance position, R hip to R hip, walk CCW 4 steps (boys forward, girls backward).
- 5-8—In closed position, pivot-turn to reverse direction, continuing in CCW direction 4 steps (girls forward, boys backward).
- 1-4—Couples split and walk 4 steps forward to meet new partners.

Part 3

- 1-4—In closed dance position with new partner, swing, using 2 two-steps (1-8) and a 4-step pivot turn.
- End with boy facing line of direction (CCW).

Review

Ask the following:

- Which dances do you like better, those with partners or without?
- What do you like about square dance?
- Don't you think it is neat to get to dance with everyone?
- Which dances allowed you to switch partners?
- Which dances did you do alone?

Salty Dog Rag

Facilities

Ventilated room with enough space for students to move freely and a floor that gives

Materials

- Sound system that can project music clearly throughout the dance space
- Music for dances learned previously (Grand March, Bingo, Pata Pata, Sevila Se Bela Loza, Hora, Saturday Night Fever Walk, Virginia Reel, La Raspa, Greensleeves, Jessie Polka, Seljancica Kola, Red River Valley, Mayim, Oh Johnny Oh, Limbo Rock, Misirlou, mambo music, Nebesko Kolo, Sicilian Tarantella, Road to the Isles, Achy Breaky Heart, Texas Star, Stepping Out, To Ting, and Teton Mountain Stomp) plus music for new dance—Salty Dog Rag
- Intermediate dance skills rubric

Performance Goals

Students will do the following:

- Use the Schottische step in the Salty Dog Rag.
- Review Teton Mountain Stomp.
- Improve their dance footwork.

Cognitive Goal

Students will learn about the versatility of the Schottische.

Lesson Safety

Make sure the emotional climate is healthy, particularly when it comes to partnering. Be available to dance with the person who is without a partner.

Motivation

Have the music on for Road to the Isles and invite students to join you as you dance it through. Then announce that the lesson will be an all-Schottische day. Review the Schottische—three steps and a hop—and discuss all the dances learned this year that have the Schottische in them (Misirlou, Road to the Isles) and last year (Sevila Se Bela Loza, Seljancica Kola). Before doing the old dances, explain that they will love the Salty Dog Rag.

Lesson Sequence

1. Teach Salty Dog Rag, an American novelty dance.
2. Do Salty Dog Rag through twice.
3. Review other dances with the Schottische.
4. If there is time, allow other requests from the floor.

Salty Dog Rag

Teach the parts then dance to the music.

Part 1

Couples are in skater's position (partners side by side), facing CCW (with R hands joined and L hands joined).

- 1-4—On R foot, grapevine Schottische to the right: step R (1), cross L behind (2), step R (3), and hop (4).
- 5-8—On L foot, grapevine Schottische to the left: step L, cross R behind, step L, and hop.
- 1-8—Take 4 step-hops forward.
- 1-16—Repeat the 2 Schottisches and 4 step-hops CCW.

Part 2

Drop R hands and females turn to face partner with L hands joined.

- 1-4—Schottische to the right, away from each other: step R, cross L behind, step R, and hop.
- 5-8—They pull joined hands and Schottische back until they are facing each other.
- 1-8—Do 4 step-hop turns in place.
- 1-16—Repeat part 2. At last step-hop, end in promenade position facing CCW.

Part 3

Couples are in promenade position facing CCW.

- 1-8—Place R heel forward (1), then in place (2), L heel forward (3), then in place (4). Rise on toes while clicking heels out and elbows out (5), click heels down and together (6), put R heel forward (7), and bring it back to place (8).
- 1-8—Turn in place with 4 step-hops, starting on the R foot and turning right.
- 1-16—Repeat all of part 3, ending so that after the last step-hop, partners are side by side in skater's position, facing CCW.

Review

Ask the following:

- Which dance was the most energetic?
- Which did the Schottische as if you were skating on a pond?
- Which dance did the Schottische in a line? To the side? With a grapevine?
- Let students know that the skills rubric is posted.

Dance
INTERMEDIATE
LESSON 9

Greek and Middle Eastern Dances

Facilities

Ventilated room with enough space for students to move freely and a floor that gives

Materials

- Sound system that can project music clearly throughout the dance space
- Music for dances learned previously (Grand March, Bingo, Pata Pata, Sevila Se Bela Loza, Hora, Saturday Night Fever Walk, Virginia Reel, La Raspa, Greensleeves, Jessie Polka, Seljancica Kola, Red River Valley, Mayim, Oh Johnny Oh, Limbo Rock, Misirlou, mambo music, Nebesko Kolo, Sicilian Tarantella, Road to the Isles, Achy Breaky Heart, Texas Star, Stepping Out, To Ting, Teton Mountain Stomp, and Salty Dog Rag)
- Intermediate dance skills rubric

Performance Goal

Students will perform a variety of dances from the Middle East and Greece.

Cognitive Goal

Students will learn how they will be graded.

Lesson Safety

Make sure the emotional climate is healthy, particularly when it comes to partnering. Be available to dance with the person who is without a partner.

Motivation

Have music for Salty Dog Rag playing as students enter and invite them to join you on the dance floor. Announce that in 2 years they have learned 24 dances. Acknowledge that it is a lot in a short time and that it would be unfair to expect everyone to do each 100% correctly. Though that would be great, getting a good grade does not depend on it. Tell them to take a look at the standards and feel free to ask any questions. If there are no questions, review some of the dances from Greece and Israel.

Lesson Sequence

1. Begin with requests from the floor. Allow one or two.
2. Go over Salty Dog Rag.
3. Review old dances from Middle East and Greece—Hora, Mayim, Misirlou.
4. If there's time, allow requests from the floor.

Review

Discuss the following:

- Can anyone identify where the Hora, Mayim, and Misirlou came from?
- If quizzing class, ask review questions that will be covered on the quiz.
- If you decide not to use the rubric, you and the class can decide how they want to be graded, such as how they dance several dances and if so, which ones, or how they learn a new dance.

Creating a Mambo Routine

Facilities

Ventilated room with enough space for students to move freely and a floor that gives

Materials

- Sound system that can project music clearly throughout the dance space
- Music for dances learned previously (Grand March, Bingo, Pata Pata, Sevila Se Bela Loza, Hora, Saturday Night Fever Walk, Virginia Reel, La Raspa, Greensleeves, Jessie Polka, Seljancica Kola, Red River Valley, Mayim, Oh Johnny Oh, Limbo Rock, Misirlou, mambo music, Nebesko Kolo, Sicilian Tarantella, Road to the Isles, Achy Breaky Heart, Texas Star, Stepping Out, To Ting, Teton Mountain Stomp, and Salty Dog Rag)
- Intermediate dance skills rubric

Performance Goals

Students will do the following:

- Review the mambo and create a 32-beat pattern with a partner.
- Focus on dances they choose to be graded on.

Cognitive Goal

Students will integrate what they have learned to make their own dance patterns.

Lesson Safety

Make sure the emotional climate is healthy, particularly when it comes to partnering. Be available to dance with the person who is without a partner.

Motivation

Put on music that students like and can perform to when they enter. Then announce that at the beginning of this unit the class spent time dancing the mambo, a Latin social dance step done in dance clubs. After a quick review, they will find partners and spend the next 15 minutes creating and practicing a 32-beat routine that they can do together and repeat until the music ends.

Lesson Sequence

1. Review the mambo beat (quick, quick, slow). Put the music on and keep it playing while students create a 32-beat dance pattern.

2. When students have established their patterns, ask them to repeat it four times without stopping. Keep mambo music playing continuously.

3. Play mambo music, having half the class perform while the other half watches. Then switch performers and audience, making sure all couples demonstrate.

4. Allow students requests. Students might choose a routine they just saw and like and ask the dancers to teach it to them, or they might like to do some dances they have been doing all unit. If the requests are not recent dances, you might review them quickly before putting on the music.

Review

If giving one, announce that a short quiz will be given in the next class.

Dance
INTERMEDIATE
LESSON 11

Dance and Assessment

Facilities

Ventilated room with enough space for students to move freely and a floor that gives

Materials

- Sound system that can project music clearly throughout the dance space
- Music for dances learned previously (Grand March, Bingo, Pata Pata, Sevila Se Bela Loza, Hora, Saturday Night Fever Walk, Virginia Reel, La Raspa, Greensleeves, Jessie Polka, Seljancica Kola, Red River Valley, Mayim, Oh Johnny Oh, Limbo Rock, Misirlou, mambo music, Nebesko Kolo, Sicilian Tarantella, Road to the Isles, Achy Breaky Heart, Texas Star, Stepping Out, To Ting, Teton Mountain Stomp, and Salty Dog Rag)
- Intermediate dance skills rubric
- One quiz for each student
- Pens or pencils

Performance Goal

Students will be tested and graded on their last day of dance.

Cognitive Goal

Students will get an idea of what they know and don't know by taking a quiz.

Lesson Safety

Make sure the emotional climate is healthy, particularly when it comes to partnering. Be available to dance with the person who is without a partner.

Motivation

As students enter, play their favorite song. Then announce that they've done a great job. After the quiz they can choose any dance they want to end the unit with.

Lesson Sequence

1. Distribute quizzes. Allow no more than 10 minutes. If students can't finish in 10 minutes, make provisions for them to finish the test while the rest of the class dances or outside of class.

2. Entertain requests from the floor.

Review

Ask the following:

- What do you think would improve the unit?
- What do you think would have improved you?

Intermediate Dance Skills Rubric

Name _____ Date _____

Teacher _____ Class _____

	0	1	2	3	4	5
Directions	No effort.	• Gets in single and double circle. • Knows CCW from CW. • Can follow a line. • Joins hands when requested.	• Forms a square. • Knows own position in square. • Knows where to find partner and corner in a square. • Knows inside from outside.	• Gets in skater's, varsouvienne, or closed dance partner position. • Has mastered basic square dance calls: circle, swing, promenade.	• Has mastered allemande left, grand right and left. • Is in correct position in relation to partner. • Has learned to star.	• Dances done more than three times in class are danced correctly. • Unfazed by change of direction. • Is a class role model and leader.
Footwork	No effort.	• Has mastered basic locomotion skills. • Has mastered the skip, leap, and gallop. • Knows the Schottische.	• Can polka in line of direction. • Can two-step in line of direction. • Stays on tempo when the tempo speeds up.	• Can dance the waltz in line of direction. • Performs a pivot turn. • Begins on correct foot.	• Can lead or follow appropriately when dancing with a partner. • Uses quick steps to turn. • Transitions from one part of a dance to another.	• Able to polka, waltz, and pivot turn with partner. • Uses proper footwork for all dances taught. • Does not need a demonstration to dance properly on cue.
Group work	No effort.	• Joins group formation on request. • Follows established class rules. • Doesn't hesitate to get a partner when needed.	• Follows line of direction but needs to watch. • Is on beat with the music. • Action is in sync with the group.	• Is courteous to partners. • Anticipates next steps and direction changes. • Behavior is not a drag on others.	• Accepts responsibility to lead or follow. • Able to stay on rhythm without musical accompaniment.	• Knows dances well enough to lead them. • Partner work is synchronized and cooperative.

From Isobel Kleinman, 2009, *Complete Physical Education Plans for Grades 5 to 12, Second Edition* (Champaign, IL: Human Kinetics).

Intermediate Dance Quiz

Name _____ Date _____

Teacher _____ Class _____

Multiple Choice

Read each question and each answer carefully. Be sure to choose the best answer that fits the statement preceding it. When you have made your choice, put the appropriate letter on the line to the left of the numbered question.

_____ 1. Dances where the instructions are typically called in a singsong fashion are

    a. partner circle dances

    b. European folk dances

    c. square dances

    d. country-western dances

_____ 2. Male partners should always

    a. bring their partner home

    b. put their partner on the right

    c. start with the left foot

    d. all of the above

_____ 3. The grand right and left is

    a. a moving human chain

    b. a way for girls to meet and join hands momentarily with boys

    c. starts with the right hand and passing right shoulders, then the left hand and passing left shoulders, then the right hand and passing right shoulders, and so on

    d. all of the above

_____ 4. The waltz is

    a. quick, quick, slow

    b. three equal steps

    c. only done forward

    d. only done in social dance position

_____ 5. A pivot turn is

    a. four equal steps

    b. done in a couple

    c. done to 4/4 time

    d. all of the above

_____ 6. The mambo step

    a. was influenced by Latin music

    b. is a step, step, bring together and hold

    c. was used in Limbo Rock

    d. all of the above

»continued

 From Isobel Kleinman, 2009, *Complete Physical Education Plans for Grades 5 to 12, Second Edition* (Champaign, IL: Human Kinetics).

»continued

_____ 7. Which of the following is not a traditional folk dance?

    a. Misirlou

    b. To Ting

    c. Achy Breaky Heart

    d. Texas Star

_____ 8. Which of the following did not require a partner?

    a. Texas Star

    b. Limbo Rock

    c. Salty Dog Rag

    d. Oh Johnny Oh

_____ 9. Choose the dance that had a silent musical passage.

    a. Nebesko Kolo

    b. Sicilian tarantella

    c. Stepping Out

    d. all of the above

_____ 10. If you were designing an aerobic unit with the dances you learned and you wanted to do an energetic dance that would significantly raise your heart rate, you would choose

    a. Salty Dog Rag

    b. Mayim

    c. Stepping Out

    d. Achy Breaky Heart

Intermediate Dance Answer Key

Multiple Choice

1. c—Square dances are called and good callers attempt to call in tune.
2. d
3. d
4. b
5. a
6. d
7. c—Square dance is considered a traditional American folk dance.
8. b—Limbo Rock was the only dance done without joining hands.
9. c—The lack of music was the challenge to this beginning soft-shoe dance.
10. a—This is the most energetic of all the dances listed.

From Isobel Kleinman, 2009, *Complete Physical Education Plans for Grades 5 to 12, Second Edition* (Champaign, IL: Human Kinetics).

Doudlebska Polka

Facilities
Ventilated room with enough space for students to move freely and a floor that gives

Materials
- Sound system that can project music clearly throughout the dance space
- Music for dances learned previously (Grand March, Bingo, Pata Pata, Sevila Se Bela Loza, Hora, Saturday Night Fever Walk, Virginia Reel, La Raspa, Greensleeves, Jessie Polka, Seljancica Kola, Red River Valley, Road to the Isles, Mayim, Oh Johnny Oh, Limbo Rock, Misirlou, mambo music, Achy Breaky Heart, Nebesko Kolo, Sicilian Tarantella, Texas Star, Stepping Out, To Ting, Teton Mountain Stomp, and Salty Dog Rag) plus music for new dance—Doudlebska Polka

Performance Goals
Students will do the following:
- Choose dances they want to review and repeat them.
- Review the polka and perform the Jessie Polka.
- Learn a Czechoslovakian dance, the Doudlebska Polka.

Cognitive Goals
Students will learn the following:
- That polka starts with a hop on the pickup beat
- The polka footwork pattern (hop, step, close, step)

Lesson Safety
- Explain that whether dancing in lines or as couples dancing freely around the room, the leader is obligated to direct the movement so there is no contact with objects or other people in the room.
- There will be a lot of partnering during the advanced dance unit. Make sure the emotional climate is healthy and that no one is left feeling awkward about not having a partner.

Motivation
Play the students' favorite music as they enter the room, encouraging them to join in and dance. Then remind them that although they don't need to dress for gym, they will be sweating so they should remove their jackets and sweaters and arrive promptly. They can put their belongings on the side of the gym or in their locker.

Tell them that as young adults with dance skills, they can expect to do a lot more partnering this year.

Lesson Sequence
1. Begin with several requests. This will set a positive tone and get the class moving quickly. Review a few measures for everyone before putting the music on.
2. Review the polka in rhythm and have the class polka around the room.
3. Review the Jessie Polka.
   a. Review the heel–toe part.
   b. Have students get in groups of 3, 4, or 5 and do the heel–toe part locked together, arms around waists, bodies leaning forward when pointing back, bodies leaning back when toes go forward.
   c. Announce that the part just practiced is preceded by four polka steps. Put the music on and dance.

4. Teach polka in couples.
   a. Review social dance position and some rules that make it work. Remind students of the reciprocity of footwork (males start on left going forward, females start on right going backward).
   b. Teach how to move as a couple.
      - Leader's job is make sure they don't crash into walls or other couples.
      - Lean away from each other but hold on to facilitate turn.
5. Teach the Doudlebska Polka.

Doudlebska Polka

Explain that it is a Czech dance and it is a mixer that starts with couples at random in social dance position. (Can also be done in CCW circle.) Teach in parts, putting the music on to show how distinct the melody is for each part. Call out instructions as they dance.

Part 1

1-64—Couples at random dance 16 polka steps traveling CCW (females on R, males on L to start).

Part 2

- Couples drop joined hands, leaving the other hands where they are (women's L hand on partner's R shoulder, men's R arm around partner's waist), and work their way into a circle, while beginning the 32 walking steps in the next segment.
- 1-32—Once there, male reaches L hand out to touch the L shoulder of the person in front and everyone moves CCW, walking 32 steps and singing.

Part 3

- 1-32—Men turn to face the center of the circle. They clap their hands once and the hands of the people to both sides once and repeat while the women dance behind them. The women put their hands on their hips, turn in reverse direction, and polka 16 polka steps CW around the outside of the men's circle.
- The ladies stop and the men turn. Each should be facing a new partner to dance away with.

Review

Ask the following:
- How many people had more than three different partners?
- Which partner was easier to move with, the one who was firm and leaned away or the one who was limp?
- Did you ever expect a law of physics to be relevant in dancing? What is the law? How is it important?
- How would you explain a mixer?

Assessment

Observe to get a sense of whether the class is keeping up. Most students should have no trouble with the basic polka and the activity level of the class should be high. If not, evaluate what needs more review and plan it for the next lesson.

Dance
ADVANCED
LESSON 2

Country-Western Dancing

Facilities

Ventilated room with enough space for students to move freely and a floor that gives

Materials

- Sound system that can project music clearly throughout the dance space

- Music for dances learned previously (Grand March, Bingo, Pata Pata, Sevila Se Bela Loza, Hora, Saturday Night Fever Walk, Virginia Reel, La Raspa, Greensleeves, Jessie Polka, Seljancica Kola, Red River Valley, Road to the Isles, Mayim, Oh Johnny Oh, Limbo Rock, Misirlou, mambo music, Achy Breaky Heart, Nebesko Kolo, Sicilian Tarantella, Texas Star, Stepping Out, To Ting, Teton Mountain Stomp, Salty Dog Rag, and Doudlebska Polka) plus country-western music for the Texas Two-Step ("If It Were Easy" or "Everything a Waltz") and Cajun music for the Cajun Two-Step

Performance Goals

Students will do the following:

- Dance the Doudlebska Polka.
- Review the two-step in a dance learned last year, Nebesko Kolo.
- Learn the Texas Two-Step and the Cajun Two-Step.

Cognitive Goals

Students will learn the following

- How dance is stylized by region
- That the Texas Two-Step is done to waltz music

Lesson Safety

- Explain that whether dancing in lines or as couples dancing freely around the room, the leader is obligated to direct movement so there is no contact with objects or other people in the room.
- There will be a lot of partnering during the advanced dance unit. Make sure the emotional climate is healthy and that no one is left feeling awkward about not having a partner.

Motivation

Have music for the Jessie Polka playing as students enter and dance it through. Then dance the Doudlebska Polka through. Review if necessary. Discuss how versatile the two-step is—it has a place in folk dance, ballroom dance, and Cajun dance. The music for each is different, and so is the style. They should watch to see how it changes.

Lesson Sequence

1. Review the two-step and pas de basque.
   a. Review Nebesko Kolo: the two-step, balances, pas de basque, stomp.
   b. Walk through without music once. Then put music on and dance.
2. Teach the Texas Two-Step, a popular partner dance using the two-step to waltz music (3/4 time).
   a. Teach the Texan variation of closed dance position—woman's left hand on man's arm (not shoulder) or hooked in her belt.
   b. Teach that couples move in line of direction (CCW).
   c. Emphasize men leading, women following.
3. Teach the Cajun Two-Step to Cajun music (similar to the jitterbug, Lindy, or swing).

Texas Two-Step

The Texas Two-Step is done with partners in the Texan variation of closed dance position. Teach the footwork and rhythm, which is quick, quick, slow, slow and is done in long, smooth gliding steps (counts 1-and, 2, 3).

- 1-3—Men walk forward on L, women go back on R in uneven rhythm (quick, quick, slow, slow).
- 1-end—Men walk L (1) R (and), L (2), R (3); then R, L, R, L; L, R, L, R; and so on, in line of direction (CCW).

Cajun Two-Step

Begin with partners in social dance position and includes a couple turn.

- 1–6—To turn, men step L sideways, close R to L, step L pivoting on the ball of the foot to complete the CW turn. They have turned halfway around. Girls follow, stepping R to side, close L to R, step on R, and pivot CW on ball of foot to finish turn.
- 1-end—Continue to dance using the two-step footwork, adding a couple turn periodically.
- Note: The footwork for the Cajun two-step is the same as in all previously learned two-steps done in 4/4 time.

Review

Ask the following:

- How can you describe the difference between the dances with the two-step?
- Which was the line dance?
- Which glided smoothly?
- Which was funkier?
- Was the rhythm for the Texas Two-Step the same as the basic two-step?

Dance
ADVANCED
LESSON 3

Reviewing the Texas Two-Step

Facilities

Ventilated room with enough space for students to move freely and a floor that gives

Materials

- Sound system that can project music clearly throughout the dance space
- Music for dances learned previously (Grand March, Bingo, Pata Pata, Sevila Se Bela Loza, Hora, Saturday Night Fever Walk, Virginia Reel, La Raspa, Greensleeves, Jessie Polka, Seljancica Kola, Red River Valley, Road to the Isles, Mayim, Oh Johnny Oh, Limbo Rock, Misirlou, mambo music, Achy Breaky Heart, Nebesko Kolo, Sicilian Tarantella, Texas Star, Stepping Out, To Ting, Teton Mountain Stomp, Salty Dog Rag, and Doudlebska Polka) plus country-western music for the Texas Two-Step ("If It Were Easy" or "Everything a Waltz") and Cajun music for the Cajun Two-Step
- Pinnies

Performance Goals

Students will do the following:

- Review the Doubleska Polka and Texas or Cajun Two-Step.
- Dance the Virginia Reel and Oh Johnny Oh.
- Learn a second break for the two-step.

Cognitive Goal

Students will review square-dance calls (corner, partner, promenade, sashay, reel, cast-off into a column right or left).

Lesson Safety

- Explain that whether dancing in lines or as couples dancing freely around the room, the leader is obligated to direct movement so there is no contact with objects or other people in the room.
- There will be a lot of partnering during the advanced dance unit. Make sure the emotional climate is healthy and that no one is left feeling awkward about not having a partner.

Motivation

Play whatever seems to be the most popular dance music as students enter and encourage them to join you on the floor. Ask what other dance they'd like to do and put that on. Then explain that once the footwork is learned and the rhythm feels natural, leaders should do new breaks, and today, everyone will learn more variations (breaks) for the two-step.

Lesson Sequence

1. Review the two-step. After time on the basic, ask the man to lift his L arm and with a little pull, initiate his partner coming under it and around to face him again.
    a. In semiopen position (two hands joined), on first step man raises L arm, on second step man pulls woman forward under his arm, on third step woman pivots to face partner.
    b. Try with music.
    c. Suggest everyone do 4 basics, 4 couple turns, one turn (women), and repeat.
    d. Emphasize the men leading, women following. Stop them to show how a man (or leader) can initiate a turn just using his left hand.
2. Make a circle. Review corner, partner, promenade and do Oh Johnny Oh.
3. Break the circle into longways sets of 4 to 6 couples.
    a. Review cast-off, sashay, and reel.
    b. Do Virginia Reel.
4. If there's time, fill dance requests. Review if the dance hasn't been done in a while.

Review

Ask the following:
- Which dance results in a change of partner?
- Which is in longways position?
- What about Oh Johnny Oh is similar to square dancing?
- What makes it different from square dancing?

Assessment

Observe to see if the majority of class can keep up with the pace of the lesson. If not, slow down, do more repetition without the music, and then do more repetition of each step with the music before letting music play through and expecting everyone to dance it to the end.

Dance
ADVANCED
LESSON 4

Vé David and the Buzz Swing

Facilities

Ventilated room with enough space for students to move freely and a floor that gives

Materials

- Sound system that can project music clearly throughout the dance space
- Music for dances learned previously (Grand March, Bingo, Pata Pata, Sevila Se Bela Loza, Hora, Saturday Night Fever Walk, Virginia Reel, La Raspa, Greensleeves, Jessie Polka, Seljancica Kola, Red River Valley, Road to the Isles, Mayim, Oh Johnny Oh, Limbo Rock, Misirlou, mambo music, Achy Breaky Heart, Nebesko Kolo, Sicilian Tarantella, Texas Star, Stepping Out, To Ting, Teton Mountain Stomp, Salty Dog Rag, Doudlebska Polka, Texas Two-Step, and Cajun Two-Step) plus music for new dance—Vé David

Performance Goals

Students will do the following:

- Learn and perform a third break for the two-step.
- Learn and perform Vé David.
- Review the Doubleska Polka and Texas or Cajun Two-Step.

Cognitive Goals

Students will learn the following:

- Why mixers are so social
- How each partner is different to dance with
- Buzz swings

Lesson Safety

- Explain that whether dancing in lines or as couples dancing freely around the room, the leader is obligated to direct the movement so there is no contact with objects or other people in the room.
- There will be a lot of partnering during the advanced dance unit. Make sure the emotional climate is healthy and that no one is left feeling awkward about not having a partner.

Motivation

Have some Cajun music playing as students enter the gym. Encourage them to join you on the floor. Begin class by teaching a new dance break.

Lesson Sequence

1. Teach continuous underarm turns.

   a. Men increase pressure on women's hand, pulling them a short step forward. Men turn CW on L while turning women CCW on R. They finish the turn so they face each other and have exchanged places.

2. Teach the buzz swing (see figure 5.6).

   a. Start without a partner. Keep one foot (R) as an anchor or pivot foot and step-push the other to generate a turn.

   b. Teach positioning.

      - L arm is up, R arm is across partner's waist.
      - Partners are side by side.

   c. Practice the buzz swing.

      - With couples side by side, R arms across each other's waist, R foot stationary, L arm raised, use L foot to propel the turn.
      - Couples should pull their upper torsos away to generate centrifugal force.

   d. Stop class to show how centrifugal force helps the swing, and practice swing again.

3. Teach Vé David in sequence, walking through instructions.

4. Do the Texas Two-Step.

5. Do the Doudlebska Polka as a mixer.

6. If there's time, fill requests.

Vé David

Couples should be in a double circle, facing CCW with inside hands joined. Teach each part then add music while cueing "Forward 4, single circle 4, in 4, out 4, girls in 4, out 4, boys in 4, turn and get a new partner." Remind anyone who loses a partner to go to the lost-and-found (center of the circle) to find a new one.

Part 1

Start each new pattern on R foot.

- 1-4—In double circle facing CCW, walk forward 4 steps—R (1), L (2), R (3), L (4).
- 5-8—Back out, joining to form a single circle in 4 steps.
- 1-8—With everyone facing center in a single circle, walk in 4 steps, then back out 4 steps.

Part 2

- 1-8—Women go forward 4 and back while men stay and clap in place.
- 1-8—Men clap as they go forward 4 steps, turn, and walk to the right of their previous partner or meet a new partner in 4 steps.
- 1-8—With new partners, do an 8-step buzz swing.

Review

Ask the following:

- Is anyone sweating?
- Do you think that dancing can be a good activity for improving fitness? Why?

Figure 5.6 The buzz swing.

Hot Lips

Facilities

Ventilated room with enough space for students to move freely and a floor that gives

Materials

- Sound system that can project music clearly throughout the dance space
- Music for dances learned previously (Grand March, Bingo, Pata Pata, Savila Se Bela Loza, Hora, Saturday Night Fever Walk, Virginia Reel, La Raspa, Greensleeves, Jessie Polka, Seljancica Kola, Red River Valley, Road to the Isles, Mayim, Oh Johnny Oh, Limbo Rock, Misirlou, mambo music, Achy Breaky Heart, Nebesko Kolo, Sicilian Tarantella, Texas Star, Stepping Out, To Ting, Teton Mountain Stomp, Salty Dog Rag, Doudlebska Polka, Texas Two-Step, Cajun Two-Step, and Vé David) plus music for new dance—Hot Lips

Performance Goals

Students will do the following:

- Choose one two-step dance.
- Learn a novelty dance based on swing, Hot Lips.

Cognitive Goal

Students will learn that a change in style with typical combination dance steps, such as the two-step, changes the nature of the dance.

Lesson Safety

- Explain that whether dancing in lines or as couples dancing freely around the room, the leader is obligated to direct movement so there is no contact with objects or other people in the room.

- There will be a lot of partnering during the advanced dance unit. Make sure the emotional climate is healthy and that no one is left feeling awkward about not having a partner.

Motivation

Have music playing as students enter and encourage them to join you on the dance floor. After everyone is assembled, ask if anyone knows what popular dance came after the Charleston and before the Twist. Here are some hints: Teenagers started it, and it was fast, athletic, and done to the big band sounds. It was swing dance, and today's dance is a takeoff on swing (some people called it the *Lindy*). This novelty dance is also a takeoff on folk dance in that the patterns repeat themselves and the dancers are organized in a group. The dance is called *Hot Lips*—don't ask why. It has breaks the class might remember from dancing the Cajun two-step.

Lesson Sequence

1. Teach Hot Lips in sections.
2. Do a circle mixer to get new partners (Vé David, Bingo, Oh Johnny Oh).
3. Do Hot Lips again with a new partner.
4. If time allows, fill requests.

Hot Lips

Begin in a double circle, with partners in closed dance position, boys' backs to center, ready to move CCW. Walk through the parts with no music, then add music. Repeat several times.

Part 1

- 1-8—On boys' L foot, girls' R foot, take 2 two-steps and 2 grapevine steps in line of direction (CCW). Do two times.
- 1-8—Holding only joined hands, do a two-step toward each other, a two-step pulling away, a two-step together, and then a two-step to turn CW. (Cue "Two-step together, two-step away, two-step together, two-step to turn.")

Part 2

- 1-4—Walk starting with inside foot and inside hands joined (1, 2, 3, 4).
- 5-8—Inside foot steps in (5), outside foot points in (6); outside foot steps out (7), inside foot points out (8).
- 1-24—Using 6 two-steps, follow this pattern: Two-step to face partner (1-4), two-step to pull away (5-8), two-step to step in (9-12), two-step to switch places and move away (13-16), two-step to go in toward partner (17-20), two-step to switch back (21-24).

Part 3

Walk through part 3, cueing, "2-step to face, 2-step to pull away, 2-step to come in, 2 step to switch, 2-step to come in, 2-step to switch."

- 1-8—Take 4 walking steps in the CW direction, reversing direction on step 4 and ending in closed dance position facing CCW.
- 1-32—Take 4 two-steps forward and 4 steps forward in CCW direction. Do two times.

Review

Ask the following:

- What dance is Hot Lips based on?
- What dance step in Hot Lips is used the most frequently?

Cha-Cha

Facilities

Ventilated room with enough space for students to move freely and a floor that gives

Materials

- Sound system that can project music clearly throughout the dance space
- Music for dances learned previously (Grand March, Bingo, Pata Pata, Sevila Se Bela Loza, Hora, Saturday Night Fever Walk, Virginia Reel, La Raspa, Greensleeves, Jessie Polka, Seljancica Kola, Red River Valley, Road to the Isles, Mayim, Oh Johnny Oh, Limbo Rock, Misirlou, mambo music, Achy Breaky Heart, Nebesko Kolo, Sicilian Tarantella, Texas Star, Stepping Out, To Ting, Teton Mountain Stomp, Salty Dog Rag, Doudlebska Polka, Texas Two-Step, Cajun Two-Step, Vé David, and Hot Lips) plus cha-cha music

Performance Goals

Students will do the following:

- Review a dance with a Latin rhythm, Limbo Rock.
- Learn a Latin ballroom dance form, the cha-cha.

Cognitive Goals

Students will learn the following:

- That the cha-cha is from Cuba and a combination of the mambo and swing
- The cha-cha steps (slow, slow, quick, quick, slow, or step, step, 1, 2, 3, hold)

Lesson Safety

- Couples dancing freely around the room are obligated to avoid contact with objects or others.
- Keep a healthy emotional climate so no one is left feeling awkward about not having a partner.

Motivation

Have music for Hot Lips playing as students enter and encourage them to dance it through. Then explain that Brazil favors the samba, Argentina favors the tango, Costa Rica loves the mambo, and Cuba invented the cha-cha.

Lesson Sequence

1. Begin with a review of Limbo Rock.
2. Teach the cha-cha, a Cuban innovation.
3. Do a mixer so students get new partners.
4. If there's time, fill requests, changing partners with every new dance.

Cha-Cha

With a partner, boys leading forward on L and girls back on R, do basic step. Walk through the step without music, then add music to learn the rhythm.

- 1-8—Step forward on L (1), back on R (2), do a cha, cha, cha L, R, L (3-and-4). Step back on R (5), forward on L (6), then do a cha, cha, cha R, L, R (7-and-8).
- 1-8—Break right by doing a forward cha-cha step on L foot. On next cha-cha, step on R back, release R hold on girls. Step L in place, step R in place turning 1/4 turn to right and ending side by side with partner.

Review

Discuss the following:

- Using the words *slow* and *quick,* what is the rhythm for the cha-cha?
- If you want to turn your partner, do you do it on the slow or the quick steps?
- Announce that next class they're having a hoedown and going American square all the way.

Square Dance

Facilities

Ventilated room with enough space for students to move freely and a floor that gives

Materials

- Sound system that can project music clearly throughout the dance space
- Music for cha-cha, Red River Valley, Oh Johnny Oh, Texas Star, Promenade the Ring, Arkansas Traveler, and Gents Star Right
- Microphone that will allow instructions to be heard clearly over the music
- Pinnies if you do not have an equal number of girls and boys

Performance Goals

Students will do the following:

- Dance up to six square dances.
- Dance to as many square-dance calls as time permits.

Cognitive Goals

Students will increase their square-dance vocabulary (see page 122 for definitions):

- Shuffle
- Do-si-do
- Promenade
- Swing
- Allemande left
- Grand right and left
- Star

Lesson Safety

Space each square so students can move without hitting an obstruction or each other.

Motivation

Put on a student favorite to get them moving. When everyone is assembled, explain that today the class will not have to learn any complicated steps, though they will have to listen to instructions and follow them correctly once they hear them, or they will be going to the wrong place.

Lesson Sequence

1. Have students form squares.
    a. Review head couples (1 and 3) and side couples (2 and 4).
    b. Review going halfway 'round the ring.
    c. Review line of direction (CCW).
    d. Review promenade.

e. Tell them to listen, wish them luck, and put on music for Promenade the Ring. Use the following calls:

- Bow to your partner.
- Heads promenade, go halfway 'round the ring.
- Sides up to the middle and back.
- Sides promenade, go halfway 'round the ring.
- Head up the middle and back.
- All join hands and circle left.
- Go halfway 'round.
- When you get home, face your own.
- Do-si-do your partner.
- Same lady swing and promenade.
- Promenade single file.
- Go back home and face your own.
- Bow to your partner, corner, too.
- Wave at the little girl across from you.

2. Review the swing.

a. Discuss position of couples and how they should lean away, where to find their corner and their partner, and what to do when told to promenade while dancing with someone other than their partner.

b. Put on an oldie—Oh Johnny Oh.

c. After they dance it through put on a new one—Arkansas Traveler—and use the following calls.

- Couples 1 and 3 go forward and back.
- Forward again.
- Turn your opposite right arm 'round.
- Your partner, left, left arm 'round.
- Corners right, right arm 'round.
- Partner left, left arm 'round.
- Promenade your corner as she comes around.

3. Talk about the social merits of square dance.

a. Dancing with everyone in the square

b. When the man goes home with the partner he started with

c. When he must take a new one home as his partner

4. Review by doing each of the following calls as they are needed in the dances.

a. Walk through allemande left, grasping left forearms.

b. Walk through grand right and left.

c. Review the call, "Head couples head down the valley."

d. Put on music for the simple version of Red River Valley and dance it through.

e. Review the distinction between "Head couples head down the valley" and "Side couples head down the valley." (See beginner unit for instructions.)

f. Put on the more complex version of Red River Valley, which has everyone dancing all the time.

5. Review a star.

a. Discuss what going halfway means in a square-dance call.

b. Put on music for Gents Star Right and use the following calls:

- Gents star R, just halfway 'round.
- Turn to your opposite left.

- Now star back home and here we go.
- Meet your partner and do-si-do.
- Now gents star left, go all the way 'round.
- Meet your partner, right arm 'round.
- To the corner, allemande left.
- Back to the partner, do a grand right and left.
- Hand over hand until you find your own.
- Promenade, come right on home.

   c. Review and walk through star promenade.

   d. Dance Texas Star. (See intermediate unit.)

6. If there's time, fill requests.

Review

Ask the following:

- If you are a girl, is your corner to your right or left?
- If a square is told to join hands, what happens?
- If you are couple 3 and are told to go left, which couple are you headed toward?
- When you begin a grand right and left, to whom do you reach out your right hand?

Assessment

This year students should decide how they want to be graded on performance. The skills rubric is posted. They should look it over and decide if they want to use that to grade performance or if they want to base the grade on any or all of the following:

- Three specific dances learned this year, one dance of each type (folk, social, and square)
- Ability to perform specific instructions on cue
- Ability to create their own dance

Dance
ADVANCED
LESSON 8

More Square Dance

Facilities

Ventilated room with enough space for students to move freely and a floor that gives

Materials

- Sound system that can project music clearly throughout the dance space
- Music for the cha-cha, Red River Valley, Oh Johnny Oh, Texas Star, Promenade the Ring, Arkansas Traveler, Gents Star Right, Split the Ring and Around Just One, Bend It Tight, and Four in the Middle
- Microphone that can be heard over the music
- Pinnies

Performance Goal

Students will dance a variety of square dances.

Cognitive Goals

Students will learn the following:

- Up to three new square dances using the new calls:
  - Split the ring
  - Around just one

- Pass through
- Bend the line
- The general rules of square dance:
  - Movement is continuous. If waiting for a call, keep the feet moving.
  - Calls are ahead, so while executing one, listen for what's next.
  - Keep the square a normal size.
  - If you are inactive while others are moving outside the square, move in.
  - Unless specifically told to promenade a fraction of the way around, men should take whomever they are dancing with home.
  - Dances end with dancers home.
  - If there is a mix-up, everyone goes home, waits, and picks instructions up after the promenade ends.
  - The caller is moving everyone around, so go by direction, not the person with whom you think you should be dancing.
  - A call to take a lady directs the man to take the lady.

Lesson Safety

Space each square so students can move without hitting an obstruction or each other.

Motivation

Put on music that everyone loves so they dance as they enter the room. Then tell the class that they are going to learn more advanced calls. You'll teach them first and then it is up to their listening skills to follow the dance once the music is on. Explain that first you are going to teach some optional moves that the leader can choose to do or not—the twirl and the courtesy turn.

Lesson Sequence

1. Teach the twirl.
   a. Have students partner and form a circle.
   b. Demonstrate the male moving in line of direction while twirling his partner under his right arm.
   c. Practice with a partner, and then a new partner. Be careful that the girl doesn't get dizzy.
2. Have students form squares.
   a. Review the grand right and left.
      - Point out how the female turns CW to face partner.
      - Teach the courtesy turn and when to do it.
      - With couples side by side, male takes female's L hand in his, puts his R arm around her waist, and guides her forward as he backs up, turning in place.
      - Do the grand right and left again. Conclude it with the courtesy turn.
   b. Let students request a square dance, asking them to use the twirl during promenade and courtesy turn when the female's direction must change.
   c. Choose another square dance for this practice.
3. Teach how to split the ring and walk each couple though it—the head couple join hands, walk between the couple they face, turn out, and wait for next call.
4. Teach how to go around just one and walk it through for each couple.
   a. Do it after couples split the ring or pass through.
   b. Boys go left, girls go right. They pass one person and come back to the center of the square. If the call is "around two," they do the same, but walk around two instead of one.
5. Teach the pass-through, where two couples face and move toward each other, passing right shoulders and waiting for next call.

6. Put on music for Split the Ring and Around Just One.
   a. Walk through the dance.
      - Couples 1 and 3 bow and swing.
      - Up to the center and back to the ring.
      - Pass through, separate.
      - Come around just one.
      - Go down the middle, pass through.
      - Split the ring, separate.
      - Go down the middle.
      - Pass through, separate.
      - Come around one, pass through.
      - Meet your corner, left allemande.
      - Right to your partner, do a right and left grand.
   b. Remind students how to handle a mix-up and put the music on. Allow it to play through unless students are hopelessly confused. If they are, stop the music and walk them through it again. If they still are confused, stay with the square that is mixed up. Ask people in the know to reach for people getting confused so they can keep them going in the correct direction.
7. Teach how to bend the line. Demonstrate and do a walk-through.
   a. A line, usually of four people, breaks in the middle.
   b. The ends move forward and the middle moves back until one half of the line faces the other half.
8. Teach how to bend it tight.
   a. Couples 1 and 3 do a pass-through.
   b. Split the ring and go around two.
   c. Hang on tight to form two lines.
   d. Go forward and back, keep in time.
   e. Pass through and bend the line.
   f. Pass through and bend it tight.
   g. Circle up eight and keep it right.
9. Ask if they want a walk-through since they already know the calls. Put the music on for Bend It Tight and stop only if everyone is hopelessly confused.
10. Put on music for Four in the Middle, a new dance that uses all calls just learned.
   a. Ask if students want a walk-through.
      - Four ladies chain across the way
      - Couples 1 and 3 roll away to a half sashay
      - Couple 1 down the middle
      - Split couple 3 around 1 to a line of four
      - Forward to the middle of the ring
      - Bend the line and face those two
      - Double pass through, that's what you do
      - First couple California twirl
      - Guess who, the corner girl
      - Left allemande
   b. When ready, put music on.
11. If there's time, fill requests.

Review

Discuss the following:

- Draw a map in the air of your path for split the ring, go around one.
- What does the man do while twirling?
- Why courtesy turn your partner?
- Tell students to expect a 10-minute quiz next time (if giving a quiz).

Dance and Assessment

Facilities

Ventilated room with enough space for students to move freely and a floor that gives

Materials

- Sound system that can project music clearly throughout the dance space
- Music for dances learned previously (Grand March, Bingo, Pata Pata, Sevila Se Bela Loza, Hora, Saturday Night Fever Walk, Virginia Reel, La Raspa, Greensleeves, Jessie Polka, Seljancica Kola, Red River Valley, Road to the Isles, Mayim, Oh Johnny Oh, Limbo Rock, Misirlou, mambo music, Achy Breaky Heart, Nebesko Kolo, Sicilian Tarantella, Texas Star, Stepping Out, To Ting, Teton Mountain Stomp, Salty Dog Rag, Doudlebska Polka, Texas Two-Step, Cajun Two-Step, Vé David, Hot Lips, cha-cha, Promenade the Ring, Arkansas Traveler, Gents Star Right, Split the Ring and Around Just One, Bend It Tight, and Four in the Middle)

Performance Goal

Students will perform as many dances as possible within the class.

Cognitive Goal

Students will recognize that dancing is active, healthy, and fun.

Motivation

Put on a favorite energetic dance and encourage everyone to join you on the floor. Then explain that they have learned a lot and that it is time to think about grading. Talk about options. Let the class dance to their requests. Observe and grade as they do.

Lesson Sequence

1. Receive requests.
2. Once students have decided how they want to be evaluated, review if they want.
3. Keep the music on, trying to keep students moving the whole class.

Review

Ask the following:

- How many of you found yourselves sweating more than you ever did for badminton, for volleyball, or for softball?
- What does that tell you about the fitness potential of dance?
- Ask if students have questions, and remind them that there is a quiz next class.

Dance and Assessment

Facilities

Ventilated room with enough space for students to move freely and a floor that gives

Materials

- Sound system that can project music clearly throughout the dance space
- Music for dances learned previously (Grand March, Bingo, Pata Pata, Sevila Se Bela Loza, Hora, Saturday Night Fever Walk, Virginia Reel, La Raspa, Greensleeves, Jessie Polka, Seljancica Kola, Red River Valley, Road to the Isles, Mayim, Oh Johnny Oh, Limbo Rock, Misirlou, mambo music, Achy Breaky Heart, Nebesko Kolo, Sicilian Tarantella, Texas Star, Stepping Out, To Ting, Teton Mountain Stomp, Salty Dog Rag Doudlebska Polka, Texas Two-Step, Cajun Two-Step, Vé David, Hot Lips, cha-cha, Promenade the Ring, Arkansas Traveler, Gents Star Right, Split the Ring and Around Just One, Bend It Tight, and Four in the Middle)
- Quiz for each student
- Pens or pencils

Performance Goals

Students will do the following:

- Take a short quiz.
- Perform as many dances as possible within the class.

Cognitive Goal

Students' understanding of dance will be measured by a quiz.

Lesson Sequence

1. Put on some music to dance to as the class assembles.
2. Distribute the quiz and writing implements and allow 10 minutes. Make provisions for students who can't finish or were absent.
3. Collect quizzes and fill all dance requests possible.
4. While students perform, observe and grade.

Review

1. Entertain questions from the quiz.
2. Remind students that although you loved having their dressing time for class activity, it all ends after this unit. Once they start their next activity, they have to be ready for all kinds of things they didn't have to worry about during dance. Tell them to dress in their regular exercise clothing for next class.

Advanced Dance Skills Rubric

Name _____ Date _____

Teacher _____ Class _____

	0	1	2	3	4	5
Directions	No effort.	• Goes to assigned formation on cue. • Follows line of direction. • Knows to find partner if lost and get into the promenade.	• Knows head and side couples. • Identifies corner and partner and knows where to find them. • Able to take a variety of couple positions.	• Has mastered basic square dance calls. • Does not get lost in the square. • Is always in correct position in relation to partner.	• Has mastered the allemande left and grand right and left. • Can safely dance with a partner at random. • Has learned square-dance terms done three times.	• Dances correctly all dances done three times or more. • Recognizes dance by music and can perform dance properly. • Unfazed by direction changes.
Footwork	No effort.	• Has mastered basic locomotion and basic dance steps when moving forward.	• Is on correct foot. • Stays on beat through tempo change.	• Has mastered dancing with a partner in line of direction. • Connects movement patterns as they flow together.	• Turns as a couple. • Uses combination steps and turns on the quick step.	• Uses centrifugal force to spin partner turns. • Performs proper footwork after being given verbal instructions.
Group work	No effort.	• Follows established class rules. • If watching, can follow line of direction. • Gets in position on request.	• Follows dancing rules of etiquette. • Follows dance instructions and does the expected during mixers. • Can stay in rhythm with or without music.	• Works with partners to learn breaks. • Can safely dance randomly in the room with a partner. • Is courteous to all partners.	• Works with others to follow square dance calls. • Practices dance steps with partner without being told.	• Knows all dances well enough to lead. • Partner work is synchronized and cooperative.

From Isobel Kleinman, 2009, *Complete Physical Education Plans for Grades 5 to 12, Second Edition* (Champaign, IL: Human Kinetics).

Advanced Dance Quiz

Name _____ Date _____

Teacher _____ Class _____

True or False

Read each statement carefully. If the statement is true, write a *T* in the column to the left. If the statement is false, write an *F*. If using a grid sheet, blacken in the appropriate column for each question, making sure to use the correctly numbered line for each question and its answer.

_____ 1. If a square dance caller sings, "Swing your corner and promenade home," you must return to your partner to promenade home.

_____ 2. If the head couple are supposed to be closest to the music, in square dance they would have their backs to the music.

_____ 3. Ve David, Texas Star, Teton Mountain Stomp, Doubleska Polka, and Oh Johnny Oh are all mixers.

_____ 4. When splitting the ring, head couples separate their opposites and turn in the opposite direction.

_____ 5. When a man leads forward with his left foot in closed dance position, the woman should move back with her right.

_____ 6. The two-step is the basic dance step used in Doubleska Polka.

_____ 7. To get the best swing, couples should lean away from each other.

_____ 8. The polka is the predominant basic dance step used in Hot Lips.

_____ 9. When a group puts left hands together, they star left but walk right.

_____ 10. A man's corner is always on his left because his partner is always on his right.

Matching

Read one item at a time from the left-hand column. Read all the choices in the column on the right and pick the one that most closely matches the left-hand item. Write the letter that represents your choice on the blank space to the left of the column, next to the appropriate item.

_____ 1. hop, step, close, step

_____ 2. quick, quick, slow (or) step, step, step-hold

_____ 3. step, step, step

_____ 4. couples with hands joined in front

_____ 5. couples with L hands joined in front, R hands joined behind woman's R shoulder

_____ 6. man's L hand holds woman's R, man's R arm across woman's back, woman's L hand on man's shoulder

_____ 7. group with joined hands

_____ 8. facing to the right of the center of a circle

_____ 9. ladies face partners, take R hand and pass by, extend left hand to the next gent and pass by, R to next, L to next, and so on

_____ 10. walking

a. circle

b. shuffling

c. skater's position

d. grand right and left

e. closed dance position

f. two-step

g. counterclockwise (CCW)

h. polka

i. varsouvienne position

j. waltz

 From Isobel Kleinman, 2009, *Complete Physical Education Plans for Grades 5 to 12, Second Edition* (Champaign, IL: Human Kinetics).

Advanced Dance Answer Key

True or False

1. T
2. T
3. T
4. T
5. T
6. F—The polka is the basic dance step in Doudlebska Polka
7. T
8. F—The two-step is the predominant basic dance step in Hot Lips.
9. T
10. T

Matching

1. h
2. f
3. j
4. c
5. i
6. e
7. a
8. g
9. d
10. b

Educational Gymnastics

Chapter Overview

1. Educational gymnastics provides students with movement problems they work to resolve according to their own abilities. Students will examine the elements of movement.

   - Space—how they move through space and the many ways they can take up space, being low, or high, or big, or small, or turning, or twisting

   - Time—whether their rhythm is slow or fast, staccato or sustained; whether they can perform simultaneously with others or start where others left off; whether they can accelerate or decelerate

   - Weight—how to balance weight to sustain all kinds of shapes and poses, how to take their weight off the floor and bring it back, how to move heavy or move light, how to take the weight of others or use their weight with others to come to balance

   - Flow—controlling several tasks and joining them together to make them a continuous movement

2. Students will learn what good movement entails, how to critique it, and how to value it.

Educational Gymnastics Study Sheet

History

- The Greeks instituted a regimen of exercise for military training and physical conditioning credited as the beginning of gymnastics. In ancient Greece, gymnastics was considered central to the proper development of the public.

- Artistic gymnastics has its roots in Germany. Friedrich Ludwig Jahn (1778–1852), the father of gymnastics, developed a set of exercises to be performed with or without stationary equipment. The purpose was to develop strength and discipline. Around the same time, the Swedes developed a program using small balls, hoops, and clubs that since has evolved into rhythmic gymnastics.

- Inspired by Rudolf Laban's dance principles and pragmatic enough to use the World War II army training equipment that littered the countryside, the British took a creative approach to exploring the plentiful stationary equipment. Educational gymnastics took hold and slowly wandered to American shores with the help of immigrants. The British use of the open movement system developed by Laban is called *movement education*.

Fun Facts

Pilobolus and Momix are two thriving American modern dance companies that were originally inspired by creative gymnastics. Their performances are a palette of wonderfully controlled unusual and unconventional movement that one can imagine started in a push–pull, over–under, or fast–slow movement education lesson. Cirque du Soleil, the famous French Canadian troupe, thrives on creative use of gymnastics skills to dazzle audiences all over the world.

Benefits

Educational gymnastics activities will improve physical fitness, body awareness, spatial awareness, and balance while inspiring creativity, aesthetic appreciation, and small-group cooperation.

From Isobel Kleinman, 2009, *Complete Physical Education Plans for Grades 5 to 12, Second Edition* (Champaign, IL: Human Kinetics).

Educational Gymnastics Extension Project

Name _____ Date _____

Teacher _____ Class _____

What equipment do you need to do these activities on your own?

Where can you participate outside of school?

Do you have friends who would join you? List their names.

What are the health benefits of participating in a gymnastics program?

Educational Gymnastics Student Portfolio Checklist

Name _____ Date _____

Teacher _____ Class _____

_____ Can complete a 5-minute gross-motor cardiorespiratory workout daily.

_____ Can roll in any direction on the floor.

_____ Can absorb momentum by curling into a ball.

_____ Can balance long enough to stretch all body parts.

_____ Can balance and move on all different levels.

_____ Can make body move fast or slow.

_____ Can move in unison with a partner.

_____ Can change direction or that of a partner's by pushing or pulling.

_____ Can use partner to help balance in ways that would not be possible alone.

_____ Can accelerate or decelerate during motion.

_____ Can make changes in direction by twisting or turning.

_____ Can feel flight and control landings.

_____ Can roll out of or into a balance.

_____ Can put different movements and balance positions together.

_____ Can do a sequence of movements and make them flow.

_____ Can work with a partner to form a symmetrical appearance of positions that are asymmetrical.

_____ Can tell the difference between rocking and rolling and use both to move.

_____ Has found many ways to be inverted and can describe what inversion means.

_____ Can go over or under objects or people in different ways.

_____ Can be bent or be arched.

_____ Can take the weight of a partner.

_____ Has been on many pieces of gym equipment.

_____ Can get on or off any piece of equipment in the gym.

_____ Can find a way to move while on the equipment in the gym.

_____ Can balance while off the floor.

_____ Can control movement so it makes no sound.

From Isobel Kleinman, 2009, *Complete Physical Education Plans for Grades 5 to 12, Second Edition* (Champaign, IL: Human Kinetics).

Educational Gymnastics Learning Experience Outline

Contents and Procedure

1. Few physical programs engage the body and mind as this one does. Students move almost 100% of the time, perform movements of their choosing, gain movement confidence, become aware of their personal space, gain body awareness, learn the options for locomotion, and become appreciative of movement aesthetics. Those who do not feel engaged by individual and team sport will now have a forum they can work independently in. Equally important, by encouraging choice and creativity, the fear factor—a major concern for many students during gymnastics—is almost eliminated or most certainly greatly reduced.

2. Lessons focus on contrasting movements, encourage exploration, work toward greater control, and aim for refinement. They include a 5-minute gross-motor warm-up followed by exploration of movement options either on the floor (mats) or on the apparatus.

3. Floor work can be adapted to a dance curriculum. After students create a theme-based movement sequence, they can introduce music, combine their routine with others, add entrances and exits, change levels, change directions, disrupt the flow, work in unison, work in contrast, work in mirror images, and so on.

4. Movement safety comes first. Early emphasis is on getting students round like a ball—with nothing sticking out—and rolling in all directions. The first lesson makes students comfortable with rolling. The second teaches them to use momentum to melt into a ball and roll out. By stressing the curling or melting reflex and providing lots of opportunity to practice it, fear of injury from insecure landings is avoided.

5. Lessons encourage exploration. Time is set aside at the end of most lessons for students to use their discovered moves to make a short routine. After developing the sequence, students are asked to repeat it to gain control of their weight during balance and transfers, to stretch when they are not intending to bend, and to have their motion flow.

6. Students work alone, in groups, or in pairs; observe and offer movement advice to others; perform; and become a discerning audience. They learn that there is no one right way to roll, stretch, bend, arch, fly, travel, land, go over, go under, pull, push, change directions, choose a level, twist, turn, take weight, go fast, go slow, invert, balance, rock, roll, or work in unison with one or more people. They come to appreciate variety, love being allowed to be themselves, enjoy the noncompetitive environment, and learn that despite individual variables and skill levels, they all can improve the control and quality of their work.

7. This program lends itself to exhibition and motivates students to excellence. Plan a schoolwide culminating activity.

Teaching Tips

- The gymnastics lessons in this chapter use movement education to guide students in their movement choices and teach them better control. Teachers who have not been trained in movement education and have not seen it implemented during gymnastics may find it intimidating because so many students are moving at once and doing many different things. This does not mean you should avoid a theme-guided approach to teaching gymnastics.

- Classes function on all cylinders, which gives them a playground look. Students are asked to do their own thing and usually do. That means everyone is doing something different at the same time. To an untrained eye, such an environment may look chaotic. Rest assured, what appears to be complete freedom and chaos is perfectly structured.

- Structure comes from what drives students to move the way they do. Despite the obvious differences that personal choice results in, all the movement is honed by ongoing teacher instruction, redirection, and feedback. Feedback is constant. It comes from the teacher as well as peers. The environment is active, creative, and supportive.

- A successful class depends on students trusting that the teacher says what is meant. With that confidence, students will be willing to follow instruction that allows them to freely explore their limitations without worrying they might be ridiculed.

- A successful teacher must remember the goals of each lesson:
  - Generate a lot of physical activity.
  - Teach an appreciation of the elements of movement.
  - Teach an understanding of what it takes to control movement better.
  - Provide constant encouragement, feedback, and cues to help students improve their movement.

- Success is *not* about raising a student's level of difficulty. Teachers who communicate this clearly will enable their students to perform at their own level, reduce risk of injury, and encourage lots of healthy activity. This is not to say that you should refrain from encouraging students to move beyond their immediate comfort zone, but it does mean that the focus of each lesson is getting students to move without fear while encouraging them to explore their parameters, learn how to do what they are capable of, and learn to appreciate good movement.

- The emotional climate should be one where students feel free to be themselves, where they feel free to try new things, and where asking for help when trying something new is the obvious thing to do. It is not productive to have timid students freeze, striving students imitate the class gymnast just to get an *A,* or risk takers try something new and difficult without the teacher by their side.

- Lessons have three segments. Each focuses on one movement theme: The gross-motor warm-up (5 minutes) introduces the movement characteristics that will be explored, and work on the floor (20 minutes) explores and refines that theme. Then work on the apparatus (25 minutes) takes the theme to another level. Since most physical education classes do not meet for the time necessary to set up and break down equipment and follow the lesson segments as suggested, a 1-hour lesson has been expanded to cover the content during two class sessions. Each session starts with the theme-oriented warm-up. The first lesson follows with work on the floor and the second lesson with work on the apparatus. It is highly suggested that lessons be introduced in the order in which they are written.

- The typical cues given during the lesson are as follows:
  - Can you find another way?
  - Can you make your body extend so that it takes up more space?
  - Can you do that without stopping?
  - Can you do that so no one hears your landing?

Facilities

The gym must be clean—the students' skin will touch the floor.

Materials

- It is best to have one mat per student. If this is impossible, have students define their own space and learn to work within it.
- One apparatus station is needed for four to six students, such as traditional gymnastic apparatuses or English equipment such as ladders, boxes, bars, and climbing ropes.
- Equipment should not be set up as it is for formal gymnastics.
  - If possible, get English equipment.
  - If not, combine pieces so students are challenged to use them creatively.

- When the equipment is set up, mats must cover the landing area so no mat overlaps another and so that there are no spaces between adjacent mats.

Unit Safety

When taking students off their normal base of support, safety can be a concern. In educational gymnastics, students respond to teacher direction by doing things they can do and then are encouraged to improve on them. This does not eliminate creative students from trying something new and daring that requires someone nearby to make sure their landing is safe. Since the variety occurring in a class that is asked to explore is endless, students must get in the habit of asking for teacher assistance, which means they must feel comfortable doing so. Teachers need to keep reminding the students that they are there to help.

Apparatus setup must be done so that all landing areas are covered with mats and so that mats do not overlap and there are no spaces between adjacent mats.

Remember that stretching should be done after the muscles are warm—at the end of class during review.

Apparatus Floor Plan

You will probably have to use what you have. To break students away from formal gymnastics training, set up the apparatus by trying to combine pieces so students are challenged to find new ways to navigate them. If students look at the pieces differently, it is hoped they will use them creatively. As you create your configuration, make sure the stations are set up so that dismounting and mounting areas do not overlap. Also, you should have enough stations to keep everyone busy. That means you need enough stations so that when the class is using them, there are no more than four to six students at any one station at once. Here are some potential combinations of the usual gymnastic equipment:

- Ropes and bleachers
- Swedish box and stall bars
- Springboard and crash mat
- Balance beam and horse (no pommels)
- Parallel bars and crash pad
- Pommel horse
- Buck and rings
- Practice beam followed by a row of mats
- Ropes
- Rings
- Uneven parallel bars

Unit Timeline

This chapter has three units:

- 13 lessons for beginner students
- 14 lessons for intermediate students
- 14 lessons for advanced students

Suggested Resources

ClearLead Inc. 2008. History of gymnastics. www.clearleadinc.com/site/gymnastics.html.

Dance Spirit Magazine. www.dancespirit.com.

Infoplease. 2008. Pilobolus Dance Theater. www.infoplease.com/ce6/ent/A0907272.html.

McDermott, D. 2004. "Fungi-Form": The story of Pilobolus Dance Theater. www.criticaldance.com/magazine/200403/articles/pilobolus-dmcdermott.html.

Morison, R. 1975. *Educational gymnastics.* London: Dent.

Moving and Learning. 2008. www.movingandlearning.com.

Murray, N. 1994. *Children and movement: Physical education in the elementary school.* Dubuque, IA: McGraw-Hill College.

Nontraditional Gymnastics. 2008. Defining nontraditional gymnastics. www.geocities.com/colosseum/stadium/7261/DEVGYM2.HTM.

Pilobolus. 2008. http://people.tribe.net/wendy/photos/0617abfc-360f-4521-b1bb-b0624586ef6c.

Saskatchewan Schools and School Divisions. www.saskschools.ca/.

Williams, J. 1987. *Themes for educational gymnastics.* London: Lepus.

Educational Gymnastics
BEGINNER
LESSON 1

Rolling (Floor)

Facilities
Clean floor

Materials
One mat per student

Performance Goals
Students will do the following:
- Spend most of the class moving.
- Change the shape of their bodies.
- Roll in different ways and different directions.

Cognitive Goals
Students will learn the following:
- In order to roll, nothing can break the circumference.
- There is no one way to roll.
- Rolling does not hurt.

Lesson Safety
- Keep the floor empty of equipment and obstructions during warm-ups.
- Provide mat space for students to work at the same time but independently.

Motivation
Some people think there is only one way to roll, but there are many. Today the class will try to find the many ways, shapes, and directions they can roll in.

Warm-Up (10 Minutes)
1. Students stand and spread out so that they take up the entire gym space.
2. Have them look right, left, in front, and in back, getting a sense of the space between them and the students nearest them and the walls.
   - Ask them to memorize the space and carry it with them as they move around the room.
   - Ask students to walk to different places in the gym so their space gets no smaller.

3. Stop and have them check to see if they have that same space around them.

4. They probably won't, so space them out again and continue walking.

5. Stop them regularly, asking them to acknowledge what happened to their space and to get it back again if it shrank. Spend several minutes stopping and starting them, attending to their space as they move, encouraging them to move to open areas so that whenever you tell them to stop, they have as much space around them as they had when they started.

6. Ask them to run, keeping their space. Do a space check regularly.

7. Stop them and ask them to melt to the ground in place.
   - Spend a few minutes explaining and practicing melting.
   - Ask them to melt and jump up out of the melt.
   - Ask them to jump and melt from the jump.

8. Tell them to run and when there is enough space to stop and melt as small as they can.

9. Start and stop students every few seconds.

Lesson Sequence

1. Have students place their mats and mark out the area they will be working in. Explain that since they will all be working at once, they must stay in their own space.
   a. Ask students to make themselves as small as possible and roll in every direction. Allow time to experiment.
   b. If they are smaller, can they roll without stopping? Let them try.

2. What about if someone rolls them—can they be rolled without stopping? Have students get in groups of four and get on one mat.
   a. Have one person curl up in the center. Everyone else at the mat rolls the person curled up in the center without rolling off the mat. Signal when you want them to stop and switch.
   b. Switch so everyone in the group gets to be the ball in the middle.
   c. Give everyone one more turn in the middle. Check that no part of their body is sticking out and that they are as round and curled as possible.

3. Have each person in the group go to a corner of the mat.
   a. Ask that someone begin rolling to an empty space on the mat so that one person at each mat is rolling and someone is constantly rolling.
   b. Without talking or using any other signal, can they make sure there is always someone in motion on the mat?
   c. Signal when you want them to stop.

Review and Stretching

1. Ask the following questions as students stretch.
   - What is a ball?
   - Why is it easier to roll when you are a ball?
   - When you couldn't roll, what part of the body usually stopped you?
   - What does it mean to be balanced?

2. Have students return the mats when finished.

Melt and Roll (Apparatus)

Facilities

Clean floor

Materials

- Create a minimum of one apparatus station for every group of four to six students. This is your chance to be creative about placing your equipment with the objects in your gym so that you use everything. Remember, you will want students to approach the equipment merely as obstacles to get on, get over, move on, and get off. You can combine pieces with the bleachers, a crash pad, a springboard, ropes, the stall bars, rings, or anything that will hold students' weight and make them think outside the box when they are answering the movement questions you present to them.
- Have a minimum of four apparatus stations no matter how small the class is.
- Make sure mats cover the landing area and do not overlap or have spaces between them.

Performance Goals

Students will do the following:

- Be assigned to set up one apparatus station for the entire unit.
- Spend 5 minutes in a gross-motor warm-up that focuses on getting low to the ground and then rolling.
- Find ways to get on and off all equipment.
- Handle momentum safely by using the melt-and-roll on landing.

Cognitive Goals

Students will learn the following:

- How to set up their apparatus and mats so the area is safe
- Class rules for using the apparatus:
  - Wait for instructions before using the equipment.
  - Allow the previous person to exit before going on the equipment.
  - Do not wander to other equipment.
  - Take care not to enter the approach or dismounting area of other stations.
- To get low to the ground and curl like a ball before rolling
- To safely use their momentum to roll

Lesson Safety

- Apparatus layout should be designed and implemented to allow student traffic to flow without obstruction.
- Mats should be placed so that they do not overlap and that all the possible landing areas are covered.
- Equipment must be stable.
- Students must stay with their group so as not to obstruct anyone's mount or dismount.
- To guarantee that the equipment is set up correctly every time, assign different groups of students to each station, make sure they have set up the equipment and mats correctly, and make sure that they know what to do each time it is a day for setting up the equipment.

Motivation

This is the first day students are using the apparatuses. After learning to set up the equipment safely, they will use it to climb on. They should remember the virtues of being round when they want to roll, because today when they get off, they are going to jump, melt, and roll.

Warm-Up

1. Have students spread out.
   - Ask them to imagine that a large glass dome is around each of them.
   - Tell them to imagine how to move so no one bumps into their glass dome.
   - Have students walk with their imaginary glass dome.
2. Ask students to run with their imaginary glass dome.
3. Stop after about 15 seconds, checking that their glass dome is distant from the others. If it isn't, have them relocate before running again.
4. Stop regularly to make sure the space around the students has not shrunk. If it has, they should relocate.
5. Tell students to run, jump, and land so they melt into a ball, get up, and continue.
6. If students cluster, stop them, remind them of their dome, and continue.
7. After a few minutes, ask them to jump up from the melt and begin running again.
8. Focus on the space around them after melting.
9. Focus on melting to the ground in one move.
10. Ask them to melt and roll.
11. Run, jump, land, melt, and roll in any direction. Get up and do it again.

Lesson Sequence

1. Set up apparatus stations (if not already set up).
   a. Divide class into groups.
   b. Assign each group to a station for the entire unit.
   c. Show each group how and where the equipment and mats go.
   d. Explain that they are always responsible for this station.
      - Teach the groups to sit when they are done setting up.
      - Check each area, particularly that the mats are properly arranged.
2. Explain class rules about using equipment and waiting.
   a. Students must stay in their area until told to switch.
   b. One student goes at a time. Students should not stand on the mats or apparatus unless it is their turn.
   c. No one goes twice until everyone goes once.
   d. If students want help, they should ask the teacher, not other students.
3. Tell students that they can find all kinds of ways to get on or over the equipment, but to get off, they are to jump, melt, and roll.
4. Circulate, encouraging students to try different ways to get on and off before they melt and roll and to try to make the melting and rolling all one move.
5. Rotate groups after 5 minutes so they can try different equipment.

Review and Stretching

1. Ask the following questions as students stretch.
   - What is the difference between falling and melting?
   - Which one makes noise?
   - Why do you think one makes noise when the other doesn't?
   - Which is better, one part of your body landing on the floor or all parts?
2. Have students put away equipment (or leave it up if another is class coming in).

Stretch and Balance (Floor)

Facilities

Clean floor

Materials

One mat per student

Performance Goals

Students will do the following:

- Perform a gross-motor warm-up introducing the difference between big and small.
- Feel the difference between being big and stretching in a variety of shapes.
- Begin developing a movement memory by memorizing a sequence of moves and building a movement routine.

Cognitive Goals

Students will learn the following:

- The difference between being big and being stretched
- To appreciate the amount of space they can take up
- The idea of movement contrasts

Lesson Safety

- Remind students to stay within their space while moving.
- Encourage students who want to try something they are not sure of to ask you for help.

Motivation

All movement takes place in space. As students concentrate on using space to move or pose, they will make the everyday version of their motion into a stretched-out motion that looks more pleasing.

Warm-Up

1. Have students spread out.
2. Remind them of the glass dome and taking it with them as they run. Have them begin running.
3. Stop and ask if their glass is in danger of being broken. If so, relocate.
4. Start and stop, making sure they are not clustered.
5. Ask them to run at top speed.
   - If they make contact with anyone, have them freeze while the rest of the class continues.
   - Continue until almost everyone is frozen.
   - Try it again.
6. Reduce the size of the space students can move in by half and ask how much of their original space they are in now. (They are in half of their original space.)
7. Continue with the rule that if they make contact with anyone, they are to freeze. Ask them to walk, then run, then run at top speed.
8. Stop them and again reduce the size of the space they can move in by half.
9. Ask them to move as quickly as they can without bumping into anyone.

A student demonstrates how to get into a position that takes up the smallest space.

Lesson Sequence

1. Have students get a mat and bring it to the largest space possible.
2. Using three parts of their body, ask them to support themselves so they don't move.
   a. Encourage them to balance five ways while small.
   b. Ask them to balance five ways while large.
3. Have students watch half of their classmates perform all they have done, and then switch.
4. Ask students to try something they haven't done. If they need help, they should get you.
5. Ask them to repeat their balances and try to stretch while in them.
6. Do the same using two parts of the body for support.
   a. Encourage them to find other ways.
   b. Ask them to repeat, stretching in each way they can remember.
7. Do same with one part of the body for support.
8. Take five balances, stretch them, and when in the greatest stretch, try another. Hold each for a few seconds.
   a. Can they do the same again but roll out of one to get into the other? Let them practice.
   b. Have students find a partner and perform the five-balance routine for each other, asking where they could extend more.
9. Take time to practice, using partner comments to perfect the routine.
10. Demonstrate: Half the students watch as the other half perform, and then switch.
11. If time permits, pick out a routine or two that best emphasize extension. Ask those students to repeat what they did, explaining why you chose their routines.

Review and Stretching

1. Ask the following questions as students stretch.
   * What was the difference between the routines that were chosen and the ones that were not?
   * Could everyone in the class try to do that with their routines?
2. Put away mats.

Stretch and Balance (Apparatus)

Facilities

Clean floor

Materials

Keep the same setup for the apparatus as before so that there is one apparatus station for each group of four to six students.

Performance Goals

Students will do the following:

- Set up their stations and sit when done.
- Perform a gross-motor warm-up that focuses on being big and small.
- Find ways to stretch in a variety of shapes on different bases of support.

Cognitive Goals

Students will learn the following:

- How to find ways to safely feel big while on several limiting bases of support
- How to use the momentum from their dismount to safely melt and roll

Lesson Safety

Review the rules of the area:

- Taking turns
- Staying in own area until told to switch
- Calling for the teacher if experimenting with something they are unsure of

Motivation

Today, they'll experiment with being big on the equipment. That will be challenging, because being big on equipment is different from being big on the floor. Why? The area is smaller, they'll be off the floor, and some equipment moves (ropes and rings). They will try to get to all the equipment today.

Warm-Up

1. Students should spread out, taking the largest space possible.
2. Ask them to begin moving and to freeze if they bump into anyone. Stop them if the space around them is smaller and have them relocate.
3. Tell them to run, jump, land softly, get up, and continue running.
4. Ask them to jump big in the air and land softly.
   - Jump big in the air, land, and melt to the ground and roll.
   - Jump big, melt and roll, and try to jump out of the roll.
5. Ask them to jump small in the air, landing softly.
6. Ask them to be aware of their space as they run.
   - Run and when they have enough space around them, jump, melt and roll, and continue.
   - Can they do the same but jump out of the roll?

Lesson Sequence

1. Students set up stations. Check that they are stable and that mats are well placed.
2. Have students rotate in the reverse direction of the day before so they are beginning on equipment they didn't use the last time the equipment was up.

3. Ask students to get on the equipment any way they want, but once on, they should get in a stretched position before getting off. As during the last class, when they touch the ground, melt and roll.

   a. Encourage students to find their own way to get on and off and be large while on.

   b. Leave time so each student gets two turns at each station, and then rotate groups.

   c. On each rotation, encourage students to find their own ways to approach equipment.

   d. Stop with 5 minutes left. Pick a student who was really extended while on the equipment and ask the student demonstrate.

   e. Have each group pick the person who was most stretched while on equipment, and have those students demonstrate.

4. Ask the class which on-stretch-off-melt-roll routine had the best look.

Review and Stretching

1. As students stretch, ask what made the difference in the routines they chose:
   - Stretch?
   - Flow?
   - That they didn't make a noise when they landed?

2. Put the equipment away.

Fast and Slow (Floor)

Facilities
Clean floor

Materials
One mat per student

Performance Goals
Students will do the following:
- Elevate their heart rate throughout the class using gross-motor movement.
- Find ways to change the natural rhythm of their movement.
- Continue to use movements that they are comfortable with to build a routine that emphasizes time, developing a movement memory.

Cognitive Goals
Students will learn the following:
- The difference between fast and slow movement
- That some movements are easier to do fast and others slow
- The idea of contrasts in time

Lesson Safety
- Remind students to stay within their space while moving.
- Encourage students who want to try something they are not sure of to ask you for help.

Motivation
Today the class will use familiar movement in an unfamiliar way. The warm-up is a clue. For instance, can students jump slowly? Playing with how much time it takes to do things should be

fun, if sometimes difficult. To be slow, students have to fight the acceleration of gravity. Sometimes being slow simply prevents them from finishing a move.

Warm-Up

1. Have students spread out. Remind them about taking their space with them.
2. Ask them to run. Stop them, and if their space is cluttered, have them relocate.
3. Ask them to run as fast as they can.
4. Ask them to walk as slowly as they can.
5. Run. Can they run faster? Can they sustain each step and run slow?
   - Can they run fast and jump slow?
   - Can they run slow and jump fast?

Lesson Sequence

1. Have students bring a mat to the largest space possible.
2. Work on time changes during rolling.
   a. Ask them to roll as fast as they can. Try rolling fast with other rolls.
   b. Now, try sustaining the movement so they are going as slow as they can.
3. Using the stretch–curl routine they used last class, have them do the following:
   a. Try the routine again, going as slowly and controlled as they can.
   b. Repeat the routine as fast as they can.
4. Talk about sustaining movement to make it slow and speeding it up to make it fast, and ask students to identify the parts of the routine that work better as fast or slow movement.
   a. Have them practice the routine, making the sustained movement slower and the parts that work better with speed faster so the movement looks sudden.
5. Students partner up, watch each other's routine, and decide which to do.
6. Have partners practice one of the routines so they don't compromise the fast–slow (sudden–sustained) sections and so they do them the same way at the same time.
7. Have half of the pairs in the class demonstrate while half of the pairs watch. Switch.

Review and Stretching

1. Ask the following while students stretch:
   - Can anyone explain why it is sometimes hard to make movement really slow?
   - Can anyone explain what makes it difficult to make movement fast?
   - Why were certain moves easier to do slowly?
   - Why were others necessary to do fast?
   - Does anyone have a word to use for when you do things at the same time?
2. Put away mats.

Educational Gymnastics
BEGINNER
LESSON 6

Fast and Slow (Apparatus)

Facilities

Clean floor

Materials

Keep the apparatus setup the same so there is one apparatus station for every four to six students.

Performance Goals

Students will do the following:

- Set up their stations and sit when done.
- Perform a gross-motor warm-up that focuses on sudden and sustained movement.
- Experiment with how speed affects the mount and dismount on equipment.

Cognitive Goals

Students will learn the following:

- Ways to force rhythm changes on their movement
- Safe procedures when using equipment

Lesson Safety

Continue using the rules of the area.

Motivation

Today, students will experiment with sudden and sustained movement on the apparatuses.

Warm-Up

1. Have students spread out before running. If they cluster, stop them, point it out, and start them again.
2. Run, run at top speed, run faster.
3. Jump and melt slowly.
4. Run slowly and jump and melt quickly.
5. Run and jump slowly, but land and melt quickly.
6. Run and jump quickly, but land and melt slowly.
7. Run and jump quickly, but melt and roll slowly.

Lesson Sequence

1. Have student groups set up their stations. Check for stability and mat placement.
2. Ask students to get on fast and off slow.
   a. Circulate, encouraging students to try as many ways as they can.
   b. Have groups rotate after students get several turns at their station.
3. If you see something unique or especially illustrative, ask the student to demonstrate.

Review and Stretching

1. As students stretch, ask what about the routines stood out.
   - Simply that it was slow?
   - Was it stretched or small?
   - Did it move smoothly with flow?
   - Did the performer make a sound?
2. Put the equipment away.

Push and Pull (Floor)

Facilities

Clean floor

Materials

One mat per student

Performance Goals

Students will do the following:

- Raise their heart rate for most of the class.
- Begin to find ways to control their transfer of weight.
- Experiment with the push and pull of moving and achieving balance.

Cognitive Goals

Students will learn the following:

- How their center of gravity works
- How to start and stop movement by pushing and pulling

Lesson Safety

- Remind students to stay within their space while moving.
- Encourage students who want to try something they are not sure of to ask you for help.

Motivation

The students seemed to enjoy partner work, so they will be trying it again. This time, they will be pushing and pulling friends. Partners will create a routine that moves by taking each other's weight by pushing or pulling.

Warm-Up

1. Have students spread out. Then ask them to run.
   - Ask them to run so their toes are pushing off the ground.
   - Ask them to run as if the ground is pulling them back.
   - Ask them to demonstrate ways to move within their own space by pushing the floor.
2. Do the same, this time moving by pulling.
3. Explain the difference between pushing and pulling:
   - Pushing is moving body weight away from point of contact.
   - Pulling is moving body weight toward point of contact.
4. Have half of the class watch the others travel by pushing and pulling. Switch.
5. Give a minute more to try some new ways of travel that they haven't tried before.

Lesson Sequence

1. Have students partner up. On a mat in the largest space possible, they should find ways to come to a stationary position by pulling away from each other.
2. Do the same, this time by pushing toward each other.
3. Discuss what happens when the center of gravity is reached by balancing weight of both people. Then ask students to try pushing or pulling so that the weight of one helps the other move away from the center of gravity.
4. Have half the class watch what the others are working on. Switch.
5. Give students time to try something new or something they were having trouble with.
6. Ask partners to move from one of their balanced positions to another until they have connected four stationary positions.

Review and Stretching

1. As students stretch, ask the following questions.
   - What made your weight stop when both of you were pushing? Pulling?
   - Does it have to do with your center of gravity? Where is it when you are together?
   - Does your center of gravity change when you are alone and trying to balance?
   - How do you get yourself to move again?
2. Put away mats.

Push and Pull (Apparatus)

Facilities

Clean floor

Materials

Use the same setup as in previous lessons, one apparatus station for every four to six students.

Performance Goals

Students will do the following:

- Set up their stations and sit when done.
- Perform a warm-up that will raise their heart rate while focusing on pushing and pulling.
- Students will mount and dismount equipment by controlling their weight transfer.

Cognitive Goals

Students will learn the following:

- How to see the apparatus in different ways and use it as an obstruction.
- How to push and pull to control their mount and dismount
- How to use safe procedures when using equipment

Lesson Safety

Continue using the rules of the area.

Motivation

Today they'll try using the idea of pushing and pulling on the apparatus. This time when they get to the apparatus, they should see if they can find a way to pull to get on and push to get off.

Warm-Up

1. Have students set up their stations. Check stability and mat placement.
2. Ask them to spread out and run, avoiding everyone in the room and the equipment.
3. This time, avoid the hanging equipment, but if they run near stationary equipment, they can push off it, land, and keep going.
4. Do the same, this time jumping before pushing on the equipment, landing, and continuing.

Lesson Sequence

1. Have students choose one piece to work at.
2. Circulate, helping if needed and encouraging them to try something different.
3. If there's time, rotate from stationary equipment to hanging equipment.
4. Ask the groups to choose someone to demonstrate a solution for pulling on and pushing off.

Review and Stretching

1. As students stretch, ask the following:
   - How did you feel when getting on the equipment by pulling? Would you have preferred to get on by pushing?
   - Was some of the equipment harder to push off than others? Why?
2. Put the equipment away.

Connecting Moves (Floor)

Facilities

Clean floor

Materials

One mat per student

Performance Goals

Students will do the following:

- Raise their heart rate for most of the class.
- Begin to learn how to connect different movements so they look as if they are one.

Cognitive Goals

Students will learn the following:

- How to make movements flow
- How controlling rhythm and weight transfer creates flow

Lesson Safety

- Remind students to stay within their space while moving.
- Encourage students who want to try something they are not sure of to ask you for help.

Motivation

In the last class, students created a push–pull partner routine composed of four positions moving from one to the other. The attention in this lesson will be connecting moves that make different movements of the routine look as if they are flowing from one to another.

Warm-Up

1. Have students spread out and ask them to run.
   - Run and without stopping, leave the floor off one foot, landing on two.
   - Run and without stopping, leave the floor off two feet, landing on one foot.
   - Run and leave the floor off one foot, landing on the other.
2. Get a partner and decide who will sit. Those standing are to run and jump over the people sitting. Switch. Repeat.

Lesson Sequence

1. After students bring a mat to the largest space possible, explain what *flow* means.
2. Have the students repeat the partner routine, asking them to concentrate on the quality of their position while in each balance position and how to smooth the transition from one to another.
3. Have half of the class demonstrate and then switch. Point out routines with extension and flow.
4. Have students return to their mats to improve their extension and flow.
5. Ask partners to work with another pair to critique where flow breaks down and where to extend more.
6. Practice a few more minutes, using the advice that was given.
7. Demonstrate the perfected version.

Review and Stretching

1. As students stretch, ask the following:
   - What does it mean to have flowing movement?
   - Can you control flow if you cannot control the following?
     - Weight transfer
     - The time it takes to do each move
     - The space your body moves through
   - What would improve your transfer of weight from one position to another?
2. Put away mats.

On and Off With Flow (Apparatus)

Facilities

Clean floor

Materials

Use the same setup, one apparatus station for every four to six students.

Performance Goals

Students will do the following:
- Set up their stations and sit when done.
- Perform a gross-motor warm-up that focuses on continuous motion.
- Keep motion flowing as they leave the floor, use the equipment, and return to the floor.

Cognitive Goals

Students will learn the following:
- Safe procedures when using equipment
- That the body can moderate speed to control movement flow

Lesson Safety

Continue using the rules of the area.

Motivation

Today, they will see how when they take their weight off the floor, move on the equipment, and return to the floor, they can make the effort look seamless.

Warm-Up

1. Have students spread out and stop them if they begin to cluster.
2. Tell students to run, moving under or around the equipment.
3. Ask students if they can touch the equipment without stopping their forward motion while they are running.

Lesson Sequence

1. Have students set up stations. Check that they are stable and mats are well placed.
2. Ask them to choose a station where they would like to stay for the class. Have them find ways to get on, form a balance position on, and get off. Give them time to experiment.

3. Students select a movement they can control and try it several times, making sure to keep their motion continuous into and out of the balance and dismount. Circulate, encouraging students to control their transfers so they flow.

4. Each group selects the person who has the best flow of movement and that person demonstrates. Have the class watch one group at time.

Review and Stretching

1. As students stretch, ask the following:
   - How did you feel getting on and off the equipment this time?
   - What did you do differently?
   - Did you have to work harder to control your motion, its time, the weight, and the stretch?
   - Did you feel that your movement was flowing?

2. Put the equipment away.

Educational Gymnastics
BEGINNER
LESSON 11

Levels (Floor)

Facilities

Clean floor

Materials

One mat per student

Performance Goals

Students will do the following:
- Raise their heart rate for most of the class.
- Explore space by seeking to move at different levels.

Cognitive Goals

Students will learn the following:
- What a base of support is
- The difference between being above or below a base of support

Lesson Safety

- Remind students to stay within their space while moving.
- Encourage students who want to try something they are not sure of to ask you for help.

Motivation

By the time this lesson is over, students will really understand what a base of support is and how to control their balance by controlling the center of their base of support no matter how high or low to the ground they are.

Warm-Up

Have students spread out and ask them to run.
- Run and jump as high as they can, landing softly.
- Find a way to move low to the ground, find another way, and so on.
- Find ways to move at a level between the highest jump and lowest locomotion.

Lesson Sequence

1. After students bring a mat to the largest space possible, ask them to find as many balances on a low level as they can.
   a. Now ask them to decrease their base of support.
   b. Ask them how they maintained their balance with a shorter base.
2. Do the same for balances high off the ground, encouraging them to find five or six.
   a. Ask them if they can reduce their base of support and still maintain balance.
   b. Discuss their center of gravity and where it is.
   c. Have them move their weight past their center to see what happens.
3. Do the same for balances at a medium level.
   a. Ask them if they can maintain their balance by extending all free parts of their body.
   b. Ask them to let their weight move past their center of gravity to move out of balance.
4. Have students take one high, one low, and one medium balance and create a routine that moves from one to the other.
5. Half of the class demonstrates. Switch.
6. Point out routines with distinct differences between levels that also show control, extension, and flow and ask those students to demonstrate again.

Review and Stretching

1. As students stretch, ask the following:
   - How can you make it easier to balance?
   - If your body is fully balanced, what can you do to move out of that balance?
   - What does finding your center of gravity mean?
2. Put away mats.

Levels (Apparatus)

Facilities

Clean floor

Materials

Use the same setup, one apparatus station for every four to six students.

Performance Goals

Students will do the following:
- Set up their stations and sit when done.
- Raise their heart rate for most of the class.
- Explore space by moving at different levels while on the equipment.

Cognitive Goals

Students will learn the following:
- What a base of support is
- The difference between being above or below their base of support

Lesson Safety

- Remind students to stay within their space while moving.
- Encourage students who want to try something they are not sure of to ask you for help.

Motivation

Now that they understand what a base of support is, let's find a way to balance above their base of support while on the equipment as well as a way to balance while their body is beneath their base of support. If they have any doubt that they can control something they want to try, remind them to get your attention so you can help.

Warm-Up

1. If the equipment is not set up, have the students set it up.
2. Have students spread out and ask them to run.
   - Run so that when they get near stationary equipment, they push away from it.
   - Run so that when they get to equipment, they move under it.
   - Run so that when they get to equipment, they go over or around it.

Lesson Sequence

1. Allow students to go to their apparatus of choice.
2. Circulate, encouraging exploration and being available to help.
3. After everyone has had several turns at the equipment, ask them to extend their body while in their balance positions.
4. Ask them if they can get on, extend their two balance positions, and get off with flow.
5. Half of the class demonstrates, then switches.
6. Point out routines that satisfied the problem and had control, extension, and flow. Ask those students to demonstrate again.

Review and Stretching

1. As students stretch, ask the following:
   - What is another word for balancing when your body is below your base of support?
   - Is there a value in balancing at different distances from your base of support? What is it?
2. Clean up if there is no following class.

Final Floor Routine

Facilities

Clean floor

Materials

- One mat per student
- Sound system that can be heard in the gym
- Simon and Garfunkel's "Bridge Over Troubled Waters"

Performance Goals

Students will do the following:

- Raise their heart rate for most of the class.
- Explore space by using four parts of their body to propel them.
- Move in conjunction with their partner.
- Plan and execute their final routine of the unit.

Cognitive Goals

Students will learn the following:

- What bridges and arches are
- That synchronizing movement does not always mean doing movements at the same time
- What goes into great movement

Lesson Safety

- Remind students to stay within their space while moving.
- Encourage students who want to try something they are not sure of to ask you for help.

Motivation

Today students are going to use movement not only as their final routine of the unit, but they will be making it so that it is good enough to show an audience. Their routine should demonstrate all the things they've learned about good movement.

Warm-Up

1. Have students spread out and ask them to run.
2. Can they move quickly using three parts of the body to propel them?
3. Can they use four? How many ways can they use all four parts?
4. Can they leave the ground using four parts of their body?
5. Can they move while they are arched?

Lesson Sequence

1. What does a bridge do? It connects two places. See how many positions they can hold that connect two places on the floor.
2. Get a partner and a mat.
    a. Find positions that both students can hold where they connect two places.
    b. Try another, and another, and so on.
    c. Watch what half of the class has figured out to do.
    d. If they see anything they want to try, go ahead.

Ask students to practice different ways they can use their bodies to bridge two places on the floor.

211

3. Partners create a routine that uses three bridges so that to move from one position to another, they pass over or under each other before striking their next pose.
4. Practice this so it moves with flow.
5. Practice it so they extend all the parts of their body when they've reached their balance.
6. Practice so they can control their center of gravity and don't lose their balance.
7. Watch everyone's completed routines.

Review and Stretching

1. As students stretch, ask if they liked the unit and why.
2. Put away mats.

Beginner Educational Gymnastics Skills Rubric

Name _____ Date _____

Teacher _____ Class _____

	0	1	2	3
Level of activity	No effort.	Begins on signal.	Continues until told to stop.	Willingly rehearses until has to stop.
Instructions	Does not follow instructions.	Acts on cue.	Adheres to rules.	Movements follow theme.
Space	Does not change shape at all.	Shows differences between big and small.	Extends free parts of body.	Extends through neck, back, fingers, and toes.
Weight	Does not move.	Moves with sound.	Moves without sound.	Controls center of gravity to balance in a variety of poses.
Time	Does not make any effort to move.	Moves with change of tempo.	Shows sudden and sustained movement.	Synchronizes movement with one or more people.
Flow	Does not move.	Moves from one pose to another.	Changes poses by using connecting moves.	Can connect different movements and poses so movement looks like one sentence.

From Isobel Kleinman, 2009, *Complete Physical Education Plans for Grades 5 to 12, Second Edition* (Champaign, IL: Human Kinetics).

Beginner Educational Gymnastics Quiz

Name _____ Date _____

Teacher _____ Class _____

True or False

Read each statement carefully. If the statement is true, write a *T* in the column to the left. If the statement is false, write an *F*. If using a grid sheet, blacken in the appropriate column for each question, making sure to use the correctly numbered line for each question and its answer.

_____ 1. All movement has space, time, weight, and flow.

_____ 2. The base of support is the parts of the body that stretch into space.

_____ 3. The opposite of moving fast is moving suddenly.

_____ 4. A person hanging on a bar has her base of support in her hands.

_____ 5. Falling is a more controlled way of landing then melting.

_____ 6. When you roll, your whole body touches the ground at the same time.

_____ 7. Stretching is hard work because it means being bigger than big.

_____ 8. The flow of your routine improves if you stop between every balance.

_____ 9. A light person can make a heavy sound when he lands; conversely, a heavy person can make no sound when he lands.

_____ 10. Pulling means bringing weight closer.

From Isobel Kleinman, 2009, *Complete Physical Education Plans for Grades 5 to 12, Second Edition* (Champaign, IL: Human Kinetics).

Beginner Educational Gymnastics Answer Key

True or False

1. T
2. F—The base of support is the parts of the body being used to balance.
3. F—The opposite of moving fast is moving slowly.
4. T
5. F—Melting is a more controlled way of landing.
6. F
7. T
8. F—To improve the flow of your routine, you should move smoothly between the balances.
9. T
10. T

Balance and Roll (Floor)

Facilities

Clean floor

Materials

One mat per student

Performance Goals

Students will do the following:

- Spend at least 5 minutes in the specified warm-up.
- Spend most of the class moving.
- Curl.
- Roll from a variety of positions.
- Use the roll as a connecting move.

Cognitive Goals

Students will learn the following:

- What *inversion* means
- That a roll can take them from one position to another
- That rolling does not hurt

Lesson Safety

- Keep the floor empty of equipment and obstructions during the warm-up.
- Provide mat space for students to work all at the same time but independently.

Motivation

Tell students that they were great during the warm-up and that you loved how they tried to keep their space while they continued to move. Today they're going to see if they can translate the idea of smooth, flowing movement by finding ways to connect forms that don't move.

Warm-Up

1. Have students spread out so that they take up the gym and instruct them to do the following.
   a. Memorize the space: Look right, left, in front, and back, getting a sense of the space around them.
   b. Move as if taking the memorized space with them.
2. Walk. Stop students if they get clustered.
   a. Have them continue for a minute, sensing their space, building up speed, and slowing down but not stopping.
   b. As they go, ask them to melt, get up, and keep walking.
3. Run. Stop them if they get clustered.
   a. Run, jump, and melt on landing. Without stopping, get up and continue.
   b. Continue, this time jumping up and running the moment they land.

Lesson Sequence

1. Have students space their mats out and mark out the area they will be working in. Explain that since everyone is working at once, they must stay in their own space.
   a. Ask students to find ways to roll. Allow time to experiment.
   b. Have half of the students watch what their classmates came up with. Switch.
   c. Take a few minutes to try some rolls that they haven't tried before.

2. Take a couple of those rolls and see if they can walk out of them.

3. Can they jump out of their roll?

4. Can they transfer their weight to their hands as they complete their roll and bring their hips above their hands?

5. Find ways to balance while inverted:

   a. With hips higher than hands

   b. With hips higher than head

6. Have students take one of the inverted balances they are comfortable with and:

   a. Roll out of it.

   b. Roll into it.

7. Create a routine that moves in and out of three balance positions.

8. Have a quarter of the class at a time demonstrate their routine.

9. Ask the class to choose a few routines that they'd like to see again, and have students demonstrate those routines again.

Review and Stretching

1. Discuss why the repeated routines stood out.

   - Did they show smooth, continuous, flowing movement?

   - Were they able to control their momentum so nothing looked jarring?

   - Were the performers taking time to extend? Did they get full extension?

2. Put away mats.

Educational Gymnastics
INTERMEDIATE
LESSON 2

Inversion (Apparatus)

Facilities

Clean floor

Materials

- As in the beginner level, the equipment setup should be creative so students do not approach it as formal gymnastics equipment. Take a look at the English system for ideas. Create combinations of pieces that usually stand alone if you have only formal equipment. Use the bleachers, rings, stall bars, springboards, crash pads, boxes that can support weight, or anything that is safe and gives students a new way to travel. When you set up the equipment, make sure you have one station for every four to six students.

- Have at least four apparatus stations no matter how small the class is.

- Make sure mats cover the landing area and do not overlap or have spaces between them.

Performance Goals

Students will do the following:

- Assume responsibility to set up an apparatus station for the unit.

- Spend 5 minutes in a gross-motor warm-up.

- Get on and off all equipment.

- Roll out of their landing regardless of dismount.

Cognitive Goals

Students will learn the following:

- How to set up their apparatus station so the area is safe
- Rules for using the apparatus
- How to get low to the ground before rolling
- How to safely use their momentum to roll

Lesson Safety

- The apparatus should be arranged to allow traffic to flow without obstruction.
- Mats should cover the landing area with no overlapping or gaps.
- Equipment must be stable (except for ropes and rings, which should be securely fastened before use).
- Students are to wait away from the mounting and dismounting areas.
- Encourage students to call for help if they are trying something new and challenging.

Motivation

This is the first day students are using the apparatus. Tell them that you're going to assign them to one station and they must learn it well—they will be setting it up each time they meet. That doesn't mean they have to stay and work there every day, only that they need to know how to set it up safely and quickly each day they use equipment. Students should sit when they think their station is ready.

Warm-Up

1. Have students spread out, finding the largest area around them.
2. Ask students to run. Stop them if they cluster and have them relocate.
3. Instruct them to do the following:
   - Run and jump, melt (curl) on landing, get up, and continue.
   - In place, jump and curl in the air, land softy, and curl into a ball.
   - Run, jump, curl in the air, land softly, and keep running.
   - Run, jump, melt on landing, roll, and get up to continue.

Lesson Sequence

1. Divide class into groups.
   a. Assign each group to set up one station.
   b. Show each group how and where the equipment and mats go.
   c. Explain that they are always responsible for this station.
   d. Teach the groups to sit when they are done setting up.
   e. Ask students to join you in checking that the mats are properly arranged so that no mats overlap and that all the landing areas under and around the equipment are covered.
2. Explain rules for using equipment while in a group.
   a. Students must stay in their area until told to switch.
   b. One student goes at a time.
   c. No one goes twice until everyone goes once.
   d. If students want help, they should ask the teacher, not other students.
   e. They should not stand on the mats or apparatus unless it is their turn.
   f. Be careful not to get in the approach or dismount area of another station.
   g. The maximum number of students at any station is six if the class is large, four if smaller.

3. Tell students to get on and off, and when they touch the ground they should melt and roll.
    a. Circulate, encouraging students to melt and roll in one move.
    b. Encourage students to find different ways to get on and off.
4. On rotation (after everyone in a group has had several turns), ask students to get on and off in one continuous move.
5. Rotate the class after students have had two or three turns. Ask them to go to a new station if it has fewer than six people.

Review and Stretching

1. As students stretch, ask the following:
    • What is your body doing when it melts? When it falls?
    • Does each part of your body touch the floor when you roll?
2. Put away equipment. (Leave it up if another class is coming in and run your warm-ups around it.)

Educational Gymnastics
INTERMEDIATE
LESSON 3

Twist and Turn (Floor)

Facilities
Clean floor

Materials
One mat per student

Performance Goals
Students will do the following:
• Raise their heart rate for the entire class.
• Change direction by twisting or turning.

Cognitive Goals
Students will learn the following:
• The difference between twisting and turning
• How to control their movement

Lesson Safety
• Keep the floor empty of equipment and obstructions during the warm-up.
• Provide mat space for students to work all at the same time but independently.

Motivation
Ask if anyone can put into words the difference between twisting and turning. Discuss that twisting is a sequence of body parts following the same path, and turning is when all of the body follows the same path at the same time. Now they're going to try some twisting and turning.

Warm-Up
1. Students spread out and memorize their space.
2. Instruct students to do the following:
    a. Carry space as they run.
    b. Run, jump, and land softly.

    c.   Run, jump, and land so that they face a new direction and continue.

    d.   Use one part of their body to change direction in the air so they are letting their body follow that part. Land softly and continue.

- Follow their hand.
- Follow both arms.
- Follow their head.

    e.   Run and jump so that their whole body changes direction at one time.

Lesson Sequence

1. Students get their mat and fix one part of the body as a base of support:
   a. Feet—Walk around the feet with the hands.
   b. Shoulders—With knees to chest, transfer weight to kneeling position.
   c. Knees and one hand—Let free hand lead the body through fixed parts.
2. Find other ways to transfer weight from hands to feet by making feet return to the ground in a different place than where they started.
3. Do the same with bases of support other than the hands.
4. Have half of the class demonstrate what they did that was a twist. Switch.
5. Have half of the class demonstrate what they did that was a turn. Switch.
6. Give students time to copy something they saw.
7. If there's time, allow students to perform a routine that has them balance, twist out of the balance into another position, and turn out of that position.

Review and Stretching

1. As students stretch, ask the following:

- When one part of your body follows a path at a time, what is it called?
- Doesn't a roll have one part follow another?
  - Is that a twist?
  - Can we refine our definition of a twist?

2. Put away mats.

Twist and Turn (Apparatus)

Facilities

Clean floor

Materials

Use the same setup as in previous lessons, with one apparatus station for every four to six students.

Performance Goals

Students will do the following:

- Set up their stations and sit when done.
- Elevate their heart rate for most of the class.
- Get on and change the direction while on or getting off.

Cognitive Goals

Students will learn the following:

- How their apparatus station needs to be set up for safety
- The right way to share the apparatus
  - One person gets on and off the apparatus at a time.
  - Remain in one area until told to switch.
  - Avoid moving into the approach and dismounting area of other stations.
  - Await a second turn until everyone gets a first.
- How to get low to the ground before rolling
- How to safely use their momentum to roll

Lesson Safety

- Apparatus should be arranged to allow traffic to flow without obstruction.
- Mats should cover the landing area with no overlapping or gaps.
- Equipment must be stable.
- Students are to stay in their area and not obstruct anyone's mount or dismount.
- Encourage students to call for help if trying something new and challenging.

Motivation

See how many ways students can get on the equipment and then get off facing a different direction by twisting or turning.

Warm-Up

1. Have students spread out, finding the largest area around them.
2. Ask students to do the following:
   - Run. Stop students and relocate them if clustered.
   - Run, changing direction when facing someone else.
   - Run, jump, change direction in the air, and land softly.
   - During the jump, make the arms start their change of direction.
   - Do the same, but see if one leg can lead the change of direction.
   - How about the head?
   - Can they turn a quarter of the way around? Half? Three-quarters? All the way? More?
   - Can they change direction starting from their hands?

Lesson Sequence

1. Set up stations.
2. Let students go to equipment they'd like to work at, as long as there are no more than four to six at a station.
3. Circulate, encouraging students to try different ways to change directions. Be available to help.
4. Rotate stations after half the time is up.

Review and Stretching

1. As students stretch, ask the following:
   - Is it challenging to control movement when you twist? Turn?
     - What makes it difficult? (landings)
     - Why? (balance and stopping momentum)
   - What must you do to control your balance while changing direction?
2. Have students put away equipment. (Leave it up if another class is coming in and run the warm-up around it.)

Flight (Floor)

Facilities

Clean floor

Materials

One mat per student

Performance Goals

Students will do the following:

- Raise their heart rate for the entire class.
- Amplify time in the air (flight) and control the landing.

Cognitive Goals

Students will learn the following:

- That pushing off the ground gives them elevation
- How to control a longer descent to the ground
- How to keep their center of gravity over their feet for landing

Lesson Safety

- Keep the floor empty of equipment and obstructions during the warm-up.
- Provide mat space for students to work all at the same time but independently.

Motivation

Students have been running and jumping for days now. Today, they are going to consider what the body does in flight—how they get there, how they are in the air, and how they can return to the ground with control.

Warm-Up

1. In their space, have students bounce.
2. As they do, they should give in to the floor a little more each time.
3. Run before bouncing, land softly, and continue.
4. Can they bounce using their hands?
   - Move into the air.
   - Move forward.
   - Move backward.
   - Move sideways.
5. Develop some momentum and bounce off the feet as high as possible.
6. Can they do the same, land softly, and keep running quietly?

Lesson Sequence

1. Students partner up and get mats.
2. With one of the partners acting as a base, the other finds ways to push off the base so that she goes up into the air, taking flight. Switch.
3. Could they increase their flight if their partner assists them? Remind them that if they have an idea they are unsure of, they should call for you to help them.
4. Have half of the class demonstrate what they did. Switch.
5. Give students time to copy something they saw or work on something they'd like to improve on.
6. If there's time, have students put together a routine. Alternating who takes flight, create a four-part routine.

Review and Stretching

1. As students stretch, ask the following:
   - What is flight?
   - What do you have to do to increase it?
   - To control it?
2. Put away mats.

Flight (Apparatus)

Facilities

Clean floor

Materials

Use the same setup as in previous lessons, with one apparatus station for every four to six students.

Performance Goals

Students will do the following:
- Set up their stations and sit when done.
- Elevate their heart rate for most of the class.
- Experience flight.

Cognitive Goals

Students will learn the following:
- Rules for safety
- How difficult it is to control oneself while flying

Lesson Safety

- Apparatus should be arranged to allow safe traffic flow.
- Mats should cover the landing area around the equipment without overlapping or gaps.
- Students are to stay in their area and not obstruct anyone's mount or dismount.
- Encourage students to call for help if trying something new and challenging.

Motivation

Students have been working on being in the air and returning to the ground—flight. They need to make some changes to the equipment setup since they will be trying to lengthen their time in the air when they leave the equipment and go to the floor. Remind them to ask for your help if they are trying something they are not sure of.

Warm-Up

1. Have students get into the largest space they can find.
2. Ask them to bounce and land softly, bouncing higher each time.
3. Partner up.
   - One forms a stable obstacle.
   - The other runs and jumps, pushing off the obstacles in the room (e.g., other partners or the apparatus).
   - Switch who is the obstacle on the gym floor and who is moving.
4. Continue, cueing students to run quietly, land softly, and not hesitate to jump.

Lesson Sequence

1. Set up apparatus stations and check that they are correct for this assignment.
2. Let students go to equipment they'd like to work at, as long as there are no more than four to six students at a station.
3. Circulate, encouraging students to try different things and being available to help.
4. Rotate after half the time is up.

Review and Stretching

1. As students stretch, ask the following:
   - What makes flight so challenging? (landing)
   - What must you do to control your landing?
2. Have students put away equipment. (Leave it up if another class is coming in and run the warm-up around it.)

Acceleration and Deceleration (Floor)

Facilities

Clean floor

Materials

One mat per student

Performance Goals

Students will do the following:

- Spend at least 5 minutes in the specified warm-up.
- Spend most of the class moving.
- Speed up (accelerate) and slow down (decelerate).

Cognitive Goals

Students will learn the following:

- What *accelerate* and *decelerate* mean
- What they need to do to control the time it takes to move

Lesson Safety

- Keep the floor empty of equipment and obstructions during the warm-up.
- Provide mat space for students to work all at the same time but independently.

Motivation

This is not the first time students have tried making their movement very fast or very slow, but this time there was a difference. What was the difference? Instead of suddenly going fast, they gradually got faster and faster. They did the same with being slow—they didn't suddenly go slowly; they gradually got slower.

Warm-Up

1. Have students spread out.
2. Have them walk, keeping their space as they go.
3. Walk faster, now faster, now as fast as they can while still walking.
4. Without stopping, can they keep walking but slow down? Can they continue walking slower, slower, and even slower?

5. Now, increase their speed until they are running faster, faster, and fastest.

6. Without stopping, can they reduce their speed while still running? Continue running slower, slower, and as slowly as they can.

Lesson Sequence

1. Within a single roll, can they bring about a time change?
   a. Try gathering speed.
   b. Try losing speed.

2. Try doing the same with other rolls.
   a. First gather speed.
   b. Then try reducing speed

3. Attach a stretch to the roll.
   a. Can they reach a stable position if they gather speed to get into it?
   b. How about if they reduce speed? Can they get into a balance stretch?

4. Once they find a roll and stretch that they can control, can they work it so that they can keep the flow of movement so that it either accelerates or decelerates?

5. Have half of the class demonstrate their combination.

6. Ask the class to choose the routines that showed acceleration best and deceleration best. After the discussion, have the other half of the class demonstrate their routines and repeat discussions of the best examples.

7. Have the best examples perform their routines again and discuss briefly.

8. Ask students to return to their mats, add a roll and stretch to what they've done, and create a routine that shows acceleration and deceleration.

Review and Stretching

1. As students stretch, discuss the following:
   - How acceleration or deceleration helped or hindered rolls and stretches
   - How using the tempo change made it easier or more difficult to manage the following:
     - Flow
     - Stretch
     - Transfer of weight

2. Put away mats.

Educational Gymnastics
INTERMEDIATE
LESSON 8

Acceleration and Deceleration (Apparatus)

Facilities

Clean floor

Materials

Use the same setup as in previous lessons, with one apparatus station for every four to six students.

Performance Goals

Students will do the following:

- Set up their stations and sit when done.
- Spend at least 5 minutes in a gross-motor warm-up.

- Spend most of the class moving.
- Use acceleration and deceleration to navigate the equipment.

Cognitive Goals

Students will learn the following:

- The meaning of acceleration and deceleration
- What they need to do to control the time it takes to move

Lesson Safety

- Apparatus should be arranged to allow safe traffic flow.
- Mats should cover the landing area around the equipment without overlapping or gaps.
- Students are to stay in their area and not obstruct anyone's mount or dismount.
- Encourage students to call for help if trying something new and challenging.

Motivation

Let's review. What happens to their movement when they accelerate? Decelerate? After the last class, they all should have an idea of how doing each can help or hinder their ability to complete their move or reach their balance. Knowing that, when they use the equipment today they should see how they can get on or off with more control while either accelerating or decelerating their motion.

Warm-Up

1. Have students spread out.
2. They begin walking, keeping their space as they go.
3. Have them walk faster, now faster, now as fast as they can while still walking.
4. Without stopping, can they keep walking but slow down?
5. Can they continue walking slower, slower, and even slower?
6. Have them increase their speed until they are running faster, faster, and as fast as they can.
7. Without stopping, can they reduce their speed while still running? Run slower, slower, and as slowly as they can.

Lesson Sequence

1. Have the students set up their stations.
2. Allow them to go to any station they want as long as there are no more than six at the station.
3. Allow students to experiment, circulating to encourage focus on gathering or reducing speed.
4. Five minutes before cleanup, ask everyone to sit.
   a. Have one person at each station at the same time show his best demonstration of acceleration or deceleration.
   b. When everyone has demonstrated, pick a few routines that outshone the rest.

Review and Stretching

1. Discuss why those routines were chosen.
2. Put mats away.

Push and Pull (Floor)

Facilities

Clean floor

Materials

One mat per student

Performance Goals

Students will do the following:

- Spend at least 5 minutes in the specified warm-up.
- Spend most of the class moving.
- Enhance movement by concentrating on pushing and pulling.

Cognitive Goals

Students will learn the following:

- What pushing and pulling are
- How to collaborate by pushing and pulling

Lesson Safety

- Keep the floor empty of equipment and obstructions during the warm-up.
- Provide mat space for students to work all at the same time but independently.

Motivation

We use the words *pushing* and *pulling* all the time, but for this minute ask students to think about what they are actually doing when they push or pull. Does anyone want to explain? If they use the term *center of gravity* in their explanation, what is done when they push? When they pull? Today they are going to do something that they haven't done in a while—they are going to work in partners and see how they can move each other by pushing or pulling.

Warm-Up

1. Have students spread out.
2. Ask them to find a way to push their body off the ground.
3. Try to push off the ground using another part of the body to push.
4. Try another part.
5. Try another (encourage them to try about eight different ways).
6. How about traveling along the ground by pushing?
7. Can they travel by pulling?
8. What if they took a few steps before they pushed? Could they get higher?
9. Have half of the class demonstrate and then switch.
10. If they see anything they want to try or to improve on, take a few minutes.

Lesson Sequence

1. Students partner up, get a mat or two, and find a space.
2. Now that they understand what pushing and pulling are, they can see how many ways they can change their partner's position by pulling or pushing.
3. Stop after 5 minutes for demonstration of what they've tried so far. If they see anything they want to try, take some time to try it.
4. By pushing or pulling, partners try to prevent each other from moving.

Students practice pushing and pulling.

5. Using pushing or pulling, partners move each other into a balanced position and out into another balanced position.

6. Use the following cues as they work on their routines:
   - Reach for full extension when balanced.
   - Reach for extension while moving.
   - Make the sequence flow.

Review and Stretching

1. As students stretch, ask the following:
   - When two people are trying to stop their movement by pushing or pulling, where is their center of gravity?
   - What happens when the center of gravity shifts?
   - How can you make the center of gravity shift?

2. Put the mats away.

Push and Pull (Apparatus)

Facilities

Clean floor

Materials

Use the same setup as in previous lessons, with one apparatus station for every four to six students.

Performance Goals

Students will do the following:
- Set up their stations and sit when done.
- Spend at least 5 minutes in a gross-motor warm-up.

- Spend most of the class moving.
- Explore the push–pull mechanics of mounting and dismounting.

Cognitive Goals

Students will learn the following:

- The meaning of pushing and pulling
- How the center of gravity works

Lesson Safety

- Apparatus should be arranged to allow safe traffic flow.
- Mats should cover the landing area around the equipment without overlapping or gaps.
- Students are to stay in their area and not obstruct anyone's mount or dismount.
- Encourage students to call for help if trying something new and challenging.

Motivation

In the spirit of working with partners and moving their center of gravity with their partner's assistance, today students are going to work on the equipment to find as many ways as time allows for them to assist each other getting onto the apparatus from above or below, which would have been impossible without a partner's help.

Warm-Up

1. Students spread out and begin to move, accelerating to a run.
2. When they have the space, push up off the ground and continue.
3. If the equipment is up, they do the following:
   - When they get to stationary equipment, push away from it and continue.
   - Push to increase their flight.
   - Push to change direction.
4. If the equipment is not up, they do the following:
   - One partner creates a stationary base that can support weight.
   - The other runs and pushes off the base. (Switch several times.)
   - Push to increase flight.
   - Push to change direction.

Lesson Sequence

1. Have the students set up their stations.
2. Allow them to go to any station they want as long as there aren't more than six people.
3. Allow students to experiment.
4. With 5 minutes of activity time remaining, have partners go to the equipment they like best and perfect the mount that they did best, attending to all aspects of movement in terms of form and balance.
5. Ask everyone to sit. Pick a few students to demonstrate.

Review and Stretching

1. As students stretch, ask the following:
   - Why do you think I chose these routines?
   - Were these the qualities you saw?
     - Creativity
     - Pulling and pushing
     - Full extension during movement
     - Control of weight
   - Did any demonstrations include all of these factors?
2. Put equipment away.

Symmetry and Asymmetry (Floor)

Facilities

Clean floor

Materials

One mat per student

Performance Goals

Students will do the following:

- Spend at least 5 minutes in the specified warm-up.
- Spend most of the class moving.
- Show the difference between symmetrical and asymmetrical.

Cognitive Goals

Students will learn the following:

- What *symmetrical* and *asymmetrical* mean
- How the center of gravity affects balance

Lesson Safety

- Keep the floor empty of equipment and obstructions during the warm-up.
- Provide mat space for students to work all at the same time but independently.

Motivation

During warm-ups, students have started exploring the difference between symmetrical and asymmetrical shapes. Now they are going to explore what it feels like to find and maintain their balance when the base they are working on is either symmetrical—what they have been doing since they started this program—*or* asymmetrical. What do they suppose the problem will be when they are using an asymmetrical base (finding the center of gravity)?

Warm-Up

1. Students spread out and run, maintaining the space around them.
2. Explain *symmetrical* and *asymmetrical*.
3. Students run, jump, and make a symmetrical shape in the air.
4. Do the same, this time making the shape in the air asymmetrical.

Lesson Sequence

1. Students get a mat and find a space.
   a. Discuss what a base is.
   b. Discuss what symmetry and asymmetry are.
2. Students find as many ways as possible to support their weight in a balanced position over a symmetrical base.
3. Stop after 5 minutes for a demonstration of what they've tried so far. If they see anything they want to try, give them some time to try it.
4. Students move their base of support so that it is asymmetrical and see if they can still find and maintain their balance.
5. Stop after 5 minutes for a demonstration.
6. Students partner up and teach each other one of their asymmetrical balances so that they are doing two. They practice doing one and then the other together.
7. See if they can improve the flow and form.
8. Have the students demonstrate their routines.

Review and Stretching

1. As students stretch, ask the following:
   - Did you notice something strange about seeing two asymmetrical shapes together?
   - Didn't doing them simultaneously make them look symmetrical?
   - Why is that?
2. Put mats away.

Symmetry and Asymmetry (Apparatus)

Facilities

Clean floor

Materials

Use the same setup as in previous lessons, with one apparatus station for every four to six students.

Performance Goals

Students will do the following:

- Set up their stations and sit when done.
- Spend at least 5 minutes in a gross-motor warm-up.
- Spend most of the class moving.
- Concentrate on asymmetry on the equipment.

Cognitive Goals

Students will learn the following:

- The meaning of symmetry and asymmetry
- How the center of gravity works

Lesson Safety

- Apparatus should be arranged to allow safe traffic flow.
- Mats should cover the landing area around the equipment without overlapping or gaps.
- Students are to stay in their area and not obstruct anyone's mount or dismount.
- Encourage students to call for help if trying something new and challenging.

Motivation

From the floor work during the last class, the students should have a pretty good understanding of what it means and how it feels to try to balance when their base is asymmetrical. In order to balance on some equipment, they need to find their center of gravity while using an asymmetrical base of support, and on other equipment it is almost natural for the base of support to always be symmetrical. Today, they will play with this concept of symmetry and asymmetry while they use the equipment.

Warm-Up

1. Students spread out and run.
2. While running, can they use their arms in an asymmetrical way?
3. Can they use their feet in an asymmetrical way?
4. Can they run symmetrically but jump asymmetrically?
5. Can they run asymmetrically but jump and form a symmetrical shape in the air?

Lesson Sequence

1. Have students set up their stations.

2. Allow them to go to any station as long as there are no more than six people.

3. Allow experimentation, encouraging students to try different asymmetrical bases on which to balance.

4. Have students rotate, changing equipment every 5 minutes or so.

Review and Stretching

1. Review the terms used:
   - Base of support
   - Asymmetrical shape
   - Balance
   - Center of gravity

2. Put equipment away.

Change of Direction (Floor)

Facilities

Clean floor

Materials

One mat per student

Performance Goals

Students will do the following:

- Spend at least 5 minutes in the specified warm-up.
- Spend most of the class moving.
- Try various methods of changing direction while moving.

Cognitive Goal

Students will learn that there are multiple methods of changing direction.

Lesson Safety

- Keep the floor empty of equipment and obstructions during the warm-up.
- Provide mat space for students to work all at the same time but independently.

Motivation

This is another day to try to be completely original. After all, how many times are they ever expecting to move where they aren't looking? Besides, halfway through the class, there will be a little surprise in the form of partner work.

Warm-Up

1. Students spread out and run, maintaining the space around them.

2. Students find ways to move in different directions

3. Run so that they are moving in a different direction from the one they are facing.

4. Run and jump so that when they land they face a different direction, land, and continue.

Lesson Sequence

1. After students get a mat, they find ways to travel along the floor so that they move in directions other than the one they are facing.
2. Try ways to move so they end up facing a different direction than when they started.
3. See if they can come up with some other ways.
4. Have half of the class demonstrate. Switch.
5. Let students try something they saw but have never tried before.
6. Have students put together three methods of moving that end in a direction different than the one they started in.
7. Have students teach a partner their three-part routine.
8. Partners choose one of the routines and practice for form, flow, and control.
9. Partners find another pair to critique their routine so that they help synchronize form and time—same extensions, same flexions, and same timing.
10. After everyone has used the critique to improve their routines, have half of the class demonstrate at a time.

Review and Stretching

1. Ask the class to choose one or two routines that stood out and have them justify why.
2. Put mats away.

Educational Gymnastics
INTERMEDIATE
LESSON 14

Change of Direction (Apparatus)

Facilities

Clean floor

Materials

Use the same setup as in previous lessons, with one apparatus station for every four to six students.

Performance Goals

Students will do the following:

- Set up their stations and sit when done.
- Spend at least 5 minutes in a gross-motor warm-up.
- Spend most of the class moving.
- Experiment with methods of getting on or off equipment in a different direction than the one they're facing.

Cognitive Goal

Students will learn how the body changes directions.

Lesson Safety

- Apparatus should be arranged to allow safe traffic flow.
- Mats should cover the landing area around the equipment without overlapping or gaps.
- Students are to stay in their area and not obstruct anyone's mount or dismount.
- Encourage students to call for help if trying something new and challenging.

Motivation

Today, instead of concentrating on getting on or off, students will concentrate on traveling while on. While they travel, though, they should try to change direction once.

Warm-Up

1. Students run, and when they get to a person or a piece of equipment, change direction.
2. Run and jump, landing in a different direction than when they left the ground.
3. Move sideways.
4. Move backward.
5. Move upward.
6. Move down.
7. Run and jump, letting themselves melt to the ground, roll in a different direction, and get up and continue running in that new direction.

Lesson Sequence

1. Have the students set up their stations.
2. Allow them to go to any station as long as there are no more than six people.
3. Allow experimentation, encouraging students to try different asymmetrical bases on which to balance.
4. Have students rotate, changing equipment every 5 minutes or so.

Review and Stretching

Put equipment away.

Intermediate Educational Gymnastics Skills Rubric

Name _____ Date _____

Teacher _____ Class _____

	0	1	2	3
Level of activity	Does not move.	Makes minimum effort to move.	Movement is limited and not on task.	Rehearses until told to stop.
Collaboration	Does not relate to others.	Self-engaged and self-indulgent. Insists that partner does things their way though the partner is afraid to.	Willingly partners with others.	Adapts to partner's abilities.
Form in space	Does not participate.	Extends appendages when stationary.	Extends appendages while moving and stationary.	Extends through the neck, back, fingers, and toes at all times.
Weight	Does not participate.	Moves along the ground without sound.	Returns to the ground without sound.	Changes direction and altitude without losing control.
Time	Does not participate.	Changes the tempo of a move.	Builds up or builds down speed.	Synchronizes movement with one or more people.
Flow	Does not move.	Can put together a sequence of moves.	Uses connecting moves to move from one pose to another.	Can make a movement sequence look like one sentence.

From Isobel Kleinman, 2009, *Complete Physical Education Plans for Grades 5 to 12, Second Edition* (Champaign, IL: Human Kinetics).

Intermediate Educational Gymnastics Quiz

Name _____ Date _____

Teacher _____ Class _____

Matching

Identify which comment in the right-hand column most closely reflects an explanation for the word or words in the left-hand column.

_____ 1.	twisting	a.	if cut in half, each side would look the same
_____ 2.	center of gravity	b.	moving weight away
_____ 3.	flight	c.	getting slower a little bit at a time
_____ 4.	acceleration	d.	a body in space with no base of support
_____ 5.	deceleration	e.	one part of the body after another turns
_____ 6.	symmetrical	f.	each half looks dissimilar
_____ 7.	asymmetrical	g.	getting on by bringing weight to apparatus
_____ 8.	pushing	h.	must center it over the base of support to balance
_____ 9.	pulling	i.	speeding up
_____ 10.	curling	j.	getting round

 From Isobel Kleinman, 2009, *Complete Physical Education Plans for Grades 5 to 12, Second Edition* (Champaign, IL: Human Kinetics).

Intermediate Educational Gymnastics Answer Key

Matching

1. e
2. h
3. d
4. i
5. c
6. a
7. f
8. b
9. g
10. j

Stretch and Curl (Floor)

Facilities

Clean floor

Materials

One mat per student

Performance Goals

Students will do the following:

- Spend 5 minutes warming up.
- Spend most of the class moving.
- Show a dramatic change in movement size.

Cognitive Goals

Students will learn the following:

- How to become more aware of their center of gravity and balance
- How to tuck and roll to get from one position to another
- That rolling does not hurt

Lesson Safety

- Keep the floor empty of equipment and obstructions during the warm-up.
- Provide mat space for students to work all at the same time but independently.

Motivation

Speak about controlling balance by making sure weight is equal on either side of their center of gravity, no matter how large or small they are. Explain that during this class, students will be experimenting with large and small balances.

Warm-Up

1. Have students spread out and memorize their space
2. Get them moving, walking to begin, keeping the space around them as they go.
3. Stop if they get clustered.
4. Continue, building speed until they are running.
5. Make certain they don't cluster. Stop them when they do.
6. Ask them to run and jump when they have space to land.
7. While in the air, ask them to form a large shape, land softly, and continue.
8. Ask them to tuck in the air, land softly, and continue.
9. They should be getting a bit tired. Stop them and talk briefly about finding their center of gravity.

Lesson Sequence

1. Have students get their own mat and find a space.
2. Using only large body parts, do the following:
   a. Have students find many balance positions. (This can be guided by asking students to find one, then another, then another, then another, and so on.)
   b. Have them stretch parts that are not part of their base of support so those parts move away from their center.
3. Take time for half of the class to show what they worked on for large balance positions.

4. Do the same with small parts of the body as the base of support.
   a. Encourage students to find another, another, and another position.
   b. Ask them to try the positions again, stretching every free body part they have.
   c. Ask them to remember their necks and fingers and toes while stretching.
5. Connect a large, small, and large balance position by tucking and rolling into the next.
6. Have a quarter of the class demonstrate routines at a time.
7. Ask the class to choose a few routines that they'd like to see again, and have those routines performed again.

Review

1. Discuss why the routines that were chosen stood out.
   - Did they show a distinction between large and small as assigned?
   - Were students able to control their weight over their center of gravity?
   - Were the performers taking time to extend? Did they get full extension?
   - Was the movement flowing?
2. Put the mats away.

Stretch and Curl (Apparatus)

Facilities

Clean floor

Materials

- As stated in each of the previous units, create combinations of equipment that will encourage creative use. Take advantage of all equipment that bears weight in your gym, such as bars, horses, rings, ropes, bleachers, boxes that can support weight, crash pads, springboards, and so on. Set up the equipment so that there is an apparatus station for every four to six students.
- Have at least four apparatus stations no matter how small the class is.
- Make sure mats cover the landing area and do not overlap or have spaces between them.

Performance Goals

Students will do the following:

- Assume responsibility for setting up an apparatus station for the unit.
- Spend 5 minutes in a gross-motor warm-up.
- Get on, form a stretched balance position, and get off a variety of equipment.

Cognitive Goals

Students will learn the following:

- How to set up their apparatus station so the area is safe
- The routine for using the apparatus
- The importance of getting low to the ground before rolling
- How to safely use their momentum to roll

Lesson Safety

- The apparatus will be arranged to allow traffic to flow without obstruction.
- Mats should cover the landing area with no overlapping or gaps.

- Equipment must be stable (except for ropes and rings, which should be securely fastened and have mats covering all possible landing areas).
- Students are to wait away from the performer's mounting and dismounting areas.
- Encourage students to call for help if trying something new and challenging.

Motivation

Last time, students worked on balances on the floor and on feeling extension through the neck, back, fingers, and toes. Today, they will use the equipment. This changes things a bit because the area to balance on is smaller and off the ground, making it more challenging. After they set up the equipment and get the signal to go, they should see what they feel comfortable translating to the equipment. It's the first day on the equipment, so they should try to get on several pieces before the end of the lesson.

Warm-Up

1. Have students spread out, finding the largest area around them.
2. Ask students to run. Stop them if they cluster and have them relocate.
3. Instruct them to do the following:
   - Run, jump, melt upon landing, and continue.
   - Jump in place, curl in the air, melt into a ball upon landing, and continue.
   - Jump, stretch in the air, land softly, get up, and continue.
   - Repeat but roll out of the landing, jump up, and continue.
   - Now, run, jump, melt on landing, roll, get up, and continue.
   - Run, jump, melt on landing, roll, jump out of the roll, and continue.

Lesson Sequence

1. Divide the class into groups.
   a. Assign each group to set up one station.
   b. Show each group how and where the equipment and mats go.
   c. Explain that they are always responsible for this station.
   d. Teach the groups to sit when they are done setting up.
   e. Ask students to check that the mats are properly placed.
   f. Check the setup yourself.
2. Explain rules about using equipment while in a group.
   a. Students must stay in their area until told to switch.
   b. One student goes at a time.
   c. No one goes twice until everyone goes once.
   d. If students want help, they should ask the teacher, not other students.
   e. Do not stand on the mats or apparatus unless it is their turn.
   f. Students must be careful not to get in the approach or dismount area of another station.
   g. The maximum number of students at any station is six if the class is large, four if it is smaller.
3. Tell students to get on the equipment in a tuck, stretch while on, and get off large.
   a. Circulate throughout, encouraging students to try something different.
   b. Ask them to sustain their balance in order to fully stretch.
   c. Remind the class to try to extend while moving.
4. Rotate after everyone in a group has had several turns.

Review and Stretch

1. As students stretch, ask if it is easier to balance and stretch on the equipment, and if so, why.
2. Have students put away equipment. (Leave it up if another class is coming in and run the warm-up around it.)

Inversion (Floor)

Facilities

Clean floor

Materials

One mat per student

Performance Goals

Students will do the following:

- Raise their heart rate for the entire class.
- Perform a variety of inversions.

Cognitive Goals

Students will learn the following:

- What *inversion* means
- How to control their movement

Lesson Safety

- Keep the floor empty of equipment and obstructions during the warm-up.
- Provide mat space for students to work all at the same time but independently.

Motivation

Most of us feel most comfortable using our eyes when we choose to move in one direction or another. Perhaps that is why doing otherwise is so uncomfortable—you cannot see where you are going, and for some people that is scary. Today, students are going to work on being inverted. Can anyone put into words what we do when we are inverted?

Warm-Up

1. Have students spread out.
2. Instruct them to begin to move, carrying the space around them as they do so.
   a. If they bump into anyone, they should freeze on the spot.
   b. After several students are frozen in place, instruct them to be conscious of moving to open areas and have them begin again.
   c. Emphasize maintaining their space as they move.
3. Begin to run.
4. Move backward.
   a. Pick up the pace.
   b. Run backward.
5. Move sideways.
6. Run forward and jump. Upon landing, they change direction, not always running in the direction they face.
7. This time, change direction in the air, land, and run backward.

Lesson Sequence

1. Students get a mat and space it properly.
2. They find balance positions where the head is lower than most of the body.
   a. Encourage students to find 10 different balance positions.
   b. Half of the class watches the 10 balance positions of the others.

3. Allow time for students to work on balance positions they saw and hadn't tried or want to control better.
   a. Remind them to move away so their center of gravity remains in the center.
   b. Allow them to get a partner to help them stabilize.
4. Ask students to repeat their balance positions with extension, stretching their body away from their head and base of support while still maintaining balance.
5. Make a routine that alternates three inverted balances with three erect balances, trying to move from one to another seamlessly.
6. Have a quarter of the class show their routines at a time.
7. Ask students to pick routines that stood out, and have those students demonstrate their routines for the class.

Review

1. Discuss why the routines they chose stood out.
2. Put mats away.

Educational Gymnastics
ADVANCED
LESSON 4

Inversion (Apparatus)

Facilities

Clean floor

Materials

Use the same setup as in previous lessons, with one apparatus station for every four to six students.

Performance Goals

Students will do the following:

- Set up their stations and sit when done.
- Elevate their heart rate for most of the class.
- Find ways to invert while getting on or off equipment.

Cognitive Goals

Students will learn the following:

- The importance of getting low to the ground before rolling
- How to safely use their momentum to roll

Lesson Safety

- Apparatus should be arranged to allow traffic to flow without obstruction.
- Mats should cover the landing area with no overlapping or gaps.
- Equipment must be stable.
- Students are to stay in their area and not obstruct anyone's mount or dismount.
- Encourage students to call for help if trying something new and challenging.

Motivation

Review what the body does to invert and explain that the task for the day is to find ways to invert while on equipment. Explain that the students will be rotating to several pieces so they can find lots of ways to be on the equipment with their head lower than most body parts.

Warm-Up

1. Have students spread out, finding the largest area around them.
2. Ask students to do the following.
   - Run, changing direction when they find themselves facing someone else.
   - Run, jump, and upon landing, move in a direction different than the one they're facing.
   - Find a way to move that is at a medium level. Move backward.
   - Find a low level way to move. Move away from their line of vision.
   - Find other ways to move where their eyes don't face where they are going.

Lesson Sequence

1. Set up stations.
2. Let students go to equipment so there are no more than four to six students per station.
3. Circulate around the room.
   a. Encourage students to try different inversions.
   b. Be available to help.
   c. If you see something stunning, stop the class and have them look.
4. Rotate stations every 8 minutes or so.

Review and Stretching

1. As students stretch, ask the following:
   - What's inversion?
   - Do you have the same center of gravity when in the same position and erect?
2. Have students put away equipment. (Leave it up if another class is coming in and run the warm-up around it.)

Bend and Arch (Floor)

Facilities

Clean floor

Materials

One mat per student

Performance Goals

Students will do the following:

- Raise their heart rate for the entire class.
- Connect two places by bridging and arching.

Cognitive Goals

Students will learn the following:

- That bending is folding or flexing at the joints
- That arching is overextending some joints to form a C
- How their body can bend or arch

Lesson Safety

- Keep the floor empty of equipment and obstructions during the warm-up.
- Provide mat space for students to work all at the same time but independently.

Motivation

Today's lesson plays with the concept of bridging as the students bend or arch. A bridge has a function—what is it? When used in movement, what could it symbolize? Usually people and things pass over bridges and under arches. Do arches connect two places? If we refer to arching our body, what would we have to do? If we added an arch to a bridge and wanted people to pass over it, would it be right side up or inverted? Today students are going to explore exactly what part of the body arches, how they can use the arch in movement, and how they can use bending or arching to create bridges that they can go over or under.

Warm-Up

1. Students begin walking (5 seconds), increasing speed until running (15 seconds).
2. At top speed, jump, arch in the air, and land by bending into a ball; get up to continue.
3. Do the same, but jump straight up, land by bending into a ball, and continue (5 seconds).
4. Find ways to cover ground by moving on all fours. Find another and another.
5. Find ways to use four parts of the body to move so two of the parts move to the other two parts.

Lesson Sequence

1. If overextending is arching, have students find the parts of their body that overextend.
2. Find three positions that balance on four parts of the body.
   a. Can they bend while in the positions and still hold their balance?
   b. Can they arch in them and maintain their balance?
3. Find three positions that balance on three parts.
   a. Arch while in them.
   b. Bend while in them.
4. Find three positions on two parts.
   a. Bend while in them.
   b. Arch while in them.

Students find a position that balances on three parts using a bend.

5. Find three positions on one part.
    a. Bend and hold.
    b. Arch and hold.
6. Find a partner and go over or under each other by forming bridges over or under each other.
7. Have half of the students demonstrate what they did. Switch.
8. Put a routine together that has three bridges with partners switching who is over and under.

Review and Stretching

1. As students stretch, ask the following:
    - What is the difference between bending and arching?
    - What do you have to do to arch?
    - What is a bridge?
2. Put the mats away.

Bend and Arch (Apparatus)

Facilities

Clean floor

Materials

Use the same setup as in previous lessons, with one apparatus station for every four to six students.

Performance Goals

Students will do the following:
- Set up their stations and sit when done.
- Elevate their heart rate for most of the class.
- Translate the concepts of bridging and arching to an apparatus.

Cognitive Goal

Students will learn how to bend or arch to connect spaces on an apparatus.

Lesson Safety

- Apparatus should be arranged to allow safe traffic flow.
- Mats should cover the landing area around the equipment without overlapping or gaps.
- Students are to stay in their area and not obstruct anyone's mount or dismount.
- Encourage students to call for help if trying something new and challenging.

Motivation

Today the students will see how many ways they can form an arch that bridges two parts of the equipment together. Remind them to try to do their own thing, but as always, if they see someone doing something they'd like to try, by all means, they should give it a try. Also remind them to call you if they are unsure of something.

Warm-Up

1. Students run, jump, arch in the air, land softly, and continue.
2. Leave one partner as a stable bridge.
   a. Standing partners run and either pass over or under bridges in their path.
   b. Switch every 15 seconds.
3. Continue for several minutes.

Lesson Sequence

1. Set up equipment and check that stations are correct.
2. Let students go to equipment they'd like to work at, as long as there are no more than six students at the station already.
3. Circulate, encouraging students to try different things and being available to help.
4. Have students rotate to another station so they get to at least three.

Review and Stretching

1. As students stretch, ask the following:
   - What made bending or arching more challenging today? (height and limited space)
   - Why do you feel you must be more careful on equipment than on the floor?
2. Have students put away equipment. (Leave it up if another class is coming in and run the warm-up around it.)

Educational Gymnastics
ADVANCED
LESSON 7

Taking Weight, Part 1 (Floor)

Facilities

Clean floor

Materials

One mat per student

Performance Goals

Students will do the following:

- Spend at least 5 minutes in the specified warm-up.
- Spend most of the class moving.
- Collaborate with a partner.

Cognitive Goals

Students will learn the following:

- How to take the weight of a classmate safely and with control
- That you don't have to be strong to support someone bigger

Lesson Safety

- Keep the floor empty of equipment and obstructions during the warm-up.
- Provide mat space for students to work all at the same time but independently.

Motivation

Students have worked on using a partner as a bridge or arch to go over or under. Today they will experiment with ways to take and support their partner's weight. And since this is an equal opportunity class, they're going to do something that is becoming popular in the dance world everywhere—the bigger person being lifted by the smaller person. Tell students to alternate taking the weight. This will be quite an adventure!

Warm-Up

1. Students spread out and begin walking.
2. They move forward without using their feet.
3. Allow other parts of the body to take their weight.
4. How many different parts of their body can they use to move?
5. How many different parts of their body can they use to push off the floor?

Lesson Sequence

1. Students partner up, get mats, find a space, and begin to experiment.
   a. Cue them to find several ways to take each other's weight.
   b. Give them time to experiment.
   c. Have half of the class watch what the other half did and then switch.
   d. Give them more time to try some new things.
2. Create a short routine of four positions, alternating who is on top and who is on bottom.
3. While students create and practice, remind them of the following:
   a. They must control their weight; if they do, no one will hear their landings.
   b. They should extend through their moves.
   c. The transitions should flow.

Review and Stretching

1. Discuss how they can tell when performers are in control of their weight.
   a. They make no noise because landings and transfers are gradual.
   b. Their movement flows because weight is controlled and thus transfers are gradual.
2. Put the mats away.

Taking Weight, Part 2 (Floor)

Facilities

Clean floor

Materials

One mat per student

Performance Goals

Students will do the following:

- Spend at least 5 minutes in a gross-motor warm-up.
- Spend most of the class moving.
- Perfect routines they began last class.

Cognitive Goals

Students will learn the following:

- How to control their own weight and the weight of others
- How to cooperate with one another to get a finished product
- How to critique and coach their peers

Lesson Safety

- Keep the floor empty of equipment and obstructions during the warm-up.
- Provide mat space for students to work all at the same time but independently.

Motivation

Tell students that they looked as if they were having so much fun and doing such creative things with their partner during the last class that you decided to give them another day to work on their routines together. Last class you asked them to start building a routine that had four transitions, but this time you want them to add two so they'll have six altogether. The problem is the same—alternate who takes the weight. But, since they are getting this extra time, they should focus on performance-level work. As advanced students, they should already know what that means in terms of space, time, weight, and flow.

Warm-Up

1. Students start walking and build up their pace until they are at top speed.
2. At top speed, run like a big, heavy elephant.
3. Continue moving as fast as possible but move like a feather.
4. Run like a feather but jump and land like a rock.
5. Run like an elephant but jump and land like a feather.
6. Run, jump, and land like an elephant.
7. Run, jump, and land like a feather.

Lesson Sequence

1. Students will get their mats, set up in their space, and begin work.
2. As they practice, talk to them individually with hints and suggestions that will improve their performance.
3. Have each group find another group to evaluate their routine.
4. Let them have a few more minutes of practice.
5. Have half of the class demonstrate at a time. Switch.

Review

1. After the class demonstration, ask the following:
   - Which routine seemed the most creative?
   - Which flowed best?
   - If they only had one routine to see again, which would they choose?
2. Put mats away.

Educational Gymnastics
ADVANCED
LESSON 9

Push and Pull (Floor)

Facilities

Clean floor

Materials

One mat per student

Performance Goals

Students will do the following:

- Spend at least 5 minutes in the specified warm-up.
- Spend most of the class moving.
- Enhance movement by concentrating on pushing and pulling.

Cognitive Goals

Students will learn the following:

- How to define pushing and pulling in reference to their center of gravity
- How to collaborate by pushing and pulling

Lesson Safety

- Keep the room empty of equipment during the warm-up.
- Provide mat space for students to work independently at the same time.

Motivation

We use the words *pushing* and *pulling* all the time, but for this minute students should think about what they are actually doing when they push or pull. Does anyone want to explain? If they use the term *center of gravity* in their explanation, what is done when they push? When they pull? Today they are going to try to see how many ways they can move by pushing away from their center of gravity or pulling toward it so that they change position or change where they are on the floor.

Warm-Up

1. Students spread out and run as quietly as they can.
2. Using two feet, push off the ground.
3. Using one foot, push off the ground.
4. Push off using anything other than the feet.
5. They should find as many ways as they can to push off the ground without using their feet.

Lesson Sequence

1. From a low level, have students push to travel in several ways.
2. Now have them see how they can travel by pulling in several ways.
3. Push from their center of gravity to change positions in several ways.
4. Pull toward their center to change position.
5. Try the same from a medium level.
6. How can they use pushing or pulling to travel from a high level?
7. Construct a routine that alternates both elements so they change position and travel, arriving in three different balance positions by pushing and pulling.

Review and Stretching

1. As students stretch, ask the following:
   - What do you do to push?
   - What do you do to pull?
   - Which action is likely to allow you to extend most, pushing or pulling?
   - Which action is likely to make you curl?
2. Put mats away.

Push and Pull (Apparatus)

Facilities

Clean floor

Materials

Use the same setup as in previous lessons, with one apparatus station for every four to six students.

Performance Goals

Students will do the following:

- Set up their stations and sit when done.
- Spend at least 5 minutes in a gross-motor warm-up.
- Spend most of the class moving.
- Explore the push–pull mechanics of mounting and dismounting.

Cognitive Goals

Students will learn the following:

- The meaning of pushing and pulling
- How their center of gravity works

Lesson Safety

- Apparatus should be arranged to allow safe traffic flow.
- Mats should cover the landing area around the equipment without overlapping or gaps.
- Students are to stay in their area and not obstruct anyone's mount or dismount.
- Encourage students to call for help if trying something new and challenging.

Motivation

Having worked on the theme of pushing and pulling, today they're going to experiment with using it on the equipment and see how many ways they can come up with to get on the equipment by pulling on. Once they are on, they should push to get off. Tell students that today they will stay at one piece of equipment for the duration of the class so they can experiment all they want.

Warm-Up

1. Students begin to walk, accelerating to a straight run.
2. When at stationary equipment or a wall, push off to change direction.
3. Slow down to a walk.
4. Walk to whomever their eyes meet. Grab hands, holding tight but pulling away while continuing to move. Let go slowly and move toward the next person whose eyes they meet.
5. This time connect at the elbow, hold tight, and pull away but keep moving. Let go slowly and move on.

Lesson Sequence

1. Have students set up their stations.
2. Allow them to go to any station they want, as long as it's not crowded.
3. While they work on their own, suggest other ways to approach this task:
   - Use different parts of their body to hold with.
   - Use different parts to push with.
   - Approach from different angles—backward, sideways, or upside down.
4. Pick a few students who solved the problem in a unique way and have them demonstrate their solution to pulling to get on and pushing to get off.

Review and Stretching

1. As students stretch, ask the following:
   - Why do you think I chose these routines?
   - Were these the qualities you saw?
     - Creativity
     - Pulling and pushing
     - Full extension during movement
     - Control of weight
   - Did any of the demonstrations include all of these factors?
2. Put mats away.

Sudden and Sustained Movement (Floor)

Facilities

Clean floor

Materials

One mat per student

Performance Goals

Students will do the following:

- Spend at least 5 minutes in the specified warm-up.
- Spend most of the class moving.
- Show the difference between sudden and sustained movement.
- Collaborate by constructively critiquing each other's performance.

Cognitive Goals

Students will learn the following:

- What sustained movement means and how to do it
- What sudden movement is

Lesson Safety

- Keep the floor empty of equipment and obstructions during the warm-up.
- Provide mat space for students to work all at the same time but independently.

Motivation

Rather than continuing to experiment with new movement, this lesson will take the floor routine from the last lesson—the push–pull lesson—and repeat the routine. This time, however, they will concentrate on maximizing or minimizing the time it takes to complete each phase of the routine so that the movement alternates between sudden and sustained.

Warm-Up

1. Students walk normally, as they do every day.
2. Now, have them sustain each step, gradually transfering their weight from the heel of the foot to the ball.
3. As they sustain walking, ask them to think about their normal arm swing and sustain that, too.
4. When they hear the whistle, they run at top speed. When they hear it again, they sustain their run, making each running step take as long as possible without making it a walk.
5. This time, run. When they hear a whistle, they collapse instantly. Get up to continue so each muscle unfolds gradually. Once up, begin again.
6. Can they stop instantly from a top-speed run? Try.

Lesson Sequence

1. Once students have a mat, they run through their push–pull routine the way it was done previously.
2. Repeat the routine in an effort to sustain it throughout. Try it again.
3. Repeat the routine, trying to make all the movement sudden. Try it again.
4. Thinking about what part was too difficult to do with sustained movement, try doing that section with sudden movement. Practice the routine a few times through, making all movement either sudden or sustained.
5. Students get someone to watch and critique each other's routine, paying attention not just to the speed but the flow, extension, and control of weight transfer.

6. They return to their space, and using the suggestions, practice the routine until it is performance quality.

7. Spend the remainder of class time watching the performances. Have the class choose the outstanding routines to see again.

Review and Stretching

1. As students stretch, ask the following:
   - Does sustained movement require more strength than sudden movement? Why?
   - Are there some moves that simply cannot be sustained? Why?
   - Did forcing a change in rhythm make your movement better? Worse?
2. Put mats away.

Sudden and Sustained Movement (Apparatus)

Facilities

Clean floor

Materials

Use the same setup as in previous lessons, with one apparatus station for every four to six students.

Performance Goals

Students will do the following:
- Set up their stations and sit when done.
- Spend at least 5 minutes in a gross-motor warm-up.
- Spend most of the class moving.
- Concentrate on speeding up or slowing down normal movement.

Cognitive Goal

Students will learn that speeding up or slowing certain movements makes them easier to perform.

Lesson Safety

- Apparatus should be arranged to allow safe traffic flow.
- Mats should cover the landing area around the equipment without overlapping or gaps.
- Students are to stay in their area and not obstruct anyone's mount or dismount.
- Encourage students to call for help if trying something new and challenging.

Motivation

Taking what was learned last lesson onto the equipment, today's goal will be to arrive on the equipment suddenly, sustain motion while on in order to arrive in and out of a stretch, and then dismount quickly.

Warm-Up

1. Students jog and as they wish, suddenly go at top speed and then suddenly change their pace until each running step is sustained.

2. Walk and as they wish, jump, land, and suddenly begin to run at top speed. Jump and melt, getting up with sustained motion and beginning to walk.

Lesson Sequence

1. Have students set up their stations.
2. Have them choose a station that is not crowded.
3. Allow students about 10 minutes to decide on their sequence.
4. Once they have arrived at a sequence of moves, encourage them to smooth out the flow, make sure they reach extension, and push the rhythm extremes without losing control. Allow 10 more minutes to perfect the sequence.
5. Have one student at each station demonstrate so that the class can watch.

Review

1. Discuss the best routines and why they were good.
2. Put equipment away. (Leave it up if another class is coming in and run the warm-up around it.)

Twist and Turn (Floor)

Facilities

Clean floor

Materials

One mat per student

Performance Goals

Students will do the following:

*   Spend at least 5 minutes in the specified warm-up.
*   Spend most of the class moving.
*   Explore methods of changing direction while moving.

Cognitive Goals

Students will learn the following:

*   What twisting is (one part rotates, followed by the other)
*   What turning is (entire body rotates around)

Lesson Safety

*   Keep the floor empty of equipment and obstructions during the warm-up.
*   Provide mat space for students to work all at the same time but independently.

Motivation

Explain to students that they are reaching the end of the unit. They have explored stretching, curling, rolling, bridging, arching, inversion, sudden movement, sustained movement, pushing, pulling, taking weight, and now twisting and turning in order to change direction. They tried to extend their body in space and control the transfer of weight so their movement was controlled and flowed, and now they are at the end. It is time to take everything they've learned and put it together for their final sequence of moves done the very best they can. Here is their last floor-work assignment: Make a routine that has six changes. It should have three stretched balances and include at least one twist and one turn.

Warm-Up

1. Students run, jump, and turn in the air, and continue in the direction they face when they land.
2. Run, jump, and twist in the air, letting the arms lead the body's rotation.
3. Turn one-quarter, half, three-quarters, and full turn. Can they do more than a full turn?
4. What parts of the body can lead the twist? Try a leg, head, knees, and so on. Experiment.

Lesson Sequence

1. Allow students to get their mats and space and get to work.
2. Walk the room, occasionally reminding them to make sure they have their movement sequence before they can work on improving the quality of their performance.
3. As they work, remind them that they need the following:
   - Six distinct moves
   - A definite twist
   - A definite turn
   - Well-extended balance positions
   - Extending while moving wherever possible
   - Flowing movements
4. Begin the grading process for those who are ready.

Educational Gymnastics
ADVANCED
LESSON 14

Performance Assessment

Facilities

Clean floor

Materials

Use the same setup as in previous lessons, with one apparatus station for every four to six students.

Performance Goals

Students will do the following:

- Spend at least 5 minutes in a gross-motor warm-up.
- Spend most of the class moving.
- Experiment with methods of getting on or off equipment in directions different than the one they face.

Cognitive Goal

Students will learn how the body changes directions.

Lesson Safety

- Apparatus should be arranged to allow safe traffic flow.
- Mats should cover the landing area around the equipment without overlapping or gaps.
- Students are to stay in their area and not obstruct anyone's mount or dismount.
- Encourage students to call for help if trying something new and challenging.

Motivation

Tell students that as they finish being graded on the floor routine, they can use the equipment to explore how to use the twist while on the equipment.

Warm-Up

1. Walk, prance, jog, run, skip, and hop.
2. Have students find a space to practice the floor routine they worked on last class for a grade.

Lesson Sequence

1. Have some stations set up, leaving area for floor-work practice and grading.
2. Allow students who have been graded to work on the equipment.

Review

Put away equipment. (Leave it up if another class is coming in and run the warm-up around it.)

Advanced Educational Gymnastics Skills Rubric

Name _____ Date _____

Teacher _____ Class _____

	0	1	2	3
Level of activity	Does not move.	Makes minimum effort to move.	Movement is limited and not on task.	Rehearses until told to stop.
Collaboration	Does not relate to others.	Self-engaged and self-indulgent. During partner or group activities, wants every decision to go his or her way even if this results in movements their partner cannot do.	Willingly partners with other students.	Adapts to partner's abilities.
Form in space	Does not participate.	Extends appendages when stationary.	Extends appendages while moving and stationary.	Extends through the neck, back, fingers, and toes at all times.
Weight	Does not participate.	Moves along the ground without sound.	Returns to the ground without sound.	Changes direction and altitude without losing control.
Time	Does not participate.	Changes the tempo of a move.	Builds up or builds down speed.	Synchronizes movement with one or more people.
Flow	Does not move.	Puts together a sequence of moves.	Uses connecting moves to move from one pose to another.	Makes a movement sequence look like one sentence.

From Isobel Kleinman, 2009, *Complete Physical Education Plans for Grades 5 to 12, Second Edition* (Champaign, IL: Human Kinetics).

Advanced Educational Gymnastics Quiz

Name _____   Date _____

Teacher _____   Class _____

True or False

Read each statement carefully. If the statement is true, write a *T* in the column to the left. If the statement is false, write an *F*. If using a grid sheet, blacken in the appropriate column for each question, making sure to use the correctly numbered line for each question and its answer.

_____ 1. The reason that people of all body types, large and small, can land without a sound is because on impact they allow their body to absorb their weight.

_____ 2. If two people do an asymmetrical routine at the same time, they no longer look asymmetrical.

_____ 3. When the center of gravity moves to the right of the base of support, movement will go to the left.

_____ 4. Acceleration, deceleration, sustained movement, sudden movement, and simultaneous movement all fit in the category of controlling time.

_____ 5. When you invert, you keep your head above most of your body parts.

_____ 6. Arching makes the body look like a *V*, whereas bending makes it look like a *C*.

_____ 7. If you change direction by moving your head first, you will be twisting.

_____ 8. A five-part routine with extra steps between each part flows better than a routine where one move seems to go directly into the next.

_____ 9. Only the larger of a pair of performers can take the weight of her partner.

_____ 10. The neck is one of the parts that performers forget about when they are asked to stretch.

   From Isobel Kleinman, 2009, *Complete Physical Education Plans for Grades 5 to 12, Second Edition* (Champaign, IL: Human Kinetics).

Advanced Educational Gymnastics Answer Key

True or False

1. T
2. T
3. F—Moving the center of gravity to the right of the base of support will cause movement to go to the right.
4. T
5. F—When you invert, your head will be below most of your body parts.
6. F—Arching forms a *c* and bending forms a *v*.
7. T
8. F—To create a routine with good flow, each move should go directly into the next.
9. F—You don't have to be strong to support someone bigger.
10. T

PART IV

Team Sports Units

Basketball

Chapter Overview

1. Teach a short history of basketball and its evolution.
2. The body mechanics of each skill are introduced, practiced, and used in some type of game situation:
   - Pass—chest, bounce, one arm
   - Catch
   - Dribble—right hand, left hand, strategy
   - Shot—inside (layup), outside (jumper)
3. Rules are taught in relationship to the skill being taught.
   - Illegal dribble—discontinued dribble, traveling, palming
   - What happens if the ball goes outside the boundaries and how to put it back in
   - What happens during a tie ball or if the feet keep moving with the ball in hand
   - Scoring
   - Three-second rule
   - Fouls when covering driving to the basket or defending against the opposition
4. Teach court positions—center, guard, and forward.
5. Before games, teach guarding and the rules against blocking and holding.
6. Teach defensive strategies—shifting, boxing out, double-teaming, pressing.
7. Teach systems of defense—zone (2-1-2, 1-3-1, 2-2-1) or person-to-person.
8. During tournament play, lessons focus on offensive strategies and skills—cutting or making a quick change of direction, passing and going, pivots and turns, feint screens, and picks.
9. As students progress, skills are combined:
   - Catching—run to catch, run to catch and shoot, turn to catch.
   - Jumping—turn to jump and shoot, jump to shoot.
10. Each lesson includes some kind of contest to excite, motivate, and emphasize the point of the lesson.

Basketball Study Sheet

Fun Facts

- The highest single scorer, Wilt Chamberlain, scored 100 points in one game in 1962.
- Dr. James Naismith of Springfield College, Massachusetts, created the game of basketball in 1891.
- The first record of a college basketball team was that of Geneva College, who played and defeated a YMCA team in Beaver Falls, Pennsylvania, in 1893.
- In the first intercollegiate game, on February 9, 1895, the Minnesota State School of Agriculture defeated Hamline College by a score of 9 to 3.
- The first intercollegiate game using the five-player format occurred in Iowa City on January 18, 1896, when the University of Chicago defeated the University of Iowa, 15 to 12.

Skills

- Dribble—Push the ball to the ground and slightly in front in order to move forward to meet it again (at waist height).
- Shooting:
    - Layup—Reach up toward the backboard with the ball and release it so it banks off the backboard and into the basket
    - Outside shot—A shooter shoots from anywhere outside the basketball key while focusing and following through to the back of the rim.
    - Foul shot—Take a free shot unhindered at the top of the key.
    - Jump shot—Release the ball in the air.
- Defending—Maintain a space between the ball carrier and the basket with the intention of catching a pass, blocking a shot, or causing the ball carrier to make an error.
- Rebounding—Get into the key before the shot is taken, jump with arms stretched as high as possible, and catch the ball coming off the rim or backboard.
- Screen—Stand between a teammate and an opposing defender.
- Pick—An offensive player stops to block a defender from following the ball carrier.

Rules

- Boundaries—Balls landing on the lines are out of bounds.
- Scoring—A basket made during play is worth 2 or 3 points; foul shots are worth 1 point.
- Violations:
    - Traveling (taking more than two steps with the ball in hand)
    - Palming (carrying the ball on the dribble)
    - Double or discontinued dribble (continuing the dribble after placing two hands on the ball)
    - Holding the ball more than 5 seconds when closely guarded
    - Taking longer than 5 seconds to throw the ball in from out of bounds
    - Entering the free-throw lane before the ball is released
    - Remaining inside the key for more than 3 seconds (offensive players)
    - Being the last one to touch the ball before it goes out of bounds

»continued

»continued

- Fouls:
  - Charging—Ball carrier contacting an opponent in an established position
  - Blocking—Defender attempting to interrupt the path of the ball carrier
  - Elbowing, hitting, pushing, tripping, or punching
  - Unsportsmanlike conduct
  - Illegal substitution

Positions

- Guards—The guard is considered the team's playmaker. Guards need good dribbling skills, the ability to throw as they run, the selflessness to pass to open teammates, the courage to drive to the basket if the lane to the basket is open, and the insight to know when to take an outside shot. Guards usually position themselves at the top of the key.
- Forwards—The forwards are the shooters of the team. They must get down to either side of the basket before the ball does. Their job is to get open and shoot. If their center is inside the key on the offensive boards, they must either shoot or pass the center the ball. Forwards must position themselves for the rebound if they are not taking the shot.
- Centers—The centers need to be able to get higher than anyone else on their team. They should be prepared to dominate the backboards at either end of the court. They have to be able to sense when someone is about to shoot so they can position themselves inside the key to retrieve a possible rebound. If on the offensive boards, they must rebound and follow up the rebound with a shot.

Defensive Systems

- Person-to-person—Player takes responsibility for covering one opponent, making it difficult for the opponent to get an open shot at the basket. Usually, players do not pick up their person until the ball has reached the opposite side of the court. Sticking with a player for the full court is called a *full-court press*.
- Zone 2-1-2—In this system, defenders create a large box around the basketball key and put their center in the center. As opponents shift the ball from side to side, so should the box. Players are responsible for their area of the box. When offensive players come into it, the defenders try to block their shots or intercept their passes. When the players leave, the defenders let them go, understanding that someone else on their team will assume responsibility for covering them in other areas.

From Isobel Kleinman, 2009, *Complete Physical Education Plans for Grades 5 to 12, Second Edition* (Champaign, IL: Human Kinetics).

Basketball Extension Project

Name _____ Date _____

Teacher _____ Class _____

What equipment do you need to play basketball on your own?

Is there a basketball team at school? Who is the coach?

Is there an intramural basketball program? Who is in charge?

Where can you participate in basketball outside of school?

Do you have friends who would join you? List their names.

What are the health benefits of participating in a basketball program?

From Isobel Kleinman, 2009, *Complete Physical Education Plans for Grades 5 to 12, Second Edition* (Champaign, IL: Human Kinetics).

Basketball Student Portfolio Checklist

Name _____ Date _____

Teacher _____ Class _____

_____ Can pass and catch the ball.

_____ Can dribble with the dominant hand.

_____ Can dribble with the nondominant hand.

_____ Can shoot and score from inside the basketball key.

_____ Can shoot outside shots and hit the rim or backboard.

_____ Can play a game while following the rules of basketball.

_____ Can jump to catch and rebound.

_____ Can pass from the dribble without having to stop first.

_____ Can guard an opponent of equal ability.

_____ Knows common violations and the procedure for returning ball to play.

_____ Knows what causes fouls to be called and their penalties and procedures.

_____ Has learned to pass and go.

_____ Understands how a screen or pick is used.

_____ Knows the responsibilities of guards, forwards, and centers.

_____ Exhibits responsibility and good sportsmanship during competition.

From Isobel Kleinman, 2009, *Complete Physical Education Plans for Grades 5 to 12, Second Edition* (Champaign, IL: Human Kinetics).

Basketball Learning Experience Outline

Contents and Procedure

1. Give a short history of basketball and its evolution.
2. Present one skill at a time, citing applicable rules as students practice.
   a. Passing and catching
      - Skills: chest pass, bounce pass, one-arm pass
      - Relevant rules: balls going out of bounds, tie balls, moving the feet with the ball in hand
   b. Dribbling
      - Skills: using dominant hand, using nondominant hand
      - Strategy: slowing the game, taking advantage of a pathway
      - Relevant rules: illegal and discontinued dribbles, traveling, palming
   c. Shooting
      - Skills: layup, outside shot, jump shot, driving to the basket
      - Relevant rules: scoring, 3-second rule

     d. Rebounding
- Skills: jumping to catch, positioning, boxing out
- Relevant rules: loose-ball fouls, 3-second rule

     e. Defense
- Skills: positioning, backpedaling, anticipation
- Relevant rules: blocking, pushing, holding

     f. Game
- Positions and their responsibilities
- Strategies
- Fouls and violation rules not already covered

3. As students progress, combine skills.

     a. Catching: run to catch, run to catch and shoot, turn to catch

     b. Jumping: turn to jump and shoot, jump to shoot

4. Once teams are made, teach court positions.

     a. Center

     b. Guard

     c. Forward

5. When entering competition, teach defensive skills.

     a. Shifting

     b. Boxing out

     c. Double-teaming

     d. Pressing

6. Once teams are formed, teach a system of defense.

     a. Zone (2-1-2, 1-3-1, 2-2-1)

     b. Person-to-person

7. With tournaments under way, focus on offensive strategies.

     a. Cutting and quick change of direction

     b. Pass and go

     c. Pivots and turns

     d. Feint screens

     e. Picks

Teaching Tips

- Lessons break down the skills, rules, and strategies as they are introduced. If you are using the intermediate or advanced units and have questions about skills, rules, strategies, and drills that are not fully explained in the later units, check earlier units to see how the material was introduced.

- Lessons might be too ambitious for the time allotted and the experience of the class. If so, repeat them before introducing new material. It is more important that students have plenty of repetition, master the basics, and digest the concepts than it is that they learn skills that they are not ready for. If choosing not to continue using the lessons as they unfold, make sure to provide plenty of game-playing opportunities so students use their skills in context and continue to enjoy the learning and practicing experience.

- Until 90% of the class is ready to move on, do not create competitive pressure.

- Students come with a wide range of abilities, with many feeling they are no match for classmates with previous basketball experience. Size differences in the close quarters of a basketball court can be intimidating. Effort should be made to spot students who have unrealistic goals and encourage them to set goals they can reach. It goes without saying that teachers must be vigilant to make sure everyone has equal playing time.

- The nonaggressive and nonathletic players must not be overrun by others on the team. To make sure that interpersonal factors elicit sustainable student growth for all, follow these guidelines:
  - Teach students that everyone can score and under what circumstances.
  - Once the game starts, don't allow the dribble until everyone gets the idea of passing to the open person.
  - Coach the one who assumes point-guard responsibilities that her role is to set up the team, not just herself.
  - Make sure that personal fouls are called.
- Every effort should be made for students to be involved in play every day.
  - Every student should have a team and every team a court to play on.
  - If substitution is necessary because of large classes, make a rule that no one is out more than 5 minutes, until everyone is out 5 minutes.
- Develop a tournament that encourages skills growth, teamwork, and excitement.
- Everyone likes to shoot a basketball, but surprisingly, not everyone likes to play the game. Too often if students' skills are not up to those of their classmates, they are made to feel bad. This problem can be avoided if teams are divided equally and the more experienced players don't make fools of the less experienced ones. With teacher guidance, students who do not feel quick enough or accurate enough to make a contribution to their team will learn that they can and the students who scorned them will learn to appreciate their teammates' efforts and growth. Showing the class that everyone can score is a good starting point.
- Students with disabilities or problems that exclude them from playing a typical basketball game can be taught aspects of the game that do not lead to contact or compromise their health. If the whole class is disabled, teach basketball skills that provide a sense of participation in basketball but are entirely safe, such as shooting games (e.g., 21 or Around the World) or relays using basketball skills that are modified to the students' needs. There are some forms of basketball where students can team up and safely play on their feet, in wheelchairs, or on scooters. Games that prevent contact, such as six-court basketball, separate opponents yet allow participants to be part of a team and play the game.
- If students needing modified activity remain in regular classes, consider letting them practice their skills during practice time or warm-ups. When games begin, those students can be involved by officiating, calling boundary lines, and keeping score. This will give them a place in the tournament where they will play a valuable role and their safety will not be compromised.
- Students who must temporarily sit out can provide their team with advice by identifying the following:
  - The most consistent scorer
  - The most effective pass the guard has used
  - The person to try to box out
  - The teammate who rushes and forces an outside shot
  - The teammate who passes off when he should shoot
  - The guard who gives the best assists
- After a book is published, rules, skills, and strategies may change. Check Internet sites listed in suggested resources to keep up with the changes.

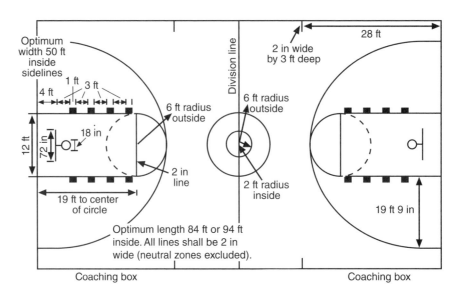

Figure 7.1 Basketball court.

Facilities

Daily lessons stipulate setup if something differs from the setup in figure 7.1. Practice backboards are necessary, and a full basketball court or one half-court is required for every two teams, marked with a basketball key, 3-point shooting zones, and side and end boundary lines.

Materials

- One ball for every two students
- Pinnies
- Whistles for student officials
- Clipboards and pencils for student scorers
- Tournament schedule and team standings
- Blackboard, marker board, or other visual aid

Unit Timeline

The units for beginner, intermediate, and advanced levels include the following:
- 3 to 5 lessons to develop enough skill to enjoy a low-level game
- 1 to 3 lessons to work with new teams in a cooperative learning environment
- 8 to 11 lessons for class round-robin tournament
- 1 lesson for quiz and assessment during a culminating activity

Assessment

Knowing whether the lessons are in tune with the class depends on the observation skills of the teacher. It is not essential to teach all the skills that are planned. Developing essential skills while having the pleasurable experience of learning how they relate to the game is more important than learning something new every day. The students' ability to derive a sense of mastery of a few basic skills is far more important than their feeling unaccomplished at a lot of them. Gauge whether to move on to the next lesson or slow down and give students more time with the previous one, but whatever you decide, students should see the relevance of their skills in terms of how the skills help them enjoy the game.

Each unit has objective tools for assessing student growth.
- Quizzes appear for each skill level.
- A detailed performance rubric concludes the unit for each skill level and general performance rubrics are available in appendix B.

- Students can record their progress by updating the student portfolio checklist at the beginning of the chapter.

Suggested Resources

Coach's Clipboard. 2008. www.coachesclipboard.net/index.html.

Goldstein, S., and D. Brown. 1994. *The basketball coaches bible: A comprehensive and systematic guide to coaching.* Philadelphia: Golden Aura.

Howard, M. 1991. *Basketball basics: Drills, techniques, and strategies for coaches.* Lincolnwood, IL: NTC Contemporary.

International Basketball Federation (FIBA). 2008. www.fiba.com.

Kraus, J., D. Meyer, and J. Meyer. 1999. *Basketball skills and drills.* Champaign, IL: Human Kinetics.

National Collegiate Athletic Association (NCAA). 2008. *Basketball rules.* www.ncaa.org/wps/ncaa?ContentID=804.

Williams, J. 1993. *Youth league basketball: Coaching and playing.* Indianapolis: Masters Publishing.

Women's National Basketball Association (WNBA). 2008. *Official rule book.* www.wnba.com/media/2006_WNBA_OFFICIAL_RULE_BOOK.pdf.

Basketball
BEGINNER
LESSON 1

Passing and Layup Shot

Facilities

Wall with no obstructions and cleared floor space with one backboard for every four students

Materials

- One ball for every two players
- Stopwatch or watch with second hand

Performance Goals

Students will do the following:

- Pass and catch a basketball.
- Perform the layup shot.

Cognitive Goals

Students will learn the following:

- Brief history of basketball and its evolution
- What constitutes a good pass
- The effect spin has on the flight of the ball
- Why layup shots are desirable

Lesson Safety

- Practice drill teams should be separated by a minimum of 6 feet (2 meters).
- Groups need their own backboard.

Motivation

Basketball is an American invention conceived in Springfield, Massachusetts. Though basketball is popular worldwide, U.S. teams have dominated international competition for many years. The games for men and women originally were vastly different. The rules and standards for women restricted players from taking more than two dribbles, playing the full court, and being both an offensive and defensive player. Instead, women played with six players and could either stay on the defensive end or on the offensive end. Sometime in the early 1960s, women were allowed to have one roving guard and one roving forward. Only those two players could cross into the other half of the court. At the time, the writers of the rules rationalized that women were not strong enough to use the same rules as men. Clearly, things have changed and the games for men and women are almost the same. There are still a few differences. Does anyone know what they are? The size of the ball is smaller for women. The time given to take a shot also varies by age and sex.

This lesson will get students started learning the most important thing—how to get the ball in both hands and how to send it where they want it to go.

Warm-Up

1. Leave the balls out and let students shoot when they come into the gym.

2. Lead the class in mimetics (the ball for mimetics is imaginary) for the following:

    a. Chest pass

      • Spread the fingers and make the palms of the hands face each other so the fingers point forward with thumbs in back, and then extend arms out and forward (5 times).

      • Step forward and extend arms (5 times).

      • As if throwing far or fast, step and lean forward on extension (5 times).

      • Reach out to catch a chest pass and bring the ball in (5 times).

    b. Layup shot

      • Spread fingers of the throwing hand, then roll them forward (5 times).

      • Extend the arm up, and at its height, roll the fingers forward (5 times).

      • As if bringing the ball up from waist with two hands, bring the arms up past the face. Extend the throwing arm and roll the fingers forward (5 times).

      • Step-hop forward on the opposite foot, bringing both arms up. On the hop, the shooting arm extends, reaching as high to the hoop as possible. At the height, let the ball roll off the fingers (5 times).

Lesson Sequence

1. Teach and demonstrate the chest pass to a desired target.

    a. Students pass back and forth with a partner 6 feet (2 meters) away (5 times).

    b. Increase the distance between partners until they are comfortable at 12 feet (3.5 meters).

    c. When it looks as if students are passing easily, have a contest; for example, see who can pass and catch 10 passes first.

2. Teach the bounce pass and discuss the following.

    • Advantages and disadvantages of bounce pass

    • Distance from target the pass should hit the floor

    • Importance of follow-through for a solid pass

3. Demonstrate how spin affects the flight and speed of the ball.

    a. Students aim for a spot on the wall and throw the ball there.

    b. See what happens when they throw it hard.

    c. See what happens when they let it come off their fingertips.

4. Teach the layup shot (see figure 7.2) and how many points a successful shot is worth.

    a. Review step-hop footwork and arm position as learned in warm-up.

    b. Demonstrate where the ball should touch backboard.

c. Practice shooting layups.

- After students have shot three balls in, rotate. Allow three turns.
- In 10-second turns, see how many shots each student can drop in.
- Ask for the highest score at each basket.
- Have highest scorer demonstrate shooting technique.
- Repeat trials.

d. Have a layup contest and see who can score the most baskets in 15 seconds.

Review and Stretching

Have students proceed with their stretching routine as you ask the following questions:

- When you throw a pass, where is the best place for your teammate to catch it?
- Why do you want passes that are quick and short?
- At what point in your throwing motion is spin imparted?
- Will a ball thrown with underspin go farther than one thrown without it?
- Will a ball thrown without underspin bounce back off the backboard or drop down into the basketball hoop?
- How do you get underspin on the ball?

Assessment

Observe progress to determine what in the lesson needs repetition.

Figure 7.2 Right-hand layup.

Dribble

Facilities

Cleared floor space with one backboard for every four students

Materials

- One ball for every two players
- Stopwatch or watch with second hand

Performance Goals

Students will do the following:

- Dribble.
- Follow up the dribble with a pass.

Cognitive Goals

Students will learn the following:

- What constitutes a good dribble and its uses
- Why it is important not to look at the ball when dribbling
  - They can see the open person and pass on the move.
  - They can see the basket on approach and shoot from the dribble.

Lesson Safety

- Practice teams should be separated by a minimum of 6 feet (2 meters).
- Groups need their own backboard.
- Before having students do the dribble maze, make sure they have basic control of their dribble, and warn them that looking where they are going is more important than getting there quickly.

Motivation

It's time to learn why the dribble is used in a basketball game and how to do it effectively. Before starting, ask students which is faster, a game that moves the ball ahead by passing it to someone down the court or by having someone dribble it down the court. The challenge in this lesson is learning to dribble so they are not blind to what is happening around them. If dribbling players can see the court because they don't have to stare at the ball, they'll see teammates they can pass to, they'll sense when they are close enough to shoot and score, and they'll be better players.

Warm-Up

1. Leave basketballs out so students practice basketball skills as they arrive.
2. Lead mimetics for the chest pass and layup shot.
3. Use mimetics to introduce the dribble.
   - Spread fingers of the dominant hand and push down from waist height.
   - Make sure the hand is pushing slightly in front of the body.
   - Start to jog, pushing down in front each time the right foot hits the ground.

Lesson Sequence

1. Demonstrate the dribble.
2. Practice the dribble first by walking straight ahead.
   a. Remind students to see the ball coming back from the floor to waist height.
   b. Increase the pace, reminding students that the ball returns at waist height.
   c. Challenge them to take their eyes off the ball to look where they're going.
   d. Create obstacles so they have to see where they are going.
   e. Gradually change the drill until it becomes the dribble maze (see figure 7.3).
      - Begin with students going in the same direction.
      - Split the lines into shuttle formation and give each side of the line a ball. Students will be dribbling from two different directions at the same time so that it will be necessary to look where they are going instead of at the ball. Warn them to proceed with care. Explain that if they need to stop to avoid a collision, they should stop their feet but keep dribbling to avoid a discontinued dribble. (This drill works wonders to teach students to keep their eye off the ball, to eliminate the discontinued dribble, and to increase stamina.)
      - Send three or four of the best ball handlers to either side of the gym. Have them dribble back and forth across the gym so they are moving perpendicular to the rest of the students, who are dribbling.

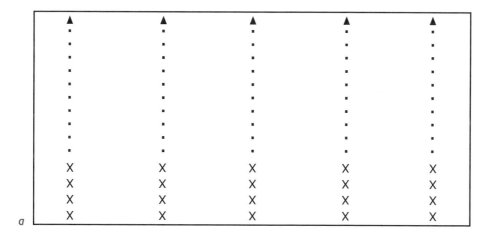

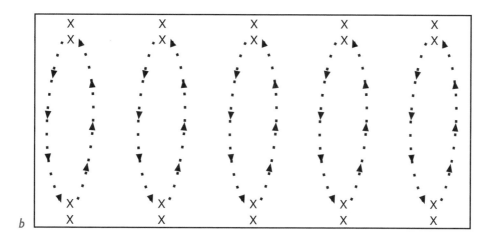

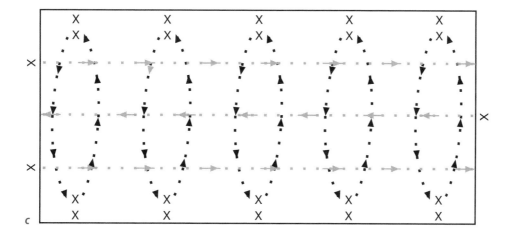

Figure 7.3 Progression of the dribble maze.

271

3. Have students use their nondominant hand to dribble.
4. Combine the dribble with throwing skills.
    a. Students dribble to zone, take two steps, and pass.
    b. Students dribble to basket, take two steps, and shoot.
5. Set up contests, using the dribble before each pass or shot.

Review and Stretching

Get students accustomed to doing their stretching routine as you review:

- Where should your hand meet the ball?
- What should your eyes be looking at?
- Is it better to have a stiff or loose wrist when you dribble?
- Should the ball be pushed out to the side or in front? Why?
- Can you explain why and when the dribble should be used in a game?

Assessment

Observe students as they dribble to determine the best ways to improve.

Layup Approach

Facilities

Cleared floor space with one backboard for every four students

Materials

- One ball for every two players
- Stopwatch or watch with second hand

Performance Goals

Students will do the following:

- Dribble and shoot.
- Shoot from outside the basketball key.

Cognitive Goals

Students will learn the following:

- More dribbling violations (palming, traveling, discontinued dribble)
- What the basketball key is
- What an outside shot is

Lesson Safety

- Each practice group should have its own backboard.
- Lanes to the basket should not conflict with other groups.

Motivation

Sometimes players are so excited to have the ball, all they do is dribble. Eventually they lose the ball before anyone could take a shot. Remind students that they cannot win unless they can score one more point than the other team. Dribbling has a purpose. If the person doing the dribbling has a clear path to the basket, she should take it and shoot. The class will learn to associate the use of the dribble for its primary goal—getting the ball closer to the basket to score.

Warm-Up

1. Leave the balls out and let students practice basketball skills when they come into the gym.
2. Use mimetics to introduce the footwork for the layup approach.
   - Have students hop as if to catch and step-hop, extending the shooting arm to shoot (10 times).
   - Concentrate on which foot catches (foot on side of shooting arm) and repeat the hop to catch and step-hop to shoot (10 times).
   - Repeat the entire sequence, asking students to reach up and imagine the ball rolling off their fingers to the backboard.

Lesson Sequence

1. Divide students by the number of backboards so each group is equal.
   - Practice just the shot from inside the key at 10-second intervals.
   - Demonstrate the layup with a hop to catch and step-hop to shoot from just in front of the foul line.
   - Ask students to do the same, going through their lines five times.
2. Discuss dribbling violations and how to recognize them.
   - Traveling—moving feet without dribbling or unplanting the established foot while still in possession of the ball
   - Discontinued dribble—dribbling, putting two hands on the ball, and then dribbling again
   - Palming—putting hand under the ball and carrying it while dribbling
3. Have groups line up 50 feet (15 meters) from their backboard so they are not in the way of another group coming in to shoot at their backboard or passing to get to their backboard (see figure 7.4).

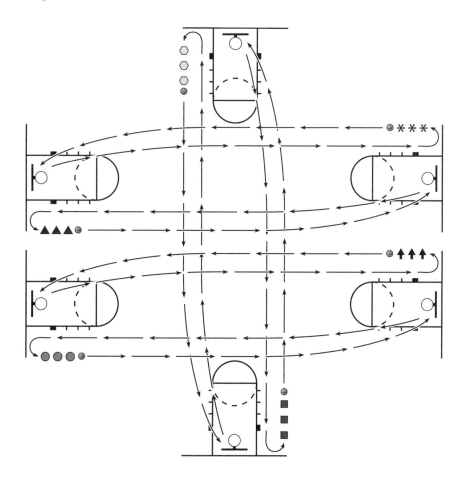

Figure 7.4 Setting up the layup activity.

Students must wait their turn behind a designated area so as not to interfere with the approaching ball carrier coming to take a shot from another group.

- Students dribble to the basket and shoot. They do not come back until they sink a shot.
- Dribble to the basket and shoot. If it does not go in, dribble to the next basket and try again, and so on.
- Dribble to the basket and take one shot. If it goes in, the student's team scores 2 points. In or not, the shooter comes back and hands the ball to the next person. The lines keep going until the whistle blows.

The idea is to see which group scores the most points in the time allotted. This is exciting for students, who will want more chances to get higher scores. Give those chances to them. What they are learning during this time is that everyone can score in the right environment, not just the stars.

Review and Stretching

Have students proceed with their stretching routine as you ask if they can explain the following violations:

- Palming
- Traveling
- Discontinued dribble

Basketball
BEGINNER
LESSON 4

Outside Shot

Facilities

Cleared floor space with one backboard for every four students

Materials

One ball for every two players

Performance Goals

Students will do the following:

- Shoot from outside the key.
- Improve their layup shot.

Cognitive Goal

Students will learn to aim and follow through while shooting outside shots.

Lesson Safety

- Each practice group should have its own backboard.
- Lanes to the basket should not conflict with other groups.

Motivation

If all players knew that the only shot the offense would take was from the easiest spot, what would they do? They would stay inside the basketball key so a shooter could never get close enough to have an unguarded shot. How can the offense team keep them honest and make them cover more than just the inside of the basketball key? The offense can make them need to guard people outside the key. That means learning to score from farther away. Shooters can find a special place on the court, an outside place to shoot from where they can reach the basket easily and have enough control to sometimes score.

Warm-Up

1. Leave the balls out and let students practice dribbling and shooting when they come into the gym.
2. Lead students through mimetics for the layup approach.
   - Bring hands to the eyes, extend shooting arm, and roll fingers forward (10 times).
   - Hop to catch, step-hop toward basket, lift off, and lay it in (10 times).
   - Right-handed shooter: Hop-to-catch on right foot, step-hop, and shoot off left foot (10 times). (Reverse for left-handed shooter.)
3. Lead students through mimetics for the outside shot using one hand.
   - Point the shooting side of the body toward the basket, bring both arms up, extend the arm, and roll the wrist forward so the fingers finish pointing at the target (10 times).
   - Jump while extending the shooting arm (10 times).
   - Jump, and when in the air, extend the shooting arm (10 times).

Lesson Sequence

1. Teach and demonstrate the outside shot, covering these points:
   - Point the shooting side of the body toward the basket.
   - As in the layup, bring the arm up, guiding the ball in both hands.
   - Focus on the back of the rim of the basket.
   - As the arm reaches extension, roll the wrist forward so the ball rolls off the fingers and the fingers finish pointing to the target.
2. Allow every ball available to be used for practicing the outside shot the way basketball teams do. Have someone behind the backboard who will return the balls to shooters—no waiting turns, just getting the ball and shooting. Do not continue the lesson until everyone has taken at least 20 shots.
3. Make the number of groups equal to the number of backboards.
   a. As in the previous lesson, line up 50 feet (15 meters) from the backboard.
   b. Do the dribble-to-layup drill that they worked on last time, seeing if they can better their scoring record.
4. Do the same drill, but this time have students dribble to their outside shot position, jump, and shoot when they get there.
   - Allow several trials.
   - Vary by rebounding a missed shot and taking a layup.
5. Once groups are comfortable with the sequence, have them keep a team score for the time allotted.

Review and Stretching

As students stretch, ask the following:

- Who found that your outside shot dropped in when you dribbled, looked, and released? Were you surprised? Did it happen again?
- How many people scored one basket? Two? Three?
- How many points is each shot?
- Did anyone get in your way? Next class someone will!

Defense

Facilities

Cleared floor space with one backboard for every four students

Materials

- One ball for every two players
- Pinnies

Performance Goals

Students will do the following:

- Improve shooting.
- Learn guarding techniques.

Cognitive Goals

Students will learn the following:

- Why and how to deny opponents an easy shot
- Violations and fouls that can occur with a defense in place

Lesson Safety

- Each practice group should have its own backboard.
- Lanes to the basket should not conflict with other groups.

Motivation

If players could shoot during games as well as they do in practice, the typical game score would be 80 points in one class. However, that type of score is unusual. Does anyone know why? Usually someone is there to try to stop the shooter from being successful. The goal of that person is not to prevent opponents from taking a shot; it is to make them take a difficult shot so they miss and to be ready to get the ball when they do.

Warm-Up

1. Leave the balls out and let students practice basketball skills when they come into the gym.
2. Do drill footwork: backpedaling, side to side, jumping up and coming straight down

Lesson Sequence

1. Teach and demonstrate what it takes to guard an opponent successfully.
   - Body position—Maintain a wide stance with weight over the balls of the feet, ready to move, square to opponent, and arms spread to block or intercept passes and close down passing lanes.
   - Focus—If opponent has the ball, concentrate on the ball in order to move arms level with it.
   - Footwork—Maintain a 2- to 3-foot (.5- to 1-meter) margin of safety between ball carrier and the defender. Move between the opponent and his objective, the basket.
2. Teach students to move between an opponent and the basket.
   - Try without the ball.
   - Try with the ball.
3. Teach typical violations and fouls that can occur when guarded.
   - Violations from holding the ball more than 5 seconds when closely guarded
   - Traveling when sliding the pivot foot
   - Fouls from contacting the ball carrier instead of the ball

4. Play keep-away—send two teams (three to five players each) to a backboard.
   - Assign pinnies to the shooters; the others are defenders.
   - Shooters get 2 minutes to score as many points as possible.
   - If nonshooters get the ball, they should use up time without shooting. After 2 minutes, switch and allow new shooters 2 minutes. Who scored most on offense?
   - Repeat the game, providing feedback and coaching based on how play went before. Give teams equal time on offense.

Review and Stretching

As students stretch, ask the following:

- Were you as successful shooting today as the last time? Why?
- During the game, did you feel pushed or held? Is that legal?
- Discuss that personal fouls, like pushing and holding, are penalized differently than violations of the rules and that if a team commits repeated fouls, the team they fouled gets not only the ball but free throws from the foul line.
- Can you hold on to a ball until someone gets open?
- Once you have the ball in both hands, can you start running with it?

Half-Court Basketball

Facilities

One marked half-court game playing area that includes the following:

- Designated basketball key
- Three-point shooting range
- Sidelines and end lines
- Backboard that is not flush with the wall

Materials

- Basketballs for practice (ideally one per student)
- Game balls
- Pinnies

Performance Goal

Students will play a game.

Cognitive Goal

Students will learn the rules for a half-court game (or full court if class has that option).

Lesson Safety

- Each practice group should have its own backboard.
- Lanes to the basket should not conflict with other groups.

Motivation

It's time to play, but first, students need to learn the ground rules for the class game.

Warm-Up

1. Leave the balls out and let students practice basketball skills when they come into the gym.
2. Do footwork drills for backpedaling, moving side to side, and jumping and coming straight down. These drills will make students better prepared to play defense.

3. Lead mimetics.
   - Jump to rebound or catch, palms facing each other and arms going up (10 times).
   - Layup approach (10 times).
   - Jump with the outside shot motion (10 times).

Lesson Sequence

1. Teach half-court basketball rules.
   - Discuss boundaries.
   - Explain when teams must bring the ball back, where, and why.
   - To simulate a full-court game, when opponents get the ball, they must bring it beyond the top of the key before shooting.
   - After violations, the opposite team gets to take the ball out but must throw it in within 5 seconds.
2. Assign equally skilled teams to courts to play each other, and tell the teams with the pinnies that they get the ball first.
3. Play games, but stop the class halfway through to answer questions or to share a class problem and its solution.

Review and Stretching

As students stretch, ask the following:
- Why do you have to bring the ball back in half-court basketball?
- What basketball skill should be used least when near the basket you shoot for (dribble)? Why?

Teacher Homework

Make up teams so that each is equal, accounting for skill, sex, height, and speed.

Creating Teams

	Team 1	Team 2	Team 3	Team 4
Rebounder (tall)				
Outside shooter				
Ball handler				
Fast				
5th player				

From Isobel Kleinman, 2009, *Complete Physical Education Plans for Grades 5 to 12, Second Edition* (Champaign, IL: Human Kinetics).

Tournament Teams

Facilities

Marked half-court playing areas

Materials

- Basketballs for practice
- Game balls
- Pinnies

Performance Goal

Students will play games.

Cognitive Goal

Students will learn to play with their teams.

Lesson Safety

- Each practice group should have its own backboard.
- Lanes to the basket should not conflict with other groups.

Motivation

Tell students that your homework was making up teams that are as even as possible. Every team has someone tall. Every team has someone who dribbles fairly well. Every team has a good shooter or two or three—teams might not think so now, but they do. So, before the tournament starts, teams have work to do. They have to learn the skills each member has and how to take advantage of them. Once teams are announced, the practice games can get under way. But today, until told otherwise, they should play a half-court game without using the dribble.

Warm-Up

1. Leave the balls out and let students practice basketball skills when they come into the gym.
2. Do footwork drills for backpedaling, side to side, and jumping and coming straight down.
3. Do mimetics for jumping to catch, layup approach, and shooting motion.

Lesson Sequence

1. Announce teams and assign courts.
2. Go over tournament procedure.
   - The team getting the ball must wear pinnies.
   - A no-dribble game means that players can't get a ball and keep it after moving the first foot they planted or else they will be traveling.
3. Begin a no-dribble game. The no-dribbling game forces players to look at their teammates in order to move the ball legally. It prevents ball handlers from hogging the ball. It prevents useless dribbling. It enables the reticent player to feel a part of the team as soon as the second pass comes to her. And it gets the kids to move once they get rid of the ball. In short, the no-dribble game requires more involvement of every team member and more court movement.
4. Go from court to court, officiating or coaching.

Review and Stretching

1. Have teams pick a captain and cocaptain and record their names.
2. As students stretch, ask the following:
   - Does the dribble slow down a game or speed it up?
   - Did the game feel faster?
   - If you want to shoot a layup but can't dribble, what must you do after passing the ball? (Go to the basket and hope for a pass.)
   - Raise your hand if you got a pass when you were inside the basketball key.
   - Raise your hand if you shot for a basket. Did you score?
   - Did anyone block a shot?

Teacher Homework

Make and post game schedule and tournament chart (see examples in appendix A).

Basketball
BEGINNER
LESSON 8

Pass and Go

Facilities

Marked half-court playing areas

Materials

- Basketballs for practice
- Game balls
- Pinnies
- Team chart with captains' names, team numbers, and the record to date
- Game schedule

Performance Goals

Students will do the following:

- Learn the pass-and-go strategy.
- Play games while improving their skills.

Cognitive Goals

Students will learn the following:

- How to work as a team unit
- What being evasive means and why it is important

Lesson Safety

As students begin to gather as a team unit, arrange activities so that each person on the team has a job and that no single player can dominate the ball, leave bad feelings, or undermine a teammate's sense of self. React immediately to stop belittling by refocusing the goals each team should be working toward. If that doesn't work, discipline is in order.

Motivation

When 10 people are going to the same space around the basket, it is difficult to get open and even more difficult to score. Before starting the tournament, work on an evasive skill that makes opponents watch the ball, not the ball carrier, allowing the player to slip away and get open. It's a simple trick called *pass and go,* and it makes most people want to look at the ball that got passed, not the player who just passed it. If a ball carrier is covered and passes the ball, he momentarily loses his guard's attention and has a perfect moment to cut for an open space so he can receive the ball again and try to score.

Warm-Up

Leave the balls out and let students practice basketball skills when they come into the gym.

Lesson Sequence

1. In shuttle formation, demonstrate the pass-and-go drill using one team to help.
   a. Have the class begin and continue, stopping only to do the following:
      - Remind students that they must pass before they go to avoid traveling.
      - Change the type of pass.
      - Address violations that are endemic to the group.
2. When traveling violations are under control, assign courts and begin round 1.
3. Go from court to court, officiating or coaching.

Review and Stretching

1. If there was a general class problem during the games, discuss it.
2. Talk about the pass-and-go strategy.
   - Have students raise hands if they changed position on the court after passing.
   - Have them raise hands if after they passed, they got the ball back.
   - Have them raise hands if when they got it back, they took a shot.
3. Collect scores and congratulate students for their good efforts.

Fouls

Facilities

Marked half-court playing areas

Materials

- Basketballs for practice
- Game balls
- Pinnies
- Team chart with captains' names, team numbers, and the record to date
- Game schedule

Performance Goals

Students will do the following:

- Play round 2 with more attention to safety.
- Improve skills while learning to work with others.

Cognitive Goals

Students will learn the following:

- How to compete as a team
- What personal fouls are

Lesson Safety

No player should create bad feelings or undermine a teammate's sense of self. React immediately to stop bullying, belittling, or unsportsmanlike behavior by refocusing the group. If that doesn't work, decisive discipline is in order. No successful class has an environment that allows bad feelings to fester.

Motivation

A defender's job is to prevent an easy shot, not prevent a player from taking a shot. The idea is to give opponents the hard shot and rebound their misses. Sometimes players think they have to stop their opponents from getting where they want to go. That usually works, but most of the time, the effort is illegal. Players cannot physically hold opponents. They cannot even get in their path. Some on-court behaviors are dangerous, and others are aggravating. Such behaviors are fouls. As class competition continues, players must try to avoid committing fouls.

Warm-Up

1. Leave the balls out and let students practice basketball skills when they come into the gym.
2. Line up the teams in shuttle formation and do a quick pass-and-go drill.

Lesson Sequence

1. Explain how fouls are different than violations. Discuss these fouls.
   a. Charging—Offensive player runs into player in an established position.
   b. Blocking—Includes stopping a moving player's progress, pushing, tripping, holding, or elbowing.
2. Begin round 2.
3. Go from court to court, officiating or coaching.

Review and Stretching

1. As students stretch, ask the following:
   - What is the difference between a foul and a violation?
   - What is the difference between a charge and a block?
2. If class is having a general problem, discuss it.
3. Collect scores and congratulate all students for their good efforts.

Assessment

At this point in the unit, it is important to decide whether giving students more information is diluting what they can assimilate as beginners. Remaining lessons on the procedures for taking foul shots, boxing out, and taking advantage of screens can be tabled for another year. Teach them only if students are ready to learn more. If they are not ready, continue to emphasize positioning on defense, cutting into open lanes to receive a pass, and using the pass-and-go strategy.

Basketball
BEGINNER
LESSON 10

Penalizing Fouls

Facilities

Marked half-court playing areas

Materials

- Basketballs for practice
- Game balls
- Pinnies
- Team chart with captains' names, team numbers, and the record to date
- Game schedule

Performance Goals

Students will do the following:

- Play round 3 of the tournament.
- Implement penalties for personal fouls during games.

Cognitive Goal

Students will learn the appropriate penalties for fouls.

Lesson Safety

As competition heats up, make sure you react immediately to any negative behavior. Refocus teams on the fact that each player makes a contribution. If the positive approach doesn't work, use alternatives to guarantee the emotional, social, and physical safety of all students in your class.

Motivation

Having learned about fouls and how they can be dangerous, it is time to learn the penalties for such behaviors. Players cannot keep endangering the safety of others without penalty. For the penalty to have some sting, students should start learning to sink their foul shots.

Warm-Up

Leave the balls out and let students practice basketball skills when they come into the gym.

Lesson Sequence

1. Go over rules and technique of foul shooting, the most practiced outside shot.
    a. Teach how the shooter and teammates line up.
    b. Each student practices five foul shots.
    c. Teach students to move into the key when the ball leaves the shooter's hand to try to rebound and take a layup shot and have them practice this while their teammates practice foul shooting.
2. Explain class penalties for fouls.
    a. If team is fouled five times, the fifth player fouled participates in a one-and-one foul shot. (Teams line up for a foul shot. They rebound a shot that doesn't go in and play continues, but if the first shot goes in, the shooting team gets 1 point and they get to shoot another foul shot.)
    b. If fouled in the act of shooting, the shooter takes two foul shots.
    c. Players who commit five fouls are benched for the day.
3. Begin round 3.
4. Go from court to court, officiating or coaching.

Review and Stretching

1. As students stretch, ask the following:
    - Is traveling more serious than pushing?
    - If you are dribbling in for a layup shot and someone is already in your path, who should be charged for a foul if contact is made?
    - Can you put your hand in the path of a dribbler to stop her from moving?
2. Collect scores and congratulate students for their good efforts.

Boxing Out

Facilities

Marked half-court playing areas

Materials

- Basketballs for practice
- Game balls
- Pinnies
- Team chart with captains' names, team numbers, and the record to date
- Game schedule

Performance Goals

Students will do the following:

- Play round 4 of the tournament.
- Try to incorporate boxing out in their game.

Cognitive Goal

Students will learn the concept of boxing out.

Lesson Safety

Make sure you react immediately to any negative behavior. Refocus teams on the fact that each player makes a contribution. If the positive approach doesn't work, use alternatives to guarantee the emotional, social, and physical safety of all students in your class.

Motivation

Though fouls are penalized, players know that doesn't mean they have to give up position. If they are on defense and they have position inside the basketball key, they may keep it and box out the other team. That means that they are in position to more easily rebound. It also means that when the other team tries to get there, they should use their body to take as much space as they can so their opponents have no room. While practicing fouls shots, students should get their waiting teammates to run into the key, make as if they are boxing out opponents, grab the rebound, and follow up with a layup shot. Be sure to mention that foul shots are the most practiced outside shot in basketball.

Warm-Up

Leave the balls out and let students practice basketball skills when they come into the gym.

Lesson Sequence

1. Demonstrate boxing out with one team (see figure 7.5). Practice outside shooting with nonshooters moving into the key in anticipation of the shot, taking a large gait, and rebounding the ball.
2. Begin round 4 of the tournament.
3. Go from court to court, officiating or coaching.

Review and Stretching

1. As students stretch, ask the following:
   - What is the purpose of boxing out opponents?
   - Where should your arms be to box out effectively?
   - Should your feet be wide apart or close together to box out effectively?
   - What should you do after you box out the other team and get the ball?
2. Collect scores and congratulate students for their good efforts.

Figure 7.5 Boxing out.

Screens

Facilities

Marked half-court playing areas

Materials

- Basketballs for practice
- Game balls
- Pinnies
- Team chart with captains' names, team numbers, and the record to date
- Game schedule

Performance Goal

Students will play round 5 of the tournament.

Cognitive Goal

Students will learn the concept of setting up a screen.

Lesson Safety

Make sure you react immediately to any negative behavior. Refocus teams on the fact that each player makes a contribution. If the positive approach doesn't work, use alternatives to guarantee the emotional, social, and physical safety of all students in your class.

Motivation

Before announcing the standings, explain how a nonshooting teammate can help the shooter by screening him from an opponent's reach. Challenge players to have the sense to help their teammate, especially when a teammate wants to shoot. Announce the standings for first, second, and third place, as well as who has to win today in order to change the standings.

Warm-Up

Leave the balls out and let students practice basketball skills when they come into the gym.

Lesson Sequence

1. Demonstrate a screen and explain its advantage.
2. Begin round 5 of the tournament.
3. Go from court to court, officiating or coaching.

Review and Stretching

1. Draw attention to the kind of accomplishments noted on the beginner skills rubric (e.g., during the games, they get free; shooters are reaching the backboard; players are catching passes).
2. Ask students the purpose of the screen and if any instances occurred in their games.
3. Collect scores and congratulate students for their good efforts.

Tournament Continues

Facilities

Marked half-court playing areas

Materials

- Basketballs for practice
- Game balls
- Pinnies
- Team chart with captains' names, team numbers, and the record to date
- Game schedule
- Beginner skills rubric

Performance Goal

Students will play rounds 6 through 10.

Cognitive Goal

Students will learn what they should be able to do as beginners in basketball.

Lesson Safety

Make sure you react immediately to any negative behavior. Refocus teams on the fact that each player makes a contribution. If the positive approach doesn't work, use alternatives to guarantee the emotional, social, and physical safety of all students in your class.

Motivation

Announce the standings for first through third place and what teams need to win or tie for the standings to change. Announce your pleasure with their effort and growth. No matter what, they are all winning because they have learned so much, are playing as a team, and are having a good time doing it. Tell students that if they are curious about the grades, the standards are posted so they can see what you are basing their skills grades on.

Warm-Up

Leave the balls out and let students practice basketball skills when they come into the gym.

Lesson Sequence

1. Go over the goals that appear on the skills rubric for beginners.
   - Offense: Get open, be able to catch a pass, shoot if open or close enough to hit the backboard.
   - Defense: Stay between your player and basket.
2. Play rounds 6 through 10 of the tournament.
3. Go from court to court, officiating or coaching.

Review and Stretching

Collect scores and congratulate all students for their good efforts.

Assessment

Observe for standards stated on the beginner skills rubric.

Tournament Conclusion

Facilities

Marked half-court playing areas

Materials

- Basketballs for practice
- Game balls
- Pinnies
- Team chart with captains' names, team numbers, and the record to date
- Game schedule
- Beginner skills rubric

Performance Goals

Students will play the last round of the tournament.

Cognitive Goal

Students will use halftime to try to turn the game around.

Lesson Safety

Make sure you react immediately to any negative behavior. Refocus teams on the fact that each player makes a contribution. If the positive approach doesn't work, use alternatives to guarantee the emotional, social, and physical safety of all students in your class.

Motivation

The class has completed 10 rounds of a double round-robin tournament. Announce the standings for first through third place and that today is the last day of the tournament. The next class there will be a short quiz, and as soon as it is over, the teams will play. Leave it to the students to decide how they want to play the last game—they can choose from facing their closest competition for the final basketball game, making new teams and playing with friends, or having a battle of the sexes.

Warm-Up

Leave the balls out and let students practice basketball skills when they come into the gym.

Lesson Sequence

1. Begin round 11 of the tournament or the play-off game.
2. Go from court to court, officiating or coaching.
3. Stop halfway through so students can use the 2-minute rest and coaching time-out.

Review and Stretching

Collect scores and congratulate students for their good efforts.

Assessment

Observe for skills standards and record observations.

Quiz and Last Playing Day

Facilities

Marked half-court playing areas

Materials

- Updated team charts
- One quiz for each student
- Pens and pencils
- Basketballs for practice
- Game balls
- Pinnies

Performance Goals

Students will do the following:

- Complete a quiz on basketball.
- Play a game of basketball with teams of choice.
- Perform a minimum of 20 minutes of activity.

Cognitive Goals

Students will demonstrate their knowledge of the following:

- Rules and basic concepts via a short quiz
- How to play games according to the option they chose in the previous lesson

Lesson Safety

Make sure you react immediately to any negative behavior. Refocus teams on the fact that each player makes a contribution. If the positive approach doesn't work, use alternatives to guarantee the emotional, social, and physical safety of all students in your class.

Motivation

Congratulate the first-, second-, and third-place winners. Assign courts for the last day of basketball team play.

Warm-Up

Leave the balls out and let students practice basketball skills when they come into the gym.

Lesson Sequence

1. Ask if there are any questions about the rules or strategies and answer them.
2. Set aside 10 minutes for the quiz, 1 minute per question.
   - If students complete the quiz before time is up, collect them.
   - For students who need more time, make individual arrangements for them to complete the quiz while classmates are playing or outside of class (during study hall, during lunch, after school, or in presence of resource-room teacher).
3. Assign courts and send students to play.

Review and Stretching

Recognize students who performed with excellence and explain why you thought so. Indicate the students who made the most dramatic improvement. Congratulate all students for their good efforts.

Assessment

Complete grading for the skills portion of the physical education grade in basketball, giving extra credit to students who performed with excellence.

Beginner Basketball Skills Rubric

Name _____ Date _____

Teacher _____ Class _____

	0	1	2	3
Shooting	No effort.	• Uses proper body mechanics. • Focuses to aim. • Meets backboard.	• Will shoot when open. • Sometimes successful inside key. • Developing an outside shot.	• Frequently successful inside key. • Makes outside shots. • Follows in outside shots.
Pass	No effort.	• Uses proper body mechanics. • Accurate to 10 ft (3 m). • Uses proper follow-through.	• Pass arrives accurately. • Can pass to someone on move. • Varies passes: bounce, chest.	• Passes to open person. • Passes on the run. • Pass arrives with speed.
Dribble	No effort.	• Has proper fundamentals. • Begins dribble when moving.	• Makes effort to keep eyes off ball. • Stops to defend the ball. • Dribbles only to gain ground.	• Rarely breaks dribble rules. • Developing both hands. • Uses dribble offensively.
Defense	No effort.	• Attempts to stay between hoop and opponent. • Uses hands to block ball.	• Anticipates change of direction. • Attempts rebound. • Jumps to block shots.	• Goes to person or position on change of possession. • Does not allow anyone near an open shot.
Teamwork and sportsmanship	No effort.	• Gets to court on time. • Gets along with teammates. • Hogs ball or blames others.	• Tries to play within rules. • Does not hog ball. • Makes effort to improve weaknesses.	• Leads team constructively. • Plays within the rules. • Is the go-to person.

From Isobel Kleinman, 2009, *Complete Physical Education Plans for Grades 5 to 12, Second Edition* (Champaign, IL: Human Kinetics).

Beginner Basketball Quiz

Name _____ Date _____

Teacher _____ Class _____

True or False

Read each statement carefully. If the statement is true, write a *T* in the column to the left. If the statement is false, write an *F*. If using a grid sheet, blacken in the appropriate column for each question, making sure to use the correctly numbered line for each question and its answer.

_____ 1. If you dribble to a stop in two steps, you are allowed to move the front foot as often as you like as long as you keep the back foot stationary.

_____ 2. Players who are fouled while they are shooting get two foul shots if their first shot misses the basket and only one if it goes in.

_____ 3. A layup shot is worth 2 points.

_____ 4. When a player travels with the ball, an opponent takes the ball and puts it back in play with a pass from outside the court.

_____ 5. Boxing out helps teams take a good rebounding position near the hoop.

_____ 6. Meeting the dribble at shoulder height is good technique and is also legal.

_____ 7. To play the pass-and-go strategy correctly, you should pass the ball and stay.

_____ 8. When guarding an opponent, keep your eyes on the backboard.

_____ 9. Stopping an opponent's pass or shot is poor sportsmanship.

_____ 10. For the best ball control, spread out the fingers of your hands on the ball.

Beginner Basketball Answer Key

True or False

1. T—The pivot turn is perfectly legal.
2. T—This is the procedure for taking foul shots after being fouled while shooting.
3. T—A layup shot is a regular field goal.
4. T—Violations are followed by the opposing team going out of bounds and putting the ball back in play with a pass.
5. T—Both those things are a necessity: position and jumping.
6. F—Good dribbling technique requires that you meet the ball at the waist. A high dribble is considered palming.
7. F—The pass-and-go strategy requires that you change your place on the court immediately after passing the ball.
8. F—If you watch the basket when you are guarding, you won't be able to stay with your player.
9. F—It is good team play and the proper goal of any team player on defense to stop the score and try to get the ball.
10. T—Spreading the hand on the ball yields better ball control.

Review

Facilities

Cleared floor space with one backboard for every four students

Materials

- One ball for every two players
- Stopwatch or watch with second hand

Performance Goals

Students will do the following:

- Shoot layups.
- Perform pivot turns.
- Dribble.

Cognitive Goal

Students will review rules and the purpose of the dribble.

Lesson Safety

- During layup drill, use only one ball at each basket at a time.
- Much of basketball takes place in crowded spaces. This lesson attempts to train students to be aware of where they are going, look where they are going when dribbling, and make them especially cautious while doing the dribble maze, which has people dribbling in four directions at one time.
- When sending dribblers down for a layup, limit the basketballs to the number of backboards and have groups line up behind each ball in equal numbers.

Motivation

Some students hate playing basketball in class because they fear getting hurt in the crowd around the basket. The hurt is not always physical; it can also come from the know-it-all teammate who hogs the ball and ridicules others he thinks cannot make a contribution. Anyone who thinks that he has teammates who cannot contribute to the team effort does not understand the game or its fundamentals. If he did, he would know better. This lesson will convince the class that everyone is capable of getting the ball in the basket. Start with the layup shot and discuss where the ball must hit the backboard to make sure it drops in.

Warm-Up

1. Leave the balls out and let students practice shooting skills when they come into the gym.
2. Do footwork drills:
   - Running to a two-step stop
   - Sticking the first foot to land and using the second foot to make the turns
3. Lead the mimetics for a layup shot.
   - Start with arms coming up, shooting arm extending, and rolling the fingers forward.
   - Add the footwork—hop to catch on shooting foot, step-hop to shoot on opposite foot.

Lesson Sequence

1. Demonstrate the point of aim for a successful layup shot and explain the spin.
   a. Have students take two or three shots each.
   b. In 10-second trials, have students see how many shots they can make.
   c. Have the most successful shooters demonstrate their technique.
   d. Give students a few more 10-second trials

2. Review essentials of the dribble.
   a. Set up a dribble drill.
      - Remind students to meet the ball at the waist and push the ball out in front.
      - After students look comfortable with the dominant hand, instruct them to use the weaker one.
      - Remind students to look where they are going, not at the ball.
   b. As students improve, progressively set up the dribble maze drill.
      - Split the class so half dribble in the opposite direction.
      - Put the best dribblers on the side so they dribble perpendicularly to the main lines.
   c. Explain that one purpose of the dribble is to get to the basket to score.
      - One student in each group dribbles to each basket around the gym and shoots, staying until she sinks the shot, then going on to the next basket.
      - Repeat, moving after one shot and scoring 2 points for each success. Groups keep team cumulative score.

Review and Stretching

As students stretch, ask the following:
- When you throw accurately but hard, can you expect to score a basket?
- Why is it important to dribble without looking at the ball?
- Can anyone score when the ball is being dribbled?
- What is the purpose of the dribble?

Assessment

Observe the ball control of the groups, making sure they are ready to move on to the next aspect of the lesson or even the next lesson before moving ahead. There is no rush; do not move on until 90% of the students look as if they are making good progress.

Outside Shooting

Facilities
Cleared floor space with one backboard for every four students

Materials
- One ball for every two players
- Stopwatch or watch with second hand

Performance Goal
Students will practice shooting from outside the basketball key.

Cognitive Goals
Students will learn the following:
- Essentials of successful outside shooting
- Purpose of the dribble

Lesson Safety
Use every ball for outside shooting, having a few people retrieve and feed back the balls to shooters. Students should avoid running under the basket and getting bopped in the head with a ball.

Motivation

Small players who don't get fast break opportunities can rarely get inside the basketball key without looking up to shoot and seeing towers of arms over their heads ready to block their shots. Because balls won't go through the wall of arms over their head, it is best to learn the outside shot, which will give them the most scoring opportunities. The outside shot has additional advantages. Teams can get up to 3 points if the shot occurs in the 3-point zone. Also, being successful from the outside keeps the opponents honest—if they fear a score from the outside, they won't clog up the basketball key. With a team able to take both shots from the outside and shots from the inside, everyone is a potential scorer.

Warm-Up

1. Leave the balls out and let students practice basketball skills when they come into the gym.
2. Do footwork: Run to two-step stop, then pivot, reverse direction, and run more.
3. Lead mimetics for the outside jump shot.
   - Feet on the ground with arm action only
   - Same arm action while leaving the ground
   - Same arm action once in the air
4. Lead mimetics for a layup shot: arm and step-hop footwork.

Lesson Sequence

1. Demonstrate the outside shot and how it will be practiced as a group.
   a. Teach students to identify the basketball key.
   b. Have them focus on the back of the rim as they release the ball.
   c. Demonstrate the effect of spin.
      - Show that accurate shots don't always drop in.
      - Show how fingers control the spin.
   d. Have students find their spot. (Use every ball and feed them back, allowing shooters to shoot for several minutes continuously.)
2. Set up a drill that has one student dribble and pass to a shooter who is on her outside spot. The shooter shoots and rebounds. If the outside shot goes in, the shooter should send the ball back to the group and go back to the end of the dribbler's line. If not, the shooter should take a layup, retrieve the ball, send it back, and go to end of the dribbler's line.
3. Move lines across the gym so outside shooters have to dribble to their spot, stop, take an immediate shot, rebound, and shoot or retrieve the ball.
4. Now it's time for a little game. Assign a relay group to every backboard and have teams line up across the gym from the backboard they are assigned to (make certain that groups have a clear path to basket and don't run the risk of colliding with other moving groups).
   a. Dribble to the basket and take one shot. Whether the shooter scores or not, he returns to the back of the line. Keep team score (2 points for every basket).
   b. Do the same, but stop and shoot from the shooter's outside spot. Whether it goes in or not, the shooter returns to the line.

Review and Stretching

As students stretch, ask the following:
- Which spin is helpful in shooting: flat (no spin), topspin, or underspin (backspin)?
- If you use too much underspin, will the ball fall short?
- How many people scored more than three baskets?
- How many scored by dribbling straight to your outside spot and getting it in from there?
- How many were surprised that the ball dropped in?

Assessment

Observe to determine how much more repetition is necessary before going on.

Rebounding and Foul Shots

Facilities

Cleared floor space with one backboard for every four students

Materials

- One ball for every two players
- Stopwatch or watch with second hand

Performance Goals

Students will do the following:

- Successfully rebound.
- Shoot foul shots.

Cognitive Goals

Students will learn the following:

- What causes fouls and why foul shots are awarded
- The significance of a basketball key
  - Where most points get scored
  - Timing entrance to the key because offensive time inside is limited to 3 seconds at a time

Lesson Safety

Use every ball for outside shooting, having a few people retrieve and feed back the balls to shooters. Students should avoid running under the basket and getting bopped in the head with a ball.

Motivation

If all students realized that missed shots might still result in their team getting the ball, they would consider shooting more often. Turning a missed shot into a 2-point score depends on the art of rebounding. It gives teams a second, third, or even fourth chance to score when they are on offense. If they are on defense, it prevents their opponents from having extra chances. Of course, it is easiest for the tallest players to be successful, but good timing, anticipation, court position, and jumping ability are equally important. Although not everyone will be the designated rebounder, there are many occasions for everyone to rebound. Today students will learn how to rebound and remember that taking an outside shot when a teammate is in the key and they can hit the backboard or rim is a good thing to do. The best scenario is that it goes in. The next best is that their teammate rebounds the ball and puts it in.

Warm-Up

1. Leave the balls out and let students practice basketball skills when they come into the gym.
2. In attendance lines, do the pass-and-go drill and a dribbling drill.
3. Lead mimetics for rebounding.
   - Jump and reach up as high as possible with hands facing each other (5 times).
   - Jump and reach to snatch the ball, pulling it down on landing (5 times).
   - Jump to rebound, landing with feet in a wide stance with ball protected (5 times).
   - Jump to rebound a ball going slightly off to the right, reach with right hand, pull it into the other hand, and land as before (5 times).
   - Jump to rebound a ball off to the left, reach with left hand, pull the ball into the other hand, and land as before (5 times).

Lesson Sequence

1. Demonstrate rebounding by jumping to catch the ball while in the air.
   a. Have students line up at a wall.
      - One person throws to a wall target with underspin.
      - Rebounder jumps when the ball hits, reaches up, and catches the ball, landing with the ball pulled down and feet spread apart.
   b. Repeat, encouraging students to reach and pull the ball into body.
2. Bring group to the basketball key and have them sit on the line of the key.
   a. Explain the 3-second rule (no players from the offensive team may stay inside the key for more than 3 seconds at a time unless the ball has been passed to them or has been shot for a basket before the 3 seconds expire).
   b. Have students alternate taking three foul shots with the others slipping into the key to rebound and take a layup shot once they do.
3. Line up groups across the gym and have them dribble to their outside shot spot, take their shot, assume it will miss, rebound the miss, and follow with a layup.
4. For excitement, challenge teams: In 3 minutes, see how many points teams can make by dribbling to an outside shot, coming back after it scores, or rebounding the miss and following up with one layup shot. Teams keep their score.
   a. After 3 minutes, get the scores and allow the enthusiasm to build.
   b. Remind students that they are great but something is missing—defense.

Review and Stretching

As students stretch, ask the following:

- Did you score more points on the outside shot or the follow-up layup?
- When playing a game, is it better to take an inside shot or an outside one? Why?
- If taking an outside shot, what should you wait for?

Basketball
INTERMEDIATE
LESSON 4

Half-Court Games

Facilities

Cleared floor space with one backboard with half-court markings for every four students

Materials

- One ball for every two players
- Pinnies
- Whistles for student officials

Performance Goal

Students will play half-court basketball games using the bring-back rules.

Cognitive Goal

Students will review half-court bring-back rules and strategies.

Lesson Safety

Game situations in crowded spaces can result in lots of accidental bumping. Make sure that students do not take the bumping personally. Also, make sure that those who are running into each other realize that such activity is a foul and penalized heavily in a game. Teach that it is the responsibility of all players to play with enough skill that they don't go crashing into people.

Motivation

Games on TV are full court. Teams have to defend their basket, get the ball, and go to the other basket to shoot. With only enough space to have games on one backboard, the class will play a bring-back rule when playing half-court in order to get a full-court experience (getting the ball from opponents and changing baskets). Playing at one key makes the 3-second rule a little tricky. This lesson will sort it out and get students ready for a game.

Warm-Up

1. Leave the balls out and let students practice basketball skills when they come into the gym.
2. Lead mimetics: jump to rebound, hop to catch, and step-hop to shoot.
3. In attendance lines, do the shuttle pass-and-go drill followed by a dribbling drill.

Lesson Sequence

1. Bring group to one half-court basket and teach the following.
   a. Boundary lines
   b. Half-court rules and the reason for them
   c. When the 3-second rule applies
2. Assign courts and pinnies. The pinnies team starts the game with a throw-in from half-court.
3. When all games are under way, go from court to court, officiating the 3-second rule and bring-back rules.

Review and Stretching

1. Compliment play. If teams used a defense, compliment them specifically, particularly since they have not had a lesson on defense yet this year and were savvy enough to set one up themselves.
2. Ask if students have any questions.

Teacher Homework

Make teams that are as equal as possible. Use the chart from lesson 6 of the beginner level on page 278.

No-Dribble Game

Facilities

Cleared floor space with one backboard with half-court markings for every four students

Materials

- One ball for every two players
- Pinnies
- Whistles for student officials

Performance Goals

Students will do the following:

- Emphasize pass-and-go skills.
- Play a no-dribble half-court basketball game.

Cognitive Goals

Students will learn the following:

- The purpose of the dribble
- The advantage of the pass-and-go strategy
- Typical rules that poorly executed pass-and-go skills might violate
    - Traveling
    - Holding the ball too long (5-second rule)
- How to play with their tournament teams

Lesson Safety

Students may be disappointed as the teams are announced. The no-dribble game will work to avoid hurt feelings and help students realize that all the players on their team can be of help since the elimination of dribbling also eliminates the ability of one player to hog the ball. Good teamwork and effort will flow from that.

Motivation

After announcing the tournament teams, the class will try to stop the automatic reflex some players have of getting a ball and dribbling it. The reason for dribbling is twofold. First, the dribble is supposed to slow down the game and give teammates a chance to get to the other end of the court and set up their offense. However, in a half-court game, everyone is already there. The other reason for a dribble is to take the ball to the basket and score. Unless there is an open lane and the ball handler is going to the basket or threatening to go, though, dribbling in a half-court is simply wasting time. Today, teams will be introduced and their first game together will be a no-dribble game on a half-court.

Warm-Up

1. Leave the balls out and let students practice basketball skills when they come into the gym.
2. Do mimetics with attention to the following:
    - Step-hop and throw (5 times)
    - Throw-and-go footwork (5 times)
3. In attendance lines, do a pass-and-go drill and a dribble drill.

Lesson Sequence

1. Review the pass-and-go strategy, and warn about traveling and a need for accurate passes to the open person.
2. Announce the teams, assign a court, and declare which team wears pinnies.
3. Direct students to play no-dribble games.
4. Travel from game to game, reinforcing the no-dribble rule for the day and reminding students to go (as in pass and go) after they pass.

Review and Stretching

As students stretch, ask how many of them realized that they have a lot more scoring opportunities during half-court if they rely on the pass instead of the dribble.

Basketball
INTERMEDIATE
LESSON 6

Center

Facilities

Cleared floor space with one backboard with half-court markings for every four students

Materials

- One ball for every two players
- Pinnies
- Whistles for student officials

Performance Goal

Students will play a half-court basketball game with tournament teams.

Cognitive Goals

- Students will learn the following:
  - The job of the center
  - The appropriate time to shoot (when open and close enough to hit the rim)
  - That each player can contribute to the team
- Students will pick their own center and leaders (captains and cocaptains).

Lesson Safety

Continue to demand good sportsmanship and require each player to make the effort to play without contact. A healthy emotional climate is crucial to success.

Motivation

Basketball is one of the few games where players have to master offense and defense. Since it can get confusing and things can happen quickly, the necessary jobs are broken down and players become specialists. Today's lesson will focus on the job of the center. A great center can take advantage of a team's missed shots by rebounding those shots and laying the ball back up and in. There are rules in place that make being in position to do that quite a challenge. Discuss the 3-second rule again.

Warm-Up

1. Leave the balls out and let students practice basketball skills when they come into the gym.
2. Lead mimetics: jump to rebound, jump to shoot, and layup shot.

Lesson Sequence

1. Explain the center's job and how teams can take advantage of an active center.
   a. Get to the basket before the ball does.
   b. On offensive side, go into the key when anticipating a shot, rebound and shoot or rebound and set the team up again by passing out and getting out.
   c. Try to secure all defensive rebounds and get the ball to one of the guards.
2. Assign courts and pinnies for a regular practice game (dribbling allowed).
3. Travel from game to game, reinforcing the following:
   a. Three-second rule
   b. Teammates waiting to take outside shot until center can slip into key
   c. Center learning to sense when teammates are shooting

Review and Stretching

1. As students stretch, ask the following:
   - Where did the most points get scored today?
   - How many rebounds did your center cash in on?
2. Before students leave, make sure they tell you their team captains and cocaptains. They should try to pick people who are not always captains.

Teacher Homework

Prepare the tournament schedule and team standings.

Guards

Facilities

Cleared floor space with one backboard with half-court markings for every four students

Materials

- One ball for every two players
- Pinnies
- Whistles for student officials

Performance Goal

Students will play a half-court basketball game with tournament teams.

Cognitive Goals

Students will learn the following:

- The job of the guard
- To shoot when open and close enough to hit the rim
- That they can make a team contribution
- Which teammates will be guards

Lesson Safety

Maintain a healthy competitive environment, eliminating reckless physical, social, or emotional play and working toward getting all players to respect the skills, effort, and sensitivity of others.

Motivation

In a full-court game, it is usually the person with the best dribbling skills that brings the ball down the court. That person happens to be very important, not because she is the best scorer, but because she knows when to dribble and when to pass. A good ball handler can see an open teammate and get the ball to him so he can use it to score. A good ball handler sets up his whole team. The best ball handler is the point guard. The point guard and another guard play the back-court while their teammates get into a threatening scoring position. Today, games will give teams more time to tune up, pick their guards, and learn to leave the guards to their job while getting ready for the job that remains—scoring.

Warm-Up

1. Leave the balls out and let students practice basketball skills when they come into the gym.
2. Lead mimetics for jump to rebound. Emphasize jumping straight up and landing where they took off (so they have the skills not to foul around the backboards).

Lesson Sequence

1. Explain the role of a guard and what skills guards need most.
   a. Necessary skills—dribbling, passing on the move, outside shooting, and fearless layups
   b. Their job—bringing the ball down the court, taking it out, and setting up plays
   c. Lucky chances—usually the guard who gets to fast break
2. Ask teams to decide which of their players should play the guard position. Assign courts and pinnies and get the games under way.
3. Travel from game to game.
   a. Reinforce all rules.
   b. Remind guards to get the ball for takeouts and take-backs.

   c. Coach guards to do the following:

- Look for open teammates.
- Sometimes force a play by coming in for a layup.
- Shoot from outside when the center is in the key.

Review and Stretching

As students stretch, ask them to think about whether their team's guards set them up or hogged the ball.

- How many people were open but no one ever sent them a pass?
- How many guards didn't throw a pass because their open teammate was standing still and was too easy to be picked off?
- How many people felt that there was too much dribbling in the game?
- How many of your guards drove to the basket and took a layup shot?

Forwards

Facilities

Cleared floor space with one backboard with half-court markings for every four students

Materials

- One ball for every two players
- Pinnies
- Whistles for student officials

Performance Goal

Students will play the last practice game before the tournament.

Cognitive Goals

Students will learn the following:

- The job of the forward
- To shoot when open and close enough to hit the rim
- That every team member has a role to play
- Which teammates will be forwards

Lesson Safety

Maintain a healthy competitive environment, eliminating reckless physical, social, or emotional play and working toward getting all players to respect the skills, effort, and sensitivity of others.

Motivation

There are five people on a basketball team. There is one center, two guards, and two more players—the forwards. Today students will learn about the role of a forward.

Warm-Up

1. Leave the balls out and let students practice basketball skills when they come into the gym.
2. Lead mimetics in skills that students would most profit from practicing.
3. Line teams up and have them practice layups with a dribbling approach.

Lesson Sequence

1. Teach about the forward.
   a. Necessary skills—getting open, shooting, rebounding
   b. Jobs—setting screens or picks, boxing out, rebounding
2. Assign courts and pinnies. Have teams decide who plays which position before starting the games.
3. Travel from game to game.
   a. Reinforce all rules.
   b. Remind forwards to do the following:
      - Get open.
      - Take advantage of shooting opportunities.
   c. Coach guards to feed the ball to their open forwards.

Review and Stretching

1. As students stretch, ask the following:
   - How do you feel about breaking down the court offensive responsibilities?
   - Whose primary job is to shoot and to score?
   - To set up plays?
   - To rebound?
2. The tournament starts next time class meets. Have students check the posted game schedules.

Teacher Homework

Post the tournament charts.

Zone Defense

Facilities

Cleared floor space with one backboard with half-court markings for every four students

Materials

- One ball for every two players
- Pinnies
- Whistles for student officials
- Tournament schedule and team standings

Performance Goal

Students will play round 1.

Cognitive Goals

Students will learn the following:

- The value of taking a halftime rest to reorganize
- The value of defense
- That they should do their own jobs the best they can

Lesson Safety

Maintain a healthy competitive environment, eliminating reckless physical, social, or emotional play and working toward getting all players to respect the skills, effort, and sensitivity of others.

Motivation

No words have been said in all this time about defense. It is time to think about not letting opponents run up the score. Legally preventing them from scoring is essential. Before starting today, make sure everyone knows their defensive responsibilities—who they cover in person-to-person defense or what place on the court they cover in zone defense.

Warm-Up

1. Leave the balls out and let students practice basketball skills when they come into the gym.
2. Lead mimetics—jump to block, jump to catch, and jump to rebound.

Lesson Sequence

1. Explain zone defense and demonstrate (either the 2-1-2 or the 1-2-2). The 2-1-2 stations the forwards by the backboard, the center in the center, and the guards by the foul line, forming a box. The 1-2-2 stations the point guard at the top of the key with two players on either side of the foul line and two more on either side of the backboard.

   a. Help students understand that they guard a zone, moving to cover people entering their zone and leaving them when the opponents enter someone else's zone.

   b. Explain how the zone shifts, keeping its integrity, with the ball.

   c. Explain the rebounding advantages of the zone and the difficulty teams have in getting into the key and taking unguarded layup shots.

2. Direct students to their courts for round 1.
3. Stop games halfway through and ask the teams the following:

   a. Is your defense breaking down?

   b. Are you giving up the ball to the other team without scoring? Why?

   c. Allow teams time to resolve these issues (2-3 minutes) and resume.

4. Travel from game to game, officiating.

Review and Stretching

1. As students stretch, tell them that the games looked great, even better after the halftime adjustments. Unfortunately, there is always a loser even when people play the best they can. Often, though, with a little attention to some things that can be changed, a team can turn a loss to a win. Discuss some strategies for correcting breakdowns that can help teams be more successful.
2. Collect scores from winning captains.

Defensive Strategy

Facilities

Cleared floor space with one backboard with half-court markings for every four students

Materials

- One ball for every two players
- Pinnies
- Whistles for student officials
- Tournament schedule and team standings

Performance Goals

Students will do the following:

- Play round 2.
- Take a halftime strategy session of 2 to 3 minutes.

Cognitive Goals

Students will learn the following:

- Whether to play a zone defense or person-to-person defense
- How to better perform their positions on the court

Lesson Safety

Maintain a healthy competitive environment, eliminating reckless physical, social, or emotional play and working toward getting all players to respect the skills, effort, and sensitivity of others.

Motivation

Some excellent teams have trouble maintaining person-to-person defense because they can't match the speed and agility of their competitors. As a result, opponents can slip away from their coverage and become a scoring threat. Fortunately, there is another option. It's the old approach of going where the fish are—if you know where the ball is going, get there first and be ready to block it when it heads for the basket. If the defense gets there first, it makes shooting more difficult. It also makes rebounding difficult. The defense is the zone defense the students saw last time. It might be the right thing for their teams to use.

Warm-Up

1. Leave the balls out and let students practice basketball skills when they come into the gym.
2. Lead mimetics: jumping to catch, jumping to shoot, and jumping to rebound.

Lesson Sequence

1. Demonstrate the 2-1-2 zone defense again, using players on the court.
   a. Show where the forwards, guards, and center usually set up.
   b. Show how the whole team shifts in the direction of the ball.
   c. Show how a big hole in defense occurs if someone chases the ball.
2. Direct students to begin round 2 and let them determine possession and pinnies.
3. Stop games halfway through, asking teams to decide the following.
   a. Should they stick to person-to-person defense or convert to zone?
   b. Are passes getting to the player on the run?
4. Allow teams some time and then resume games.
5. Travel from game to game, officiating.

Review and Stretching

1. As students stretch, ask the following:
   - What is the advantage of the zone defense?
   - Which zone did you learn today?
   - Who guards the top of the key by the foul line?
   - Who is in the middle of the key? Where are the forwards?
2. Have winning captains stand so you can get the scores and update standings.

Boxing Out and Screens

Facilities

Cleared floor space with one backboard with half-court markings for every four students

Materials

- One ball for every two players
- Pinnies
- Whistles for student officials
- Tournament schedule and team standings

Performance Goal

Students will play round 3.

Cognitive Goal

Students will review the importance of boxing out and screens.

Lesson Safety

Maintain a healthy competitive environment, eliminating reckless physical, social, or emotional play and working toward getting all players to respect the skills, effort, and sensitivity of others.

Motivation

Before beginning the games, students need to know how to use their body to prevent opponents from blocking a teammate's shot, or in other words, screening them from the block. Equally, students can use their body to prevent opponents from getting a good position in the key to get a rebound, which is called *boxing out*. Each strategy can help a team add points to their overall count.

Warm-Up

1. Leave the balls out and let students practice basketball skills when they come into the gym.
2. Practice footwork for shifting in the direction of the ball, keeping the same space between classmates.

Lesson Sequence

1. Demonstrate how a screen can enable an unguarded shot.
2. Show how boxing out can take up so much room in the key that opponents have a hard time getting into rebounding position.
3. Direct students to begin round 3.
4. Stop halfway through for a couple of minutes. Be available to provide coaching hints, and then resume play.
5. Travel from game to game, officiating.

Review and Stretching

1. As students stretch, ask the following:
   - Did anyone screen for a teammate?
   - Did anyone score off a rebound?
   - Did a guard drive for the basket?
2. Collect scores and update tournament standings. Congratulate students on their play.

Performance Goal Review

Facilities

Cleared floor space with one backboard with half-court markings for every four students

Materials

- One ball for every two players
- Pinnies
- Whistles for student officials
- Tournament schedule and team standings

Performance Goal

Students will play round 4.

Cognitive Goal

Students will learn the performance goals for their level.

Lesson Safety

Maintain a healthy competitive environment, eliminating reckless physical, social, or emotional play and working toward getting all players to respect the skills, effort, and sensitivity of others.

Motivation

Before starting, explain the highest level standards on the skills rubric so students know that they are all within reach and that they can aim for the reachable *A*.

- Offense
    - Able to score.
    - Move so able to receive pass.
- Defense
    - Stay between opponent and basket.
    - Jump to block or rebound.

Then announce the standings after three rounds.

Warm-Up

Leave the balls out and let students practice basketball skills when they come into the gym.

Lesson Sequence

1. Direct students to the court for round 4.
2. Stop games halfway through playing time and allow teams to talk; then resume play.
3. Travel from game to game, officiating.

Review and Stretching

1. Review what students will be graded on and why. Next time the skills rubric will be posted so they can read it at their leisure.
2. Have the winning captains report to you.

Tournament Round 5

Facilities

Cleared floor space with one backboard with half-court markings for every four students

Materials

- One ball for every two players
- Pinnies
- Whistles for student officials
- Tournament schedule and team standings
- Intermediate skills rubric

Performance Goal

Students will play round 5.

Cognitive Goal

Students will review the skills that will be graded.

Lesson Safety

Maintain a healthy competitive environment, eliminating reckless physical, social, or emotional play and working toward getting all players to respect the skills, effort, and sensitivity of others.

Motivation

Announce that from now until the unit is over, you will be grading achievement in class based on the intermediate skills rubric that is posted. Remind students that on offense, they need to constantly move to get open and should shoot when they are open and can reach the basket. Remind them that on defense, they need to stay between the opponent and the basket and make sure to jump to block a shot or to try to rebound. Then announce standings after four rounds.

Warm-Up

Leave the balls out and let students practice basketball skills when they come into the gym.

Lesson Sequence

1. Direct students to courts for round 5.
2. Stop halfway through, allowing teams to regroup; then resume play.
3. Travel from game to game, officiating and observing for achievement.

Review and Stretching

1. Compliment the best guard in the class and explain why. Do the same for a center and a forward.
2. Collect scores and update standings.

Tournament Rounds 6, 7, and 8

Facilities

Cleared floor space with one backboard with half-court markings for every four students

Materials

- One ball for every two players
- Pinnies
- Whistles for student officials
- Tournament schedule and team standings
- Intermediate skills rubric

Performance Goal

Students will play rounds 6 through 8.

Cognitive Goal

Students will learn that a quiz is coming up and be given an opportunity to ask questions.

Lesson Safety

Maintain a healthy competitive environment, eliminating reckless physical, social, or emotional play and working toward getting all players to respect the skills, effort, and sensitivity of others.

Motivation

Announce standings. If this is the final round of the class tournament, announce that during the next class they will take a short quiz and spend the remainder of the class in play-offs or fun games. Before beginning, entertain questions about rules, positions, strategies, and penalties.

Warm-Up

Leave the balls out and let students practice basketball skills when they come into the gym.

Lesson Sequence

1. After a review of a rules, positions, strategies, or penalties, direct students to courts for rounds 6, 7, and 8.
2. Stop games halfway through playing time.
3. Allow teams some time to talk (1 minute) and then resume games.
4. Travel from game to game, officiating and observing for achievement.
5. Record skills after class.

Review and Stretching

1. Compliment students for the most incredible improvement since the beginning of this unit.
2. Entertain questions.
3. Collect scores and remind the class about the short quiz.

Teacher Homework

Make sure you have enough quizzes for each student.

Quiz and Final Game

Facilities

Cleared floor space with one backboard with half-court markings for every four students

Materials

- One quiz for each student
- Pens and pencils
- One ball for every two players
- Pinnies
- Whistles for student officials
- Tournament schedule and team standings
- Intermediate skills rubric

Performance Goals

Students will do the following:

- Take a basketball quiz.
- Play the last basketball game of the unit.
- Perform a minimum of 20 minutes of activity.

Cognitive Goal

Students will demonstrate their understanding of what was taught by taking a quiz.

Lesson Safety

Allow students a bit of warm-up time after they complete their quiz.

Warm-Up

After students finish the quiz, allow them time to pick up a ball and practice before sending them into a game.

Lesson Sequence

1. Distribute quizzes as students come in.
   a. Have students sit in their attendance spots to take the quiz.
   b. Collect tests in 10 minutes, making provisions for those needing more time.
2. Direct students to the court for their last basketball game.
3. Travel from game to game, officiating the rules and observing achievement.

Review and Stretching

Give compliments for whatever seems worthy.

Teacher Homework

Complete performance assessments.

Intermediate Basketball Skills Rubric

Name _____ Date _____

Teacher _____ Class _____

	0	1	2	3
Offensive skills	No effort.	• Passes to open player. • Succeeds at inside shots. • Catches passes.	• Always works to get open. • Scores when open. • Can pass or catch on the go. • Developing a specialty.	• Usually scores. • Able to evade opponent. • Creates opportunities.
Defensive skills	No effort.	• Finds zone or opponent on change of possession. • Uses hands to block the path of the ball. • Makes legal contact with ball.	• Stays between hoop and opponent. • Is legally able to break up opponents' plays.	• Can block shot in air. • Will rebound if not guarding shooter.
Court transition	No effort.	• Not confused by change of possession. • Does not shoot at wrong basket or pass to opponent.	• Has good anticipation of role change. • Gets into new position quickly. • Avoids fouls during exchange. • Gets open on offensive side.	• Leads directional changes with dribble or leading passes. • Creates legal changeovers.
Team strategy	No effort.	• Starting to learn position. • Developing specific skills.	• Fulfills team plan smoothly. • Plays both offense and defense.	• Has excellent skills to meet team role.

From Isobel Kleinman, 2009, *Complete Physical Education Plans for Grades 5 to 12, Second Edition* (Champaign, IL: Human Kinetics).

Intermediate Basketball Quiz

Name _____ Date _____

Teacher _____ Class _____

Multiple Choice

Read each question and each answer carefully. Be sure to choose the best answer that fits the statement preceding it. When you have made your choice, put the appropriate letter on the line to the left of the numbered question.

_____ 1. What makes the job of the center difficult is

    a. dribbling

    b. blocking an outside shot

    c. timing the entrance to the key when on offense

    d. taking the ball out

_____ 2. A good guard

    a. uses the dribble to slow down the game so the team can get organized

    b. feeds the ball to open forwards

    c. takes advantage of an open lane by driving in for a layup shot

    d. all of the above

_____ 3. The foul shot is

    a. the most practiced outside shot in basketball

    b. must be taken with the feet stationary

    c. is taken when a shooter is fouled in the act of shooting

    d. all of the above

_____ 4. A forward's important offensive role is

    a. dribbling the ball around the court

    b. boxing out opponents

    c. rebounding

    d. shooting and scoring

_____ 5. The 3-second rule applies to

    a. all players in the key

    b. defensive players in the key

    c. offensive players in possession of the ball

    d. all of the above

_____ 6. The 3-second count ends when

    a. someone shoots

    b. a defensive player gets the ball

    c. players from both teams have the ball at the same time

    d. all of the above

_____ 7. The best kind of spin to use when shooting is

    a. underspin

    b. no spin

    c. topspin

    d. all of the above

»continued

»continued

_____ 8. A defense that makes you responsible for opponents entering your area is
    a. a 2-1-2 zone defense
    b. a person-to-person defense
    c. double-teaming their best shooter
    d. all of the above

_____ 9. The best way to play a zone defense is to
    a. chase the ball as it is coming down the court
    b. go to your zone as soon as the other team gets the ball
    c. follow the ball carrier even when the carrier leaves your zone
    d. all of the above

_____ 10. The advantage of a screen is
    a. it protects the shooter from being blocked
    b. it prevents the dribbler from losing the ball
    c. it enables the center to get into the key for a rebound
    d. all of the above

Intermediate Basketball Answer Key

Multiple Choice

1. c—What makes the center's job difficult is the 3-second rule (a challenge to timing).
2. d
3. d
4. d
5. c
6. d
7. a
8. a
9. b
10. a

From Isobel Kleinman, 2009, *Complete Physical Education Plans for Grades 5 to 12, Second Edition* (Champaign, IL: Human Kinetics).

Skill Review

Facilities

Cleared floor space with one backboard with half-court markings for every four students

Materials

- One ball for every two players
- Stopwatch or watch with second hand

Performance Goals

Students will do the following:

- Pass and dribble.
- Shoot layups.
- Take outside shots.
- Rebound.

Cognitive Goals

Students will review the following:

- Rules for and strategies of the dribble
- Playing on a full court

Lesson Safety

- Use only one ball at each basket during layup 10-second drill.
- Help students take into account that 10 players under a hoop makes for a crowded court in general, and this lesson will help them be aware of where they are going. Make them particularly aware of the necessity to look up during the dribble maze.
- Before the dribble-to-shoot drill begins, collect extra basketballs, leaving one per backboard. Make certain that each group has a route to the basket that does not intersect with the other groups.

Motivation

Students have been playing half-court basketball for years. They have learned the dribble and been discouraged from using it because there is rarely a need for it in half-court games seeing as no one is needed to bring the ball down to the other basket. They learned it anyway, though, as a way to go to the basket if a lane was open to shoot. This year, however, they will have the opportunity to play a full-court game. Being able to dribble on the run, pass from the dribble, and avoid opponents will be necessary. Today students will take time to get the feel of the basketball again and tune up their skills. Ask those who played basketball all year to please bear with the rest of the class. Others have not had the same opportunity and will be on their team eventually, so it is in their interest to help their future teammates feel comfortable on the court.

Warm-Up

1. Leave the balls out and let students practice basketball skills when they come into the gym.
2. Practice footwork: Have students run around the gym perimeter. On the whistle, they stop (two-step stop) and pivot, moving only the front foot without dragging the rear (pivot) foot.
3. Lead mimetics for the jump to catch, block and rebound, and the layup shot:
   a. Practice arm motion and release independently first.
   b. Practice hop-catch, step-hop, and release.

Lesson Sequence

1. Demonstrate layup shooting, focusing on point of aim and soft one-hand release.

    a. Divide the class so that every backboard is used.

    b. Give everyone at least two trials of 10 seconds each.

2. Review essentials of the dribble and progress the drill until it becomes the dribble maze drill (see beginner lesson 2, page 269).

3. Set up relay lines, safely routing students who will dribble to shots:

    a. Layup shot

    b. Outside shot

4. Using a three-person drill (one on the left, one on the right, one in the middle), have students progress down the court with the pass (no dribble) and shoot when they get to the key.

Review and Stretching

While students stretch, ask the following:

- Where should the dribbler's hands meet the ball? (in front at waist height)
- Should the ball handler look at the ball while dribbling?
- Which uses up the clock more, dribbling or passing?
- How can a right-handed person dribble and protect the ball with his body when someone is approaching him from the right?
- How can a person with the ball protect the ball with her body when she has stopped to pass and her opponent is in front of her?

Assessment

This lesson is chock full of skills and is very ambitious, even for the higher grade levels. Observe to see if your students need more time before moving on. If their performance is awkward, they will benefit from an extra day. Make sure you do not move on until they are ready.

Full-Court Strategies

Facilities

One full court for every 10 players or the opportunity to play on full court for half the class and play on half-court the rest of the class

Materials

- One ball for every two players
- Pinnies
- Whistles for student officials

Performance Goal

Students will improve dribbling, shooting, and passing skills.

Cognitive Goals

Students will learn the following:

- What to do to go from offense to defense on full court
- What a press is

Lesson Safety

Help students take into account that 10 players under a hoop makes for a crowded court in general and that they have two obligations:

- They must play clean, meaning that they need to develop enough skill to go after the ball, not the person, a feat that will be more difficult when they have to cover more territory on a full court.
- They should understand that contact is usually not personal and that they should not take offense.

Motivation

The goal of the advanced unit is to provide as much full-court playing experience as possible. Though no one is a beginner, initially the full-court game will feel different. However, the only difference between the two games is that everyone must get to the other side of the court when possession of the ball changes. Beginners often get caught chasing the ball instead of getting into position at the other end, which is when midcourt problems occur. Focus on these problems and how to avoid them.

Warm-Up

1. Leave the balls out and let students practice basketball skills when they come into the gym.
2. In attendance lines, do drills.
   - Practice dribbling and then dribbling and passing.
   - Split the lines to shuttle formation and do a pass-and-go drill.

Lesson Sequence

1. Discuss the following:
   a. Options to get the ball down the court (pass or dribble)
      - Dribbling when forwards are open and in position to shoot
      - Chasing the dribbler and causing fouls
      - Losing the ball in midcourt
   b. Need for the off-the-ball players to set up before the ball arrives
   c. Danger of a sluggish defense arriving after the ball does
2. Divide into groups of five and assign a court for full-court play. If there are not enough full courts available, send some teams to play on half-courts until they rotate to the full court.

Review and Stretching

As students proceed with their stretching routine, discuss the following:

- How many of you thought that the dribble was overused?
- Who was open and never got the ball?
- Which of you caused your opponents to lose the ball before they could shoot?
- Raise your hand if your team decided who would be the guards, forwards, and center.

Basketball
ADVANCED
LESSON 3

Positions

Facilities

One full court for every 10 players or the opportunity to play on full court for half the class and play on half-court the rest of the class

Materials

- One ball for every two players
- Pinnies
- Whistles for student officials

Performance Goals

Students will do the following:

- Improve their transition from offense to defense.
- Play full-court games for all or part of the class.

Cognitive Goals

Students will review the following:

- The role of each position during offense and defense
- Why they need to make quick transitions to defense

Lesson Safety

To discourage fouls and dangerous physical contact, begin calling fouls and awarding penalties.

Motivation

The first thing that happens in unskilled games is that fouls occur more frequently. Everyone wants the same ball and as soon as someone gets it, unskilled players crash into the ball carrier. In skilled games, the most obvious flaw is not going back for defense. Discuss defensive responsibilities, how anticipation can avoid the fouls, and how in full-court games, players have to avoid sticking around the basket they are at when the ball changes possession.

Warm-Up

1. Leave the balls out and let students practice basketball skills when they come into the gym.
2. Practice footwork: backpedaling, side to side, squaring shoulders, and change of direction.
3. Lead mimetics for the jump to block and jump to rebound.

Lesson Sequence

1. Discuss the following:
   a. Positions in zone defense and when to get into them
   b. When and where they pick up their person in person-to-person defense
   c. What a full-court press is
   d. The difference between charging and blocking fouls
2. Let students get into groups of five and assign full-court play for every two teams. If there are not enough full courts, assign others to play on half-courts and rotate them onto the full court.

Review and Stretching

If students played 2-1-2 zone defense, ask:

- Who covers the person coming down the middle if she stops at the foul line and takes a shot?
- Did anyone get a chance to take an inside shot against the zone? Where were most of your shots taken?

If students played person-to-person defense, ask:

- When the other team got the ball, was it easy to catch up with your person to cover him? What suggestions could you come up with to make getting to your coverage more predictable?

Teacher Homework

Make up teams that equitably divide player skills.

Team Organization

Facilities

One full court for every 10 players or the opportunity to play on full court for half the class and play on half-court the rest of the class

Materials

- One ball for every two players
- Pinnies
- Whistles for student officials

Performance Goal

Students will play full-court games for all or part of the class.

Cognitive Goals

Students will do the following:

- Meet their tournament teams.
- Review offensive roles and offensive strategies.
- Decide who will play which position with their new teammates.

Lesson Safety

Be vigilant about any negative social and emotional behavior and react to stop it immediately.

Motivation

The students are not complete strangers to one another or to the game of basketball. Some of them play on outside teams. To fit the needs of that team, they may play a position that would not fit the needs of the class team they are on now. For instance, if they are forwards on an outside team but because of their experience and speed and skill level would be the most likely candidate to play guard on the class team, they should reconsider what position to play. The tallest person on a class team would be quite an asset as the center, even though on her outside team she doesn't play that position. When students meet their class teams, they should use the day to get a sense of where each person fits best and a sense of team organization.

Warm-Up

1. Leave the balls out and let students practice basketball skills when they come into the gym.
2. Practice footwork: backpedaling, side to side, squaring shoulders, and change of direction.
3. Lead mimetics: jump to block, jump to rebound, and jump to shoot.

Lesson Sequence

1. Announce teams.
2. Discuss the following:
   a. Skill needs of a point guard and the other guard and their strategies
      - They bring the ball down slow enough to allow their team to get in position.
      - As playmakers, they can pass, drive to the basket, and shoot outside.
      - They take the ball out and return it to play.
   b. Scoring potential of a team if their center is successful
   c. Role of forward—getting open, setting screens, and rebounding
3. Give students time to get pinnies and decide who plays what position.
4. Play full-court games.

5. Pause the games after about 10 minutes to consider position changes.
6. Continue games.

Review and Stretching

As students stretch, discuss the following:

- How does the 3-second rule affect offensive rebounding?
- Is everyone clear on your offensive responsibilities?
- Who tends to bring the ball down most often? What skill does that person need?
- Whose rebounding skills are a gold mine if they can cash in on missed shots from team-mates?
- Which position has to think, get open to score, get inside, and score, score, score?

Basketball
ADVANCED
LESSON 5

Fouls and Their Penalties

Facilities

One full court for every 10 players or the opportunity to play on full court for half the class and play on half-court the rest of the class

Materials

- One ball for every two players
- Pinnies
- Whistles for student officials

Performance Goal

Students will play basketball games, full court when possible.

Cognitive Goals

Students will do the following:

- Review fouls on and off ball and penalties for fouling (shooter and nonshooter).
- Choose their leaders (captains and cocaptains). Encourage them to choose someone who has not captained a team before.

Lesson Safety

- Focus students on how to help their team and the contributions they make when they all have a function and try to do their job. This focus will defuse negative competitive behavior within teams and help students feel good about themselves, whether they score or not.
- Make students play by the rules, calling fouls, penalties, and violations. Keeping games fair and square eliminates flare-ups and keeps the competition more fun for everyone.

Motivation

Basketball has more players in a concentrated area than any other game. Physical contact is almost the rule rather than the exception, yet it is illegal. Why? It results in injury and is the prime reason that some students dread the game. It is each player's responsibility to limit body contact and use skill to win rather than do whatever it takes to survive. When students don't do so, they should be penalized.

Warm-Up

1. All equipment should be immediately available for practice as students enter.
2. In attendance lines, have students dribble with their nondominant hand.

Lesson Sequence

1. Discuss the following (these might be the most practical for class use):
   a. Fouling—Contact with an opponent is usually illegal, but who is at fault?
      - Determining who has position, the ball carrier or defender
      - Determining the path in the air and on the ground
      - Determining if the foul occurred while in the act of shooting
   b. Penalties for fouling
      - Personal fouls and fouling out
         - Fouled shooters receive 2 or 3 shots if they missed, 1 if they scored.
         - In class, a player will foul out after three personal fouls.
      - Team fouls
         - The team fouled puts the ball in play from out of bounds closest to where the foul occurred, and the offending team is charged with one team foul.
         - On the fifth team foul, the penalty situation is in effect and the team fouled shoots one free throw, and if successful, another.
   c. Procedure for taking foul shots
      - Players from each team alternate on the line, with the shooter's opponents in both spots closest to the backboard.
      - All players must stay outside the lane until the ball is released.
2. Have teams pick captains and cocaptains, encouraging them to pick someone who has not been captain or cocaptain before.
3. Play full-court games.
4. Stop the game at halftime to make suggestions.
5. Continue games.

Review and Stretching

1. As students stretch, discuss the reason why fouling is so harshly penalized. Survey the teams:
   - Did anyone accumulate 5 team fouls?
   - Was anyone in a one-and-one free-throw situation?
   - Were fouled shooters given their two free throws?
   - Did teams increase their score because of successful free throws?
2. Collect the names of captains and cocaptains.

Teacher Homework

Make up tournament schedule.

Basketball
ADVANCED
LESSON 6

The Pick

Facilities

One full court for every 10 players or the opportunity to play on full court for half the class and play on half-court the rest of the class

Materials

- One ball for every two players
- Pinnies
- Whistles for student officials
- Tournament schedule chart

Performance Goal

Students will play practice basketball games, full court when possible.

Cognitive Goal

Students will learn how to set a pick and its purpose.

Lesson Safety

Work to keep the emotional, social, and physical environment safe and positive throughout the tournament.

Motivation

During the tournament, which starts next time, class time will be purely for playing the game. As a team, students will use what they have learned to organize themselves, to coach themselves, and to make progress on the court. Though they will be in charge of themselves, tell them that you will be available to offer advice and will be officiating part of each game. Announce that the schedule is posted, that their win–loss record will be recorded next to their team or captains' names, and that for this last practice game, you are going to teach them how to use a pick so they can practice using it.

Warm-Up

1. Leave the balls out and let students practice basketball skills when they come into the gym.
2. Before games, have each team shoot and rebound foul shots.

Lesson Sequence

1. Discuss and demonstrate setting a pick.
   a. A pick uses a teammate's position to block the path a guard must take to keep up with the ball handler.
   b. The ball handler dribbles toward a teammate as close as possible and past her to head for the basket.
   c. The teammate who screens out the defender must stop a step or two before the guard gets there, lining his chest up with the shoulder of the moving guard, and sticking that position with arms down by the sides, feet parallel and knees bent, until his teammate dribbles by. Then he may roll to a better court position.
2. Play full-court games.
3. Stop at halftime to offer advice or discuss a teachable moment.
4. Continue games.

Review and Stretching

As students stretch, do the following:
- Review what a pick is.
- Entertain their questions.
- If there are none, let teams discuss plans for their next game.

Teacher Homework

Prepare and post team standings.

Tournament Round 1

Facilities

One full court for every 10 players or the opportunity to play on full court for half the class and play on half-court the rest of the class

Materials

- One ball for every two players
- Pinnies
- Whistles for student officials
- Tournament schedule chart
- Team records with captains' names

Performance Goal

Students will play round 1 of their tournament.

Cognitive Goals

Students will learn the following:

- How to follow the tournament chart and assume responsibility
  - For arriving on correct court
  - For choosing for possession, which means wearing pinnies
  - For getting pinnies
- How to play well while exhibiting good sportsmanship

Lesson Safety

Be vigilant about the emotional, social, and physical environment. React immediately to any negative behavior.

Motivation

This is round 1. Have captains direct their teams to their courts, choose who gets the ball first, and remember, whoever gets first possession wears the pinnies. The other team can choose which side of the court they want.

Warm-Up

Leave the balls out and let students practice basketball skills when they come into the gym.

Lesson Sequence

1. Entertain questions and begin round 1.
2. Have students play full-court games, officiating at each court equally.
3. Stop the games at halftime and allow reorganization and change of basket.
4. Continue games until 3 minutes before dismissal.

Review and Stretching

Entertain questions and collect scores.

Assessment

Observe, using observations to provide students with personal suggestions and coaching.

Basketball
ADVANCED
LESSONS
8-11

Tournament Rounds 2, 3, 4, and 5

Facilities

One full court for every 10 players or the opportunity to play on full court for half the class and play on half-court the rest of the class

Materials

- One ball for every two players
- Pinnies
- Whistles for student officials
- Tournament schedule chart
- Team records with captains' names
- Advanced skills rubric

Performance Goal

Students will complete rounds 2, 3, 4, and 5.

Cognitive Goals

Students will assume responsibility for the following:

- Daily expectations
- Seeking out or trying to make strategic adjustments to new opponents
- Playing hard but still exercising good judgment and sportsmanship

Lesson Safety

Be vigilant about the emotional, social, and physical environment. React immediately to any negative behavior.

Motivation

Announce the standings, your positive observations of previous contests, and items that were not covered enough or need review, and wish the students good luck and lots of fun.

Warm-Up

Leave the balls out and let students practice basketball skills when they come into the gym.

Lesson Sequence

1. Answer questions and then begin.
2. Have students play full-court games, officiating for equal time on each court.
3. Stop the games at halftime to allow reorganization and change of basket.
4. Continue games until 3 minutes before dismissal.

Review and Stretching

1. Entertain questions.
2. Announce that if students are curious, the skills rubric is posted.
3. Collect scores and compliment whatever you can.

Performance Goals and Tournament Round 6

Facilities

One full court for every 10 players or the opportunity to play on full court for half the class and play on half-court the rest of the class

Materials

- One ball for every two players
- Pinnies
- Whistles for student officials

- Tournament schedule chart
- Team records with captains' names
- Advanced skills rubric

Performance Goal

Students will play round 6 while being graded.

Cognitive Goal

Students will learn the performance standards for grades.

Lesson Safety

Be vigilant about the emotional, social, and physical environment. React immediately to any negative behavior.

Motivation

As the unit is closing, remind students that a quiz is coming up, as well as grading. Explain that grading will break down how they play their position on offense and how they assume defensive responsibilities. In short, it is how they try to do the right thing, even if their shooting or timing is off, that will be graded. Remind them that what you will be looking for is posted. Then announce standings and wish them a good game.

Warm-Up

Leave the balls out and let students practice basketball skills when they come into the gym.

Lesson Sequence

1. Answer questions and then begin.
2. Have students play full-court games, officiating for equal time on each court.
3. Stop the games at halftime to allow reorganization and change of basket.
4. Continue games until 3 minutes before dismissal.

Review and Stretching

1. Entertain questions.
2. Collect scores.
3. Compliment whatever you can.

Assessment

Use the advanced skills rubric or grade by team responsibility.
- Guards—bringing the ball down, feeding their teammates, and using their shooting options occasionally
- Centers—getting into key on offense, putting the ball up again on the offensive boards, and getting into position quickly on defense and boxing
- Forwards—getting down to the other side before ball does, getting open, and taking open outside shots when team is in position to rebound
- Defense—positioning and being prepared to jump to block and rebound

Basketball
ADVANCED
LESSON 13

Tournament Round 7

Facilities

One full court for every 10 players or the opportunity to play on full court for half the class and play on half-court the rest of the class

Materials

- One ball for every two players
- Pinnies
- Whistles for student officials
- Tournament schedule chart
- Team records with captains' names
- Advanced skills rubric

Performance Goal

Students will play round 7.

Cognitive Goal

Students will understand that the pressure of the competition does not entitle them to inappropriate behavior.

Lesson Safety

Be vigilant about the emotional, social, and physical environment. React immediately to any negative behavior.

Motivation

As you continue officiating and determining grades, remind students that they should just get out there and do their best. They are playing so well with their teams that they will have no problem getting full credit because doing their job for their team, not being great scorers, dribblers, or rebounders, is what's important.

Announce the standings and wish everyone a great game.

Warm-Up

Leave the balls out and let students practice basketball skills when they come into the gym.

Lesson Sequence

1. Answer questions and then begin round 7.
2. Have students play full-court games, officiating for equal time on each court.
3. Stop the games at halftime to allow reorganization and change of basket.
4. Continue games until 3 minutes before dismissal.

Review and Stretching

1. As students stretch, review their jobs:
   - Guards—bringing the ball down, feeding their teammates, and using their shooting options occasionally
   - Centers—getting into key on offense, putting the ball up again on the offensive boards, and getting into position quickly on defense and boxing
   - Forwards—getting down to the other side before ball does, getting open, and taking open outside shots when team is in position to rebound
   - Defense—positioning and being prepared to jump to block and rebound
2. Collect scores and compliment play.

Final Tournament Round

Facilities

One full court for every 10 players or the opportunity to play on full court for half the class and play on half-court the rest of the class

Materials

- One ball for every two players
- Pinnies
- Whistles for student officials
- Tournament schedule chart
- Team records with captains' names
- Advanced skills rubric

Performance Goal

Students will play round 8, the last competitive round of the tournament.

Cognitive Goal

Students will enjoy their last game and learn how much they improved.

Lesson Safety

Be vigilant about the emotional, social, and physical environment. React immediately to any negative behavior.

Motivation

Compliment the class on their all-around play as a team. Tell them that win or lose, you are delighted with how each team learned to work together, how they took up their court responsibilities, and how some have improved so much since they started that you are amazed. Tell them to enjoy their last tournament game and remind them that next class they will have a short quiz before playing in a special event. Announce the standings and possibilities and send them out for a great last round.

Warm-Up

Leave the balls out and let students practice basketball skills when they come into the gym.

Lesson Sequence

1. Answer questions and begin round 8.
2. Have students play full-court games, officiating for equal time on each court.
3. Stop the games at halftime to allow reorganization and change of basket.
4. Continue games until 1 minute before dismissal.

Review and Stretching

Collect scores and compliment achievements.

Quiz and Play-Offs

Facilities

One full court for every 10 players or the opportunity to play on full court for half the class and play on half-court the rest of the class

Materials

- One quiz for each student
- Pens and pencils
- One ball for every two players
- Pinnies
- Whistles for student officials
- Tournament schedule chart
- Team records with captains' names
- Advanced skills rubric

Performance Goals

Students will do the following:

- Take a quiz.
- Perform a minimum of 20 minutes of activity.

Cognitive Goal

Students will measure how well they understand the game of basketball.

Lesson Safety

Allow some time to warm up after students conclude their quiz.

Warm-Up

Have students pick up a ball after taking the quiz and practice before the last game.

Lesson Sequence

1. Distribute tests as students enter and collect after 10 minutes.
2. Allow students to decide how they want to play the last day of basketball.
   a. Assign courts to play-off teams if play-offs are necessary.
   b. If not, it's a day to play pickup games.
3. Continue games until 3 minutes before the end of class.

Review and Stretching

Announce final standings and compliment students:

- Most improved player
- Most improved team
- Most valuable players
- Any other accomplishments you can find to compliment

Advanced Basketball Skills Rubric

Name _____ Date _____

Teacher _____ Class _____

	0	1	2	3	4	5
Skills	No effort.	• Finds legal ways to move the ball. • Selects appropriate times to shoot. • Has stamina to play offense and defense. • Takes responsibility for a position.	• Makes fast, accurate passes. • Jumps to rebound, catch, shoot, or block. • Runs to get open on offense and to close in on defense. • Stays between opponent and hoop.	• Shots from outside are not forced and are sometimes successful. • Can catch while on the go. • Won't let opponent take an unguarded shot.	• Is scoring threat. • Gets open. • Effective on defense and rarely fouls. • Anticipates teammates' cuts and can pass to the person cutting to the inside of the key.	• Can drive to basket to score. • Makes offensive rebounds that usually lead to a score. • Feeds open player for score. • Has developed outside shot for score. • Causes turnovers.
Position and transition	No effort.	• Does not concentrate on play. • Hardly plays position. • Does not drop back for defense as necessary.	• Tries to assume assigned position. • Does not cause unforced turnovers. • Attempts to get to defense position. • Has stamina on both ends.	• Changes direction as needed. • Moves to cover defensive position before the ball arrives. • Plays offensive role. • Plays person-to-person without making unnecessary fouls.	• Gets open on offense. • Anticipates transition and tries to get there early. • Can execute full-court press. • Can switch from person-to-person or zone defense.	• Screens for the ball carrier. • Either slows down the ball on transition or gets to position ahead of it. • Has skills to keep possession when double-teamed.
Teamwork and attitude	No effort.	• Blames others. • Needs supervision to stay on task. • Interferes with other team. • Tries to take over.	• Gets to court on time. • Warms up with team. • Plays within the rules.	• Works well with teammates. • Plays within the rules. • Takes responsibility for position.	• Consistently tries to play at personal best. • Recognizes good teammate effort and success. • Shows good sportsmanship.	• Inspires team. • Backs up instead of taking over for teammates. • Shows reliable, consistent leadership. • Helps individual team members improve.

From Isobel Kleinman, 2009, *Complete Physical Education Plans for Grades 5 to 12, Second Edition* (Champaign, IL: Human Kinetics).

Advanced Basketball Quiz

Name _____ Date _____

Teacher _____ Class _____

True or False

Read each statement carefully. If the statement is true, write a *T* in the column to the left. If the statement is false, write an *F*. If using a grid sheet, blacken in the appropriate column for each question, making sure to use the correctly numbered line for each question and its answer.

_____ 1. The 3-second rule limits the time defensive players may stay in the basketball key.

_____ 2. Once the ball is in the air, it is free, no team is in possession, and everyone can remain in the key to block or to rebound or to shoot.

_____ 3. If your shot hits the backboard and comes right back to you, you are imparting too much underspin.

_____ 4. A player who fouls too often is ejected from a basketball game.

_____ 5. If you decide to dribble to the basket to take a layup shot because the lane is clear, but suddenly someone is there and there is contact, you are charged with a foul called *charging*.

_____ 6. When one team is responsible for six team fouls during a playing quarter, opponents take a foul shot, and if successful, they take another one.

_____ 7. Letting the tips of your fingers touch the ball as it rolls out of your hands imparts underspin.

_____ 8. When the ball changes possession, forwards and centers should change sides of the court as quickly as possible.

_____ 9. If the center is playing her team role, she will be taking lots of outside shots.

_____ 10. The point guard can speed up the game by dribbling.

Advanced Basketball Answer Key

True or False

1. F—The 3-second rule only applies to the offense when they are in possession of the ball.

2. T

3. F—Underspin will make the ball drop, not come straight back at you.

4. T—A limit is set to how many fouls a player can have in one game. Class, interschool, club, and professional limits may vary.

5. F—The person who entered the lane is charged with a foul called *blocking*.

6. T—Teams line up for a foul shot and the referee instructs that the shooter has one and one.

7. T

8. T—The faster forwards and centers make their transition to the other side, the more options offensive guards have and the less likely it is for opponents to easily score.

9. F—The center should be positioned to rebound everyone else's outside shots.

10. F—The game is slowed down by the dribble.

 From Isobel Kleinman, 2009, *Complete Physical Education Plans for Grades 5 to 12, Second Edition* (Champaign, IL: Human Kinetics).

8

Field Hockey

Chapter Overview

1. Introduce equipment and relevant rules.
   a. Stick
   b. Grip
   c. Shin guards
2. Explain, demonstrate, and practice common offensive and defensive skills.
   a. Dribble
   b. Push-pass
   c. Drive
   d. Stop
3. Explain, demonstrate, and practice defensive skills.
   a. Straight-on tackle
   b. Left-hand lunge
4. Diagram field positioning and explain the major responsibilities of each position.
   a. Forwards—wings, centers, inners (strikers)
   b. Halfbacks (midfielders)—right, left, and center
   c. Fullbacks—right and left
   d. Goalie
5. Teach both types of standard rules and use them during game play
   a. Procedural rules
   b. Starting play
   - Ball is put in play with a back-pass by a player in the midfield circle.
   - Return ball from out-of-bounds.
     - From the sideline, use a pass where it went out.
     - From the goal line, use a corner hit if sent out by defense; use a sideline pass if hit out by offense

»continued

»continued

- Restarting play after a goal is same as starting a game.
- For simultaneous penalties, ball is put in play with a bully.

c. Fouls
- Obstruction—shielding the ball with the stick or the body
- Illegal use of the stick—advancing the ball with the round side of the stick
- Illegally advancing the ball with anything other than the stick

d. Playing unsafely
- Avoid unsafe play and penalties.
- Drive the ball so it stays close to the ground.
- End the swing at the knees.
- No hooking or holding the opponent's stick.

6. Teach procedures used after penalties and personal fouls.
7. Teach how strategy and skills differ on different sides of the field.

Field Hockey Study Sheet

History

Drawings in a tomb in the Nile Valley that are over 4,000 years old show the earliest evidence of the sporting use of curved sticks. The ancient Greeks held competitions using sticks during the Olympics, thousands of years later. Centuries later, French shepherds played a stick game called *hoque*. Despite these early starts, modern field hockey is credited to the British for their efforts to create uniform rules during the 19th century.

The Irish, Scots, British, and Welsh played hurley, shinty, hockie, and ban, games that all used sticks but had their own rules. The British standardized them in the late 1800s, which is when field hockey began looking like the game played today.

The British love of the game crossed the Atlantic Ocean in 1901 with Constance Applebee. Horrified by what she saw as passing for women's activity at a summer seminar at Harvard, Applebee introduced field hockey to the Harvard women. She is also credited with introducing field hockey to Wellesley, Smith, Radcliffe, Mount Holyoke, and Bryn Mawr.

Official competitions began in Philadelphia at the Merion Cricket Club. Since 1902, the Merion Cricket Club has hosted an annual competition between their club and players from Bryn Mawr.

Field hockey is an international game. It is played at all levels by all ages and by both sexes. The Internet is a wonderful source of information on the many organized clubs and leagues that specialize in field hockey.

Fun Facts

- Men's field hockey began in 1928 when the Westchester Field Hockey Club of Rye, New York, played the Germantown Cricket Club near Philadelphia.

- Field hockey did not allow substitutions until 1992. Until then, the only time fresh players could enter the game was at halftime.

- Unlike most games, field hockey requires shooters to be inside a strike zone. The strike zone is marked by a semicircle 16 yards (14.5 meters) from the goal.

- One side of the stick is curved and the other is flat. Players can only advance the ball using the flat side of the stick.

- In field hockey, it is illegal to shield the ball with your body or stick.

- At one time, the game began with a bully. During the bully, two opposing players stood in the center of the field on either side of the ball. On the signal, they alternately tapped their sticks to the ground and then together. After the third tap, they could attempt to gain control of the ball. Now the only time the bully is used to put the ball back into play is after the two teams on the field commit simultaneous penalties. In that event, the bully only requires one tap.

Benefits

- Field hockey provides a great workout.
- It is great fun to be part of a team.
- Playing outdoors on a grassy field is exhilarating.

Field Hockey Field With Starting Positions

The positions on this diagram (see figure 8.1) are the positions each player should go to at the start of the game and after a goal is scored.

»continued

From Isobel Kleinman, 2009, *Complete Physical Education Plans for Grades 5 to 12, Second Edition* (Champaign, IL: Human Kinetics). **333**

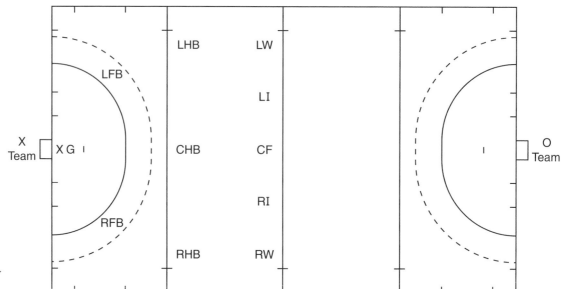

Figure 8.1 Field hockey field with starting positions.

Positions

Forwards

- Left wing—The left wing receives most passes, needs good foot speed, must have a good dribble, and must be able to drive the ball to the right.

- Left inner—This shooter needs to be in front of the goal during the inlet pass and to deflect or drive the ball into the goal. The left inner also must be able to push the ball off to the right.

- Center forward—This is the leader of the attack, who directs it left, right, or center. The center forward must be in front of the goal to shoot when the inlet pass crosses the goal.

- Right inner—The primary job of the right inner is to score.

- Right wing—The right wing is the beneficiary of interceptions from opponent's left wing and needs foot speed and good dribbling skills.

Halfbacks

- Right halfback—Must keep up with opponent's left wing, trying to stay between the left wing and the goal. Also needs good tackling skills.

- Left halfback—Needs good tackling skills and to be able to pass forward and to the right.

- Center halfback—The leader of the defense converts offense to defense and vice versa. The center halfback directs the attack to the left or right wings. Under special circumstances, the center halfback can go all the way into the striker's circle to score.

Fullbacks

- Right—The right fullback must be able to clear the ball down and out with a strong drive and have a sense of where the goalposts are. The right fullback must also be prepared to cover for the halfback if the halfback is being overrun by opponents' left wing.

- Left—Same as right halfback, but on opposite side.

Goalie

- Must wear a helmet and leg, chest, and hand padding, and can legally block the ball with body and hands when inside the strikers' circle.

- Goalies may only use their stick or feet to clear it.

»continued

From Isobel Kleinman, 2009, *Complete Physical Education Plans for Grades 5 to 12, Second Edition* (Champaign, IL: Human Kinetics).

»continued

Rules

Procedures

- Start of game and after a goal begins in the center circle with a pass-back
- Balls going out of bounds
  - Over the sideline—hit-in from where it went out
  - Over the goal line
  - By attacking team—put into play with a 16-yard (14.5-meter) hit
  - By defending team (accidentally)—penalty corner
  - By defending team (intentionally)—penalty shot at goal

Fouls

- Obstruction (using body or stick to shield the ball)
- Using the round side of the stick
- Unsafe play caused by charging, hitting, pushing, tripping, or shoving
- Playing the ball with the stick in a dangerous way such as high sticks
- Interfering with opponent's stick by hitting, hooking, or holding the stick
- Advancing the ball with anything other than the stick
- Stopping or deflecting the ball with the body
- Using the round side of the stick
- Shooting for goal outside the striker's circle

Penalties

- When the violation occurs on the playing field, a free hit is awarded to opponents on the spot.
  - Opponents must be 5 yards (4.5 meters) off the ball.
  - The ball must be stationary when struck.
  - The hitter cannot replay the ball until another player touches it.
- When the violation occurs inside the striker's circle by the offense, the defense gets a 16-yard (14.5-meter) hit. When it occurs by the defense, the offense gets a penalty corner.
- When the violation is intentional, the offense gets a penalty shot.
- When the defense hits the ball over their goal line, the offense getes a corner hit.
- When the defense violates the rules to prevent a sure goal, the offense gets a penalty shot on goal.
- A player who exhibits a flagrant disregard for the safety of others can be suspended from play.

Field Hockey Extension Project

Name _____ Date _____

Teacher _____ Class _____

What equipment do you need to do these activities on your own?

Where can you participate outside of school?

Do you have friends who would join you? List their names.

What are the health benefits of participating in a field hockey program?

 From Isobel Kleinman, 2009, *Complete Physical Education Plans for Grades 5 to 12, Second Edition* (Champaign, IL: Human Kinetics).

Field Hockey Student Portfolio Checklist

Name _____ Date _____

Teacher _____ Class _____

_____ Can hold hockey stick.

_____ Can dribble the ball forward slowly.

_____ Can move the ball to a teammate with a push-pass.

_____ Knows how to reverse grip so can play ball to the right.

_____ Knows how to receive the ball with hockey stick.

_____ Often able to stop opponents if they dribble nearby.

_____ Can drive the ball 15 yards (14 meters).

_____ Can drive the ball 25 yards (23 meters).

_____ Can drive the ball 40 yards (36.5 meters).

_____ Knows what to do when playing position.

_____ Knows how the forwards count on their halfbacks and fullbacks.

_____ Can sense when to go back to get a pass.

_____ Can pass the ball to the right.

_____ Can use the left-hand lunge to stop a ball that is ahead.

_____ Knows how the game starts.

_____ Knows how to return a ball to play after it goes over the sideline.

_____ Knows where players must be to legally shoot for goal.

_____ Knows what the obstruction rule is trying to prevent.

_____ Can dribble at top speed without losing the ball.

_____ Knows how to line up for a penalty corner.

_____ Knows why teams get awarded a free hit.

_____ Can dodge opponents and keep control of the ball.

From Isobel Kleinman, 2009, *Complete Physical Education Plans for Grades 5 to 12, Second Edition* (Champaign, IL: Human Kinetics).

Field Hockey Learning Experience Outline

Contents and Procedure

1. Introduce equipment.
   a. Stick
   b. Grip
   c. Shin guards

2. Teach skills common to offense and defense.

   a. Dribble

   b. Push-pass

   c. Drive

   d. Stop

3. Teach defensive skills.

   a. Straight-on tackle

   b. Left-hand lunge

4. Teach putting the ball in play.

   a. Starting play—Ball is put in play with a back-pass by a player in the midfield circle.

   b. Returning ball from out-of-bounds from the sideline by taking a free hit where the ball crossed the line.

   c. Putting it in play if it passes over the goal line.

      • Corner hit from the 5-yard mark if sent out by defense.

      • Sideline free hit if hit out by offense.

5. Fouls

   a. Obstruction (shielding the ball with the stick or the body)

   b. Illegal use of the stick (advancing the ball with the round side of the stick)

   c. Illegally advancing the ball with anything other than the stick

6. Teach field positioning and the major responsibilities of each position.

   a. Forwards—wings, centers, and inners (strikers)

   b. Halfbacks (midfielders)—right, left, and center

   c. Fullbacks—right and left

   d. Goalie

7. Teach standard rules.

   a. Procedural rules

      • Restarting play after a goal—Same as starting a game.

      • Simultaneous penalties—Ball is put in play with a bully. (Two opponents alternately hit the ground and then the flat side of their sticks once before putting the ball, which is on the ground between them, back into play.)

   b. Playing unsafely

      • To avoid unsafe play and penalties, drive the ball so it stays close to the ground and end the swing at the knees.

      • Hooking or holding the opponent's stick is unsafe.

8. Teach what procedures to use after penalties and personal fouls.

9. Teach how strategy and skills differ on different sides of the field.

Teaching Tips

It is essential that every student in class have access to a field hockey stick and shin guards throughout the lesson. Since moving is more important than the actual activity, being short of equipment makes field hockey an unacceptable curriculum choice.

This unit integrates basic field hockey skills, basic game strategies, and the rules all players should know so that measured learning takes place in every lesson. New material might be a skill, a strategy, or a rule. Almost every minute of the lesson is dedicated to having students move. As students assemble, time is set aside to warm up by practicing the skills they learned in previous classes.

Students must wear shin guards as soon as defensive skills are introduced. Leave them near the sticks and balls, and have the students get accustomed to putting them on before they come out to the field.

Although the goal of the game and how it is accomplished is similar to soccer, try not to teach field hockey by comparing the two. Such an approach works only if the students know soccer and are able to move the ball in field hockey as far as they were able to in soccer. Introduce game concepts as if students are beginners and do so when students show they are able to pass the ball to a person 15 yards (14 meters) away, stop it, and dribble it legally.

Students will enjoy field hockey if they are capable of changing the direction of play. To do that, they need to hit solid drives. The drive and stop can never be overpracticed. Allow lots of repetition. This can be done by allowing students to come right to the field to practice as soon as they are dressed. Their warm-up should include driving, stopping, and dribbling the ball.

Involve students in a game once they have covered the dribble, drive, push-pass, and stop. An unorganized game can begin by the end of the third lesson if students have moved through the previous lessons easily. In many cases, especially for younger students, planning an unorganized game by the end of the third lesson is too hasty. So if students are not losing interest in skills acquisition, do not rush into a game situation. Lessons can be repeated for young players. Keep the enthusiasm high by creating challenges and varying the skills students are practicing and how they are practicing them. Spending an entire class on the dribble is extremely taxing for most students. It might even make them take an instant dislike to field hockey. To make practice challenging without spending an undue amount of time reorganizing, ask students to see who can do the following:

- Drive the ball the farthest.
- Hit and receive the most passes from their partner in 2 minutes.
- Get the ball from someone dribbling straight at them the most times (5 chances).
- Get the ball from someone running away (5 chances).
- Dribble from the right inner's position on the centerline, shoot, and get the ball in an unprotected goal (5 chances).

After a book is published, rules, skills, and strategies may change. Check Internet sites listed in suggested resources to keep up with the changes.

Teaching Tips for Students With Special Needs

Students who are unable to play should still have some responsibilities. For most, it is best to stay with the class; learn technique, rules, and strategies; and do what they are capable of doing. They should be able to walk to the field. They might be able to practice during warm-ups, or act as game officials, team coaches, or statisticians. Encourage them to do what they can.

Students with a long-term disability probably would be better served by placement in an adaptive physical education class. If there is no adaptive physical education program, students should do something else that is relevant. For instance, they can write a research report on the game and its history, equipment, and rules. They can draw charts that explain how each skill is executed. They can create an appropriate bulletin board with material they researched or drew. Or they can research the problem that keeps them from playing, cite medically suggested remedies, explain what would be acceptable movement for someone in their situation, and write about preventative care.

Facilities

Lined field with goalposts (see figure 8.2)

Materials

The lessons in this unit leave the goal cage empty and encourage all students to play a moving position.

- Set of goals for each field
- Cones
- Shin guards for every student
- Field hockey stick for every student
- Pinnies for half the class
- Ball for every student
- Blackboard, magnetic board, or other visual aid
- Two sets of goalie equipment for each game fielded at one time

Unit Safety

- Students must wear shin guards.
- If students play goalie, they must wear goalie pads, gloves, and helmet.

- Students exhibiting a dangerous use of sticks must be given immediate feedback to
  - stop endangering others,
  - learn the proper follow-through,
  - develop consideration for their classmates, and
  - learn to play by the rules.
- If students continue to play dangerously, the rules of the game (and of the class) should be exercised. Under the rules, players would be suspended for dangerous play.
- Lessons will always start with a skill-specific warm-up.
- Stretching should be done after the muscles are warm—at the end of class during review.

Rainy Days

Much can be accomplished during rainy days.

Warm-Ups

If used well, the warm-up can be a reinforcing activity as well as a learning activity. By using mimetics (movement rehearsals) for the push-pass, dribble, stop, drive, dodge left, dodge right, left-hand lunge, and reversing the grip (with or without the stick), students get into good habits. Have students go through the movement pattern,

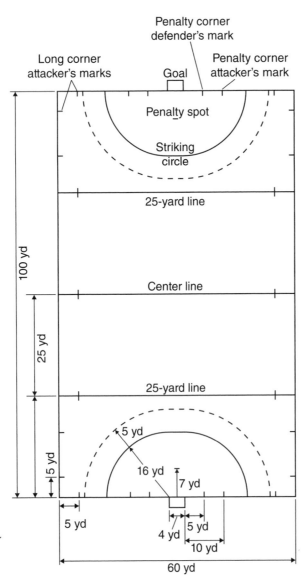

Figure 8.2 The markings of an official field hockey field.

repeating the motion at least 10 times. While doing so, have them practice the correct footwork, stick motion, and body positioning relative to an imaginary ball. Once they get the preparatory motions, have them practice following through to an imaginary target. In later classes, complicate your directions to them by asking that they practice getting ready to hit to the right (a tricky action in field hockey), to the left, or straight ahead.

Teach Fielding

Diagram and explain the unique responsibilities of each position and how they relate. Then use them in a modified game. When students understand their job, they will be much more comfortable on a big field and be better able to play as part of a team.

Teach Rules

Although students need not learn to be officials, they should learn the basic rules. A healthy respect for the rules of play should be expected. Some rules will need more review, and some will be learned on the field during teachable moments. Students will have the most difficulty understanding obstruction, so spend a bit more time on it.

Modified Games

Sometimes games must be modified. This will occur when you have too few or too many players, when the size of the space is suddenly reduced because you must field more teams, or when you have to come indoors because of inclement weather. Just because the game is modified does not mean you cannot continue to teach the same concepts. For instance, you may use outdoor field positions even though you might have to come indoors. By operating on a smaller scale without letting go of the need to communicate and play as a team, students will still be learning and having fun. If you have enough scooters, play scooter hockey (using knock hockey sticks). Students sit on the scooters and advance the ball (use a sponge or Wiffle ball) by dribbling or passing with a knock hockey stick. If you don't have scooters, have students play on the ground with a smaller stick and a smaller ball. Check out broomball.

Unit Timeline

This unit is designed to be used over 6 to 8 weeks and is made up of:

- 3 lessons for introduction of skills,
- 3 lessons for introducing new skills and beginning to use them in competition,
- 5 lessons for game strategies and teamwork,
- 6 lessons for a tournament, and
- 1 lesson for assessment and review.

Suggested Resources

Anders, S., and S. Myers. 1998. *Field hockey: Steps to success.* Champaign, IL: Human Kinetics.

Australian Sports Commission. 1991. *Level 0 coaching manual.* Reservoir, Victoria: Tecprint Australia.

Champion's Edge. 2008. Field hockey. www.ce-fieldhockey.com.

Fieldhockey.com. 2008. www.fieldhockey.com.

International Hockey Federation. 2008. www.fihockey.org.

Mitchell-Taverner, C. 2005. *Field hockey techniques and tactics.* Champaign, IL: Human Kinetics.

National Collegiate Athletic Association (NCAA). 2008. Women's field hockey. www.ncaa.com/fieldhockey/default.aspx?id=188.

Planet Field Hockey. 2005. www.planetfieldhockey.com.

USA Field Hockey. 2008. www.usfieldhockey.com.

wikiHow. 2008. Field hockey. www.wikihow.com/Special:LSearch?fulltext=Search&search=field+hockey.

Dribble and Push-Pass

Facilities

Grass field

Materials

- One hockey stick for every student
- One ball for every student

Performance Goals

Students will do the following:

- Grip the hockey stick properly.
- Advance the ball with their stick:
  - Using a dribble
  - Using a push-pass
- Improve their physical fitness.

Cognitive Goals

Students will learn the following:

- About the stick:
  - It has a flat side, which is the only side they can use.
  - It is best to contact the ball at the heel of the stick and not the toe.
- How to pass the ball to a teammate that is close by
- The advantages of both a tight and loose dribble:
  - When each are used in a game
  - How to change from loose to a tight dribble

Lesson Safety

1. Teach respect for the proper use of the field hockey stick.
2. Explain how in the course of the game, going for the ball might accidentally translate into hitting another player's stick or even legs near the ball, and that is why students wear shin guards.
3. Set up rules about the misuse of sticks. Dangerous students must either learn to curb their tendencies (whether it is a lack of skill or another problem causing it) or be removed from play until they can learn to play correctly.

Motivation

After students have run the field one and a half times, they are likely to be tired, out of breath, and hating you, so address that immediately. Their being tired works in your favor, because you have some teaching to do and will have their undivided attention while you explain that the stick has a flat side and that the rules allow players to use only the flat side to advance the ball. That means they cannot kick or use their feet to advance the ball, so they need to find out how to hold the stick so they can dribble down the field without feeling lopsided. They also need to learn how to get the ball to a nearby teammate using the push-pass. Tell them that though you'd like to teach the dribble first, you will let their heart rates come down a little while they learn the push-pass, which uses the same grip as the dribble, making an easy transition to the dribble.

Warm-Up (10 Minutes)

1. Ask students to take a stick and run once around the field holding it in their left hand.
2. When they return, have them put their right hand lower on the stick, palm facing out, and run halfway around the field so that the stick grazes the grass as they go.

3. Lead the mimetic for the dribble. Students come to attendance spots, holding the stick firmly with their right hand 6 inches (15 centimeters) below the left. Ask them to make the clubhead touch the grass with gentle taps generated by pulling the top of the stick back slightly and forward with their left hand.

4. Lead the mimetic for a push-pass to the right. Students step forward on their right foot (very unusual but necessary), and holding the left hand firm, push the stick with the right hand so the head stays along the ground until the right arm comes to full extension, pointing to its target. Have them recover to a standing position (5 times).

5. Have students repeat the push-pass with the left leg forward (5 times). Note how the grip is different for the push pass in figure 8.3 and how separated the hands are on the stick.

6. During the first day of the unit, set up a class routine that has students practicing and warming up while you take care of procedural tasks, students who have individual problems, and those in need of extra help.

a

b

Figure 8.3 The push-pass.

Lesson Sequence

1. After distributing one ball to every two students, check that they have the appropriate grip. The top of the left hand faces the direction of follow-through, and the palm of the right hand wraps completely around the stick about 6 inches (15 centimeters) lower than the left.

2. Students learned the lever action during warm-up. Now they have to address the ball.

   a. Place the heel of the clubhead behind the ball.

   b. Ask them to practice short, accurate passes to a partner stepping forward with the right foot (10 times) and then switch so they are stepping on their left (10 times).

3. As they practice, circulate, making sure

   a. the stick stays in contact with the ball as long as possible,

   b. the grip is not too tight,

   c. the right foot moves forward,

   d. they use no backswing, and

   e. the pushing arm extends toward their target.

4. Encourage students to use the stick to stop the ball.

   a. Remind them that they can only use the flat part of the stick.

   b. Let them experiment.

5. Gather students around to explain that a tight dribble uses the lever action in the push-pass, but it consists of gentle taps so they can keep the ball one step in front and to their right as they move forward.

   a. Students take turns dribbling, walking one way, and jogging on their return.

   b. Allow students several trips to become comfortable (they will be getting tired).

   c. Each trip, ask them to go faster as they come back.

   d. Before the third trip, explain the loose dribble.

      • Used in open field.

      • Allows players to run at top speed.

      • Players should be able to get to the ball within three steps.

   e. Have them use a loose dribble to go to the sideline and a tight dribble to come back.

   f. Afterward, ask them to push-pass the ball to their waiting partner.

Review and Stretching

1. Set up a routine to be done during the review that stretches these muscle groups:

   • Hamstrings

   • Quadriceps

   • Low back

   • Shoulders

2. Ask questions:

   • Can you legally stop a ball with your foot?

   • What is the only thing you can use to make the ball advance?

   • What can happen if the loose dribble gets too loose?

   • Where should the ball be during a loose dribble?

3. Tell students that next time, they should get equipment, dribble a lap, find a partner, and practice the push-pass.

Drive and Stop

Facilities

Grass field with a striker's circle marked in front of each goalpost

Materials

- One hockey stick for every student
- One ball for every student

Performance Goals

Students will do the following:

- Get a stick and a ball and go directly out to practice the dribble and push-pass.
- Advance the ball with their stick:
  - Using a dribble
  - Using a push-pass
  - Using a drive
- Stop the ball with their stick.
- Improve their physical fitness.

Cognitive Goals

Students will learn the following:

- The difference between a loose dribble and a tight dribble
- The difference between a drive and a push-pass
- Several rules
  - That swinging the stick high is considered dangerous
  - That it is illegal to take a shot outside the striking circle

Lesson Safety

Monitor the setting, curbing any dangerous tendencies, whether it be failure to put on shin guards or misuse of the field hockey stick.

Motivation

The students are looking more proficient at their dribble and push-pass and should be complimented for their success. Many are probably interested in hitting the ball a bit farther, and today they will learn how. As they learn how to drive the ball, they have to do so without endangering anyone around them. They also need the skill to legally stop the ball. The field hockey drive is not only used when shooting for goal, but it is also a long pass that players must learn to receive and control.

Warm-Up

1. Students take a lap around the field, dribbling as they go.
2. Students get a partner and practice their push-pass and stop (see figure 8.4). (This would be a good time to begin checking attendance, either as they practice or while they are doing mimetics.)
3. Lead mimetics:
   a. Dribble
   b. Push-pass
   c. Stop
      - Separate hands on the stick, the bottom hand going almost to the edge of the binding.
      - Lean the top of the stick forward so the face of the stick closes over the ball.
      - Give a little on imaginary stop to prevent ball from rebounding.

Figure 8.4 The stop.

Figure 8.5 Hand position and swing for the drive.

4. Do mimetics for the drive (see figure 8.5).
   - Bring hands together and to the top of the stick.
   - Step forward so the left shoulder faces the direction of the hit.
   - Take a backswing with elbows extended; follow through with stick, wrists, and elbow forming a straight line pointing in the direction of the target.

Lesson Sequence

1. Have students partner up and practice the drive and the stop, which they just learned during the mimetics warm-up.
2. As they practice, circulate, making sure
   - students only use the flat side of the stick to strike the ball,
   - the positioning is a side-stride to the ball (as a batter in baseball),
   - the left foot moves forward with hands together on the stick, and
   - the ball is slightly in front and to the left of the left foot on contact.

3. Have students use only the stick to stop the ball.
   - Remind them that they can only use the flat part of the stick.
   - Emphasize the separate hand positioning and the give on contact.
4. Gather students around to explain that the rules restrict the swing so no one gets hit in the face. Therefore, the backswing and follow-through are nothing like a golf swing and are penalized if the stick goes high.
5. Allow a few more minutes of practice before holding a little contest.
   - See which partners can legally drive (and stop) the most passes in 2 minutes.
   - If the students are excited, do this contest one more time.
6. End the session by asking student partners to dribble from the right wing and right inner position, passing back and forth to each other and shooting for goal once they enter the circle. If there is time, have them go down the other side of the field, switching who is the wing and inner and shooting within the circle.

Review and Stretching

While students do their stretching routine, ask:
- How does the grip on the hockey stick differ between a push-pass and a drive?
- Which foot should step forward on a drive? On a push-pass to the right?
- Which pass should be used when you want the ball to go farther and with more speed?
- Does anyone know why you were asked to wait to shoot until you entered the striking circle? (In field hockey you can only shoot for goal from within the striking circle.)

Straight Tackle

Facilities
Lined field

Materials
- Shin guards
- Pinnies
- Field hockey sticks (one for each student)
- One ball for every two students

Performance Goals
Students will do the following:
- Practice taking the ball away from its carrier.
- Improve skills:
  - Loose and tight dribble
  - Push-pass
  - Drive
  - Stop
- Improve their physical fitness.

Cognitive Goals
Students will learn the following:
- That getting a ball from an opponent means stopping it
- To use shin guards

- Several rules:
  - Shooting must take place inside the striker's circle.
  - The game begins with a pass-back from the circle on the center line.
  - Dangerous use of sticks is penalized.

Lesson Safety

Monitor the setting, curbing any dangerous tendencies, whether it be failure to put on shin guards or misuse of the field hockey stick.

Motivation

Students are improving their ability to move the ball. Compliment them on their accomplishments frequently. The only thing left to do before actually using the skills in a game is learning how to get the ball from someone who has it. How else can a player come up with a ball when the other team controls it? Intercepting. Opponents will not make getting the ball easy. To get the ball, the opponent's ball control must be challenged. That's what the straight-on tackle will do. Tell students not to get nervous about the word *tackle*. This is not football—no contact is allowed.

Warm-Up (5 Minutes)

1. Students go to the field, take a lap (dribbling and passing with a partner), and practice their drive and stop.
2. In attendance spots, lead mimetics for the push-pass, drive, and stop.
3. Introduce the straight-on tackle as moving in front of a loose dribbler to stop the ball.
   a. Have students separate their hands so they have a wide grip.
   b. Ask them to move forward directly in line with an imaginary dribbler and put the clubhead on the ground so the flat side is angled to block the ball from continuing on with the dribbler.
   c. Keep the stick down to block the ball from moving forward with the dribbler.

Lesson Sequence

1. Practice and review the loose and tight dribble.
   a. Have students dribble to sideline with a tight dribble and come back at top speed.
   b. Stress that they stay within a couple of strides of the ball when running fast.
   c. Allow two turns.
2. Teach how and why to use shin guards, and have students put them on.
3. Explain and demonstrate how to practice the straight-on tackle:
   a. Ask the dribbler not to be evasive but to dribble straight ahead as practiced.
   b. Have the partners switch so they practice five times on offense, five on defense.
   c. Circulate, praising aspects that are good and correcting those that need to be corrected.
      - Grip should be wide.
      - Positioning relative to the dribbler should be directly in front.
      - Position of clubhead should be down on ground and angled forward.
      - Hold firm until the dribbler overruns the ball.
4. Organize for a game.
   a. Divide the class in half and issue pinnies to half.
   b. Tell them guidelines for this field game.
      - The pinnies team will begin with a pass-back from the center circle.
      - Shooting can only be done inside the circle.
      - The stick is only for hitting the ball, not people.
   c. Ask them to take the field and let the game begin.

5. When the students, who will probably all be following the ball, get clustered, have them freeze in place.

    a. Ask them to look around and see how close they are.

    b. Ask some to stay back to stop an attack, some to take the right side of the field, and some to take the left side of the field.

6. Let the game continue after the adjustment. Stop the game as necessary.

Review and Stretching

1. Have students gather to return equipment.

2. As students stretch using the previous routine, ask questions.

    - What is a straight-on tackle?
    - When is the tackle likely to be most successful: when opponents use a loose dribble or a tight dribble?
    - Does the game start with a forward pass?
    - Should you follow the ball?

Basic Game

Facilities

Marked field hockey field for every two teams

Materials

- One hockey stick for every student
- One ball for every student
- Pinnies

Performance Goals

Students will do the following:

- Put on shin guards before coming out to the field.
- Begin a game.
- Improve skills:
    - Loose and tight dribble
    - Push-pass
    - Drive
    - Stop
- Improve their physical fitness.

Cognitive Goals

Students will learn the following:

- That they should not try to cover the whole field themselves
- How to return the ball to play after the game is stopped:
    - Out of bounds on the sidelines
    - Out of bounds on the end lines
    - After a goal

Lesson Safety

Monitor the setting, curbing any dangerous tendencies, whether it be failure to put on shin guards or misuse of the field hockey stick.

Motivation

What the students really need to learn is that with more team organization, they'll have teammates to pass to and others who can get the ball back for them when they lose it. After team organization is explained, they will be playing the game.

Warm-Up (5 Minutes)

1. Students go directly to the field to practice dribbling and passing to a partner (1 lap).
2. Practice the drive and stop.

Lesson Sequence

1. Organize for a game.

    a. Make sure shin guards are on.

    b. Issue pinnies to half the class.

    c. Remind them of guidelines:

    - The pinnie team begins with a pass-back from the center circle.
    - Shooting can only be done inside the striking circle.
    - The stick is only for hitting the ball, not people.
    - When the ball goes out of bounds, they have to learn how to put it back in.

    d. Ask them to take the field and let the game begin (no goalie).

2. After a few minutes of play, stop the class and ask some players to take the left, the right, or the middle of the field.

3. After a few more minutes of play, ask those on the left to divide up so they are forwards, halfbacks, or fullbacks.

    a. Forwards are to get the ball in the striker's circle to shoot.

    b. Halfbacks need to stop the other team and, once they get the ball, to feed it back to their forwards.

    c. Fullbacks are first defenders if opponents get the ball to the centerline quickly and last defenders if opponents pass their halfbacks.

4. As the game continues, use teachable moments for balls rolling out of bounds.

    a. Sideline

    - A push-pass or drive sends the ball in from where it went out by opponents.
    - Other players must stand at least 5 yards (4.5 meters) from the ball.

    b. End line

    - If sent out by offense, defense takes a 16-yard (14.5-meter) hit in line with the exit point.
    - If sent out by defense, the following occurs:
        - The ball is placed on end line, 10 yards (9 meters) from the goalpost.
        - Offensive team must stand outside the striking circle.
        - A shot on goal cannot be taken directly until the ball travels outside the circle.
        - Up to five defenders may stand behind the goal line.

Review and Stretching

As students stretch, comment on fielding weaknesses that occurred during the game and ask questions:

- How did people on the left feel when having to pass to the right?
- Which is easier, hitting to the left or hitting to the right?
- Who actually received a ball because your teammate passed it to you?
- What other ways were there to receive a ball?

Left-Hand Lunge

Facilities

Marked field hockey field for every two teams

Materials

- One hockey stick for every student
- One ball for every student
- Pinnies
- Visual aid showing several examples of obstructions

Performance Goals

Students will do the following:

- Continue improving the skills of driving, stopping, and dribbling.
- Perform a second defensive skill, the left-hand lunge.
- Improve their physical fitness.

Cognitive Goals

Students will learn the following:

- The obstruction rule (not allowed to shield the ball with stick or body)
- What behaviors are considered fouls
- Necessary attributes of the wing
- How to play as a team and not follow the ball

Lesson Safety

Monitor the setting, curbing any dangerous tendencies, whether it be failure to put on shin guards or misuse of the field hockey stick.

Motivation

Remind students how frustrating it is when someone gets past them and there is no one in sight to stop them. It is frustrating when an opponent escapes a straight-on tackle and they can't get in front of the opponent to get the ball back. That's why students will love the left-hand lunge. It gives them another chance at getting the ball when their opponent is not kind enough to accidentally lose control of the ball and send it to a teammate. Students will learn the left-hand lunge and take a little time to practice it before getting into a short game.

Warm-Up (10 Minutes)

1. Students go directly to the field to practice:
   - One lap around the field, dribbling and passing to a partner
   - Drive and stop
2. Do mimetics for the drive and push-pass.
3. Do mimetics for the left-hand lunge:
   - With two hands on the stick, the right hand pushes the stick out front and to the left so the left arm is extended and the right is no longer holding on (5 times).
   - Step forward with left leg and begin the stick motion (5 times).

Lesson Sequence

1. Explain and demonstrate the left-hand lunge (see figure 8.6). From a two-handed carrying position, the player uses the right hand to help the left arm swing the stick out in a low arch until the left hand is the only hand on the stick, the arm is fully extended, the stick is as far forward as possible, the body is lunging forward on the left foot, and the stick

has met the ground a few inches in front of the ball so that the ball rolls into it. Proper placement will result in the ball stopping when it rolls into the stick and the opponent overrunning the ball.

 a. Approach from behind and on the stick side of the ball carrier.

  • Aim the stick about 4 inches (10 centimeters) in front of the ball.

  • Keep the one-hand grip and wrist firm to hold the ball in place.

 b. Avoid hitting the ball or hooking sticks with the opponent.

 c. If the tackle is near the opponent, use two hands on the stick.

2. Have partners practice trying to stop and get the ball until each has five successes.

 a. Player 1 begins to run and dribble across the field.

 b. Player 2 tries catching up, but before doing so, uses the left-hand lunge to stop the ball.

3. Explain the obstruction rule.

 a. Illegal for ball carriers to protect the ball by turning their back so opponent can't reach it, blocking the ball with the stick, or getting someone to screen out opponents.

 b. When an obstruction is called, the other team gets a free hit on the spot.

 c. Show examples. Either demonstrate or use a visual aid.

4. Distribute pinnies to half the class.

5. Tell students that if they are really fast, they should play the left or right wing.

  • The defense should clear the ball to the outside of the field.

  • The outside is less crowded so fast players can use their speed more.

  • The wing might have to drop back to help the defense.

6. Stop the game for dangerous play or otherwise illegal play.

 a. Teach the fouls during teachable moments (only if they happen).

  • Obstruction—shielding the ball from opponents with the body or stick

  • Using the round side of the stick

  • Personal fouls such as charging, hitting, shoving, or tripping an opponent

  • Playing the ball or using the stick in a potentially dangerous way

  • Advancing the ball with anything other than the stick

Figure 8.6 Performing a left-hand lunge on the right foot results in a shorter reach.

AP Photo/Ivan Sekretarev

- Stopping or deflecting the ball with the body
- Interfering with the opponent's stick by hitting, hooking, or holding it
    b. Teach what happens after a routine field penalty is called.
        - A free hit is awarded to opponents on the spot the penalty occurred.
        - Opponents must be 5 yards (4.5 meters) off the ball.
        - The ball must be stationary when struck.
        - The hitter cannot replay the ball until another player touches it.

Review and Stretching

As students stretch, ask questions.

- When you try to take a ball away from an opponent legally, what are you trying to do?
- If an opponent gets by you with the ball, what can you do with your stick?
- Why should the right and left wings have good foot speed and a great dribble?
- What players have to learn to pass to their right?
- Can anyone explain how to obstruct an opponent's access to the ball?
- After a call, how is the ball put back into play?

Teacher Homework

Make up team rosters when you feel you know the students well enough to create evenly skilled teams. Consider the following:

- Speed
- Stick work
- Ability to move the ball long distances
- Stamina

Do not put more than 11 players on any team. If you have more students, make smaller teams and make more of them.

Field Positioning

Facilities

Marked field hockey field for every two teams

Materials

- One hockey stick for every student
- One ball for every student
- Pinnies
- Visual aid (blackboard, chart, or magnetic board) to diagram positions at the start of a game (see figure 8.1 on page 334) and teams when the ball is left of the striker's circle (see figure 8.7 on page 354)

Performance Goals

Students will do the following:

- Continue improving the skills of passing, receiving, dribbling, and tackling.
- Play a designated role for their team during the game.
- Improve their physical fitness.

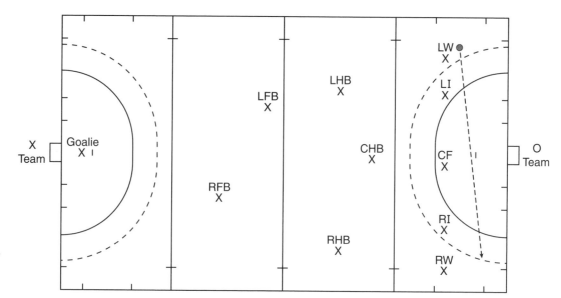

Figure 8.7 Team X moves down to attack their opponent's goal. Here the left wing centers the ball with an inlet pass.

Cognitive Goal

Students will learn how players divide responsibilities on the field.

Lesson Safety

Monitor the setting, curbing any dangerous tendencies, whether it be failure to put on shin guards or misuse of the field hockey stick.

Motivation

An awful lot of work goes into having one person score a goal. Without the defense backing up their forwards, there would be no offense. Talk about field positions, their special responsibilities, and how each position helps the others out.

Explain that when teams are announced, players should choose a position and begin playing it. So students are knowledgeable about the demands of each position, at halftime the class will go over what the positions do and where they should be at different times during the course of the game.

Warm-Up (5 Minutes)

Students go directly out to practice:

- Do one lap around the field, dribbling and passing to a partner.
- Practice the drive and stop.
- Practice left-hand lunge and straight-on tackle.

Lesson Sequence

1. Announce the teams. (This can be delayed a lesson or two, though students should still play and start getting an understanding of positioning.) Check that students have shin guards and then send two teams to each field.
2. Start the game, using the teachable moment to call fouls.
3. Call a halftime. Go over positions. Show the 11 positions of an official team.
   a. Forwards—left and right wing, left and right inner (shooters), and center forward
   b. Halfbacks—right, left, and center
   c. Fullbacks—left and right
   d. Goalie (no goalie for class games)
4. Go over positioning when the ball is in different locations on the field.
   a. Forwards are responsible for getting the ball in the striker's circle and scoring.
   b. Halfbacks should be 25 to 30 yards (23-27 meters) from the forwards so they can stop opponents from getting into attacking position and redirect the ball while the forwards are still in a position to score.

c. Fullbacks, as the last line of defense before the goalie, never cross the centerline but stop the attack before it closes in on the goalie. They have to sense where the goalposts are so they don't drive their shots across them when clearing the ball to a halfback or forward.

5. Start the second half using the teachable moment to remind students who wander out of position where they should be. Try to do this without stopping the game to coach them.

Review and Stretching

As students stretch, ask questions:

- If you are a forward, raise your hand. What is your main job?
- If you play the left side of the field, raise your hand. What direction do you generally have to pass to, right or left?
- Does anyone have a guess about whose job on the field might be the most confusing?

Pass to Right and Games

Facilities

Marked field hockey field for every two teams

Materials

- One hockey stick for every student
- One ball for every student
- Pinnies

Performance Goals

Students will do the following:

- Continue improving their skills and fitness.
- Practice passing from left to right.
- Play the game in their designated position.

Cognitive Goals

Students will learn the following:

- How footwork and stick work differ in order to send a ball right
- How players divide responsibilities on the field

Lesson Safety

Monitor the setting, curbing any dangerous tendencies, whether it be failure to put on shin guards or misuse of the field hockey stick.

Motivation

Not much time will be spent on anything new so the class can get into the game, but students will be sensitized to the difficulty that players on the left of the field face when they try to pass. Students who play on the left have an entire team and the direction of the goal on their right. To gain options so they are capable of surprising their opponent by passing right, and to develop an appreciation for the difficulties the left wing and left halfback in particular have to put up with, the whole class will spend a little pregame time learning how to drive the ball to the right.

Warm-Up (5 Minutes)

1. Students go directly to the field to practice.
2. Lead mimetics and footwork of passing to the right.
   a. Practice reversing the stick in the grip so the flat side faces right. Turn the stick, using the left hand to rotate it, so the toe faces the feet.
   b. Practice the motion for a reverse stick push-pass.
      - The right foot and shoulder face the direction of the target.
      - The left hand is the lever, and the right hand steadies the stick and extends right.
   c. Practice the motion for hitting a normal drive to the right.
      - Stop to hit the ball when it is off the rear foot.
      - Plant the left foot to the right and use the normal drive.
      - Explain a possible problem—obstruction.

Lesson Sequence

1. Set up a practice drill for passing to the right.
   a. Ask students to use the push-pass first (10 passes each).
   b. Enlarge the practice distance and have them drive the ball right.
2. Distribute pinnies and get into starting positions for the game.
   a. Call out the names of the positions and ask whoever is in the positions to raise their hand.
   b. Ask players responsible for defense to raise their hand.
   c. Ask which players must get the ball in the striker's circle and shoot.
   d. Start the game.
3. Use teachable moments to emphasize positioning relative to the ball and team responsibility.

Review and Stretching

1. Ask the teams to choose a captain and cocaptain and record the names of the captains.
2. Have the captain and cocaptain lead their team in the stretching routine. Ask review questions while students are stretching.
   - What foul can occur if you turn to the right to hit the ball to the right?
   - Which hand is on top when you reverse your grip?
   - Which is the power hand when hitting the ball to the right?

Field Hockey
BEGINNER
LESSON 8

Defensive Strategy and Games

Facilities
Marked field hockey field for every two teams

Materials
- One hockey stick for every student
- One ball for every student
- Pinnies
- Blackboard, magnetic board, or other visual aid

Performance Goals

Students will do the following:

- Continue improving skills and fitness.
- Play the game in their designated position.

Cognitive Goals

Students will learn the following:

- How halfbacks help the team
- How to put a ball in play after a foul in the striker's circle

Lesson Safety

Monitor the setting, curbing any dangerous tendencies, whether it be failure to put on shin guards or misuse of the field hockey stick.

Motivation

Before starting the game, talk about the confusing job that halfbacks have. Remind students that the wings should be the fastest players on the field and therefore need the best stick work. Then explain that because of their positioning, it is up to the right and left halfbacks to stop them. Tell students that as they learn more about each position, they might feel better suited to play a different one than they started in. Suggest that as they learn more about positions, they might change so their team can take advantage of their strengths.

Warm-Up (5 Minutes)

1. Students go directly to the field. Remind them to practice passing to the right.
2. Lead students in mimetics:
   - Push-pass (right and left)
   - Drive (right and left)
   - Left-hand lunge

Lesson Sequence

1. Explain the job of halfbacks, using a visual aid to help students understand the following:
   a. When halfbacks move up and why
      - To feed the ball back to forwards while forwards are able to shoot
      - To stop opponents while still in favorable field position
   b. How they have to stay between opponents and the goal they defend
   c. Why the center halfback has the most complex job
      - Directs which side of the field the attack will start on.
      - Sometimes becomes a sixth forward.
      - Must recover back to the goal if opponents get past the 50-yard (46-meter) line.
   d. How the right halfback will probably face the fastest player on the field
   e. How the left halfback will need to receive the ball and pass it off either straight ahead or to a teammate on the right
   f. How the halfbacks are a team within a team and that along with the fullbacks they have to stop the other team
2. Begin the game, using the teachable moment to coach each team's halfbacks.
3. Use halftime to teach the penalty corner.
   a. Setup
      - The ball is set up on the 10-yard (9-meter) marker on the end line.
      - The offense must stand outside the circle.
      - Five defensive players may stand behind the end line.
      - Remaining defensive teammates must drop back behind the center line.

b. Strategy
- Wings take corners, sending the ball to someone outside the circle.
- When the ball passes the circle, the offense is allowed to shoot.
- On the hit, the defenders may enter the striker's circle.

4. Continue the game, using teachable moments to instruct individuals while the game flows.

Review and Stretching

While team captains lead the stretching, ask questions:
- Which side of the field is it easiest to hit to?
- If the left side of the field is easiest to hit to, which halfback will see the most action?
- Why is the center halfback in a leadership position on the field?
- Why would a team be awarded a penalty corner?
- Where must the defense stand on a penalty corner?
- Where must the offense stand on a penalty corner?

Field Hockey
BEGINNER
LESSON 9

Dodge and Games

Facilities

Marked field hockey field for every two teams

Materials

- One hockey stick for every student
- One ball for every student
- Pinnies

Performance Goals

Students will do the following:
- Continue improving skills and fitness.
- Practice evasion techniques.
- Play the game in a designated position.

Cognitive Goal

Students will learn that dribblers can keep the ball if they dodge their opponent.

Lesson Safety

Monitor the setting, curbing any dangerous tendencies, whether it be failure to put on shin guards or misuse of the field hockey stick.

Motivation

Remind students that players cannot always depend on getting the ball from opponents without trying. Yes, they can get it by intercepting a pass or reaching a ball that has been dribbled too loosely, but once they have it, they have to know what to do to keep it. Sometimes passing it off to teammates is not the best thing. In that case, they have to learn to dodge their opponents.

Warm-Up (5 Minutes)

1. Students go directly to the field to practice.
2. Lead mimetics.
   - Dodge left
   - Dodge right

Lesson Sequence

1. Explain and demonstrate all three techniques. Then send students to practice.
   a. Right dodge—Push ball to the right of opponent (use partners for practice) using a light touch so the ball isn't pushed so far that it cannot be caught up with. Partners alternate roles (5 times each).
   b. Dodge left—Students run toward opponent and at the last minute drag the ball and themselves left, keeping control of the ball as they move left to get by (5 times each).
   c. Scoop under the ball to bring it up over opponent's stick (5 times each).
2. Set up for the game.
3. Use the teachable moment to coach positioning and teach the rules.

Review and Stretching

As students stretch, ask questions:

- Raise your hand if you successfully dodged an opponent during this game. What method did you use—pulling left, pushing right, or scooping over?
- To dodge successfully, what skills do you need? (good tight dribble, good timing to know when it is the right time to make the move, good footwork to catch up to the ball, finesse so you don't overhit it)

Games in Designated Position

Facilities

Marked field hockey field for every two teams

Materials

- One hockey stick for every student
- One ball for every student
- Pinnies
- Blackboard, magnetic board, or other visual aid

Performance Goals

Students will do the following:

- Continue improving skills and fitness.
- Play the game in their designated position.

Cognitive Goal

Students will understand how fullbacks coordinate with each other and halfbacks.

Lesson Safety

Monitor the setting, curbing any dangerous tendencies, whether it be failure to put on shin guards or misuse of the field hockey stick.

Motivation

Ask students if they've ever seen someone score for the wrong team—accidentally, of course. It happens when the defense doesn't trust the backs to move up and help them out. Today the class will clear up the interaction between fullbacks and halfbacks.

Warm-Up (5 Minutes)

Students go directly to the field to practice.

Lesson Sequence

1. Explain the fullback position using diagrams (see figure 8.8).
   a. Interact with other fullback.
      - Fullback moves to the center line if ball is on her side of the field.
      - The other fullback drops back, preparing to switch sides of field if necessary.
      - Each recovers by switching sides of the field if his side is covered.
   b. Attack the ball.
      - Move up to tackle approaching opponent when uncovered.
      - Early tackle may not come up with the ball, but it may cause opponents to make an error, allowing teammates to get the ball, or it may slow down their progress and allow teammates to reposition.
   c. Pass the ball to the closest sideline (outlet pass).
2. Begin games, using teachable moments.
3. At halftime, go over the ideas that need reviewing.
4. Switch sides and continue the game.

Review and Stretching

As students stretch, ask questions:

- Why is it important that fullbacks don't retreat when the goal is under attack? (Attacking early slows down opponents, giving teammates time to realign, and causes opponents' hits and dodges to give way to errors, cutting down the possible successful angles.)
- If the halfback is already on the ball carrier, should the fullback move up too?
- When someone moves to cover your side of the field, should you reposition yourself?

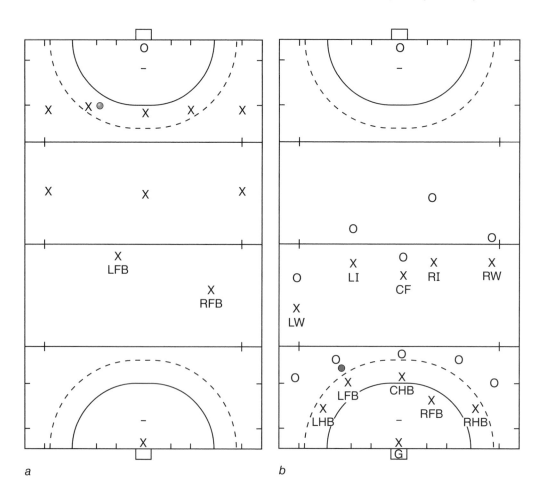

Figure 8.8 (a) Fullbacks on offense and (b) dropping back to defend their goal when they have been unable to stop the opponent's advance.

a

b

360

Outlet and Inlet Pass and Games

Facilities

Marked field hockey field for every two teams

Materials

Blackboard, magnetic board, or other visual aid

Performance Goals

Students will do the following:

- Continue improving skills and fitness.
- Play the game in their designated position.

Cognitive Goal

Students will understand that the offense and defense should use different directions when passing in the goal area.

Lesson Safety

Monitor the setting, curbing any dangerous tendencies, whether it be failure to put on shin guards or misuse of the field hockey stick.

Motivation

The outlet pass was discussed when talking about fullbacks, but it was not fully explained. Today the class will see why the outlet pass is imperative for the defender and how the inlet pass is just as imperative for the attacker. This is the last practice day before the class tournament, so the teams will probably want to get this concept straight.

Warm-Up (5 Minutes)

Students will go directly to the field to practice.

Lesson Sequence

1. Diagram and explain the outlet pass (see figure 8.9a).
   a. Show that the right fullback's outlet pass is to the right.
   b. Explain the reasons for sending the ball out to the sideline.
      - Opponents have no clear shot at goal.
      - Fast wings are out there and can pick it up and move down a relatively empty lane.
      - Hitting to the farthest sideline sets up opponents since the ball crosses the goal.
   c. Explain that if the saying "When in doubt, hit it out" is done over the goal line, it is a serious violation that results in a penalty shot on goal.
2. Diagram and explain the inlet pass (see figure 8.9b).
   a. Show that left wings have the hardest job passing in since they have to hit right.
   b. Show how inlet passes cross in front of the goal so teammates can deflect it in.
   c. Remind the inners and center forwards to be in position for the inlet pass.
3. Begin the game. Use teachable moments to reinforce what has been taught.

Review and Stretching

As students stretch, ask questions:

- Can anyone explain the advantages of using an outlet pass if you are a defender?
- Which wing usually sees the most action from an outlet pass?

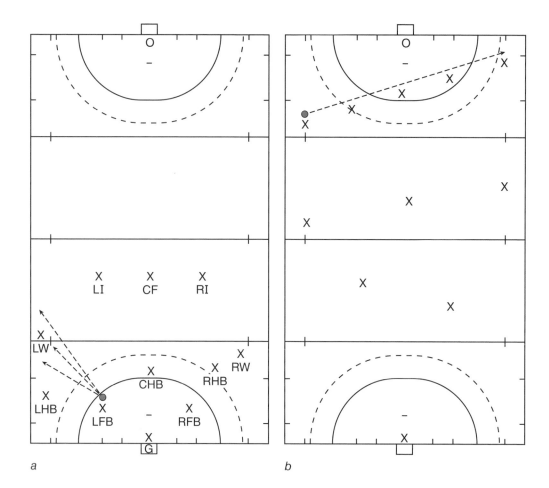

Figure 8.9 *(a)* Outlet passes to the closest sideline and *(b)* inlet passes through the strikers' circle so teammates can deflect the ball into the goal.

a

b

- Which fullback has the most difficult clear?
- If the defense keeps the ball centered but gets it out of the striker's circle, can opponents shoot for goal if they intercept?

Teacher Homework

- Depending on the number of teams in each class, set up a round-robin tournament to take place over the next six lessons.
- Post the schedule.
- Post a sheet that will show the standings.

Field Hockey
BEGINNER
LESSON 12

Major Penalties and Tournament Round 1

Facilities

Marked field hockey field for every two teams

Materials

- One hockey stick for every student
- One ball for every student
- Pinnies

Performance Goals

Students will do the following:

- Continue improving skills and fitness.
- Begin the class tournament, playing in a designated position.

Cognitive Goals

Students will learn the following:

- The penalties and awards for fouling inside the striker's circle
- How to organize themselves and use the teacher as a resource and referee

Lesson Safety

- Continue to monitor the setting, curbing any dangerous tendencies, whether it be failure to put on shin guards or misuse of the field hockey stick.
- Competition brings out the best in some students and the worst in others. This is an educational setting. In this unit, the point of competition is to enhance and motivate increased effort, teamwork, and enthusiasm. There is no place for negative behavior, whether players are simply overplaying a position or bullying teammates who don't perform. Take all opportunities to model and praise good sportsmanship and eliminate bad behavior.

Motivation

Before beginning, go over penalties that occur in the heat of the match, inside the striker's circle.

Warm-Up (5 Minutes)

1. Students go directly to the field to practice.
2. Meet with captains so they can choose whose team gets the ball to begin the game (and the pinnies). The team that does not get the ball chooses side of the field.

Lesson Sequence

1. Explain the penalty stroke, a shot against the goalie 7 yards (6 meters) from the goal line, and when it is awarded.
   a. Unintentional foul that stopped a sure goal
   b. Intentional foul inside the striker's circle
   c. How to set up for it (use teachable moments to explain):
      - The goalie stands on the goal line until the ball is struck.
      - The shooter stands on the 7-yard (6-meter) line.
      - Everyone else must stand outside the 25-yard (23-meter) line.
2. All other offenses in the circle result in
   a. penalty corner awarded to shooting team if defense errs, or
   b. 16-yard (14.5-meter) hit from edge of striker's circle if attackers erred.
3. Begin the game. Give a 2-minute halftime and then finish the game.

Review and Stretching

1. At the end of the game, have the captains lead their teams in stretching.
2. Collect the scores.
3. Entertain questions.

Tournament Round 2

Facilities

Marked field hockey field for every two teams

Materials

- One hockey stick for every student
- One ball for every student
- Pinnies

Performance Goals

Students will do the following:

- Continue improving skills and fitness.
- Continue the class tournament, playing a designated position.

Cognitive Goal

Students will organize themselves and use the teacher as a resource and referee.

Lesson Safety

Monitor the setting, curbing any physically or socially dangerous tendencies.

Motivation

Comment on the previous games, giving as many positive comments as possible. Also make some general suggestions. Then announce standings after round 1 using a scoring system that awards

- 3 points for a win,
- 2 points for a tie, and
- 1 point for competing.

Let students know that they can find their team schedule and results posted, and then begin round 2 of your tournament.

Warm-Up (5 Minutes)

1. Students go directly to the field to practice.
2. During the warm-ups have captains choose pinnies and pass-back or side of field.

Lesson Sequence

1. Begin the games. Referee.
2. At halftime, ask if anyone has questions. Offer the following teamwork suggestions:
   a. Have the halfback closest to the sideline where the ball went out take the hit in.
   b. Let your fullback take the 16-yard (14.5-meter) hits.

Review and Stretching

1. At the end of the game, have the captains lead the teams in stretching.
2. Collect the scores.
3. Ask if anyone knows why teams would have the halfbacks and not the wings take the hit-ins.

Tournament Round 3

Facilities

Marked field hockey field for every two teams

Materials

- One hockey stick for every student
- One ball for every student
- Pinnies

Performance Goals

Students will do the following:

- Continue improving skills and fitness.
- Continue the class tournament, playing a designated position.

Cognitive Goal

Students will organize themselves and use the teacher as a resource and referee.

Lesson Safety

Monitor the setting, curbing any physically or socially dangerous tendencies.

Motivation

Before announcing the standings, you might compliment their previous play and review the suggestion for having fullbacks take 16-yard (14.5-meter) hits and the closest halfback take the hit-ins from out of bounds.

Announce standings after two rounds. Encourage students to feel free to ask for coaching hints during halftime, and remind them that you will be on the field officiating at least part of their game.

Warm-Up (5 Minutes)

1. Students go directly to the field to practice.
2. During the warm-ups have captains choose pinnies and pass-back or side of field.

Lesson Sequence

1. Begin the games. Referee.
2. At halftime, ask if anyone has a question. Offer suggestions based on the weaknesses that are appearing in the game.

Review and Stretching

1. At the end of the game, have the captains lead teams in stretching.
2. Collect the scores.
3. Entertain questions.

Tournament Round 4

Facilities

Marked field hockey field for every two teams

Materials

- One hockey stick for every student
- One ball for every student
- Pinnies

Performance Goals

Students will do the following:

- Continue improving skills and fitness.
- Continue the class tournament, playing a designated position.

Cognitive Goal

Students will organize themselves and use the teacher as a resource and referee.

Lesson Safety

Monitor the setting, curbing any physically or socially dangerous tendencies.

Motivation

Review some common problems from previous games and compliment play and effort where possible. Ask if there are any questions. Then announce the standings after three rounds.

Warm-Up (5 Minutes)

1. Students go directly to the field to practice.
2. During the warm-ups, have captains choose pinnies and pass-back or side of field.

Lesson Sequence

1. Begin the games. Referee.
2. At halftime, ask if anyone has questions. Offer suggestions based on the weaknesses that are appearing in the game.

Review and Stretching

1. At the end of the game, have the captains lead teams in stretching.
2. Collect the scores.
3. Entertain questions.

Field Hockey
BEGINNER
LESSON 16

Tournament Round 5

Facilities

Marked field hockey field for every two teams

Materials

- One hockey stick for every student
- One ball for every student
- Pinnies

Performance Goals

Students will do the following:

- Continue improving skills and fitness.
- Continue the class tournament, playing a designated position.

Cognitive Goal

Students will organize themselves and use the teacher as a resource and referee.

Lesson Safety

Monitor the setting, curbing any physically or socially dangerous tendencies.

Motivation

As always, compliment whenever possible. Encourage the teams who are having difficulty prevailing and then announce standings. Remind students to feel free to ask you for coaching hints and that you will be on the field officiating.

Warm-Up (5 Minutes)

- Students go directly to the field to practice.
- During the warm-ups, have captains choose pinnies and pass-back or side of field.

Lesson Sequence

1. Begin the games. Referee.
2. At halftime, ask if anyone has questions. Offer suggestions based on the weaknesses that are appearing in the game.

Review and Stretching

1. At the end of the game, have the captains lead teams in stretching.
2. Collect the scores.
3. Entertain questions and comment on what they should be trying to do as a team.

Tournament Round 6

Facilities

Marked field hockey field for every two teams

Materials

- One hockey stick for every student
- One ball for every student
- Pinnies

Performance Goals

Students will do the following:

- Continue improving skills and fitness.
- Continue the class tournament, playing a designated position.

Cognitive Goal

Students will organize themselves and use the teacher as a resource and referee.

Lesson Safety

Monitor the setting, curbing any physically or socially dangerous tendencies.

Motivation

After five rounds, announce standings. Remind students to feel free to ask you for coaching hints and that you will be on the field officiating.

Warm-Up (5 Minutes)

- Students go directly to the field to practice.
- During the warm-up, have the captains choose pinnies and pass-back or side of field.

Lesson Sequence

1. Begin the games. Referee.
2. At halftime, ask if anyone has questions. Offer suggestions based on the weaknesses that are appearing in the game.

Review and Stretching

1. At the end of the game, have the captains lead the teams in stretching.
2. Announce the upcoming quiz and entertain questions.

Quiz and Defense-Offense Switch

Facilities

Marked field hockey field for every two teams

Materials

- Quiz for every student
- Pens and pencils
- One hockey stick for every student
- One ball for every student
- Pinnies

Performance Goals

Students will do the following:

- Continue improving their field hockey skills and fitness.
- Play the position that opposes the position they usually play.

Cognitive Goals

Students will learn the following:

- How much they've learned about field hockey by completing a short quiz
- What it is like to switch from offense to defense and vice versa

Lesson Safety

Monitor the setting, curbing any physically or socially dangerous tendencies.

Motivation

Compliment each team for their performance thus far and announce the results of the tournament. Then, just for fun, announce the idea of switching positions from defense to offense for the last day of field hockey. It is also possible to split the teams so that the team 1 offense plays against the team 2 defense and the team 2 offense plays with the team 1 defense, but let the class decide if they want to do that.

Warm-Up (5 Minutes)

After turning in their completed quizzes, students go to the field to warm up.

Lesson Sequence

Begin games and referee.

Review

At the end of the game, entertain questions.

Beginner Field Hockey Skills Rubric

Name _____ Date _____

Teacher _____ Class _____

	0	1	2	3
Level of activity	No effort.	Begins on signal.	Continues activity until told to stop.	Willingly practices until told to stop.
Instructions and rules	No effort.	Arrives with equipment and begins to practice.	Follows procedures to begin play and return out balls to play.	Does not commit personal fouls.
Dribbling	No effort.	• Can move with the ball while walking. • Dribbles during practice.	• Can dribble on the run. • Will use the dribble in the game.	• Dribbles during the game. • Tightens the dribble when in a crowd. • Can move with the ball at top speed.
Passing	No effort.	• Has proper body mechanics. • Can pass left or forward accurately up to 10 yd (9 m).	• Accurate to 20 yd (18 m) when passing left or forward.	• Can pass left or right. • Capable of hitting the ball across the field.
Receiving and stopping	No effort.	• Has proper body mechanics. • Lines up to stop balls.	• Can slow balls down that are within reach. • Able to get ball off a left-hand lunge.	• Gets to and controls balls within 3 yd (1 m). • Able to redirect the ball off the stop.
Teamwork	No effort.	• Prepared to play daily. • Gets into position on time. • Tends to follow the ball.	• Changes forward–back positioning as the team goes from offense to defense. • Can be trusted to be in position. • Will pass to teammate to avoid opponent.	• Can begin the team attack after getting the ball from an opponent. • Backs up, but does not interfere with, teammate playing the ball. • Will move to cover an uncovered position when off the ball.

From Isobel Kleinman, 2009, *Complete Physical Education Plans for Grades 5 to 12, Second Edition* (Champaign, IL: Human Kinetics).

Beginner Field Hockey Quiz

Name _____ Date _____

Teacher _____ Class _____

Multiple Choice

Read each question and each answer carefully before deciding on an answer. Be sure to choose the best answer that fits the statement preceding it. When you have made your choice, put the appropriate letter on the line to the left of the numbered question.

_____ 1. The surest, most accurate pass to a teammate is
   a. taking a left-hand lunge
   b. when, with separated hands on the stick, you push the ball toward a target
   c. when you run with the ball to the goal
   d. during a penalty shot on goal

_____ 2. An inlet pass is
   a. putting a ball back on the field after it went out of bounds
   b. best used by the forward line as they get near the striker's circle
   c. an attempt to get the ball out of the opponent's scoring position
   d. all of the above

_____ 3. The reason every position on the field should be covered is because
   a. the teacher will get mad if everyone does not get a chance
   b. it gives the ball carrier more options for a pass if he is in danger of being stripped of the ball
   c. defensive players are not allowed to shoot for goal
   d. all of the above

_____ 4. To receive a ball,
   a. you should use the flat side of your stick
   b. your stick should give on contact
   c. your stick should be angled to trap the ball between it and the ground
   d. all of the above

_____ 5. When a ball goes out of bounds at a sideline, the game stops and an opponent must
   a. run out of bounds, put it down on the line, and hit it back into the field
   b. run out of bounds, get it, and dribble it into play
   c. run to get it and throw it in using both hands with both feet on the ground
   d. wait for the official to roll it into play

_____ 6. The striker's circle is
   a. the area in which a goalie may stop a ball with her hands
   b. where a penalty shot is awarded the offense if the defense purposely fouls them or if the defense stops a sure goal
   c. the only area in which it is legal for players to shoot
   d. all of the above

»continued

 From Isobel Kleinman, 2009, *Complete Physical Education Plans for Grades 5 to 12, Second Edition* (Champaign, IL: Human Kinetics).

»continued

_____ 7. The game begins with a
  a. kick-off
  b. bully
  c. pass-back at the center of the field
  d. none of the above

_____ 8. To properly keep a ball from opponents,
  a. turn your back to them while keeping the ball in front of you
  b. put your foot on top of the ball so opponents can't get it
  c. push the ball slightly beyond your opponent's nonstick side and run to catch up to it
  d. hit their stick until the ball is exposed and you can take it away

_____ 9. The fastest person with the best stick skills should be the left wing because
  a. it is easiest for teammates to hit the ball to the left, so most passes wind up going to the left wing
  b. the field is less crowded on the sides than in the middle, so the wing has fewer players to stop him
  c. if the wing can break away from the defender, she can dribble straight to the goal
  d. all of the above

_____ 10. The player most likely to play defense and also have offensive opportunities is the
  a. goalie
  b. center halfback
  c. fullback
  d. all of the above

Extra Credit

Eleven players on the X team are diagrammed as if spread out during play. Find the correct number on the diagram to correspond with the questions on the left.

_____ Which is the team goalie?
_____ Which is the team left wing?
_____ What is the name of X8?
_____ What is the name of X3?
_____ Which is the right halfback?

Beginner Field Hockey Answer Key

Multiple Choice

1. b
2. b
3. b
4. d
5. a
6. d
7. c
8. c
9. d
10. b

Extra Credit

1. X11
2. X1
3. right inner
4. left fullback
5. X7

From Isobel Kleinman, 2009, *Complete Physical Education Plans for Grades 5 to 12, Second Edition* (Champaign, IL: Human Kinetics).

Flag Football

9

Chapter Overview

1. Lessons introduce the body mechanics of each skill, provide repetition to enhance performance, and introduce rules and strategies as students acquire experience and are able to understand them.

2. Teach throwing grip, stance, arm motion, and follow-through.

3. Teach catching hand position, eye contact, and footwork from a stationary position, and applicable rules (completed pass, pass interference).

4. Run the hook, square-right, square-left, and post football patterns, learning to throw ahead of the player and catch on the move.

5. Teach offensive options—quarterback sneak, handoff—as well as pass plays and applicable rules.

6. Teach defensive skills, such as how to legally use flags, break up pass plays, block, and stop the ball-carrying runner.

7. Teach football terminology—line of scrimmage, downs, fumble, rushing the quarterback, dead or downed ball.

8. Introduce the strategies appropriate to the skill as it is taught.

9. Once the games begin, introduce whatever rules were not introduced during skills lessons. The following should be included: onsides and offsides, how to keep possession, the boundaries, and scoring.

10. Teach common penalties for rules violations (so students can assist officiating in the games of others and monitor their own games):

    - Holding, offensive and defensive—10 yards (9 meters)
    - Pass interference—automatic completed pass
    - Unnecessary roughness—disqualification
    - Illegal belts—15 yards (14 meters) and loss of down (disqualification)
    - Flag guarding—10 yards (9 meters)
    - Offsides—10 yards (9 meters)

11. Teach fundamental game strategies for offense and for defense.

Flag Football Study Sheet

History and Fun Facts

When William Ebb Ellis, a student at Rugby School in England, broke all rules in 1823 and picked up the soccer ball and ran with it, British football was about to change from a form of the ancient Greek game known as *harpaston* to a modernized British version. Later in the 1800s, British football eventually became two games: rugby and soccer (soccer is known as *football* outside of the United States). In America, a variety of rough games were played on college campuses, but it wasn't until after the Civil War when colleges, led by Princeton, began drawing up some basic rules and American football was developed and patented that football as we know it in America began to take shape.

In the United States, applying the name *football* to the game probably more refers to the unusual shape of the ball than using the feet to play the ball. Clearly, American football is more a game of throwing and catching than fielding the ball from a kick.

Princeton and Yale played the first collegiate football game in 1879. Much of what makes American football distinctive can be attributed to Walter Camp, a Yale player, coach, and athletic director who was central to the evolution of the rules and rulebooks from the late 1880s until his death in 1925. Professional football had its start with the National Football League (NFL) in 1920.

Skills

- Grip the football by putting the forefinger on the seam and three fingers on the laces so there is a *V* between the forefinger and the thumb.

- Pass so the ball reaches receivers in the numbers (where jersey numbers would be on the chest) as they arrive where they are anticipated to go. Avoid throwing to a stationary player.

- Catch with eyes on the ball so that you see it into your hands. For high passes, catch with palms open and fingers up, watching the tip of the ball into the window between your forefingers and thumbs. For low passes, do the same with fingers down. Run pass patterns without looking for the ball until you have made the cut.

  - Hook (or hitch) pattern—The receiver runs forward and then turns in an almost about-face to come back to the ball.

  - Square in—The receiver lines up on the outside of the line, runs downfield, and cuts toward the inside of the field to run in front of the quarterback.

  - Square out—The receiver lines up near the quarterback, runs straight ahead, and cuts to continue movement toward the sideline of the field.

  - Slant—After running forward about 4 yards (3.5 meters), the receiver cuts in a diagonal, running at a 45° angle from the line of scrimmage.

  - Post—The receiver runs toward the goalpost.

Rules

- Games start with a throw-off or punt from a line delineated by your ground rules. If the ball bounces into the end zone, it comes out to the equivalent of the 20-yard (18-meter) line. If it bounces in and then goes out on the sideline, it is put in play in line with where it went out.

- Players must line up on the line of scrimmage behind the ball on their own side of the field before each new play. If they are offside, the play is repeated and their team suffers a loss of 5 yards (4.5 meters).

- Ball carriers can only be stopped by pulling one of their flags. If the flags are not flying, the team loses a down, 5 yards (4.5 meters), and the play is called back. Intentional physi-

»*continued*

 From Isobel Kleinman, 2009, *Complete Physical Education Plans for Grades 5 to 12, Second Edition* (Champaign, IL: Human Kinetics).

»continued

cal contact will result in the loss of a down, possible ejection from the game, and either a 15-yard (14 meter) penalty if committed by the offense or halfway to the goal line if committed by the defense.

- There can be no forward passes in front of the line of scrimmage.
- The defensive team cannot cross the line of scrimmage until one of the following happens: the count has reached 7 Mississippi ("1 Mississippi, 2 Mississippi, 3 Mississippi . . .") or the quarterback is no longer in possession of the ball. Once the ball is off the ground, the count to 7 Mississippi begins.

From Isobel Kleinman, 2009, *Complete Physical Education Plans for Grades 5 to 12, Second Edition* (Champaign, IL: Human Kinetics).

Flag Football Extension Project

Name _____ Date _____

Teacher _____ Class _____

What equipment would you need to play football on your own?

Is there a football team at school? Who is the coach?

Is there intramural football after school? Who is in charge?

Where can you participate in football outside of school?

Do you have friends who would join you? List their names.

What are the health benefits of participating in a football program?

What types of football games can you be involved in?

From Isobel Kleinman, 2009, *Complete Physical Education Plans for Grades 5 to 12, Second Edition* (Champaign, IL: Human Kinetics).

Flag Football Student Portfolio Checklist

Name _____ Date _____

Teacher _____ Class _____

_____ Able to throw a football to a person 5 yards (4.5 meters) away.

_____ Able to throw 10-yard (9-meter) passes.

_____ Able to pass to someone running a pass pattern.

_____ Able to catch a football thrown from 10 yards (9 meters) away.

_____ Can run a hook football pattern.

_____ Can run a square left or right or a square out or in.

_____ Can catch while on the run.

_____ Understands the goals of the team in possession of the ball.

_____ Understands the goals of the team without the ball.

_____ Understands basic football terminology (downs, safety, touchback, touchdown, blocking, kickoff, throw-off, snap, line of scrimmage).

_____ Understands the contributions made by offensive players without the ball.

_____ Knows how to and can attempt to disrupt the successful play of opponents.

_____ Follows basic flag football rules.

_____ Exhibits sportsmanship during competition.

_____ Plays without endangering the safety of others.

From Isobel Kleinman, 2009, *Complete Physical Education Plans for Grades 5 to 12, Second Edition* (Champaign, IL: Human Kinetics).

Flag Football Learning Experience Outline

Contents and Procedure

1. Warm-ups introduce proper skill mechanics and provide additional opportunity to practice the proper motion without the ball.

2. As students acquire and enhance skills, lessons introduce applicable rules and strategies.

   - With the throw and catch, students learn the concepts of a completed pass, yardage gained, moving forward at least 10 yards (9 meters) in four downs, and gaining a first down.

   - With the hook, square-left, square-right, and post patterns, students learn what it means to leave the line of scrimmage, catch on the move, and throw ahead of receiver.

   - With offensive options, they learn the choices (quarterback sneak, handing off and blocking for ball carrier) and the rules to protect the quarterback from the rush.

   - With defensive skills and effective positioning, they learn rules about pass interference, legally stopping the ball carrier, and breaking up pass plays.

3. When beginning game play, students are taught the following:
   a. Terminology (fumble, rushing the quarterback, dead or downed ball)
   b. Rules (onside and offside, boundaries, scoring, coed rule modifications)
   c. Common penalties for rules violations
      - Holding, either offensive or defensive—10 yards (9 meters)
      - Pass interference—automatic completed pass
      - Unnecessary roughness—disqualification
      - Illegal belts—15 yards (14 meters) and loss of down (disqualification)
      - Flag guarding—10 yards (9 meters)
      - Offside violation—10 yards (9 meters)

Teaching Tips

- When introducing new skills, start with a goal that everyone can meet. Success breeds confidence, which is a necessary ingredient for students to want to keep learning.
- Allow noncompetitive practice time each lesson so students can improve without performance pressure (practice at the beginning of each class).
- Use football footwork, specific skills, and terminology during the warm-up phase of the lesson when students are in an on-and-off-the-ball drill.
- After you know the abilities of the class, make teams of five or six players that equally divide players with good football handling skills, speed, and previous experience, as well as gender if teams are coed. Encourage teams to work as a unit. Promote leadership, feelings of belonging, and feelings of being needed within the team.
- Develop a tournament that involves all students. Give jobs of officiating, marking the ball, and keeping score to anyone unable to participate in the regular program.
- After a book is published, rules, skill and strategies changes may occur. Check Internet sites listed in suggested resources to keep up with the changes.

Teaching Tips for Special Considerations

- Students will have different experiences with football. Athletes whose experience far exceeds that of their classmates should be encouraged to help others and improve their own skills. While complying with class instruction, the advanced athletes should be trying to improve their consistency, accuracy, distance, time, and speed.
- Students who are medically unable to play should be given assignments that keep them involved in their team and the unit. Assignments can be providing coaching hints to teammates, developing strategies and plays for the next down, spotting the ball and setting up the next line of scrimmage, being the game official, or keeping score. If they are unable to join players on the field, have them write a report that leads to their better understanding of football and its value as an activity for developing fitness.
- Every effort should be made to reassure students that improvement is what is valued, not a predisposition to being a great football player.

Facilities

- Large, unencumbered space that permits moving 30 yards (27 meters) forward and 10 yards (9 meters) right and left without running into a wall, a person, or obstructions
- Clear boundaries for each game (see figure 9.1)

Materials

- One football for every two students
- One belt for every student with matching flags

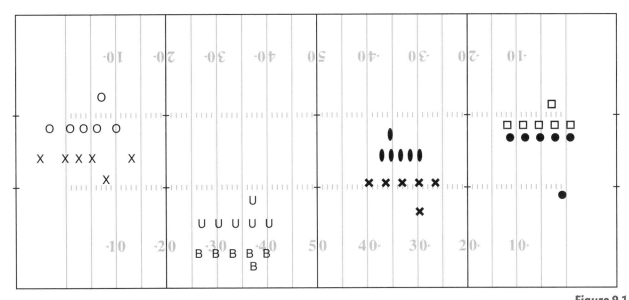

Figure 9.1 Diagram of a football field designed for class use and multiple games.

- Two sets of different-colored flags so teams can identify themselves
- Visual aid

Unit Timeline

There are three units in this chapter.

1. Beginner unit has 16 lessons.
   - 6 lessons to focus on fundamental skills and building basic game concepts
   - 6 to 10 lessons to take the fundamentals and challenge students to use them in a game situation and class tournament
2. Intermediate unit has 10 lessons.
   - 4 lessons to review skills, terminology, rules, and football strategies
   - 1 lesson to meet new teammates and organize teams for a tournament
   - 5 lessons to challenge students in a small class tournament
3. Advanced unit has 8 lessons.
   - 2 lessons to review skills, terminology, rules, and strategies
   - 1 lesson to meet new teammates and organize teams for a tournament
   - 5 lessons to challenge students in a small class tournament

Assessment

Students will conclude each unit with a quiz. Their performance will be assessed using a skills rubric included at the end of each unit.

Suggested Resources

American Football Coaches Association. 1996. *Football coaching strategies.* Champaign, IL: Human Kinetics.

American Sports Education Program (ASEP). 1996. *Coaching youth football.* Champaign, IL: Human Kinetics.

eHow. 2008. Football articles. www.ehow.com/sublist_2188.html.

Flores, T., and B. O'Connor. 2005. *Coaching football.* Indianapolis, IN: Master Press.

Wikihow. 2008. How to throw a football. www.wikihow.com/Make-a-Football-Spiral.

Throw and Catch

Facilities

Clear area large enough for class to be able to safely move in

Materials

One football for every two students

Performance Goal

Students will hold, throw, and catch a football.

Cognitive Goals

Students will learn the following:

- How to grip the peculiar shape of a football
- How to throw with reduced wind resistance
- How to direct the ball where they want it to go
- What a complete pass is and why it is important

Lesson Safety

- Have practice groups separated by a minimum of 5 yards (4.5 meters) per group with a ball.
- Throwing and running should take place in the same line of direction.

Motivation

American football is different from international football; when the world speaks of football, they are referring to what Americans call *soccer*. Ask students how many play soccer. Do they use the foot to move the ball in soccer? Explain that although we call the game *football,* American football depends on running with the ball in the hands or passing it to someone else who catches it with their hands and then runs with it. Before doing anything else, everyone has to learn to throw and catch this strangely shaped ball we call a *football.*

Warm-Up

1. Jog the playing area.
2. Lead football throwing mimetics, adding next steps as they appear, one at a time.
   - Grip—Make a wide *V* with the index finger and the thumb and bring thumb near the ear. Use other hand to help bring imagined ball to a position above and behind the ear.
   - Follow-through with wrist snap—Begin forward motion from behind the ear. At height of the throwing motion, imagine letting the ball come off the fingers as the wrist snaps forward. Continue the motion until the arm extends forward with fingers pointing to the target (10 times).
   - Step forward—Shift weight forward on foot that is opposite the throwing arm as the throwing motion begins. Finish as before (10 times).
   - Backswing—Bring the elbow back and let the shoulder follow until shoulders are parallel to the target and the weight is leaning over the same foot, which is now slightly to the rear (10 times).
   - Practice whole motion (10 times).
3. Lead the class through mimetics for catching a football.
   - Hand position for catching high balls—Make a triangle with both hands so the palms face the ball, fingers pointing up for high balls (3 times).
   - Hand position for catching low balls—Hold hands with the pinkies touching and the fingers pointing down (3 times).

- Alternate hand positions (1 time high, 1 time low, 1 high, 1 low).
- Watch the ball into hands—Keep eyes on the ball, watching as the tip of it comes into the open triangle space made by the hands and the hands close around it (3 times).
- Pull ball into body—As hands close around the ball, bring the ball into the body and tuck it away so it can't get loose (5 times).
- Line up behind the path of the ball—Throw an imaginary ball and have the class move to catch it (10 times).

Lesson Sequence

1. Teach the throw and catch (the mechanics were learned during the warm-up). Check that the forefinger is on the seam, three fingers are on the laces, and there is a V between the forefinger and the thumb (see figures 9.2 and 9.3).

   a. Demonstrate a proper throw and how the ball should spiral.

   b. Have students partner and practice throwing back and forth.

      - Begin from 5 feet (1.5 meters) away, emphasizing getting a spiral.
      - When students are successful, have them move apart a few feet at a time.
      - Have students then concentrate on getting the ball in the numbers.

2. As they practice and get farther apart, emphasize the catch.

   a. Teach what is considered a completed pass.

   b. Teach that to move a team forward, passes must be caught.

3. To prevent boredom while students continue to improve this important skill, hold a contest that reinforces the practice, such as the following:

   a. Who can catch 10 passes first?

   b. The passers begin from the line of scrimmage (use the sideline of the field) and pass forward to their partner. If the pass is complete, the passer moves up to where it was caught and passes forward again. See which partnership gets farthest in four passes. Remind them that if the ball is not caught, the next pass must be from the same spot as before.

   c. Which group can move forward with legal passes and get to the opposite side of the field first?

Review and Stretching

1. If the students do not already have a stretching routine, take time now to teach one to them. The stretching routine for football should include a stretch of the upper arms and shoulders.

2. As students stretch, ask:

   - How should fingers be aligned on the ball?
   - Who can show a proper follow-through?
   - Why is stepping forward on the opposite foot to throw so important?
   - What is a completed pass?
   - Why is a completed pass important?

Figure 9.2 Proper grip on football.

Figure 9.3 Fingers positioned to catch a pass into the numbers.

Assessment

Observe as students throw and catch, coaching throughout the lesson. If students can reach each other in the numbers (chest) with a spiral at 5 yards (4.5 meters), move on to the next lesson. If not, repeat this lesson.

Flag Football
BEGINNER
LESSON 2

Hook Pass

Facilities

Clear area large enough for class to be able to safely move in

Materials

One football for every two students

Performance Goals

Students will do the following:

- Throw 5 yards (4.5 meters) and 10 yards (9 meters) to a stationary receiver.
- Catch while stationary.
- Run, catch, and throw to someone running a hook pattern.

Cognitive Goals

Students will learn the following:

- To become more confident in their accuracy and ability to catch a football
- What a hook pattern is and how to perform it

Lesson Safety

- Have practice groups separated by a minimum of 5 yards (4.5 meters) per group with a ball.
- Throwing and running should take place in the same line of direction.

Motivation

Explain that no one stands still to catch a football and ask why that might be. Then explain that the class is going to learn to throw to someone running away from the passer, as well as how to catch the ball while on the run. In games, the passer—the quarterback—wants to know where the receiver is running, so he tells the receiver where to run. Each running pattern has a name. The one the class will work on in this lesson is a hook pattern.

Warm-Up

1. Practice throwing and catching with a friend as the class assembles. Allow 10 minutes for this, coaching as they warm up. Seek out those having difficulty and work with them independently while the rest practice with friends.

2. Lead mimetics for throwing and catching as done in the previous lesson.

3. Lead class through agility moves, having them respond to your direction.

   - Call for change of direction (run forward, back, to the right, to the left).

   - Have them run and plant the foot to make a sharp directional turn (right, left, and about face).

   - Have students run 6 yards (5 meters) forward and without breaking stride, plant their forward foot, pivot, and run back (5 times).

Lesson Sequence

1. Demonstrate running the hook pattern so students see how it looks. Then emphasize the following:

   a. The receiver running with back to the passer (quarterback), then planting forward foot to turn

   b. The receiver watching the ball into the hands

   c. The passer anticipating the need to throw the ball less than 5 yards (4.5 meters)

2. In pairs, have students alternate being passer and receiver from 5 yards (4.5 meters). After success, have the students increase the running and throwing distance.

3. Group two pairs together so the passer can throw to several receivers and the players in the line can practice receiving when they are waiting for their turn to become the passer. (See figure 9.4, which shows the passer as first in line, the second going out for the pass, and two players waiting their turns to become the receiver.) When the passer throws to each person in line, the next person becomes the new passer and the passer joins the receiving line.

4. After some practice, stop class to emphasize the receiver's need to

   a. watch the flight of ball into the window made by the forefinger and thumb,

   b. run straight forward and away from the ball without looking back,

   c. take advantage of turning on a dime,

   d. run back to the ball, and

   e. complete the catch.

5. Combine two practice pairs for a group of four and continue this way: quarterback 1 throws to each of the three people in her group who go out, one at a time, running a hook pattern. Quarterback 1 becomes a receiver and quarterback 2 passes to the three others, who also run a hook pattern. When everyone has been a quarterback and every quarterback has thrown to every receiver, the group rotation is done. Using this arrangement, go through the rotation with challenges:

   - Which group is done first?

   - Which quarterback can move the line of scrimmage the farthest in three passes?

   - Can a passer and receiver make a completion on a 10-yard (9-meter) hook pattern?

   - Which quarterback and receiver can complete a pass at 15 yards (14 meters)?

   - Which group can get to the opposite side of the field first?

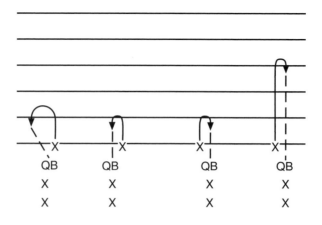

Figure 9.4 Groups of four practicing passing to someone running a hook pattern.

Review and Stretching

As students go through their stretching routine, ask questions:

- What is the difference between passing to someone in a hook pattern and passing to someone standing in front of you?
- Why should you learn how to throw to someone who is moving?
- What should the receiver concentrate on while running the pattern?
- What should the receiver concentrate on while trying to catch the ball?
- What does the quarterback need to do differently when passing?

Assessment

Observe each student, coaching throughout the lesson. Students need to hold on to the ball at 5 and 10 yards (4.5 and 9 meters) and have the stamina to run the plays. More work will be done on this in the next lesson.

Flag Football
BEGINNER
LESSON 3

Squaring Right and Left

Facilities

Clear area large enough for class to be able to safely move in

Materials

One football for every two students

Performance Goals

Students will do the following:

- Throw to a moving target 5 to 10 yards (4.5-9 meters) away.
- Catch on the run.

Cognitive Goals

Students will learn the following:

- To square a running pattern
- To become more confident in throwing, catching, and running a hook pattern

Lesson Safety

Before asking students to square left or right, have them identify their left from their right to avoid collisions with classmates or someone else's pass.

Motivation

If everyone ran only hook patterns during a game, the opponent would not be confused and would soon learn to break up the play. This lesson will practice other patterns so each offensive team has more passing choices.

Warm-Up

1. As students assemble, encourage practicing with partners.
2. Lead mimetics for the football throw, high catch, and low catch.
3. Lead footwork drills for running forward and planting the pivot foot to come back, to turn right, and to turn left.

Lesson Sequence

1. Demonstrate the square left, showing how the pattern looks to the quarterback and how the quarterback has to guess where the ball should go so that it and the receiver arrive in the same place at the same time.
2. In groups of two with pairs separated by at least 5 yards (4.5 meters) along a sideline, have partners alternate between running the pattern to receive and being the quarterback. Work in pairs until students have been both a passer and receiver at least five times and look successful.
   a. Have receivers run forward six steps before cutting left.
   b. Increase running distance a few yards after everyone has success at 5 yards (4.5 meters).
   c. Stop the class to correct common mistakes only. Otherwise, use the teachable moment to fix individual problems.
      * Coach the receiver to remember to plant the right foot to cut left.
      * Coach passers to throw ahead of receivers so receivers can run to the ball.
      * Emphasize watching the ball into the hand.
3. Have partners practice squaring to the right.
4. Combine pairs so that they are in groups of four.
   a. Practice so the quarterback throws to everyone in the group before switching quarterbacks.
   b. Now that the class has succeeded in hook patterns and squaring left and right, call the play for the class to stimulate interest and make them listen and think.
      * Vary the pattern.
      * Vary the distance, telling students which pattern to run and how far to go before they cut.

Review and Stretching

As student perform their stretching routine, ask:
* Why is it important to have different patterns?
* Does anyone know what an interception is?
* What probably would happen if the quarterback tells his receiver to go 10 and square left and the receiver runs 5 and squares right?
* It is important to throw where the receiver is going, not where she is. Why?
* Who would rather be a quarterback?
* Who would rather be a receiver?

Handoff and Use of Flags

Facilities

- Area large enough for class to move in safely
- Game areas bounded by lines or cones that indicate sidelines, end zone, and first downs

Materials

- One football for every two students
- One belt with two flags for every student
- Three cones for each game area and each squad of students

Performance Goals

Students will do the following:

- Practice defensive techniques.
- Practice the handoff.

Cognitive Goals

Students will learn the following:

- Why passing accuracy is important (throwing against a defense)
- Priorities when playing person-to-person defense

Lesson Safety

Clearly and decisively disallow all rough play.

Motivation

Explain that though the class has been practicing throwing and catching, there are other options for moving a ball. Before getting into those options, it is important to know what to do if they are in the game and don't have the ball but want it. Unlike when players are in protective equipment and tackling the opponents to make them stop running, in class they will be stopping the ball carriers by pulling one of their flags. Before dealing with the flags, explain that the class needs to learn how to give and receive a handoff. Then they will learn to use the flags.

Warm-Up

1. Make footballs available and encourage practice as students assemble.
2. Go through mimetics for the high catch, low catch, and throw.
3. Run a few pass patterns without the ball, having students plant their right foot to turn left and to turn around and plant their left foot to turn right.

Lesson Sequence

1. Demonstrate a handoff, how to receive it, and how to tuck it in (see figure 9.5).
   a. Practice in partners so each is quarterback and receiver.
   b. Have receiver take handoffs and run several steps with the ball tucked in.
2. Demonstrate how a proper belt and flag ensemble looks.
   a. Players should put on belts and then get team flags in matching color.
   b. Explain applicable rules.
      - The flags must be loose and unobstructed. They cannot be wrapped around the belts, covered, tied down, held down by arms, or blocked from view. If not worn correctly, there is a 10-yard penalty and the loss of a down.
      - Ball carriers cannot stiff-arm their opponents.

3. Teach and practice the defensive drill as shown in figure 9.6. Use three cones, one to mark the line of scrimmage, the second to show a first down, and the third to show another first down.

   a. The drill should rotate the job of quarterback, receiver (ball carrier), and defender.

   b. Explain that the goal for the receiver is to get to or pass a cone (10 yards [9 meters]) with both flags. The defender's job is to get a flag before the receiver succeeds.

   c. During practice, coach the defense:
      - Stay between receiver and cone.
      - Focus on the runner's hips to know where he is going.
      - Reach for flags only.

4. Teach defending against the pass by explaining what each player wants.

   a. Receiver—Catch the ball and run by a cone without losing a flag.

   b. Defense—Pull the flag of the ball carrier as soon as possible, get in position so the receiver doesn't get closer to the end zone than the defense, and try to prevent a completed pass by
      - catching the ball,
      - batting the ball down, or
      - pulling the receiver's flags when the ball is caught.

   c. Quarterback—Pass accurately.

Review and Stretching

While students complete their stretching routine, ask:

- How do you legally stop a player from advancing the ball?
- Can players run after they catch the ball? How can you stop them?
- Is there only one right way to wear the belt and flags? How?
- Are there penalties if they are not worn properly? What are they?

Figure 9.5 The hand-off.

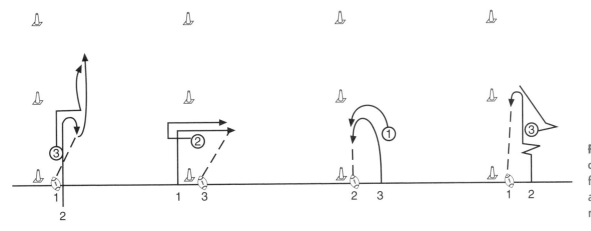

Figure 9.6 Defensive drill with three cones for line of scrimmage and first-down markers.

387

Playing a Game

Facilities

- Area large enough for class to move in safely
- Game areas bounded by lines or cones that indicate sidelines, end zones, and first downs

Materials

- One football for every two students to warm up with
- One belt with two flags for every student
- Eight cones per game, marking game boundaries and first downs

Performance Goals

Students will do the following:

- Play a flag football game.
- Continue improving skills and confidence.
- Play by the possession rules, giving up the ball to opponents if
  - the ball is intercepted, or
  - the team could not go to first-down marker or 10 yards (9 meters) in four carries.

Cognitive Goals

Students will learn the following:

- To line up with own team on own side of the ball (line of scrimmage)
- Relevant rules and penalties (offside)
- How to maintain possession and attempt to score
  - First down
  - Fourth down
  - End zone
  - Touchdown
- Consequence of not getting to first-down marker in four attempts

Lesson Safety

Clearly disallow rough play and explain the following:

- Rules are in place for safe, equitable play and will be enforced
- Students who flagrantly disregard safety will be removed until they apologize and are mindful of what to avoid (or until the next lesson).

Motivation

It's time to try the game. Explain that the purpose of learning all these skills is using them to out-play, outwit, and outsmart their opponents by getting to the end zone with both their flags and the ball in their teammates' hands.

Warm-Up

1. On arrival, students practice their football skills.
2. Lead the class through mimetics for the throw, high and low catch, square-left pattern, 5-yard (4.5-meter) hook pattern, and square-right pattern.

Lesson Sequence

1. Give color-coordinated flags to five or six students, putting experienced students on each team if you have them.
   a. Give students time to put the belts on properly.

b. Go over possession rules for the day.
   - Red has the ball first today.
   - Games will begin at midfield for red's first down.
   - After a touchdown, yellow takes over at midfield for first down.
c. Quickly review these everyday rules:
   - A play ends when the ball is on the ground or when the ball carrier's flag has been pulled.
   - A pulled flag should be dropped where it is pulled and that becomes the next line of scrimmage.
   - After a play, all players must get behind the line of scrimmage.
   - Opponents take over when the offensive team is unable to reach a first down marker in four plays.
d. Entertain questions, assign fields, and start games, reminding everyone that there will be no kickoff today and that play begins at midfield with red in possession.
2. As games are played, go from field to field, using the teachable moment and explaining what students don't understand.

Review and Stretching

As students stretch, ask:

- Having played games for the first time, do you have any questions?
- How many teams scored?
- How many teams used the pass only to gain yardage on the field?
- Did any team use the handoff and run to gain yardage?
- Who caught the ball? Which receiver was able to gain yardage after the catch?

Assessment

Observe for common problems that can be addressed in the review or at the beginning of the next class.

Teacher Homework

- Make teams, dividing students:
  - With football experience
  - Who can throw accurately
  - Who can catch on the run more than 10 yards (9 meters) away
  - With running speed
- Create and post a tournament schedule that assigns team colors and fields.

Working as a Team

Facilities

- Area large enough for class to move in safely
- Game areas bounded by lines or cones that indicate sidelines, end zones, and first downs

Materials

- Blackboard, chart, or visual aid with a scheduling example
- One football for every two students to warm up with
- One belt with two flags for every student
- Eight cones per game, marking game boundaries and first downs

Performance Goals

Students will do the following:

- Meet and play with their tournament teams.
- Begin a daily preparation routine.

Cognitive Goals

Students will learn the following:

- The reason for a preparation routine and what it is
- To assign defensive responsibilities based on size, speed, and knowledge
- Rules about scoring and how to start the game.
  - Scoring and point after
  - Starting the game and its rules
- To identify a team leader

Lesson Safety

React to and disallow rough play or arguments.

Motivation

Explain that you did your homework by making equally skilled tournament teams and that in today's games, their job will be to learn to work together, choose a captain and cocaptain, and figure out who would be best to put in the quarterback position.

Warm-Up

As students assemble, have them put on a belt and practice to warm-up.

Lesson Sequence

1. Organize for games.
   a. Announce teams.
   b. Have students put on belts, announcing that they should do so when they come to class to save time for playing
   c. Show how the posted game schedule assigns team color and field.
2. Review and teach the following:
   a. Kickoff rules (throw-off until punt is taught)
   b. Point value for each touchdown, no point after
   c. Importance of setting a good defensive match based on speed, size, and knowledge of the game
3. Direct opposing teams to fields for game.
4. Start games with a throw-off and play.

Review and Stretching

1. Have teams elect captains and cocaptains, encouraging students to pick someone who has not been captain before, and collect their names.
2. As students stretch, summarize the following:
   - How to return belts and flags properly
   - How to report scores
   - Rules for a throw-off and scoring
3. Answer all questions.

Teacher Homework

Make and post the tournament schedule and tournament standings chart.

Tournament Begins

Facilities

- Area large enough for class to move in safely
- Game areas bounded by lines or cones that indicate sidelines, end zones, and first downs

Materials

- Round-robin schedule (see appendix A) with field and flag assignments
- List of teams on which to make daily entries of wins, losses, or ties
- Blackboard, chart, or visual aid with a scheduling example
- One football for every two students to warm up with
- One belt with two flags for every student
- Eight cones per game, marking game boundaries and first downs

Performance Goals

Students will do the following:

- Try to rush the quarterback legally.
- Begin first round of their tournament.

Cognitive Goals

Students will learn the following:

- The strategy behind the quarterback rush and the rules about it
- Behavior expectations during competition

Lesson Safety

Be available to disallow rough play and arguments.

Motivation

The first round of the tournament begins as soon as students learn about rushing the quarterback and go over behavior expected during competition. They will be excited to play.

Warm-Up

As students assemble, they will practice passing and receiving to warm-up. While they do, remind them to put their belts on.

Lesson Sequence

1. Teach the strategy and rules for rushing the quarterback.

    a. Explain why they would want to pull the quarterback's flags (to cut the time to for the quarterback to find an open receiver).

    b. Explain when it is legal to go after the quarterback (after the opposing center counts to 7 Mississippi, anyone can rush the quarterback).

    c. Explain what happens once 7 Mississippi is counted out loud.

    - The player covering the quarterback crosses the line of scrimmage to grab the quarterback's flag while the quarterback still has the ball.

    - The quarterback can run (or throw if she hasn't crossed the line of scrimmage).

    d. Make up a penalty if the rush is too early such as moving the opponents forward 10 yards and repeating the down.

    e. Let students know that if the quarterback gives the ball to someone else behind the line of scrimmage, they can go after the ball carrier.

2. Discuss the behavioral expectation that they play with sportsmanship and by the rules. Honest disagreements should be worked out between captains, and you are always available to help settle disputes.

3. Send teams to their field, have captains choose sides and possession, and begin.

4. Start games with throw-off.

5. Attend each game, coaching, calling the downs, and inviting teams to work out their problems without arguments.

6. Call out a last minute of play warning so teams can use time wisely.

Review and Stretching

1. While students stretch, ask:

   - Why should teams leave someone back to count to 7 Mississippi?

   - Why would anyone want to cross the scrimmage line to rush the quarterback?

   - What is the penalty for going in too soon?

2. Review problems or rules questions and compliment players' good judgment and sportsmanship.

3. Collect game scores for the first round of tournament.

Flag Football
BEGINNER
LESSON 8

Round 2 and Defense Against the Pass

Facilities

- Area large enough for class to move in safely

- Game areas bounded by lines or cones that indicate sidelines, end zones, and first downs

Materials

- Updated round-robin tournament standings chart (see appendix A) with field and flag assignments

- List of teams on which to make daily entries of wins, losses, or ties

- Blackboard, chart, or visual aid with a scheduling example

- One football for every two students to warm up with

- One belt with two flags for every student

- Eight cones per game, marking game boundaries and first downs

Performance Goals

Students will do the following:

- Defend against the pass and play by relevant rules.

- Play round 2 of their tournament.

Cognitive Goals

Students will learn the following:

- The strategy for defending against the pass

- What pass interference is and how it is penalized

- That good sportsmanship and playing by the rules is valued

Lesson Safety

Be available to stop rough play and arguments and follow up with game penalties and explanations or more severe measures if necessary.

Motivation

Announce that this is round 2 and what the standings are after one round. Remind students that the team that plays best together wins. If you have an anecdote to help make the point, use it.

Warm-Up

Students practice throwing and catching with a friend.

Lesson Sequence

1. Teach defense against the pass in terms of priorities and relevant rules.
   a. Stay behind the receiver (between the receiver and the end zone) to be able to grab his flags if he gets the ball.
   b. If just able to reach the ball, knock it to the ground, not in the air.
   c. If able to use two hands, catch it for an interception.
   d. Avoid pass interference (interfering with an attempt to catch a forward pass by holding, pulling, pushing, or tripping). Penalty is an automatic first down.
2. Announce field assignments and begin round 2.
3. Coach each game, praising good positioning, good defense, good effort, or whatever a student does that is positive.
4. Alert the class to the last minute of play so teams can use the time wisely.

Review and Stretching

1. As students stretch, ask:
   - What three ways can a player defend against receivers gaining yardage?
   - What is the difference between knocking down the ball and pass interference? How is it penalized?
2. Review problems or rules questions. Compliment good judgment and sportsmanship.
3. Collect results for round 2.

Round 3 and Quarterback Options

Facilities

- Area large enough for class to move in safely
- Game areas bounded by lines or cones that indicate sidelines, end zones, and first downs

Materials

- Updated round-robin tournament standings chart (see appendix A) with field and flag assignments
- List of teams on which to make daily entries of wins, losses, or ties
- Blackboard, chart, or visual aid with a scheduling example
- One football for every two students to warm up with
- One belt with two flags for every student
- Eight cones per game, marking game boundaries and first downs

Performance Goals

Students will do the following:

- Review and use quarterback options.
- Play round 3 of the tournament.

Cognitive Goals

Students will learn the following:

- Quarterback options
- How to mix strategies to keep the defense guessing

Lesson Safety

Be available to stop rough play and arguments and follow up with game penalties and explanations or more severe measures if necessary.

Motivation

Announce the results after round 2 and spur all teams on to victory in the third round.

Warm-Up

Students put on their belts and warm up by practicing passing and receiving.

Lesson Sequence

1. Review three quarterback options:
   a. Handoff
   b. Quarterback running after 7 Mississippi
   c. Passing
2. Explain why mixing plays, options, and receivers is a good strategy.
3. Direct students to their fields for round 3 and start games as soon as possible.
4. Coach each game. Praise variety in offensive play making and good plays.
5. Call out the last minute of play so teams can use the time wisely.

Review and Stretching

1. As students stretch, ask what three choices are available to every team on every play.
2. Review problems or rules questions and compliment good judgment and sportsmanship.
3. Collect results for the third round of tournament.

Round 4 and Playing With a Safety

Facilities

- Area large enough for class to move in safely
- Game areas bounded by lines or cones that indicate sidelines, end zones, and first downs

Materials

- Updated round-robin tournament standings chart (see appendix A) with field and flag assignments
- List of teams on which to make daily entries of wins, losses, or ties
- Blackboard, chart, or visual aid with a scheduling example
- One football for every two students to warm up with
- One belt with two flags for every student
- Eight cones per game, marking game boundaries and first downs

Performance Goals

Students will do the following:

- Play with a defensive safety.
- Play round 4 of their tournament.

Cognitive Goal

Students will learn flexible defensive strategy and the need for considering it.

Lesson Safety

Be available to stop rough play and arguments and follow up with game penalties and explanations or more severe measures if necessary.

Motivation

Announce the standings after three rounds. Make some suggestions for teams that want to stop the ball handlers but always let them get away. Explain that by using a safety, they might have a better chance to stop their scoring.

Warm-Up

1. As students assemble, they put on a belt and practice passing and receiving.
2. Lead them in footwork drills for agility and moving backward.

Lesson Sequence

1. Teach the strategy behind using a safety (leaving a player back) and explain that they should use it when an opponent is too fast to be covered by a person on the team.
2. Direct students to their fields for round 4.
3. Coach each game, encouraging the use of a safety and praising good moments.
4. Call out the last minute of play so teams can use the time wisely.

Review and Stretching

1. As students stretch, ask:
   - Does person-to-person defense always work?
   - Is your team helpless if opponents have a faster player than anyone on your team?
2. Review problems or rules questions that occurred during the games. Compliment good judgment and sportsmanship.
3. Collect the results for the fourth round of the tournament.

Tournament Conclusion

Facilities

- Area large enough for class to move in safely
- Game areas bounded by lines or cones that indicate sidelines, end zones, and first downs

Materials

- Updated round-robin tournament standings chart (see appendix A) with field and flag assignments
- List of teams on which to make daily entries of wins, losses, or ties
- Blackboard, chart, or visual aid with a scheduling example

- One football for every two students to warm up with
- One belt with two flags for every student
- Eight cones per game, marking game boundaries and first downs

Performance Goals

Students will do the following:

- Plan and play as a team.
- Complete the round-robin tournament.
- Continue improving their football skills, confidence, and understanding.

Cognitive Goals

Students will understand the following:

- Routine class procedure, evidenced by their self-direction
- Good sporting and ethical behavior
- The strengths and weakness of teammates and how to adapt to them

Lesson Safety

Be available to stop rough play and arguments and follow up with game penalties and explanations or more severe measures if necessary.

Motivation

Announce the standings before each new round, and explain what the teams out of first place have to do to change the outcome. Encourage them to do so and invite them to ask you for coaching hints that might get them into a winning mode.

Warm-Up

Students practice passing and receiving as they assemble.

Lesson Sequence

1. Direct students to fields for games.
2. Get to each game to coach and officiate, drawing attention to individual achievements (e.g., good coverage, good pass, good blocking, great patterns, good cuts, great hands) and teamwork while you are there.
3. Call out the last minute of play so teams can use the time wisely.

Review and Stretching

1. As students stretch, announce that there will be a short quiz on football on the next rainy day.
2. Discuss problems or rules questions that occurred during games and compliment good judgment and sportsmanship.
3. Collect results.

Assessment

Post the beginner football skills rubric. Observe as students play to see what level they reach on the rubric.

Assess their knowledge of basic rules, strategy, and movement fundamentals with the beginner football quiz.

Beginner Flag Football Skills Rubric

Name _____ Date _____

Teacher _____ Class _____

	1	2	3	4	5
Throw	• Uses proper body mechanics during mimetics. • Has correct grip, forward foot, and follow-through.	• Ball wobbles in flight. • Ball drops before reaching stationary 5 yd (4.5 m) target.	• Ball reaches stationary 5 yd (4.5 m) target. • Pass has spin.	• Ball reaches moving 5 yd (4.5 m) target. • Throw is accurate to a 10 yd (9 m) stationary target.	• Throw is accurate to variable moving targets at 10 yd (9 m) or more. • Can change speed and maintain accuracy.
Catch	• Changes position to be in line with ball. • Watches ball in flight. • Has proper hand position to receive ball.	• Brings ball into body. • Catches accurate 10 yd (9 m) pass while standing still. • Watches ball into hands.	• Can run and catch a ball thrown accurately to 5 yd (4.5 m) target. • Can catch 10 yd (9 m) pass if feet are set.	• Can adjust to inaccurate throw up to two steps from target area. • Does not need to stop running in order to catch.	• Can catch a ball thrown over head. • Can catch while running full stride. • Can catch ball thrown with speed or for distance.
Patterns	• Runs hook or squares left and right on command. • Turns in proper direction.	• Makes clean cuts. • Doesn't watch for the ball until the cut is made.	• Can lose opponent and still keep pattern. • Can reliably run 10 yd (9 m) pattern and catch ball thrown accurately.	• Knows when to cut back to the ball. • Can run short and long patterns well.	• If the quarterback changes the running pattern, follows the call without confusion. • Fakes opponent before making the cut. • If open, will catch a ball on target.

From Isobel Kleinman, 2009, *Complete Physical Education Plans for Grades 5 to 12, Second Edition* (Champaign, IL: Human Kinetics).

Beginner Flag Football Quiz

Name _____ Date _____

Teacher _____ Class _____

True or False

Read each statement carefully. If the statement is true, write a *T* in the column to the left. If the statement is false, write an *F*. If using a grid sheet, blacken in the appropriate column for each question, making sure to use the correctly numbered line for each question and its answer.

_____ 1. A team able to move the line of scrimmage forward at least 10 yards (9 meters) in four downs maintains possession of the ball.

_____ 2. Offensive players must line up on either side of the line of scrimmage for the next play.

_____ 3. Passes, handoffs, running plays, and blocking for the ball carrier are plays made by the defensive team.

_____ 4. A touchdown is scored when a team has the ball in the opponent's end zone.

_____ 5. Once a ball is ahead of the line of scrimmage, it can be passed forward.

_____ 6. If the ball changes hands behind the line of scrimmage, the defense may rush the ball carrier even though "7 Mississippi" has not yet been called.

_____ 7. In order to legally stop a ball carrier, you must pull her flag.

_____ 8. Defensive players should not let the person they cover get behind them.

_____ 9. If a pass is not caught, the line of scrimmage does not move and players must return to where the line of scrimmage was in the previous play.

_____ 10. If a player runs out of bounds with the ball, the new line of scrimmage is in line with where the ball was taken out of bounds.

Extra Credit

Match the columns (1 point each)

_____ 1. catch the ball   a. illegal in class

_____ 2. interception   b. push off left foot

_____ 3. tackling   c. watch the ball into your hands

_____ 4. square right   d. starting the game

_____ 5. kickoff or throw-off   e. the defense catches the ball

 From Isobel Kleinman, 2009, *Complete Physical Education Plans for Grades 5 to 12, Second Edition* (Champaign, IL: Human Kinetics).

Beginner Flag Football Answer Key

True or False

1. T
2. F—This is an offside violation. There is a penalty for whoever is at fault.
3. F—Each strategy requires possession of the ball, which means the team is on offense.
4. T
5. F—Forward passes must be made from behind the line of scrimmage.
6. T—Counting to 7 Mississippi protects the quarterback. Once the quarterback gives up the ball, the defense should go after the flag.
7. T
8. T
9. T
10. T

Extra Credit

1. c
2. e
3. a
4. b
5. d

Pass Pattern Review

Facilities

Area large enough for the class to move in safely

Materials

One football for every two students

Performance Goals

Students will do the following:

- Review and practice throwing and catching.
- Review and practice the footwork for different football patterns.

Cognitive Goal

Students will know what hook, square-left, and square-right pass patterns are.

Lesson Safety

Set up a practice area so each group

- is a minimum of 5 yards (4.5 meters) from one another,
- all groups are moving in the same line of direction, and
- everyone has the same line of scrimmage.

Motivation

Remind the class that passing and pass patterns were worked on in previous years. Now that they are older and stronger, they should strive to attain greater accuracy, the ability to move the ball longer distances, and the confidence to expect that when a play to go out 10 yards (9 meters) and square left is called, teammates will know what is meant and how to do it.

Warm-Up

1. Allow students to practice throwing and catching in pairs when they arrive.
2. Lead the class in mimetics for throwing, catching, footwork to cut left, and footwork to cut right. (See the beginner unit for details.)

Lesson Sequence

1. Have students line up behind a designated line of scrimmage.
2. Demonstrate and practice a square left:
   a. For the receiver, emphasize running a set number of steps forward, planting the right foot, pushing off to the left, and watching the ball into the hands.
   b. For the passer, emphasize passing to the left and ahead of the running receiver.
   c. Allow several turns as the pairs trade off being passer and receiver.
   d. Ask students to reverse the foot planted and practice square-right patterns.
3. Demonstrate the hook pattern and have students practice in pairs.
   a. For the receiver, emphasize running from the passer without looking, cutting to come back to the ball, and watching the ball into the hands.
   b. For the passer, emphasize waiting to throw until the cut and throwing shorter so the receiver can run back to the ball to make the catch.
4. In groups of four behind the same line of scrimmage, call the plays for the class, mixing the calls (hook, square left, square right) and the distances. Each person is the quarterback for the others in the group before rotating.
5. If time remains, let the quarterback call the plays, telling the receiver how far to go and what pattern to run.

Review and Stretching

If necessary, review the class stretching routine. If not, as the students stretch, answer questions they might have. Then ask the following:

- When may the offense move over the line of scrimmage? The defense?
- To cut left, what foot should be planted? To cut right?
- Why is it necessary to watch the ball into your hands?

Assessment

Continue practicing one pass pattern until most students demonstrate mastery before changing the patterns. Determine this by observation. If the class needs more time with the patterns, repeat the lesson.

Slant Pattern

Facilities

Area large enough for the class to move in safely

Materials

One football for every two students

Performance Goals

Students will do the following:

- Run another short pattern—the slant.
- Practice throwing at increasing distances.
- Be responsible for calling their own patterns and following their own quarterback.

Cognitive Goal

Students will understand what to do when told to run a slant or post pattern.

Lesson Safety

Set up a practice area so each group

- is a minimum of 5 yards (4.5 meters) from one another,
- all groups are moving in the same line of direction, and
- everyone has the same line of scrimmage.

Motivation

Ask if anyone has seen a football game in person. Comment on how different it looks in person than on TV because when looking at the whole field, you can see the receivers and how many places they are going, and so you can see the choices the quarterback has. That is why quarterbacks tell a primary receiver what to run and have a backup receiver if the primary receiver cannot shake his defender. If a quarterback tells one receiver to hook at 15 and another to square out at the 10, will it happen? Make sure everyone can follow directions given by the quarterback by spending a little more time practicing before getting into real competition.

Warm-Up

1. As students assemble, they practice throwing and catching in pairs.
2. Lead the class through mimetics for the short pass, the deep pass, catching high, catching low, tucking the ball in, and running backward.

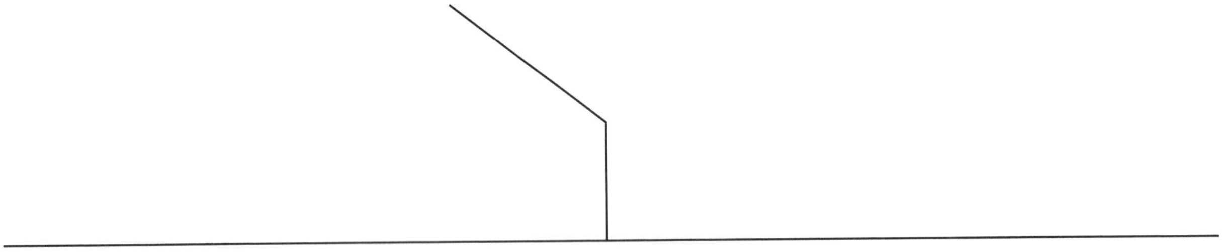

Figure 9.7   Slant
pattern.

Lesson Sequence

1. Have students line up behind a designated line of scrimmage.
2. Demonstrate the slant pattern (see figure 9.7) and have students practice just the footwork:
   - Receiver runs down the field 4 yards (3.5 meters) and then slants toward the center at a 45° angle, running at least 6 more yards (5 meters) on slant before receiving pass.
3. Practice running the slant and having a passer throw to it, emphasizing the passer throwing ahead of the receiver.
4. Call the snap for the class, mixing the patterns and distances.
5. Leave 10 minutes so each quarterback can make the calls, deciding how far the receiver should go and what pattern to run.

Review and Stretching

As student stretch, ask:
- What pattern has the receiver run across the center?
- Should receivers expect to get the ball as soon as they make their cut?
- Why is making a clear cut so important?

Assessment

Look for mastery from 90% of the class before teaching anything new.

Flag Football
INTERMEDIATE
LESSON 3

Snap and Defense

Facilities

Area large enough for the class to move in safely

Materials

- Belt and flags for every student
- Cones for marking a goal to run to after making a catch
- One football for every two students

Performance Goals

Students will do the following:
- Snap the ball to the quarterback.
- Wear flags and belts.
- Run patterns against a defender.

Cognitive Goals

Students will learn the following:

- Focus of the defense
- Rules of possession, the start of game, and playing in the end zone
- How to wear belts and flags legally and penalties for not doing so

Lesson Safety

Students will need more space between groups to be able to work safely. Be prepared to double the usual space and to make adjustments during the course of this lesson.

Motivation

If the receiver is running close to an opponent, is the quarterback able to thread the needle, which means getting the ball into an almost impossibly small space without its being intercepted? Can the opponent intercept the pass? If not, can the opponent pull the receiver's flag, stopping the receiver exactly where she made the catch? Today's lesson allows the class to answer those questions because there will be someone else there who wants the ball, too.

Warm-Up

1. As students assemble, they practice passing and receiving in pairs.
2. Lead students through footwork drills, having them run backward, and change direction following your lead.

Lesson Sequence

1. Review the legal method of wearing belts and flags.
   a. Explain that belts should be on comfortably and flags should hang.
   b. Assign a penalty for shielding the flags and explain it. For example, if a player shields his flag, the play should be called back and the down should be lost.
2. Demonstrate and teach the two-handed snap.
   a. Allow several practices between partners.
   b. Teach relevant rules.
      - The snap begins the count to 7 Mississippi.
      - With fumbles, a ball hitting the ground is dead.
3. In groups of three (quarterback, receiver, and defender) with a cone marking the line of scrimmage and another marking the goal the receiver wants to reach (see figure 9.6 on page 387), have students practice, alternating roles.
   a. The player snapping is the eligible receiver.
   b. The quarterback decides the pass pattern.
   c. The defender intercepts, bats down the ball, or pulls the flag of the receiver trying to stop the receiver from reaching the cone with the ball.
4. Set up a contest focusing on defensive skills, such as the following.
   a. Which defender can score the most points?
      - Interception—4
      - Batted-down ball—3
      - Pulled flag on catch—2
      - Pulled flag before opponent reached the cone—1
   b. Which receiver can score the most points?
      - Catches—1
      - Catches and makes it to the cone—2
   c. Which quarterback can score the most points?
      - Snap received without fumble—1
      - Completed throw—2

Review and Stretching

As students stretch, ask questions:

- What are the penalties for tied-on flags and illegal belts? For obstructed flags? For pass interference?
- What usually happens when a defender goes for the ball but comes up empty?

Teacher Homework

Make up teams that are equally skilled. If you do not know the skills of the class well enough, wait another day. It is important to make sure that no team is too strong or too weak to compete. Divide good passers, good receivers, students with good foot speed, and those who know the game and place them on separate teams.

Game

Facilities

One game area for every two teams bounded by lines or cones that indicate sidelines, end zones, and first downs

Materials

- Belt and flags for every student
- Cones for marking a goal to run to after making a catch
- One football for every two students

Performance Goal

Students will play a scrimmage game with their assigned teams.

Cognitive Goals

Students will learn the following:

- Rules for rushing the quarterback, fumble, unnecessary roughness, and kickoff
- Who is on their tournament team
- How to choose a team captain and cocaptain

Lesson Safety

Clearly marked lanes for each game will help prevent games from overlapping and students from colliding with players on another field.

Motivation

If the teams are ready, announce the tournament teams. If not, announce that the students will be playing a full game. In either case, they need to decide who will be the quarterback and defensive coverage.

Warm-Up

1. As students assemble, they practice passing and receiving in pairs.
2. Practice footwork, running several pass patterns without the ball, and running backward.

Lesson Sequence

1. Review skills:
   - Throw-off process to start game
   - No rushing or quarterback sneaks until 7 Mississippi

- Penalties for unnecessary roughness
  - Offense—loss of a down and sent back 10 yards (9 meters)
  - Defense—opponents advance 15 yards
  - Person involved—one warning; second time, out
2. Make teams and have them pick up belts and flags.
3. Assign fields and begin games right away.
4. Get to each group, officiating where necessary and providing positive feedback whenever possible.

Review and Stretching

As students stretch, share something that came up that might be useful to know and then ask questions:

- Did a team use the handoff instead of pass?
- Who caught a pass?
- Who got a flag?
- Whose game had close scores?

Assessment

Make sure teams are relatively equal. If they're not, switch players. Look for common problems in skill, strategy, or rule observation that can be addressed during the review or at the beginning of the next class.

Blocking

Facilities

One game area for every two teams bounded by lines or cones that indicate sidelines, end zones, and first downs

Materials

- Belt and flags for every student
- Cones for marking a goal to run to after making a catch
- One football for every two students

Performance Goal

Students will play another practice game.

Cognitive Goals

Students will learn the following:

- To block for a ball carrier
- How to get points in the end zone
  - Scoring a touchdown
  - Point after play and how to set up for the 2-point play option
  - Scoring a safety
- How to take part in the offense when not carrying the ball

Lesson Safety

Clearly marked lanes for each game will help prevent games from overlapping and students from colliding with players on another field.

Motivation

Announce another practice game (and that the class will play this game with their tournament teams if the teams were announced previously). This gives students more time to get to know teammates, figure out how best to organize, put into practice things not done last year, go for the points after a touchdown, and block for the ball carrier.

Warm-Up

1. As students assemble, they practice passing and receiving in pairs.
2. Lead a footwork drill by having class run in pairs, side to side, and back and front.

Lesson Sequence

1. Explain that students should do the following:
   a. Routinely put on belts without flags when they arrive so as not to waste time.
   b. Block or screen for their ball carrier (show what it is and how it helps).
2. Review scoring for a touchdown and safety.
3. Introduce the point-after option and that it is played from the next-to-last cone.
4. Assign fields and begin games. Cover all games, one at a time. Remind students about blocking and the point-after option, encourage good defensive matches, and praise anything noteworthy (e.g., good blocks, pass coverage, containing the quarterback).

Review and Stretching

As students stretch, ask:
- Where is the point-after taken? Did any team get a point-after?
- What does a block do for the ball carrier? Did anyone block for your teammate?

Teacher Homework

Prepare and post charts of game schedules and team standings.

Flag Football
INTERMEDIATE
LESSON 6

Round 1

Facilities

One game area for every two teams bounded by lines or cones that indicate sidelines, end zones, and first downs

Materials

- Posted roster of teams, captains, game assignments, and tournament standings
- Belt and flags for every student
- Cones for marking a goal to run to after making a catch
- One football for every two students

Performance Goal

Students will play round 1 of the tournament.

Cognitive Goals

Students will learn the following:
- How the quarterback can become a receiver
- Other options for moving ball:
  - Handoff
  - Quarterback sneak
  - Pass

Lesson Safety

With the tournament starting, be vigilant about preventing excessive aggression since it will compromise the emotional and physical environment of your class. Respond promptly. If persuasion does not work and the behavior is the responsibility of one student, remove the student until he apologizes and alters his behavior.

Motivation

Announce that during round 1, you will be getting to each game, but if there is a problem or question, students should get your attention.

Warm-Up

Students will put on their belts and practice passing and catching in pairs.

Lesson Sequence

1. Review strategies:
   a. Quarterback option to become a receiver
      - Ask how that is possible. (The quarterback hands off and runs out to become a receiver.)
      - Discuss how the defense can react. (Center should yell as soon as the ball leaves the quarterback's hands and go after the ball carrier. If the carrier passes, the center should yell "Up" when the ball is in the air, which will release the team to go after the intended target.)
   b. Other quarterback options (pass, handoff, and run)
2. Captains pick up team flags and meet on assigned fields to begin games.
3. As games are being played, coach and encourage teams to control the ball and use a variety of options.

Review and Stretching

1. As students stretch, ask:
   - Which quarterbacks rushed for yardage?
   - What was most successful, the run, long pass, or short pass and run?
   - Is it better to go for the touchdown or the first down?
2. Gather the scores and dismiss the class.

Round 2

Facilities

One game area for every two teams bounded by lines or cones that indicate sidelines, end zones, and first downs

Materials

- Updated tournament standings charts
- Posted roster of teams, captains, game assignments, and tournament standings
- Belt and flags for every student
- Cones for marking a goal to run to after making a catch
- One football for every two students

Performance Goal

Students will play round 2 of the tournament.

Cognitive Goals

Students will learn the following:

- Defensive priorities:
    - Pull the flags of the ball carrier.
    - Knock down an aerial ball if it can't be caught.
    - Intercept a pass intended for the other team.
- That they are improving their endurance and fitness

Lesson Safety

With the tournament starting, be vigilant about preventing excessive aggression since it will compromise the emotional and physical environment of your class. Respond promptly. If persuasion does not work and the behavior is the responsibility of one student, remove the student until he apologizes and alters his behavior.

Motivation

Comment on how much less winded and more energetic everyone is looking since the beginning of the unit and how good it is to be in better shape. Point out that playing flag football has been not only fun, but has increased their aerobic capacity and overall fitness as well. A sure sign is how much better they are feeling despite the fact that they are working harder. Announce the standings after round 1, encouraging students to go out for round 2 and try their best.

Warm-Up

Students will practice passing and catching before the games.

Lesson Sequence

1. Review how to be more effective on defense. The priority for each play should be to get the flag as soon as they know who the ball carrier is, knock the ball down to the ground if they can't catch it, and intercept if possible.
2. Students get their flags, go to assigned fields, and begin games.
3. Get to each game and act as a coach and game official.

Review and Stretching

1. As students stretch, ask:
   - Who gained yardage after the catch?
   - Who caught a ball and had a flag ripped off almost as soon as you did?
   - Who grabbed a flag?
   - Who knocked a pass to the ground that was intended for your opponent?
   - Did anyone intercept? What is the advantage of an interception?
2. Gather the scores.

Assessment

Evaluation should be as objective as possible and take place over several days. Tools for assessing performance standards are defined in the intermediate football rubric at the end of the unit. There is also a short written quiz at the end of the unit, which can be given on the first rainy day of the tournament.

Round 3 Until Tournament Conclusion

Facilities

One game area for every two teams bounded by lines or cones that indicate sidelines, end zones, and first downs

Materials

- Footballs, flags, and cones as usual
- Updated tournament standings charts
- Posted intermediate skills rubric

Performance Goal

Students will play the remaining rounds of the tournament using a variety of offensive and defensive strategies.

Cognitive Goal

Students will learn to adjust their defense and offense to the strengths of different teams.

Lesson Safety

Be vigilant over competitive behavior, making sure it is safe and emotionally appropriate.

Motivation

Announce the standings after each round, spending a little time sharing what wins and losses can change the standings and challenging everyone to outperform the team that is in the lead. Make it clear that you are there if anyone needs some friendly advice and that you will be at each game to officiate, coach, and cheer them on.

Warm-Up

Assembling students get their belts and a football and practice passing in pairs.

Lesson Sequence

1. Before beginning each round, discuss some strategic alternatives losing teams can consider:

   a. Defensive alternatives

      - Switch to zone if opponents constantly outrun you.
      - Leave a safety back.
      - Don't leave a person back to call "7 Mississippi."

   b. At least one offensive strategic change

      - Go short since short passes are easier to catch.
      - Go for the first down and short yardage rather than going long.
      - Pass to the least expected receiver.
      - Use the run more.
      - Send blockers out with the ball carrier.

2. Captains bring out flags, meet on assigned fields, and begin games.

3. Act as coach and official, and praise everything worthy of recognition, such as team strategy (even if it doesn't work out), team cohesiveness, skills during play, sportsmanship, reliability, and so on.

4. Alert class to the last minute of play.

Review and Stretching

1. As students stretch, ask:
   - What can you do when an opponent is the fastest person on the field?
   - How can you stop someone who can outrun everyone on your team?
   - Why do you want someone equally fast to stay back with the quarterback?
   - Did someone on your team block for you when you carried the ball?

2. Let students know that if they are interested in how they are being evaluated, the intermediate skills rubric is posted, and announce you will be giving a short quiz (if you intend to) on the first rainy day.

Intermediate Flag Football Skills Rubric

Name _____ Date _____

Teacher _____ Class _____

	1	2	3	4	5
Offensive skills	• Can generally direct or control the football. • Knows the team's general objective and uses skills to help meet it. • Gets back to line of scrimmage at the end of each play.	• If given the ball, can maintain possession. • Can assist the team in maintaining possession by faking, blocking, or getting open.	• Can play the game within the context of the rules. • Has a good sense of the boundaries, the end zone, and first-down markers. • Able to implement team strategies.	• Can adapt to short or long plays. • Will block for ball carrier. • Uses speed and agility to avoid flag pull. • Can play a flowing game.	• Understands responsibility and how it relates to the rest of the team. • Able to call plays and adjust if play does not work the way planned. • Finds a way to get the next first down.
Defensive skills	• Knows to stop the ball carrier by pulling flags or tagging. • Will leave the line of scrimmage on the snap. • Will use hands to reach for ball carrier or ball.	• Capable of covering a person of equal speed and size. • Covers assigned zone. • Able to occasionally interrupt opponents' play.	• Can react to a handoff at the line of scrimmage. • Does not let opponent get behind. • Will drop person or zone once the ball is up and go after the ball carrier. • Plays within the rules.	• Knows how to use positioning to cut off opponents' lanes. • If unable to prevent a completed pass, prevents additional yardage. • Will run down the ball carrier who gets away from teammates.	• Able to intercept passes and change direction of the game. • Effective in regaining possession of the ball. • Can anticipate opposition. • Helps teammates focus on the things to stop.
Run, catch, pass	• Very reliable up to 5 yd (4.5 m) on offense. • Very reliable up to 10 yd (9 m) on defense. • Prepares for game (flags) and arrives on correct field in a timely fashion.	• Offensively effective to 10 yd (9 m). • Defensively effective to 15 yd (14 m) if the person covered is the ball carrier or if the ball carrier enters the zone covered.	• Leaves own defensive assignment only if the ball is up and not going to the person covered. • Has the stamina to play aggressively. • Reliable to go to the ball when open. • Will get open and run evasively.	• Plays aggressively within the rules. • Can run a variety of plays in front and behind the line of scrimmage. • Can focus and catch balls in a crowd. • Though not designated quarterback, can pass accurately down field.	• Can throw accurately long or short. • Can catch a ball thrown fast, high, low, or off target a few steps. • Handles power, speed, and long distances with ease. • Can change direction immediately.

From Isobel Kleinman, 2009, *Complete Physical Education Plans for Grades 5 to 12, Second Edition* (Champaign, IL: Human Kinetics).

Intermediate Flag Football Quiz

Name _____ Date _____

Teacher _____ Class _____

True or False

Read each statement carefully. If the statement is true, write a *T* in the column to the left. If the statement is false, write an *F*. If using a grid sheet, blacken in the appropriate column for each question, making sure to use the correctly numbered line for each question and its answer.

_____ 1. Teams should throw off on fourth down when on their own 20-yard (18-meter) line.

_____ 2. A player who is ahead of the ball before the play begins is offside.

_____ 3. Receivers squaring in should line up closer to the sideline than the center of the field.

_____ 4. The defense scores when an opponent's flag is pulled while holding the ball inside his own end zone.

_____ 5. Once the ball is in front of the line of scrimmage, the ball carrier can pass to someone behind her or next to her.

_____ 6. The player staying back to count to 7 Mississippi gives the opposing quarterback unlimited time to find an open receiver.

_____ 7. A player unable to intercept a pass but able to touch the ball should bat the ball to the ground.

_____ 8. Defensive players should keep their own end zone to their back and the player they are responsible for in front of them.

_____ 9. It is better to throw off so that the ball lands in-bounds at the 10-yard (9-meter) line and bounces out than it is to have it land in the end zone.

_____ 10. No one on the offensive team can pass if the quarterback gives the ball to a team-mate and runs in front of the line of scrimmage.

Extra Credit

Match the columns. (1 point each)

_____ 1. pass interference   a. moving the ball from the ground to the quarterback

_____ 2. snap   b. protects quarterback without a defensive line

_____ 3. safety   c. illegal, loss of yardage, play repeated

_____ 4. 7 Mississippi   d. pushing the receiver away from the ball

_____ 5. hidden flags   e. person on defense staying deep

Intermediate Flag Football Answer Key

True or False

1. T—If opponents take over, they are only 20 yards (18 meters) from the end zone.
2. T—Penalties result when a team breaks a rule, in this case the offside rule.
3. T—Squaring in requires running across the middle.
4. T—Touchback.
5. T—No forward pass is allowed; these are not going forward.
6. F—The count to 7 Mississippi is the limited time the quarterback has without fear of being rushed.
7. T—If the ball hits the ground, there is no chance of the opponent getting a completion.
8. T—Never let your person get behind you.
9. T—No chance of a run back.
10. F—Quarterback or anyone else can receive a forward pass as long as the ball is thrown from behind the line of scrimmage.

Extra Credit

1. d
2. a
3. e
4. b
5. c

From Isobel Kleinman, 2009, *Complete Physical Education Plans for Grades 5 to 12, Second Edition* (Champaign, IL: Human Kinetics).

Punt and Review

Facilities

Area large enough for class to safely move in

Materials

One football for every two students

Performance Goals

Students will do the following:

- Improve the depth and accuracy of their passing.
- Punt a football.

Cognitive Goal

Students will learn how to use the punt to put the ball in play.

Lesson Safety

- Space out students so there are no collisions.
- Practice in the same line of direction, using the same scrimmage line for all.

Motivation

Announce that after a few years of flag football under their belts, the students will spend awhile reacquainting themselves with the football, learning a new skill or two, and being introduced to ideas they might not be familiar with. If the consensus is that more practice is needed, there is no rush to get into games—it's their choice.

Warm-Up

1. Have students jog the field.
2. Then make balls available to throw and catch in pairs.
3. Lead the class in mimetics for the punt, breaking it down for right-footed kickers this way:
   - Hold both arms out with left arm slightly bent as if the ball is in both hands and angled to the left.
   - Kick right foot, with left arm to the side and right arm down to drop the ball (5 times).
   - Step left, step right, step left, letting the left arm let go of the ball (5 times).
   - Step left, step right, step left as before, and as the right leg comes up, the right hand drops down to let the ball down on the foot.

Lesson Sequence

1. On the sideline of a field, have students work in pairs throwing 5 yards (4.5 meters), then 10 yards (9 meters), then 15 yards (14 meters), and then as far as they think they can throw to a stationary partner.
2. Gather the class to demonstrate the punt (see figure 9.8). Have them practice in pairs.
   a. Hold the ball between the chest and the waist with arms extended and the imaginary ball angled slightly to the left so laces show while taking the first two steps.
   b. As the third step on left foot begins, drop left hand from the ball, keeping it out for balance.
   c. As the right foot comes up to kick, let right hand drop and release the ball.
   d. Right leg should follow through.

413

Figure 9.8 Kicking a punt.

a

b

3. In groups of four, with one quarterback passing to each receiver and then alternating, call pass patterns and distances, checking that the class knows what is meant by hooking in at the 10, squaring left on the 5, or running a slant. If there is confusion, stop and explain.

4. Remind the class of the options for moving the ball forward. Then lead practice of the following, stopping to discuss the skill, its relevance, the associated rules, and the problems to anticipate.

   a. Snaps with quarterback dropping back

   b. Handoffs

   c. Long and short passes

   d. Lateral passes

Review and Stretching

As students stretch, invite questions, review problems, and compliment good performance, effort, and improvement.

Assessment

Observe students' comfort with each skill and rule to decide whether to move to the next lesson.

Teacher Homework

If you are familiar with your students and their skills, make up teams, distributing talents so teams are as competitively equal as possible. If you are not familiar with the class, delay this process or elicit help from the students who seem most aware and have been in the school the longest time.

Flag Football
ADVANCED
LESSON 2

Fakes and More Review

Facilities

Area large enough for class to safely move in

Materials

One football for every two students

Performance Goals

Students will do the following:

- Improve the depth and accuracy of their passing.
- Practice previously learned pass patterns with a fake before the cut.

Cognitive Goals

Students will learn the following:

- Why they want to fake out defenders and how to do it
- The advantage of a zone defense

Lesson Safety

- Space out students so there are no collisions.
- Practice in the same line of direction, using the same scrimmage line for all.

Motivation

Announce that you want to take a little more time to figure out the teams and let everyone get back into a football rhythm. You also want to take a few minutes to teach them something you haven't covered before—the fake.

Warm-Up

1. Practice in the same line of direction, using the same scrimmage line for all.
2. Lead the class in mimetics for the punt (5 times).
3. Lead the class in footwork for the fake:
   a. Run forward, shift right as if about to cut right, then shift left, go right (3 times).
   b. Reverse (3 times).
   c. Run forward, shift right, run forward (3 times).

Lesson Sequence

1. Gather the class to explain the fake.
   a. Explain the fake used by the quarterback, and run a few action fakes so quarterbacks look as if they are handing off.
   b. Explain how using footwork to fake out a defender buys a receiver time, and run several patterns, using the fake before making the cut.
2. In groups of four, with a quarterback, a receiver, a center playing an eligible ball carrier, and a defender (rotate all the positions), let the quarterback call a play and distances and see if the play fakes out the defender.
3. Gather the class and discuss the advantages and disadvantages of playing person-to-person or zone defense.
4. If time remains, create groups of four for a one-hand touch game, asking them to split the defensive area into zones and have one person cover each area.

Review and Stretching

As students stretch, invite questions, review problems, and compliment good performance, effort, and improvement.

Assessment

Observe the level of comfort with each skill and rule to decide whether to move to the next lesson.

Teacher Homework

If you are familiar with your students and their skills, make up teams, distributing talents so teams are as competitively equal as possible. If you are not familiar with the class, delay this process or elicit help from the students who seem most aware and have been in the school the longest time.

Teams and Scrimmage Game

Facilities

Marked game areas with clearly defined boundaries

Materials

- Belt and flags for every student
- Cones to divide the field into game stations, enough for every two teams
- One football for every two students

Performance Goals

Students will do the following:

- Review rules and procedures for flag football games.
- Find out who their teammates are for the class tournament.
- Work on team skills.

Cognitive Goals

Students will review the following:

- Rules:
    - Use of flags
    - Kickoff
    - Rushing the quarterback
    - Offside
    - Unnecessary roughness
- Defensive strategies and the advantages of each:
    - Zone
    - Person to person
    - Person to person with safety

Lesson Safety

Monitor play for unnecessary roughness.

Motivation

Announce that you will be telling students their teams and giving them the job of deciding who will lead them, what their responsibilities are on offense and defense, and how to organize so they can play with all the skills and knowledge they have.

Warm-Up

1. As students assemble, they practice passing and catching.
2. Lead students in mimetics for the punt, the throw, pulling the ball in on a high catch, and pulling it in on a low catch.
3. Lead footwork drills for agility and backpedaling.

Lesson Sequence

1. Review rule and procedure differences for games in advanced football classes.
    a. Instead of throwing off to start, use a punt.
    b. Captains choose to either receive or take a side of the field.
    c. Counting to 7 Mississippi is not an option.
2. Announce teams, assign fields, and begin a scrimmage game.

Review and Stretching

As students stretch, entertain questions and review problems or misinterpretation of rules questions that occurred during the practice games. Be sure to compliment good performance, effort, and improvement.

Teacher Homework

Prepare and post a tournament schedule and team standings.

Tournament

Facilities

One game area bounded by lines or cones for every two teams

Materials

- One football for every two students
- Color-coded belts and flags for every student on a team
- Cones to divide the field
- Team standings and posted tournament schedule

Performance Goals

Students will do the following:

- Use their skills to the advantage of their team.
- Play by the rules and follow regulations for flag football.
- Play up to five rounds of a football tournament over five classes.

Cognitive Goal

Students will understand their weaknesses and learn how their team can overcome them by refocusing team strategies.

Lesson Safety

Monitor games for unnecessary roughness and emotionally stressful behavior.

Motivation

The teams that usually do well are the ones with everyone involved and contributing. Tell students that those who only have eyes for the biggest and fastest player on the team will learn quickly—if they play only one player, that player can easily be shut down by alert opponents. Everyone can contribute to a team, and smart teams make sure everyone does. Smart teams have players score when you'd least suspect them to be given the responsibility. Announce that the tournament is purely for fun. Students are their own masters, so they should go out there and see if their wits and skills can keep them in the running for first place.

Warm-Up

1. Students put on their belts and begin passing and catching.
2. Drill footwork for cutting left and right, quick footwork change, and running backward.
3. Practice mimetics for jumping to pull down a high pass.

Lesson Sequence

1. Discuss what the posted tournament schedule includes:
   a. Round of the tournament
   b. Team identity numbers and which team they play (e.g., team 1 plays team 4)

417

    c. Color of flags their team will be wearing

    d. Which field the game will be played on

2. Discuss what the posted standings include:

    a. Team-identifying number

    b. Captain's and cocaptain's names

    c. Game record

3. Each day before the games, change the focus to one of the following for each position and responsibility.

    a. Quarterback

- Throwing to the open player
- Using short passes to retain possession
- Exercising all options to avoid predictability
- Learning that it is better to run than to throw and be intercepted

    b. Defense

- Pressuring the quarterback
- Not letting person get behind you
- Alerting teammates that the ball is moving so they can drop their person and chase the carrier
- Using zones or a safety when playing person to person

    c. Receiver

- Eye on ball
- Breaking to the outside
- Making cuts and faking to lose opponents
- Running behind teammates so they block or screen

    d. Offense—making a plan that includes everyone, even if not ball carrier

4. During games, act as an official and coach, reminding students to focus on the strategies introduced at the start of class.

Review and Stretching

1. As students stretch, review how you thought the day's strategy played out.

- Which team incorporated it and if it was successful
- How to make the strategy work better
- How the strategy breaks down and possible examples

2. Answer questions and collect scores.

Assessment

This unit is short. Testing knowledge of rules, strategies, and fundamentals of movement in football follows, although testing football alone is questionable since football will only be part of the quarter. It is probably best to select questions from all activities done in the quarter before taking the time to quiz the students. Grading performance can be based on minimal standards:

- Proper positioning on defense
- Moving to the open field on offense
- Cutting to lose opponent on offense
- Screening teammates
- Catching accurate passes
- Responding to the team game plan

You might also consider letting advanced students evaluate themselves against the advanced performance rubric.

Advanced Flag Football Skills Rubric

Name _____ Date _____

Teacher _____ Class _____

	1	2	3	4	5
Offense	• Can generally direct or control the football. • Knows the team's general objective and uses skills to help meet it. • Gets back to line of scrimmage at the end of each play.	• If given ball, can maintain possession. • Can assist the team in maintaining possession by faking, blocking, or getting open.	• Can play the game within the context of the rules. • Has a good sense of the boundaries, end zone, and first-down markers. • Able to implement team strategies.	• Can adapt to short or long plays. • Will block for ball carrier. • Uses speed and agility to avoid flag pulled. • Can play a flowing game.	• Understands responsibility and how it relates to the rest of the team. • Able to call plays and adjust if play does not work the way planned. • Finds a way to get the next first down and score.
Defense	• Knows to stop the ball carrier by pulling flags or tagging. • Will leave the line of scrimmage once ball is snapped. • Will use hands to reach for ball carrier or ball.	• Capable of covering a person of equal speed and size. • Covers assigned zone. • Able to occasionally interrupt opponents' play.	• Can react to a handoff at the line of scrimmage. • Does not let opponent get behind. • Will drop person or zone once the ball is up and go after carrier. • Plays within the rules.	• Knows how to use positioning to cut off opponents' lanes. • If unable to prevent the completed pass, prevents additional yardage. • Runs down the ball carrier who gets away from teammates.	• Able to intercept passes and change direction of the game. • Effective in regaining possession of the ball. • Anticipates opposition. • Helps team focus on the things to stop.
Skill	• Generally successful in uncrowded field. • Competent up to 10 yd (9 m).	• Occasionally successful in competitive, crowded field. • Competent up to 15 yd (14 m).	• Undeterred from primary objective. • Does not compromise team. • Relatively consistent to 20 yd (18 m).	• Can perform despite distractions. • Consistent at most distances. • More competent on either offense or defense.	• Plays offense and defense equally well. • Is one of strongest and fastest on team. • Is the big play maker.

From Isobel Kleinman, 2009, *Complete Physical Education Plans for Grades 5 to 12, Second Edition* (Champaign, IL: Human Kinetics).

Advanced Flag Football Quiz

Name _____ Date _____

Teacher _____ Class _____

True or False

Read each statement carefully. If the statement is true, write a *T* in the column to the left. If the statement is false, write an *F*. If using a grid sheet, blacken in the appropriate column for each question, making sure to use the correctly numbered line for each question and its answer.

_____ 1. When on the opponents' 10-yard (9-meter) line, teams should punt if it is their fourth down.

_____ 2. Grabbing an opponent's clothes or tackling him is unnecessarily rough play for flag football and penalized as such.

_____ 3. A receiver intending to square in will line up closer to the sideline than to the center of the field.

_____ 4. Stopping an opponent who is playing the ball in her own end zone results in a score for the defending team whether or not they have the ball.

_____ 5. A ball in front of the line of scrimmage can be passed as long as the pass is a lateral or backward.

_____ 6. The player counting to 7 Mississippi should count with his hands at his sides.

_____ 7. Players able to touch the ball but unable to intercept it should bat it to the ground.

_____ 8. Defensive players should keep their own end zone to their back and the player they are responsible for in front of them.

_____ 9. It is better to punt so that the ball lands inbounds at the 10-yard (9-meter) line and bounces out of bounds than it is to have it land in the end zone.

_____ 10. If the quarterback gives the ball to a teammate behind the line of scrimmage and then runs in front of the line of scrimmage, the defense should go after the new ball carrier because no one on the offensive team can pass the ball.

Match the Columns

_____ 11. safety

_____ 12. offside

_____ 13. blocking

_____ 14. defensive center

_____ 15. right foot

a. ahead of the ball before it is snapped

b. counts to 7 Mississippi while being ready to bat the ball down on the scrimmage line

c. a runner should plant it before cutting left

d. the player covering an area well behind the rest of his team's defense

e. creating a moving wall between a teammate and an opponent

»*continued*

From Isobel Kleinman, 2009, *Complete Physical Education Plans for Grades 5 to 12, Second Edition* (Champaign, IL: Human Kinetics).

»continued

Diagram

In the following figure, identify the running pattern that best describes the question and then put the correct number on the line to the left.

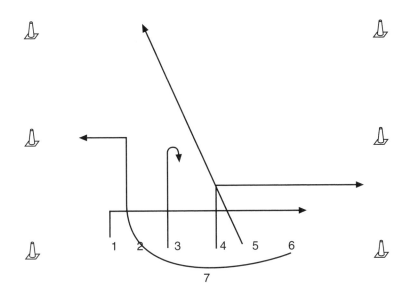

_____ 16. Which is a slant pattern?

_____ 17. Which pattern allows the quarterback to either hand off or throw to the runner later?

_____ 18. Which pattern has the receiver running in front of the quarterback?

_____ 19. If the cone represents a first-down marker, which receiver is running to receive the ball for the next first down?

_____ 20. Which receiver is expecting to come back to the ball?

Advanced Flag Football Answer Key

True or False

1. F—They cannot hope to get their opponents any farther back than they already are and they can use the fourth down to possibly score.
2. T
3. T
4. T
5. T
6. F—The player should always use the arms to block the throwing lanes of the quarterback
7. T
8. T—Good defense means never letting your opponent get behind you.
9. T—If the ball bounces in the end zone, the touchback brings it up to the 20-yard (18-meter) line.
10. F—A ball behind the line of scrimmage can be passed by anyone. The defense should continue to cover their person until the ball is up to or over the line of scrimmage.

Match the Columns

11. d
12. a
13. e
14. b
15. c

Diagram

16. 5
17. 6
18. 1
19. 6
20. 3

From Isobel Kleinman, 2009, *Complete Physical Education Plans for Grades 5 to 12, Second Edition* (Champaign, IL: Human Kinetics).

Lacrosse

10

Chapter Overview

1. Lessons provide repetition to enhance performance and introduce equipment, the body mechanics of each skill, and rules and strategies as students acquire experience and are able to understand them.

2. Teach how to effectively control the ball in the lacrosse stick: the cradle, pick-up, overarm throw, catch.

3. Teach evasive techniques: the dodge, the pivot, controlled checking (crosse to crosse contact).

4. Teach field positions and responsibilities (based on non-contact modified girls' rules).

5. Teach standard rules: starting play, returning the ball to the field, minor fouls of illegally advancing the ball, the 3-second rule, the third player obstruction rule, entering restraining area illegally.

6. Teach major fouls: playing unsafely (uncontrolled shots at the goal, checking anything but the stick, checking in the 7-inch area around the player's head, body checks.

7. Teach procedures for penalties and personal fouls.

8. Teach the strategy and skills on different sides of the field.

Lacrosse Study Sheet

History

Lacrosse, the oldest game in North America, was played by Native American males. It is believed that the game held a ceremonial role far more serious than the leisure activity we use it for today. Named by early French settlers, lacrosse was used for healing purposes, is steeped in ceremony, and is part of Indian legend. As the Native American culture was eroded by nonnative settlers, the game saw an increase in wagering and violence, all of which provoked strong opposition from missionaries and government officials. Finally, when the Oklahoma Choctaw began affixing weights to their sticks and calling them *skull-crackers,* the sport was banned.

In the mid-1800s, some English-speaking Montrealers decided to adapt lacrosse for white Canadians. They created rules and amateur playing clubs. Once the game became popular in Canada, it was exported to the rest of the British Commonwealth.

Fun Facts

- American Indian players from the Southeast held two short 2.5-foot (76-centimeter) sticks, one in each hand, and retrieved the ball between them. In other parts of the continent, the game was played with one 3-foot (1-meter) stick.
- A game between the Creek and the Choctaw was played to settle a territorial dispute around the 1790s.
- The game was originally played in a natural field, with no boundaries and no protective equipment.

Benefits

- Practice and play provide a great workout.
- It is fun to play with a team.
- Playing outdoors on a field of grass is exhilarating.

Field

Lacrosse is typically played in an open field, using only natural boundaries. Strangely, each division has slightly different field sizes and lengths. Included for school use is a girls' modified field, its markings, and the starting positions (see figure 10.1).

Positions

Offense

- The center is primarily a defensive player but begins play and sometimes plays offense. Centers need speed and endurance.
- Left attack wings and right attack wings need speed and endurance so when they get the clears (shots that are hit to the side, away from their opponents) they can run the ball and open the field as they begin the attack. They should be as good as running with the ball as passing it.
- Third home is the transition person who goes from offense to defense and swings to fill in the wing areas.
- Second home is the playmaker. The second home needs to be able to shoot from every angle and all distances and needs good anticipation.
- First home shoots more than anyone else. First homes need to cut often, either to get into position to score or to cut away from the goal to make room for someone else. They need a good cradle and to be able to shoot from every angle.

»continued

 From Isobel Kleinman, 2009, *Complete Physical Education Plans for Grades 5 to 12, Second Edition* (Champaign, IL: Human Kinetics).

»continued

Defense

- Right defense wings and left defense wings, who mark attack wings, need speed and endurance and to be able to bring the ball to the attack area.

- Third man, who marks the third home, needs to be quick, to intercept, and to clear the ball.

- Cover point must be able to receive clears, mark the second home, run fast, and have good anticipation and communication.

- Point marks the first home and needs courage in the critical scoring area to anticipate and stop most shots on goal.

- Goalie must wear a helmet and leg, chest, and hand padding. Goalies can legally block the ball with their body and hands when inside the striker's circle. They may only use their stick or feet to clear it. They need quick reflexes, confidence, and the willingness to wear a helmet, pads, and gloves and carry a big stick.

Rules

Procedures

- The draw starts the game and play after a goal.
- A ball going out of bounds is brought back into play by the closest player.

Fouls

- Unsafe play caused by charging, hitting, pushing, tripping, shoving
- Body checking
- Holding on to the ball when closely guarded for more than 3 seconds (moving stick to the other side to restart the clock)
- Dangerous use of sticks
- Checking the stick within 7 inches (18 centimeters) of the head
- Gaining an advantage by moving or stopping the ball with anything other than the stick

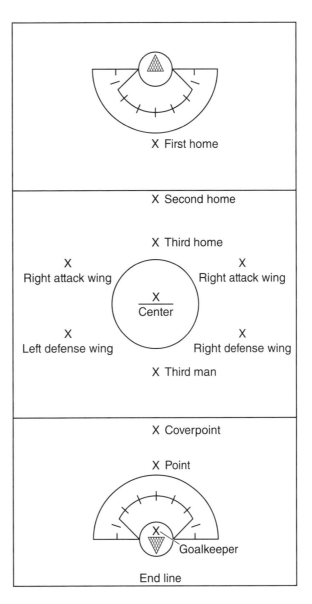

Figure 10.1 Lacrosse positions on a marked field.

»continued

»continued

Penalties

- Minor violation on the playing field
  - A free position is awarded to opponents.
  - Offender must move 4 meters off in the direction from which she approached. Offending teammates must be 4 meters away.
  - The player taking the free position can run or pass.
- Major violation inside the critical scoring area
  - The offender stands 4 meters behind the player taking the free position.
  - The player may run, shoot, or pass.
- Flagrant disregard for the safety of others (suspension from play)

From Isobel Kleinman, 2009, *Complete Physical Education Plans for Grades 5 to 12, Second Edition* (Champaign, IL: Human Kinetics).

Lacrosse Extension Project

Name _____ Date _____

Teacher _____ Class _____

What equipment do you need to do these activities on your own?

Where can you participate outside of school?

Do you have friends who would join you? List their names.

What are the health benefits of participating in a field-hockey program?

Lacrosse Student Portfolio Checklist

Name _____ Date _____

Teacher _____ Class _____

_____ Can hold crosse.

_____ Can run with the ball slowly.

_____ Can pass the ball to a teammate with an overarm throw.

_____ Knows how to reverse grip to play the ball to the right.

_____ Knows how to receive the ball with crosse.

_____ Often able to catch a ball sent straight.

_____ Can throw the ball 15 yards (14 meters).

_____ Can throw the ball 25 yards (23 meters).

_____ Can throw the ball 40 yards (37 meters).

_____ Knows what to do when playing position.

_____ Knows how the offense counts on the defense.

_____ Can sense when to go back to get a pass.

_____ Can pass the ball to the right.

_____ Can legally pick up balls that are on the ground.

_____ Knows how the game starts.

_____ Knows how to return a ball to play after it goes over the sideline.

_____ Knows that the defense cannot hang around in the critical scoring area.

_____ Does not hold stick close to head and body.

_____ Can run at top speed without losing the ball.

_____ Knows what to do if an opponent is awarded a free position.

_____ Knows why teams are awarded a free position.

_____ Can dodge opponents and keep control of the ball.

_____ Can explain and execute an outlet pass.

_____ Can explain and execute an inlet pass.

From Isobel Kleinman, 2009, *Complete Physical Education Plans for Grades 5 to 12, Second Edition* (Champaign, IL: Human Kinetics).

Lacrosse Learning Experience Outline

Contents and Procedure

1. Introduce equipment
2. Skills
   a. Cradle
   b. Pickup
   c. Overarm throw
   d. Catch
   e. Dodge
   f. Pivot
   g. Controlled checking (crosse-to-crosse contact)
3. Field positions and responsibilities (based on noncontact modified girls' rules)
4. Standard rules
   a. Procedural rules
      - Starting play with a draw
      - Returning the ball to the field
   b. Minor fouls
      - Illegally advancing the ball.
      - Three-second rule—Defender cannot stay in the critical 8-meter shooting area for more than 3 seconds unless closely marking an opponent.
      - A third player obstructing the free space to the goal—The player marking the shooter only may stay between the shooter and the goal.
      - Entering restraining area when not allowed.
   c. Major fouls
      - Playing unsafely
        - Wild, uncontrolled shots at the goal
        - Checking anything but the stick
        - Checking in the 7-inch (18-centimeter) area around the player's head
        - Body checks
5. Procedures for penalties and personal fouls
   a. Minor fouls—an indirect pass from a free position, opponent 4 meters away
   b. Major fouls by defense inside 8-meter arc—free position from the closest hash mark and the right to shoot when the whistle signals play to resume
6. Strategy and skills on different sides of the field

Teaching Tips

It is essential that every student in class have access to a lacrosse stick, a mouthpiece, and safety glasses. Since being active safely is more important than a particular activity, if you are short the necessary equipment, lacrosse is an unacceptable curriculum choice.

The lessons that follow integrate basic skills, game strategies, and rules in an effort to keep students moving as they learn. Goals in each lesson are measured so that students will attain a sense of accomplishment as they work toward mastering basic skills, concepts, and rules. Every lesson will increase students' lacrosse abilities as well as their level of fitness.

Field marking, positions, and even many basic rules differ in girls' and women's games. They also differ in boys' and men's games. Students with previous experience might get confused, so it will be important to explain that this unit will follow noncontact rules. Students will enjoy the openness of the game. Lacrosse has few rules and until recently, it didn't even have boundaries. There are simple procedures for returning the ball to play and few reasons to blow the whistle and stop the game.

The throw, catch, and cradle are the essential skills and can never be overpracticed. The use of repetition and lots of hands-on experience is enabled by using all the time available for practicing and moving. Have students pick up their equipment and go to practice once they are dressed. Using all the time available to them to move means extra practice and more success. Teachers who hesitate to do this should read the introductory chapter in this book, which explains the pros and cons of allowing students to perform as soon as they arrive for class.

If students are not losing interest in working on skills and the class has reached the lesson that introduces the game but it feels too rushed, repeat earlier lessons by adding challenges that vary how the skills are practiced and what the students focus on. Such practice can be challenging without taking an undue amount of time to reorganize.

- Who can throw the farthest?
- Who is the most accurate against a target?
- Who receives the most passes from a partner in a certain number of minutes?
- Who has the most success when given a certain number of chances to get the ball?
- Who scores the most when running to the crease and shooting at an unprotected goal?

Teaching Tips for Students With Special Needs

Students who are unable to play the game should have class responsibilities. For most, it is best to stay with the class; learn technique, rules, and strategies; and do what they are capable of doing. If they are able to walk to the field, they should stay with the class. Some might be able to do the warm-up exercises. Some might be able to participate in part of the practice. During the games, they can learn to act as officials, team coaches, or statisticians. All students should be encouraged to do what they can.

Students who have a long-term disability may be better served by placement in an adaptive physical education class. If there is no adaptive physical education class, have the students do something relevant. For instance, in addition to the previous suggestions, they could do the following:

- Write a research report on the game, including its history, equipment, and rules.
- Draw charts that explain how each skill is executed.
- Create an appropriate bulletin board with material they researched, drew, or cut out.
- Research the problem that keeps them from playing, citing the medically suggested remedies, explaining what would be acceptable movement for someone in their condition, stating what can be done for preventative care, and drawing up a plan to keep them as fit as possible.

Facilities

Lacrosse is typically played in an open field, using only natural boundaries. Strangely, each division has slightly different field sizes and lengths. Included for school use is a girls' modified field, its markings, and the starting positions (see figure 10.1, page 425).

Materials

The lessons in this unit leave the goal cage empty and encourage students to play a moving position in class.

- Set of goals for each field
- Cones
- One lacrosse stick for each student
- Personal mouthpiece and safety glasses for each student
- Pinnies for half the class
- One ball per student
- Visual aid (blackboard, magnetic board, or chart)
- Two sets of goalie equipment for each game fielded at one time

Unit Safety

- Students exhibiting a dangerous use of sticks must be given immediate feedback to stop endangering others.
- Teach the proper follow-through.
- Teach students to have consideration for classmates.
- Play by the rules.
- Checking when the crosse is near the head or using any body contact will not be allowed.
- If students play goalie, they must wear a helmet, leg pads, and gloves.
- Students must wear protective glasses and mouthpiece.
- Lessons will always start with skills-specific warm-ups.

Rainy Days

Much can be accomplished when classes come indoors because of inclement weather.

- Warm-up—If used well, the warm-up can be a reinforcing activity as well as a learning one. If the students practice the movement patterns they use in lacrosse (mimetics) as a warm-up, they will develop good movement patterns. Have students repeat the proper movement patterns with a stick in hand up to 10 times. As they get comfortable with the correct stick movement, have them start concentrating on the correct footwork. Over the course of the unit, have them practice getting into the right body position relative to a particular game situation. Once they have acquired the correct preparatory motion, have them practice following through to an imaginary target on the right, left, or straight ahead. Such warm-ups not only get the body ready for the game, but get the students ready to play with proper mechanics.

- Teach fielding—The acoustics, the closeness, and the availability of a blackboard make using a diagram and explaining the unique responsibilities of each position and how they relate much easier than trying to cover this information outdoors. After an explanation, have students use what you taught in a modified game. When students understand the job they do for the team, they will be much more comfortable on a big field and better able to play as part of a team.

- Teach rules—The most important rules are introduced in each lesson, but rainy days allow review. Although students need not learn to be officials, they should learn the basic rules and how to abide by them. A healthy respect for rules should be expected.

Modified Games

Sometimes games must be modified. This occurs when there are too few or too many players or when the size of the space is suddenly reduced because you must field more teams or because you have to come indoors. Despite the need to modify, you can still teach team concepts, strategies, and rules and expect them to be used. It is possible to use the same outdoor field positions indoors. It works well if students use a smaller implement, a smaller ball, or are themselves made smaller (by being on their knees or on scooters), or if their movement is made more difficult when they have to pass (have them sit on the floor) and work with their teammates. In a smaller context, players still need to communicate and play as a team. Despite the smaller scale, they will continue learning game essentials and having fun with teammates.

Unit Timeline

This unit is designed to be used over 6 to 8 weeks. There are 17 lessons in this introductory unit to lacrosse:

- four lessons focus on skills acquisition,
- one introduces the game,
- five lessons combine skills acquisition and practice with game play,
- six lessons are designed for tournament play and learning teamwork and strategy, and
- one is left for completing performance and knowledge assessment

Suggested Resources

e-Lacrosse. 2008. www.e-lacrosse.com.

Laxhistory.com. 2008. Lacrosse history. www.laxhistory.com.

Trafford, B., and K. Howarth. 1989. *Women's lacrosse: The skills of the game.* Wiltshire, England: Crowood Press.

U.S. Lacrosse. 1998. *Women's lacrosse drills: A manual.*

U.S. Lacrosse. 2008. www.lacrosse.org.Stretching will be done after the muscles are warm, at the end of class during review.

Cradling, Picking Up, and Pivoting

Facilities

Grassy field

Materials

- One modified lacrosse stick for every student (Modified sticks are shorter, easier for youngsters to handle, and have a slightly larger net [crosse])
- One ball for each student

Performance Goals

Students will do the following:

- Stop on every whistle.
- Grip the lacrosse stick properly.
- Legally advance the ball while cradling it.
- Legally pick up the ball in their crosse.
- Improve their physical fitness.

Cognitive Goals

Students will learn the following:

- That lacrosse rules require every player to stop in place on the whistle
- That the modified stick has a slightly larger pocket than a regulation stick
- Why they must cradle the ball when running with it

Lesson Safety

- Follow the unit guidelines for safety, making sure that students get in the habit of wearing all protective equipment. It is essential that every student in class have access to a mouthpiece and safety glasses.
- Make clear to students that the lacrosse stick is not a weapon but a tool to be used skillfully, and any misuse will result in forfeiture.
- Space students out so that they can move freely without worrying about running into anyone.

Motivation

During the warm-up, the students dash around the field and swing their sticks away from imaginary opponents to protect an imaginary ball. Now it's time for the real thing—doing it all with a ball—as well as an explanation about the importance of cradling.

Warm-Up (10 Minutes)

Set up a class routine that has students practicing skills as they warm up while you take care of procedural tasks. This is a good time to work with students in need of extra help or those who have individual problems such as medical excuses.

1. Students take a stick and run around the field holding the stick in both hands so that the stick head is above their shoulders.
2. Ask them to take another lap, rotating the stick from their right side to their left side (top hand moves from ear to ear and bottom hand moves from hip to hip).
3. While in attendance spots, review proper grip using lacrosse terminology for the parts of the stick:
   - Dominant hand should be at the throat of the stick and under the crosse.
   - Other hand should be at the butt end of the stick.
   - Head of the stick should be at eye level.
   a. Ask students to practice cradling an imaginary ball in the pocket of their stick.
      - They should start so that they are staring at the face of the crosse.
      - To cradle, they should swing the cross from side to side, allowing the wrists to roll so that the face of the crosse is open at either side (see figure 10.2).
      - Coach them:
        - Have both hands move in unison.
        - Keep the crosse upright.
        - Keep a firm grip but let the wrists roll.
   b. Ask students to pivot so they turn a quarter to the right (then half, then three-quarters).
      - Have them keep the stick upright as they pivot.
      - Maintain balance by planting the front foot and having the rear foot move in the new direction.
      - Once they have the footwork, ask them if they can cradle as they pivot, pretending that they are swinging their crosse away from an opponent.

Lesson Sequence

1. Distribute a ball to every student and ask them to walk with it in their crosse to a line.
   a. When students drop the ball, have them pick it up and continue, reminding them to continue cradling it as they go.
   b. Repeat, counting the number of times the ball is dropped.
   c. Repeat, asking who can get to the other side without dropping it at all.

Figure 10.2 Cradling.

2. Teach how to pick up dropped balls legally. (To see the pickup, go to www.expertvillage.com/videos/lacrosse-ground-ball.htm.)

    a. Explain and demonstrate. With the front foot next to the ball and the player's head over the ball, push the crosse under the ball with the lower hand and begin cradling as soon as the ball is lifted off the ground.

    b. Ask students to try it while they are standing still (5 times).

    c. Given 20 seconds, who can pick up the ball the most?

3. Ask students to run, drop the ball, pick it up, and continue to the line (5 times).

4. Set up shuttle lines with at least four and no more than six students in each group.

    a. Have students run to the people on the other side of their shuttle, leaving the ball on the ground for the next person to pick up and run back with. Go through the lines several times, coaching students:

      • Push the stick under the ball with the butt end of the stick.

      • Start the cradle right away.

      • Bend down over the ball.

      • Watch the ball all the way into the crosse before trying to run with it.

      • Get the stick in an upright position right away.

    b. Run a few relay races to increase enthusiasm.

      • Following the practice instructions, see which line finishes first.

      • Have students form one line. Each person runs down, pivots, runs back, and exchanges possession of the ball.

Review and Stretching

1. Set up a stretching routine to be done during the review. Include the following:

    a. Hamstrings

    b. Quadriceps

    c. Lower back

    d. Shoulders

    e. Neck

2. As students stretch, ask questions:
   - Which hand should be on the top of the stick, your strong one or your weak one?
   - Why is it necessary to cradle the ball if you want to keep possession of it?
   - Will pivoting help you keep your opponent from getting the ball from you? Why?
   - Can anyone guess why it is necessary to learn these skills in order to advance the ball? (It is illegal to gain advantage by moving the ball with any part of the body.)
3. Announce that next time, everyone should get a stick and a ball, run a lap, and then practice picking up a ball.

Overarm Throw and Catch

Facilities

Grassy field

Materials

- One modified lacrosse stick for every student
- One ball for each student

Performance Goals

Students will do the following:

- Get a stick, a ball, and go directly out to practice.
- Advance the ball:
  - Running with it in their crosse
  - Using the lacrosse stick to make an overarm pass
- Catch the ball with their lacrosse stick.
- Improve their physical fitness.

Cognitive Goals

Students will learn the following:

- Why they must cradle on reception of the ball
- That they gain strength and power by using their stick as a lever
- That their follow-through determines the direction of their pass

Lesson Safety

- Follow the unit guidelines for safety, making sure that students get in the habit of wearing all protective equipment. It is essential that every student in class have access to a mouthpiece and safety glasses.
- Make clear to students that the lacrosse stick is not a weapon but a tool to be used skillfully, and any misuse will result in forfeiture.
- Space students out so that they can move freely without worrying about running into anyone.

Motivation

Students will all have the proper throwing and catching mechanics because they will learn them as they warm up. They have the mechanics for catching, throwing, and cradling but still have to try them with the ball and a real target. They will be excited to try.

Warm-Up (10 Minutes)

1. Students run around the field, keeping the ball in their possession as they go.
2. Students get a partner and practice picking up the ball while their partner's stick is over it.

435

3. Have students go to their attendance spots and begin mimetics.
    a. Ask students to hold sticks up and in front of their body to catch.
        • Reach with the widest part of the stick for the imaginary ball.
        • Wrap the crosse around the ball and begin cradling immediately.
        • Make hands soft, keep wrists and elbows flexible, and keep a firm grip.
        • Watch the imaginary ball into the top of the crosse and give.
        • Repeat with coaching hints (10 times).
    b. Now that they have learned to catch, they need to learn to throw.
        • Cradle the stick to the dominant side (where the hand is highest on the grip) and step forward with opposite leg (5 times).
        • Slide the top hand behind the stick (5 times).
        • Using just the top hand, bend the top elbow back, and using an overarm throwing motion, follow through toward the target (5 times).
        • Place the bottom hand back on the butt end of the stick and pull it while throwing with the top hand until the crosse points toward the target (10 times).

Lesson Sequence

1. Demonstrate catching from a high thrown toss.
2. Have partners take turns tossing the ball to each other by hand. Circulate, making sure they are
    a. watching the ball into their cross,
    b. reaching to catch it as high as possible,
    c. wrapping the stick around the ball with the top of the crosse,
    d. cradling right away, and
    e. positioning themselves so the catch is not directly in front of their body.
3. Have students do the same, but this time, toss it high to themselves.
    a. Remind them to reach for the ball, wrap, and cradle in one motion.
    b. Remind them to give on contact.
4. Have students catch a low toss.
5. Practice the lacrosse overarm throw and catch (see figure 10.3).
    a. If there is a wall, use it. If not, line partners up on the field.
        • Begin a high throwing practice with students about 5 yards (4.5 meters) apart. If they cannot reach each other on a fly, have them get closer until they are at a distance where they can throw and catch without the ball touching the ground first.
        • As they progress, have them move farther apart.
    b. Circulate, coaching them:
        • Use the stick as a lever and pull the bottom arm.
        • Make sure the elbow of the throwing arm goes back, as if preparing to throw a ball.
        • Snap the wrist on the follow-through.
        • Keep the head of the crosse above the ears.
6. Allow more practice and introduce a challenge to keep interest high.
    • Which pair can legally catch the most passes in 30 seconds?
    • You might repeat this if students are excited.
7. To get them moving, make time for relays.
    a. In relay formation, have players run about 20 feet (6 meters) away, turn, and pass back to the next member of their team. As soon as that member either catches or picks up the ball legally, she does the same. Meanwhile, the person who passed should run back to the back of his team line. The relay continues until the entire group has gone once and everyone is in original positions. When the last person finishes, have the line sit.

a   *b*

c   *d*

Figure 10.3 The overarm throw.

    b. Or, with everyone beginning from the same place, see who can get to the farthest sideline first with the ball in their crosse.

Review and Stretching

As students stretch, ask:

- What slowed your team? Bad throws, inability to catch, losing the ball while running?
- If you don't have the ball when you think you do, what should you do with your eyes?
- Can someone demonstrate how to wrap the stick around the ball to catch it?
- Why must you cradle after catching the ball?
- Which action creates most of the force during a throw?
- If you want to add power, what must you do with your wrists? Feet?
- Where should the butt of your crosse point when you begin to throw?
- What should be pointing toward the target when the throw is complete?

Moving to Pass

Facilities

- Crease marked and a set of goalposts
- Grassy field

Materials

- One modified lacrosse stick for every student
- One ball for each student

Performance Goals

Students will do the following:

- Begin integrating movement with throwing, catching, and shooting.
- Improve their physical fitness.

Cognitive Goals

Students will learn the following:

- How the lever action of their pass helps with power
- How to change the direction of their pass

Lesson Safety

- Follow the unit guidelines for safety, making sure that students get in the habit of wearing all protective equipment. It is essential that every student in class have access to a mouthpiece and safety glasses.
- Make clear to students that the lacrosse stick is not a weapon but a tool to be used skillfully, and any misuse will result in forfeiture.
- Space students out so that they can move freely without worrying about running into anyone.

Motivation

The students are improving their ability to move the ball and should be complimented for their accomplishments. They have yet to learn how to pass and catch while on the move and how to obtain the ball when others control it. Once they do so, they will be ready to try out their skills in a game.

Warm-Up (10 Minutes)

1. Students take a warm-up lap, cradling the ball as they run. Then practice passing and catching.
2. Lead mimetics:
   - Pass (5 times)
   - Pass with specified direction—forward (5 times), left (5 times), right (5 times)
   - Five running steps forward (while cradling), pivot, and pass right (5 times)
   - Five running steps forward (while cradling), pivot, and pass left (5 times)
   - Five running steps forward (while cradling), pivot, and pass back (5 times)
   - Catch high (5 times)
   - Catch low (5 times)

Lesson Sequence

1. Practice passing and catching on the move:
   a. Partners go down the right side of the field, passing back and forth. At the end line, switch sides, alternating who is nearest the center lane on the way back.
   b. Repeat, but when nearing the goal, shoot.

2. While they are catching their breath, try a contest:
   a. Who has the farthest throw?
   b. Who can catch the longest pass?
3. Play monkey in the middle, switching who is in the middle. Conclude by explaining that one way to get the ball is to intercept it.
4. Set up several goals (or targets).
   a. Have students run toward the goal and shoot.
   b. Divide students into two lines per goal. One line will go and shoot. The other will mark the shooter (stay between the shooter and goal to intercept, pick up, or hinder a good shot). If they can, the defense should carry the ball back to their line before the shot is taken. After everyone gets a turn in offense and defense and seems to be feeling comfortable with those responsibilities, keep score:
      - 1 point for offense to take the shot
      - 2 points if offense gets it in
      - 1 point for the marking team to bring it back to their line

Review and Stretching

1. When students gather at the end of class, have them return equipment.
2. As students stretch, ask questions:
   - What does *marking* mean?
   - What does *intercept* mean?
   - If you want to throw to the right and are going forward, what must you do?

Checking and Keep-Away

Facilities

One 50- by 25-yard (23- by 46-meter) field area for every 10 to 12 students

Materials

- Sets of goalposts, flags, or cones for each small field
- Mouthpieces and safety glasses for each student
- Pinnies for half the class
- One modified lacrosse stick for every student
- One ball for each student

Performance Goals

Students will do the following:

- Use a stick check.
- Start a keep-away game.

Cognitive Goals

Students will learn the following:

- Why they must wear the mouthpieces and eye guards
- More rules:
  - For returning the ball to the field, the player closest to it puts it back in play.
  - When closely guarded (a stick's length), a player cannot hold the ball longer than 3 seconds.

- Penalty for illegal contact is a free position to run, pass, or shoot with offending player 4 meters away.

Lesson Safety

- Checking can be dangerous. Students either intentionally go for the ball carrier or accidentally hit the ball carrier when they check. Consider omitting this skill if you feel your students are not skilled enough to play cleanly.
- Follow the unit guidelines on safety, making sure that students wear their mouthpiece and safety glasses.
- Students are not to use the lacrosse stick as a weapon. Misuse will result in forfeiture.

Motivation

Students have had 3 days of practicing the most essential skills in lacrosse and have done well. They are ready to have some fun with their skills. In a game, it is important to wear protective equipment and learn how to legally dislodge a ball from an opponent's stick.

Warm-Up (5 Minutes)

1. Students take a lap with the ball before practicing passing and catching.
2. Lead mimetics. While they practice, check that students have mouthpieces and eye guards.
   - Catching a pass from the right (3 times)
   - Catching a short pass (3 times)
   - Catching a high pass (3 times)
   - Passing to a teammate 10 yards (9 meters) to the right (3 times)
   - Passing to a teammate across the field on the left (3 times)
   - Shooting for goal (3 times)
   - Pickups

Lesson Sequence

1. Review what players can do to get ball from opponents without causing harm:
   - Position themselves to intercept.
   - Mark opponent (person to person) to impede a good pass or shot.
   - Pick up a loose ball from the ground.
   - Check their opponent's stick so the check
     - is not in the 7-inch (18-centimeter) area around the head, and
     - is away from the opponent's body.
2. Explain that unlike other sports, if the ball goes off the field, the player closest to it puts it back in play.
3. Have students partner up and take turns legally checking each other.
4. Issue pinnies to half the class and set up a routine for their use.
   - Return them at the end of the game.
   - Pinnies team has choice of side (or ball if the game being played does not use a draw).
5. Organize several small keep-away games (five or six players), asking players to play within their lanes.
   a. Award the ball to the pinnies team and have them defend for 2 minutes, trying not to give up the ball. Only the other team can shoot for goal.
   b. After 2 minutes, switch.
   c. Repeat, reminding defenders that they cannot shoot but asking them to record the scores for each shooting team.

6. As they play, circulate.
   a. Ask offensive players not to get closer to their teammates than 10 yards (9 meters).
   b. Make sure that the stick checking is legal.
   c. Do not allow body contact at all.
7. If time remains, have the teams play the keep-away game with a different group.

Review and Stretching

While students are stretching, ask:

- What did you have to do to keep the ball?
- What made you lose the ball?

Draw and Minigame

Facilities

Properly marked fields for every two teams

Materials

- Visual aid such as a blackboard, magnetic board, or chart
- Mouthpieces and safety glasses for each student
- Pinnies for half the class
- One modified lacrosse stick for every student
- One ball for each student

Performance Goals

Students will do the following:

- Start the game with a draw.
- Continue improving the throw, catch, and cradle.
- Play on the full field while improving their physical fitness.

Cognitive Goals

Students will learn the following:

- Why they shouldn't try to cover the whole field themselves
- That different positions have different team responsibilities
- The procedure for starting a modified game—the draw

Lesson Safety

- Make certain students are wearing their protective equipment.
- Do not allow students to use the lacrosse stick as a weapon.

Motivation

During the last class, students played a keep-away game and got the feeling of passing to their teammates and controlling the ball while on defense. Today, the class will play a minigame of lacrosse where the ball carriers can shoot if they are in the right place and facing the correct goal.

Warm-Up (8 Minutes)

1. Students go directly to the field to practice passing.
2. While still in attendance spots, have students do a pass-and-go shuttle drill (5 times).
   - Divide lines into shuttle formation with one ball to each line
   - Students pass to whomever they face and run to the back of the line they face.

Lesson Sequence

1. Teach the draw.

   a. The ball is placed between the back of two sticks, held horizontally at waist height, with players in any position they choose as long as the back of their stick is facing the goal their team attacks. The whistle signals when players may pull their sticks up and apart, sending the ball in the air.

      • Used to begin the game.

      • Used to continue the game after a score.

   b. Let students partner up and try a draw (3-5 times).

2. Give pinnies to half the teams of five or six students and send them to one of the lanes for a minigame of lacrosse.

   a. Remind students of the rules.

      • No checking or body contact.

      • Must wear protective equipment.

      • If the ball goes out, the closest player gets it and puts it back in play.

   b. Have them choose which goal they defend, start with a draw, and enjoy.

   c. Use teachable moments to suggest the following:

      • They should try not to be closer than 10 yards (9 meters) to a teammate.

      • Have some of the team stay back to stop an attack.

      • Have half go right, left, or center to give the ball carrier passing options.

      • Call the rules—no fouls.

Review and Stretching

As students stretch, ask:

• How is a lacrosse game started?

• What is the purpose of a legal check?

• Is it legal to check a stick that is close to a person's head?

• When you don't have the ball, is it better to join the people carrying it or go to open field?

Lacrosse
BEGINNER
LESSON 6

Positions on the Full Field

Facilities

Marked field for every two teams

Materials

• Visual aid such as a blackboard, magnetic board, or chart

• Mouthpieces and safety glasses for each student

• Pinnies for half the class

• One modified lacrosse stick for every student

• One ball for each student

Performance Goals

Students will do the following:

• Play a game on the full field.

• Improve their physical fitness.

Cognitive Goals

Students will learn the following:

- That they should not try to cover the whole field themselves
- That positions have different team responsibilities
- That seven attacking players are allowed over the restraining line (modified girls' game)
- That only eight defending players can be inside the restraining line (modified girls' game)

Lesson Safety

- Make certain students are wearing their protective equipment.
- Do not allow students to use the lacrosse stick as a weapon.

Motivation

The students have learned so much already, but most have never been on a whole field, with a whole team, and with the proper field markings. For students who have, let them know that the field and rules the class will be following are modified for noncontact lacrosse. So even if they have seen a men's game, they probably have never seen the critical scoring areas marked by the 8-meter fan and another 12-meter fan around the goal. They have not seen the restraining line or learned that no more than seven attacking players and only eight defenders are allowed in it. They have not had the support of 11 teammates. Today they will. And while they do, they will learn that each player does something slightly different to help each other.

Warm-Up (10 Minutes)

1. Students go directly to the field to practice passing.
2. While still in attendance spots, do a pass-and-go shuttle drill (5 times).
   a. Divide lines into shuttle formation with one ball to each line.
   b. Students pass to whomever they face and run to the back of the line they face.

Lesson Sequence

1. Organize for a game.
   a. Create teams of 11 and ask them to divide into offense and defense (12 allows a goalie). Review positions during the draw.
   b. Use a visual aid to show where each position lines up for the draw (see figure 10.1 on page 425).
   c. Have students line up and respond to the name of their position.
2. Begin with a whistle and stop the game for dangerous or otherwise illegal play.
   - Personal fouls (charging, hitting, shoving, or tripping an opponent)
   - Using the stick in a potentially dangerous way
   - Getting advantage by advancing, stopping, or deflecting the ball with anything other than the stick
   - Checking the opponent
3. Halfway through, stop the game to review defensive positions and to get the defense to mark the person on the other team who is lined up for the draw near them. (In boys' and men's lacrosse, the 10 positions are more similar to other field sports—attack, midfield, defense.)
   - Right defense wing and left defense wing mark attack wings and need speed and endurance to be able to bring the ball to the attack area.
   - Third man marks the third home and needs to be quick, to intercept, and to be able to clear the ball.
   - Cover point must be able to receive clears, mark the second home, run fast, and have good anticipation and good communication.
   - Point marks the first home, needing courage in the critical scoring area to anticipate and stop most shots on goal.

- Goalie needs quick reflexes, courage and confidence, and the willingness to wear a helmet, pads, and gloves and carry a big stick.

4. Continue the game, reminding defense not to lose their person. Use teachable moments to enforce rules.

Review and Stretching

As students stretch, ask:

- Who can remember how many running players are on a team?
- How many play defense?
- Can the center go inside the defensive restraining area?
- Which position is the last running defender of the goal?
- Which position takes the draw?
- Which defenders are around the circle during the draw?

Attack Positions

Facilities

Marked field for every two teams

Materials

- Visual aid such as a blackboard, magnetic board, or chart
- Mouthpieces and safety glasses for each student
- Pinnies for half the class
- One modified lacrosse stick for every student
- One ball for each student

Performance Goals

Students will do the following:

- Continue improving skills as they play a designated role in a lacrosse game.
- Improve their physical fitness.

Cognitive Goal

Students will learn how players divide responsibilities on the field.

Lesson Safety

- Make certain students are wearing their protective equipment.
- Do not allow students to use the lacrosse stick as a weapon.

Motivation

A lot of work from a lot of people goes into each goal. Without the defense working to recover the ball from their opponents and feed it back to their offensive players so they can move toward the goal, the offense would find it almost impossible to score. Defensive positions were named in the last class but not explained. Simply speaking, the defensive player's job is to make the offense's job difficult, which is to score. By understanding that the offense wants an open path to the goal and how they work together to get that open path, the defense's job gets easier.

Warm-Up (5 Minutes)

1. Students go directly out to practice passing and catching with a partner.
2. In their attendance spots, practice a pass-and-go drill while formalities are taken care of (attendance, checking for protective equipment).

Lesson Sequence

1. Introduce offensive positions and their most important job and skills.

   a. Center is primarily a defensive player but begins play and sometimes plays offense. The center needs speed and endurance.

   b. Left attack wing and right attack wing need speed and endurance so when they get the clears, they can run the ball and open the field as they begin the attack. They should be as good at running with the ball as passing it.

   c. Third home is the transition person who goes from offense to defense and swings to fill in the wing areas.

   d. Second home is the playmaker. The second home needs to be able to shoot from every angle and all distances and needs good anticipation.

   e. First home shoots more than anyone else. The first home needs to cut often, either to get into position to score or to cut away from the goal to make room for someone else. The first home also needs a good cradle and to be able to shoot from every angle.

2. Start the game.

   a. Use teachable moments to call fouls.

   b. Encourage teammates to stay at least 10 yards (9 meters) from one another.

3. Call a halftime.

   a. Review what it means to mark an opponent and how important it is for the defense to try to stay between their person and the ball.

   b. Take the most glaring weakness and discuss a solution, such as the following:

   - Clustering up
   - Not moving to an open space when wanting the ball
   - Getting so excited on the catch that they forget to cradle

4. Start the second half using teachable moments to coach without stopping the game.

Review and Stretching

As students stretch, ask:

- If you are on offense, raise your hand. What is your main job?
- If you play on the left side of the field, raise your hand. If you are on defense, what should guide where you go on the field?
- What should offensive players do when they want someone to pass them the ball?

Teacher Homework

Make up team rosters if you know the students well enough to create evenly skilled teams. (After teams are made, attendance can be taken by team roster.) To make sure that teams are equally skilled, consider the following:

- Speed
- Stick work
- Ability to move the ball long distances
- Stamina

No more than 12 students should be on a team. If you have more, make smaller teams.

Cutting and Dodging

Facilities

Marked field for every two teams

Materials

- Visual aid such as a blackboard, magnetic board, or chart
- Mouthpieces and safety glasses for each student
- Pinnies for half the class
- One modified lacrosse stick for every student
- One ball for each student

Performance Goals

Students will do the following:

- Practice cutting to receive a pass and passing where teammates are expected to move.
- Continue improving their skills and fitness.

Cognitive Goals

Students will learn the following:

- Why they should pass to where a teammate is going
- Who their tournament teammates will be

Lesson Safety

- Make certain students are wearing their protective equipment.
- Do not allow students to use the lacrosse stick as a weapon.

Motivation

It's time to get permanent teammates and begin learning to work together as a team.

Warm-Up (8 Minutes)

1. Students go directly to the field to practice.
2. Lead mimetics for dodging left and right.
   - Head fake left, push off left foot, and run right three steps, cradling as they go.
   - Crosse fake right, push off right foot, and run left three steps, cradling as they go.
   - Body fake left, run right three steps, cradling as they go.
   - Foot fake right, run left three steps.
3. Repeat several times before getting organized for the game.

Lesson Sequence

1. Announce teams.
2. Distribute pinnies and have students take a starting position for the game.
   a. Call out the names of the positions and ask the people holding the position to raise their hand.
   b. Ask everyone responsible for defense to raise hands.
   c. Ask the people who work together to score to raise hands.
   d. Ask the people who might be defense one minute and starting to attack the next to raise their hand.
3. Start the game.
4. Use teachable moments to coach. Play through, leaving extra time for closure.

Review and Stretching

1. Ask the teams to choose a captain and cocaptain.
2. Have the captain and cocaptain lead the stretching while you record the captains' names and begin the review with the following questions:
   - Which position probably has the greatest responsibility for shooting?
   - Which position has the responsibility for covering the first home?
   - Which is preferable, passing to someone cutting into open territory or passing to someone who is open and standing still? Why?
   - What are you hoping to achieve by making a fake move left and then running right?

Three-Second Rule

Facilities

Marked field for every two teams

Materials

- Visual aid such as a blackboard, magnetic board, or chart
- Mouthpieces and safety glasses for each student
- Pinnies for half the class
- One modified lacrosse stick for every student
- One ball for each student

Performance Goal

Students will continue improving skills and fitness as they play in designated positions.

Cognitive Goals

Students will learn the following:

- The value of cutting
- That the defense has to move out of the critical scoring area within 3 seconds unless closely marking an opponent

Lesson Safety

- Make certain students are wearing their protective equipment.
- Do not allow students to use the lacrosse stick as a weapon.

Motivation

There is one rule in this sport that is reminiscent of basketball—the 3-second rule. There is a 3-second rule for players in possession of the ball who are closely guarded. But this rule is different and unlike basketball, it applies to the defense. In short, it makes it impossible for the defense to clog up the critical scoring area in order to prevent a shot at goal. A defensive player is not allowed inside the crease unless closely marking an opponent. If not closely marking, the player must move out of the crease within 3 seconds.

Apply the 3-second rule. It will make the net more open, make players move more often, and challenge the defense to enter the area briefly if they're not with the player they mark.

Warm-Up (5 Minutes)

1. Students go directly to the field to practice.
2. Lead mimetics for alternate dodging left and right:
   - Head fake and cradle (5 times)
   - Body fake and cradle (5 times)

- Crosse fake and cradle (5 times)
- Foot fake and cradle (5 times)

Lesson Sequence

1. Explain the role of the defense:
   a. Mark players who are not in scoring position by moving between them and the ball carrier.
   b. Mark ball carriers in position to score by moving between them and the goal.
2. Explain the role of the offense:
   a. Nonmoving offenses lose opportunity to open up a shooting lane and are not going to get a pass.
   b. If they lose their defender, they should go to the goal and shoot.
   c. If someone new tries to stop them, it means that defender has left his person open. They should find and pass to the open teammate.
3. Begin the game, using teachable moments to coach.
4. Use halftime to
   a. go over the 3-second rule,
   b. address the frequent errors on the field, and
   c. encourage ball carriers to use eye contact to decide to whom to pass.
5. Continue the game, using teachable moments to instruct players while they play.

Review and Stretching

While team captains lead the stretching, ask:

- What would allow the defensive player to stay in the crease longer than 3 seconds?
- How do you know when you should make a pass to a teammate?
  - You've made eye contact.
  - Her basket is facing you.
  - She's uncovered.

Choosing the Right Position

Facilities

Marked field for every two teams

Materials

- Visual aid such as a blackboard, magnetic board, or chart
- Mouthpieces and safety glasses for each student
- Pinnies for half the class
- One modified lacrosse stick for every student
- One ball for each student

Performance Goal

Students will continue improving skills and fitness as they play the game.

Cognitive Goal

Students will learn that some positions require more throwing accuracy, others more stamina, others more speed, others more of a sense of what is about to happen so they can stop it, and others the ability to pass to opposite sides of their dominant hand.

Lesson Safety

- Make certain students are wearing their protective equipment.
- Do not allow students to use the lacrosse stick as a weapon.

Motivation

It is the third day that students are playing with their teacher-chosen teams. At this point, they should either stay in the position they have been playing or assess the needs of the team and make slight changes. Review the qualities that are important for each position so they can either play them better or make the necessary changes.

Warm-Up (5 Minutes)

1. Students go directly to the field to practice.
2. Lead mimetics:
   - Dodge fake (left, front, right)
   - Passing (left, right, front) with body facing forward
   - Catching a pass from behind and beginning a cradle

Lesson Sequence

1. Review the special abilities required by each position and ask students to consider adjustments.
2. Let the games begin. During the game, officiate and coach.
3. At halftime,
   a. remind the offense that their off-the-ball running is important and why, and
   b. encourage the defense to stick to their person.
4. Complete the games.

Review and Stretching

As the teams stretch, ask:

- What are six positions that should never be in open field?
- What are six positions that strive to get into open field?
- The game starts with three attackers lined up with the goal. Should they stay in the middle?

Announce that a round-robin tournament will begin next time and explain that in a round-robin, teams play each other. Remind students that their team needs them.

Teacher Homework

- Based on the number of teams, schedule a round-robin that can be completed in six lessons.
- Create and post a tournament schedule with field and pinny assignments.
- Create and post a chart of captains and cocaptains and the record of wins, ties, and losses.

Tournament Round 1

Facilities

Marked field for every two teams

Materials

- Tournament charts posted in accessible area
- Visual aid so all students can learn to read posted charts
- Mouthpieces and safety glasses for each student
- Pinnies for half the class

- One modified lacrosse stick for every student
- One ball for each student

Performance Goal

Students will continue improving skills and fitness playing in designated positions.

Cognitive Goals

Students will learn the following:

- How to read the tournament schedule and follow its instructions
- How to use their accumulated knowledge to be self-directing

Lesson Safety

- Make certain students are wearing their protective equipment.
- Do not allow students to use the lacrosse stick as a weapon.

Motivation

The class is about to start a tournament, which means that every minute is going to be used for the captains to get their teams organized, warmed up, and into their positions against the correct team, on the correct field, and with the correct equipment (pinnies, mouthpieces, eye guards, and sticks). All the necessary information is posted.

Warm-Up (5 Minutes)

Students go directly to the field to warm up.

Lesson Sequence

1. Explain how to read the tournament charts and what captains have to do to start the game. Have captains choose side of field.
2. Begin games. Use teachable moments to coach and officiate as necessary.
3. At halftime, go over the ideas that need reviewing.
4. Switch sides of the field and continue.

Review and Stretching

As students stretch, ask why it is important that the defense not move back when the goal is under attack.

- Slows down opponents and gives teammates time to realign.
- Alternately, makes opponent rush, which gives way to errors.
- Cuts down on the possible shooting angles.
- Eliminates the need to worry about the 3-second rule.

Lacrosse
BEGINNER
LESSON 12

Tournament Round 2 and Outlet Pass

Facilities

Marked field for every two teams

Materials

- Tournament charts posted in accessible area
- Mouthpieces and safety glasses for each student
- Pinnies for half the class
- One modified lacrosse stick for every student
- One ball for each student

Performance Goals

Students will do the following:

- Continue improving skills and fitness.
- Organize themselves, using the teacher as a resource and referee.

Cognitive Goal

Students will learn the advantage of fast attack wings and using an outlet pass to get the ball to them.

Lesson Safety

- Make certain students are wearing their protective equipment.
- Do not allow students to use the lacrosse stick as a weapon.

Motivation

Before beginning round 2 and announcing team standings, point out the advantages of an outlet pass and of having the fastest players on the sidelines. Explain that when the defense clears the ball to the side of the field, it is great to have a fast wing there to pick up possession and run downfield to start the attack before the opponents can shift to stop it from happening. This can put teams in the winning column or keep them there. With that in mind and with 3 points for a win, 2 points for a tie, and 1 point for competing, announce the standings.

Remind students where they can find the tournament schedule and results and begin round 2 by telling them to enjoy themselves and wishing them good luck.

Warm-Up (5 Minutes)

1. Students go directly to the field to practice.
2. Captains choose side of field.

Lesson Sequence

1. Diagram and explain the outlet pass.
   a. What happens to the defense when the ball goes to the side
   b. What happens to the offense if the left or right attack player breaks free
2. Begin the game. Use teachable moments to reinforce what has been taught.
3. Call a halftime. Allow the students to catch their breath, ask questions, regroup, and get water.
4. Continue the game.

Review and Stretching

As students stretch, ask:

- If your person doesn't have the ball, where should you position yourself to mark him?
  - In relation to the ball?
  - In relation to the goal?
- What does the point have to worry about when her person has the ball?
- What is the advantage of having a left and a right attack when everyone else seems to be lined up down the middle?

Tournament Round 3 and Penalties in the Fan

Facilities

Marked field for every two teams

Materials

- Tournament charts posted in accessible area
- Mouthpieces and safety glasses for each student
- Pinnies for half the class
- One modified lacrosse stick for every student
- One ball for each student

Performance Goal

Students will continue improving skills and fitness as they organize themselves and use the teacher as a resource and referee.

Cognitive Goal

Students will learn the penalties for fouls occurring inside the critical scoring area.

Lesson Safety

- Make certain students are wearing their protective equipment.
- Do not allow students to use the lacrosse stick as a weapon.

Motivation

Fouling inside the critical area is serious. Before continuing, everyone should know the penalties for major and minor fouls. After discussing fouls, announce tournament standings and what teams need to do to change them.

Warm-Up (5 Minutes)

1. Students go directly to the field to practice.
2. Captains choose side of field.

Lesson Sequence

1. Explain fouls and their penalties.
   a. Major fouls—A free position is awarded and the offending player must go 4 meters behind the player taking the free position.
   b. Minor fouls—A free position is awarded with the offending player moving 4 meters off in the direction she approached. If it occurred inside the 12-meter fan, the player given the ball gets an indirect position (must pass or be checked by an opponent).
2. Begin the game, being available as an official.
3. At halftime, answer questions and offer suggestions.
4. Complete the game.

Review and Stretching

1. Have captains lead their team in stretching.
2. Entertain questions.
3. Collect scores.

Tournament Round 4

Facilities

Marked field for every two teams

Materials

- Tournament charts posted in accessible area
- Mouthpieces and safety glasses for each student
- Pinnies for half the class
- One modified lacrosse stick for every student
- One ball for each student

Performance Goal

Students will continue improving skills and fitness while playing the class tournament.

Cognitive Goal

Students will use their knowledge to organize and coach themselves.

Lesson Safety

- Make certain students are wearing their protective equipment.
- Do not allow students to use the lacrosse stick as a weapon.

Motivation

Comment on the previous games, giving as many positive comments as possible. Also make some general suggestions. Then announce standings.

Warm-Up (5 Minutes)

1. Students go directly to the field to practice.
2. Captains choose side of field.

Lesson Sequence

1. Begin the games. Referee.
2. At halftime, ask if anyone has a question and offer coaching hints.
3. Complete the games, making sure to referee at all games.

Review and Stretching

1. Have captains lead their team in stretching.
2. Entertain questions.
3. Collect scores.

Tournament Round 5

Facilities

Marked field for every two teams

Materials

- Tournament charts posted in accessible area
- Mouthpieces and safety glasses for each student

- Pinnies for half the class
- One modified lacrosse stick for every student
- One ball for each student

Performance Goal

Students will continue improving skills and fitness as they play the class tournament.

Cognitive Goal

Students will organize themselves and use the teacher as a resource and referee.

Lesson Safety

- Make certain students are wearing their protective equipment.
- Do not allow students to use the lacrosse stick as a weapon.

Motivation

After four rounds, announce standings. Encourage students to ask for coaching hints during half-time. Make sure they understand that you will be on their field officiating at least part of their game.

Warm-Up (5 Minutes)

1. Students go directly to the field to practice.
2. Captains choose side of field.

Lesson Sequence

1. Begin the games. Referee.
2. At halftime, ask if anyone has a question and offer suggestions based on the weaknesses that are appearing in the game.
3. Complete the game.

Review and Stretching

1. Have captains lead their team in stretching.
2. Entertain questions.
3. Collect the scores.

Lacrosse
BEGINNER
LESSON 16

Tournament Round 6

Facilities

Marked field for every two teams

Materials

- Tournament charts posted in accessible area
- Mouthpieces and safety glasses for each student
- Pinnies for half the class
- One modified lacrosse stick for every student
- One ball for each student

Performance Goal

Students will continue improving skills and fitness as they play the class tournament.

Cognitive Goal

Students will organize themselves and use the teacher as a resource and referee.

Lesson Safety

- Make certain students are wearing their protective equipment.
- Do not allow students to use the lacrosse stick as a weapon.

Motivation

Review some common problems from previous games. Compliment the play, teamwork, strategy, and effort where possible. Ask if there are questions. Announce standings after five rounds and the possibilities of different outcomes once the final round is over. Tell the students to enjoy the final round and wish them luck.

Warm-Up (5 Minutes)

1. Students go directly to the field to practice.
2. Captains choose side of field.

Lesson Sequence

1. Begin the games. Referee.
2. At halftime, ask if anyone has a question and offer suggestions based on the weaknesses that are appearing in the game.
3. Complete the games.

Review and Stretching

1. Have captains lead their team in stretching.
2. Entertain questions.
3. Collect the scores.
4. Announce a short quiz and a final but unusual game for the next class.

Quiz and Reverse Playing Roles

Facilities

Marked field for every two teams

Materials

- Tournament charts posted in accessible area
- Pencils or pens so there is one for each student
- A quiz for each student
- Mouthpieces and safety glasses for each student
- Pinnies for half the class
- One modified lacrosse stick for every student
- One ball for each student

Performance Goals

Students will do the following:

- Complete a short quiz.
- Continue improving their skills and fitness during a new game setup.

Cognitive Goal

Students will see what it is like to switch from offense to defense and vice versa.

Lesson Safety

- Make certain students are wearing their protective equipment.
- Do not allow students to use the lacrosse stick as a weapon.

455

Motivation

Compliment each team for their performance thus far and announce the results of the tournament. Then, announce the idea of switching positions from defense to offense for the last day o the unit. It is also possible to split the teams so that the defense of team 1 plays with the offense of team 2 and the offense of team 1 plays with the defense of team 2, but let the students decide if they want to do that.

Warm-Up (5 Minutes)

After turning in their completed quizzes, students go to the field to warm up.

Lesson Sequence

Referee games.

Review and Stretching

At the end of the game, stretch and entertain questions.

Beginner Lacrosse Skills Rubric

Name _____ Date _____

Teacher _____ Class _____

	0	1	2	3
Level of activity	No effort.	Begins on signal.	Continues activity until told to stop.	Energetically practices until told to stop.
Instructions, rules	No effort.	Arrives with equipment and begins to practice.	Follows procedures to begin play and return out balls to play.	Does not commit personal fouls.
Moving with the ball	No effort.	• Moves with the ball while walking. • Can cradle during practice.	• Can advance the ball on the run. • Will cradle during the game.	• Can run with the ball when challenged. • Able to change direction while in possession of the ball.
Passing	No effort.	• Has proper body mechanics. • Can pass left or forward accurately to 10 yd (9 m).	Accurate to 20 yd (18 m) when passing left or forward.	• Can pass to a player cutting to open field. • Capable of passing long.
Receiving, stopping	No effort.	• Has proper body mechanics. • Lines up to catch balls. • Has successful pickups during practice.	• Uses stick to slow balls within reach. • Able to catch and maintain possession for a few steps. • Can pick up the ball in the heat of the game.	• Can move easily to a ball going to open space. • Able to receive a long pass. • Can redirect the ball off the catch.
Teamwork	No effort.	• Is prepared to play daily. • Gets into position on time. • Still tends to follow the ball.	• Changes field positioning relative to opponent as team goes from offense to defense. • Passes to teammate to avoid opponent.	• If on defense, marks person. • If on offense, cuts to open space to receive a pass. • Will move to cover a player who broke away from person.

From Isobel Kleinman, 2009, *Complete Physical Education Plans for Grades 5 to 12, Second Edition* (Champaign, IL: Human Kinetics).

Beginner Lacrosse Quiz

Name _____ Date _____

Teacher _____ Class _____

Multiple Choice

Read each question and each answer carefully before choosing an answer. Be sure to choose the best answer that fits the statement preceding it. When you have made your choice, put the appropriate letter on the line to the left of the numbered question.

_____ 1. It is safe to say that without a cradle
   a. the baby has no chance of growing up
   b. it will be difficult to run while in possession of the ball
   c. you cannot shoot
   d. you will be penalized and your opponents will take a free position

_____ 2. An outlet pass
   a. is a throw downfield
   b. is intended for the attack wings
   c. requires the closest person to get it and return the ball to play
   d. all of the above

_____ 3. The reason every position on the field should be covered is that
   a. the teacher wants everyone to be safe
   b. the ball carrier has more options if she is in danger of being checked
   c. defensive players are not allowed to shoot for goal
   d. all of the above

_____ 4. To receive a ball
   a. you need to reach for the ball with the fat part of the crosse
   b. your stick should give on contact
   c. your stick should wrap the ball on contact and begin the cradle
   d. all of the above

_____ 5. When a ball goes out of bounds at a sideline, the game stops and
   a. an opponent must run out of bounds, bring it back, and throw it in
   b. the closest player gets it and returns it to play
   c. the opponent should throw it in using both hands, with both feet on the ground
   d. everyone waits for the official to roll it into play

_____ 6. The critical scoring area is
   a. the circle surrounding the goal cage
   b. the 12-foot (3.5-meter) arc in front of the goal
   c. the only area in which it is legal for players to shoot
   d. all of the above

_____ 7. The game begins with
   a. a kickoff
   b. a bully
   c. a pass back at the center of the field
   d. a draw

»continued

»continued

_____ 8. To properly keep a ball from opponents,

    a. you can turn your stick away so they cannot check it

    b. you can pass the ball to an open teammate

    c. you can run away, cradling the ball as you go

    d. all of the above

_____ 9. Making the fastest person with the best stick skills an attack wing is a reasonable strategy because

    a. the ball is safely away from the critical scoring area when the wing receives it

    b. it is less crowded on the sides so fast wings have fewer players to stop them

    c. his speed can create a breakaway, enabling him to go straight to the goal

    d. all of the above

_____ 10. The player most likely to play both defense and also have offensive opportunities is

    a. the first home

    b. the center

    c. the point

    d. all of the above

 From Isobel Kleinman, 2009, *Complete Physical Education Plans for Grades 5 to 12, Second Edition* (Champaign, IL: Human Kinetics).

Beginner Lacrosse Answer Key

Multiple Choice

1. b
2. b
3. b
4. d
5. b
6. b
7. d
8. d
9. d
10. b

11

Soccer

Chapter Overview

1. Give students the chance to learn a skill by providing a lot of repetition with the ball as well as encouraging them to understand the advantage of using their skills within game rules and strategies.

2. Teach the instep kicking pass (footwork, point of contact, firm leg), the foot trap (heel-down position, lining up behind the ball), and the applicable rules (such as not using hands).

3. Teach the soccer positions and their special responsibilities (forward line, midfielders, fullbacks, goalies) and applicable rules (offsides, penalty area, lineup on kickoff).

4. Teach the place kick, body trap, knee trap, and heading.

5. Teach the goalie's punt and the drop kick.

6. Incorporate soccer terminology while the skills are being learned.

7. Introduce whatever rules have not been introduced during skills lessons (throw-in, penalty kick, direct kick, indirect kick, corner kick, goal kick).

8. Teach the common penalties for rule violations so that students can assist in the games of others or monitor their own games, knowing when something is illegal and what penalty is awarded the violated team.

9. Teach the fundamental game strategies for defense:
   - Zone or person-to-person defense
   - Outlet pass

10. Teach the fundamental offensive strategies:
    - Centering the ball
    - Moving forward with the ball or moving ahead of the ball with two opponents between the player and the goal

Soccer Study Sheet

History

The earliest record of people using their feet in a contest is in 300 BC in a Chinese military challenge called *ts'uh kúh* where participants had to kick a ball filled with feathers into a 16-inch (40-centimeter) hole in a 1-foot (30-centimeter) net that was raised 30 feet (9 meters) above the ground. In 600 AD, the Japanese played a circle game where they tried to keep the ball in the air. Similar activities were taking place in the Mediterranean and in the Americas. Around 800 AD, soccer is said to have had its birth in England with a game called *mob football* that was played during celebrations where the participants tried to force a ball into the market square of an opposing village. It is said that the only restriction was murder or manslaughter and that it was so violent that people barricaded their windows during matches. The sport was so loved that instead of practicing military skills, people were out kicking around balls. It is questionable whether this practice is what infuriated King Edward III or whether it was the lack of Christian rules, but in 1314 he tried to suppress the game by banning it. The ban never held, though—too many people loved the game and took their chances.

In the 1863, as the industrial revolution took people from farms to cities and outdoor recreation needed more organization, the London Football Association was formed. It separated mob football into two sports—rugby and football (American soccer). Then it developed the first set of rules for each.

Soccer Positioning

One ball but eleven people on a team? Should everyone run after the ball? No, they should not. Each player has a different job on the field and each works with their 10 other teammates to cover the field. See figure 11.1 to see how players line up for the kickoff, and read on to see what each position specializes in doing.

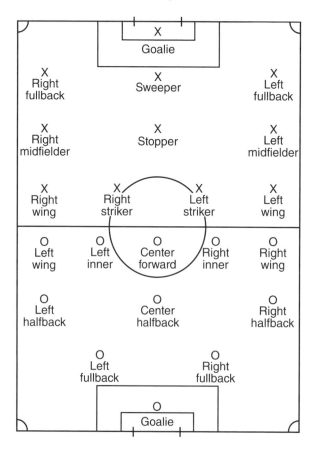

Figure 11.1 Soccer field and positions.

Offense

- Forward line—Has the job of scoring.

- Wings—Cover the outside of the forward line and should be fast and have good dribbling skills. The left wing should be able to pass to the right and should have excellent foot speed.

- Inners (strikers)—Should try to position themselves so they are in front of the goal when the ball is centered so they can shoot.

- Center forward—Sometimes there are only four forwards, in which case this position would not exist. When it does, the center is aligned to be in shooting position when the ball is in front of the goal. Passes received from the center determine which side of the field the attack comes from, so a center should be able to pass both right and left.

»continued

From Isobel Kleinman, 2009, *Complete Physical Education Plans for Grades 5 to 12, Second Edition* (Champaign, IL: Human Kinetics).

»continued

Defense

- Halfbacks or midfielders—Try to keep the forwards on offense by following them downfield but keeping their distance so they can stop opponents should the opponents come up with the ball.
  - Left halfback—Has to neutralize the speed of the other team's right wing; should be able to pass to the right and straight ahead. The left halfback will probably receive most of the team's outlet passes because passing left is easier than passing right; should be able to gain control of long passes.
  - Right halfback—Must neutralize the fastest player on the field, the opponent's left wing, and try to keep the ball out of the penalty area.
  - Center halfback—Has the most complex job on the field because sometimes must take the moment and threaten to take a shot on goal, and other times must get back to stop opponents from scoring. The center halfback usually controls the direction of the game (right, left, or down the center). Center halfbacks need a keen sense of everyone's positioning and the ability to pass to the open field so teammates can generate an attack.
- Fullbacks—Work together to stop the attack as if they were an accordion. If the ball is on the left, the left fullback moves up and the right fullback stays deep and vice versa. Fullbacks should slow down the attack if they cannot stop it. Their efforts give halfbacks time to drop back and reposition themselves so that there are six people defending the goal instead of two. Fullbacks need a strong clearing pass that will get the ball downfield.
  - Left fullback—Should try not to pass the ball right when near the penalty area; otherwise the ball is centered for the opponents, giving them another shot at the goal. Fullbacks should talk to their halfback so that they don't wind up playing the same ball and blocking each other's outlet pass.
  - Right fullback—Should try not to pass to the left when near the penalty area. Outlet passes should go either down the field or angled to the right; need a strong clearing pass.
- Goalies—Need a great sense of angle, good reaction time, the fearlessness to block shots, and the ability to stay warm and alert when the play is downfield and far away from them. They're the only players on the field who may use their hands, dress differently, and would do better with basketball skills.

Skills

- Dribbling—Moving with possession of the ball.
  - Tight dribble—Small pushes of the ball with the foot so it stays close to you, enabling you to pass or to dodge or control the ball when being challenged for it.
  - Loose dribble—Sending the ball two or three steps in front of you so you can run at top speed to take advantage of the open field.
- Trapping—Using any part of your body to put the ball down to the ground so you can use your feet to redirect it.
  - Foot trap—Raising the toe while the heel remains down so you can put the sole of your foot on the ball and stop it.
  - Knee trap—Bending at the knees to trap a bouncing ball between your knees and the ground.
  - Body trap—Caving in to let your body absorb the force of the ball so it drops at your feet.

»continued

From Isobel Kleinman, 2009, *Complete Physical Education Plans for Grades 5 to 12, Second Edition* (Champaign, IL: Human Kinetics).

»continued

- Tackling—Legally attempting to get the ball from your opponent.
  - Straight-on (front) tackle—Attempting to stop the ball so that the dribbler overruns it and you can take possession.
- Passing—Sending the ball with a kick or volley to someone else.
  - Instep kick—Kicking the ball with the inner part of either foot. Works best for passes to the right or left. To direct the ball straight ahead, kickers must turn so their side faces their target.
  - Place kick—Using the top of the arch of the foot to send the ball in the direction you are facing.
  - Foot, knee, shoulder, or head volley—The part of the body used depends on the height of the ball when the player tries to hit it while it is in the air.

Rules

- Kickoff—Each playing time begins with a kickoff, at which time players must be on their own side of the field with the receiving team outside the circle until the kick. The kicker may not touch the ball again until someone else does.
- Putting the ball back into play—There are different rules for different situations.
  - After a score, use a kickoff.
  - After it goes over a sideline, the ball must be thrown in from out of bounds with two hands from above and behind the head and both feet on the ground.
  - After a shooter sends it out on the goal line, the defender, usually the back, kicks a goal kick from anywhere inside the goal box. No one may play it until it clears the penalty area.
  - After the defensive teams sends it out on the goal line, the attacking team takes a corner kick anywhere on the corner arch. Others have to stay 10 yards (9 meters) away.

Fouls and Their Penalties

- Direct kicks (kicks for goal that need not be touched by any other player before they score) are awarded after
  - endangering the opposite team (charging, tripping, hitting, kicking, pushing, jumping into, using excessive force),
  - holding an opponent, or
  - deliberately using one's hands on the ball.
- Indirect kicks (must be touched by someone other than the kicker before it enters the goal) are given after
  - endangering oneself (e.g., low heading a ball that someone is trying to kick),
  - using one's body to impede the progress of an opponent,
  - preventing the goalie from releasing the ball,
  - unsportsmanlike behavior, or
  - offside violations (a player gets ahead of the ball so that there are not two defenders between the player and the goal).
- Penalty kicks are free shots on goal given to the attacking team when the defenders commit a foul that would normally result in a direct kick had the infraction not been inside the penalty box. The goalie must stand on the goal line until the kick and then try to stop the goal. The kicker must stand on or behind the 10-yard (9-meter) line to take the kick. All teammates must be out of the penalty area until the ball comes out or is scored.

 From Isobel Kleinman, 2009, *Complete Physical Education Plans for Grades 5 to 12, Second Edition* (Champaign, IL: Human Kinetics).

Soccer Extension Project

Name _____ Date _____

Teacher _____ Class _____

List three places where you can play soccer other than in class.

What kind of equipment do you need? Itemize and estimate the cost of each.

What can you do to practice by yourself?

List the names of friends who would play soccer with you.

What is the least number of people you need to get up a game?

From Isobel Kleinman, 2009, *Complete Physical Education Plans for Grades 5 to 12, Second Edition* (Champaign, IL: Human Kinetics).

Soccer Student Portfolio Checklist

Name _____ Date _____

Teacher _____ Class _____

_____ Is able to stop a ball from a dribble.

_____ Is able to stop a ball from a 10-yard (9-meter) pass.

_____ Is able to gain control of a ball coming from a long pass.

_____ Is able to pass a soccer ball 10 yards (9 meters) to the right.

_____ Is able to pass a ball 10 yards (9 meters) to the left.

_____ Can use a tight soccer dribble.

_____ Uses a loose dribble only in an open field.

_____ Uses different parts of the body to trap or volley a high ball.

_____ Positions self correctly when the team has possession of the ball.

_____ Adjusts positioning when the team loses possession of the ball.

_____ Follows coaching hints when they use basic soccer terminology.

_____ Actively repositions self to be effective though not playing the ball.

_____ Knows how to and can attempt to disrupt the successful play of opponents.

_____ Able to follow basic soccer rules.

_____ Exhibits good sportsmanship.

_____ Plays without endangering the safety of others.

From Isobel Kleinman, 2009, *Complete Physical Education Plans for Grades 5 to 12, Second Edition* (Champaign, IL: Human Kinetics).

Soccer Learning Experience Outline

Contents and Procedure

1. Teach skills, providing a lot of repetition, and introduce applicable rules.
   a. Instep kicking pass (footwork, point of contact, firm leg)
   b. Foot trap (heel-down position, line up behind the ball) and rules applicable (illegal to use hands)
   c. Place kick, body trap, knee trap, heading
   d. Goalie's punt and drop kick
2. Have students use skills while learning rules and strategies in game context.
   a. Teach positions and their responsibilities (forward line, midfielders, fullbacks, goalies) with applicable rules (offsides, penalty area, lineup on kickoff).
   b. Incorporate soccer terminology while skills are being learned.

    c. Introduce rules not introduced during skills lessons (throw-in, penalty kick, direct kick, indirect kick, corner kick, goal kick).

    d. Teach the common penalties for rule violations so students know when something is illegal and what penalty is awarded so they can be self-sufficient or assist in officiating other games.

    e. Teach fundamental game strategies for defense.

- Zone or person-to-person defense
- Outlet pass

    f. Teach fundamental offensive strategies.

- Centering the ball
- Moving forward with the ball or moving ahead of the ball with two opponents between you and goal

3. Allow sufficient noncompetitive practice time so students can learn and improve without additional performance pressure.

4. Use movement specific to soccer during the warm-up.

5. Avoid making teams until you know the skill of the class and can divide the class into equal teams on the basis of skill, sex, and number.

6. Once teams are made, encourage them to work together as a unit, develop their own peer leadership, and give everyone a feeling of belonging and of being needed.

7. Conclude with a short tournament that has all students involved in team play. If some are unable to play, they can officiate, mark the ball, or keep score.

Teaching Tips for Special Considerations

- When numbers are short, consider not using a goalie and having all students take moving positions. When they object, remind them that there is no goalie for either team.

- Students will have different levels of experience with soccer. Advanced soccer athletes should be encouraged to help others while improving consistency, accuracy, distance, time, and speed.

- Students who are temporarily unable to play should be given alternative assignments that keep them involved with the class, their team, and learning the unit. Assignments can be to provide coaching hints to teammates; develop strategies; take notes of instruction, rules, and summary provided during lessons; become officials; keep score; or write a report that will develop a better understanding of soccer and its value for developing fitness.

- Students with disabilities that preclude full participation will need adaptation that allows physical participation without endangering them. If able, they should participate in warm-ups and most aspects of skills acquisition. Other modifications depend on their disability. For instance, if they are not mobile, a lesson might be developed that hampers the mobility of the whole class so they can compete equally (get down on scooters, play with two people bound together, eliminate the ability to kick in order to move the ball).

- Every effort should be made to reassure students that improvement is what is valued, not a predisposition to be a great athlete.

Facilities

- Indoors—large unencumbered space that allows moving a minimum of 30 yards (27 meters) forward and 10 yards (9 meters) to the right and left without running into walls, a person, or temporary obstructions

- Outdoors—Clear boundaries and field markings for each concurrent game for every group of 22 players (see figure 11.2)

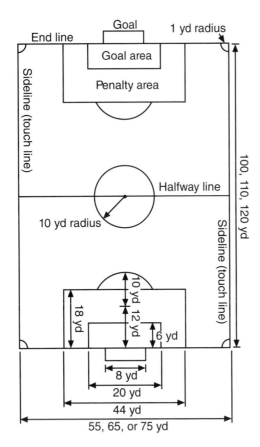

Figure 11.2 Markings for the soccer field.

Materials

- One soccer ball for every two students
- Pinnies to identify opposing teams
- Visual aid (blackboard, chart, marker board)

Unit Timeline

There is one unit of 12 to 14 lessons for younger age groups, which includes the following:

- 6 lessons for skill development and learning basic game concepts
- 6 to 8 lessons for fun and challenging tournament play

Assessment

The unit concludes with a short written quiz and a beginner soccer skills rubric.

Suggested Resources

BBC Sport. 2008. Football skills. http://news.bbc.co.uk/sport1/hi/football/skills.

Expert Football. 2008. Training techniques. http://expertfootball.com/training/techniques.php.

Herbst, D. 1999. *Soccer: How to play the game—The official playing and coaching manual of the United States Soccer Federation.* Englewood, NJ: Universe.

McGettigan, J. 1989. *Soccer drills for individual and team play.* Englewood, NJ: Prentice Hall Direct.

Rees, R., and C. Van Der Meer. 1996. *Coaching soccer successfully.* Champaign, IL: Human Kinetics.

Scottish Football Association. 2008. www.scottishfa.co.uk/index.cfm.

Soccer
BEGINNER
LESSON 1

Dribble, Pass, and Trap

Facilities

Clear area large enough for class to be able to safely move in

Materials

One soccer ball for every two students

Performance Goals

Students will do the following:

- Use their foot to pass and trap a soccer ball.
- Practice the loose and tight dribbles.

Cognitive Goals

Students will learn the following:

- That passing with the left or right instep gives them choices
- Why they should not lift their foot to trap a ball
- Several ways to advance the ball

Lesson Safety

- Separate each group by a minimum of 5 yards (5 meters).
- Keep students practicing in the same line of direction.

Motivation

Ask if anyone can guess what they might be trying to learn today. Remind them that when a ball has come rolling their way, they have kicked it out of the way, and today they will begin learning to use their foot to get the ball to go with them so they don't lose it. Ask if anyone knows why they would not want to lose it.

Warm-Up

1. Rehearse soccer mimetics.
   a. Dribbling
      - Have students turn instep forward and imagine pushing a ball forward with it with first the right instep, then the left instep.
      - Walk and tap every third step.
      - Run and tap every third step.
   b. Instep kick (practice with right and left foot)
      - With foot in same position as the dribble, firm up the leg and extend the leg swing, keeping the supporting leg slightly bent.
      - Pass with right foot following through to left (5 times).
      - Pass with left foot following through to right (5 times).
   c. Foot trap
      - Move behind the ball and lift toe up while keeping the heel down and balancing on the opposite foot (see figure 11.3).
      - Alternate three steps right and trapping with right foot (5 times) with moving left and trapping with left foot (5 times).

Lesson Sequence

1. Demonstrate a tight dribble (see figure 11.4).
   a. Ball is kept under their nose.
   b. They want it close enough so it can be kicked at will and so it will be difficult for opponents to get it.
2. In shuttle groups of four, have students do the following:
   a. Walk forward 50 feet (15 meters) with the ball under their nose (3 times).
   b. See how fast they can go while still keeping the ball close (3 times).
3. Give the groups an extra ball and have partners practice passing and trapping.
   a. Start close so passes are accurate.
   b. Increase the distance a few feet at a time until 20 feet (6 meters) apart.
   c. Ask who can stop five passes first.

Figure 11.3 Trapping the ball with the sole of the foot.

469

Figure 11.4 Tight dribble.

4. Demonstrate a loose dribble.
   a. Used when no one is around and the path is open.
   b. Used so players can run at top speed.
   c. It's tricky because the ball goes farther away, but they don't want it to go too far or they will lose it.
5. Re-form the shuttle groups that they practiced in earlier.
   a. Practice dribbling at top speed (3 times).
   b. Move the groups into relay formation and have them dribble to a line 30 yards (27 meters) downfield, turn, and dribble back, sending the ball to the next person in line. Ask them to sit when the line is back to starting position.
6. If time remains, change the goal to maintain interest. For example, have everyone with a ball line up on the sideline and ask who can wind up with the ball on the opposite sideline first.

Review and Stretching

If this is the first unit of the year and you haven't created a stretching routine, create a routine that students can stretch to as you ask questions:

- Where should your foot contact the ball on the dribble?
- What must you do to change the dribble to a pass?
- Why is keeping the heel down is so important when trapping the ball?
- What is the advantage of a tight dribble?
- What is the advantage of a loose dribble?

Assessment

Observe and provide individual coaching hints to improve the tight and loose dribbles. Check that on the kick, students have a low kicking motion and meet the ball firmly.

Soccer
BEGINNER
LESSON 2

Straight-On Tackle and Body Trap

Facilities
Clear area large enough for class to be able to safely move in

Materials
One soccer ball for every two students

Performance Goals
Students will do the following:

- Practice a straight-on tackle, using their foot to trap a ball an opponent is dribbling.
- Perform a body trap.
- Practice passing the ball with both their instep and top of foot.

Cognitive Goals

Students will learn the following:

- Rules relevant to a body trap—no hands may touch the ball.
- Rules relevant to the straight-on tackle—it's illegal to
  - kick opponents,
  - slide tackle, or
  - use unnecessary roughness.

Lesson Safety

- Make certain practice groups are 5 yards (5 meters) apart for simple drills.
- Once the minicompetition starts, separate groups by 10 yards (9 meters).

Motivation

Tell the class that there are a few skills they absolutely need to play soccer. For instance, they have to know how to move the ball forward. They learned one way when they practiced the dribble, and there are other ways to move it forward. But realism requires them to understand that they won't always have the ball unless they learn how to get it legally. That is what they are going to find out today.

Warm-Up

1. Arriving students pick up a ball and dribble around the field.
2. Gather the class and lead them through mimetics.

   a. Pass:
      - Step on left, leaving knee bent, and kick left with right instep (5 times).
      - Step on right, leaving knee bent, and kick right with left instep (5 times).
      - Step forward on either foot and kick forward, imagining kicking the ball with the shoestrings (5 times).

   b. Body trap: Tap stomach as if it were the ball hitting it and cave in so that the body gives with the impact of the imagined ball (5 times).

   c. Straight-on tackle: Raise the toe while keeping heel down. Flex at the heel to make the sole of the foot stop the imaginary ball while keeping the weight on the opposite foot (5 times).

   d. Do the same while reaching for a ball to the right (5 times).

   e. Do the same while reaching for a ball to the left (5 times).

Lesson Sequence

1. Teach the straight-on tackle (see figure 11.5).

   a. Demonstrate.

   b. Have students partner up. The one with the ball should dribble slowly to the other, and the one without the ball should

Figure 11.5 A successful straight-on tackle stops the ball's forward momentum so the dribbling player overruns it.

471

stop it while the partner is dribbling. Have them try slowly at first and repeat their efforts several times. Increase the speed once students can do it slowly.

2. Demonstrate a place kick (top of foot contacts ball) and practice.

3. To maintain interest, try the following:

    a. See who can kick a place kick (top of foot) farthest.

    b. Can they dribble the ball halfway and pass to their partner accurately?

    c. In groups of four, count 1, 2, 3, 4, so that each person has an assigned number. Then begin an odd–even drill. Give the ball to the odd team, whose job is to dribble from their cone to a cone on the other side. If they do, they get a point for their team. While they are trying to do that, the even team must try to get the ball for themselves using the straight-on tackle. If they do so and can dribble to the opposite cone, they get a point. The group has 20 seconds.

Review and Stretching

1. As students stretch, ask where their foot should contact the ball on the following:

    • Forward pass

    • Pass to the right

    • Pass to the left

    • Straight-on tackle

2. Announce that the next time they come, they should help themselves to equipment, get a partner, and do a lap around the field, dribbling and passing back and forth with their partner. When they have finished, practice passing.

Soccer
BEGINNER
LESSON 3

Knee Trap and Knee Volley

Facilities

Goalposts and a game area for every two teams

Materials

• One soccer ball for every two students

• Pinnies for half the class

Performance Goals

Students will do the following:

• Move the ball by knee volleying.

• Play a game.

Cognitive Goals

Students will learn the following:

• Why, when, and where they use their knees to contact the ball

• A legal way to redirect a ball coming at their body

• Why jobs on the soccer field are differentiated

Lesson Safety

The fields should be clean of debris and set up with visible goalposts.

Motivation

Explain that to some athletes who have played all kinds of other sports, it feels weird to start playing soccer because in soccer it is possible to use every part of the body to control the ball except the part they are most used to using—the hands. This lesson will teach everyone how to use a few more parts of the body. Then they will try to do what everyone else tries to do when they play soccer—score.

Warm-Up

1. As students arrive, they partner up and take a ball. They do one lap around the field, dribbling and passing to their partner as they go. After that, they practice passing with their partner.

2. Lead mimetics for the following:

   - Pass left (5 times), right (5 times), and straight ahead (5 times).
   - Body trap (5 times).
   - One-leg knee trap—Bend knee over ball and lean forward (5 times).
   - Two-leg knee trap—Bend both knees over the ball and lean on it (5 times).
   - Knee volley—Raise the right knee to meet the ball and send it in another direction (5 times), then left knee (5 times).

Lesson Sequence

1. Demonstrate the knee volley (see figure 11.6).

   - In partners, alternate who tosses the ball and who knee volleys it back (5 times each).

2. Demonstrate the knee trap. Have partners practice it (5 times each).

3. Organize for a quick game. It's a good idea to leave the goal empty so all players have running positions. I do this until we get into the tournament, and if we are short players, I leave the goalie out even then.

   a. Divide the class.

   b. Indicate boundaries and point out the goals.

   c. Have one team wear pinnies and assign them to kick on your whistle.

   d. Let them play with no other instructions.

Review and Stretching

As students stretch, comment on how difficult it looked out there on the field and discuss the following:

- Can you dribble in a crowd?
- How did you know when to go after the ball?
- Did you think all of you had to go after the ball all at once?
- Say that 22 people are trying to get the ball. What are their chances of succeeding?
- How could you get the ball out of the crowd? If you can kick it out and everyone is with you, trying to get the ball, who will get the pass?
- Explain that it is confusing, but during the next class you will teach them how to divide responsibilities on the field so that they are not all so frustrated.

Figure 11.6 Knee volley.

Dividing Offense and Defense

Facilities

Goalposts and a game area for every two teams

Materials

- One soccer ball for every two students
- Pinnies for half the class
- Visual aid (blackboard, chart, marker board) or diagram of team positions at kickoff

Performance Goals

Students will do the following:
- Begin games with a proper kickoff.
- Be in position at kickoff and play positions during a game.

Cognitive Goals

Students will learn the following:
- Why jobs differ on the field
- How to do one job
- Rules for a throw-in

Lesson Safety

- The fields should be clean of debris and set up with visible goalposts.
- Be prepared to stop any dangerous play, particularly once competition starts.

Motivation

Explain that if every player tried to do it all on the field, there would be 22 people around the ball, no one to pass to, and no way to move forward against another team. When the ball can travel 5,000 square yards (4,181 square meters) in any given moment, no one player can do it all. That is why teams divide responsibilities, back each other up, and try to get the ball to someone in the open who can challenge the goal. Explain that you will teach how soccer teams divide jobs.

Warm-Up

1. Students take a lap, dribbling and passing to a partner as they go around the field.
2. When they are done, they practice passing to a partner.

Lesson Sequence

1. Explain a diagram of team positions at kickoff.
   a. Show where players start at kickoff and after every score. (To see two systems of setting field positions, see figure 11.1 on page 462.)
   b. Name positions and explain their general responsibility.
      - Forwards work together to score.
      - Halfbacks (or midfielders) sometimes join the forwards but mostly try to get the ball once it is lost to opponents.
      - Backs (fullbacks) stop the ones who get away and who are a scoring threat.
      - Goalies are the last line of defense.
2. Change the diagram to show each position when the ball is down the field.
3. Divide into teams, have one team put on pinnies, and start with a kickoff.
4. During games, coach students to remember to cover their side of the field.

5. After 10 minutes, stop the game.

    a. Demonstrate a proper throw-in.

    b. Explain when it is used and what happens if it is not done correctly.

6. Continue the game until time for review.

Review and Stretching

As students complete their stretching routine, ask the following:

- What should you do when the ball goes out-of-bounds on the sidelines?
- Who played on the forward line? As wings? Strikers? Who shot at the goal?
- Who were the midfielders? Did you remember to defend your own goal before you worried about scoring?
- Did backs move up or were they glued to the penalty area?

Assessment

If this is too much to cover in one day, spend a second day on it before going to the next lesson.

Heading

Facilities

Goalposts and a game area for every two teams

Materials

- One soccer ball for every two students
- Pinnies for half the class

Performance Goals

Students will do the following:

- Volley a ball with their head.
- Play a game.

Cognitive Goals

Students will learn the following:

- What skills work best for people on the left or right side of the field
- What skills are more useful in different soccer positions
    - Fast runners with good ball-handling skills—wings
    - Good basketball skills with no fear of being hit—goalies

Lesson Safety

- The fields should be clean of debris and set up with visible goalposts.
- Be prepared to stop any dangerous play, particularly once competition starts.

Motivation

Explain that everyone is different and can make unique contributions. People who are strong footed on one side and not the other, people with great anticipation of their opponents, people with good reach and quick reflexes with their hands, people who have long driving kicks, and people with good foot speed and a love of keeping the ball to themselves as they razzle-dazzle everyone with good footwork all would fit well in different positions on the soccer field. Today they are going to learn where their strengths can be taken advantage of.

Figure 11.7 Heading.

Warm-Up

1. Students practice passing and dribbling with a partner.

2. Have class do mimetics for the following:

   a. Body trap

   b. Knee volley

   c. Heading

   - Redirect a high ball with the head by looking up at the ball and meeting it at the hairline with firm neck muscles (see figure 11.7).

   - Extending to the ball or jumping into it gives extra power.

   d. Shoulder volley

   - If the ball is in the air and is too low for the head, it can be redirected with the shoulder.

   - Fold the arm of the hitting shoulder to the body and tilt the head away from the ball while focusing on the ball, then jump toward the ball to meet it with the top and side of the shoulder.

Lesson Sequence

1. Demonstrate heading.

   a. Allow students to first head the ball from a self-toss (5 times).

   b. Have partners alternate tossing the ball to each other so they can head (5 times each).

2. Explain how individual assets can be used more easily in certain positions.

   a. Those able to kick right should play positions on the left side of the field.

   b. If the breakaway position is the wing, the fastest dribbler with the best footwork should be the wing.

   c. The most complex job on the field is the center halfback, so assign the best, most knowledgeable player on the team to that position.

   d. Goalies use their hands to get everything near the goal and get down to stop balls that opponents want to shoot for goal. They need guts and good basketball skills.

   e. The least amount of running is done by backs, who need a strong kick. People in the middle must pass well to the right and left, so they should be able to kick well with both feet.

3. In teams from before, have the other team put on pinnies and start the kickoff after team members go to the position they feel most suited for.

4. Coach from the sidelines.

   a. Remind students about positions and where the players should be on the field.

   b. Call obvious rule violations.

Review and Stretching

While students stretch, ask the following:

- Who seemed fast on your team? Did they play wing? Did they get to use their speed?
- Who feels stronger kicking to the right? Were you on the left side of the field?
- Who has a long kick you can clear downfield? Were you a back?

Teacher Homework

Begin dividing the class into equally skilled tournament teams.

Putting a Ball Back Into Play

Facilities

Goalposts and a game area for every two teams

Materials

- One soccer ball for every two students
- Pinnies for half the class
- List of teams
- Diagram that shows how a player can be ahead of the ball with fewer than two opponents between the player and the goal

Performance Goals

Students will do the following:

- Properly return the ball to play.
  - After a score (kickoff)
  - After a failed shot for goal that leaves the boundaries (goal kick)
  - After it goes out on the sideline (throw-in)
  - After personal fouls
- Play a game.

Cognitive Goals

Students will learn the following:

- What high kicking, dangerous play, sliding tackles, pushing, holding, and offside are and that each is illegal
- Rules for the goal kick, kickoff after a score, and throw-in
- Why penalties are sometimes harsh (e.g., penalty shot for goal)

Lesson Safety

- The fields should be clean of debris and set up with visible goalposts.
- Be prepared to stop any dangerous play, particularly once competition starts.

Motivation

Rules make it possible for everyone to play a fair and safe game. Tell them that today they're going to review them, especially now that they are getting ready to start the tournament, and then you will announce teams.

Warm-Up

1. As students arrive, they will pick up equipment and do a lap, dribbling and passing to a partner.

2. Perform mimetics for several traps (body, knee, foot) and several volleys (using head, knees, and shoulders).

Lesson Sequence

1. Explain situations that stop the game.
   a. Fouls
      - High kicking and why it is dangerous
      - Dangerous play, especially around the goalie
      - Sliding tackles
      - Personal violations (pushing, holding, kicking, tripping)
      - Offside (use diagram)
   b. Out-of-bounds
      - Sideline
      - Goal line

2. Explain how to put the ball back into play.
   a. On penalties (direct kick, indirect kick, penalty shot for goal)
   b. After the ball goes out of the field (throw-in, goal kick, corner kick)

3. Announce tournament teams.

4. Start games with a kickoff.

5. Coach positions and call obvious rule violations.

Review and Stretching

As students stretch, ask the following:

- If someone shoots and scores, how does the ball get put back into play?
- If someone shoots and misses, how does the ball get put back into play?
- What would cause a penalty shot for goal?
- Would offside be dangerous?
- Who can explain offside?
- Can you be offside when you are no closer to the goal than the ball?
- Can you be offside if you dribble past everyone on the field?

Soccer
BEGINNER
LESSON 7

Working as a Team

Facilities

Goalposts and a game area for every two teams

Materials

- One soccer ball for every two students
- Pinnies for half the class

Performance Goals

Students will do the following:

- Properly return the ball to play.
- Choose captains and cocaptains.
- Play a game.

Cognitive Goal

Students will learn to work together as a team.

Lesson Safety

- The fields should be clean of debris and set up with visible goalposts.
- Be prepared to stop any dangerous play, particularly once competition starts.

Motivation

Before beginning, it is best to take a little time choosing captains and deciding where it would be best for everyone to play. Before they do, they are going to review the positions and their responsibilities.

Warm-Up

1. As students arrive, they will do a lap, dribbling and passing to a partner.
2. Then they should do mimetics for traps (body, knee, foot) and volleys (head, knee, shoulder).

Lesson Sequence

1. Choose captains and cocaptains. As students are grouped in teams, review the following:
   a. Attributes of each position on the forward line and how the line works together
   b. The concept of the midfielder backing up forwards, moving up behind them and dividing the width of the field
   c. How backs should move up if the ball is on their side of the field to stop the attack early and how they and the midfielders should anticipate the need to scramble back to keep the ball out of the penalty area if opponents still have the ball after a teammate tried to get it
2. Have the kickoff team wear the pinnies.
3. Start games. While games are in progress, coach students to play their position and make obvious rule calls.

Review and Stretching

As students stretch, review rules that they don't seem to understand and share vignettes from the games that provide a learning experience for the class.

Outlet and Inlet Passes

Facilities

Goalposts and a game area for every two teams

Materials

- One soccer ball for every two students
- Pinnies for half the class
- One game ball for every game

- Posted tournament schedule
- Posted team standings
- Visual aid (blackboard, chart, marker board)

Performance Goals

Students will do the following:
- Play a practice game.
- Assume responsibility for one position.
- Play by the rules.
- Exhibit good sportsmanship.

Cognitive Goals

Students will learn the following:
- How team interaction works
- What an outlet pass and an inlet pass are and when to use each

Lesson Safety

Correct and redirect competitive behavior that takes a negative turn and starts to endanger the physical and psychological health of the students.

Motivation

Sometimes when we get caught up in the action, we do things that do not help us or our team. Explain that students should have a clear picture of the field so that when they pass, they are not defeating themselves.

Warm-Up

Students practice passing, trapping, and dribbling with a partner.

Lesson Sequence

1. Explain by diagramming the following:
    a. Value of the outlet pass while on defense
    b. Value of the inlet pass while on offense
2. Have captains choose sides or pinnies (pinnies team wins the kickoff).
3. Start games with a kickoff, coach positions, and call obvious rule violations.

Review and Stretching

As students stretch, ask the following:
- What rule might be invoked if a forward gets ahead of the ball in anticipation of being able to receive a pass and score?
- What is the danger of a left fullback passing to the right when he's near the goal?
- Where should a left fullback pass if she and her opponents are near the goal?
- Would it be proper for a left wing to pass left? Where should a left wing be able to pass?

Tournament

The number of lessons will vary based on how long it takes until everyone gets a turn at being a captain.

Facilities

Goalposts and a game area for every two teams

Materials

- One soccer ball for every two students
- Pinnies for half the class
- One game ball for every game
- Posted tournament schedule
- Posted team standings
- Offside diagram

Performance Goals

Students will do the following:

- Play one match each day.
- Play their positions and assume team responsibilities.
- Play by the rules.
- Exhibit good sportsmanship.

Cognitive Goals

Students will improve their understanding of the following:

- Team interaction
- Offensive and defensive strategies
- Soccer rules
- How to play a round-robin tournament

Lesson Safety

Correct and redirect competitive behavior that takes a negative turn and starts to endanger the physical and psychological health of the students.

Motivation

Review the rules or strategies that are difficult for the class to grasp, starting with being offside. Each class, announce the tournament standings. If you have several games going on, remind students that you will be at every game but if you are not there when they need you, they should not hesitate to call for you. Wish them a good game.

Warm-Up

Students practice passing, trapping, and dribbling with a partner.

Lesson Sequence

1. Review offside violations with a diagram.
2. Announce standings, new team match-ups, and assigned fields.
3. Have captains choose sides (pinnies team wins the kickoff).
4. Start games with a kickoff, coach positions, and call obvious rule violations.

Review and Stretching

As students stretch, collect results and entertain questions.

Assessment

- Observe and compliment good passes, anticipation, field positioning, stops, assists, attempts, sportsmanship, team leadership, and so on.
- If giving a written test, save it for a rainy day if possible; otherwise give it on the last day of the unit.
- Post defined performance goals as they appear in the beginner soccer skills rubric and observe for those standards.

Beginner Soccer Skills Rubric

Name _____ Date _____

Teacher _____ Class _____

	0	1	2	3
Trapping	No effort.	• Has proper body mechanics. • Lines up with ball.	• Foot traps accurate pass. • Blocks inaccurate ball up to 3 ft (1 m) away.	• Successfully uses body traps. • Gains control of ball off a long pass.
Dribble	No effort.	• Has proper body mechanics. • Moves ball forward.	• Uses tight dribble. • Moves ball at top speed.	• Chooses to use a loose or tight dribble at proper times.
Pass	No effort.	• Has proper body mechanics. • Accurate up to 10 yd (9 m).	• Moves ball forward, left, and right. • Passes from a dribble. • Moves ball to 30 yd (27 m).	• Uses many body parts to pass. • Follows up a trap with an accurate pass. • Varies speed and distance.
Position and direction	No effort.	• Knows where to go to score. • Tries to move ball in correct direction.	• Uses outlet pass on defense or inlet pass on offense. • Shifts in direction of play. • Maintains distance between teammates.	• Interchanges position. • Senses when help is needed. • Anticipates opponents.
Teamwork and sportsmanship	No effort.	• Gets to court on time. • Gets along with teammates. • Hogs ball or blames others.	• Tries to play within rules. • Does not hog ball. • Makes effort to improve weaknesses.	• Leads team constructively. • Plays within the rules. • Is the team's go-to player.

From Isobel Kleinman, 2009, *Complete Physical Education Plans for Grades 5 to 12, Second Edition* (Champaign, IL: Human Kinetics).

Beginner Soccer Quiz

Name _____ Date _____

Teacher _____ Class _____

Multiple Choice

Read each question and each answer carefully. Be sure to choose the best answer that fits the statement. When you have made your choice, put the appropriate letter on the line to the left of the numbered question.

_____ 1. The soccer dribble is a skill that allows
   a. the player to bounce the ball from her hands to the ground
   b. the player to move with the ball by tapping it with his instep
   c. the player to kick the ball to the goal for a possible score
   d. the ball to get clean while the top of the player's sneakers get dirty

_____ 2. An outlet pass
   a. is out-of-bounds
   b. is best used by the forward line as they get closer to the goal
   c. is an attempt to get the ball out of the opponents' scoring position
   d. all of the above

_____ 3. The reason every position on the field should be covered is that
   a. the teacher will get mad if everyone does not get a chance
   b. it gives players more places to pass when in danger of being stripped of the ball
   c. defensive players are not allowed to shoot for goal
   d. all of the above

_____ 4. The body trap should result in the ball
   a. dropping near your feet so that you can dribble or pass it if you want to
   b. bouncing away from your body
   c. hitting your shoulder before bouncing on the ground
   d. being covered by the goalie until everyone clears the penalty area

_____ 5. When a ball goes out-of-bounds at a sideline, the game stops and an opponent must
   a. run out of bounds, put it down on the line, and kick it in
   b. run out of bounds to get it and dribble it into play
   c. run to get it and throw it in using both hands, with both feet on the ground
   d. wait for the official to roll it into play

_____ 6. The penalty area is
   a. the area in which the goalie may pick up the ball with hands
   b. where penalty shots are awarded the offense because the defense fouled them
   c. the area in which the goal box is marked
   d. all of the above

_____ 7. The kickoff
   a. is used at the beginning of the game
   b. starts play at the beginning of each play time and after a team scores
   c. is awarded to the team that did not just score
   d. all of the above

»continued

»continued

_____ 8. To properly head the ball, you should
    a. drop your head just before the ball touches it
    b. keep your eyes up, get under the ball, and allow it to meet your hairline
    c. be prepared to scream a lot but feel good about helping the team
    d. believe that using your head for anything other than to think with is nuts

_____ 9. The left wing position should be taken by the fastest person on the team because
    a. most people kick left more easily than right, meaning that more passes go to the left wing
    b. the field is usually emptier on the sides than in the middle and there is room for the wing to use his speed
    c. when the wing gets a breakaway, she can outrun everyone to the goal
    d. all of the above

_____ 10. The players most likely to play defense and also score are the
    a. goalie and fullback
    b. center halfback and center midfielder
    c. stopper and fullback
    d. all of the above

Extra Credit

Eleven players on the X team are diagrammed as if spread out during play. Find the correct number on the diagram to correspond with the questions.

1. _____ Which is the X goalie?
2. _____ Which is the X left wing?
3. _____ Which is the X stopper?
4. _____ Which is the X left striker?
5. _____ Which is the X right midfielder?

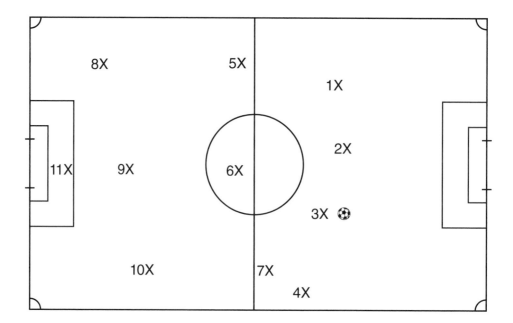

From Isobel Kleinman, 2009, *Complete Physical Education Plans for Grades 5 to 12, Second Edition* (Champaign, IL: Human Kinetics).

Beginner Soccer Answer Key

Multiple Choice

1. b—A dribble is intended to move but keep control of the ball.
2. c—Outlet passes move the ball away from the goal to the side of the field, getting the ball out of scoring position.
3. b
4. a—The purpose of trapping a ball is so that you can get control of it.
5. c—A throw-in is the required method of returning a ball that goes out-of-bounds on the sideline.
6. d
7. d
8. b
9. d
10. b

Extra Credit

1. 11X
2. 1X
3. 6X
4. 3X
5. 7X

12

Softball

Chapter Overview

1. Introduce and develop one new concept each lesson. The early lessons tend to practice more than one skill, which avoids muscle overuse and flattening of the learning curve due to boredom.

2. Teach skills by providing a lot of repetition with the ball. Teach the advantages of using skills within a game, as well as rule strategies:
   - Throwing—grip, stance, arm motion, and follow-through for accuracy, speed, and distance
   - Catching—glove position, eye contact, and footwork for grounders, fly balls, and drives
   - Pitching terminology, rules, and strategies; the strike zone
   - Batting—full swing, bunt
   - Baserunning—tagging inside of the bag, overrunning first, sliding, and leading off
   - Fielding strategies and rules:
     - Going for the automatic out at first
     - Force plays
     - Squeeze plays
     - Throwing ahead of the runner to get the out
     - What to do after catching a fly ball
     - Anticipating coverage
     - Limiting the bases run by throwing to second
     - The cutoff person
     - When a tag is necessary
   - Offensive strategies—batting-order strategies and baserunning
   - Game rules and coeducational rule modifications

Softball Study Sheet

History

After hearing that Yale prevailed in the 1887 Thanksgiving Day Harvard–Yale football game, a Harvard student picked up a boxing glove and tossed it at someone, who hit it with a pole. George Hancock, considered the founder of softball, tied the glove into a ball and said, "Let's play ball," which they did by breaking a broom handle for a bat.

Despite its Harvard start, the birthplace of softball is said to be Chicago, where a fire chief used it to keep his men occupied during their free time in a small lot next to their firehouse.

Softball is a wonderful summertime game. Leagues are available in slow pitch or fast pitch for all age groups in all localities.

Materials

- Catchers must wear a mask and chest protector.
- All fielders must wear a glove.

The Game

- Official teams have nine players and play seven innings.
- Runs score after the base runner touches all bases and home before the third out.
- A strike occurs when the ball passes into the strike zone (over part of home plate between the batter's knees and armpits) without being hit in fair territory, unless a foul ball is hit on what would have been the third strike. (Batters cannot foul out when using full swings.)
- Pitches thrown outside the strike zone are called *balls*. If a pitcher pitches four balls, the batter walks to first base and becomes a base runner and a scoring threat.

Field Coverage

Figure 12.1 shows the areas players are responsible for covering and where player coverages overlap.

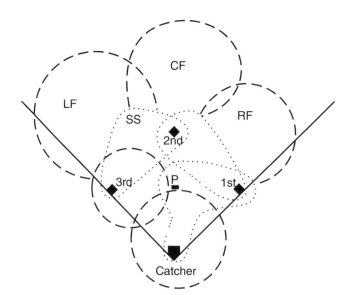

Figure 12.1 Softball field coverage.

»*continued*

From Isobel Kleinman, 2009, *Complete Physical Education Plans for Grades 5 to 12, Second Edition* (Champaign, IL: Human Kinetics).

»continued

Batting
- Batters must stand in the batter's box and must follow the batting order.
- Batters are out when the following occur:
  - They strike out.
  - Their hit is caught on a fly.
  - The catcher catches the third-strike pitch.
  - Their foul hit is caught.
  - They bunt foul on the third strike.
  - They hit an infield fly ball with a runner on first (in advanced games).
- Batters can run to base when the following occur:
  - They get a hit.
  - The catcher drops the third strike and first base is empty.
  - Or, they can walk if they are hit with a pitched ball while they are in the batter's box.

Base Runners
- Base runners must touch bases in legal order and run inside the baselines.
- They may advance to the next base after the following:
  - The ball leaves the pitcher's hand.
  - The ball is hit into fair territory.
  - An overthrow occurs.
- Base runners must return to base if the following occurs:
  - The batter hit a foul.
  - The batted ball was caught on a fly.
- When base runners are forced to move to the next base, they need not be tagged to be put out. They must be tagged if they are not forced to advance to the next base.
- Runners are allowed to overrun first without fear of being tagged out.
- Base runners may try to advance to the next base after a fly ball is caught (tag up).
- Base runners are out if they are hit with a fairly batted ball before fielders touch it.

Pitching
- The ball is dead when the pitcher holds it in pitching position with the catcher ready to catch at the plate.
- Pitchers must stop with squared shoulders, both feet on the pitcher's mound, and both hands on the ball with it in front of their body for between 1 and 20 seconds before pitching. Before pitching, they must make sure all base runners are on base.
- The pitch must be underhand.
- Pitchers are allowed one step forward and must throw while taking that step.

Fielding
- Fielders must have control of the ball to tag a runner out.
- A hit ball is fair if it remains in fair territory until it passes first or third base.
- Fielders may not stand in the baseline to block the runner. A free base is given to the runner when there is obstruction by a fielder.

»continued

From Isobel Kleinman, 2009, *Complete Physical Education Plans for Grades 5 to 12, Second Edition* (Champaign, IL: Human Kinetics). **489**

»continued

Coaching Hints

- Throwing—The ball should roll out of three fingers without resting in the palm of your hand.

- Catching—The palm of the glove should face the incoming ball and you should move in to meet it at chest height. Allow your fingers to touch the ground to stop grounders. Most importantly, keep your eyes on the ball and watch it into your glove.

- Hitting—Choose a bat you can control. Keep your hands together, knuckles aligned with each other and your dominant hand on the top. As you take your stance at home plate, make certain that if you stretch the bat out, it meets the outer edge of the plate.

- Bunting—Turn your feet so your body faces the pitcher without your back foot moving out of the batter's box. As the ball contacts the bat, give with it. Make certain to get out of the way of the ball so you don't run into it. Remember not to bunt if you already have two strikes, because if you bunt foul, you are out.

 From Isobel Kleinman, 2009, *Complete Physical Education Plans for Grades 5 to 12, Second Edition* (Champaign, IL: Human Kinetics).

Softball Extension Project

Name _____ Date _____

Teacher _____ Class _____

List three places where you can play softball other than in class

What kind of protective equipment do you need to play softball? Itemize and estimate the cost of each.

Is there any other equipment you need?

What can you do to practice by yourself?

List the names of friends who would play softball with you.

Softball Student Portfolio Checklist

Name _____   Date _____

Teacher _____   Class _____

_____ Throws accurately to 30 feet (9 meters).

_____ Throws accurately to 40 feet (12 meters).

_____ Throws accurately to 60 feet (18 meters).

_____ Can trap the ball in the pocket of a softball glove.

_____ Is able to catch a softball.

_____ Can catch a ball that is 5 feet (1.5 meters) off target.

_____ Can run the bases.

_____ Can stop ground balls.

_____ Can catch pop-ups within a four-step radius.

_____ Has learned and can assume responsibility for one defensive position.

_____ Has learned softball rules.

_____ Has learned the batter's stance and how to swing and meet the ball.

_____ Can identify the strike zone.

_____ Exhibits sportsmanship.

_____ Plays without endangering the safety of others.

From Isobel Kleinman, 2009, *Complete Physical Education Plans for Grades 5 to 12, Second Edition* (Champaign, IL: Human Kinetics).

Softball Learning Experience Outline

Contents and Procedure

1. The beginner, intermediate, and advanced units in this chapter introduce skills and game strategies.
2. Lessons explain skills, indicate how they can be practiced, and use them in context with their applicable rules.
   a. Throwing—grip, stance, arm motion, and follow-through for accuracy, speed, and distance
   b. Catching—glove position, eye contact, and footwork for grounders, fly balls, and drives
   c. Pitching—terminology, rules, and strategies; the strike zone
   d. Batting—full swing, bunt
   e. Baserunning—tagging inside of the bag, overrunning first, sliding, and leading off

3. Lessons introduce fielding strategy and rules.
    a. Going for the automatic out at first
    b. Forced plays
    c. Squeeze plays
    d. Throwing ahead of the runner to get the out
    e. What to do after catching a fly ball
    f. Anticipating coverage
    g. Limiting the bases run by throwing to second
    h. The cutoff person
    i. When a tag is necessary
4. Lessons introduce offensive strategies.
    a. Batting order
    b. Baserunning (to first, rounding bases, tagging up, sliding, stealing)
5. Students will learn game rules (full innings, three outs, scoring, knowing when a game is over).
6. Students will also learn coed rule modifications, if necessary (gender equity in field positions and batting order, girls pitching to girls and boys pitching to boys).
7. Penalties for rule violations are introduced (balk, interfering with the base runner, batting out of batter's box, overrunning the bases).
8. Lessons provide a lot of noncompetitive practice so students can improve without performance pressure.
9. Units all end with a short tournament.

Teaching Tips and Special Considerations

• The elementary grades should stick to the first lessons in the beginner unit. When ready to move into game play, consider lead-up games that do not include a pitcher. If there are no gloves for the fielders, play punchball, a game where the batter punches a ball about the size of a fist and has to be put out at base. This game is usually played on a basketball court or in a gym. Another alternative is to play Throw Softball using a tennis ball or a blooper softball. These games will allow you to focus on defense.

• Avoid boredom and muscle overuse by practicing a variety of skills while exploring one concept.

• Teach and practice the proper muscle sequence and footwork as part of the warm-up.

• Delay making teams until you know the skills of each student. Divide the class into teams on the basis of skill and sex so teams are equal. Encourage teams to work as a unit. Promote leadership within the group and feelings of belonging and of being needed.

• Students come to class with different levels of experience. Advanced players should be encouraged to help others while also improving their consistency, accuracy, distance, time, and speed as their classmates work at lower levels.

• Students who are unable to play should have alternative assignments. For example, they can help their teams by coaching their team's baserunning and fielding; developing strategies for a team lineup and field coverage; taking notes to summarize the instructions, rules, and strategies; or umpiring or keeping score. If these tasks are not appropriate, they can write a report that helps them better understand softball, its place in American history, and the significant attributes necessary to play well.

• Every effort should be made to assure that improvement is what is valued, not a student's predisposition to be a great athlete.

- After a book is published, rules, skills, and strategies may change. Check Internet sites listed in suggested resources to keep up with the changes.

Facilities

- Lessons require a large space, free of obstructions and rocks.
- If a real softball field is not available, the location should have a minimum of a backstop (wall) and a first and third baseline (see figure 12.2).

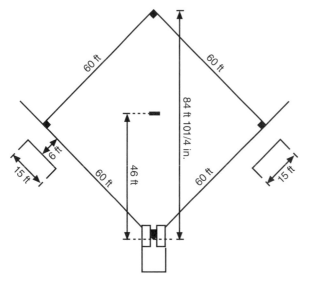

Figure 12.2 Softball field.

Materials

- One softball for every two students
- One glove for every student
- Catcher's equipment for each game (mask, chest protector, glove)
- Set of bases and a pitcher's mound for each field
- Bats of varying lengths and weights (one set for every team)
- Visual aid (blackboard, marker board, softball magnetic board, or chart)

Unit Safety

- The catcher must wear protective equipment.
- Fielders should each have a softball glove.
- Sliding will not be allowed during class. If students are disappointed or in doubt as to why, suggest that they watch *A League of Their Own,* where a player gets horribly scraped from sliding without the proper uniform.
- Practice throws and catches are restricted to the beginning of class and each inning.
- Practice swings are restricted to whoever is on deck.
- Stretching should be done after the muscles are warm—at the end of class during review.

Unit Timeline

There are three units in this chapter.

1. The beginner level has 15 lessons:
   - 6 lessons to develop the basic skills
   - 4 lessons to learn to use them in a game
   - 5 lessons to play three games of a class tournament and take a quiz
2. The intermediate level has 13 lessons:
   - 7 lessons for skills and game practice
   - 6 lessons for a small class tournament of three games
3. The advanced level has 11 lessons:
   - 5 lessons for skills and game practice
   - 6 lessons for three official games

Assessment

Units include a short quiz and skills rubric designed for each level.

Suggested Resources

American Sport Education Program (ASEP). 1996. *Coaching youth softball.* Champaign, IL: Human Kinetics.

Craig, S. 1985. *The softball handbook.* Champaign, IL: Human Kinetics.

Meyer, G.C. 1984. *Softball for girls and women.* Boston, NY: IDG Books Worldwide.

Pitch Softball. 2008. www.pitchsoftball.com.

Potter, D., and G. Brockmeyer. 1999. *Softball: Steps to success.* Champaign, IL: Human Kinetics.

Softball
BEGINNER
LESSON 1

Throw and Catch

Facilities

- Designated field large enough to safely move in
- Practice lanes separated by a minimum of 5 yards (4.5 meters) per pair of students
- Four bases in a diamond, 60 feet (18 meters) from each other, preferably on a softball field.

Materials

- One softball (or hand-sized ball) for every two students
- One glove (or none if using a simple hand-sized ball) per person
- Blooper softballs (or small-sized handballs) if there are not enough gloves to go around

Performance Goals

Students will do the following:

- Hold and throw a softball.
- Catch with their nondominant gloved hand.
- Run around and tag the bases.

Cognitive Goals

Students will learn the following:

- Short history of softball
- How to give the ball direction and speed
- Why the catch is so important when fielding
- Why they should tag the inside corner of the base when rounding it

Lesson Safety

- Practice should be in the same line of direction.
- Students should have softball gloves. Those who do not should practice with a softer ball. If you do not have softball gloves, teach the concepts using a small ball the size of a tennis ball.

Motivation

Americans invented baseball in the early 1800s, and then the game of indoor baseball was created in Chicago. Using an oversize ball made up of a wrapped up glove, a smaller infield because it was played in a gym, and a broken broomstick for a bat, eventually indoor baseball became softball and has been played outdoors ever since. The first organized softball league was created in Toronto, Canada. To date, baseball and softball are similar, but some differences remain: the size of the field and ball, the number of innings that make up a game, when runners are allowed to lead off and steal base, how the pitch is thrown, and what defensive player is in position to throw the stealer out.

Explain why fielding is important. Use your own story to make the point, or use mine. I was one of a few teachers who agreed to be part of a gung-ho teachers' group that challenged our girls' softball team to play one hot May afternoon. We chose last licks, so the girls got up to bat and stayed there for what seemed forever. They kept hitting our pitches as if we were giving them batting practice, and of the teachers in the field, only three of us could catch and throw. So, we were out on the sunny, hot field for over an hour before we could not get our girls out and get to bat, and what we all really wanted to do was hit, not field.

Warm-Up

1. Jog the bases, having students tag the inside corner of the bag.
2. Lead softball throwing mimetics.
   a. Grip and wrist snap—Ball should rest between three or four fingertips and students should snap toward the target (5 times).
   b. Throwing motion—Bent arm straightens as it comes forward, ending with the wrist snap in direction of the target (5 times).
   c. Backswing with shoulder rotation—Rotate shoulder so the bent elbow moves back and weight has transferred over the back foot (5 times).
   d. Throw—Rotate upper body forward from the waist until the throwing arm has fully extended (5 times).
   e. Leading the throwing motions with a forward step—Step forward and unwind the body until the throwing arm (with wrist) is fully extended (5 times).
3. Catching mimetics—Rehearse reaching with the nondominant hand.
   a. Practice proper hand position for high ball—Reach with nondominant hand so fingers are up and the palm faces the incoming (imaginary) ball (5 times).
   b. Position for low balls—Nondominant hand turns fingers down with the palm open to the ball (5 times).
   c. Watch ball into the glove—Imagine seeing the ball land in the glove by using the free hand to hit inside the pocket (5 times).
   d. Lining up behind the path of a ball—Have students run three or four steps in, right, left, or back to practice adjusting to balls that are not coming directly to them (5 times).

Lesson Sequence

1. Having learned the throwing motion during warm-ups, emphasize catching.
   a. Have students get one partner and practice throwing back and forth.
      - Emphasize using the glove to reach for the ball.
      - Remind students to trap the ball in the glove with their free hand.
      - Teach students to remove the ball from the glove quickly.
   b. Start at distances that everyone can master easily and move out 5 feet (1.5 meters) at a time.
2. Use a contest to emphasize accuracy and speed and to make practice more fun.
   - From the sound of the glove, see who throws to their partner fastest.
   - See which partner catches the most throws in 10 seconds.
   - Do the same contests over a larger distance.

3. Be careful not to overdo the throwing muscles—change the skills and teach moving to grounders and scooping them up. Have people sending the grounders use an underarm motion to give their throwing arm relief.

    a. Position—Line up behind the ball, bending down so the body blocks a grounder that takes a bad hop.

    b. Move in to get the ball (don't wait for the ball, go to it).

    c. Practice scooping the ball up and then throwing it quickly back.

Review and Stretching

In addition to the normal stretching routine the students have been taught, make sure to include a stretch for the shoulder joint. As students stretch, ask the following:

- Should the ball rest in your hand when you want to throw it?
- Who can show a proper throwing follow-through?
- Explain why stepping forward on the opposite foot is important.
- What makes the catch important?
- What should you do when going after a ground ball?

Fielding Game

Facilities

- Designated field large enough to safely move in
- Practice lanes separated by a minimum of 5 yards (4.5 meters) per pair
- Four bases in a diamond, 60 feet (18 meters) from each other, preferably on a softball field

Materials

- One softball (or hand-sized ball) for every two students
- One glove (or none if using hand-sized ball) per person
- Blooper softballs (or small, hand-sized balls) if there are not enough gloves to go around

Performance Goals

Students will do the following:

- Improve their throwing and catching.
- Simulate a softball game but only use throwing and catching skills.

Cognitive Goals

Students will learn the following:

- The virtue of accurate throwing and being able to catch
- How catching a fly ball affects baserunning, forces, and tags
- That three outs is half an inning and what a full inning is

Lesson Safety

Use the same line of direction for a well-spaced-out practice. Begin developing proper safety habits by having the batter's team stay at least 10 yards (3 meters) from the first or third baselines and no one from their team but the batter inside the backstop.

Motivation

Tell the class how pleased you were with their work last time and that you think they might be ready to put some of that throwing and catching to a test. Tell them that after more practice today, they will play an interesting game. (You might think that getting students into a modified game so early is rushed, but students lose interest in fielding until they see a need for it. Playing Throw Softball will reinforce the need to throw and catch consistently while teaching some softball rules.)

Warm-Up

1. As students enter, have them take equipment and practice.
2. Have them jog the bases, then run them, making sure to tag the inside corner of the bag.
3. Lead throwing and catching mimetics with footwork as taught in previous lesson.

Lesson Sequence

1. Practice throwing and catching fly balls and grounders (10-15 minutes).
2. Teach Throw Softball, where the batter catches a throw and throws (instead of bats) to become a base runner. (This is where you might note that a pitch in softball is usually underhanded, but since no one has practiced underhand pitching, for now pitchers can use any throw they want that can get the ball to home plate.)
   a. Fielders follow the rules of softball.
      - Ball must beat the runner to the base if the runner is forced.
      - Runners rounding first with no one behind must be tagged out.
      - Caught fly balls make the batter out, and advancing runners must return.
   b. Batters have one chance to catch a controlled throw to the plate. If they drop the ball, they are out.
      - Batters must go in order.
      - Once the pitch is caught, the batter can throw it anywhere in fair territory. Foul throws will be out.
      - If a pitch is wild or higher than the batter's head, the batter walks.
      - Batters can strike out, fly out, or be put out on base.
3. Send half the class to the field and half to the batter's area. Play the game, continuing to have the batter simply throw the ball into the field and then run the bases as far as possible.
4. When both teams have gotten three outs, announce the end of the inning and that softball games usually have seven innings. Then continue making sure that all students get up to bat once before anyone gets up a second time.

Review and Stretching

As students stretch, ask the following:

- Why is it better to catch a ball than let the ball drop?
- Can you overrun a base without being afraid of being tagged out? Which one?
- What does it mean if someone is forced to the next base?
- Do both teams have to bat and be put out before an inning is over?

Softball
BEGINNER
LESSON 3

Fly Balls

Facilities

- Designated field large enough to safely move in
- Practice lanes separated by a minimum of 5 yards (4.5 meters) per pair
- Four bases in a diamond, 60 feet (18 meters) from each other, preferably on a softball field

Materials

- One softball (or hand-sized ball) for every two students
- One glove (or none if using hand-sized ball) per person
- Blooper softballs (or hand-sized balls) if there are not enough gloves to go around

Performance Goals

Students will do the following:

- Throw for distance.
- Catch pop-ups.
- Simulate a softball game using only throwing and catching skills.

Cognitive Goals

Students will learn the following:

- Rules that apply to fly balls (runners go back, automatic out)
- What a batting order is and how to follow it

Lesson Safety

- Practice should be in the same line of direction.
- Students should have softball gloves. Those who do not should practice with a softer ball. If you don't have softball gloves, teach the concepts using a small ball.

Motivation

The students can probably guess what they will be working on today—catching fly balls. Explain what is so special about catching a fly (automatic out, advancing runners must go back) and how if they throw the ball to the base that a runner left before they caught the fly, they might actually get the runner out, too. Tell them that the nicest part of fly balls is that for every second the ball stays in the air, they have more time to get under it to catch it.

Warm-Up

1. Arriving students take equipment and practice.
2. Lead mimetics for catching and throwing, emphasizing high balls.
   a. Throw long balls.
      - Make the throwing motion follow through up (5 times).
      - Run forward as throwing motion follows through up (5 times).
   b. Catch a pop-up—Reach the glove hand up above the eyes. Close the pocket around and trap the (imaginary) ball inside the pocket with the free hand.
   c. Catch a short pop-up—Run forward to get under the ball, and reach up to trap it as it looks as if it is falling in the eyes.
   d. Catch a deep pop-up—Run back to get behind the path of the ball. Reach up with the glove, squeeze it closed, and use the free hand to trap the ball in the pocket of the glove.

Lesson Sequence

1. Practice throwing pop-ups and catching them.
2. Review Throw Softball.
   a. Review how to put the batter out.
      - Thrown ball must beat the runner.
      - If runner is not forced or has rounded first with no one behind her, she must be tagged out.
      - Caught fly balls are out and advancing runners must return to base.
   b. Review rules for batters.
      - Batters must catch a controlled throw to home plate. If not, they are out.
      - They can throw the ball anywhere on the field, but they must throw it high.

- The batter must be thrown out at base or tagged out if the ball is not caught.
- A ball thrown foul by the batter is an automatic out.

3. Continue the previous game with the students who did not get up to bat.
   a. Help students anticipate what to do in the field if they catch the ball.
      - Ask the fielding team where the lead runner is going.
      - Ask them where the runner should be if the ball is caught on a fly
   b. Compliment everything they did right—the way they ran, caught, got ready, and so on.
4. Announce the top- and bottom-of-the-inning scores, reinforcing the concept of complete innings.

Review and Stretching

As students do their stretching routine, ask the following.
- Why do fielders love fielding pop-ups?
- What should be done with the pop-up ball in the following situations?
  - You catch it and the runner from second ran to third and is still there.
  - You drop it. The runner was on first base before the hit.
  - No runner is on first. The runner from second is heading for third even though you just caught the ball.

Softball
BEGINNER
LESSON 4

Pitching

Facilities

Painted, chalked, or taped strike-zone targets on a wall, or setup where catchers have their back to a wall, fence, or backstop

Materials

- One softball (or hand-sized ball) for every two students
- One glove (or none if using hand-sized ball) per person
- Blooper softballs (or hand-sized balls) if there are not enough gloves to go around

Performance Goals

Students will do the following:
- Pitch to a target.
- Swing the bat.

Cognitive Goals

Students will learn the following:
- What the strike zone is
- How to get someone out at home plate
- The danger of being a pitcher with no control

Lesson Safety

- Practice should be in the same line of direction.
- Students should have softball gloves. Those who do not should practice with a softer ball. If you don't have softball gloves, teach the concepts using a small ball.

Motivation

It is time to learn how to hit the ball, but before they can hit, there has to be someone who can throw the ball somewhere near the strike zone, so they're going to work on pitching first.

Warm-Up

1. As students arrive, they pick up equipment and begin practicing.
2. Perform mimetics for pitching and batting.
    a. Pitching—Fingers of both hands are on the ball with arms holding it out in front. The feet are almost squared. Bring the throwing arm straight back. When it is as far back as it goes, step forward on the opposite foot and begin the downward pendulum underhand motion. Release just past the front knee (10 times).
    b. Batting—Stand inside the batter's box with the opposite hip facing the pitcher. Put hands, one on top of the other, as low on the bat as possible while maintaining control. Swing back, keeping the elbows and bat up. Step toward the ball and swing. During the swing, the arms should straighten with the bat parallel to the ground. The swing should carry the bat around the body while the feet remain stationary (10 times).

Lesson Sequence

1. Go to the wall where the targets are visible.
    a. Have each student pitch three pitches, fast, aiming for the target.
    b. Rotate after every three pitches.
    c. Continue until the line has had three turns each.
    d. Give five pitchers a turn to see who hits the target most in 15 pitches.
2. Explain pitching rules.
    a. The strike zone is over part of home plate between the batter's knees and armpits.
    b. One of the pitcher's feet must be on the pitcher's mound until the release.
    c. Once the pitching motion starts, it cannot be stopped without penalty.
    d. Hitting a batter with the ball when he is inside the batter's box is illegal and results in automatically sending the batter to first base.
3. Continue the Throw Softball game with the pitcher using an underhand pitch.

Review and Stretching

As students stretch, ask the following:

- If your pitch is too high, what should you change?
- Where is the strike zone?
- Must a foot remain on the pitcher's mound during the pitch?
- Does a ball have to come down the middle of the plate to be a strike?

Batting

Facilities

Third baseline for setting up batters

Materials

- One softball for every group of four students
- One glove per person
- Two different-sized bats for every group

- Plate for every group
- Pitching mound (or tee) for every group

Performance Goal

Students will bat, either by hitting a ball on a tee or hitting from a slow pitch.

Cognitive Goals

Students will learn the following:

- How to address the plate
- How to choose a bat that is right for them
- How to swing a bat
- Where the point of contact should be (see figure 12.3)

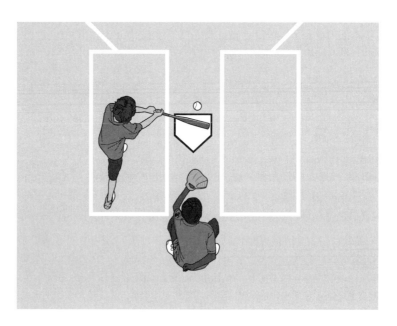

Figure 12.3 Proper form and contact point when batting.

Lesson Safety

- Batters must be all on the same line with their catchers well behind them since there is no catcher's equipment for the catchers.
- Students must learn to keep two hands on the bat at all times so that they don't fling or let go of the bat while swinging.
- Groups should be at least 20 yards (18 meters) from one another.
- All fielders wear a softball glove. If there are not enough gloves, do not do this lesson and restrict the remainder of the unit to hand-sized balls.

Motivation

The class is finally going to bat and be successful at hitting the ball. It is going to be exciting! (If this is a young group, you might want to use a tee and have students hit off it for the first day of batting.)

Warm-Up

1. As students arrive they take equipment and begin practicing.
2. Lead mimetics for pitching (10 times), batting (10 times), catching grounders that are three steps to the right (5 times), dropping back three steps to catch a deep pop-up (5 times), and throwing the ball accurately to a target after a catch (5 times).

Lesson Sequence

1. Explain the following.
   a. Choosing a bat—The head of the bat should not drop when it is swung. If it does, it is either too heavy or too long.

b. Addressing the plate—The batter should be able to reach the far edge of the plate with the bat from inside the batter's box.

c. Grip and stance—Hips should be perpendicular to the pitcher and the nondominant hand should grip the bottom of the bat handle. The dominant hand should be right above it so the knuckles of each hand are aligned.

d. Swing—As practiced in mimetics, the swing begins when the ball is about a bat's length in front of home plate.

2. Divide the class into groups of four. (For slow pitch, they would be the catcher, batter, pitcher, and fielder. If hitting off a tee, two would field, one would stay back to put the ball on the tee, and one would bat.) Distribute equipment and explain the practice.

a. After three successful hits, the group rotates one position. If the pitching is short or wild, have groups let the best pitcher pitch so batters have more hittable balls.

b. Ask pitchers to loop the ball over the plate so hitters can get the feel of the hit. (Save the strike-outs for the game.)

c. Use a line or pitching mound to keep the pitcher away from batter.

d. Have the catchers stay well back of the batters, but ask them to give pitchers a hand as a target to focus on.

e. Explain that getting the ball back to the pitcher quickly will give everyone more turns at bat and ask all outfielders to relay stray balls to the pitcher calling for them. Class cooperation will make the practice more meaningful.

3. Coach each group.

a. Encourage swinging at everything they can reach with their bat in the beginning so they get a feel for their hitting zone.

b. Show the batters where the ball must be for them to begin their swing and how it will drop as it arrives. Help them anticipate the path of the ball dropping so they focus on it and can hit it.

Review and Stretching

As student stretch, ask:

- How do you address the plate?
- If you are right-handed, which hip faces the pitcher?
- Are the feet supposed to help give the swing more power? Both? One? Which one?
- Is a ball coming across your knees hittable? If you don't hit it, will it be a strike?

More Batting

Facilities

Third baseline for setting up batters

Materials

Batting equipment for each group of four

Performance Goal

Students will bat a pitched ball.

Cognitive Goals

Students will learn the following:

- How to adjust to faster pitches
- Batting rules

Lesson Safety

- Batters must be all on the same line with their catchers well behind them since there is no catcher's equipment for the catchers.
- Students must learn to keep two hands on the bat at all times so that they don't fling or let go of the bat while swinging.
- Groups should be at least 20 yards (18 meters) from one another.
- All fielders wear a softball glove. If there are not enough gloves do not do this lesson and restrict the remainder of the unit to hand-sized balls.

Motivation

Compliment the class on their batting last time and explain you'd like them to have some more turns to work their magic at the plate. Also suggest that the ball being delivered might be a little tougher to hit—you want the pitchers to try for more speed while aiming for the strike zone.

Warm-Up

1. As students arrive, they take equipment and begin practicing.
2. Lead mimetics for pitching (10 times), batting (10 times), catching grounders that are five steps to the left (5 times), running forward to get a short pop-up (5 times), and throwing the ball accurately to a target after a catch (5 times).

Lesson Sequence

1. Discuss how to change timing when the ball is coming in faster. Review choosing a bat and addressing the plate.
2. Distribute equipment to groups.
   a. The rule is still three hits before the group rotates positions.
   b. Ask pitchers to see if they can control the ball when throwing.
   c. Set a pitching mound to keep the pitcher at the correct distance from the plate.
   d. Have the catcher stay behind the batter and set a hand target for the pitcher to focus on.
   e. Encourage speedy fielding so the ball gets back to the pitcher and everyone gets more hits.
3. Coach each group.
   - Work with students who are having trouble meeting the ball.
     - Show the zone the ball must move into before they should swing.
     - Make sure they do not move their feet during the swing.
     - Encourage them not to chase after the ball.
     - The single most important hint is to watch the ball.
4. Teach the rules that apply to batters.
   a. Batters must follow the same order throughout the game.
   b. The batter is out if the following occurs.
      - Three strikes have been called.
      - A fly ball is caught.
      - The batter moves out of the batter's box and is tagged.
      - You might add this ground rule—the batter is out if he flings the bat.

Review and Stretching

As students stretch, ask:

- How do you address the plate?
- If you are right-handed, which hip faces the pitcher?
- Are the feet supposed to help give the swing more power? Both? One? Which one?
- Is a ball coming across your knees hittable? If you don't hit it, will it be a strike?

Teacher Homework

Divide class into teams of equal ability.

Field Positions

Facilities

Designated softball field for each game

Materials

- Blackboard or chart of fielding positions and coverages
- Bases and pitcher's mound for each game
- Catcher's mask and softball equipment for each game
- 1 softball glove for each student
- 1 ball for every 2 students
- 3 different-sized bats for each field or game
- List of each team's players

Performance Goal

Students will play a softball game in set teams.

Cognitive Goals

Students will learn the following:

- Fielding positions and coverage responsibilities
- How to fit into a nine-member team

Lesson Safety

- Catchers must wear safety equipment.
- All fielders must wear a softball glove.
- There is to be no sliding.

Motivation

Compliment the class on their improvement and explain that with all the catching, throwing, pitching, and batting they have done, they are now ready for a softball game. Explain that you spent the evening doing homework to make equal teams so that today you could explain the fielding positions and help teams organize. Remind them that the quicker they start and the better they pay attention, the sooner they can get out on the field.

Warm-Up

As students arrive, they practice throwing and catching with all equipment available.

Lesson Sequence

1. Announce teams and have them sit together and select a captain.
2. Diagram where fielders position themselves to anticipate the hit.
    a. Indicate how broad of an area each person covers.
    b. Indicate how fielders move in several scenarios.
        - Grounders hit toward right field.
        - Line drives hit to left field.
3. Send the teams to their fields to use the information you just taught.
4. Begin games. (You might want to modify pitching rules and distances. For example, shorten the distance between the pitcher's mound and home plate, don't call balls and strikes, or use a batting tee instead of a pitcher.)

Review and Stretching

1. As students stretch, ask:
   - Should a baseman stand on base when the pitcher is pitching? Why not?
   - Is it true that only one person is responsible for fielding the ball?
   - If you are a baseman and the ball is not coming anywhere near you, should you move after the ball is hit?
   - Where is the base where the runner is always forced?
   - Does a forced runner have to be tagged?
2. Ask students to come out next class and practice the skills they need to field the game: pitching, catching a ball with their foot on a corner of the base, catching pop-ups, and throwing accurately to a baseman.

Softball
BEGINNER
LESSON 8

Field Responsibilities and Game

Facilities

Designated softball field for each game

Materials

- Blackboard or chart of fielding positions and coverage
- 1 softball glove for each student
- 1 ball for every 2 students
- 3 different-sized bats for each game
- Bases and a pitcher's mound for each game
- Catcher's equipment

Performance Goal

Students will play a softball game.

Cognitive Goal

Students will review the field positions and responsibilities.

Lesson Safety

- Catchers must wear safety equipment.
- All fielders must wear a softball glove.
- There is to be no sliding.

Motivation

Acknowledge that covering such a large field with so few players when batters are able to hit the ball is difficult and requires team effort. Explain that once they understand how their team can cover the field, they will be able to get three outs. Then they can get up to bat without letting the other team run away with a huge score.

Warm-Up

As students arrive, they practice throwing or pitching and catching with all equipment available.

Lesson Sequence

1. Using a visual aid, show how basemen must be fielders first.
   a. Show how they must cut off the ball before it gets out in the field.
   b. Show who takes the base when they are running for the ball.
   c. Show how the throw in from the outfield should go to second, not first.
   d. Explain that it is great to get the lead runner out, but when that is not possible, go for the forced out at first.
2. Begin games. Assign someone to call balls and strikes at each field.

Review and Stretching

As students stretch, ask:

- Does anyone have any questions?
- How different is it to play with someone calling balls and strikes?
- Did anyone get to first without hitting the ball? Have you ever heard the saying, "A walk is as good as a hit?" Does that mean if you see a bad pitch, you hit it anyway?

Making a Lineup

Facilities

Designated softball field for each game

Materials

- Blackboard or chart with lineup
- Clipboard, pencil, and lineup sheet
- Blackboard or chart of score sheet
- 1 ball for every 2 students
- 3 different-sized bats for each game
- Softball glove for each student
- Catcher's equipment
- Bases and a pitcher's mound for each game

Performance Goal

Students will play softball.

Cognitive Goal

Students will learn how to create a lineup and follow it.

Lesson Safety

- Batting team members must remain outside the backstop until their turn to bat.
- Catchers wear all safety equipment.
- All fielders wear a softball glove.
- No sliding or bat flinging.

Motivation

Every team has players who can always get on base somehow or hit the ball out of the park, while the other players will always do something surprising. Teams have learned this about each other and try to take the predictable and turn it into scoring opportunities. For instance, teams with a great hitter (a cleanup batter) want to have players on base when their cleanup batter comes up.

Arranging the batting lineup is pretty important. Look at the blackboard to see what is suggested; both the fielding positions and the lineup suggestions are on the board. Let students know they can check them when they like.

Warm-Up

As students arrive, they practice throwing and catching with all equipment available.

Lesson Sequence

1. Diagram and explain the lineup chosen and what it looks like on a score sheet.
   a. Lead off with player strengths (will walk, bunt, or get a piece of the bat on the ball almost all the time).
   b. Discuss third and fourth batters and rationale for placing them there (they make the big hits that drive in runs if other people are on base).
   c. Explain how the score sheet shows who is up next.
2. Begin games. Use a student-leader or nonparticipant to call balls and strikes.

Review and Stretching

As students stretch, ask:

- Does anyone have any questions?
- Why don't you put your best hitter up first?
- What qualities would you like in your leadoff hitter?
- Why is the fourth hitter considered the cleanup hitter?
- How many innings did you complete today?
- If an official game is seven innings, will you ever complete a game during class?

Teacher Homework

Make and post tournament schedules and standings.

Softball Score Sheet

Name _____   Date _____

Teacher _____   Class _____

	1	2	3	4	5	6	7		1	2	3	4	5	6	7
1								1							
2								2							
3								3							
4								4							
5								5							
6								6							
7								7							
8								8							
9								9							
Runs in inning								Runs in inning							
Cumulative score								Cumulative score							

Score Sheet Box Codes

Got to first: O

Got to second: >

Got to third: ⌐

Scored: ■

Out: /

From Isobel Kleinman, 2009, *Complete Physical Education Plans for Grades 5 to 12, Second Edition* (Champaign, IL: Human Kinetics).

Scoring

Facilities

Designated softball field for each game

Materials

- Catcher's mask and chest protector
- Softballs
- Softball glove for each student
- 3 different-sized bats for each game
- Bases and a pitcher's mound
- Clipboard, pencil, and lineup sheet
- Posted tournament schedule and standings
- Blackboard or large chart with a score sheet

Performance Goal

Students will play part of a softball game.

Cognitive Goals

Students will learn the following:

- That full games are seven innings, or two class days
- How to resume a game where it left off
- How to record games that are called because of time so they can resume the next day

Lesson Safety

- Batting team members must remain outside the backstop until their turn to bat.
- Catchers must wear safety equipment.
- All fielders must wear a softball glove.
- There is to be no sliding.

Motivation

Announce that the winner is the team that is ahead at the end of the last complete inning, and that official games are usually seven innings, five if the game is called because of weather, dark, or time. For that reason, starting today and continuing the next time class meets, class games will span two meetings. Because we need to know exactly how to continue the game, we are going to learn how to keep a score sheet and start keeping one today so we can continue today's game next time we meet. Compliment how everyone has done to date and wish them all a good experience with their teams.

Warm-Up

As students arrive, they practice throwing and catching with all equipment available.

Lesson Sequence

1. Using a visual aid that everyone can see, show the following:
   a. Who made each of three outs
   b. What people are on base
   c. What the score is
2. Begin games, reminding students that they should ask any questions they need to in order to keep an accurate score sheet which will determine who is on base, who is at bat, and what the score is the next time class meets.

Review and Stretching

1. As students stretch, ask if they have questions.
2. Have students turn in their score sheets so they know who will be the batter, who is on base, and what the last score was before the game was stopped.

Class Series

Facilities

Designated softball field for each game

Materials

- Softballs
- Softball glove for each student
- Bases and a pitcher's mound
- Catcher's equipment
- 3 different-sized bats for each game
- Clipboard, pencil, and lineup sheet
- Updated tournament schedule and standings
- Beginner skills rubric

Performance Goals

Students will do the following:

- Keep and follow an official score sheet.
- Complete the game started in lesson 10 and then play two more games, each of which will take two lessons to complete.

Cognitive Goals

Students will learn the following:

- That fielding responsibilities mean backing up teammates
- A batting strategy
- How to coach themselves
  - On defense, learn to remind each other:
    - Where the next fielding play is
    - Who the lead runner is
    - Where the force is
    - If they can go for a double play
    - If they need pitching changes
  - On offense, coach:
    - Baserunning
    - Designing their own lineups
- How to come back from a deficit to try to turn the tables

Lesson Safety

Special attention should be given to unsportsmanlike conduct. Behavior that endangers the class either physically or psychologically should be stopped immediately. Maintain the usual safety rules:

- Batting team members must remain outside the backstop until their turn to bat.
- Catchers must wear safety equipment.

- All fielders must wear a softball glove.
- There is to be no sliding.

Motivation

Encourage teams to get out there and warm up so when they are in the field, they can be effective.

Warm-Up

As students arrive, they practice throwing, catching, and pitching with all equipment available.

Lesson Sequence

Begin games right away.

Review and Stretching

1. As students stretch, ask if there are any questions.
2. Remind students to be prepared for a quiz on the first rainy day.
3. Collect score sheets.

Assessment

This unit includes a softball quiz and a skills rubric for objective assessment.

Beginner Softball Skills Rubric

Name _____   Date _____

Teacher _____   Class _____

	0	1	2	3
Throwing	No effort.	• Has proper body mechanics. • Keeps eye on target. • Can reach a target 30 ft (9 m) away.	• Accurate up to 45 ft (14 m). • Throws with speed. • Smooth transition from catch to throw.	• Throws fast. • Accurate 60 ft (18 m) and more. • Quick release after catch.
Catching	No effort.	• Has proper body mechanics. • Catches soft throws. • Aligns body with ball.	• Moves forward for pop-ups. • Blocks grounders with body.	• Moves backward for pop-ups. • Can catch on move.
Batting	No effort.	• Uses proper grip, stance, and swing. • Keeps eye on ball. • Swings at balls in the strike zone.	• Connects with ball. • Can take a walk. • Does not fling bat.	• Hits grounders on demand. • Undeterred by varied pitches.
Fielding	No effort.	• Gets to position quickly. • Attempts to stop ball.	• Backs up plays in sector. • Moves to cover ball. • Is frequently successful.	• Effective at putting opponents out. • Reliable in position.
Baserunning	No effort.	• Runs to first base after hit. • Runs in correct order. • Touches each base.	• Holds up on fly balls. • Leads after each pitch. • Aware of base runner in front.	• Tags inside of corner. • Rounds base aggressively. • Takes advantage of rules.

From Isobel Kleinman, 2009, *Complete Physical Education Plans for Grades 5 to 12, Second Edition* (Champaign, IL: Human Kinetics).

Beginner Softball Quiz

Name _____ Date _____

Teacher _____ Class _____

True or False

Read each statement carefully. If the statement is true, write a *T* in the column to the left. If the statement is false, write an *F.* If using a grid sheet, blacken in the appropriate column for each question, making sure to use the correctly numbered line for each question and its answer.

_____ 1. A ball hit in foul territory is usually a strike.

_____ 2. After each hit, at least one force play is usually to first base.

_____ 3. Runners leaving base before a ball is caught on a fly must return.

_____ 4. You may overrun third base without fear of being tagged out.

_____ 5. Basemen should always try to stop the batted ball from going into the outfield.

_____ 6. Most people at bat miss the ball because they do not watch it drop over the plate.

_____ 7. A ball that passes above the outside corner of home plate at waist level is a ball.

_____ 8. The shortstop covers second base almost as often as the second baseman does.

_____ 9. The cleanup batter is usually the first person in the lineup.

_____ 10. Batters cannot get on first base unless they have a fair hit.

_____ 11. There are seven complete innings in an official softball game.

_____ 12. To field a grounder, get down so your body blocks a ball that takes a bad bounce.

_____ 13. Right-handed players wear a softball glove on their right hand.

_____ 14. When catching a ball below the waist, your fingers should point to the ground.

_____ 15. The game was called after the top of the sixth inning. The team leading 10 to 5 claimed the win, though they scored six of their runs during the top of the sixth inning. However, their opponents are the actual winners. (Be careful—this question is tricky.)

Beginner Softball Answer Key

True or False

1. T
2. T
3. T
4. F—You may only overrun first base without fear of being tagged out.
5. T
6. T
7. F—Any ball that passes over part of home plate between the batter's knees and armpits is a strike.
8. T
9. F—The cleanup batter is usually the fourth person in the lineup.
10. F—Batters can also get on first base if they are walked.
11. T
12. T
13. F—The softball glove is worn on a player's nondominant hand.
14. T
15. T

 From Isobel Kleinman, 2009, *Complete Physical Education Plans for Grades 5 to 12, Second Edition* (Champaign, IL: Human Kinetics).

Fielding Skills

Facilities

- Undefined space large enough for the class to practice on safely
- Designated softball field

Materials

- One softball for every two students
- One glove per student
- Blackboard, magnetic board, or chart of field positions
- Bases

Performance Goals

Students will do the following:

- Practice and improve their softball throw.
- Practice catching pop-ups, grounders, and fastballs.
- Run the bases.

Cognitive Goals

Students will learn the following:

- Fielding skills, knowledge, and rules
- The importance of being able to catch

Lesson Safety

- Use same line of direction when practicing.
- Space out practice groups so there is a minimum of 10 feet (3 meters) between groups.

Motivation

Remind students that most of them haven't touched a softball or put on a softball glove in a year, so warming up their throwing arm, getting familiar with the glove again, and digging into their memory banks for what they have already learned is a good thing to do on the first day out.

Warm-Up

1. Have equipment available so students begin practicing as they arrive.
2. Practice the motions of throwing, catching grounders, dropping back to catch a pop-up, throwing long throws, batting, pitching, and picking the ball out of the glove and quickly releasing it with an accurate throw to a baseman (10 times each).

Lesson Sequence

1. Practice fast throwing to a partner, increasing the distances 10 feet (3 meters) at a time until everyone is doing well at 60 feet (18 meters).
2. Take a time-out from throwing to do the following:
   a. Run the bases.
      - Tag the inside corner of the bag.
      - Overrun first.
   b. Stretch the shoulder as seen in figure 3.7, a and b, on page 46.
3. Explain the need to throw farther (to get the ball in from the outfield, for the shortstop to throw to first, or for the catcher to throw to second to stop the stealer) and teach how to get greater distance.
   a. Add momentum with steps.
   b. Raise the angle of trajectory up to 45°.

4. Take a time-out from throwing.
   a. Run the bases.
   b. Stretch the shoulder again.
5. Practice getting down for grounders and releasing the ball quickly and accurately. Be careful not to overuse this muscle group.
6. Using a visual aid, review the following:
   a. Baseman's stance before the hit
   b. Fielders' positioning before the hit
   c. The changes each fielder and baseman should make on hits up the right-field line, the left-field line, and the infield
   d. Coverage for basemen going after the batted ball
   e. Coverage for plays into home plate
   f. The objective of the fielding team—getting three outs quickly

Review and Stretching

As students stretch, ask:
- Which position on the field almost never throws the ball?
- Which infielders have the longest throw to first?
- If an outfielder picks up the batted ball, should she throw to first or second?

Assessment

The progress of this lesson depends on the skill level of the class. Unless the skills are good and the practice seems routine, it might be best to make this two lessons. If your class needs two lessons, you might want to work on fly balls first and have a Throw Softball game, allowing the batters to throw only fly balls. On the next day, work on grounders and have the batters only throw grounders.

Softball
INTERMEDIATE
LESSON 2

Throw Softball Game

Facilities
- Undefined space large enough for the class to practice on safely
- Designated softball field

Materials
- One softball for every two students
- One glove per person
- Set of bases for each game

Performance Goal
Students will improve their defensive skills.

Cognitive Goal
Students will concentrate on defensive strategies.

Lesson Safety
- Use same line of direction when practicing.
- Space out practice groups so there is a minimum of 10 feet (3 meters) between groups.

Motivation

Explain that the power of the throw and catch will be in play for the day. After a little warm-up, the class will break into a fielding Throw Softball game.

Warm-Up

1. Have equipment available so students can begin practicing as they arrive.
2. Practice the motions of throwing, catching grounders, dropping back to catch a pop-up, throwing long throws, batting, pitching, and picking the ball out of the glove and quickly releasing it with an accurate throw to a baseman (10 times each).

Lesson Sequence

1. Practice fast throwing, catching pop-ups, stopping grounders and quickly releasing the ball back to partners, and pitching (10 of each).
2. Divide students into teams of nine and send them out to play Throw Softball.
    a. Batters must catch a pitch thrown near home plate and must throw the caught ball anywhere they want as long it goes into fair territory.
    b. Pitchers must throw underhand and the ball must pass over home plate.
    c. Baserunning and all fielding plays are the same as softball.

Review and Stretching

As students stretch, ask:

*   If a team has someone who is rock steady at catching anything within a stretch nearby him but can't throw, which position should he take?
*   Which player needs to be especially good at stopping grounders and making long throws?
*   What player needs the guts to watch the ball even though a bat is swinging right in front of his face?

Softball
INTERMEDIATE
LESSON 3

Bunting and Batting

Bunting can be saved for a rainy day since it can be safely done in the gym.

Facilities

Designated field large enough to safely move in

Materials

*   One softball for every two students
*   One glove per person
*   One long and one short bat for every four people
*   Two plates for each practice group

Performance Goals

Students will do the following:

*   Improve their throwing and catching.
*   Learn how to bunt.
*   Practice batting.

Cognitive Goals

Students will learn the following:

- Rules relating to bunting
  - Striking out if bunt goes foul
  - Footwork in relationship to the plate
- Batting strategy

Lesson Safety

- Separate batting groups by 10 yards (3 meters).
- Have each home plate set up on the same horizontal plane.
- Do not allow anyone to swing away if the class is learning to bunt.

Motivation

Most people get up to bat and hope to drive in the runners on base by hitting a home run, and then they hit a fly ball and are out. Batting has its own strategies. Among them is the option to advance the runner and possibly be thrown out, which can be executed by hitting a soft, slow-moving infield ball—the bunt.

Warm-Up

1. Have equipment available so students can begin practicing throwing and catching skills as they arrive.
2. Lead mimetics of the long throw, quick throw, running in for grounders, backing up for pop-ups, pitching, and batting (5 times each).
3. Lead mimetics of bunting (5 times).
   - Back foot steps forward so it faces second base without being square to the pitcher.
   - The upper hand slides up the grip on the bat so the hand stays hidden behind the bat and doesn't get bruised by the ball.
   - Angle the barrel or fat part of the bat so it hits the ball down to the ground and toward the target.

Lesson Sequence

1. Introduce the bunt.
   a. Demonstrate the grip (see figure 12.4), stance, and deadened soft contact.
   b. Explain rationale for direction and the strategy of purpose.
   c. Discuss who covers the bunt to first, third, and straight ahead.
   d. Explain that third base is the suicide position by explaining the batter's choice of bunting or hitting away.

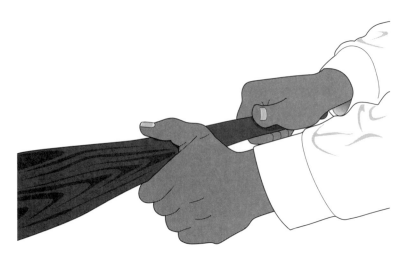

Figure 12.4 Hand position for the bunt.

2. Send out groups in fours—baseman, pitcher, batter, and catcher—and coach as they practice.

    a. Insist on three successes before everyone rotates.

    b. Encourage catchers to play the bunt and throw the ball to a baseman.

    c. Explain pitcher's responsibility if the bunt goes more than halfway to the mound.

    d. Allow several group rotations for a minimum of six successes per student.

3. Call groups in. Review full swing mimetics.

    a. Practice hitting away.

    b. Switch first baseman to the outfield.

    c. Ask all outfielders to retrieve and return balls from other groups if the ball is hit in their alley.

Review and Stretching

As students stretch, ask:

- What are some mechanical differences between a bunt and full swing?

- How do the stance and footwork differ between the two?

- If the bunt is directed up the first-base line, who gets the bunt and who covers the base? What if a bunt is up the third-base line?

- If a bunt is a sacrifice out to advance a runner, where would you bunt to send an unforced runner home?

Stealing

Facilities

Designated field with backstop for each game

Materials

- One softball for every two students

- One glove per person

- One long and one short bat for every four people

- Set of bases with a pitcher's mound

- Catcher's equipment

Performance Goals

Students will do the following:

- Improve their skills.

- Legally steal bases.

- Play a game.

Cognitive Goals

Students will learn the following:

- When it is legal to take a lead in softball and how it differs from baseball

- How to steal a base

- How to defend against stolen bases

- What a balk is

Lesson Safety

Only the batter, the catcher, and the official are allowed inside the backstop.

Motivation

Explain that spectators watching a game of baseball probably think they know how to steal bases in softball, but they would be wrong. If they tried to steal bases in softball the way they do in baseball, they would be out. There is stealing in softball; it just has to be done legally.

Warm-Up

1. Have equipment available so students can begin practicing fielding skills as they arrive.
2. Students will do mimetics for pitching, bunting, running right to pick up a grounder and throw it down to a base, and full batting swing with step.

Lesson Sequence

1. Explain rules for leading up and stealing bases in softball.
   a. Runner cannot leave the base until the ball is out of the pitcher's hand.
   b. A started pitcher's motion must be completed or a balk is called.
   c. Runner advances a base.
   d. Batter gets a ball added to the count.
   e. Only the catcher is in the position to throw the stealer out. (No stealer can leave the base legally until the ball is pitched.)
   f. The batter cannot interfere with the catcher.
2. Divide into teams and begin games. Use teachable moments to coach.

Review and Stretching

As students stretch, ask the following:

- What is the difference between stealing in baseball and softball?
- Why is only the catcher able to throw out the stealer?
- Why steal? (Better scoring position and must be tagged out.)

Softball
INTERMEDIATE
LESSON 5

Strike Zone

Facilities

Designated softball field with backstop for every two teams

Materials

- Bases and pitcher's mound
- Bats of varying sizes for each game
- Catcher's equipment
- Softball gloves for each student
- Softballs
- Visual aid diagramming field (see figure 12.2 on page 494) and diagramming home plate (see figure 12.3 on page 502)

Performance Goal

Students will learn how to back each other up on the field.

Cognitive Goals

Students will learn the following:

- Their secondary responsibilities in the field
- To anticipate and shift for anticipated hits

Lesson Safety

Set these safety rules for all class games:

- Catcher must wear protective equipment.
- Fielders should each have a softball glove.
- Sliding is not allowed.
- Fielding practice is restricted to the beginning and end of the inning.
- No one can practice batting.
- Swinging is restricted to the player on deck.

Motivation

The great thing about playing on a team is, if you make a little mistake, someone should be there to get the ball before it keeps running farther away. Students shouldn't feel bad when they miss a ball they tried to cut off early. They were doing the right thing. However, if they have to turn to run after the ball and do not have a teammate coming in for it, then someone else did do something wrong. Review everyone's secondary field responsibilities.

Warm-Up

1. Have equipment available so students can begin practicing throwing and catching as they arrive.
2. Complete mimetics for running forward to catch a pop-up immediately followed by a long throw to second, pitching, full swing, picking up a grounder and throwing across the field, and bunting.

Lesson Sequence

1. Review coverages.
    a. Outfielders
    b. Third, shortstop, and second
    c. Pitcher, catcher, and first
2. Explain shifting with the ball; depending on where the fielded ball is going, coverage changes.
3. Ask students if they can remember the direction a batter generally hits and shift there.
4. Play games with same groups as last class.

Review and Stretching

As students stretch, review confusing plays during the games—review the play and what should have been done. See if anyone could spot a consistency in the batter's hitting pattern.

Teacher Homework

Make equal teams—split good pitchers, hitters, outfielders, and basemen.

Lineups and Score Sheets

Facilities

Designated field with backstop for every two teams

Materials

- Team lists
- Clipboards with pens and pencils and team score sheet
- Softballs

- Softball glove for each student
- Bats of varying sizes
- Catcher's equipment
- Bases and pitcher's mound

Performance Goal

Students will play with a designated team.

Cognitive Goals

Students will learn the following:

- How to choose and follow a team leader
- The concepts involved in making and following a lineup

Lesson Safety

Follow safety routines and rules set in previous lessons.

Motivation

Explain that you did your homework—making equal teams—so that winning is no sure bet. Everyone will have to use all their skills, plan well, and work as a team to come out ahead. Talk about creating a lineup that works for each team. Promise that games will get started as soon as everyone can fill out and read a score sheet. Keeping an accurate score sheet is important because the games need to continue where they left off, and the only way to do that is to have an accurate score sheet to follow.

Warm-Up

Students practice fielding skills as their warm-up.

Lesson Sequence

1. Announce teams and have them pick a captain and cocaptain.
2. Review the following:
   a. Making a lineup and the need to follow it
   b. Entering positions on base, runs, and outs
   c. The aim to play five or more innings in two class lessons before declaring a winner
3. Distribute clipboards with score sheets.
4. Play games with new teams.

Review and Stretching

As students stretch, ask:

- Do they have questions about keeping the score sheet?
- Did anyone try stealing a base? (Review rules.)
- Did anyone get tagged out trying to steal a base? (Review rules.)

Softball
INTERMEDIATE
LESSON 7

Baserunning

Facilities

Designated field with backstop for every two teams

Materials

- Softball
- Softball glove for each student

- Bats of varying sizes
- Bases and pitcher's mound
- Catcher's equipment
- Clipboards with pens and pencils
- Team lists
- Clean team score sheet

Performance Goals

Students will do the following:

- Lead off and try stealing bases.
- Play games with tournament teams.

Cognitive Goals

Students will learn the following:

- How to coach their base runners:
  - Taking a proper leadoff
  - When to hold (overrun first, stop on the bag, when to go)
- Penalties for a balk and leading off too soon
- How to stop the steal (who throws the ball, who covers the base, who backs up the base, if a tag is necessary)
- Tagging up

Lesson Safety

Follow safety routines and rules set in previous lessons.

Motivation

Ask students if they think they could get to first base faster if they ran without being afraid to overrun it or if they thought they needed to turn to go to second base. Would their baserunning be faster if they turned to check how the fielders were handling the ball or if they focused on running? Do they think it is better for a base runner to just go or if runners are slowed by having to decide whether to go to the next base? Let them know that good coaching helps the runner because it leaves the decisions to someone who can see the whole field. Explain that teams might want to have someone coaching runners from the first and third bases.

Warm-Up

Students throw and catch to warm up fielding skills.

Lesson Sequence

1. Teach the strategy of baserunning (overrunning first, rounding bases, leading off, tagging up, stealing).
2. Teach rules that apply to coaching the base runners (be off the field, can't touch runner).
3. Distribute clipboards with score sheets to the batting team on each field.
4. Play games.

Review and Stretching

As students stretch, ask:

- Did you find coaches helpful?
- Did a reluctant runner score after being coached to go on?
- Can anyone explain tagging up?
- Who has to throw the stealer out? Whose job became much more difficult now that stealing is allowed?

Teacher Homework

Create and post the game schedule.

Third-Strike Rule

Facilities

Designated field with backstop for every two teams

Materials

- Team lists
- Clipboards with pens and pencils and team score sheet
- Bats of varying sizes
- Softballs
- Softball glove for each student
- Bases and pitcher's mound
- Catcher's equipment

Performance Goals

Students will do the following:

- Play the first half of the first game of the tournament.
- Coach their own base runners.
- Exhibit good sportsmanship by either helping to officiate or accepting the calls of the designated umpires.

Cognitive Goals

Students will learn that players can strike out and still get to base (third-strike rule).

Lesson Safety

Follow safety routines and rules set in previous lessons.

Motivation

Explain that the tournament starts today and if they are nervous about getting up to bat and striking out, they should think about this: Unless the play represents the third out of the team, a batter who strikes out is not out if the catcher drops the third strike. The batter can run to first and has to be put out either by the catcher tagging her before she reaches first base or by the ball reaching first base before she does. Remind everyone to keep that rule in mind.

Warm-Up

Students throw and catch to practice their field skills and get warmed up.

Lesson Sequence

1. Students practice throwing or pitching once in position on the field.
2. Games commence as soon as possible.

Review and Stretching

1. As students stretch, ask if there are any questions.
2. Review a situation that occurred that will help students understand the game better.
3. Collect the completed score sheets.

Class Series

Facilities

Designated field with backstop for every two teams

Materials

- Bats of varying sizes
- Softballs
- Softball gloves
- Bases and pitcher's mound
- Catcher's equipment
- Team lists
- Clipboards with pens and pencils and team score sheet
- Updated team standings

Performance Goal

Students will complete the first game and play two additional games.

Cognitive Goal

Students will learn to be team players.

Lesson Safety

Follow safety routines and rules set in previous lessons.

Motivation

Games and standings will be the motivation.

Warm-Up

Students throw and catch as soon as they get to the field.

Lesson Sequence

1. Students practice specific skills as they take position on the field.
2. Games commence as soon as possible.
3. Use teachable moments, reacting to an event during the game to teach or reinforce something taught before.

Assessment

Observe to determine what needs to be reemphasized. Post the standards for grading skills. If giving a written quiz, save it for a rainy day. Since it only takes a few minutes, continue games afterward. If it is raining, you might still continue the tournament, using Wiffle balls and bats.

Intermediate Softball Skills Rubric

Name _____ Date _____

Teacher _____ Class _____

	0	1	2	3
Offensive skills	No effort.	• Has good batting form. • Moves forward on hit.	• Gets to base with a hit or a walk. • Runs bases aggressively.	• Consistent at bat. • Able to direct hits or bunts.
Defensive skills	No effort.	• Blocks ball from getting deeper into outfield. • Inconsistent catching.	• Has good catching and throwing skills. • Aware of base runners. • Throws ahead of lead runner.	• Moves to properly cover on hits. • Makes big plays.
Fielding	No effort.	• Gets to position. • Focuses on game.	• Throws ahead of lead runner. • Anticipates hits.	• Tries for double plays. • Backs up teammates.
Team strategy	No effort.	• Understands basic game. • Improving specific skills.	• Keeps chances for scoring alive. • Uses baserunning rules.	• Sets goals that individual teammates can meet.
Sportsmanship	No effort.	• Frequently in disagreements. • Blames others. • Breaks rules to win.	• Tries to improve. • Works well with team. • Violations are unintentional.	• Plays within rules. • Team leader. • Helps others.

From Isobel Kleinman, 2009, *Complete Physical Education Plans for Grades 5 to 12, Second Edition* (Champaign, IL: Human Kinetics).

Intermediate Softball Quiz

Name _____ Date _____

Teacher _____ Class _____

Multiple Choice

Read each question and each answer carefully. Be sure to choose the best answer that fits the words preceding it. When you have made your choice, put the appropriate letter on the line to the left of the numbered question.

_____ 1. When the batter hits down the first-base line, what should occur?

    a. The first baseman should get the ball and run back to cover first.

    b. The first baseman should stay on first. The pitcher and catcher have to deal with the ball.

    c. Shortstop should cover second. The second baseman should cover first. Both the pitcher and the first baseman should try to field the hit ball.

    d. Everyone should move to get the ball. Whoever gets it should cover first.

_____ 2. The second-base runner takes off after the pitch. To throw the stealer out, what should occur?

    a. The catcher should throw the ball to second base.

    b. The third baseman covers third, while the shortstop backs up the catcher's throw to third.

    c. The shortstop should run into the baseline to slow down the runner.

    d. All of the above.

_____ 3. To take a sacrifice out in order to advance a base runner on second, what should occur?

    a. The batter should bunt to third.

    b. The batter should bunt to first.

    c. The batter should hope to get walked.

    d. All of the above.

_____ 4. A ball is hit long and high into right field.

    a. The runner on third should go home no matter what.

    b. The runner on third should stay on third and wait for the next batter to come up.

    c. The runner on third should run home after the ball is caught.

    d. The runner on third should go back to second.

_____ 5. The count is two strikes and three balls. Which strategy should not be one that the batter chooses to use?

    a. The batter should swing at the ball if he thinks he can hit it.

    b. The batter should leave a ball that looks out of the strike zone.

    c. The batter should bunt.

    d. The batter should fake a bunt and swing away.

»continued

From Isobel Kleinman, 2009, *Complete Physical Education Plans for Grades 5 to 12, Second Edition* (Champaign, IL: Human Kinetics).

»continued

Matching Questions

Read one numbered item at a time. Then look at each of the possible choices in the column on the right. Decide which item in the right-hand column best matches with that of the left-hand column. Put the corresponding letter on the blank space left of the number it best matches.

_____ 6. tagging up   a. over the plate, above the knees, and below the armpits

_____ 7. bunting   b. suicide position

_____ 8. catcher   c. advancing after a ball is caught on a fly

_____ 9. strike   d. makes the throw to put the stealer out

_____ 10. third baseman   e. sliding the hands up the grip

 From Isobel Kleinman, 2009, *Complete Physical Education Plans for Grades 5 to 12, Second Edition* (Champaign, IL: Human Kinetics).

Intermediate Softball Answer Key

Multiple Choice

1. c
2. b
3. b
4. c
5. c

Matching Questions

6. c
7. e
8. d
9. a
10. b

Squad Skills Work

Facilities

Designated field large enough to set up several squad areas (see figure 12.5)

Materials

- One softball for every two students
- One glove per student
- Bats in several sizes
- Set of bases for each group of 11 students working on a field
- Catcher's equipment
- Blackboard, magnetic board, or chart of fielders' positions

Performance Goals

Students will do the following:

- Practice catching pop-ups, grounders, and fastballs.
- Practice batting.

Cognitive Goal

Students will review fielding and batting skills.

Lesson Safety

Make sure the line of direction of throws and hits does not compromise safety or interfere with squads working on different skills in neighboring areas.

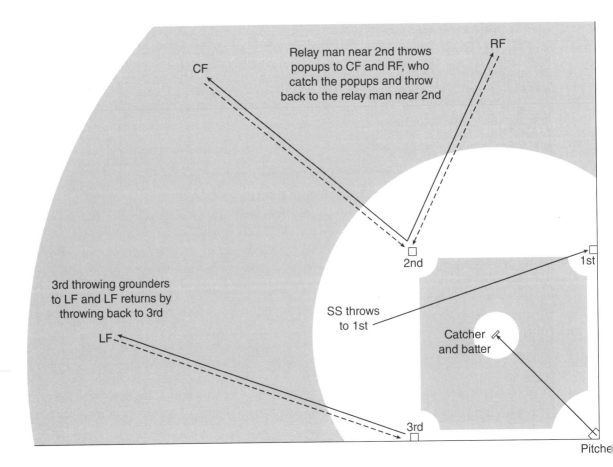

Figure 12.5 Working on a field in four squads.

Motivation

Explain that since most of the students haven't touched a softball or glove in a year, it is important to warm up their throwing arm, get familiar with the glove again, and review what has already been learned.

Warm-Up

Make gloves and balls available as students arrive to warm up their throwing arm.

Lesson Sequence

Divide students to work at varying practice stations that cover each of the skills being reviewed. Rotate every 8 minutes or so.

- Pitching, bunting, catching
  - Batter hitting into the backstop
- Catching grounders and throwing to first or third base
- Catching pop-ups and throwing to base

Review and Stretching

1. As students stretch, pay particular attention to the shoulder joint.
2. Review the rules.
   - Baserunning, when to advance, when to return, tagging up
   - Forced plays and reason for tags
   - Strike zone
   - Fouls and fouling out when bunting
   - Stealing

Assessment

Observe to determine how much practice is necessary and if the class would do well to repeat this lesson the next time. If not, get right into the next lesson.

Third-Strike Rule

Facilities

Softball field cleared of garbage and rocks with a backstop for each game

Materials

- One softball for every two students
- One glove per person
- Bats in several sizes
- Complete set of bases for each game
- Catcher's equipment

Performance Goal

Student will play a game.

Cognitive Goal

Students will review the third-strike rule and see if they can take advantage of it.

Lesson Safety

Students should observe game rules that are meant for their safety.

- Catchers must wear protective equipment.
- All fielders must wear softball gloves.
- Only the batter, catcher, and official belong in the backstop.
- Spectators and at-bat team should sit 10 feet (3 meters) outside of the baseline.
- There is no batting warm-up.
- Fielding warm-up can take place before the first batter comes up.

Motivation

As upperclassmen, most students will think that they know everything, but ask if they knew that they can get to base without a hit and without having four balls pitched to them. Did they know that they can even swing and miss a third strike and still not be out? They probably don't remember, so explain the third-strike rule.

Warm-Up

Have equipment available as students arrive for throwing and catching practice.

Lesson Sequence

1. Divide the class into teams and send them out to play.
2. Make an appearance at each game. Use the teachable moment to reinforce rules and coaching hints for fielding.

Review and Stretching

As students stretch, ask if the third-strike rule came up.

- Did someone who thought they struck out make it to base?
- When is the third-strike rule in effect?
- If there are runners on base, can they also advance?
- Can the batter leave the batter's box and then decide to run to first?

Softball
**ADVANCED
LESSON 3**

Squeeze Play

Facilities

- Clear area for practicing in small groups
- Softball field with backstop for every game

Materials

- Bats of varying sizes
- Softballs
- Softball glove for each student
- Catcher's equipment
- Bases and pitcher's mound

Performance Goals

Students will do the following:

- Practice a squeeze play.
- Play a game.

Cognitive Goals

Students will learn the following:

- How to strand unforced runners and make it easier to tag them out
- How to steal bases

Lesson Safety

Have the squeeze-play drill groups work in the same line of direction.

Motivation

Ask how many students have turned the corner to drive to the next base only to find the baseman waiting there with the ball. What do they do? They turn back if unforced and hope to get back to base before the tag. Ask how many basemen found themselves throwing behind the runner only to watch their throw go awry and the runner make it back to base. Some know how to trap someone between bases from watching baseball, but others do not have the foggiest idea. For a squeeze play to work, both basemen have to do the same thing. To learn what to do and how it feels, the class will practice monkey in the middle to get the feel of squeezing the runner between two basemen until someone is able to reach out to make the tag. Running a squeeze play is an important defensive skill.

Warm-Up

1. Students pick up equipment as they arrive and practice throwing and catching.
2. Lead students through mimetics for throwing, batting, and pitching (10 times each).

Lesson Sequence

1. Demonstrate a squeeze and send groups of three to practice, rotating the monkey in the middle. (This makes a wonderful rainy-day lesson, so you might want to save it until it rains.)
2. Review stealing rules and strategies.
3. Send the same teams to play, changing the field and opponent.

Review and Stretching

As the class stretches, ask:

- Was there a squeeze play in any game today?
- What should the defenders do to execute a squeeze play?
- Did the third-strike rule come up?
  - Can anyone explain when it is in effect?
  - Did the batter remember to go to first?
  - Was the catcher able to get the batter out at first?

Relay Throws and Sliding

Facilities

- Practice area for sliding (mats and indoor space)
- Softball field for every outdoor game

Materials

- Bases and pitcher's mound
- Softball
- Softball glove for each student

- Bats of varying sizes
- Catcher's equipment

Performance Goals

Students will do the following:

1. Slide.
2. Play a game.

Cognitive Goals

Students will learn the following:

- Why sliding is done and the difficulty of the tag
- How to use a relay person to feed balls to home from the outfield

Lesson Safety

Because of the potential for abrasions, this lesson should not be practiced outdoors unless students are wearing the appropriate clothing to protect their legs.

Motivation

Explain that sliding is a runner's attempt to tag the base before and under the fielder, who is trying to catch the ball and tag the runner. Sliding is a great strategy that can be dangerous if not done properly—runners have even broken their legs sliding—and it should be used sensibly. Ask if sliding into first makes any sense. Make it clear that although students will see a proper slide, unless they are wearing pants, you don't recommend practicing it in the dirt. Instead, they can practice sliding on mats indoors.

Warm-Up

1. As students arrive, they pick up equipment for throwing and catching practice.
2. Lead students through mimetics of bunting, picking up grounders, throwing to a target, and backpedaling to catch a fly ball (5 times each).

Lesson Sequence

1. Demonstrate and explain the slide. (You might want to save this skill for a rainy day since it can be done indoors on mats.)
   a. Explain that it attempts to evade a tag.
   b. Explain that it helps the runner stop on the bag.
   c. Do not practice unless indoors using mats, or students want to try it and are wearing long pants.
2. Review all new rules learned this year and answer questions about old ones.
3. Reinforce the use of a relay person when the ball is hit into the outfield.
4. Send same teams out to play, changing the field and opponent.

Review and Stretching

As students are stretching, ask:

- Why do runners slide?
- Is it sensible to slide into first base? Why not?
- What is the purpose of a relay person?
- What strategies changed the catcher's job from the easy one that it was in the beginner units to one of the hardest jobs on the field? (Stealing and the third-strike rule make it harder.)

Teacher Homework

- Divide the class into teams that are equally skilled.
- Write a team list on top of score sheets for distribution to each team next class.

Procedure and Teams

Facilities

Softball field with a backstop for each game

Materials

- Blackboard or enlarged score sheet
- Clipboard with score sheet for each team and pens or pencils
- Bats of varying sizes
- Softballs
- Softball glove for each student
- Bases and pitcher's mound
- Catcher's equipment

Performance Goals

Students will play a practice game.

Cognitive Goals

- Students will learn the following:
  - How to read and make entries on the score sheet
  - Who their teammates are
- Students will understand and exhibit the following:
  - Leadership
  - Responsibility
  - Sportsmanship
  - Teamwork

Lesson Safety

Observe game rules that are meant for their safety, including wearing all appropriate protective gear.

Motivation

Remind students that they have been with each other long enough to know who their cleanup batters are; who will get on base; who should pitch; who should play first, cover shortstop, or center field; and who should take on the massive job of catcher. Explain that if they follow your procedure, they will get the most out of their class time, so you will go over it quickly and then announce teams so they can play. Games will take place over 2 days. Give the selected captains the clipboards so they can insert their lineups and keep score, but first, show them a score sheet and how to use it.

Warm-Up

Have equipment available as students arrive for throwing and catching practice.

Lesson Sequence

1. Announce procedure for the tournament.
   a. Read game schedule and assigned fields for warm-up.
   b. Games start after the pitcher is warmed up.
   c. Fielding teams are responsible for setting up and breaking down the field. (They must bring out three or four balls.)
   d. Batting teams are responsible for bringing bats in several sizes, clipboards, pens, and score sheets.

e. Balls and strikes are either called by a neutral umpire or a person from the batting team.

   f. Students are responsible for coaching their base runners.

   g. Games will continue for a second day from the exact position they stopped in.

2. Announce teams.

3. Give teams their score sheet with their team roster on it.

4. Use a visual aid to go over the score sheet and type of entries necessary (lineup, outs, runs).

5. Have teams choose captains and cocaptains before starting their last practice game.

6. Use teachable moments for input on strategy, coverage, rules, and mechanics.

Review

Ask the following:

- Are there are any questions? (They will have to be prepared for a rainy-day quiz, so they shouldn't sit with unanswered questions.)
- Are score sheets up to the minute?

Softball
ADVANCED
LESSONS
6-11

Class Series

Facilities

Softball field with a backstop for each game

Materials

- Bats of varying sizes
- Softballs
- Softball glove for each student
- Bases and pitcher's mound
- Catcher's equipment
- Clipboard with score sheets for each team and pens or pencils

Performance Goal

Students will compete in a tournament of three games over six days.

Cognitive Goals

Students will understand and exhibit the following:

- Self-sufficiency
- Leadership
- Responsibility
- Sportsmanship
- Teamwork

Lesson Safety

Be vigilant that students continue wearing protective equipment. As the tournament begins, also be vigilant about keeping the emotional climate under control so that the psychosocial environment is healthy and motivating. Respond quickly and assertively to any bullying, name-calling, or unsportsmanlike behavior.

Motivation

The start of the tournament will be the motivation.

Warm-Up

Have equipment available as students arrive for throwing and catching practice.

Lesson Sequence

1. Give each field a score sheet for each game.
2. Encourage fielding teams to set up and warm up in position.
3. Begin games after a 5-minute warm-up.
4. Use teachable moments for input on strategy, coverage, rules, and mechanics.

Review and Stretching

As students stretch, cover the following:

- Ask if anyone has questions.
- Use a moment to share an important issue that came up in class.
- If you intend to give a quiz, ask them to be prepared for a rainy-day quiz.
- Collect score sheets.

Assessment

- Give quiz on the first rainy day.
- Consider having the students grade themselves or someone on their team using the advanced skills rubric on the last fully active day of the unit.

Advanced Softball Skills Rubric

Name _____ Date _____

Teacher _____ Class _____

	0	1	2	3	4	5
Skills	No effort.	• Has proper swing. • Has proper mechanics. • Has erratic throws. • Walks instead of running.	• Bat meets ball. • Blocks the batted ball in the field. • Has slow, accurate throw to 60 ft (18 m). • Catches slow balls thrown accurately.	• Gets to base. • Moves to the ball quickly. • Swings at pitches in the strike zone. • Runs the bases legally.	• Has fast, accurate throws. • Makes solid hits. • Has smooth release of ball after catch. • Moves to the ball instead of waiting for it.	• Hits in runs. • Plays position well. • Assists in securing the out. • Uses knowledge to make the most of baserunning.
Teamwork	No effort.	• Argues about assigned position. • Doesn't cooperate with the team.	• Plays assigned position. • Forgets to back up teammates. • Forgets where the lead runner is.	• Responds to coaching hints. • Backs up team. • Remembers where to play the ball.	• Anticipates hits and necessary coverage in field. • Uses skill to advance the team, not self.	• Helps keep the team focused. • Takes leadership role.
Sportsmanship	No effort.	• Blames others. • Needs supervision to stay on task. • Interferes with other team.	• Gets to field on time. • Warms up with team. • Plays within rules.	• Works well with team. • Takes responsibility for position.	• Consistently tries to play at personal best. • Recognizes good team effort and successes. • Exhibits good sportsmanship.	• Allows team members to play their position and backs them. • Demonstrates reliable, consistent leadership. • Helps teammates improve.

From Isobel Kleinman, 2009, *Complete Physical Education Plans for Grades 5 to 12, Second Edition* (Champaign, IL: Human Kinetics).

Advanced Softball Quiz

Name _____ Date _____

Teacher _____ Class _____

True or False

Read each statement carefully. If the statement is true, write a *T* in the column to the left. If the statement is false, write an *F*. If using a grid sheet, blacken in the appropriate column for each question, making sure to use the correctly numbered line for each question and its answer.

_____ 1. Batters who bunt foul on the third strike are out.

_____ 2. Taking a lead *before* the pitch is legal.

_____ 3. A third-base runner should stay after a fly has been caught in deep center field.

_____ 4. With runners on second and third and two outs, the fielder should throw to first.

_____ 5. The only position on the field where catching is everything and the need to throw is almost nonexistent is the first baseman's position.

_____ 6. With runners on first and second, the shortstop catches a line drive and wisely throws to first.

_____ 7. With an unforced runner between two bases, the leading baseman should stay on base, waiting for the runner and throwing.

_____ 8. Bunting toward first with a runner on third is a strategy to help the third-base runner score.

_____ 9. The third baseman is usually the relay person.

_____ 10. Sliding when you are forced to run to a base is taking a risk for no reason.

Matching Questions

Read one numbered item at a time. Then look at each of the possible choices in the column on the right. Decide which item in the right-hand column best matches that of the left-hand column and put the corresponding letter on the blank space to the left of the number it best matches.

_____ 11. What a right-hand batter generates power from   a. second baseman

_____ 12. Covers first base on grounders to right field   b. lead runner

_____ 13. Advancing to the next base after a ball is caught on a fly   c. tagging up

_____ 14. Conditions allowing batter to run after striking out   d. left hand

_____ 15. Runner closest to scoring   e. third-strike rule

Diagram Questions

The following diagram represents a score sheet turned in after one day of play. Each question is based on the information in the diagram. Read each question and choose the best answer based on all the rules you know and the information in the diagram. When you have made your choice, put the appropriate letter on the line to the left of the numbered question.

_____ 16. Nancy has

   a. advanced to second each time she got up to bat

   b. been left stranded on base

   c. never been put out

   d. all of the above

»continued

Softball

»continued

Stars	1	2	3	4	5	6	7	Heroes	1	2	3	4	5	6	7
1. Sue	①	◆	/					1. Carol	◆	②					
2. Mike	/	③						2. Lisa	>	/					
3. Hugh	②		◆					3. Mark	/	③					
4. Roger	③		②					4. Steve	①						
5. Cathy		①	◆					5. Alan	②						
6. Iris		◆	◆					6. Daryl	③						
7. Marcus	_	②	◆					7. Kisha		①					
8. Nancy		>	>					8. Ari		◆					
9. Anna		/	①					9. Mohammed		◆					
Runs in inning	0	2						Runs in inning	1	2					
Cumulative score	0	2						Cumulative score	1	3					

_____ 17. The Stars believe they are officially winning the game.

    a. true

    b. false

_____ 18. Who leads off for the Heroes?

    a. Carol

    b. Ari

    c. Steve

_____ 19. The cleanup hitter for the Stars is

    a. Iris

    b. Marcus

    c. Roger

_____ 20. When this game resumes,

    a. the Stars go into the field.

    b. the Stars are up, Sue is on first, Nancy is on second, and Mike is up

    c. Alan from the Heroes leads off

    d. none of the above

 From Isobel Kleinman, 2009, *Complete Physical Education Plans for Grades 5 to 12, Second Edition* (Champaign, IL: Human Kinetics).

Advanced Softball Answer Key

True or False

1. T—A bunt that goes foul is considered a strike, even if it is the third strike.
2. F—It is illegal to leave the base before the ball is pitched in softball.
3. F—The runner should tag up and try to score.
4. T—Go for the force play.
5. T—First basemen rarely throw. Their ability to catch with a foot on the plate is worth its weight in gold!
6. F—The shortstop would be wiser yet to go for second and a possible double play.
7. F—This is a classic squeeze-play situation where both basemen want to get closer until the tag is easy.
8. T—A sacrifice out at first allows a runner from third to score.
9. F—The relay is usually to shortstop when the ball is thrown from center or left field.
10. T—As soon as the ball gets to base, you are out. There is no need for a tag or a slide.

Matching Questions

11. d
12. a
13. c
14. e
15. b

Diagram Questions

16. a
17. b—The official score is that of the last complete inning. In that case it was Stars 2, Heroes 3.
18. c
19. c
20. b

Team Handball

Chapter Overview

1. Teach the basic skills of soccer, basketball, and handball that apply to this game: throwing, catching, hand dribbling, hitting, and volleying using knees, shoulders, and head.

2. Teach familiar rules that apply and how:
   - Holding should be for no more than 3 seconds.
   - If the player is still moving with the ball after three steps, the following choices must be made for it to be legal:
     - Basketball dribble
     - Basketball dribble followed by three steps
     - Passing the ball
     - Shooting the ball
   - The following are legal passes (note, no kicking):
     - Jump pass
     - Bounce bass
     - Overhand pass
     - Wrist pass

3. Teach the boundaries and field marking and how the rules apply:
   - Players cannot use the "when in doubt, it's out" strategy.
   - They cannot enter the goal area unless playing goalie.
   - They may shoot from anywhere, including off the field when throwing in.

4. Teach the goalie's limitations:
   - While inside the goalie area, the goalie cannot grab a stationary ball or rolling ball outside of the goalie area.
   - The goalie cannot intentionally deflect the ball out of bounds once gaining control of it.

5. Teach violations, fouls, and penalties—for example, a player cannot intentionally send the ball out of bounds.

Team Handball Study Sheet

Fun Facts

Team handball is a relatively young sport, having begun in Europe around 1920. For many years, it was called *European handball,* but now that it is popular worldwide, it is called *team handball.*

Sixteen years after its introduction, it became an Olympic sport, making its first worldwide appearance at the Olympic Games in Berlin in 1936. It took almost 50 years for the United States to send a women's handball team to the Olympics.

Though it sees limited play in the United States, it is said that team handball is the second most popular sport in the world. It is also a popular sport in the Special Olympics.

Skills

All the skills necessary for successful team handball play are skills that are common to basketball, volleyball, and soccer:

- Overarm throw
- Catch
- Rolling the ball
- Volleying with the arms, wrist, torso, and knees
- Pat-down dribble (not as controlled as the dribble in basketball)

Rules

- There are seven players on each team, including the goalkeeper.
- When in possession of the ball, follow these rules:
    - The ball may be thrown, hit, or caught (not kicked) with hands, thighs, knees, and torso.
    - Players may not hold the ball more than 3 seconds.
    - Offensive players are not allowed to charge into opponents.
- To keep possession of the ball, players must do the following:
    - Take no more than three steps.
    - Use a pat-down dribble instead of a controlled basketball dribble.
    - Roll the ball.
    - Consider a pivot step as one of the three steps.
    - Avoid having a discontinued dribble.
- The ball is legally passed when the following occurs (note, no kicking allowed):
    - It's thrown.
    - It's volleyed with any part of the body above the knee.
    - It's struck.
- Following are rules for boundaries and field marking:
    - Field players cannot enter the goal area.
    - Players may shoot from anywhere, including when off the field, for a throw-in.
- Following are the goalie's limitations:
    - The goalie cannot grab a stationary ball or a ball rolling outside of the goalie area.
    - The goalie cannot intentionally deflect a ball out of bounds once gaining control of it.
- Free throws are awarded for rules violations. Goals may be scored directly from a free throw.

 From Isobel Kleinman, 2009, *Complete Physical Education Plans for Grades 5 to 12, Second Edition* (Champaign, IL: Human Kinetics).

Team Handball Extension Project

Name _____ Date _____

Teacher _____ Class _____

What equipment would you need to play team handball on your own?

Is there a handball team at school? Who is the coach?

Is there intramural team handball after school? Who is in charge?

Where can you participate in team handball outside of school?

Do you have friends who would join you? List their names.

What are the health benefits of participating in a team handball program?

What types of team handball games can you be involved in?

From Isobel Kleinman, 2009, *Complete Physical Education Plans for Grades 5 to 12, Second Edition* (Champaign, IL: Human Kinetics).

Team Handball Student Portfolio Checklist

Name _____ Date _____

Teacher _____ Class _____

_____ Has reviewed all methods to legally advance the ball while in possession of it.

_____ Has reviewed legal methods to pass or shoot the ball.

_____ Knows the rules of scoring.

_____ Knows the boundaries for the player and the goalie.

_____ Understands specific restrictions for the goalie and the goal area.

_____ Knows common violations and the procedure for returning the ball to play.

_____ Knows violations and fouls and their penalties and procedures.

_____ Has developed offensive and defensive strategies.

_____ Exhibits responsibility and good sportsmanship during competition.

From Isobel Kleinman, 2009, *Complete Physical Education Plans for Grades 5 to 12, Second Edition* (Champaign, IL: Human Kinetics).

Team Handball Learning Experience Outline

Contents and Procedure

1. Review the skills of soccer, basketball, and handball that apply to this game: throw, catch, hand dribble, hit, and volley using knees, shoulders, and head.
2. Teach the rules that seem familiar but are different.
   a. Players may not hold the ball more than 3 seconds.
   b. To keep possession of the ball, players must
      - take no more than three steps,
      - use a pat-down dribble instead of a controlled basketball dribble,
      - roll the ball,
      - consider a pivot step as one of the three steps, and
      - avoid having a discontinued dribble.
   c. The ball is legally passed when the following occurs (note, no kicking allowed):
      - It is thrown.
      - It is volleyed with any part of the body above the knee.
      - It is struck.
   d. Discuss boundaries and field marking and how the rules apply.
      - Field players cannot enter the goal area.
      - Players may shoot from anywhere, including when off the field, for a throw-in

e. Discuss goalie's limitations.
  * The goalie cannot grab a stationary ball or a ball rolling outside the goalie area.
  * The goalie cannot intentionally deflect a ball out of bounds once gaining control of it.

f. Teach violations, fouls, and penalties for each. Note that players cannot hit or pull a ball out of an opponent's arms.

Teaching Tips

* Follow the lessons. They combine skill, knowledge acquisition, and game play.
* Review skills, acknowledging that students might know the skills from another sport, but when they use them in this one, there is a difference.
* Get students into the game immediately.
* Develop a short tournament, changing teams daily and having a different person assume the captainship so that each student in class is a captain for a day.
* After a book is published, rules, skills, and strategies may change. Check Internet sites listed in suggested resources to keep up with the changes.

Teaching Tips for Students With Special Needs

* Students with disabilities or temporary medical problems that exclude them from playing the regular game can be taught aspects that do not lead to contact or in any way compromise their health.
* Participation can involve the following:
  - Learning skills outside the game so students feel safe participating
  - Using skills in noncontact, competitive ways
  - Playing shooting games
  - Holding relays in wheelchairs or on scooters
* Students can also be taught to officiate and score, giving them a safe place to be and giving them a valuable role in the tournament.
* Students who must temporarily sit out can provide their team with strategy advice or statistical analysis, recording what rules and violations come up the most, who has the most assists, who makes the most stops, and so on.
* As a last resort, students can do library work. They can research the history and development of team handball and make a presentation to the class at the end of the unit.

Special Considerations for Team Handball

This unit is for students who have played soccer and basketball and have developed the skills necessary for getting immediately into team handball. The unit is short; there are only enough lessons to allow each player an opportunity to be a team captain and lead the decision-making process. You might consider omitting the assessment phase of the unit, although a written quiz and general skills rubric are included.

This game will equalize the soccer and basketball players who excelled in their own sport during their season. Those players might even experience difficulty because what comes naturally in their sport might be illegal and need redirection in team handball

Facilities

Court with goals and a goalie restraining area for every two teams

Materials

* One ball for every two students
* Pinnies for half the class

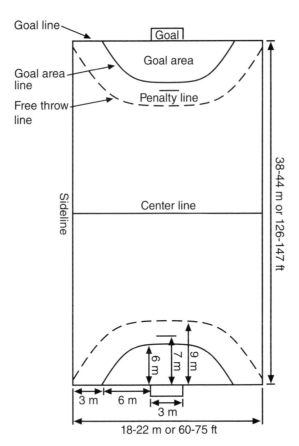

Figure 13.1 The team handball court.

Unit Safety

- Make certain that participants have a minimum of 6 feet (2 meters) separating them from others.
- Arrange a court and set of goals of their own for every two teams (see figure 13.1).
- Stretching should be done after the muscles are warm—at the end of class during review.

Unit Timeline

There is one unit for the beginner team handball player who has already developed soccer, basketball, and handball skills.

- 2 lessons for adapting skills from basketball and soccer to team handball
- 4 lessons for a class tournament
- 1 lesson for a quiz (not recommended in this short unit) and culminating activity

Suggested Resources

Clanton, R.E., and M.P. Dwight. 1996. *Team handball: Steps to success.* Champaign, IL: Human Kinetics.

Hamil, B.M., and J.D. LaPoint. 1994. *Team handball.* Dubuque, IA: Eddie Bowers.

International Handball Association. 1995. Rules of the game. www.ihf-online.info/upload/PDF-Download/rules_english.pdf.

Sportplan. 2008. What is handball? www.coachinghandball.com/userapp/pages/whatIsHandball.jsp.

Team Handball
BEGINNER
LESSON 1

Adapting Skills

Facilities

Area with no obstructions and a court with goals and a goalie restraining area for every 14 players

Materials

- One ball for every two players
- Pinnies in a different color for six players on every team of seven

Performance Goal

Students will learn how to legally advance a ball.

Cognitive Goals

Students will learn how soccer and team handball rules differ.

- Size of team (six field players and one goalie)
- Moving ball
    - Cannot use anything below knees to direct ball
    - Cannot palm or double dribble
    - Cannot pass to self
- Can shoot from anywhere
- Boundaries and using them
    - Cannot delay the game
    - Cannot hold the ball more than 3 seconds
    - Players cannot go inside goalie area

Lesson Safety

- Participants with a ball should be separated by a minimum of 6 feet (2 meters).
- Two teams need a set of goals and their own court on which to play.

Motivation

Team handball has a big following, but learning to play is a trick of adjustment. Students already have the skills; they learned them playing soccer and basketball. So, instead of focusing on skills, everyone needs to learn how the rules and skills differ from the games they know so well. The ball cannot be propelled by the body below the knees, and the dribble must be patted rather than controlled.

Warm-Up

Have students take a short jog, hand dribbling and hand or body passing a ball to a partner.

Lesson Sequence

1. Review the allowed skills by calling them out and having partners practice each three times.
    a. Hand dribble—Pat the ball to the ground.
    b. Hand roll—Roll the ball on the ground with the hand.
    c. Throw to partner who practices catching, three times with feet on the ground and three times with a jump throw.
    d. Volley with partner practicing throwing and catching. Volley by hitting the ball out of the air with the arms, part of the torso, or the thighs or knees.
    e. Take three steps with the ball and then dribble it, roll it, or pass it with a throw.
    f. Head, knee, shoulder volleys—Do the allowable soccer skills (not allowed to use feet).
2. Go over boundaries, point out the goalie area, and discuss applicable rules.
    a. Players are not allowed inside the goalie area, though they can land in it after taking a shot.
    b. Goalie can come out to play the ball and dribble it back in.
    c. Pushing, tripping, holding, and hitting are fouls penalized by a free throw where they happened.
3. Divide into teams of seven and play.

Review and Stretching

As students do their stretching routine, ask the following:

- Did you like it?
- How many people got mixed up?
- What was the most difficult skills transition for you to make?

Playing the Game

Facilities

Area with no obstructions and a court with goals and a goalie restraining area for every 14 players

Materials

- One ball for every two players
- Pinnies in a different color for six players on every team of seven

Performance Goal

Students will play team handball.

Cognitive Goals

Students will learn the following:

- How rules keep the game fair and safe
- Rules and penalties
  - Size of team
  - Violation of skills
    - Taking too many steps
    - Forwarding the ball with a part of the body below the knees
- Penalties (free throws with opponents 3 meters away)

Lesson Safety

- Participants with a ball should be separated by a minimum of 6 feet (2 meters).
- Every two teams need a set of goals and their own court on which to play.

Motivation

Explain that after a quick question-and-answer session about the rules, they will play a team handball game because they have already learned all the skills in soccer, volleyball, and basketball.

Warm-Up

Have students go once around the field using any legal pass to send the ball back and forth to a partner.

Lesson Sequence

1. Review violations and fouls.
   a. Skills—Players cannot double dribble, palm, air dribble, or advance the ball with contact below the knees.
      - A free throw is taken on the spot of the violation.
      - Penalty throws are on the 7-meter line after a foul during a scoring opportunity.
   b. Boundaries—Only the goalie can play inside the goal area.
2. Play.
   a. Game starts with a throw-on at midcourt.
   b. A point is awarded for a goal that is legally propelled inside the goal and over the goal line.

Review and Stretching

As students do their stretching routine, ask the following:

- Can you roll the ball with your foot?
- Can you pass by kicking?

- What is the penalty if you do either?
- Can you score from off the field?
- Can you score from inside the goalie area?
- What is the usual penalty?

Teacher Homework

Prepare and post a list for students to include their win–loss record and whether they have been captain.

Tournament With Rotating Captains

Note that the number of lessons will vary based on how long it takes until everyone has been a captain.

Facilities

Area with no obstructions and a court with goals and a goalie restraining area for every 14 players

Materials

- One ball for every two students
- Pinnies in a different color for each team
- Posted student roster

Performance Goal

Students will play team handball.

Cognitive Goals

Students will do the following:

- Learn to work with a variety of teammates and adapt to each new change
- Rotate the responsibility of choosing teams and being captains
- Have an opportunity to play a leadership role

Lesson Safety

Teams need a set of goals and their own field on which to play.

Motivation

Announce that you thought it might be interesting for everyone to see what it is like to be captain and that in this unit, everyone is going to be one. As captain, they will have an opportunity to pick a cocaptain and one other player. In other words, they will be picking half their team. You will send out the other half of their team. Explain that captains will take charge of assigning field positions and coordinating team strategy once the team is assembled. Because new teams are being picked each day, students will get individual scores. They will win 1 point when they play and 2 if they win. They will win 3 points for playing while they are captain and 4 points if their team wins while they are captain. At the end, the person with the most points will be class champion.

Warm-Up

Have students take a warm-up lap. Select captains and have them choose teams while the others practice.

Lesson Sequence

1. Pick captains each day (make sure they have equal skill and leadership ability).
2. Assign a team color.
   - Let captains choose their cocaptain and one other person.
   - Do this during the warm-up so the rest of the class is practicing.
   - Hand color-coded pinnies to groups of three students at a time, directing them to the captain with the same color. (Try to divide skills equally.)
2. Play team handball.

Review and Stretching

As students do their stretching routine, ask for questions. Answer them and collect scores, making sure to credit the right number of points to each student.

Teacher Homework

- Update and post scores after each class.
- This is a short unit since handball is dependent on what students have learned in other sports. With a unit this short, specific grading is contraindicated; however, a short quiz follows.

Beginner Team Handball Skills Rubric

Name _____ Date _____

Teacher _____ Class _____

	0	1	2	3	4	5
	No effort.	• Awkward • Unsuccessful • Haphazard • Unfocused	• Intentional • Focused • Occasionally successful	• Successful • Automatic reaction to the ball and team movement on the field • Consistent	• Combines skills • Proper reactions in predictable situations • Accurate and controlled	• Performs in changing conditions • Modifies approach if situation demands it • Complex performance
Catch						
Throw						
Body mechanics						
Footwork						
Defensive use of hands						
Defensive positioning						
Offensive positioning						

From Isobel Kleinman, 2009, *Complete Physical Education Plans for Grades 5 to 12, Second Edition* (Champaign, IL: Human Kinetics).

Beginner Team Handball Quiz

Name _____ Date _____

Teacher _____ Class _____

True or False

Read each statement carefully. If the statement is true, write a *T* in the column to the left. If the statement is false, write an *F*. If using a grid sheet, blacken in the appropriate column for each question, making sure to use the correctly numbered line for each question and its answer.

_____ 1. There are 11 players on an official team.

_____ 2. A player kicking the ball into the goal does not score.

_____ 3. Throwing the ball up in the air and running forward to catch is a violation.

_____ 4. On a throw-in from out-of-bounds, the thrown ball goes through the goalpost and over the goal line. This is a scored goal.

_____ 5. All the rules of soccer apply in team handball.

_____ 6. A person in possession of the ball is allowed to hold it 5 seconds before passing.

_____ 7. Once you get the ball, you may take three running steps before releasing it to dribble or before passing it off.

_____ 8. If the ball has rolled to a stop outside the goal area, the goalie cannot go out to get it and bring it back into the restraining area.

_____ 9. If you make a save, your deflecting pass is best if it stays in the middle, in front of the goal.

_____ 10. In team handball, as in basketball, players have an unlimited ability to use the pivot step.

Beginner Team Handball Answer Key

True or False

1. F—There are seven players on an official team.
2. T—Kicking is illegal in team handball.
3. T—Air dribbles are illegal. The ball must touch someone or something before a person can touch it again.
4. T
5. F—Team handball incorporates some strategies and skills of soccer, handball, and basketball but has its own rules.
6. F—The ball holder is allowed only 3 seconds to hold the ball.
7. T
8. T
9. F—Whatever the sport, defensive clearing of the ball is best done using an outlet pass, getting the ball away from the middle and its goal.
10. F—The pivot step is counted as one of the three steps a player is allowed to take.

 From Isobel Kleinman, 2009, *Complete Physical Education Plans for Grades 5 to 12, Second Edition* (Champaign, IL: Human Kinetics).

14

Volleyball

Chapter Overview

While teaching skills and strategies, conclude each lesson with a game of some kind.

1. Teach skills.
   - Serves—underhand, overhead, sidearm
   - Passes—bump and set, being able to direct both
   - Defensive skills—tip-over, net recovery, block
   - Offensive skills—offensive volley, spike, backward set
2. Teach a short history of volleyball.
3. Teach the importance of teamwork and acceptance of individual differences.
4. Teach the rules of the game as skills are being taught:
   - The difference between legal and illegal taps while learning to set and bump
   - Service rules while learning to serve
   - Legal rotation and scoring when ready for the first game
   - Rules around the net while learning net recovery, spiking, and blocking
5. Teach the ground rules (boundaries, obstructions).
6. Teach strategies.
   - Be prepared:
     - Keep eyes on the ball.
     - Good position depends on where the ball is.
     - When receiving, get behind and under the incoming ball.
     - Pay attention even when it seems the point is over.
     - It is not over until the ball hits the ground.
   - When in doubt, hit it up.
   - Offensive strategies include hitting the ball to the open court, deep, to the weakest player, with a change of direction, and with power and speed.

Volleyball Study Sheet

Fun Facts

- Volleyball is an American game that was conceived as a combination of basketball, tennis, and handball skills by William G. Morgan in Springfield, Massachusetts, in 1895.
- Volleyball was originally called *mintonette*.
- Setting and spiking skills were first used in the Philippines in 1916.
- The United States Volleyball Association (USVBA) was created in 1928 when it became apparent that players needed to follow a set of standard rules.
- The first beach volleyball association was formed in California in 1965.
- The first two-person volleyball competition occurred in 1948.
- The Olympics included two-person volleyball for the first time in 1996.

Skills

- Underhand serve—With the holding hand at waist height, the foot opposite the hitting hand forward, and the body facing the net, swing the hitting arm so that the fist or heel of the hitting hand contacts the ball below its center, or in the mouth of the imagined face.
- Overhead serve—In a forward-stride position, holding the ball in front of and slightly above the shoulder, bring the hitting elbow back and then forward, contacting the ball with the heel of the hand so the heel of the hand meets the ball on the nose of the imagined face.
- Bump, dig, forearm pass—From the ready position of arms straight, 90° away from the body, shoulders forward, hips back, and knees bent, meet the ball at hip height with the lower part of the forearm, slightly above the wrists. If an arm swing is necessary, it should be in the direction of the target.
- Setup pass—With fingers spread in an unclosed triangle over the eyes, get under the ball, face the target, and meet the ball with the fingers slightly above the forehead. On the hit, extend legs and arms up in the direction of the target.
- Net recovery—Use a bump pass and get under the ball to retrieve it. If it hits high on the net, it will roll almost straight down. If it hits in the middle of the net, it will rebound out.
- Spike—Jump off both feet with both arms swinging forward and the hitting elbow pulling back. With a relaxed, open hand, swing up to make the hit, using the heel of the hand to hit the ball, continuing the face metaphor, around its eyes. Your hand and the ball should meet in front of you with the hitting arm extended overhead.
- Block—Jump with and in front of the hitter from the other team. Go straight up off both feet, with arms extended overhead and angled slightly forward. Watch the opposing setter's hands before the set to know where the hitter will be and thus where to make the block. Watch the hitter's eyes to know where he plans to direct the hit.

Rules

- Boundaries
  - A ball landing within the court or on the line is fair
  - If the ball touches ceiling, walls, people, or objects outside the court, it is out of play.
- Serving
  - The ball must be put into play with one hand.
  - The serve must be contacted outside the court and inside the service zone.
  - Teams get the right to serve:
    - After they win the choice at the beginning of the game.
    - After they win a point when they were the receiving team.

»continued

»continued

- - Teams not following their service order lose points gained when the rotation error is discovered.
  - Rotation is clockwise.
- Scoring
  - The team that wins the rally scores a point (rally scoring system).
  - If both teams commit a fault at the same time, the point is replayed.
  - Games (sets) are won when one team gets 25 points (class rules may be different) and is ahead by 2 points.
  - Official matches require winning three games, or sets (class rules may be different).
  - In official matches, if a fifth game is necessary, the team achieving 15 points and leading by 2 has won the match.
- Hitting
  - Each team is entitled to three hits before the ball passes over the net.
  - A player cannot hit the ball twice in succession, with the following exceptions:
    - An opponent touched it simultaneously over the net.
    - The ball touching any part of the body is considered a hit.
    - A block is not considered one of the team's three hits.
- Net play
  - Blockers may touch the ball beyond the net once attackers have executed their play, not before or during opponent's hit.
  - Players may follow through over the net.
  - Players cannot go beyond the center line or go into the opponents' court.
  - When playing the ball, players cannot contact the net.
  - Back-line players may play balls at the net if the ball is lower than the net at the moment of contact, but they may not execute an attack in the front zone.
  - There can be no attack in response to an opponent's service.
  - Only frontline players may block or spike in the front part of the court.

Positions

- Rotation positions during serve (see figure 14.4 on page 572)
  - Right back (server)
  - Right forward
  - Center forward
  - Left forward
  - Left back
  - Center back (last server)
- Playing positions for advanced teams that specialize
  - Setter—Sends the second tap to the team hitter or spiker; always faces left sideline.
  - Outside hitter—Hits from the strong side, left-front position; blocks weak-side hits and assists in blocking middle hits.
  - Weak-side hitter (to the right of the setter)—Hits and blocks balls on the right side; responsible for setting if the setter plays the first tap.
  - Middle hitter—Hits and blocks balls to middle of court; assists blocks on either side.

Volleyball Extension Project

Name _____ Date _____

Teacher _____ Class _____

What equipment do you need to play volleyball on your own?

Is there a volleyball team at school? Who is the coach?

Is there a volleyball intramurals program? Who is in charge?

Where can you participate in volleyball outside of school?

Do you have friends who would join you? List their names.

What are the health benefits of participating in a volleyball program?

 From Isobel Kleinman, 2009, *Complete Physical Education Plans for Grades 5 to 12, Second Edition* (Champaign, IL: Human Kinetics).

Volleyball Student Portfolio Checklist

Name _____ Date _____

Teacher _____ Class _____

_____ Can perform the underhand volleyball serve.

_____ Can perform the bump pass.

_____ Knows the rules of service and how to rotate.

_____ Can play a game while following the rules.

_____ Can perform the setup pass.

_____ Has learned to tip the ball over the net.

_____ Will attempt to save a ball out of the net.

_____ Can direct the ball to different places on the court.

_____ Knows and understands rules involving net play.

_____ Has learned and can perform the overhead serve.

_____ Has learned the spike.

_____ Has learned the block.

_____ Is able to play an offensive game.

_____ Knows the official rules.

_____ Has learned basic volleyball strategies.

_____ Exhibits responsibility and sportsmanship during competition.

_____ Has learned to specialize and take responsibility for the team.

_____ Can interchange positions during play within the rules.

From Isobel Kleinman, 2009, *Complete Physical Education Plans for Grades 5 to 12, Second Edition* (Champaign, IL: Human Kinetics).

Volleyball Learning Experience Outline

Contents and Procedure

1. Throughout the teaching of skills and strategies, lessons conclude with a game.
   a. Cover skills.
      - Serves—underhand, overhead, sidearm
      - Passes—bump and set, being able to direct both
      - Defensive skills—tip-over, net recovery, block
      - Offensive skills—offensive volley, spike, backward set

    b. Discuss short history of volleyball.
- Originally called *mintonette.*
- In Springfield, Massachusetts, 1895, William G. Morgan combined basketball, tennis, and handball skills, creating mintonette.
- Setting and spiking first showed up in the Philippines in 1916.
- The need for standard rules resulted in the formation of the USVBA in 1928.

    c. Rules of the game are taught as the related skills are taught.
- Legal and illegal taps while learning to set and bump
- Service rules while learning to serve the ball in play
- Legal rotation and scoring when beginning the first game
- Rules at the net during net recovery, spiking, and blocking lessons
- Ground rules for your school (boundaries, obstructions)

    d. Teach strategies.
- Learning the importance of teamwork and accepting differences
- Being prepared
    - Keep eye on ball.
    - Position depends on where the ball is.
    - When receiving, get behind and under the incoming ball.
    - Be ready to play the ball until it actually hits the ground.
- Hitting the ball up when in doubt
- Placement of hits
    - To open court
    - Deep
    - To weakest player
    - With change of direction
    - With power and speed
- Specialized positions (advanced students)

2. Have some informal, noncompetitive practice during each lesson so students can improve without pressure.

3. Develop a double tournament that allows students to continue learning as they compete in the first meetings with the other class team. Then repeat the competitions so they can use their acquired skills, team concepts, and growing self-confidence and allow internal leadership to develop.

4. Assess students objectively.
    a. A performance rubric can be found at the end of each unit.
    b. There is a short written quiz at the end of each unit.

Teaching Tips for Special Considerations

- Lessons break down new skills as each is introduced. Check the beginner unit for the breakdown of basic skills.
- After a book is published, rules, skills, and strategies may change. Check Internet sites listed in suggested resources to keep up with the changes.
- Students with medical problems that prevent them from playing the game should not automatically be excluded from activity. Where possible, they can warm up and

follow the class in mimetics. They can also become an important part of the class if they are taught to officiate. This will give them a valuable role to play without endangering their safety.

- Students who sit out temporarily can do the following:
  - Identify the strengths of their team.
    - Most consistent scorer
    - Most effective person at net
    - Person with the best setup pass
    - Person with the best reflexes
    - Most attacking
  - Keep score.
  - Assist with officiating.
- Once game play begins, take an active role in officiating and coaching as students play their matches. Be proactive about eliminating bullying and intimidation and discouraging ball hogs. Do not let players stay on court when their behavior endangers the physical or psychological safety of their classmates. Volleyball is exciting enough that students will be motivated to improve their style to be allowed to stay on the court. If students are removed, address the reasons why so they understand what they should or shouldn't do.

Facilities

- Overhead obstructions should be removed.
- Courts should be marked (see figure 14.1).
- Nets should be up and taut.

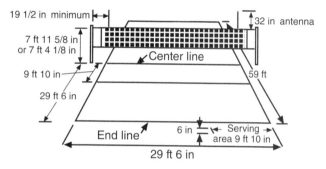

Figure 14.1   Volleyball court.

Materials

Minimum of one ball for every four students

Unit Timeline

Volleyball is a terrific team sport and as such, it is the longest unit in this book. It lends itself to large classes, being indoors, and coed participation. It is one of the few sports that require each player to react to the ball or the point simply ends. Teams cannot depend on one or two shining stars to get the work done; they have to depend on everyone. Lessons provide so much reinforcing repetition that all students will develop enough basic skills to have the confidence to enjoy the game and the competency to make a contribution to their team. Despite the length of the unit, interest will be sustained because students will find themselves more in control and a valued member of their team as the competition continues into the second round robin.

This chapter includes three units—beginner, intermediate, and advanced. Each has the following:

- 4 lessons to develop the basic skills necessary for starting a low-level game
- 1 or 2 lessons to develop a cooperative working and learning environment
- 10 lessons of a round-robin tournament, each with its own focus
- 1 lesson to quiz students and do a culminating activity

Assessment

Tools for assessment appear at the end of each unit.

- A short written quiz designed specifically for each level
- A performance rubric allowing skills assessment for each level

Suggested Resources

American Sport Education Program (ASEP). *Coaching youth volleyball.* 1996. Champaign, IL: Human Kinetics.

Asher, K., ed. 1996. *Basic elements of the game* (Best of coaching volleyball, vol. 1). Dallas, TX: Masters Press.

AthleticScholarships. 2008. History of volleyball. www.athleticscholarships.net/history-of-volleyball .htm.

Bertucci, B., and J. Peterson. 1995. *Volleyball drill book: Individual skill.* Dallas, TX: Masters Press.

Neville, W.J. 1989. *Coaching volleyball successfully: The USVBA coaching accreditation program and American coaching effectiveness program leader level volleyball book.* Champaign, IL: Human Kinetics.

Volleyball.org. 2008. Playing volleyball. http://volleyball.org/playing/index.html.

Volleyball BEGINNER LESSON 1

Bump Pass

Facilities

- Wall with no obstructions
- Large area with cleared floor space and no overhead obstruction

Materials

One ball for every four players

Performance Goal

Students will hit a bump pass.

Cognitive Goals

Students will learn the following:

- Brief history of volleyball and its evolution
- That to hit something up, you must hit from beneath it
- Why hitting a bump pass up is necessary

Lesson Safety

- Groups need a minimum of 15 feet (4.5 meters) between them.
- Establish rules for dealing with errant balls and teach students to follow them.
  - Do not run on anyone else's court to get an errant ball; wait for the person closest to the ball to throw it back.
  - Throw it back on one bounce so it can be easily caught.
  - Throw it under the net when returning it to the serving team.

Motivation

Volleyball was developed in the United States and has become so popular that it is difficult to go to any resort, beach community, or park without seeing nets up and people playing. Over the years, the original format of six on six, which is still the way volleyball is played in Olympic, class, and interscholastic activities, has evolved. Beach volleyball started the two-on-two craze. With only one teammate, the only chance to reach a pass is with time, so volleyball has a lot of hits in the air. Without a true pass—one intended for a teammate—you cannot have much of a game, so today's lesson starts with a true pass in volleyball, the bump pass.

Warm-Up

1. Do footwork for side-to-side shuffles and back-and-forward runs.
2. Do pogo springs, when students leave the ground by flexing their ankles. Do 10-20 reps.
3. Lead mimetics for the bump pass, explaining as they practice the components (see figure 14.2).
   a. Link hands palm over palm with forearms extended straight (5 times).
   b. Bend knees in a forward stride position while preparing arms (5 times).
   c. Repeat arm and leg preparation so it is one smooth, flowing motion (5 times).
   d. Continue as if contacting the ball (10 times).
      • Keep eyes on the imaginary ball as it touches the forearm.
      • Keep legs bent.
      • Move arms in the direction you want the ball to go (forward and up).
      • Finish with hands pointing to the target.
   e. Add footwork to get the ball, preparing to contact, hit, and follow through.

Lesson Sequence

1. Demonstrate the bump pass and explain that they already learned how to bump during mimetics; they just didn't use a ball. Have them try.
   a. Bump (block off forearm) to themselves (2-3 times).
   b. Bump to a wall, aiming high, and bump back what the wall returns (2-3 times).
2. Bring students together to learn rules that relate to bump passing.
   a. Open hand below the waist is illegal.
   b. Balls hitting fixtures on the ceiling or the walls are out of bounds.

Figure 14.2 Preparing for a bump pass.

3. Demonstrate hitting a bump pass from a low toss to a point high on the wall.
   a. Students line up to receive a toss and bump it back high to the wall (3 times each turn, for at least 2 turns).
   b. Receive a toss and bump it back to the thrower (3 times each turn, for at least 2 turns).
   c. In a circle, keep the ball alive by bumping it so its arch is toward the middle of the circle.
4. Start a contest to keep the enthusiasm high as they master bumping.
   a. Who can keep the ball up 5 times before losing control? What about 10 times, or 15 times?
   b. Which circle can keep it up legally the most times before it hits the floor?
   c. Can anyone beat the best score so far?

Review and Stretching

Have students do the stretching routine that you have established in previous units as you ask questions:

- Why use a bump pass for balls below the waist?
- If a pass is out of control and goes too high, what rule might be broken?
- If a bump pass is going straight ahead, how can it be corrected?

Underhand Serve

Facilities

Nets already set up

Materials

One volleyball for every four players

Performance Goals

Students will do the following:

- Serve underhand (or use other serves of their preference).
- Improve their bump pass.

Cognitive Goals

Students will learn the following:

- How to use their arm as a striking implement
- That to hit something forward, the point of contact is in the back
- Basic service rules (boundaries, foot fault, faultless flight)

Lesson Safety

When practicing serving over a net, being able to use every ball is great but can result in balls hitting students who are not expecting them. Safety is not a problem if students remember that they should be practicing to have the serve land within the court. Some get excited and try to hit the ball as hard as they can. When they do, they wind up hitting the wall or even a classmate on the other side of the net on a fly. Being hit with a hard, unexpected serve will not be welcomed. Be aware of this possibility and vigilant in guarding against it. If students are intimidated by so many balls flying and being close enough to hit them, have half the students act as servers on one side of the net so the other half can catch the served balls and serve them back.

Motivation

No game can start if players cannot put the ball into play. Today, everyone will learn to serve. Ask which is most likely to be successful, getting a ball to fly from this end of the court to the other by hitting it with a stick or hitting it with a feather?

Today, students will learn how to make their arms like a stick and how to find the right spot on the ball to get it to go anywhere they want.

Warm-Up

1. Begin with running—side to side with crossover steps, back and forward.
2. Lead mimetics.
   a. Repeat mimetics for the bump pass.
   b. Introduce mimetics for underhand serve.
      - Stand so the hip of the nonhitting hand faces the target and the nonhitting hand holds the imaginary ball below the waist. Swing using a straight arm so the swinging arm passes over the hand holding the imaginary ball (5 times).
      - Hit by having students open the hand holding the ball so they have a point of contact. Ask them to swing and hit the palm of the hand as if it is just below the middle of the back of the ball with the heel of the hitting hand (5 times).
      - Serve underhand and run three steps forward after the hit (10 times).

Lesson Sequence

1. Demonstrate the underhand serve, reviewing what was learned during mimetics.
2. Set up a short practice drill.
   a. Hit the ball underhand to a wall 10 feet (3 meters) away.
   b. Allow three chances on each turn at the wall and have students rotate so they get at least three turns practicing the underhand serve against the wall and several repetitions per person.
   c. Move students away gradually, encouraging serves that hit 12 feet (3.5 meters) high.
3. Teach service rules.
   a. To put the ball into play, a serve must pass over the net cleanly.
   b. The server must be off the court to serve.
4. Set up a serving (shooting) gallery, so that half of the class is on one side of the net and the other half on the other side.
   a. Distribute all balls. Have students behind either side of the court and allow as much repetition as possible.
   b. Here are some suggestions:
      - After 10 successes, students sit so others can get the balls and more repetition.
      - Do not spend the whole lesson on this (arms will hurt and students will get bored).
      - If a few students are having problems, let them know you will work with them during practice time next class.
5. Put groups in a circle and give them 5 minutes to practice their bump pass.
6. Afterward, ask them to count the number of legal taps in a row their group made.
   a. Remind them of the rules.
      - No open hand.
      - No one person can tap the ball two times in a row.
      - If a ball touches the wall, ceiling, or anything below the waist, it is out, even if it still goes over the net. (Note: In a game situation, balls that touch objects or the ceiling on or above the court are playable. Balls touching outside the court are out of bounds.)

7. Which team can keep the ball up the most in this class? Can anyone beat the best team of the best class?

Review and Stretching

As students stretch, ask questions:

- What part of the hand should meet the ball on a serve?
- Look at the ball as if it had a face. What part of the face should you hit on the serve?
- What constitutes a foot fault?
- Do you still believe in do-overs?

The Set

Facilities

Nets already set up

Materials

One volleyball for every four players

Performance Goals

Students will do the following:

- Legally hit a ball with an open hand.
- Improve their serve and bump pass.

Cognitive Goals

Students will learn the following:

- How to judge when to use a bump pass and when to use a set
- How to avoid illegal passes
- The importance of sending passes up

Lesson Safety

Make sure that practice time has students working in the same direction and there is no cross traffic.

Motivation

When a ball drops from a high arc, players can get under it and use a setup pass to redirect it. This is the pass that begins (sets up) the volleyball attack, since it is used to send the ball to someone or someplace specific, such as the best player on the team. Control takes time to develop, so students are going to start now.

Warm-Up

1. Practice before the class formally begins.
2. Do mimetics for the setup pass, or set (see figure 14.3).
   a. From hands at sides, have students spread fingers in the shape of a ball, making a triangular window with the forefingers and thumbs and with hands up so the eyes can see through them in the waiting or neutral position (10 times).
   b. From neutral, extend up until arms are straight up (10 times).
   c. In forward-stride position, bend at the knees and then extend arms and body up (10 times).
3. Practice mimetics for the bump pass and serve.

Lesson Sequence

1. Demonstrate the set as the movement they practiced but this time coordinated with the ball.

2. Start progressive drills.

    a. Set to self for a few seconds to get under the ball and follow through up.

    b. Set to the wall, aiming for height and continuous returns that are high.

3. Teach the rules.

    a. Both hands have to contact the ball at one time.

    b. The ball cannot appear to rest in the hands, no basketball carries allowed, and so on.

4. Continue setting practice.

    a. Receive toss and return it in a high arc that pops off the fingertips and goes directly to tosser.

    b. Divide class into several circles to practice setting high balls (bumping low ones or performing saves to keep the ball in play when necessary).

5. After a few minutes of circle practice, ask students to count the number of continuous legal taps for which their group was able to control the ball.

Figure 14.3 The set.

Review and Stretching

As students stretch, discuss the following:

- Name two types of passes.
- What pass is used if the ball is dropping from a high arc?
- Show how you prepare to hit it.
- What part of your hand touches the ball on a set?
- What part of your arm touches the ball when you hit a bump pass?

Playing the Game

Facilities

- Nets already set up
- Courts marked with lines

Materials

One volleyball for every four players

Performance Goal

Students will use skills in a game situation.

Cognitive Goals

Students will learn the following:

- How to rotate
- Game rules
    a. Three taps per team
    b. Scoring system (choose one)
        - Rally scoring (point awarded after each play)
        - Side-out scoring (point scored when serving team wins the rally)
    c. Rotation after opposing team loses serve
    d. Boundary lines

Lesson Safety

Make sure practice time has students working in the same direction and there is no cross traffic.

Motivation

Ask, "Are you ready?" You think they are, so tell them so. Explain that they need to learn the rest of the game rules so they can play.

Warm-Up

1. Give time to practice before the class formally begins.
2. Lead mimetics for the setup, bump, and serve.

Lesson Sequence

1. Teach remaining game rules.
    a. Rotation
    b. Three taps per team
    c. Staying on own side of court
2. Assign groups of six to courts.
3. Begin by volleying in a circle for a few minutes. Encourage the hitter to move under the ball and send it up.
4. Play games. Assist with rotation questions and any other questions.
5. After about 8 minutes, change the teams that play each other.

Review and Stretching

As students stretch, ask questions:

- Can anyone serve twice before everyone on the team has served?
- Can the team not scoring ever win a point?
- Is the rotation clockwise or counterclockwise?

Volleyball
BEGINNER
LESSON 5

Receiving Serves

Facilities

- Nets already set up
- Courts marked with lines

Materials

One volleyball for every four players

Performance Goals

Students will do the following:

- Receive serves with a bump pass that goes up.
- Improve skills in a game situation.

Cognitive Goals

Students will learn the following:

- How important positioning is to success
- The importance of using a controlled bump pass as a first tap

Lesson Safety

Make sure practice time has students working in the same direction and there is no cross traffic.

Motivation

Tell students that after watching the classes' games, it was clear that they can bump and set reasonably well when practicing in a circle, but once the game started, it was hard to hit a bump pass that stayed on the court, especially off an opponent's serve. Take time before the game to practice serving and blocking it up with a bump pass without it hitting the ceiling or walls.

Warm-Up

1. Allow practice time before the class formally begins.
2. Lead mimetics for the setup, bump, and serve.

Lesson Sequence

1. Demonstrate how you want partners to practice.
    a. One serves and the other receives by bumping ball up.
    b. Allow a maximum of three pairs per court.
    c. Allow enough time so each person gets to serve six times and receive six times.
2. Have students get in their own group of six and assign them to a court.
3. Begin with a few minutes of volleying in a circle.
4. Play games. Spend time at each court.

Review and Stretching

As students stretch, ask questions:

- Many times when the serve was received, the bump pass went over the net. Do you want that to happen?
- Why did it happen?
- What things can your body do to prevent it?

Teacher Homework

Make up teams of equal gender and ability.

Tournament Teams

Facilities

One marked court for every two teams

Materials

One volleyball for every four players

Performance Goals

Students will do the following:

- Use the skills taught in a game situation.
- Meet and play with their tournament teams.
- Choose captains and cocaptains (if coed, a boy and a girl).

Cognitive Goals

Students will learn the following:

- Who their teammates are
- That everyone has different abilities and weaknesses
- That the best server can get the ball over again and again
- How to build the rotation order around strengths

Lesson Safety

Make sure that practice time has students working in the same direction and there is no cross traffic.

Motivation

Announce the permanent tournament teams and that it is important to get to know each other and how they will respond to balls that fall between them. It is important to know which teammate will go the extra distance, who needs a little more backup, and who is the best server. Agree that the best server is someone who is able to get the ball over the net and onto the court over and over. By the end of the day, each team should agree on who is their best server.

Warm-Up

1. Allow time to practice before the class formally begins.
2. Practice moving forward and back, then side to side.
3. Lead mimetics that include footwork. Students run in three steps, bend down, and extend to set. Then they move back three steps, get down for the set, and set (5 times).
4. Do same but with the bump (5 times).
5. Practice the mimetic for the serve (5 times).

Lesson Sequence

1. Announce teams.
2. Assign teams to different courts.
3. Begin with a few minutes of volley practice in a circle.
4. Play games. Assist with rotation questions and any other questions.
5. Stop the games and ask teams to decide on captains. Have captains report to you.

Review and Stretching

As students stretch, ask questions:

- Who is your best server?
- Anyone have an idea where your best server should serve in a one-through-six rotation order?

Teacher Homework

Chart and post the tournament schedule (see appendix A). Make and post a chart of team captains that can be updated to show team standings.

Rotation Order

Facilities

One marked court for every two teams

Materials

- One volleyball for every four players
- Blackboard or other visual aid
- Game schedule
- Posted team standings

Performance Goals

Students will do the following:

- Set up a team rotation order.
- Encourage each other to hit the ball up.
- Play round 1 of the tournament.

Cognitive Goals

Students will learn the following:

- More about rotation order
    - Where the first server is at the start of the game
    - Where the last server is at the start of the game
    - Ideas about positioning strong players in the rotation order
- How to adjust to strengths and weaknesses of team members
- That to win, a team must lead by 2 points or else a tie is recorded

Lesson Safety

Make sure that practice time has students working in the same direction and there is no cross traffic.

Motivation

Today the class begins the first round of a double round-robin tournament. Discuss what a round-robin tournament is (each team plays all other teams in the tournament once) and what a double round-robin is (when each team plays all teams a second time). Then discuss how to take advantage of players' strengths to win. Do they remember who they thought the best server was on their team? Talk about why you'd put those servers first, not last, because you want them to be the player on the team who gets to serve more often than all the other players. Use the blackboard to show how to arrange the team to take advantage of its strengths.

Warm-Up

1. Allow time to practice before the class formally begins.
2. Lead mimetics with footwork for the bump, set, and serve.

Lesson Sequence

1. Diagram and explain rotation order for the serving and receiving teams (see figure 14.4).
2. Have each team volley in a circle on assigned courts.
3. Have captains meet to decide which team wins first serve. Remind captains to place their best server first.
4. Play round 1 games. Assist with questions and officiating.

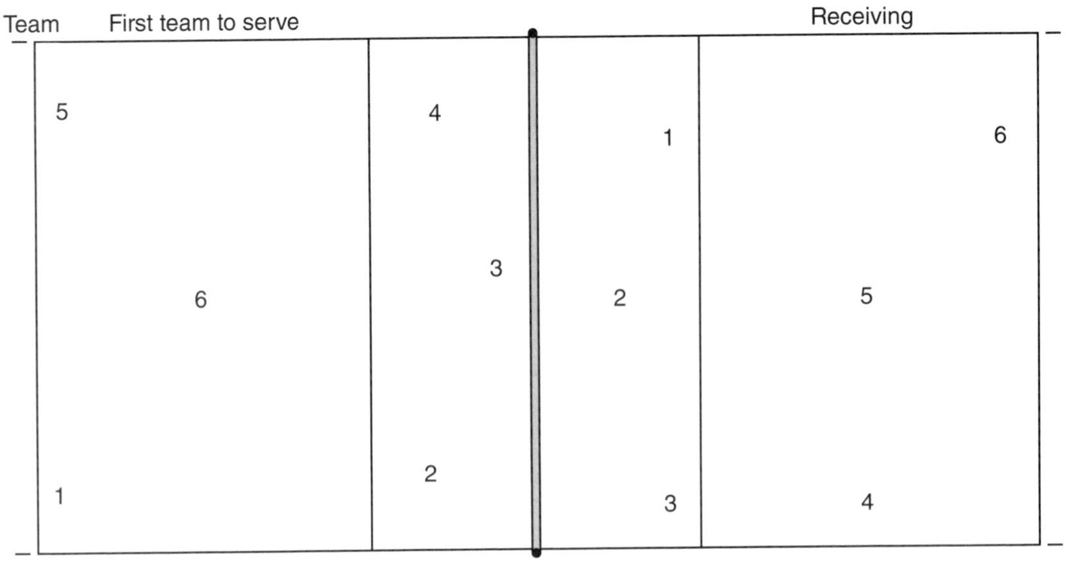
Team
First team to serve
Receiving
5
4
1
6
3
6
2
5
2
1
3
4

Figure 14.4 Rotation order.

Review and Stretching

1. As students stretch, ask them if the best server is in the right back position before the game starts and the other team serves first, what should their team do? Why?
2. Get the scores by asking winning captains to stand, and then, if there were any ties, those captains stand.

Volleyball
BEGINNER
LESSON 8

Using All Three Taps

Facilities

One marked court for every two teams

Materials

- Blackboard or other visual aid
- Game schedule
- Updated team standings
- One volleyball for every four players

Performance Goals

Students will do the following:

- Practice emergency reactions to save errant taps by teammates.
- Play round 2 of their tournament.

Cognitive Goals

Students will learn the following:

- How to deal with the excitement and pressure of wanting to win
- That even if it looks hopeless, as long as they have one tap left and the ball has not hit the floor, walls, or ceiling, they have a chance
- More about rotation order and pairing of players

Lesson Safety

- Make sure that during practice time, students work in the same direction.
- Be vigilant during competition, making sure to stop bullying, unsportsmanlike conduct, or any other negative behavior that competition might bring out in students.

Motivation

This is the second round of the tournament. Announce the leaders after one round and explain how they arrived at their tournament points: 2 for a win and 1 for a tie. Ask who on their team is able to save balls that they think are hopeless. If they can identify those players, explain that there is probably a great place to put them in the rotation order and that before the games begin, the class will try to figure it out.

Warm-Up

1. Allow time to practice before the class formally begins.
2. Lead mimetics that include forward-and-back and side-to-side footwork for the serve, set, and bump passes (10 times each).

Lesson Sequence

1. Diagram and explain more about the rotation order.
   a. Rotation order should put good servers up earlier.
   b. Divide the talent so it works best for the team.
      - Players who make great saves should be next to teammates who cannot seem to get the ball to go where they want.
      - If there are two players who are good at giving the ball the last hit and making sure it goes over the net, place them so that one is always at the net.
2. Begin with a few minutes of volleying in a circle as a team.
3. Start the games, assisting with questions about rotation and following rules.

Review and Stretching

1. As students stretch, ask questions:
   - Does your team have a good rotation order?
   - Is your best server serving first?
   - Did your best server serve more than once during the game?
   - Do you have two people who are good near the net?
   - Were they separated so that one was always rotating into a net position?
2. Get the results by asking winning captains to stand, followed by tying captains.

Volleyball
BEGINNER
LESSON 9

Tip-Over

Facilities

One marked court for every two teams

Materials

- Blackboard or other visual aid
- Game schedule
- Updated team standings
- One volleyball for every four players

Performance Goals

Students will do the following:

- Hit a ball backward over the net.
- Play round 3 of the tournament.

Cognitive Goals

Students will learn the following:

- How the follow-through can make the ball go in a direction different than the one they are facing
- How to accept their teammates' differences
- The difference between backing up teammates and taking over

Lesson Safety

- Make sure that during practice time, students work in the same direction.
- Be vigilant during competition, making sure to stop bullying, unsportsmanlike conduct, or any other negative behavior that competition might bring out in students.

Motivation

Explain how important it is for everyone on the team to hit the ball up. Not everyone will be great at controlling where it goes, but keeping it off the floor is great and by sending it up, everyone on the team has another chance to send it over. Because it is important to be ready to make saves, announce that you will teach how to save the ball that falls just short of the net so everyone can help out, even when students have their backs to the net.

Figure 14.5 The tip-over from a set.

Warm-Up

1. Allow time to practice before the class formally begins.
2. Lead the class in mimetics for a backward tip-over.
   a. Do the usual set so the follow-through ends with the fingers behind the head and back slightly arched (10 times).
   b. Do the usual bump pass but have the follow-through finish over the head so the arms are near the ears and the back is slightly arched (10 times).

Lesson Sequence

1. Demonstrate hitting a tip-over from a high set (see figure 14.5).

   a. Set up a team line practice with one person retrieving, one sending a high toss, and another hitting the tip-over over the net.
   b. Allow the person to stay at the net until she has three successes.
   c. Consider going through the line again.

2. Demonstrate saving a low pass when your back is to the net and have students practice bumping it backward and over until they have successes (see figure 14.6).

3. Announce standings and court assignments and play round 3.

Review and Stretching

1. As students stretch, ask why it is more important to back up teammates rather than having the best player jump in and take over. What does backing someone up mean? Discuss a moment that occurred on one of the courts as an example.

2. Gather scores.

Figure 14.6 Bumping a low pass backwards and over the net.

Net Recovery

Facilities

One marked court for every two teams

Materials

- Blackboard or other visual aid
- Game schedule
- Updated team standings
- One volleyball for every four players

Performance Goals

Students will do the following:

- Hit the ball out of the net.
- Play round 4 of the tournament.

Cognitive Goals

Students will learn the following:

- That it is legal to recover a ball out of the net
- To identify the different net rebounds if the ball hits high or low
- Rules involving the net:
  - Serves cannot touch the net.
  - The ball is alive if it touches the net.
  - Players cannot legally touch the net.

Lesson Safety

- Make sure that during practice time, students work in the same direction.
- Be vigilant during competition, making sure to stop bullying, unsportsmanlike conduct, or any other negative behavior that competition might bring out in students.

Motivation

The students have learned just about everything they need to in order to play well, though they have not had the opportunity to really master it all. The trouble is, no matter how much they practice and get better, they will make mistakes, one of which is to hit the ball into the net. However, all is not lost—hitting the ball into the net is a mistake that a teammate can save, too.

Warm-Up

1. Allow time to practice before the class formally begins.
2. Practice mimetics for the tip-over, bump pass backward, and running in to the net, squatting, and bumping straight up.

Lesson Sequence

1. Demonstrate hitting the ball out of the net.
   a. Show how the ball rolls down the net if it contacts the net at the top (see figure 14.7a).
   b. Show how the ball bounces back when it hits the net in the middle (see figure 14.7b).
   c. Demonstrate getting under the ball, squatting, and using the bump pass to get it up.
2. Have teams throw the ball into the net and practice recovering it. Practice until each player has three successes.
3. Announce standings, opponents, and court assignments.
4. Play round 4.

Review and Stretching

1. As students stretch, ask questions:
   - Did anyone make a net recovery during the game?
   - Which is harder, the ball that hits the net on top or in the middle? Why?
   - Which comes out of the net farther, a ball hitting the middle that hits hard or one that hits the middle softly?
   - What do you have to do to play under it?
   - Did your teammates react as if the ball hitting the net were dead?
2. Collect scores.

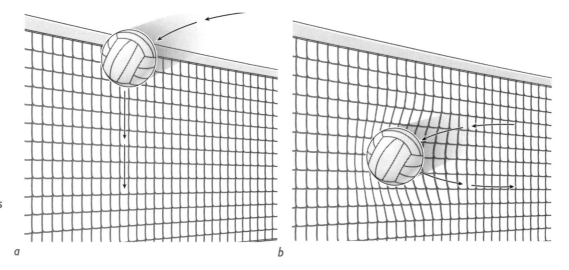

Figure 14.7
Recovery when (a) the ball hits the net near the top and drops straight down and (b) it is sent into the center of the net.

a   b

576

Directing the Bump Pass

Facilities

One marked court for every two teams

Materials

- Blackboard or other visual aid
- Game schedule
- Updated team standings
- One volleyball for every four players

Performance Goals

Students will do the following:

- Improve their teamwork.
- Bump the ball back or sideways.
- Play round 5.

Cognitive Goals

Students will learn the following:

- How to improve their sportsmanship by appreciating their teammates' improvement
- Why the follow-through is integral to the direction of the bump pass

Lesson Safety

- Make sure that during practice time, students work in the same direction.
- Be vigilant during competition, making sure to stop bullying, unsportsmanlike conduct, or any other negative behavior that competition might bring out in students.

Motivation

Round 5 of the tournament, with six teams, is the last match of a single round-robin tournament. After today, the class will have played every team. Announce standings and that this is the last chance for everyone to practice for half the class. Explain that there will be 10 minutes for teams to practice what they want; they just have to stay on their own side of the net. Choose whether to do bumps, serves, sets, net recovery, tip-overs, or a little of each. If you do net recovery or the tip-over, make sure teams don't interfere with each other when sharing the net.

Warm-Up

1. Allow time to practice before the class formally begins.
2. Lead mimetics for the set and the bump, including footwork and cues for the class to follow through so the ball goes forward, back, and right or left.

Lesson Sequence

1. Announce court assignments.
2. Give the class 10 minutes to practice before the games.
3. Play round 5.

Review and Stretching

1. Use this time to bring up problems that need addressing and entertain questions.
2. Collect scores.
3. Announce that during remaining volleyball classes, games will begin as soon as everyone is warmed up. There will be no instruction before games in order to make it possible to play more than one game. As a result, it may be possible for teams to win up to

6 tournament points in one lesson (each game won is worth 2 tournament points). That's plenty of points for a team to catch up with, so students should hurry in the next class to play as many games as possible.

Match Play

Facilities

One marked court for every two teams

Materials

- Blackboard or other visual aid
- Game schedule
- Updated team standings
- One volleyball for every four players

Performance Goals

Students will do the following:

- Improve their teamwork.
- Play round 6 of the tournament.

Cognitive Goal

Students will learn about match play.

Lesson Safety

- Make sure that during practice time, students work in the same direction.
- Be vigilant during competition, making sure to stop bullying, unsportsmanlike conduct, or any other negative behavior that competition might bring out in students.

Motivation

Explain how match play is different than the one long continuous game they played during the first round robin. Match play is more than one game. In order to play a match in class, there will be 3 games. The standings can change dramatically. In addition, students will meet teams they have already played so they can develop some strategy based on what they remember from the last time they played the team. Announce standings and that despite the standings, the tournament is still wide open. Explain that each game won is worth 2 tournament points, giving a lot of opportunities for teams to catch up. In interscholastic competition, a match is the best of five games, but class time is too short so they will play as many games as they have time for, scoring 2 points for each win and 1 for a tie.

Warm-Up

Direct students to their tournament courts for a team circle volley.

Lesson Sequence

1. Explain procedure and scoring for match play:
   a. Game is 15 points.
   b. After a game, the rotation order for second is the same as start of first.
   c. Switch sides of net for each game.
   d. Partial wins will count if a team can get a minimum of 8 points:
      - If ahead by 2, they get a win.
      - If not, they get a tie.

2. Announce court assignments and practice time. Allow 3 minutes.

3. Play round 6.

Review

Collect scores.

Second Tournament Continues

Facilities

One marked court for every two teams

Materials

- Beginner skills rubric
- Updated tournament standings
- Volleyballs for practice and game balls for each court

Performance Goals

Students will do the following:

- Improve teamwork.
- Foster leadership skills with self-direction.
- Play rounds 7 through 10.

Cognitive Goals

Students will learn basic strategies to enhance team play:

- Team organization of rotation
- Keeping the ball high on first and second taps
- Strategies to win points rather than just sending the ball over
  - Change direction.
  - Hit to the weak player.
  - Hit the ball deep.
- Other placement strategies
  - Hit where the opponent's ball hog is not.
  - If a ball hog leaves his position right away, hit to the place he vacated.
- Convince class that ball hogs reduce team effectiveness.

Lesson Safety

- Make sure that during practice time, students work in the same direction.
- Be vigilant during competition, making sure to stop bullying, unsportsmanlike conduct, or any other negative behavior that competition might bring out.

Motivation

Announce standings and explain some scenarios that could change first place.

Warm-Up

1. Allow time to practice before the class formally begins.
2. Circle volley with teams.

Lesson Sequence

1. Teach a strategy of the day. Five strategies are listed in the cognitive goals; choose the one that will do the most good for your class and work in descending order. If teams are still suffering from ball hogs, go for the strategy against ball hogs first. If teams are losing because their rotation order is leaving weak zones or starting with servers who cannot serve, start with that strategy.
2. Invite any team to request your coaching services.
3. Post court assignments and team records.
4. Have students practice setting and bumping in a circle for at least 3 minutes before the match.
5. Post minimum performance standards and explain them.
6. Play the rounds.

Review

1. Continue to relate to what happened on the courts if there is a lesson from it.
2. Respond to any questions.
3. Collect the scores.
4. After the last round, announce a short quiz for next class.

Assessment

Throughout the last few rounds, observe students' skills and effort compared with the performance standards as defined in the skills rubric. Students will take a short written quiz at the conclusion of the unit.

Quiz and Final Event

Facilities

One marked court for every two teams

Materials

- One quiz for each student
- Pens and pencils
- Two volleyballs for each court

Performance Goals

Students will do the following:

- Take a volleyball quiz.
- Play a culminating game.

Cognitive Goal

Students will get feedback on what they have learned about volleyball via a quiz.

Lesson Safety

- Make sure that during practice time, students work in the same direction.
- Be vigilant during competition, making sure to stop bullying, unsportsmanlike conduct, or any other negative behavior that competition might bring out.

Motivation

The class just finished a great tournament. Everyone should feel like winners because the real winners are all the people who had fun learning, playing with new classmates, and making new friends. Congratulate teams that made a great comeback, had the best teamwork, and had the best sportsmanship.

Remind students of how they felt when teams were announced. Most thought their goose was cooked because their friends were not on their team. Happily, it looks as if they all made some new friends and developed an appreciation for people they did not know quite as well a few weeks ago. The question now is, do the standings make a couple of play-offs necessary, do they want to stay with their teams for one last challenge, or do they want to play this last day with different teams? And if they want to play with different teams, do they want an all-star game, a battle of the sexes, or any teams of their choice? Take a quick vote.

Warm-Up

Circle volley with team.

Lesson Sequence

1. Distribute quiz and pencils as students arrive. Have them space out and begin the quiz.
2. Collect tests 10 minutes after class starts. If students are not finished, allow them to finish on the sidelines, after school, or during a free class and let the rest of the class get under way.
3. After the vote, send groups to warm up on court.
4. Begin the last volleyball game of the unit.

Review and Stretching

As students stretch, ask questions:

- If you could change anything about this unit, what would it be?
- Did any questions stump you?

Beginner Volleyball Skills Rubric

Name _____ Date _____

Teacher _____ Class _____

	0	1	2	3
Serve	No effort.	• Steps forward on opposite foot. • Uses correct arm motion. • Contacts ball in front.	• Can put ball in play.	• Serves legally. • Can serve in a game.
Bump pass	No effort.	• Prepares with proper arm position and bent knees. • Uses proper follow-through.	• Directs ball upward.	• Moves to and under the ball. • Keeps pass on the same side of the net.
Set	No effort.	• Uses proper hand position. • Bends knees to get under ball. • Follows through.	• Directs ball upward.	• Moves eyes under ball. • Pass travels in a high arc. • Ball reaches destination.
Tip-over	No effort.	• Maintains stance on contact with ball. • Uses proper follow-through.	• Directs ball backward. • Makes effort to clear the ball over net.	• Ball passes over net.
Teamwork, sporting behavior	No effort.	• Keeps eye on ball during play. • Gets to court on time. • Gets along with teammates.	• Rotates properly. • Covers ball in own zone. • Makes effort to improve weaknesses.	• Avoids touching net. • Plays within the rules. • Covers balls inside court.

From Isobel Kleinman, 2009, *Complete Physical Education Plans for Grades 5 to 12, Second Edition* (Champaign, IL: Human Kinetics).

Beginner Volleyball Quiz

Name _____ Date _____

Teacher _____ Class _____

True or False

Read each statement carefully. If the statement is true, write a *T* in the column to the left. If the statement is false, write an *F*. If using a grid sheet, blacken in the appropriate column for each question, making sure to use the correctly numbered line for each question and its answer.

_____ 1. If there are seven players on a volleyball team, only six may play at one time.

_____ 2. Rotation occurs after each point is won.

_____ 3. To follow a legal rotation order, a team must rotate in a clockwise direction.

_____ 4. A ball hitting the net during play always ends the point.

_____ 5. The left back player is the server.

_____ 6. A bump pass is used when it's as if the ball is falling into a player's eyes.

_____ 7. If Nancy hits the first tap and John hits the second, Nancy can hit the third tap.

_____ 8. A server who is off the court when serving is doing something illegal.

_____ 9. Players should open their hands and hit a setup pass if the ball is below the waist.

_____ 10. It is good team strategy to hit the ball away from the strongest player on the other team.

_____ 11. Using a firm arm is bound to be more successful than a soft, feathery arm when you hit a serve.

_____ 12. Volleyball games are 15 points, but they must be played out to find a winner if the score is 14 to 15 because teams cannot win until they are in the lead by 2 points.

_____ 13. If John hits the ball, sending it to Nancy, but she is only able to hit it so it goes straight up in the air, she should hit it again to send it over the net.

_____ 14. Servers should run onto the court as soon as they hit the ball because they are needed to cover the play on the court.

_____ 15. Neither the server nor another player is allowed to touch the net.

Beginner Volleyball Answer Key

True or False

1. T—Only six are allowed on the court at one time; substitution provisions must be made for the extra team members.
2. F—Rotation occurs after a team loses the serve.
3. T
4. F—A ball hitting the net is still in play.
5. F—The right back player is the server.
6. F—The set is used when high passes descend.
7. T—A player can tap the ball twice as long as the taps are not consecutive.
8. F—The serve must be hit from off the court. Once the serve is hit, the server should enter the court.
9. F—The bump pass should be used for balls below the waist. Hands should be closed.
10. T
11. T
12. T
13. F—Nancy cannot hit the ball twice in a row.
14. T
15. T

From Isobel Kleinman, 2009, *Complete Physical Education Plans for Grades 5 to 12, Second Edition* (Champaign, IL: Human Kinetics).

Bump and Set

Facilities

One marked court for every 12 players

Materials

One ball for every four players

Performance Goals

Students will do the following:

- Practice the bump pass.
- Practice the set.
- Play a short game.

Cognitive Goals

Students will review the following:

- The need for high passes
- How to decide whether to use a set or bump pass
- The difference between offensive hits and passing to teammates

Lesson Safety

- Practice areas should be well spaced.
- Reestablish rules for how to deal with errant balls.
    - Do not run across anyone's court to get the ball.
    - Return the ball by throwing it back to the group signaling for it.
    - Return the ball to opponents by sending it under the net.

Motivation

Many of the students enjoyed volleyball before. This unit will build on their skills so games become more exciting and require even more teamwork. Making volleyball a more strategic game is not possible unless players can control the ball on their own side of the court and unless they are able to hit the ball up so it falls near a specific place on the court. Today will be a quick review to renew skills that must have gotten rusty since they were last used. If all goes well, the lesson will end with a short game.

Warm-Up

1. Use mimetics to practice bump and set pass mechanics (see beginner unit for more detail).
    a. Practice each in a stationary position (5 times).
    b. Practice each using proper footwork (5 times).
2. Do 10 jumps, bringing arms straight up.

Lesson Sequence

1. Review the bump pass and the set pass as performed in mimetics.
    a. Choose a drill for personal repetition, such as rallying off the wall.
        - First, have students focus on meeting the ball and sending it up.
        - Second, have students focus on where it goes on the wall.
    b. Remind students of the strategy of each pass.
        - Aim for height with controlled power on the bump.
        - In a game, the bump should not go over the net.
        - In a game, the set should be predictable and accurate.

2. In groups of six, send students to one side of the net to volley in circle.
    a. Have them count their taps and tell you when they kept the ball up 10 times.
    b. If they can keep it alive 15 times, they are ready for a game.
3. Arrange for successful groups to play each other for the remainder of class.
4. Groups that are still aiming for 15 times should continue practicing in circle.

Review and Stretching

As students stretch, review rule issues that came up during the games and rules pertaining to tapping the ball:

- One person can tap it once in succession.
- Each team is allowed three taps.
- Player A can hit, player B follows, and then player A can hit again.
- The ball must clearly come off the hands or forearms without carrying.

Volleyball
INTERMEDIATE
LESSON 2

Overhead Serve

Facilities
One marked court for every 12 players

Materials
One ball for every four players

Performance Goals
Students will do the following:

- Perform an overhead serve.
- Improve their set.

Cognitive Goals
Students will learn the following:

- To think of sending offensive serves onto the court
- The value of accurate passing skills

Lesson Safety
- Practice areas should be well spaced.
- Reestablish rules for how to deal with errant balls.
    - Do not run across anyone's court to get the ball.
    - Return the ball by throwing it back to the group signaling for it.
    - Return the ball to opponents by sending it under the net.

Motivation
If students have watched highly competitive volleyball, they may want to put the ball into play so that it is more difficult for opponents to return. Today's lesson on the overhead serve gives a way to put the ball in play offensively and is also the foundation for hitting a spike—the overhead serve is the same motion with feet on the ground. This serve is more difficult than the underhand serve because the ball is usually tossed, so it is hit while moving. In addition, the arc of the ball is flatter, so it's more difficult to avoid the net and keep it inbounds. Hitting a moving object is more difficult than hitting a stationary object.

Warm-Up

1. Leave the balls out so students can practice.
2. Start mimetics to introduce the overhead serve.
   a. Hold the nonhitting hand in front of the face slightly higher than the forehead.
   b. Bring the elbow of the hitting arm back.
   c. Bring the hitting arm forward so the heel of the hitting hand hits into the palm of the holding hand.
   d. Follow through so the hitting hand ends facing a target.
   e. While stationary, repeat (5 times).
   f. Repeat the arm motion while the weight shifts over the forward foot (5 times).
3. Continue with mimetics for the bump pass and setup pass.
4. Have students rally off the wall.

Lesson Sequence

1. Using every ball, organize practice for the overhead serve (see figure 14.8).
   a. Practice contact by serving toward a target on the wall (3 successes).
   b. Send students to each side of the court to practice serving over the net.
      - Interrupt the class to remind them of the boundary lines.
      - Interrupt the class to remind them of foot-fault violations.
   c. Circulate to emphasize the following:
      - Keeping the wrist firm
      - Meeting the ball with the heel of the hand
      - Imagining a face on the ball and contacting the ball on the nose
      - Continuing the follow-through toward a target
2. Have students get in teams and practice circle volley on half court. After they have kept the ball up 15 times, they are ready for a game.
3. Play practice games, encouraging the following:
   a. Use of the overhead serve
   b. High bump passes to center of the court
   c. Using a second pass—a set

Review and Stretching

As students stretch, ask questions:

- If the ball were a face, where would the point of contact be for the overhead serve?
- Can you hit an overhead serve without tossing it in the air?
- What makes an overhead serve more difficult than an underhand serve?
- Why do you want passes to be high?
- Do you want the ball going over the net to be as high?

Figure 14.8 Overhead serve.

Spiking

Facilities

As many courts as possible for spiking practice in groups of three

Materials

One ball for every three players

Performance Goals

Students will do the following:

- Spike.
- Improve their set.
- Play a game.

Cognitive Goals

Students will learn the following:

- How angles affect spiking success
- Rules around the net:
  - Touching the net is illegal.
  - Players are not allowed to cross the center line.
  - Either player involved in a simultaneous tap or block may hit the ball again.

Lesson Safety

Have groups on one side of the court so they hit their spikes in the same direction.

Motivation

The students have been working up to spiking for 3 years, and today is the day. Even shrimps can spike, although their margin of error is small—everything has to be just right (timing, position behind the ball, being above the net while the ball still is above the net). But, have no fear. Deviations don't have to result in a wild shot. They can result in an offensive volley. So today they all will try spiking. It will be a while before they know who the great spikers of the group will be. For practice, the toss will be important. Today they'll take a look at how they can all practice.

Warm-Up

1. Leave the balls out so students can practice.
2. Lead mimetics.
   a. For the bump pass, set, and overhead serve with footwork
   b. Mechanics for the spike
      - Jump straight up (5 times).
      - During jump, bring the elbow of the hitting arm back and above the head (5 times).
      - At the height of the jump, swing the arm straight up in the air (5 times).
      - Take two steps before jumping, and at the height of the jump, swing the arm up (5 times).

Lesson Sequence

1. Demonstrate the spike (see figure 14.9) and set up for practice.
   a. Use small groups to guarantee as much repetition as possible.
      - A reliable player does all tosses, students move in to spike, and a retriever on the other side of the net returns the ball under the net.
      - Rotate after two tries.
      - Continue until each person in line has gone three or four times.

2. Gather the class to go over the rules at the net.
   - No touching net.
   - No centerline violation.
3. Send them back to spike again, avoiding rule infractions.
4. Circulate, providing coaching hints as they practice.
   - Keep the hitting hand relaxed and open.
   - Bring the hitting arm back as you jump.
   - Time the jump as the ball starts to come down.
   - Get in position so the ball looks as if it is dropping in front of you.
5. Take a few minutes to practice passing while in circles (circle volley).
6. Play practice games, encouraging students to do the following:
   a. Use the overhead serve.
   b. Send bump passes high and to center of the court.
   c. Use a second pass before sending the ball over the net, preferably a set.
   d. Try to make the third tap offensive by using a spike, a deep volley, a hit that changes direction, or by surprising opponents with a tip-over.

Review and Stretching

As students stretch, ask questions:

- What is the value of a spike?
- Is it easy for everyone to do?
- Can players spike if they haven't been set up?
- Did anyone spike during the game?
- Did you get a set from your teammate, or was it a mistake of your opponents that got the ball up for a spike?

Figure 14.9 Spike.

Assessment

- Observe, noting each student's strengths and weaknesses.
- Use weaknesses for planning the next lesson.
- Use strengths to plan how to divide the class into teams.

Setting to a Target

Facilities

One marked court for every 12 players

Materials

One ball for every four players

Performance Goals

Students will do the following:

- Practice setting to a target.
- Practice spiking.
- Play a game.

Cognitive Goals

Students will learn the following:

- That they need good footwork and timing to have a successful spike
- That teams should set to their spikers during a game
- That getting off their feet and meeting a ball above the net is a good offensive strategy even if a hard spike is not the result

Lesson Safety

- Practice areas should be well spaced.
- Follow rules for how to deal with errant balls.

Motivation

Players can't throw the ball up to a spiker in the game. They have to pass it using a set. Setting has become so specialized that many teams have only one setter, but in this lesson everyone will practice using the set so that the spiker can move to the ball, jump, and spike it. It is a shame if a team has great spikers but is unable to set to them.

Warm-Up

1. Leave the balls out so students can practice.
2. Lead mimetics:
   a. Bump pass, set, overhead serve, and spike (5 times each)
   b. Introduce the block (see figure 14.10):
      - Jump, extending arms straight up in the air (5 times).
      - Introduce the block and land with arms still straight up (5 times).

Lesson Sequence

1. Set the class up to work on the set as an offensive skill.
   a. Diagram and demonstrate where the height of the ball should be.
   b. Ask students to self-toss and set the ball at a point of aim against a wall.

c. In the smallest groups for the most repetition, bring students to the net.

- Have them toss to themselves and set to the spiker, with a retriever on the other side.
- Rotate after two tries.
- Continue this practice until everyone has three or four successes.

2. Play practice games, continuing to encourage the following:

a. Using the overhead serve

b. High bump passes to the center of the court

c. Using a second pass—a set

d. Using a third tap, either the offensive volley or spike

Review and Stretching

As students stretch, ask questions:

- Who received good sets while you practiced?
- What made a good set?
- Who received good sets during the game?
- Who was able to spike as a result of a set from a teammate?
- Who was able to spike as a result of a pass coming over the net?
- What makes accurate setting difficult?

Teacher Homework

Divide students into teams that are equal in terms of gender, spikers, setters, and good athletes.

Figure 14.10 Jumping to block.

Tournament Teams

Facilities

One marked court for every 12 players

Materials

One ball for every four players

Performance Goals

Students will do the following:

- Meet and work with new teams.
- Improve their skills.
- Play a game.

Cognitive Goals

Students will learn the following:

- Their tournament team members and their strengths
  - Who their spikers are
  - Who their strongest servers are
  - Who is least likely to control the ball
- That turning before the ball arrives rather than while trying to hit yields better directional control

Lesson Safety

- Practice areas should be well spaced.
- Follow rules for how to deal with errant balls.

Motivation

Announce the tournament teams right away, acknowledging that it will take a few days for teams to get accustomed to each other and figure out who is best at what. When teams meet, they make a circle and practice their sets.

Warm-Up

1. Leave the balls out so students can practice.
2. Lead mimetics.
   a. For the bump pass and set with proper footwork (5 times each)
   b. For the overhead service motion, taking care not to foot fault (5 times)
   c. For the spike (stepping to spot, jumping, swinging at height of jump)
      - Have students check their takeoff and landing spot.
      - Teach students to block momentum so they land where they took off.
      - Explain that they need to do so to avoid net and centerline violations.
      - Teach them to plant their feet after the approach but before jumping.
   d. For the block
      - Have students jump with their arms extended over their head (5 times).
      - Land with arms extended (5 times).
      - Extend the arms so they are slightly angled in direction of the imaginary net and make a wall above their head (5 times).

Lesson Sequence

1. Announce teams and send them to a court to practice circle volleying.
2. Teach turning under the ball to direct passes in a different direction.
   a. Explain the purpose:
      - To learn to set to a specific person
      - To keep control by turning before (not during) the hit
   b. Practice setting and getting to know the team by having students name the person their pass is intended for. If they don't know everyone's name, have them find out before they start.
3. Play practice games, encouraging the following:
   a. Use of the overhead serve
   b. High bump passes to center of the court
   c. Use of a second pass—a set
   d. Use of a third tap, either offensive volley or spike

Review and Stretching

1. Call teams together. Have them elect a captain and cocaptain (girl and boy), asking them to choose someone who has not been captain before.

2. Have captains lead their teams in stretching.

Teacher Homework

Complete and post a chart showing the class tournament schedule. Create and post a chart listing the teams and their captains, leaving space for the results.

Blocking

Facilities

One marked court for every 12 players

Materials

One ball for every four players

Performance Goals

Students will do the following:

- Learn the timing and positioning for the block.
- Play a game.

Cognitive Goals

Students will learn the following:

- Rotation concerns—setters, spikers, best servers
- How to identify spikers on their team

Lesson Safety

Now that tournament play is about to begin and players have not adjusted to their teammates, be vigilant and active about correcting anything that can be perceived as physical or emotional harassment.

Motivation

This is the last practice day before the tournament begins. The purpose of the day is to practice some blocking before trying to organize for round 1, which begins next class.

Warm-Up

1. Leave the balls out so students can practice.

2. Lead mimetics as before, but during spiking do the following:

   a. Toss the ball and ask students to jump as the ball starts to come down.

   b. On the toss, have students take two running steps forward and jump as the ball comes down.

   c. Do same thing, adding the spiking motion at the height of the jump.

   d. Do same thing, but add a foot check. Are they passing the spot on the ground they took off from?

   e. Divide the class in half and have half the class practice timing for the block.

      - Leave the ground as the hitter does (the other half of the class) with arms extended overhead, angled slightly forward.
      - Check the landing. Are students still where they took off?

Lesson Sequence

1. Explain how to make position configurations according to skill.
2. Send teams to practice the set, spike, and block.
3. The class will play rotating games. Go over rules.
   a. On new games, teams can change their rotation order or return to starting lineup.
   b. Encourage teams to do the following:
      - Feel free to change rotation order if needed.
      - Instead of keeping score, just identify the best servers, spikers, and setters and who is best on defense at the net.
4. Play practice games, rotating opponents every 8 minutes.

Review and Stretching

1. As teams stretch, entertain questions.
2. Explain that the game schedule for round 1 will be posted, along with court assignments. To get the most game time, they should meet on the court and begin to circle volley when they come in.

Assessment

- Observe the ball control of each group before class and interaction during play.
- Disrupt any possible harassment of players who are viewed as not good enough.

Volleyball
INTERMEDIATE
LESSON 7

Rotation Order

Facilities

One marked court for every two teams

Materials

- Blackboard or other visual aid to show tournament schedule
- Tournament chart with team standings
- Game and court schedules
- Practice balls and game balls for each court

Performance Goals

Students will do the following:

- Create their rotation order.
- Play round 1 of their tournament.

Cognitive Goals

Students will learn the following:

- How to read and follow the daily tournament schedule
- How to begin the rotation order for each new game
  - Remind them that the receiving team rotates before they serve.
  - Remind them that the first server on the receiving team is in the right front position when the game begins.

Lesson Safety

Be prepared to disrupt psychologically damaging comments to teammates and opponents.

Motivation

This is round 1. Do not start games until both teams are ready. Include at least 5 minutes of warm-up volleying in a circle. Choose for first serve and carefully assign serving order because teams will be stuck with them for the whole class.

Warm-Up

1. Leave the balls out so students can practice.
2. Do the circle volley before games.

Lesson Sequence

1. Post the tournament schedule, team lists, and standings. (See appendix A.)
   a. Enlarge an example for the class to see.
   b. Explain how to read and follow the chart, and announce court assignments.
2. Go over scoring rules for rally scoring.
   a. Points go to any team that won the rally.
   b. Games are over when one team has 25 points and is ahead by 2.
   c. Official matches, which there's not enough class time for, require one team to win three of five sets. If a fifth game needs to be played to decide a winner, it concludes at 15 points when one team leads by 2 points.
3. Play round 1.

Review and Stretching

1. As students stretch with their team, entertain questions.
2. Explain that winning teams get 2 tournament points per game, and tying teams get 1.
3. Collect the results from the captains.

Taking the Offense

Facilities

One marked court for every two teams

Materials

- Blackboard or other visual aid with previous lesson left on
- Updated tournament chart showing team standings
- Game and court schedules
- Practice balls and game balls for each court

Performance Goals

Students will do the following:

- Practice the block.
- Practice offensive skills before the game.
- Use offensive strategies during round 2.

Cognitive Goals

Students will learn the following:

- The importance of practice for improving their skills
- Rules around the net
  - Cannot touch the net
  - Cannot cross the center line

- Rules affecting blocking and spiking
  - A simultaneous tap is not counted as a team tap.
  - If the ball remains on a player's side of the net after a block, can the player tap it again?
  - Back-line players can only spike behind the 10-foot (3-meter) line.

Lesson Safety

Be prepared to disrupt psychologically damaging comments to teammates and opponents.

Motivation

During round 2, teams wanting a more effective offense could profit from spiking and blocking practice, so in addition to warming up their bumps and sets during the circle volley, suggest that they also practice their sets to a spiker and block, using one side of the court. Explain that those who are not designated spikers will still have occasion to hit third taps over, so the time taken to practice spiking or offensive volley (hit the ball deep, trying not to arc it over the net) is worthwhile.

Warm-Up

1. Leave the balls out so students can practice.
2. Lead mimetics.
   a. Spike
      - Include approach steps to a line or spot for takeoff.
      - Check where the feet land so students learn to stop forward motion in the air and don't cause a centerline violation.
   b. Block
      - Have students run to a spot, jump with arms fully extended, and land with arms still up.
      - Check landing. They must learn to block their forward motion so they don't hit the net or go over the center line.

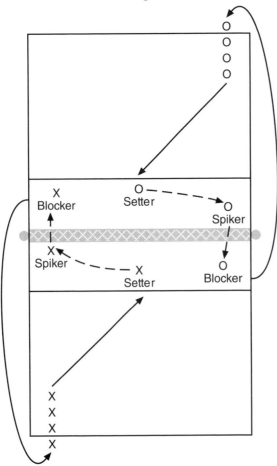

Figure 14.11 Setup for two teams at a net practicing the spike.

Lesson Sequence

1. Use the setup shown in figure 14.11 with teams practicing the set, spike, and block while sharing a court.
2. Explain the rules that affect the success of a block.
   a. Not touching the net
   b. Not landing over the center line
3. Explain what happens when the block is successful and how the rules apply:
   a. If there is a simultaneous tap or block
   b. If the blocked ball remains on the same side of the net whether they can tap it again
4. Take a few more minutes to practice spiking and blocking.

5. When each student gets a sixth shot at spiking and blocking, begin volleying counter-clockwise.

6. Play round 2.

Review and Stretching

As students stretch, do the following:

1. Share an overall problem that you observed.
   - Rushing the game by not taking advantage of all three taps
   - Setting the ball to the wrong place on the front line
   - Taking for granted the serve will go over and missing because they didn't pay attention
   - Being too eager to kill, forcing shots that result in netted balls
2. Entertain questions.
3. Collect the scores.

Ball Control

Facilities

One marked court for every two teams

Materials

- Blackboard or other visual aid with previous lesson left on
- Updated tournament chart showing team standings
- Game and court schedules
- Practice balls and game balls for each court

Performance Goals

Students will do the following:

- Practice their offensive skills before the game begins.
- Play round 3.

Cognitive Goal

Students will learn that control and strategy can make up for being too aggressive and making offensive mistakes.

Lesson Safety

Be prepared to disrupt psychologically damaging comments to teammates and opponents.

Motivation

Announce standings and that it is round 3. Talk about a team being only as strong as its weakest link, how everyone is capable of preventing the ball from hitting the ground, how everyone is capable of making it go up into the air, and how the higher in the air it goes, the better the chances are that a teammate can recover it and send it where it has to go. Remind students that competitive teams have defensive players, one setter, and a couple of spikers and that all they really need to do is depend on everyone for defense and on a couple of team members for offense.

Warm-Up

1. Leave the balls out so students can practice.
2. Lead mimetics for the set, bump, spike, and block as practiced in previous lessons. Include footwork.

Lesson Sequence

1. Have teams practice the tip-over and backward bump pass as saves (see figure 14.5 on page 574 and figure 14.6 on page 575).
   a. Explain the offensive strategy.
      * Going over the blocker and deep
      * Dropping it short if opponents are deep
   b. Practice.
2. Have teams practice volleying clockwise.
3. Gather the class together before beginning games and explain the following:
   a. Keeping the ball on the court is better than dazzling, uncontrolled hits.
   b. Effective team play begins with defense—keeping the ball up.
4. Play round 3.

Review and Stretching

1. As students stretch, share one of the overall problems you observed.
   * Rushing the game by not using all three taps
   * Setting the ball to the wrong place on the front line
   * Taking the serve for granted and missing
   * Not taking advantage when opportunity strikes (other team hits a long set that is dropping on their side of the net)
   * Forcing shots that don't exist (trying to spike when the ball is not higher than the net)
2. Collect the scores.

Assessment

Observe progress with the idea of helping those who lag during practice or for future targeted warm-ups.

Changing Direction on a Set

Facilities

One marked court for every two teams

Materials

* Blackboard or other visual aid with previous lesson left on
* Updated tournament chart showing team standings
* Game and court schedules
* Practice balls and game balls for each court

Performance Goals

Students will do the following:

* Learn to change the ball's direction by turning before the hit.
* Play round 4.

Cognitive Goals

Students will learn the following:

* That back-line players should bump pass to the center of their court
* That using three taps slows the game and gives the team a chance to set up

Lesson Safety

Be prepared to disrupt psychologically damaging comments to teammates or opponents.

Motivation

Announce round 4 and the standings. Tell them how proud you are of the development of skills, teamwork, use of offense, exceptional saves, or whatever has been happening that you can compliment. Make students smile at their own success.

Warm-Up

1. Leave the balls out so students can practice.
2. Lead mimetics.

   a. Receiving a pass, turning under the ball, facing counterclockwise, and setting to person on the right (5 times)

   b. Receiving a pass, turning under the ball, facing clockwise, and passing to the left (5 times)

   c. Three running steps and jumping to spike (5 times)

   d. Three running steps and jumping to block (5 times)

Lesson Sequence

1. Remind the back line of the following:

   a. Don't send the ball over the net.

   b. Bump to the center of the court.

2. Have teams practice volleying in a circle and direct the ball counterclockwise.
3. Play round 4.

Review and Stretching

While students stretch, do the following:

- Discuss problems, ideas, and positive situations that arose in play.
- Entertain questions.
- Collect scores.

Skill-Specific Team Warm-Up

Facilities

One marked court for every two teams

Materials

- Blackboard or other visual aid
- Practice balls and one game ball for each court

Performance Goal

Students will play round 5.

Cognitive Goals

Students will review concepts:

- Backing up a teammate, not taking over, and why
- That a ball is not dead when it hits the net; recovery is possible
- That anticipation helps
  - How to anticipate a spike and how to prepare
  - The possible winning angles a player has when hitting

599

Lesson Safety

Maintain vigilance about the psychosocial climate during competition, making sure that it is a sound, enjoyable experience for all.

Motivation

Round 5 is the last game of the first round-robin (in a six-team tournament). It is the last class where so much time will be set aside for practicing. In this pregame warm-up, each team will have two balls. Captains can decide to practice anything as long as it doesn't interfere with the team sharing the court. Some of the players might need more practice serving, setting, or bumping, whereas others might want to tone up their spike and block. Tell students to use the time wisely as they go to the scheduled court and continue practicing until they hear a signal to start the games.

Announce standings after four rounds.

Warm-Up

1. Leave the balls out so students can practice.
2. Lead mimetics for the team to set, jump and spike, jump and block, and bump to the right, forward, and back.

Lesson Sequence

1. Teams have self-directed practice on their scheduled court with captains deciding what their team needs to practice and whether they need a few work stations on their court.
2. Gather the class together at the blackboard and review the following:
   a. The difference between backing up a teammate and taking over
   b. That the ball is not dead when it hits the net; recovery is possible
   c. That anticipation is half the game
      - Is the ball is coming down in front of a spiker? What should they expect if it is?
      - What angles can the player hit the ball at?
3. Play round 5.

Review and Stretching

While students stretch, collect the scores and ask questions:
- What are the negative effects of players taking over for teammates?
- Will a ball hitting the center of the net come out or roll down?
- If the bump pass goes to the center of the court, what should the second pass be for? The third?

Assessment

Begin assessing student performance using the intermediate skills rubric.

Volleyball
INTERMEDIATE
LESSON 12

Match Play

Facilities

One marked court for every two teams

Materials

- Updated tournament standings
- Blackboard or other visual aid
- Practice balls and one game ball for each court

600

Performance Goals

Students will do the following:

- Simulate the multiple games in match play.
- Play round 6.

Cognitive Goals

Students will learn the following:

- Match play
  - Official
  - Class modifications of official match play
- How to use every minute to accumulate more tournament points

Lesson Safety

Maintain vigilance about the psychosocial climate during competition, making sure that it is a sound, enjoyable experience for all.

Motivation

Announce round 6, the tournament point accumulations and standings to date, and that match play is about to begin. Explain that match play can be fruitful for teams that started out slowly but have learned a lot since the unit began; they can win many more tournament points if they can win multiple games in one class.

Explain the following:

- Game ends at 15 points when one team is ahead by 2.
- After each game, switch sides of the court.
- Every new game should start with original starting lineup.
- If the game is incomplete when the playing time ends, score as follows:
  - A win is recorded for teams with 8 points who are ahead by 2.
  - A tie is awarded when teams have at least 8 points, with neither ahead by 2.

Warm-Up

Leave the balls out so students can practice.

Lesson Sequence

1. Warm up on court assigned for round 6.
2. Play round 6.

Review and Stretching

While students stretch, collect scores.

Tournament Matches

Facilities

One marked court for every two teams

Materials

- Performance rubric for intermediate volleyball
- Updated tournament standings
- Blackboard or other visual aide
- Practice balls and one game ball for each court

Performance Goal

Students will play multiple games, completing rounds 7, 8, 9, and 10.

Cognitive Goals

Students will learn the following:

- To value and maintain good sportsmanship
- To explore other strategies during their matches
  - Do the unexpected (look as if spiking but hit soft).
  - Change direction of hit.
  - Send ball deep.
  - Hit to the weak player on the other side of the court.

Lesson Safety

Maintain vigilance about the psychosocial climate during competition, making sure that it is a sound, enjoyable experience for all.

Motivation

Express that the class has been terrific. Tell them that over the next few lessons you will be evaluating their skills as posted on the skills rubric. Announce the standings.

Warm-Up

Leave the balls out so students can practice.

Lesson Sequence

1. Explain a strategy of the day (see examples in cognitive goals).
2. Explain and post grading standards.
3. Practice on court for rounds.
4. Play rounds.

Review and Stretching

1. As students stretch, ask questions:
   - Did anyone exercise the right to look tough and hit soft?
   - Did anyone serve to different spots on the court?
2. Entertain questions and collect scores.

Assessment

Grades will be based on the level reached in the performance rubric. The teacher, a friend, a teammate, or a third-party student may evaluate using the rubric.

Volleyball
INTERMEDIATE
LESSON 17

Quiz and Final Event

Facilities

One marked court for every two teams

Materials

- One quiz for each student
- Pens and pencils
- At least one ball for every six players

Performance Goals

Students will do the following:

- Take a quiz.
- Choose their final volleyball event.
- Play their last class volleyball game.

Cognitive Goals

Students will evaluate their understanding of volleyball via a quiz.

Motivation

Compliment the play of the tournament. Announce the standings.

Warm-Up

Leave the balls out so students can practice.

Lesson Sequence

1. Distribute the quiz while inviting final questions.
2. After 10 minutes, collect quizzes. Make arrangements with students who need more time to complete the test while the class is playing or during study hall, lunch, or after school.
3. Review standings. Pay personal compliments for play, improvement, assists, spikes, sportsmanship, leadership, and so on.
4. Assign play-off teams to their courts. Have them warm up for a few minutes with the circle volley.
5. Teams not involved in play-offs should choose how they want to play their last volleyball game and then warm up doing the circle volley. They have four choices:
   a. Play-offs if necessary
   b. All-star game
   c. Contest with friends
   d. Stick with tournament teams for a rematch against opponents of their choice
6. Play games.

Review and Stretching

While students stretch, respond to questions about the quiz.

Intermediate Volleyball Skills Rubric

Name _____ Date _____

Teacher _____ Class _____

	0	1	2	3
Serve	No effort.	• Uses proper body mechanics. • Has inconsistent success. • Serves behind service line.	• Consistently puts ball in play. • Performs legal serve.	• Has good placement. • Has good speed.
Bump pass	No effort.	• Uses proper body mechanics. • Can direct upward arc. • Makes legal contact with the ball.	• Moves under ball. • Directs ball upward after moving to it.	• Pass stays on the same side of the net. • Can direct the ball to spot or player.
Set	No effort.	• Has proper body mechanics. • Performs legal upward tap.	• Moves eyes under ball to tap legally.	• Controls direction, height, and target. • Will send over if third tap.
Strategy	No effort.	• Tries to send third tap over the net.	• Uses speed and direction for taps going over net. • Makes effort to set or to spike.	• Spikes or uses third tap offensively. • Has depth, speed, and direction.
Teamwork, sporting behavior	No effort.	• Avoids rules. • Blames others.	• Tries to improve. • Works well with team. • Violations are unintentional.	• Plays within rules. • Is a team leader. • Helps others.

From Isobel Kleinman, 2009, *Complete Physical Education Plans for Grades 5 to 12, Second Edition* (Champaign, IL: Human Kinetics).

Intermediate Volleyball Quiz

Name _____ Date _____

Teacher _____ Class _____

Referring to the diagram will help you to understand some of the questions. Read each statement carefully. If the statement is true, write a *T* in the column to the left. If the statement is false, write an *F*. If using a grid sheet, blacken in the appropriate column for each question, making sure to use the correctly numbered line for each question and its answer.

_____ 1. According to the diagram, the gold team will be serving first.

_____ 2. Player 3 on either team can legally spike a ball set up at the net.

_____ 3. Player 5 on the purple team may not spike in front of the 10-foot (3-meter) line.

_____ 4. Purple 1 will commit a service violation if remaining in place on the court when she serves.

_____ 5. The team that serves first during the first game is the team that must serve first in the second game.

_____ 6. If playing time ends when the score is 8 to 7 with the purple team in the lead, the game is a tie.

_____ 7. Volleyball players may not enter the other team's court even if they go over the center line an inch.

_____ 8. If the ball has been hit, players may contact the net on the follow-through.

_____ 9. Opposing blockers and spikers may hit the ball a second time if the ball was hit by both of them but didn't go anywhere.

_____ 10. The best first-tap strategy for the gold team is to bump the ball to area 4.

6		
	Gold team	4
	5	
	10-foot line	
1	2	3
		2
4	3	
	10-foot line	
	Purple team	
	6	
5		
		1

Matching Questions

Read one numbered item at a time. Then look at each of the possible choices in the column on the right. Decide which item in the right-hand column best matches with one in the left-hand column. Put the corresponding letter on the blank space to left of the number it best matches.

_____ 1. legal limit of taps per team   a. spike

_____ 2. number of team players on court   b. 15

_____ 3. skill used by teammate   c. 6

_____ 4. back line cannot spike closer than   d. 2 points

_____ 5. team serves twice and neither serve is returned   e. 3

_____ 6. number of points one player can get in a game   f. 10-foot line

_____ 7. kill shot   g. set

_____ 8. surprise   h. reverse set

From Isobel Kleinman, 2009, *Complete Physical Education Plans for Grades 5 to 12, Second Edition* (Champaign, IL: Human Kinetics).

Intermediate Volleyball Answer Key

Diagram Questions

1. F—Purple will be serving first; the first server is in the proper place in the rotation order.
2. T—Both are net players.
3. T—Player 5 is still a back-line player and may only spike from behind the 10-foot (3-meter) line.
4. T—The server must move off the court until the serve is hit.
5. F—Teams alternate who serves first at the beginning of each new game in a match.
6. T—Unless one team leads by 2 points, the game is a tie.
7. T—Crossing the center line is a centerline violation.
8. F—Touching the net is illegal at any time.
9. T
10. F—The best bump pass goes to the middle of the court.

Matching Questions

1. e
2. c
3. g
4. f
5. d
6. b
7. a
8. h

Review Basic Skills

Facilities

- Wall with no obstructions
- Taut net
- Court marked with boundaries and a 10-foot (3-meter) line

Materials

One ball for every four players

Performance Goals

Students will practice the following:

- Bump pass
- Set
- Overhead serve
- Playing the game

Cognitive Goals

Students will review the following:

- Need for controlling bumps so they reach the middle of the court
- Goal of setting the ball so it will drop at a specific place
- Need for a team to break down into specific defensive and offensive skills

Lesson Safety

- Leave at least 15 feet (4.5 meters) between groups.
- Reestablish rules for how to deal with errant balls.

Motivation

At the advanced level, students have the skills necessary to play and the ability to start to make that play more challenging. Since the students can all hit the ball, the goal for this unit will be to get them to hit it where they want it to go—to win. That strategy requires control, planning, and taking advantage of the individual strengths of each team member because, as they should know by now, no one player can do it all. In years past, many spikes that occurred were almost by accident. Often sets that were too long turned out to be wonderful for the front line of the opposing team. The goal for the day will be to control the sets and bumps so that they go where they are intended to go.

Warm-Up

1. Leave the balls out so students can practice.
2. Lead mimetics with footwork for the overhead serve, bump pass, set, block, and spike.

Lesson Sequence

1. Review the bump pass.
   a. Stress footwork and follow-through for control and placement.
   b. Drill from low toss, aiming to return the bump to the person tossing.
   c. Speed up the toss on each new turn.
2. Review set.
   a. Stress footwork and follow-through for control.
   b. Begin with setting to a spot on the wall, rallying the ball back.

    c. To improve footwork and speed, use the set-to-wall drill. In relay formation, player 1 sets to the wall and then runs to the back of the line. Player 2 moves under the rebounding ball, sets, and moves to back of line. Player 3 moves under the rebounding ball and sets it back to the wall, and so on.

3. Practice overhead serves (minimum of 10 serves).
4. Allow games if practice seems too long and students lose motivation.

Review and Stretching

While students are stretching, review illegal tap rules and any rules that come up during games.

Assessment

Observe students' ball control to determine if they are ready to proceed with lesson 2 and the best way to break class into teams.

Spiking

Facilities

- Marked volleyball court with 10-foot (3-meter) lines for every 12 players
- Additional practice nets for students to work in threes

Materials

One ball for every three players

Performance Goals

Students will do the following:

- Review the spike.
- Develop a spike or offensive volley.
- Play a short game.

Cognitive Goals

Students will review the following:

- Mechanics of the spike:
  - Timing of the jump
  - Sequence of footwork, jump, and arm motion
  - Why they need to block their forward motion on landing
- Rules around the net
  - No reaching over the net to meet the ball
  - No touching the net during the play
  - No crossing the center line

Lesson Safety

- Groups need a minimum of 15 feet (4.5 meters) between each other for practice.
- Reinforce established routines for dealing with errant balls.

Motivation

The only offensive skill students will practice is the spike. Other offensive efforts require thinking and outwitting the opponent. During this lesson, they will practice the set and spike with friends. Tell students to allow their friends to coach them a bit. With a hint here or there, they might be able to make adjustments that will help them be more successful. For instance, a friend might notice that another friend jumps too late or runs under the path of the ball before leaving the ground. Both of these would cause problems. The first would make the ball go into the net and the second would lead to hitting out of bounds. If friends see that another friend swings too hard and is finished before the ball arrives or notice that a friend has not adjusted the takeoff to an improperly placed set, they might be able to help. Tell students to use their insights. As always, you will also be there to offer advice. If you're not there at the moment, remind them to just ask for help.

Warm-Up

1. Leave the balls out so students can practice.
2. Lead mimetics with footwork for the bump, set, overhead serve, spike, and block.

Lesson Sequence

1. Demonstrate and review the spike. Through demonstration, teach results of the following:
   a. Overrunning the ball
   b. Jumping too late
   c. •Jumping too early
   d. Swinging too late
2. Drill in groups of three.
   a. Demonstrate positioning of setter, spiker, and retriever. (Rotate spikers after they have three spiking or offensive volley successes.)
   b. Rather than have students wait, send groups to the wall for a three-person wall-volley shuttle.
   c. Rotate stations after everyone in the spiking group has three successes.
3. Allow games if practice seems too long and students lose motivation.

Review and Stretching

As students stretch, review rules around the net:

- Centerline violations (cannot cross the center line)
- Net violation (cannot touch net)
- Taking a second tap after a block is legal
- Cannot reach over the net to hit or follow through

Assessment

This review moves rather quickly. If the students are not up to it and if you have not been able to figure out who the best spikers, setters, and defensive players are, it would be difficult to move on to lesson 3, which teaches specialization on the court.

Teacher Homework

Create tournament teams, making certain to include an equal number of spikers, setters, and defensive players on each team so that the teams are as even as possible.

Volleyball
ADVANCED
LESSON 3

Team Roles

Facilities

- One marked court for every 12 players
- Additional practice nets for students to work in threes

Materials

One ball for every three players

Performance Goals

Students will do the following:

- Meet their tournament teammates.
- Play practice games.
- Choose captain and cocaptains.

Cognitive Goals

Students will learn the following:

- To identify how their strengths fit with those of their teammates
- The concept and rules applying to interchange of positions
- To define their role on their team as defense, offense, or setter

Lesson Safety

- Groups need a minimum of 15 feet (4.5 meters) between each other for practice.
- Reinforce established routines for dealing with errant balls.

Motivation

Some students must have thought that learning all about spiking and blocking was pretty stupid; after all, there are at least four people who play with them who they think are better at it. And if they are short and near the net and they see someone jumping up on the other side of the net to spike, all they probably want to do is run away. Unless they have been on a competitive interscholastic team or have seen their games, they probably don't realize that some people on the team never set and others never spike or block. They have positions just as they do in all the other team sports they have learned. Today you're going to explain how that works and how to do it legally so that students can begin to organize in their new teams.

Warm-Up

Lead mimetics:

1. Bump a ball on the right so it goes to the left (5 times). Reverse (5 times).
2. Turn under a high pass and use set to send it in a different direction.
3. Approach (a spot), jump, spike, and land in the same place.
4. Approach (a spot), jump, block, and land in place.

Lesson Sequence

1. Announce teams and send them to a court to practice controlled passing.
   a. In a circle, pass the ball to a person whose name the passer calls before the hit.
   b. Pass the ball to the person on the right or counterclockwise.
2. Demonstrate how to interchange positions legally and explain applicable rules.
   a. Players must be in the proper rotation order before and during the serve.
   b. Players can go anywhere to play the ball once the serve is struck.
   c. Back-line players may not spike if they are in front of the 10-foot (3-meter) line.
3. Show how court is broken down—where the setter goes and where the spiker waits.
4. Play games.

Review and Stretching

1. As students stretch, entertain questions.
2. Ask teams to identify two spikers and their best setter. Declare the others the defense.

Assessment

Observe students:

- Confirm that new teams are well balanced.
- Beware of conflict and intercede to get groups working cooperatively.

Interchanging Positions

Facilities

- One marked court for every 12 players
- Additional practice nets for students to work in threes

Materials

One ball for every three players

Performance Goals

Students will do the following:

- Continue to improve their skills.
- Experiment with specialized roles as defender, setter, or spiker.
- Play games, interchanging positions.

Cognitive Goals

Students will learn the following:

- Reasons for interchanging positions
- To assume a role for their team

Lesson Safety

- Groups need a minimum of 15 feet (4.5 meters) between each other for practice.
- Reinforce established routines for dealing with errant balls.

Motivation

The objective today is to get used to changing positions as soon as the serve is hit. Getting used to moving on the serve is going to take a while, but the results will be worth the effort. The tricky part is going back to original spots in the service order when the next person serves. That means if they are server 3, they must be between servers 2 and 4 during service.

Warm-Up

1. Leave the balls out so students can practice.
2. Lead mimetics.
   a. Changing direction on sets and bumps
   b. Approach, jump, spike, and balanced landing
   c. Approach, jump, block, and balanced landing

Lesson Sequence

1. Explain the role of each position.
   a. Defense plays the deep balls, bump passing to the center of the court.
   b. Setters receive bump passes and redirect them to the corner of the court.
   c. Spikers are ready to approach sets sent to the corner of the court.
2. Announce courts and send teams to practice in a circle. Ask students to pass to the right, left, or across as they practice.
3. Play games.

Review and Stretching

As students stretch, ask questions:

- Have you identified the spikers, setter, and defense?
- The master plan hinges on execution. If the first pass isn't sent to the center of the court, the setter cannot set. Does that mean letting the ball drop?
- What should you do when the master plan doesn't work?

Assessment

Observe common problems to share during the review or next lesson.

Rotation Order

Facilities

- One marked court for every 12 players
- Additional practice nets for students to work in threes

Materials

- Blackboard or other visual aid
- One ball for every three players

Performance Goal

Students will play games, interchanging positions and rotating against opponents.

Cognitive Goals

Students will learn the following:

- The value of their role during the game
- The best rotation order for their team

Lesson Safety

- Groups need a minimum of 15 feet (4.5 meters) between each other for practice.
- Reinforce established routines for dealing with errant balls.

Motivation

On the last practice day before the tournament, answer any questions students have about taking on a job for the team. Encourage them to be their own coaches and remind them that you are there to assist. As they play their rotating games, ask them to rearrange their rotation order so they take advantage of their team assets.

Warm-Up

1. Leave the balls out so students can practice.
2. Lead mimetics.
   a. Use a ball toss so that students learn to time their jump to spike (5 times).
   b. Use a ball toss so that students learn to time their jump to block (5 times).

Lesson Sequence

1. Review considerations for rotation order.
   a. Best net player (left front should be strongest hitter)
   b. Defensive player who is a fine server (right front serves often)
   c. Second best spiker (right back so a spiker is always rotating at the net)
   d. Best setter (center front)
   e. Setter (center back)
2. Send teams to courts to play.
   a. Volley in a circle.
   b. Stop games every 8 minutes.
      - Have teams switch courts and adjust the rotation order until they feel they have the best arrangement.
      - Continue switching games every 8 minutes.

Review and Stretching

As students stretch, ask questions:

- Are you getting used to the off-the-ball movement on the court?
- Do you like it better?
- Who was confused when you had to save a ball you did not anticipate having to save because it was not your job?
- Do you have any questions?

Student Homework

Have captains write up their team lineup.

Teacher Homework

Complete and post tournament schedules and team standings.

Scoring Round 1

Facilities

One marked volleyball court for every two teams

Materials

- Three balls for every team
- Tournament charts posted and updated after each round
- One game ball for each court

Performance Goal

Students will play round 1 of a double round-robin tournament.

Cognitive Goals

Students will learn the following:

- How matches will be scored
- To take responsibility for their own performance
- To play with good sporting behavior
- To anticipate their opponents' abilities
- To enjoy their teammates' success

Lesson Safety

- During warm-up, teams must keep the balls on their side (right or left) of the court until everyone is allowed serving practice.
- Be vigilant about unsporting behavior, particularly if it threatens the physical or emotional health of the class. Students who lose control must be taught to make amends (apologize for hurting someone physically or emotionally) and correct their behavior.

Motivation

The tournament is starting and students will be excited. During the first round of the double round-robin, they will duplicate how teams warm up for games. Therefore, half the class will be a timed warm-up as teams so they can improve their advanced skills in the bump-set-spike strategy.

Warm-Up

1. Leave the balls out so students can practice.
2. Lead mimetics: Toss the ball so students learn to time the jump for the spike and block.

Lesson Sequence

1. Explain the following:
   a. Posted schedule and court assignments
   b. A winning game
      - In side-out scoring, a winning game is 15 points and ahead by 2.
      - In rally scoring, a winning game is 25 points and ahead by 2.
      - If games end early, do not start a second game. Use the time to practice the things that need improvement.
2. Send teams to their courts with three balls each for a timed practice. Give 3 minutes for serving, 3 for passing, and 3 for spiking and blocking.
3. Play games.

Review and Stretching

1. As students stretch, ask questions:
   - Did the rotation order turn out to be as good as you thought?
   - Does any team want to officially change it? Captains can legally change the rotation order but it must be designated in writing and followed throughout the game. If changing it, captains should write out the change before next class and bring it with them.
2. Entertain questions.
3. Collect game scores.

Assessment

Officiate and observe for coaching hints for specific teams.

Student Homework

Captains review service order.

Rounds 2-5 of First Round Robin

Facilities

One marked volleyball court for every two teams

Materials

- Three balls for every team
- Tournament charts posted and updated after each round
- One game ball for each court

Performance Goals

Students will do the following:

- Improve passes, spikes, blocks, and serves.
- Complete the first round-robin tournament, playing rounds 2 through 5.

Cognitive Goals

Students will learn the following:

- To take responsibility for improving their performance
- To maintain a sense of sportsmanship and fair play no matter how heated the competition
- To applaud their teammates' success

Lesson Safety

- During warm-up, teams must keep the balls on their side (right or left) of the court until everyone is allowed serving practice.
- Be vigilant about unsporting behavior, particularly if it threatens the physical or emotional health of the class. Students who lose control must be taught to make amends (apologize for hurting someone physically or emotionally) and correct their behavior.

Motivation

Announce standings and point count. Ask if any teams need help. Remind students that you will let them know when the 3 minutes for service practice is over, as well as practice for bumps, sets, spikes, and blocks.

Lesson Sequence

1. Teams meet on assigned courts.
   a. Captains choose for first serve.
   b. Teams practice serving, volleying, and spiking and blocks.
2. Play the tournament games.

Review and Stretching

As students stretch, do the following:

- Collect scores.
- Entertain questions.
- Comment about an aspect of the day's play.

Announce that in order to get the most out of match play, when students come in for the next class they should go directly to their courts and begin practicing so the matches will get under way more quickly.

Assessment

Observe while officiating. Use observations about play during the review.

Student Homework

Captains should review the service order to make it efficient.

Second Round Robin

Facilities

One marked volleyball court for every two teams

Materials

- Updated team standings
- Advanced performance rubric
- All practice balls and one game ball for each court

Performance Goal

Students will play a second round-robin tournament using match play.

Cognitive Goals

Students will learn the following:

- To focus on the future and let go of previous mistakes
- To use their knowledge about opponents to play offensive strategy
- To reinforce each other
- To recognize individual accomplishment

Lesson Safety

In the advent of match play, highly competitive students will be intense about the use of time and their scores. Guard against difficulties that might arise if tempers flare.

Motivation

Announce standings and the beginning of match play. Today there will be tournament credit for every game completed. Encourage students not to waste time. If they can win more than one game in a day, their tournament results can dramatically change the standings. From here on, games will be actively officiated. Wish them luck.

Warm-Up

Teams meet on court and begin warming up as they arrive.

Lesson Sequence

1. Students meet on their courts.
    a. Teams practice.
    b. Each day before games begin, ask a different thought question:
        - Everyone pat the person who makes the kill shot on the back. Today, acknowledge the great sets and the setter who enables the spiker to spike.
        - When was the last time you recognized the outstanding job your defenders do to keep the ball in play? Start today if you have not already.
        - What are your choices if a big blocker or spiker is facing you down on the other side of the net and you have the ball?
        - Have you recognized the accomplishment of the person on your team who is so into winning but does not explode or make you feel bad when you make a mistake?
        - Think about your teammates. Think about how you felt when the team first organized. Think about whose personal effort made the biggest leap forward during these last few weeks. Maybe you can let your teammates know how much you appreciate their effort.
2. Play matches.

Review and Stretching

As students stretch, do the following:

- Get scores.
- Review strategies that might improve their play next class.
- On the last day of the tournament, remind students that they will have a quiz and invite any questions that remain.

Assessment

- Post assessment goals and answer any questions related to it.
- Begin the skills evaluation process during match play.

Quiz and Final Event

Facilities

One marked volleyball court for every two teams

Materials

- One quiz for each student
- Pens or pencils
- Complete chart of team records
- One volleyball for each game

Performance Goals

Students will do the following:

- Take a volleyball quiz.
- Choose a culminating activity.

Cognitive Goals

Students will learn the following:

- An objective measure of their understanding of volleyball
- What they achieved in the unit via public recognition for their accomplishments

Lesson Safety

Use established rules.

Motivation

Explain that for the day, how they play and with whom is up to a class vote since this is the last day of volleyball.

Lesson Sequence

1. As students enter the gym, distribute the quiz and pencils.
   a. Students should find a place to sit alone and begin immediately.
   b. After 10 minutes, collect quizzes (students who are not done may finish on the sidelines).
2. Take a vote on how they want to play for the last day.
   a. New team
   b. All-girls and all-boys games
   c. Requests for rematches
3. Play games.

Review

1. Congratulate class on accomplishments, being as specific as possible and crediting as many students and good plays as possible.
2. Announce the final standings of the tournament.

Assessment

- Rate students' skills according to posted assessment goals.
- Grade quizzes.

Advanced Volleyball Skills Rubric

Name _____ Date _____

Teacher _____ Class _____

	0	1	2	3	4	5
Skills	No effort.	• Serves legally. • Blocks most incoming balls up. • Uses correct body mechanics.	• Has consistent serve. • Bump pass goes to center of court. • Developing a specialty.	• Can serve deep. • Interchanges position to fit team strategy. • First and second tap remain on own side.	• Varies speed, depth, and direction of serve. • Either directs pass to setter or spiker or spikes.	• Has attacking serve. • Defense is offensive when necessary. • Net person varies touch and anticipates blocks. • Setter can set backward.
Strategy	No effort.	• Hits ball over net on first or second tap. • Concentrates on play. • Tries to take over.	• Moves to prevent ball from landing on own side. • Sets up team's attacker. • Tries to send third tap over net.	• Plays a specialty in bump-set-spike strategy. • Anticipates teammates. • Varies depth, direction, and speed on hit over.	• Interchanges correctly. • Will back up, not take over. • Anticipates angles of opponent's attack.	• Helps team focus and adjust when losing. • Can detect deficiencies and redirect focus constructively.
Teamwork, sporting behavior	No effort.	• Blames others. • Needs supervision to stay on task. • Interferes with other team.	• Gets to court on time. • Warms up with team. • Plays within the rules.	• Works well with teammates. • Takes responsibility for position.	• Consistently tries to play at personal best. • Recognizes good teammate effort and success. • Shows good sportsmanship.	• Inspires team. • Will back up, not take over. • Shows reliable, consistent leadership. • Helps team members personally improve.

Advanced Volleyball Quiz

Name _____ Date _____

Teacher _____ Class _____

True or False

Read each statement carefully. If the statement is true, write a *T* in the column to the left. If the statement is false, write an *F*. If using a grid sheet, blacken in the appropriate column for each question, making sure to use the correctly numbered line for each question and its answer.

_____ 1. It is better to spike a ball dropping slightly in front of your face than to try to spike it when it drops behind your head.

_____ 2. The setter should stay in rotation and wait there for the set.

_____ 3. It is illegal to post a two-person block.

_____ 4. If the ball bounces off your shoulder and goes over the net, the other team must play it.

_____ 5. Neither the spiker nor the blocker can reach over the net.

_____ 6. A server can legally step inside the court before contacting the serve.

_____ 7. When the game seems to be going too fast, the best way to slow it down is to use one hit and send the ball back over the net immediately.

_____ 8. The right back player will be the last server if your opponents have the first serve.

_____ 9. The bump pass is the only passing skill that every person on the team must be able to execute.

_____ 10. Going down the line is a placement strategy for serves and third taps.

From Isobel Kleinman, 2009, *Complete Physical Education Plans for Grades 5 to 12, Second Edition* (Champaign, IL: Human Kinetics).

Advanced Volleyball Answer Key

True or False

1. T
2. F—Once the server has hit the ball, players should move into their positions.
3. F—It is legal, and good strategy, to post a two-person block.
4. T
5. T
6. F—The server must remain outside the court during service.
7. F—To slow the pace of the game, teams should use all three of their taps to send the ball over the net.
8. T
9. T
10. T

PART V

Individual and Dual Activity Units

Badminton

15

Chapter Overview

1. Introduce one skill at a time:
   - Short serve
   - Overhead clear
   - Long serve
   - Underhand clear
   - Smash
   - Forehand and backhand drives
   - Directing shuttlecock from left to right
   - Hairpin shot
2. Teach rules of the game as the skill being taught is presented:
   - Serve—Teach serving rules (short, out of bounds, turn of service).
   - Once game play begins—Teach scoring, boundaries, order of receiving, and positioning.
   - Once tournament begins—Review all game rules and teach court and skills strategies, such as strategies for the smash.
3. Teach the reliability of smashing from different distances.
4. Go over the laws of trajectory and angles.
5. Discuss the concept of probability with a net in the way.
   - Doubles strategies
   - Playing matches instead of games

Badminton Study Sheet

Fun Facts

- Badminton originally was played without a net with the objective of keeping a rally going as long as possible.
- Badminton evolved from a child's game in India called *battledore and shuttlecock*.
- Shuttlecocks can travel at speeds of up to 200 miles (322 kilometers) per hour.
- Badminton joined the Olympic Games in 1992.
- The shuttlecock has been often called a *birdie* because it is made of feathers.

History

Badminton did not get its name until it was played at Badminton, the country estate of the Duke of Beaufort, in 1893, though different forms of the game were played thousands of years earlier in ancient Greece and China. The game arrived in Britain in the early 1870s thanks to some military officers who served in India and returned home with equipment for a competitive game called *poona*. The Duke of Beaufort officially introduced the game to his party guests and its popularity grew among the elite who came to call it the Badminton game. By 1896, with more than 14 clubs actively playing badminton, the British standardized its rules. The International Badminton Association is still housed in England.

Skills

- Serves (putting the shuttlecock into play):
  - Short serve—With racket foot forward, handle and racket head lower than the waist, and a backhand grip, push forearm forward, hyperextending the wrist.
  - High serve—In forward stride position (non-racket-foot forward), reach the racket beneath the dropping shuttlecock. Swing so the butt of the racket leads. Finish with a sharp wrist snap. Follow through so the racket comes up across the body and the face is up.
- Clearing shots (keeping opponents in backcourt):
  - Overhead clear—Get under the dropping shuttlecock. Bring both arms up so the racket is behind the head and the racket elbow is up. On contact, extend the racket arm quickly, with the racket facing up through most of the swing. Finish with a crisp wrist snap.
  - Underhand clear—Same instructions as for the high serve.
- Attacking shot or smash (finishing the point)—Prepare as you would for an overhead clear, with both arms up as you position yourself to be slightly in back of the dropping shuttlecock. Make sure to contact the shuttlecock above and in front of your face. Swing and follow through as you would in the overhead clear. This shot cannot be successful from deep in the court because it will not clear the net.
- Touch shots:
  - Overhead drop shot—Prepare for overhead clear, arms up, weight on back foot, swing up to contact the shuttlecock above and slightly closer to the net than you. Soften grip on racket on contact, stop the wrist snap, and limit the follow-through so that the racket pushes the shuttlecock just over the net toward the sideline.
  - Hairpin shot—Run in to return a drop shot. Use an open racket face. Contact with a soft touch, flicking the wrist to make the shot barely clear the net.

»continued

 From Isobel Kleinman, 2009, *Complete Physical Education Plans for Grades 5 to 12, Second Edition* (Champaign, IL: Human Kinetics).

»continued

Rules

- Doubles serving
    - The server on the right side begins.
    - A server continues his turn of service until put out.
    - Server must alternate the box he serves from.
    - Serves must pass over the net, beyond the short line, and land on or inside the diagonal service box.
    - Both hands have a turn of service (except on the first service of each game).
    - The second hand to serve must serve from the box she was in when the serve went to her.
- Singles serving
    - If the score is even (e.g., 0, 2, 4, 6, 8), the server serves from the box on the right.
    - If the score is odd (e.g., 1, 3, 5, 7, 9), the server serves from the box on the left.

Scoring

As in volleyball, scoring can follow the side-out scoring system, in which case a team wins a point only when serving, or it can follow the rally scoring system, meaning that the team that wins the rally wins the point.

Whoever wins 15 points (side-out system; 21 in rally scoring) wins the game. However, when the score reaches 20–all, the team that leads by 2 points first wins the game. If the score gets to be 29–all, the winner is the team first scoring 30.

Match Play

- The team winning the previous game serves first.
- The best of three games wins the match.

Positioning Strategies

- Up and back (forward and back): The strongest player covers two-thirds of the court, taking a center position two-thirds back from the net. The net player plays a center position in forecourt, on or near where the short line meets the centerline.
- Side by side (parallel): Each player plays own side of the court, with shots down the center being played by the left-side player, who takes it with her forehand.

From Isobel Kleinman, 2009, *Complete Physical Education Plans for Grades 5 to 12, Second Edition* (Champaign, IL: Human Kinetics).

Badminton Extension Project

Name _____   Date _____

Teacher _____   Class _____

What equipment do you need to do this activity on your own?

Is there a badminton team at school? Who is the coach?

Is there a badminton intramurals program? Who is in charge?

Where can you participate in badminton outside of school?

Do you have friends who would join you? List their names.

What are the health benefits of participating in badminton?

 From Isobel Kleinman, 2009, *Complete Physical Education Plans for Grades 5 to 12, Second Edition* (Champaign, IL: Human Kinetics).

Badminton Student Portfolio Checklist

Name _____ Date _____

Teacher _____ Class _____

_____ Knows how to care for the badminton racket and shuttlecock.

_____ Can perform a low serve.

_____ Can perform a high serve.

_____ Knows rules of service.

_____ Familiar with the court and its markings.

_____ Has been taught the overhead clear and smash.

_____ Can perform the overhead clear.

_____ Can perform the smash.

_____ Can perform the underhand clear.

_____ Has been taught the overhead drop shot and the hairpin shot.

_____ Can perform the overhead drop shot.

_____ Can perform the hairpin shot.

_____ Can clear the shuttlecock with forehand.

_____ Can clear the shuttlecock with backhand.

_____ Can direct the shuttlecock right or left.

_____ Able to play a game.

_____ Knows the official rules of scoring badminton games.

_____ Can play singles.

_____ Can play doubles.

_____ Has exhibited responsibility and sportsmanship during competition.

From Isobel Kleinman, 2009, *Complete Physical Education Plans for Grades 5 to 12, Second Edition* (Champaign, IL: Human Kinetics).

Badminton Learning Experience Outline

Contents and Procedure

1. Discuss equipment.
   - Badminton equipment is fragile and needs attention. Elicit help by explaining the fragility and how best to have usable rackets throughout the unit.
   - Shuttlecocks do not travel the way balls do. Explain the drop on descent and that the weight and shape make the difference.

- Generating power is more difficult in badminton. Explain the laws of momentum that come into play with the lighter badminton racket.
  - Less mass requires more velocity to generate the same force.
  - Wrist snap adds to the velocity.

2. Introduce one skill at a time: short serve, overhead clear, long serve, underhand clear, smash, forehand and backhand drives, directing the shuttlecock from left to right, and hairpin shot.

3. Teach the rules as the skill is presented to the class:
   - When teaching serve, teach serving rules: short, out of bounds, and turn of service. When game play begins, teach scoring, boundaries, receiving order, and positioning on serve.
   - When the tournament begins, review rules and court strategies, and throughout the tournament teach skills, strategies, and concepts.
     - Smash
       - Reliability for smashing at various distances
       - Laws of trajectory and angles
       - Concept of probability when net is in the way
     - Doubles strategies
     - Match-play strategies

Teaching Tips

- Allow daily time for noncompetitive practice so students can improve without performance pressure.
- Lessons should end with a game or contest that emphasizes the point of the lesson and keeps the interest high.
- After a book is published, rules, skills, and strategies may change. Check Internet sites listed in suggested resources to keep up with the changes.

Teaching Tips for Students With Special Needs

- Students whose coordination makes learning the badminton serve difficult should be encouraged to forget the net and work at a wall until they are able to drop the shuttlecock and contact it repeatedly without a problem. If they worry about whether the serve passes over the net and goes in the diagonal box, their timing may be further compromised by fear of failure.

- Students with disabilities or temporary medical excuses might be able to take part in the warm-up and in the drills where they are learning the skills independent of the game. If this endangers their safety, they should be kept involved in the learning experience by helping to officiate, coach classmates to identify a better strategy, or keep score and take care of equipment.

- Maintain the flow and fairness of a tournament as well as guarantee that players have a good daily experience even if their partner is absent. The player whose partner is absent can either
  - play the whole court alone, or
  - officially forfeit but play with a substitute.

Facilities

One court is needed for every two partners. Limited space may prevent 100% of the students from playing 100% of the time once practice drills are over, but students deserve equal court time. Use an equitable rotation schedule:

1. Assign players A, B, and C to court 1.

2. Divide class time into three playing rounds.

- Playing round 1—Player A plays B while C officiates.
- Playing round 2—Player B plays C while A officiates.
- Playing round 3—Player C plays A while B officiates.

3. Courts should have nets and be marked with

- sidelines,
- service boxes,
- short lines, and
- long lines.

See figure 15.1 for official court dimensions.

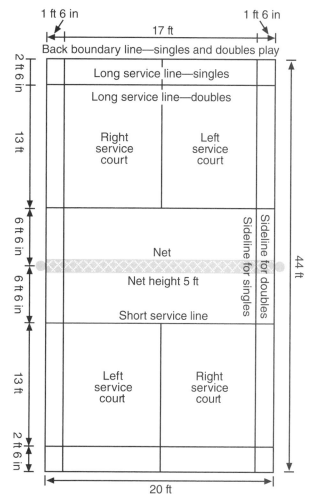

Figure 15.1 Badminton court.

Materials

- One badminton racket for each student
- One shuttlecock for every two students, with extras to replace shuttlecocks that get lodged on overhead rafters and basket backboards

Planning a Tournament

Round-robin tournaments are the best format for class. If there is a wide range of abilities, run separate skills-level tournaments concurrently. This ensures that students play on their own level with partners of their choice, that the atmosphere is competitive, and that players are encouraged to play at their best. It also guarantees more winners. See appendix A for tournament forms and charts.

Unit Timeline

There are two units, a beginner and intermediate unit. Each has

- 4 to 6 lessons to develop enough skill to enjoy a game;
- 1 or 2 lessons for noncompetitive games to use rules, scoring, and strategies;
- 6 lessons for a class tournament; and
- 1 or 2 lessons for assessment.

Assessment

Observe each lesson to decide whether to teach something new or reemphasize what was already taught. Moving forward in early lessons should depend on the ability of the majority of the class to have some success with essential skills—the serve and overhead clear.

A short written quiz for beginners and another for intermediate students can be found at the end of their respective unit.

Skills standards are suggested for performance evaluation. Beginner and intermediate performance rubrics are included in this chapter.

Suggested Resources

Ainsworth, D., ed. 1965. *Individual sports for women.* Philadelphia: Saunders.

Basic techniques. 2008. http://badminton.chorwong.com/badmintontechniques.html.

eHow. 2008. Badminton. www.ehow.com/articles_2130-badminton.html.

Miller, D., and K. Ley. 1963. *Individual and dual sports for women.* Englewood Cliffs, NJ: Prentice Hall.

Poole, J. 1982. *Badminton.* Glenview, IL: Scott, Foresman, and Company.

Sportsknowhow. 2008. History of badminton. www.sportsknowhow.com/badminton/history/badminton-history.shtml.

Badminton
BEGINNER
LESSON 1

Low Serve

Facilities

- Nets
- Short lines on every court
- Boundaries and service boxes marked on the playing surface

Materials

- One racket for each student
- One shuttlecock for each pair of students
- Replacement shuttles as necessary

Performance Goals

Students will do the following:

- Perform a low serve.
- Take care with the equipment and return it.

Cognitive Goals

Students will learn the following:

- That equipment is fragile and needs special care
- The parts of the racket and shuttlecock and how to hold both
- Some service rules:
  - Serve must be met below the waist.
  - Serve must clear the net.
  - Serve must pass a short line.

Lesson Safety

Practice wall areas should be separated by a minimum of 10 feet (9 meters) per group.

Motivation

Badminton is a popular game in Asia. People practice on the streets, in local parks, and in any space they find. A badminton racket is as common to the people of Shanghai as a softball glove is to Americans. The racket is light and so is the object it sends traveling through the air, which some call a *birdie*. Maybe they call it that because the birdie should never land, but the official name is *shuttlecock*. Because the shuttlecock is light and cone shaped, it does not play or fly like a ball. For students who are familiar with tennis, racketball, pickleball, or squash, the equipment and rules are what make badminton different. The class needs to start by learning how to get the shuttlecock into play legally.

Warm-Up

1. Do footwork, practicing change of direction:
   a. Side to side
   b. Crossover steps back and forward
2. Lead mimetics for the low backhand doubles serve (see figure 15.2).
   a. From backhand position, snap the wrist toward a target (5 times).
   b. With racket foot forward and racket hand lower than waist, exaggerate the wrist snap so it hyperextends (5 times).
   c. Using the forefinger and thumb as if holding the shuttlecock several inches below waist, push forearm forward and hyperextend the wrist.

Figure 15.2 Back-hand low serve.

Lesson Sequence

1. Discuss:
   - Lightness of equipment
   - Equipment use
2. Assign students responsibility for preserving equipment.
   - Throwing the racket ruins the frame.
   - Unraveling the grip makes it hard to hold.
   - Plucking the strings makes the racket unusable.
   - Tearing feathers or removing cork ruins the flight of shuttlcocks.
3. Teach students how to grip:
   - Racket
   - Shuttlecock
4. Demonstrate and teach the low backhand serve.
   - In lines, students practice hitting the shuttlecock to a wall.
     - Rotate after two successes.
     - Go through line a few times.
   - Gather students to teach the service rules.
     - Shuttlecock must be met below waist.
     - Shuttlecock must clear the net.
   - In pairs, serve back and forth over the net.
5. Teach the remaining service rules.
   - Serve must land in diagonal box.
   - One chance to serve properly or lose turn of service.
6. Create a skill contest that relates to the serve:
   - Who can meet the shuttlecock every time?
   - Who can get the shuttlecock to land in the service box?
   - Who can get the serve over the net and in the box three times?

Review and Stretching

As students go through the class stretching routine (teach one if they haven't learned it already), review the rules of service and concerns about equipment care.

High Serve and Underhand Clear

Facilities

- Nets
- Short lines on every court
- Boundaries and service boxes marked on the playing surface

Materials

- One racket for each student
- One shuttlecock for each pair of students
- Replacement shuttles as necessary

Performance Goals

Students will do the following:

- Improve the low serve.
- Perform an underhand clear and high serve.

Cognitive Goals

Students will learn the following:

- Remaining service rules:
    - Serve alternates from side to side after each point, starting from right to left.
    - Server whose serve does not pass over the net and enter the correct box loses chance to serve.
- That hitting up requires hitting shuttlecock from below
- How to hit shots with depth

Lesson Safety

Allow no more than four people on one court at a time.

Motivation

The building blocks of any game begin with how to start play. After receiving serves, students must learn to play the shuttlecock back without getting into trouble. That means making the opponent drop back from the net. Hitting the shuttlecock high and deep is an effective method. Clearing the shuttlecock when meeting it underhand is similar to the way a high serve is hit, so learning both at once is easy. The underhand clear is also a terrific response when receiving a low serve.

Warm-Up

1. Students practice on the court with equipment before formalities begin.
2. Do footwork drills for agility.
3. Lead mimetics (with rackets if possible):
   - Backhand low serve (10 times)
   - Steps to hit the high serve (see figure 15.3; same motion for the underhand clear)
       - With nonracket foot forward, racket head reaches beneath a dropping shuttlecock (5 times).
       - Swing forward, leading with butt of the racket. Finish with a quick, sharp wrist snap (10 times).
       - Add footwork to preparation, swing, and follow-through. Make sure the racket comes up and across the body on the follow-through (10 times).

Lesson Sequence

1. Demonstrate and teach the high serve and underhand clear.

   a. Practice the swing until the motion can be heard cutting the air.

   b. Practice the high serve over the net.

      • Have partners catch and return it using high serves (10 times).

         - Make sure they meet the shuttlecock from below it.

         - Encourage a sharp wrist snap to get the shuttlecock deep.

      • Have partners rally using an underhand clear.

   c. Practice low serve, with receiver hitting an underhand clear.

2. Discuss the specific requirements of serving.

   a. Direct the serve diagonally (demonstrate follow-through).

   b. Keep the serve low and short.

3. Practice serving straight ahead first.

   a. Try serving low so partner cannot return with an overhead.

   b. After a while, ask receivers to see if they can hit it back overhead.

4. Explain that the serve must be to the diagonal box (see figure 15.4). Allow practice.

5. End class with a contest to keep interest high:

   a. See whose high serve prevents their opponents from coming into the center of the court.

   b. See which partners can rally from baseline to baseline 10 times.

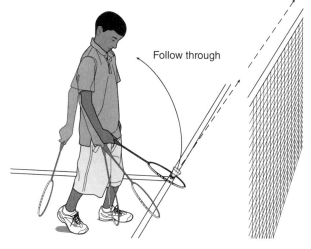

Figure 15.3 High serve.

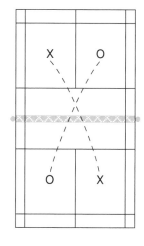

Figure 15.4 Partners practice serving to the diagonal box together.

Review and Stretching

As students perform their stretching routine, ask:

• Where do you want a clear to go? Why?

• Why do you have to swing so hard?

• Do you want your short serve to be high or low?

• If you don't send your serve into the diagonal box, what happens?

Overhead Clear

Facilities

• Nets

• Short lines on every court

• Boundaries and service boxes marked on the playing surface

Materials

- One racket for each student
- One shuttlecock for each pair of students
- Replacement shuttlecocks as necessary

Performance Goals

Students will do the following:

- Improve their low and high serves and underhand clear.
- Perform an overhead clear.

Cognitive Goals

Students will learn the following:

- The difficulty of making light objects travel fast and deep
- Doubles rules for service and receiving order

Lesson Safety

Allow no more than four people on one court at a time.

Motivation

The overhead clear is a great response to a long, high serve. It is also a great shot to use when opponents have closed in on the net. What's more, once students learn the motion, they're half-way to learning how to smash.

After a bit of practice, the class will go on to a game.

Warm-Up

1. Students practice on the court with equipment before formalities begin.
2. Do footwork—side-to-side stepping and running forward and backward.
3. Lead mimetics with a racket for low and high serves, for the underhand clear on forehand and backhand sides, and for the overhead clear, which should be done as follows:
   - Bring the racket up behind the ear so the elbow is up (5 times).
   - Bring nonracket arm up as you swing the racket arm for balance (5 times).
   - From backswing position, swing so that the racket passing through the air can be heard and so the racket arm extends up toward target, finishing with a wrist snap and follow-through diagonally across the body (5 times).
   - Run under imaginary shuttlecock, taking backswing (5 times).
   - Run, stop in forward stride (nonracket foot forward), and take full swing (5 times).

Lesson Sequence

1. Demonstrate the overhead clear. Have students rally in pairs.
2. Teach turn of service and receiving rules:
   a. Singles
      - If the server's score server's is even (2, 4, 6), the server serves from the right.
      - If the server's score is odd (1, 3, 5), the server serves from the left.
   b. Doubles
      - Whoever is in the right box is the first server.
      - The first server up switches sides after every point, continuing to serve until the team is put out. Then (except if this is the first service of the game) her partner takes her turn of service, serving from whichever box she was in at the time her partner was put out.
      - Both hands (as in both players on a doubles team) serve, except on the first turn of service.
   c. Receivers must receive all serves that are intended for their box.
3. Play a game if time remains.

Review and Stretching

While stretching, ask questions:

- What makes a clearing shot travel as deep as it does?
- When should you use a clear?
- What are two types of clears?
- When a team wins the first serve, do both players get to serve?
- In a doubles game, which player serves first, the player on the right or left?

Smash

Facilities

- Nets
- Short lines on every court
- Boundaries and service boxes marked on the playing surface

Materials

- Blackboard or premade chart diagramming contact points for the overhead clear, drop shot, and smash (see figure 15.5)
- One racket for each student
- One shuttlecock for each pair of students
- Replacement shuttlecocks as necessary

Performance Goals

Students will do the following:

- Perform the smash.
- Improve skills already introduced.
- Play a short game.

Cognitive Goals

Students will learn the following:

- That hitting down instead of up depends on contact point
- That the motion for the smash and overhead clear is the same

Lesson Safety

Allow no more than four people on one court at a time.

Motivation

The last few lessons warned of hitting the shuttlecock up and short, encouraging deep hits. A shuttlecock that is hit up and short will come back as a smash that is difficult if not impossible to return. This lesson will give students their first attacking skill—the smash. Hopefully by the end of class everyone will take advantage of short, high shots to step forward and smash.

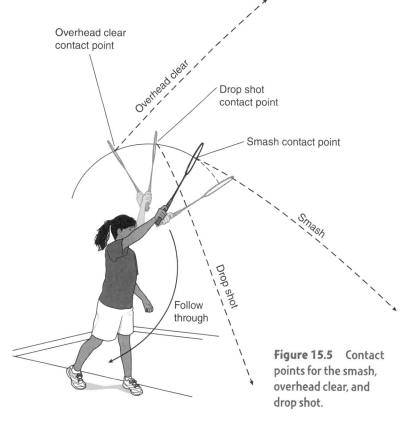

Figure 15.5 Contact points for the smash, overhead clear, and drop shot.

Warm-Up

1. Students practice on the court with equipment before formalities begin.
2. Lead mimetics for all learned skills with a racket in hand.
3. Lead mimetics to introduce the smash:
   - Bring both arms up, with the racket arm bent at the elbow and the racket head dropped behind the head (5 times).
   - As the arms come up, move to get beneath the path of a shuttlecock falling slightly in front of the elevated nonracket arm (5 times).
   - With the nonracket foot forward, swing up to the shuttlecock, striking it in front but well above the face as it falls. Snap the wrist on contact (5 times).

Lesson Sequence

1. Show contact point for overhead clear and smash (see figure 15.5).
2. Demonstrate the smash.
3. Students line up inside midcourt so that they face the net and drill.
   a. Self-toss and smash; retriever is necessary (5 times).
   b. Partner tosses and smashes (5 times).
   c. Partner hits shallow, high shot and the other smashes (5 times).
4. Play a game.

Review and Stretching

While students stretch, ask about the difference between an overhead clear and a smash.
- Is the swing different?
- Is the follow-through different?
- Is the preparation different?
- Is the contact point different? How so?

Badminton
BEGINNER
LESSON 5

Review Smash

Facilities

Lined court with nets for every two teams

Materials

- Blackboard or premade chart diagramming contact points for the overhead clear and smash
- One racket for each student
- One shuttlecock for each pair of students
- Replacement shuttlecocks as necessary

Performance Goals

Students will do the following:
- Review the smash.
- Play a game.

Cognitive Goal

Students will understand how court position defines what overhead skill to use.

Lesson Safety

Allow no more than four people on one court at a time.

Motivation

People who have great skills have to know when to use them. It is impossible to look at a dropping shuttlecock and smash it all the time, because if the hitter doesn't have the right angle, the shot will not go over the net. Before the game, the class will take some time to practice smashing from midcourt, three-fourths of the way back, and from the end line. At the end, they should be able to tell what part of the court they need to be on to use their smash and where they are when they have to abandon the smash as a plausible shot.

Warm-Up

1. Students practice on the court with equipment before formalities begin. Encourage students who are having difficulty to see you for extra help.

2. Lead mimetics for the smash and overhead clear, moving up to smash and back to clear.

Lesson Sequence

1. Set students up to drill the smash off the following:
   - Self-toss (3 times).
   - Partner hits it over the net up and short (3 times).
   - Partner hits a clearing shot three-quarters of the way to baseline (3 times).
2. Gather students to ask where they have a chance of a successful smash.
3. Play games.

Review and Stretching

While students stretch, ask:

- What makes the smash fast and low and the clear high and deep?
- When would you smash—when in deep court or in midcourt?
- What part of the hand and arm creates the power and depth?

Review Rules and Scoring

Facilities

Lined court with nets for every two teams

Materials

- One racket for each student
- One shuttlecock for each pair of students
- Replacement shuttlecocks as necessary
- Blackboard or other visual aid

Performance Goals

Students will do the following:

- Improve their skills.
- Score a game.

Cognitive Goal

Students will learn what constitutes a point and official scoring.

Lesson Safety

Allow no more than four people on one court at a time.

Motivation

After all these lessons, students are ready for full games. Some may already know the rules on how to score, but as the class prepares for a tournament, it is necessary to review them all so the games are about playing, not arguing over the score.

Warm-Up

1. Students practice on the court with equipment before formalities begin, with individual coaching.
2. Lead mimetics:
   - Low serve, high serve
   - Footwork with mimetics for the overhead clear and smash

Lesson Sequence

1. Using a diagram of badminton court (see figure 15.1 on page 629), review:
   - When a team wins a point (score only when serving)
   - When a team loses the serve (when a rally is lost)
   - Boundaries (shuttlecocks landing on the line are good)
2. Review service rules, receiving rules, and rules for when games are over (15 points if using side-out scoring, 21 if using rally scoring).
3. Have students choose tournament partners.
   - Collect the names of each team.
   - Send teams to courts to play together.
   - Rotate the opposition every 5 minutes.
4. Instruct students to make rule calls (short serve, serve contact higher than the waist, carry, reaching over the net to play the shuttlecock).

Review and Stretching

As students stretch, answer or review questions.

Assessment

Observe every court. See what problems students are having with the rules and order of play and plan to review those items at the beginning of the next lesson even if you covered them during the summary.

Teacher Homework

Divide the class by ability levels and make each level a different league. If the class has 12 or more doubles teams, create at least three leagues. Once done, plan a tournament for each. This works well using a round-robin format. Students from each ability level play among themselves. Several small round-robin tournaments run concurrently. The playing field is level; players have a chance to be competitive at their own level of ability. See appendix A for tournament charts to assist in setting up and scoring the tournament.

Badminton
BEGINNER
LESSON 7

Beginner Tournament

Facilities

Lined court with nets for every two teams

Materials

- Round-robin tournament information with game schedules and team standings
- Equipment in good repair
- Replacement shuttlecocks as necessary

Performance Goal

Students will play round 1.

Cognitive Goals

Students will learn the following:

- To be responsible for themselves during a tournament:
    - Read tournament schedule.
    - Get to their court on time.
    - Play by the rules.
    - Demonstrate good sportsmanship.
    - Report their scores.
- To rely on a partner during a competitive experience

Lesson Safety

Be vigilant about the emotional tone during competition. Be sure to address psychologically and physically unhealthy interactions and stop them before they cause damage.

Motivation

The tournament begins. For more time on the court, tell students to get to class quickly, check court assignments, go to the correct court, agree to warm up practicing clears and serves, and when ready, begin the game.

Warm-Up

Students practice on the court with equipment before formalities begin.

Lesson Sequence

1. Post round-robin schedule and team standings (see Team Standings Chart on page 640).
   - Teach students to read the schedule and court assignments.
   - Explain that the games go on when partners are absent:
     - For the games to count, the one who is present plays alone.
     - If the present partner wants a substitute, get a nonplaying class member, enjoy the game, and realize it will be recorded as a default.
2. During matches, move from court to court, giving hints or positive comments.

Review and Stretching

As the class stretches, answer any questions and gather results from round 1.

Assessment

Observe the ability of each group to be self-directed. Be available for students who are having difficulty following the tournament schedule so that their game time is not wasted by going to the wrong court or playing with the wrong opponent.

Doubles Position Strategy

Facilities

Lined court with nets for every two teams

Material

- Round-robin tournament information with game schedules and team standings
- Equipment in good repair
- Replacement shuttlecocks as necessary
- Blackboard or other visual aid

Performance Goals

Students will do the following:

- Continue improving.
- Play second tournament round.

Cognitive Goals

Students will learn the following:

- Good class habits:
  - Be responsible for themselves during a tournament.
  - Read tournament schedule.
  - Get to their court on time.
  - Play by the rules.
- How to work with a partner

Lesson Safety

- Courtside officials should be between courts or at net poles.
- Discourage inappropriate use of rackets to vent frustration.
- Students should not run on other courts because they could interrupt a point.

Motivation

Announce team standings after round 1. Remind students to call you if they have a rule question, need help with strategy, need to replace a shuttlecock, or whatever. The main thing is to go out there and have an enjoyable contest.

Warm-Up

1. Students practice on the court with equipment before formalities begin.
2. Lead mimetics, practicing all covered skills.

Lesson Sequence

1. Discuss posted tournament schedule.
2. Discuss, with the help of blackboard diagrams, how doubles players split the court responsibilities (see figure 15.6).
   - Diagram up-and-back strategy.
   - Diagram side-to-side strategy.
3. Remind students to take full swings with wrist snap.
4. Move from court to court, giving helpful hints and positive comments.

Review and Stretching

1. As students stretch, ask:
   - What happens if you intend to clear the shuttlecock but don't take a full swing?
   - What should you be prepared for if your shot travels short?
2. Receive scores.

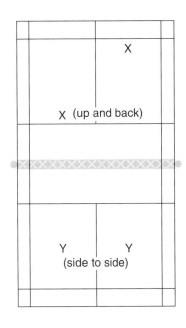

Figure 15.6 Up-and-back positioning and side-to-side positioning.

Beginner Tournament Conclusion

Facilities

Lined court with nets for every two teams

Materials

- Round-robin tournament information with game schedules and team standings
- Equipment in good repair
- Replacement shuttlecocks as necessary
- Skills rubric, posted and large enough to be easily read

Performance Goals

Students will do the following:

- Improve skills.
- Play by the rules.
- Complete a tournament.

Cognitive Goals

Students will learn the following:

- To be responsible for being where they have to be
- To be a good sport in a competitive environment
- To be responsible for their own games, scores, and standings

- Different strategies each day to help their game play
  - Hit to open court.
  - Exploit opponents' weaknesses.
  - Hit to opponents' backhand.
  - Keep opponents in the back of the court.
  - Confusion helps—hit down the middle.

Lesson Safety

- Courtside officials should be between courts or at net poles.
- Discourage inappropriate use of rackets to vent frustration.
- Students should not run onto other courts.

Motivation

Announce team standings. Tell students that you have been watching them and what you are impressed with even though most have never played this game until this year. Whatever the score, all teams should be pleased. As Yogi Berra used to say, "It ain't over 'til it's over." Many things can change. Tell students what teams have to do to change the standings. Wish students luck and remind them to call if they need your help.

Warm-Up

Students practice on the court with equipment before formalities begin.

Lesson Sequence

1. Follow the tournament schedule until its end.
2. Go over a strategy of the day, focusing on something different each day.
   a. Keep hits deep.
   b. Be ready to move up and put away any high, short shots.
   c. Make the opponent move by hitting to the empty court.
   d. Play the weaker of the two opponents.
   e. Concentrate to cut down on errors.

Review and Stretching

As students stretch, answer questions and collect scores. If something comes up that should be shared with the class, share it now.

Assessment

Observe, looking for standards as defined by the assessment rubric.

Student Homework

On the last day of the unit, remind students that after a short quiz, they will play against the opponents each team played when the tournament began.

Quiz and Final Games

Facilities

Lined court with nets for every two teams

Materials

- Rackets and shuttlecocks for every player
- Posted beginner performance rubric
- One quiz per student
- Pens and pencils

Performance Goals

Students will do the following:

- Take a written quiz lasting no more than 10 minutes.
- Sit quietly if finished early, stretching until everyone is done.
- Play a game against their first opponent in the tournament.

Cognitive Goal

Students will demonstrate conceptual knowledge on the test.

Lesson Safety

- Discourage inappropriate use of rackets to vent frustration.
- Students should not run onto other courts.

Motivation

When starting the tournament, the students were all still novices. Many have improved a lot. This is their chance to see if the improvement can turn the tables. Announce that the skills grades will be based on the posted skills rubric.

Warm-Up

Students practice on the court with equipment after turning in their quiz.

Lesson Sequence

1. Students pick up quizzes as they enter gym and begin right away.
2. Collect quizzes after about 10 minutes.
3. Send students to the courts to warm up.
4. Play for the remainder of the class.

Review

Review the questions on the quiz.

Assessment

Grades will partly be based on

- the results of a written quiz, and
- the level students have achieved on the skills performance rubric.

Beginner Badminton Skills Rubric

Name _____ Date _____

Teacher _____ Class _____

	0	1	2	3	4	5
Serve	No effort.	• Has proper grip. • Has correct stance. • Holds shuttlecock correctly.	• Makes contact below the waist. • Uses wrist on swing. • Redirects shuttlecock forward.	• Makes contact using legal swing. • Directs shuttlecock on diagonal. • Able to put shuttlecock in play legally.	• Has consistent low serve.	• Attempts to serve strategically. • Has a low and high serve.
Overhead clear	No effort.	• Uses correct mimetics. • Chooses overhead swing when shuttlecock is high.	• Uses full practice swings that whip the air. • Can redirect shuttlecock upward using overhead swing.	• Moves to get under the dropping shuttlecock. • Hits are high.	• Can run 4 steps or more and still direct a high, deep hit. • Can receive from back line and clear shuttlecock past midcourt.	• Hits deep in opponent's court from deep in own court. • Can direct shuttlecock left or right purposefully.
Underhand clear	No effort.	• Uses correct mimetics. • Correctly chooses underhand swing when shuttlecock is short or low.	• Practice swings whip the air. • Able to direct shuttlecock over the net when it arrives low.	• Sends underhand swing up. • Succeeds in redirecting on forehand side.	• Redirects low shots up on the backhand and forehand sides. • Can clear the shuttlecock high off favorite side.	• Clears shuttlecock high and deep often. • Can clear off forehand and backhand. • Can hit clear shots to the left or right side of an opponent's court.

From Isobel Kleinman, 2009, *Complete Physical Education Plans for Grades 5 to 12, Second Edition* (Champaign, IL: Human Kinetics).

Beginner Badminton Quiz

Name _____ Date _____

Teacher _____ Class _____

This diagram represents a badminton court. Each number gives a location of a player or an actual spot on the court. If the number is on a line, it refers to that line. If it is in a space, it refers to the general area. Based on the diagram, decide whether the statement is true or false and record your answer in the column to the left of the statement.

_____ 1. Players X2 and X9 think X9 should serve first.

_____ 2. Server X2 correctly serves to the box represented by 12.

_____ 3. Player Y7's serve, if left, will land on line 11. X2 must return it.

_____ 4. A serve landing in area 4 is short.

_____ 5. If team X hits a good overhead clear, the shuttlecock should land near area 5.

_____ 6. Server X9 should direct the serve to the area marked by 12.

_____ 7. If X2 hits so the shuttlecock starts falling near 7, the closest Y player should step up to smash it.

_____ 8. Team Y7's serve lands on the line marked by 3. Y gets a point.

_____ 9. If someone near 5 tries to smash, the shuttlecock will go into the net.

_____ 10. If the shuttlecock has been hit between X2 and X9 and both players are right-handed, X9 should leave it for X2 to take with the forehand.

Beginner Badminton Answer Key

Badminton Diagram

1. F—Server on the right, X2, should serve first.
2. F—Server must serve to the diagonal box; in this case, X2 must serve to 7.
3. T—If the shuttlecock lands on the line, it is a good serve.
4. T—A good serve must clear the area between the net and the short line.
5. T—Such a clear would be very deep but not out-of-bounds.
6. T—The area and its boundaries is the diagonal X9 must serve to.
7. T—The X player hit a setup for a smash; team Y should take advantage.
8. T—When a legal serve is not returned, the team that serves gets a point.
9. T—If the net is the proper height, the angle of a smash that will stay inbounds will not clear the net.
10. F—If X2 is supposed to return the shot, X2 will have to use the backhand.

 From Isobel Kleinman, 2009, *Complete Physical Education Plans for Grades 5 to 12, Second Edition* (Champaign, IL: Human Kinetics).

Skills Review

Facilities

- Nets
- Short lines marked
- Boundary lines marked on playing surface

Materials

- One racket per student
- One shuttle per pair
- Replacement shuttlecocks as needed

Performance Goals

Students will do the following:

- Perform a low and high serve and overhead clear and smash.
- Care for equipment.

Cognitive Goals

Students will review the following:

- Equipment care and responsibility for proper handling
- Mechanical difference between swings that produce the following:
    - High, deep serves
    - Low, short serves
    - Overhead clear
    - Smash
- Service rules for doubles and singles:
    - Serve must be met below the waist.
    - Serve must clear the net and pass a short line.
    - Must start from the right and direct serve to diagonal box.
    - In singles, start from the right if the server's score is an even number but start from the left if the score is an odd number.

Lesson Safety

- Practice areas should be separated by a minimum of 10 feet (3 meters) per group.
- Assign no more than four students to a court.

Motivation

It has been a while since students have touched a badminton racket. This day will be exclusively dedicated to getting the feel of the game back and doing what they already know.

Warm-Up

1. Students jog around the playing area
2. Lead mimetics (with racket) to review the low and high serves and the overhead clear and smash.

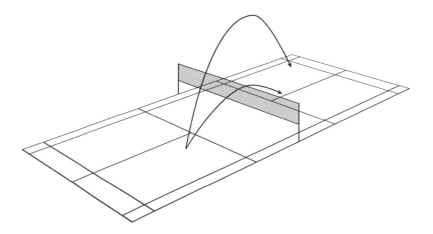

Figure 15.7 Flight pattern and good placement for low and high serves.

Lesson Sequence

1. Discuss equipment use and care.
2. Demonstrate and practice (see figure 15.7):
   a. High serve
      - Opposite foot forward, knees bent
      - Full backswing
      - Forceful wrist snap
      - Follow-through above head toward point of aim
   b. Low serve
      - Backhand stroke
      - Racket foot forward
      - Slower wrist snap
      - Little follow-through
   c. Practice low serve to partner (5 successes each).
   d. Practice high serve to partner (5 successes each).
3. Illustrate the mechanical differences between overhead clear and smash, and practice both.
4. Review service rules:
   a. Must land on the line or inside the diagonal box.
   b. Contact must be beneath waist.
   c. After winning a point, the server switches and serves to other box.
5. If time allows, play a game with practice partner.

Review and Stretching

Review rules of service and concerns about equipment as students stretch. Ask:

- Does the swing look different in the smash and clear?
- What is the biggest difference between the two?
- Does the swing look different between the short and long serve?
- What makes one travel farther?

Badminton
INTERMEDIATE
LESSON 2

Overhead Drop Shot

Facilities

Lined court with nets for every four players

Materials

- Blackboard or other visual aid
- Contact points and flight pattern of the overhead clear, smash, and drop shot (see figure 15.5 on page 635)
- One racket for each student
- One shuttlecock for each pair of students with a few extras in case of loss or tears

Performance Goals

Students will do the following:

- Improve their overhead shots.
- Perform a new overhead shot—the overhead drop shot.
- Play a short game.

Cognitive Goals

Students will learn the following:

- How contact point and follow-through make overhead shots behave differently
- Strategy for the overhead shots (smash, clear, and drop)

Lesson Safety

- Practice areas should be separated by a minimum of 10 feet (3 meters) per group.
- Assign no more than four students to a court.

Motivation

As masters of the major skills, it's time to learn to be a little sneaky. The fact that the overhead motion has three different results allows players to be quite deceptive. Once they become good at it, hitting a drop shot, a clear, or a smash, is a legal method of making opponents flinch. Players who use their brain can thoroughly confuse an opponent by doing something the opponent does not anticipate.

Warm-Up

1. Students practice on the court with equipment before formalities begin, working on the shot that needs the most work after the last lesson.
2. Lead mimetics for both serves, overhead smash, and clear.
3. Lead mimetics to introduce the overhead drop shot.
   - Prepare for overhead clear, arms up, weight on back foot (5 times).
   - Swing up to contact the shuttlecock above the head and slightly nearer the net than the hitter (5 times).
   - Soften grip on contact, stop the wrist snap, and limit the follow-through so that the racket pushes without carrying the shuttlecock just over the net toward the sideline (10 times).

Lesson Sequence

1. Discuss differing overhead mechanics for overhead shots (point of contact, wrist snap, follow-through).
2. Have students practice overhead shots.
   - Start with the drop shot (5 successes each).
   - Practice clears and smashes (5 successes each).
3. Encourage students to practice mixing up the shots.
4. Allow game in remaining time.

Review and Stretching

As students stretch, ask:

- If the shuttlecock is directly overhead, what kind of shot will you take if you do not move and simply swing at it?
- To hit offensively, what could you do to change the outcome?
- Which is the deeper shot, the smash or the drop shot?

Hairpin Shot

Facilities

Lined court with nets for every four players.

Materials

- Blackboard or other visual aid
- Contact points and flight pattern of the overhead clear, smash, and drop shot (see figure 15.5 on page 635)
- Badminton rackets for each student
- Shuttlecock for each group of two

Performance Goals

Students will do the following:

- Improve underhand shots.
- Perform the hairpin shot.
- Play games.

Cognitive Goals

Students will learn the following:

- That preparation, contact point, and follow-through can change the result when meeting the shuttlecock with an underhand swing
- When to use the hairpin shot (see figure 15.8)

Lesson Safety

- Practice areas should be separated by a minimum of 10 feet (3 meters) per group.
- Assign no more than four students to a court.

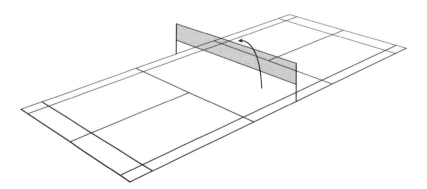

Figure 15.8 Hairpin shot.

Motivation

The sneakiness alluded to when learning the drop shot can be accomplished with underhand shots too. Show what the effect is and see if everyone can do it.

Warm-Up

1. Students practice on the court with equipment before formalities begin.
2. Do change-of-direction drills:
   - Crossover steps going backward and sideways
   - Small side-to-side steps going left to right and right to left
   - Running forward, stopping, and running backward
3. Mimetics for learned overhead strokes and underhand strokes.
4. Introduce the hairpin shot during mimetics (5 times):
   - Run in to return a drop shot near the net with an open racket face.
   - Contact is with a soft touch, flicking the wrist to make the shot barely clear the net.

Lesson Sequence

1. Demonstrate how one technique in an otherwise similar motion can cause differences in underhand shots.
   - Same backswing
   - Same point of contact but different wrist snap
   - Minimal follow-through (hairpin)
   - Trajectory barely passing over the net (hairpin)
2. Practice.
   - Partners rallying with hairpin shots over the net
   - Receiver returning drop shots with a hairpin shot
   - Mixing shots (clearing, hairpin, or smashing the shuttlecock)
3. Allow game in remaining time.

Review and Stretching

As students stretch, ask:

- Where on the court would you have to be to execute a hairpin shot—near the net or near the end line?
- Which shot has no swing and depends only on the wrist?
- Name a deep underhand shot.

Assessment

- Observe each student's control and court coverage so you can develop a fair tournament for each level of play.
- Identify weaknesses that need reviewing and review them in the next lesson.

The Backhand Clear

Facilities

Lined court with nets for every two teams

Materials

- Badminton racket for each student
- Shuttlecock for each group of two

Performance Goals

Students will do the following:

- Improve backhand shots.
- Play games.

Cognitive Goals

Students will learn the following:

- Why people have difficulty with their backhand
- Serving rules

Lesson Safety

- Practice areas should be separated by a minimum of 10 feet (3 meters) per group.
- Assign no more than four students to a court.

Motivation

People who avoid shots to their nondominant side—the backhand—usually do so because they feel more confident in the shot they learned first—the forehand. Also, they feel that by pivoting to the nonracket side, they are turning away from their target. Unfortunately, no one can always run around the backhand to hit a forehand. It might not feel comfortable at first to hit on the nondominant side, but it is worth the effort.

Warm-Up

1. Students practice on the court with equipment before formalities begin.
2. Lead mimetics for backhand clear.

   - Pivot on nonracket foot and step toward net with racket foot (5 times).
   - During pivot, bring racket back with bent elbow (5 times).
   - Shift weight to front foot as arm swings and extends forward (5 times).
   - Pivot, backswing, forward swing, wrist snap, and follow through with the palm facing up (5 times).

Lesson Sequence

1. Practice at a wall. Begin with the backhand low serve to get started and encourage students to hit higher and higher as the shuttlecock bounces off the wall.
2. Practice the full swing until it unfolds smoothly. Then send students to rally over the net with backhand clears or drives.
3. Discuss simple placement strategy—aim for a weakness, usually the backhand side.
4. Play game.

Review and Stretching

As students stretch, ask:

- When you face your opponents, should you hit to the left or right to shoot for a right-handed person's backhand?
- When your team begins to serve, who serves first?
- Does the team who wins first service get two turns of serve before the opponents gain the serve?
- Name a few errors that would cause the server to lose the serve.

Doubles Strategy

Facilities

Lined court with nets for every two teams

Materials

- Clipboard
- Paper and pencil for team sign-up
- Badminton racket for each student
- Shuttlecock for each group of two

Performance Goals

Students will do the following:

- Choose a doubles partner and sign up for the tournament.
- Improve skills while playing in a game situation.

Cognitive Goals

Students will learn the following:

- Strategies for choosing a doubles partner
- How teams divide the playing court so they can each cover it equitably (see figure 15.6 on page 641)

Lesson Safety

- Practice areas should be separated by a minimum of 10 feet (3 meters) per group.
- Assign no more than four students to a court.

Motivation

It's time to put skills to work. The class will organize for a round-robin tournament. Over 2 years, everyone has learned seven skills. That is a lot to absorb. Using them at the right time during a game considering the limited playing time everyone has had is somewhat unlikely. Most everyone needs more time before the skills, when to use them, and what to expect all come together. Suggest that students use what skills feel comfortable and what they can count on being relatively consistent. Once games start, they do not want to give opponents easy points. When playing doubles, it is not just their own skills they need to worry about, but how the team covers the whole court without getting in each other's way and without leaving empty spaces for opponents to aim for. Badminton is fast, and good team positioning helps a lot.

Warm-Up

Students practice on the court with equipment before formalities begin.

Lesson Sequence

1. Discuss attributes of a good partner and fun, fair competition.
    a. Dependable to be in class, prepared to play.
    b. Has good sportsmanship.
    c. Has a positive attitude.
2. Teach strategy for dividing the court:
    a. Up and back
    b. Side to side
3. Direct students to pick a partner and register partnership with the person holding the clipboard.
4. Rotate opponents, asking students to come to you once they win 5 points.

5. Reassign teams so winners play winners and losers play losers. Send them right on again to play someone different. Continue until the end of the class, matching winners with winners and losers with losers. (Do not call them losers; the whole purpose of this is to give them a variety of people to play against and to allow you to see what level they play at so you can draw up a more equitable tournament.)

Review and Stretching

1. As students stretch, review rules of scoring and service order.
2. Comment on equipment maintenance, keeping it in shape for the tournament.
3. Make sure everyone submitted their doubles teams.

Teacher Homework

Look at the skill range and divide the class so students with similar skill levels play each other. Create a round-robin tournament for each group, posting a game schedule, team names, and team numbers.

Intermediate Tournament Round 1

Facilities

Lined court with nets for every two teams

Materials

- Tournament schedule
- List of teams that can be updated to show tournament points as matches are completed

Performance Goal

Students will play round 1.

Cognitive Goals

Students will learn the following:

- How to read tournament chart and schedule
- To show up prepared and promptly for scheduled games
- To record scores before leaving
- Strategies:
  - Who should serve first?
  - Who should take the shot down the middle?

Lesson Safety

- Assign no more than four players to any one court to play at a time.
- Be vigilant about the psychological safety of the students as well as the physical safety.
- Be prepared to deal with poor sportsmanship and any psychologically abusive behavior that might come out during competition.

Motivation

Today is the first round. If help is needed, they should ask for it.

Warm-Up

1. Students practice on the court with equipment before formalities begin.
2. Lead mimetics with footwork that helps to quickly vary shots.

Lesson Sequence

1. Post and discuss the tournament schedule.
2. Review expected daily procedure.
3. Focus on today's strategy and decisions:
   - Who should serve first
   - Who should take the shot down the middle
4. Direct students to begin tournament.

Review and Stretching

1. As students stretch, ask:
   - Who was the strongest server on your team?
   - Did that person begin the game on the right-hand side?
   - Who serves first?
   - Should the strongest server begin on the left-hand side?
2. Make sure students have turned in their scores.

Intermediate Tournament Conclusion

Facilities

Lined court with nets for every two teams

Materials

- Updated team standings
- Game and court assignments
- Badminton rackets for each student
- Shuttlecock for each group of two

Performance Goals

Students will do the following:

- Follow tournament routine responsibly.
- Demonstrate good sportsmanship.

Cognitive Goals

Students will learn the following:

- To be self-sufficient by following daily procedures
- Strategies to focus on each day before games
  - Stepping up to low, short shots
  - Varying speed and depth
  - Identifying opponents' weaknesses and playing to them
  - Varying low and high serves
  - Staying focused so as not to lose unnecessary points

Lesson Safety

- Be vigilant about the psychological safety of the students as well as physical safety.
- Be prepared to deal with poor sportsmanship and any psychologically abusive behavior that might come out during competition.

Motivation

Announce standings daily. As always, find a way to provide positive feedback that is accurate before games begin, while they are being played, and at the end of each class. Make sure comments are not effusive or students will not take you seriously. Encourage them to use you as a resource for helping to fix a skills problem, devise a winning team strategy, or answer questions that come up during the game.

Warm-Up

Students practice on the court with equipment before formalities begin.

Lesson Sequence

1. Schedule a new round each day.
2. Focus on the strategy and decision making of the day.
3. Direct students to begin.

Review and Stretching

1. During the stretching routine, find out if anyone was able to execute the strategy of the day. Ask if the strategy helped and how.
2. When there is one round to play, or when you anticipate needing play-offs, announce that after a short quiz the next meeting, the class will begin its last match, which will be completed over 2 days.

Assessment

Observe for performance standards as delineated in the intermediate assessment rubric.

Badminton
INTERMEDIATE
LESSON 12

Intermediate Quiz and Final Event

Facilities

Lined court with nets for every two teams

Materials

*   One quiz for each student
*   Blackboard or poster of the skills rubric
*   Badminton racket for each student
*   Shuttlecocks

Performance Goals

Students will do the following:

*   Take a quiz.
*   Play the team whose ability is closest to theirs for last games of the unit.

Cognitive Goal

Students will test their knowledge of the game with a quiz.

Motivation

Announce the final standings of the tournament. This last competition in badminton is one they should enjoy.

Here are some ways to make the last day different. Evaluate your class to decide, with their help or on your own, which would be best.

*   Playing the team with the closest score
*   Playing a team in the same place but in a different round-robin

- Battle of the sexes
- Singles against own partner

Warm-Up

Students practice on the court with equipment before formalities begin.

Lesson Sequence

1. Take quiz.
   - Hand out quizzes and pens or pencils as students arrive.
   - Have them sit on the perimeter of the gym and begin immediately.
   - As they finish, allow students to begin on court warm-ups.
   - When 10 minutes are up, collect remaining quizzes.
2. Proceed to motivate and announce the culminating activity.
3. Direct students to begin games.
4. Grade skills as students play, using the posted rubric as a guideline.

Assessment

Observation will determine the qualitative score for skills based on the intermediate skills rubric. Knowledge grades will be based on the written quiz.

Intermediate Badminton Skills Rubric

Name _____ Date _____

Teacher _____ Class _____

	0	1	2	3	4	5
Serve	No effort.	• Uses proper motions during mimetics. • Able to serve legally from one side of the court.	• Capable of legally serving from both sides of the court.	• Has a consistent serve.	• Has good low serve. • Aims the serve strategically. • Occasionally can serve high.	• Varies depth, height of serve. • Very consistent. • Serve can put opponents on the defensive.
Skills	No effort.	• Uses at least one overhead stroke. • Hits an underhand stroke on one side.	• Clears often fall deep in opponent's court. • Can receive from back line and clear past midcourt. • Varies depth occasionally.	• Covers shots up to 7 ft (2 m) away. • When possible, moves up to hit a smash. • Has occasional success with smash or drop shot.	• Directs shuttlecock to open court. • Chooses to smash at proper moments. • Able to change direction of play.	• Wins points by moving opponent or using speed. • Covers large part of the court. • Has mastered one offensive shot.
Team-work	No effort.	• Arrives on time, prepared, and equipped. • Takes the left side of court if weakest of two servers. • Moves to shots within 4 ft (1 m) radius.	• Follows service and receiving rules. • Assumes responsibility for own territory on court.	• Switches sides with partner to keep court fully covered. • Keeps score legally. • Has occasional success at offensive strategy.	• Has four offensive strategies: place, smash, fake-out, or exploit weaknesses. • Backs up partner without taking over partner's position.	• Is best server on team. • Detects opponent's weaknesses and sets strategy to exploit them. • Is focused. • Demonstrates good sporting behavior.

From Isobel Kleinman, 2009, *Complete Physical Education Plans for Grades 5 to 12, Second Edition* (Champaign, IL: Human Kinetics).

Complete the Final Matches

Facilities

Lined court with nets for every two teams

Materials

- Graded quizzes
- Badminton racket for each student
- Shuttlecocks

Performance Goals

Students will do the following:

- Finish the match they began last class.
- Review their quizzes.

Cognitive Goal

Student will learn what they got wrong on their quiz.

Motivation

Review the quiz because there might be something they will learn from it that will help them play better on the last day of the unit. The matches continue from where they left off. This is the last game—enjoy it.

Warm-Up

Students practice on the court with equipment before formalities begin.

Lesson Sequence

1. Hand out graded quizzes and review.
2. Begin the games.

Review and Stretching

1. As students stretch, congratulate individuals:
   - Best overhead
   - Best record
   - Most improved
   - Best sportsmanship
   - Best ability to mix up opponents
   - Best ability to adjust in an emergency
2. Announce tournament winners.

Intermediate Badminton Quiz

Name _____ Date _____

Teacher _____ Class _____

This diagram represents a badminton court. Each number gives a location of a player or an actual spot on the court. If the number is on a line, it refers to that line. If it is in a space, it refers to the general area. Based on the statement and the diagram, decide whether the statement is true or false and record your answer in the column to the left of the statement.

_____ 1. Team Y wins the first turn of service of the game. When Y7 loses serve, Y12 becomes the next server.

_____ 2. Server X2 is in good position to hit a successful smash.

_____ 3. Team Y regains the serve. Y12 becomes the first server once the Y team gets the second turn of service.

_____ 4. A good hairpin shot lands in area 4.

_____ 5. The main difference between a shot that goes to 4 and one that lands on 5 is wrist snap.

_____ 6. If Y7 is the server, the serve most likely to be hit by a backhand is one directed to area 11.

_____ 7. A good strategy if your opponents are right-handed is to hit the shuttlecock down your right so it goes to the left side of their court.

_____ 8. Serves landing on the short line or on the line that divides the service boxes are good and should be hit back to prevent a loss of point to the serving team.

_____ 9. Attempting a smash when standing deep in the court near area 5 will result in netting the shuttle.

_____ 10. The shot whose swing most looks like a hairpin shot is an overhead clear.

Team X ... Team Y

9   8   7

11

3   2   4   12   5

Intermediate Badminton Answer Key

Badminton Diagram

1. F—The first team to serve gets one turn of service. When lost, the serve goes to the opponent in the right-hand box.

2. T—Player X2 is close enough to the net that if choosing to smash a shuttlecock dropping from overhead, the angle of clearance gives enough margin of error for the shot to clear the net.

3. F—The first person to serve when a team wins the serve back is always the person on the right side of the court.

4. T—A good hairpin shot is a short shot.

5. T—Wrist snap, not arm swing, provides the power in all badminton shots.

6. T—The serve must be returned by X2, who would have to meet the shuttlecock on the left of his body.

7. T—The left side of a right-handed player is her backhand, the weakest of the sides.

8. T—The lines are good.

9. T—The angle of the smash will not clear the height of the net if the smash is hit from deep in the court. That is why deep shots are safe shots to hit: The opponent cannot return a deep shot with a smash unless the net is too low.

10. F—A hairpin shot is underhand and an overhead clear is overhead. A hairpin is short and low and a clear is long and high.

   From Isobel Kleinman, 2009, *Complete Physical Education Plans for Grades 5 to 12, Second Edition* (Champaign, IL: Human Kinetics).

Golf

16

Chapter Overview

1. Teach the history and value of playing golf:
   - Physical benefits from hitting the ball and walking the course
   - Golf carts limiting cardiorespiratory benefits
2. Teach the accessibility of golf:
   - Public and private courses
   - Driving ranges
   - Pitch and putt courses
3. Teach the economics of golf:
   - Cost of equipment
   - Cost of course fees
4. Teach golf basics:
   - Proper grip and swing
   - Proper stance and weight transfer
   - Proper pitch, chip, putt, and drive
5. Teach golf terminology: fore, green, fairway, lie, rough, teeing up, divots.
6. Teach the rules of scoring.
7. Teach golf courtesies.

Golf Study Sheet

Fun Facts

- The Professional Golf Association (PGA) is the largest sport organization in the world.
- Yale won the first collegiate golf game.
- Walking an 18-hole golf course is the equivalent of walking 4.5 miles (7 kilometers).
- Beverly Klass, the youngest girl to tee off in a Ladies Professional Golf Association (LPGA) event, teed off at the Dallas Civitan Open in 1967 at the age of 10 years, 6 months, and 3 days.
- In 2003, at the Kraft Nabisco Championship, Michelle Wie became the youngest girl to make the cut in a major tournament. She was 13 years, 5 months, and 17 days old.
- In 1957, at 15 years, 8 months, and 20 days, Bob Panasik became the youngest male to make the cut in a major tournament, the Canadian Open.
- Players say, "Drive for show, putt for dough."
- Since 1997, Tiger Woods has been a dominant force in golf, not only for breaking the race barrier but for his incredible succession of victories.
- Annika Sörenstam heads the women's tour for her winning record.
- Michelle Wie is known for her professional start as a teenager and her attempts to get into the men's tour.
- For more fun golf facts, check out the Golf Trivia Challenge Web site at www.cincinnati .com/golf/golfquiz/html/brand.htm.

Mechanics

- Full swing—With feet shoulder-width apart, bring club up and back in a straight arc until the elbows bend, weight shift rotates hips and torso back, and front knee bends in. As the clubhead retraces its path downward, the body shifts, rotating so the front leg straightens, the rear shoulder and side follow, and the right knee comes in as the right hip pivots so that both hips face the target and the club has moved beyond the forward shoulder.
- Pitch—When 30 to 50 yards (27-46 meters) out, the clubs of choice are the 9-iron, pitching wedge, or sand wedge. Wrists should be firm, hands ahead of the ball, body in an open stance, the ball back of center, and body weight forward of the ball. A dominant left arm takes a short backswing, no wrist action, and longer follow-through. The head and legs remain still. The right arm must not roll or cross over the left.
- Chip—This short running shot with the 7-iron gets the ball onto the green from a close distance. Lower the grip to get more feel and keep the wrists firm. Stand behind the ball so you are back of center with your weight over the front foot. Use the club to hood (come down over the top) the ball and hit it on the downstroke so it jumps and bumps along the grass.
- Putt—Take a stance so your eyes are over the ball and the ball is off the left toe. Keep your shoulders and body square to the flag, though your weight favors the left side. On the stroke, keep a low clubhead and short backswing. Follow through toward an intermediate target and accelerate through the ball.

Choosing Clubs and Addressing the Ball

In general, the higher the club number, the greater the pitch and the more flying time the ball has in the air (see figure 16.1). The lower the club number, the longer the club and the farther the golfer must stand from the ball, resulting in a greater distance the ball will travel. A higher shot travels a shorter distance. Books recommend distances, but distances are relative to the power

»continued

»continued

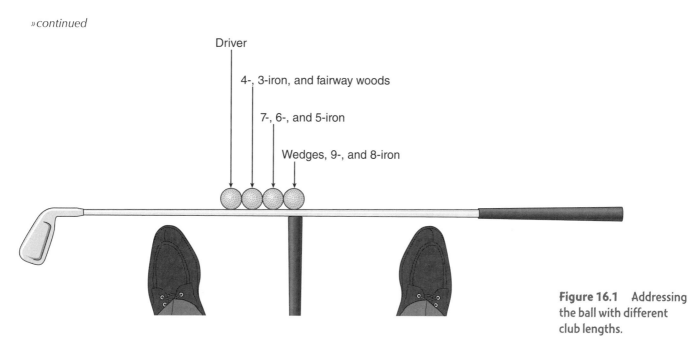

Figure 16.1 Addressing the ball with different club lengths.

of the person hitting the ball. Pros will hit farther with a 7-iron than many people will hit using a 2-wood. If you generally hit 100 yards (91 meters) with a 5-iron and need to go 75 yards (69 meters) to the green, you should take an iron with a higher pitch because you do not want the ball to travel as far on your next shot.

When addressing the ball, one must take into account the club length. The longer the club, the more forward of center the ball should be when placed on the ground relative to one's stance. "Addressing the ball" is how one aligns oneself to the ball. Balls meant to go short distances before stopping are hit off the back foot.

Rules

- Play the ball as it lies.
- You may move man-made objects. If they are immovable, you may drop within one club-length of the nearest point of relief as long as it is not nearer the hole. No penalty.
- You may drop away from ground under repair, burrowing animal holes, or casts at the nearest point of relief as long as it is not nearer the hole. No penalty.
- If you hit your ball into a water hazard and cannot play it, either take a drop behind the hazard or at the place where you played the shot. One penalty stroke.
- If you hit a ball out of bounds or lose it, add a penalty stroke, go back, and drop it at the place where you last played it. Play a provisional ball before searching for the first one.
- When you have an unplayable lie, you may drop a ball at the place where you played the previous shot, adding a penalty stroke. On the tee, you may tee the ball. Alternatively, drop within two club-lengths, no nearer the hole, or any distance behind the unplayable spot, keeping it between you and the hole. If the ball is in a bunker, you must drop in the bunker under either of the alternatives.
- On the putting green, you may repair ball marks and old hole plugs on the line of the putt, but not spike marks.

Courtesies: Behavioral Expectations on a Golf Course

- On the tee
    - The player with the honor (the player who won the last hole) goes first.
    - Tee off behind the markers.

»continued

»continued

- Do not talk or move while another player is driving.
- Wait until players in front of you have played their second shot and are well out of your way before teeing off.

- On the fairway
  - Never stand in the line of a player's shot.
  - If you are playing more slowly than the players behind you, wave them through and wait until they are out of range before you continue to play.
  - Replace and press down all divots.
  - If your ball is nearing another player, yell "Fore!"

- In sand traps
  - Leave your bag on the edge of the trap.
  - Enter and leave the trap at the point nearest the ball.
  - Rake any marks you left in the sand.

- On the green
  - Do not bring your bag on the green.
  - The player farthest out putts first.
  - Keep your shadow and body away from the other players' line.
  - Be silent while others are putting.
  - Leave the green after holing out. Record the score after getting off the green.

From Isobel Kleinman, 2009, *Complete Physical Education Plans for Grades 5 to 12, Second Edition* (Champaign, IL: Human Kinetics).

Golf Extension Project

Name _____ Date _____

Teacher _____ Class _____

List three classmates with whom you can play golf.

If you could buy five clubs, which ones would be most important to include in a starter set?

Other than golf clubs, what equipment would you need?

Where is the closest driving range? How much does a bucket of balls cost?

Where is the closest miniature golf course? How much does it cost to play 18 holes?

Where is the closest public golf course? How much does it cost to play nine holes?

Is there a pitch and putt course near you? Where?

How would playing golf benefit you?

From Isobel Kleinman, 2009, *Complete Physical Education Plans for Grades 5 to 12, Second Edition* (Champaign, IL: Human Kinetics).   **665**

Golf Student Portfolio Checklist

Name _____   Date _____

Teacher _____   Class _____

_____ Is able to grip the golf club properly.

_____ Has a smooth and complete full swing.

_____ Can transfer weight while swinging.

_____ Uses proper stance on all putts.

_____ Uses proper stance on the drive.

_____ Adjusts stance for chipping and pitching.

_____ Can consistently contact the ball.

_____ Understands when to use drives, pitches, putts, and chips.

_____ Chooses the right club for approach shots.

_____ Can putt.

_____ Can play a short game.

_____ Follows golf etiquette and common courtesy.

_____ Follows scoring rules.

_____ Knows common golf terminology.

_____ Has identified local areas that provide a golf experience.

_____ Assumes responsibility and care of equipment.

From Isobel Kleinman, 2009, *Complete Physical Education Plans for Grades 5 to 12, Second Edition* (Champaign, IL: Human Kinetics).

Golf Learning Experience Outline

Contents and Procedure

1. Teach the history and value of playing golf.
    a. Physical benefits of hitting the ball and walking the course
    b. How golf carts limit the cardiorespiratory health benefits
2. Discuss the accessibility of golf.
    a. Public and private golf courses
    b. Driving ranges
    c. Putting greens, miniature golf courses, and pitch and putt courses
3. Review the economics of the sport.
    a. Cost of equipment
    b. Cost of playing 9 or 18 holes

    c. Cost of hitting a bucket of balls at the driving range

    d. Playing a round preceded by 3 days at the range

4. Teach proper golf mechanics.

    a. Grip and stance

    b. Natural, unrushed rhythm on the swing

    c. Proper weight transfer

5. Teach that different distances call for different clubs and strokes (pitch, chip, putt, drive).

6. Teach golf terminology: fore, green, fairway, lie, rough, teeing up, divots.

7. Teach scoring and strategy (the best short game generally wins).

8. Teach golf courtesies.

Teaching Tips

- Students need to be in comfortable, unrestrictive clothing and will welcome the opportunity to wear street clothing.
- Every effort should be made for enjoyment, repetition, and lots of walking to the ball.
- Allow noncompetitive practice time with equipment.
- Use formal class warm-ups to practice proper golf mechanics and technique.
- Create end-of-lesson challenges that emphasize what students are practicing. Here are examples:
  - When working on swings, ask how many contacts they make in 10 swings, or how many swings it took to contact the ball 10 times.
  - When working on the putt, mark their first putt positions and count the number of putts it takes to drop the putt in the hole. The winner has the lowest score.
  - When practicing chipping, create a target (archery targets are great, or use cones or paint a circle) and award points for the ball landing in designated areas. Student should use the same number of balls.
- Develop a short tournament.
- Plan a field trip to a driving range, pitch and putt course, par-3 course, or golf course.
- After a book is published, rules, skills, and strategies may change. Check Internet sites listed in suggested resources to keep up with the changes.

Teaching Tips for Students With Special Needs

Golf lends itself to inclusion. Most students with disabilities and temporary medical problems are able to play golf with minor adaptations. Blind students can play when someone helps them line up and locate the ball. Wheelchair golfers can play with specially fitted clubs and adapted rules. See the United States Golf Association (USGA) Web site (www.usga.org/playing/rules/golfers_with_disabilities.html) for adapted rules for the blind, players on crutches or using canes, wheelchair players, and amputees.

Facilities

- Adapt the activity to smaller spaces or being indoors if necessary.
- Define areas for practicing:
  - Full swings
  - Putting
  - Chipping

- A putting green must be bought or created.
- Lay out a short golf course of at least four holes with the following:
  - Tee-off areas
  - Putting greens
- Find a local driving range or golf course that will work with the school.

Materials

- Irons—5, 7, 9, or sand wedge
- Putter
- One wood per student
- Minimum of six practice balls per student (yarn, paper, plastic)
- Real golf balls for putting
- Rubber mats for indoor play
- Rubber and wood tees
- Carpet for indoor golf green
- Hang cloth or golf cage
- Cups for the golf holes
- Targets for pitching and chipping to the green

Unit Safety

Safety must be addressed before anyone swings a golf club. Set up rules for

- moving around a driving range,
- where to stand and how to behave while people are hitting the ball, and
- complying with signals for ball retrieval.

Safety on the golf course should be part of the general instruction.

Unit Timeline

This introductory unit includes the following:

- 10 lessons to develop skill competency and an understanding of scoring, terminology, and course courtesies
- 3 lessons for a class tournament

Assessment

Skills will be graded based on performance standards (skills rubric).

Suggested Resources

Golf.com. 2008. Course finder. www.golfonline.com/golfonline/coursefinder.

Golfable. 2008. Course finder. www.golfable.com.

Golf Digest. 2008. www.golfdigest.com.

Golfhelp.com. 2008. Golf tips. www.golfhelp.com/golf-tips.

Golf Today. 2008. www.golftoday.co.uk/proshop/tuition.

Hogan, B. 1989. *Ben Hogan's five lessons: The modern fundamentals of golf.* New York: Simon & Schuster.

Jones, B., B. Crenshaw, R.Y. Jones, and M. Davis. 1997. *Classic instruction.* New York: Broadway Books.

USGA. 2008. www.usga.org.

USGA. 2008. USGA rules for players with disabilities. www.usga.org/playing/rules/golfers_with_disabilities.html.

Full Swing and 5-Iron

Facilities

Hitting stations that are set off from each other and foot traffic

Materials

- Music that will help students get a relaxed swinging rhythm
- One 5-iron for each student outdoors or each station indoors
- Minimum of six practice balls per student or station
- Mats, if indoors

Performance Goals

Students will do the following:

- Grip a 5-iron properly (see figure 16.2).
- Learn a full golf swing:
  - Without the club
  - With the club but without the ball
  - With the club and the ball
- Get and return their own equipment.

Cognitive Goals

Students will learn the following:

- Fitness benefits of playing golf into old age
- Respect for safety around golf clubs
- How to address the ball (position to the ball)
- Proper stance

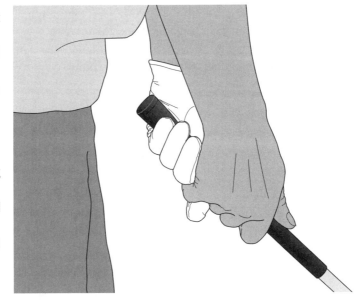

Figure 16.2 The grip.

Lesson Safety

- Facilities must be set up to minimize accidents.
  - Practice areas should be separated by a minimum of 15 feet (4.5 meters) per station.
  - There should be a clearly defined waiting area.
- Students must learn correct habits that will protect their safety.
  - Set up clear rules and procedures for retrieving balls.
  - Students can only take full swings with their clubs in specified areas.

Motivation

Some people think golf is a weak sport and that if there is no running, you can't get fit. However, lots of walking is involved when you play 18 holes. Three hours of play is actually a fast round. Many people take far more than 3 hours to walk 18 holes. When I was first invited to play 18 holes, I grabbed my tennis racket and bathing suit, convinced that when I was done, I would really want to move! Our group played the front nine holes and stopped for lunch, which was a good thing because I was really hungry. When we finished the back nine, I went to the tennis club, donned my swimsuit, did a few laps, and sat to dry off and read. In about 5 seconds I was fast asleep—that was my first nap since I was 5. Clearly, walking 18 holes while carrying clubs can be tiring!

Warm-Up

1. Walk, jog, or run the perimeter to a rhythmic beat, preferably music.
2. Using the same rhythm, lead mimetics for the full golf swing without the club:
   a. Stance: Stand on a line, feet shoulder-width apart, hips over toes, knees slightly bent, weight on the heels, eyes on a spot on the ground where the ball would be.
   b. Sense of swinging:
      - Swing the right arm back and forward, in line with the line (5 times).
      - Swing the left arm back and forward, in line with the line (5 times).
      - Put the hands together.
   c. Grip: Overlapping grip has the left hand lightly clasped with the thumb extended beneath the pad of the right thumb so knuckles are in line. Have students continue swinging in a rhythmic, relaxed motion (5 times).
   d. Weight transfer: Increase the arc, encouraging students to allow their weight to shift back and forth without moving their feet.
   e. Backswing: The arm comes back straight, and as it passes the back shoulder the elbow bends, weight shifts to the right foot, hips rotate to the right, left knee bends in, and torso rotates right. The head stays down with the eyes focused on the ball.
   f. Downswing: Begin with the clubhead retracing its path down. As it comes down, body weight shifts forward. The left leg straightens, the right shoulder and side relax to follow the swing, and the right knee bends in.
   g. Pivot for follow-through: On completion, the right hip follows the pivot until both hips face the imaginary target and the hands have moved past the forward shoulder.

Lesson Sequence

1. Focus on safety.
   a. Create awareness of the danger of being hit with a swinging golf club.
   b. Create procedures that make it clear when to swing, travel, or retrieve balls.
2. Teach and check the proper grip, this time checking it while holding a 5-iron.
   a. Explain
      - Power comes from what they consider their weak hand, the hand on top.
      - The hand they use to write is the hand that controls the clubhead.
   b. Coaching hints
      - Thumbs should be diagonally across the shaft.
      - Grip should be secure but not tight or squeezed.
      - When the right palm is open, it should face the target.
      - The clubhead should be mainly controlled by the fingers.
3. Practice the full swing with the 5-iron but without the ball (see figure 16.3).
   a. Backswing
      - Body weight shifts as practiced in mimetics.
      - The clubhead should stay low as it comes back.
      - The forward arm should remain straight through most of the swing.
   b. Downswing
      - When the backswing ends, the downswing begins unwinding.
      - The right shoulder and side should relax to follow the swing.
      - The swing should come down smoothly with no acceleration.
   c. Follow-through
      - The clubhead hits through the ball, going as far forward as the arms will permit it to.
      - Eyes stay down on the ball until after it is hit.
      - The body completes the pivot until the hips face forward.

Figure 16.3 The full swing.

4. Introduce the ball and the golf stance for addressing it for the typical 5-iron shot.

   a. The ball should be at a comfortable distance in front of the hitter and slightly ahead of the center line between the feet.

   b. Explain that a ball hit squarely will go in the direction of an extended line from the right through the left toe.

   c. Have students hit, using all of their balls before anyone is allowed to retrieve them and go again.

Review and Stretching

1. As students stretch, discuss that the most important thing any golfer can learn is a smooth, rhythmic, consistent swing. Once that comes, the rest is easy.

2. Review the grip.

   • Which hand is the power hand?

   • Which controls the clubhead?

3. Review using an iron.

   • Anyone know which number we used?

   • Where should you stand in relation to the ball?

Full Swing to a Target

Facilities

Designated hitting stations in clear area

Materials

• Music that will help students get a relaxed swinging rhythm

• One 5-iron for each student (for each indoor station)

• Minimum of six practice balls per student or station

• Mats, if indoors

Performance Goals

Students will do the following:

• Swing the golf club smoothly without the ball.

• Contact the ball with a 5-iron.

• Direct the ball to a target.

Cognitive Goals

Students will learn the following:

- The parts of the golf club (head, shaft, grip)
- The distance a typical 5-iron shot travels

Lesson Safety

Reemphasize safety rules and ball-retrieval procedures before beginning practice. Do this each lesson until the behavior is ingrained so that it has become routine.

Motivation

If all golf players knew that every time they swung, the ball would go exactly as planned down the fairway at the distance their particular club should yield, they would probably be on the pro circuit. Something always interferes, and usually it is the head because beginners are always looking up to see where their ball is going which always ruins their shot. The job for this lesson is to accomplish a smooth, relaxed swing through the ball that will result in the same hit going the same direction and distance every time.

Warm-Up

1. Run, jog, or walk the perimeter of the area to rhythmical background music.
2. Use mimetics to reinforce proper swinging mechanics:
    a. Put hands behind the neck and under the head so elbows are bent. Take a proper golf stance on a line. Acknowledge that the left hip (right-handed golfer) faces the target. The backswing mimetic rotates from the hips so that the shoulders and torso follow to the right and the left elbow follows the line. As the body reverses for the forward swing rotation, the body uncoils and the left elbow rotates back to its original position (10 times).
    b. Repeat with a golf club resting on the shoulders and the arms holding either end.
    c. As if the club is in the left hand (right-handed golfers), swing along the horizontal plane that is the invisible line one could extend through the toes (10 times).
    d. Do the same with the right hand (10 times).
    e. Take a proper grip and do the same with both hands (10 times).
    f. Grip a club behind the back and practice pivoting back and forward (10 times).

Lesson Sequence

1. Remind students of the safety rules.
    a. Do not move behind or in front of anyone playing the ball.
    b. Wait for a signal to retrieve balls so that everyone goes at once.
2. With a club in hand, swing as practiced during the warm-up.
    a. Emphasize relaxing as the clubhead drops through the ball.
    b. Don't have too tight of a grip on the club.
    c. Keep eyes on the ball.
3. Review ball placement and stance as they begin hitting.
    a. The ball should be centered with the clubhead resting on the ground.
    b. All balls should be hit before anyone goes out to retrieve them.
4. Compliment students on their smooth, rhythmic swing and making contact.
5. Set a target and compliment students on reaching the target and making repeated contact with target.
6. To maintain interest, you might try making a contest, such as seeing how many out of six shots hit the target.

Review and Stretching

It is important to have a smooth, rhythmic, consistent swing. Once that comes, the rest is easy. As students stretch, ask questions:

- Where should you stand in relation to the ball?
- Did anyone notice problems once you were aiming for a target?
- Did anyone start looking at the target before you actually hit the ball?
- What would happen if you took your eyes off the ball before hitting it?

Putting

Facilities

- Hitting station for work with 5-iron
- Separate area for the putting green

Materials

- One putter for every student
- Floor target, carpet green, or practice green with multiple holes
- Three balls per student for putting
- Six practice balls per station for practicing with the 5-iron

Performance Goals

Students will do the following:

- Putt at a variety of distances.
- Continue working with the 5-iron.

Cognitive Goals

Students will learn the following:

- The grip, stance, and motion for the putt (see figure 16.4)
- Terminology (green, lie)

Lesson Safety

Teach a new safety rule: No swinging on or near the green.

Motivation

At a driving range, people practice their drives, trying to hit the ball as hard and far as they can. That is important, but it is the short game—finally getting on the green and putting the ball in the hole—that divides great golfers from the great hitters. No matter how far the ball is hit, the hitter still has to drop it in the cup. Once on the green, golfers need to judge the lie (irregularities on the ground that might prevent the ball from traveling in a straight line), line up correctly, and sense how much speed their ball needs to reach the hole.

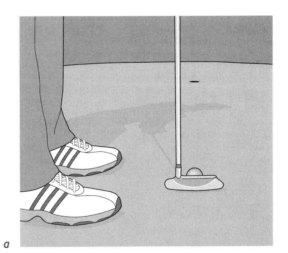

a

b

Figure 16.4 The putt.

Striking the ball (putting) so it moves on the green (closely cropped grass with a flag indicating the location of the hole) and into the hole is all about feel and alignment. Putting requires a special iron, stance, and grip. Since it accounts for 40% of all shots taken, it is a critical shot.

Warm-Up

1. Run, jog, or walk the perimeter of the area to rhythmic background music.
2. Lead the class through the mimetics of a full swing. Use music in the background if possible. Have students stand on a line so they can see if the path of their clubhead is in line. Begin with this simple exercise:
   a. With hands lightly behind the base of the head, take a proper golf stance, keep eyes down on the line, and rotate the torso so head stays down and weight shifts forward and back naturally (10 times).
   b. With same stance and eyes on the line, swing the right arm back and forward (10 times).
   c. With same stance and eyes on the line, swing the left arm back and forward (10 times).
   d. Grasping hands in a golf grip, swing both arms together (10 times).

Lesson Sequence

1. Introduce putting and allow practice (see figure 16.4):
   a. Stance—Eyes are over the ball, the ball off the left toe, shoulders and body square to the hole, and weight favoring the left side.
   b. Stroke and follow-through—Keep clubhead low with a short backswing, follow through toward intermediate target, and accelerate through the ball.
2. Stop students to discuss the variables on a green.
   a. Fast or slow surface
   b. Hitting up or hitting down
   c. Checking the lie
3. Have everyone shoot for the same target, changing the distance after six hits.
4. Emphasize safety.
5. Divide class into teaching stations, sending half to a station for putting and half to a station for hitting with the 5-iron.
6. Compliment students.
   a. Head staying down so they can keep their eyes on the ball
   b. Consistent, rhythmic swing
7. At the putting green, set up a 16-foot (5-meter) putt to see who can drop the putt in three strokes or fewer.

Review and Stretching

As students stretch, ask questions:

- What is the difference between the backswing for a drive and for a putt?
- What would you do differently at 30 feet (9 meters) away than 5 feet (1.5 meters) away?
- What helps you to line up properly for a putt?
- What does checking the lie mean?
- What is a golf green?

674

Scoring

Facilities

Designated hitting stations in clear area

Materials

- Scorecard and golf pencil for every student
- Putter and ball for every student

Performance Goal

Students will play a putting match.

Cognitive Goals

Students will learn scoring terminology and golf scoring:

- Par—perfect score for the length of the hole
- Birdie—one stroke below par
- Eagle—two strokes below par

Lesson Safety

Reemphasize that there is to be no swinging in the area of the green.

Motivation

A match requires that everyone score the same way. So, in this game, when the ball is played, it counts as a stroke. The lowest score wins. The golf course indicates where to tee off and the number of strokes it should take to make a perfect hole or par. If the hole says three strokes are par, and a player takes only two, he has scored a birdie. If a player can get a hole in one and is two strokes under par, she has scored an eagle.

Warm-Up

Lead the class in mimetics for the golf swing and the putt.

Lesson Sequence

1. Introduce scoring (see Golf Scorecard on page 676).
2. Review putting preparation:
    a. Check the lie.
    b. Line yourself up.
    c. Practice your motion before addressing the ball.
    d. Once you address the ball, any motion counts as a stroke.
3. Explain the putting contest:
    a. Explain which is the first hole and where to take the first stroke.
    b. Explain how to follow to the next hole along with the etiquette for waiting.
    c. Explain that students should record their score.
4. Have students begin at each hole so that all holes are used and they rotate to each before finishing. If the class is too big to allow everyone to putt at one time, rotate the group that cannot putt to an area to practice using their 5-iron. Halfway through, switch them to the putting greens.
5. Circulate to correct what is wrong and compliment what is right.
    a. Not lining up properly
    b. Forgetting their follow-through
    c. Taking their eye off the ball

Golf Scorecard

Name _____   Date _____

Teacher _____   Class _____

Hole	1	2	Hole handicap	Hole yardage	3	4
1			15	25 yd (23 m)		
2			8	42 yd (38 m)		
3			3	43 yd (39 m)		
4			13	12 yd (11 m)		
5			6	29 yd (26.5 m)		
6			2	63 yd (57.5 m)		
7			12	32 yd (29 m)		
8			7	55 yd (50 m)		
9			9	46 yd (42 m)		
Par 27			Front 9 total			
10			10	40 yd (36.5 m)		
11			11	30 yd (27 m)		
12			4	31 yd (28 m)		
13			14	11 yd (10 m)		
14			1	95 yd (87 m)		
15			17	40 yd (36.5 m)		
16			5	35 yd (32 m)		
17			12	29 yd (26.5 m)		
18			18	30 yd (27 m)		
Par 27			Back 9 total			
Par 54			18 total			

From Isobel Kleinman, 2009, *Complete Physical Education Plans for Grades 5 to 12, Second Edition* (Champaign, IL: Human Kinetics).

Review and Stretching

As students stretch, ask questions:

- Who was able to sink a putt in one stroke? If entitled to three strokes, what would sinking the putt in one stroke be called?
- What is par? A birdie? An eagle?

Golf
BEGINNER
LESSON 5

Pitching

Facilities

Designated area for pitching in addition to previous two stations

Materials

- One putting green
- One putter and three balls per student
- One 5-iron and six balls per student
- Several large targets that either stand or can rest on the ground

Performance Goals

Students will do the following:

- Pitch (see figure 16.5).
- Practice their full swing and putt.

Cognitive Goals

Students will learn the following:

- Terminology (pitch)
- What is meant by an approach shot

Lesson Safety

With three practice stations, students need to remain at their area until instructed to switch. Students must be careful to use their equipment only when in designated stations.

Motivation

Pitch and putt courses reach the green in 50 to 85 yards (46-78 meters). Tell students that there is no better place to practice the strokes they need to bring them onto the green when the drive leaves them short. The short shot, or the approach shot, is a pitch or a chip that gets golfers on the green so they have a short putt. Beginning golfers will remember getting 50 to 30 yards (46-27 meters) from the green and hitting the ball over the green several times before getting it to stay on so they could putt. Being able to pitch and chip eliminates that frustration.

a   *b*   *c*

Figure 16.5 Pitching.

Warm-Up

1. Walk, jog, or run the perimeter.
2. Lead mimetics:
   - Full golf swing
   - 5-foot (1.5-meter) putt
   - 15-foot (4.5-meter) putt
   - Stance—Keep eyes over the ball, the ball off the left toe, shoulders and body square to the hole, and weight favoring the left side.
   - Stroke and follow-through—Keep clubhead low with a short backswing, follow through toward intermediate target, and accelerate through the ball.

Lesson Sequence

1. Having gone through the mimetics, introduce pitching with a 9-iron.
   a. Have students practice the motion with the iron in their hands.
   b. Give them six balls and have them pitch to a target.
   c. Before sending everyone to practice, discuss the pitch.
      - Should cover up to 50 yards (46 meters).
      - Uses a wedge or 9-iron.
      - The length of the swing should relate to the distance of the shot.
      - Ball needs to pop up, hit the ground, and stop.
      - This is a touch shot.
   d. Teach when to use an open club face (getting out of sand).
2. In a large class, divide students into three groups. In smaller classes, everyone can work on the same skill at the same time. This decision should be based on space and equipment. It is best to have every student active.
   a. Send one group to the putting area.
   b. Send a second to the area for a full swing with a 5-iron.
   c. Send the third group to the pitching area.
   d. Emphasize safety.
   e. Rotate groups so everyone gets to work in the pitching area.
3. Provide feedback at the pitching area.
   a. Correct stance is open with weight on forward foot.
   b. Check alignment with the ball—the ball should be back of center.
   c. Check grip—hands should be forward of the ball with firm wrists.
   d. Head and legs should remain still on follow-through.

Review and Stretching

As students stretch, ask questions:

- What is the difference between driving the ball and pitching the ball?
  - Is the backswing different?
  - Is the foot your weight is on different?
- Which goes farther, a pitch with a 7-iron or a chip with a 9-iron or wedge? Think about what you know about angles when you answer why.

Hitting With Woods

Facilities

Three designated stations:

- Driving
- Putting
- Pitching

Materials

- One 2-wood for everyone
- Hang cloth or driving cage if working indoors
- Rubber mats if working indoors
- Putters, three balls, and a putting green for the putting station
- One 9-iron and six balls for the pitching station

Performance Goals

Students will do the following:

- Drive the ball with a 2-wood.
- Practice chipping.
- Practice putting.

Cognitive Goal

Students will learn that ball position varies with longer clubs.

Lesson Safety

Reemphasize that there is to be no swinging in the area of the green.

Motivation

Sometimes golfers must go for distance when their lie is not smooth. Woods (so called because that is what the clubhead used to be made of) are longer and have less of an angle, so they are the club of choice when teeing off. Long irons can come out of the rough more easily, so they might be better to use when distance is a factor and they are not on the fairway. The woods feel different because the balance is different. And, since the club is longer, students will have to change the placement of the ball when they address it.

Warm-Up

1. Run, jog, or walk the perimeter of the area.
2. Go through mimetics for the pitch, full swing, and putt.

Lesson Sequence

1. Introduce the 2-wood.
   a. Have students practice the swing without the ball.
   b. Explain that the ball should be left of center when they address it.
   c. Have them start ball contact with feet together, swinging slowly first.
2. Explain a divot.
   a. When it is taken
   b. That course courtesy requires replacing the divots
3. Divide the class into three groups and have groups practice driving, pitching, and putting for equal amounts of time.

4. Circulate, providing feedback on using the woods.
   a. Remind students about where the ball should be when they address it.
   b. Correct form mistakes in the full swing.

Review and Stretching

As students stretch, ask questions:

- When would you choose to use a 2-iron and not a wood? Which goes farther?
- Did anyone take a divot?
- What do you do after you see the grass fly?
- What should you do when you take a divot?

Chipping

Facilities

Hitting station, putting station, and targets for chipping

Materials

- Putters
- Woods
- 7-irons
- Wedges
- Balls

Performance Goal

Students will practice using a 2-wood, a 7-iron to chip, and a putter.

Cognitive Goal

Students will learn the difference between a pitch and a chip (see figure 16.6).

Lesson Safety

Reemphasize that there is to be no swinging in the area of the green.

Motivation

Students have worked on full swings with a short iron and a wood, used a putter, and learned how to pitch onto the green for an easy putt. This lesson will cover the chip, a shot that is used when close to the green but not close enough to use a putter.

Warm-Up

1. Walk, jog, or run the perimeter of the area.
2. Lead mimetics:
   - Chip—gripping down slightly to get more feel, wrists firm, ball back of center, weight toward the left
   - Pitch
   - Drive
   - Putt

  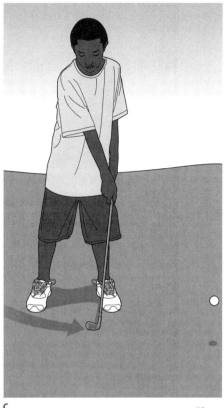

a *b* *c*

Figure 16.6
Chipping.

Lesson Sequence

1. Using a 7-iron, demonstrate and explain the chip.
    a. Use an open stance.
    b. Place the ball back of center.
    c. Keep firm wrists, as in the pitch.
    d. Look to land the ball on an intermediary target so it rolls to the hole.
    e. Hit the ball on the downswing so the club hits it before the ground (hooding the ball).
    f. Follow through is longer than the backswing.
    g. Do not roll or cross over the wrist.
2. Have students spend a third of their time practicing each stroke: chip, drive, and putt.
3. Circulate, providing coaching hints and feedback on the chip.

Review and Stretching

As students stretch, ask questions:

- What iron would you use to chip?
- Why is the ball placed behind center?
- Why would you use your club as a hood (covering the ball)?
- Should you hit under the ball to chip it?

Rules for Playing a Course

Facilities

Hitting station, putting station, and pitching and chipping station

Materials

- Putters
- Woods
- 5-, 7-, and 9-irons
- Wedges
- Balls

Performance Goals

Students will do the following:

- Perform full swings with a wood and a 5-iron.
- Putt.
- Chip and pitch.

Cognitive Goals

Students will begin to learn courtesies at a golf course:

- Honor of who goes first
- Where to stand once leaving the tee
- How to play as foursomes take approach shots
- The meaning of *fore*

Lesson Safety

Emphasize that there is to be no swinging in the area of the green.

Motivation

On a golf outing, all golfers want to make a good impression. They don't want to shoot into the water or slice into the woods. If they do, they have to look for their ball, but they don't always find it. Maybe if they took a little longer to look they could find it, but remember, people are waiting behind them and their foursome wants to play. Courtesy is a large part of golf. When they give up looking for the ball, not only do they need another ball, but they have to know what to do about the score and where to take their next shot from. Today students will learn the answers to those questions and then practice some more.

Lesson Sequence

1. Teach courtesies and how to deal with the lost ball.

    a. Duck when you hear "Fore!" It means someone's ball is headed your way.

    b. The winner on the last hole has the honor of being first up on the next.

    c. Remain quiet while players prepare to address the ball.

    d. The person farthest away from the hole putts first.

    e. No one putts until everyone is on the green.

    f. A lost ball requires you to return to where you last hit it and lose a stroke.

2. Divide class time so students have equal time for driving, putting, and chipping.

3. Provide feedback to students.

Review and Stretching

As students stretch, ask questions:

- When you hear someone call out "Fore," what should you do?
- Why carry more than one ball?
- Who takes their second shot first when leaving the tee?

Teeing Up

Facilities

Hitting station, putting station, and pitching station

Materials

- Golf mats
- Rubber tees (if indoors) or wooden tees
- Putters, balls, and green for the putting area
- Several 9-irons and balls for the chipping area

Performance Goals

Students will do the following:

- Hit the ball off a tee.
- Continue chipping and putting.

Cognitive Goals

Students will learn the following:

- How to use a tee and why
- The differences between using a wood and long iron

Lesson Safety

Emphasize that there is to be no swinging in the area of the green.

Motivation

Woods are longer and lighter and with the weight more evenly balanced than the irons, yet if golfers learn to use an iron first, they usually feel more comfortable with it. The reason is because woods are longer and people lose control coming through the ball with the longer shaft. However, the students already have been using woods. Today, they will put the ball on a tee. That will change things.

Lesson Sequence

1. Teach use of woods and tees.
    a. Teeing up is allowed on the first stroke of every hole.
    b. Tees lift the ball.
    c. The height of the tee should be higher for a driver than for a wedge.
    d. Using a tee makes it easier to hit the ball into the air.
    e. Tees are often hit, but if found they are also often reusable.
2. Divide class into three groups that practice drives, putts, and pitches equally.
3. Circulate, checking placement of the tee and correcting poor mechanics.

Review and Stretching

As students stretch, ask questions:

- When are golfers allowed to use a tee?
- What makes using woods different from using other clubs?

Seeking Local Play

Facilities

Hitting station, putting station, and pitching station

Materials

- Golf mats
- Rubber tees (if indoors) or wooden tees
- Putters, balls, and green for putting area
- Several 9-irons and balls for chipping area

Performance Goals

Students will do the following:

- Practice drives on and off a tee.
- Practice pitching and chipping.
- Practice putting.

Cognitive Goals

Students will learn the following:

- Local driving ranges and their location and the cost of a bucket of balls
- The differences between hitting a practice ball and a regular golf ball

Lesson Safety

Emphasize that there is to be no swinging in the area of the green.

Motivation

Tell students that it's silly to learn something they can never use on their own, so today you're going to talk about the easiest way to test their skills. They cannot sense how well they are doing until they get out there and hit a real ball. Can they anticipate what the difference would be? Does anyone know where the nearest driving range is? Tell them that you would like them all to go to the driving range. If possible, they will have a field trip. If not, they should go at least once by the end of the next 2 weeks.

Warm-Up

1. Run, jog, or walk the perimeter of the area.
2. Perform mimetics for the swing, pitch, chip, and putt.

Lesson Sequence

1. Discuss:
   a. Local driving ranges
   b. Cost of a hitting a bucket of balls
   c. Equipment they must bring
   d. Signing out school equipment if a field trip is impossible

2. Divide class into three groups and have students practice at all stations equally.

3. Provide feedback.

Review and Stretching

As students stretch, ask questions:

- What is the difference between the flight of a real golf ball and a practice one?
- Given the difference, which shot would fly farther, a golf ball or practice ball?
- What will you learn about your drives at a range that you could not at school?

Playing Pitch and Putt

Facilities

Short golf course of at least four holes that vary in distance from the tee-off area to the putting green

Materials

- One 9-iron, putter, and practice ball per student
- Scorecards and pencils for each hole that is set up
- Beginner golf skills rubric

Performance Goal

Students will compete, using golf skills for the entire lesson.

Cognitive Goal

Students will learn to play in a competitive situation.

Lesson Safety

Emphasize that there is to be no swinging in the area of the green.

Motivation

Tell students that today they are playing a pitch and putt game. They should tee off in a foursome, as they do at golf courses. If their shot goes astray, they should yell out "Fore!" They also should duck if they hear someone yell "Fore!" They should play the ball into the hole before proceeding to the next hole unless they have taken six strokes and haven't gotten it in. In that case, proceed. When done at the hole, record the number of strokes each person took. If they didn't sink the ball, they get a 7. Don't forget who gets the honor of starting the next hole. By the way, score-cards usually tell you the approximate distances to the green. On long courses, it is important, but this is a short course.

Warm-Up

1. Students do windmills (with a club across their shoulders and arms folded over the club, students bend at the waist and knees and rotate the shoulders from left to right – 10 times) and jog in place.

2. Practice swings.

Lesson Sequence

1. Provide students with scorecards.

2. Have each group begin at a different hole so no one is waiting.

Review and Stretching

1. As students stretch, ask questions:
   - Today you had to use golf courtesies and scoring. Did anything come up that left you puzzled?
   - How many of you found yourselves waiting before you could tee off?
   - Did anyone hear "Fore"?
   - Did all of you remember to replace your divots?
   - Who in your group had the honor most?
2. Make announcements:
   - Next class, pick up your equipment and start playing as soon as you have a foursome.
   - As you play, your performance will be graded against the skills rubric that is posted.
   - We will plan to use your skills and courtesies on a golf course. If you can go to one on your own, it will be worth extra credit.

Playing the Short Game

Facilities

Short golf course of at least four holes that vary in distance from the tee-off area to the putting green

Materials

- One 9-iron, putter, and practice ball per student
- Scorecards and pencils for each hole that is set up

Performance Goal

Students will play a course.

Cognitive Goal

Students will use their golf knowledge in a playing situation.

Lesson Safety

Students playing on a short course must follow the rules of etiquette on a golf course not only for appropriate behavior but also for safety. For instance, practice swings must be made away from any other players and any approach area for the other holes or greens.

Motivation

As the golf rounds continue, work to two putts (use only two putts to get the ball to drop into the hole).

Lesson Sequence

1. Provide foursomes with a scorecard when they arrive and have them begin immediately.
2. Assign groups to start at different holes so there is no waiting to tee off.

Review and Stretching

As students stretch, ask questions:

- Can you tell me what courtesies you had to use today?
- Were there any questions about the scoring?
- Did anyone achieve par on one hole? Two? Three? All four?

Assessment

Students will take a written quiz.

Beginner Golf Skills Rubric

Name _____ Date _____

Teacher _____ Class _____

	0	1	2	3	4	5
Chip	No effort.	• Uses proper stance and grip. • Places ball in proper position to chip. • Has smooth practice swing.	• Uses correct club. • Keeps wrists firm. • Uses short backswing with longer follow-through.	• Keeps weight forward. • Occasionally reaches target. • Contacts ball.	• Reaches a variety of targets up to 30 yd (27 m). • Has consistent ball contact.	• Has smooth swing. • Controls depth of shot. • Reaches intermediary target frequently.
Drive	No effort.	• Takes correct stance in relation to the ball. • Has good body mechanics on practice swings.	• Keeps eyes on the ball through contact. • Can contact ball. • Finishes with proper hip rotation.	• Frequently meets the ball. • Has smooth, full swing. • Keeps head down with ball in place.	• Has many straight shots. • Able to project ball 75+ yd (68.5+ m). • Can contact ball using a wood.	• Drives ball 100+ yd (91+ m). • Rarely tops ball. • Shots stay on fairway.
Putt	No effort.	• Uses proper stance and grip. • Keeps head down. • Reaches for putter.	• Aligns self correctly. • Follows through to the cup.	• Has inconsistent success on flat surface. • Follows proper etiquette on the green.	• Is developing touch. • Compensates for dips and dives. • Able to complete all 5 yd (4.5 m) shots in two putts.	• Is frequently able to sink 5 yd (4.5 m) putt. • Has accurate approach on flat surfaces.

From Isobel Kleinman, 2009, *Complete Physical Education Plans for Grades 5 to 12, Second Edition* (Champaign, IL: Human Kinetics).

Beginner Golf Quiz

Name _____ Date _____

Teacher _____ Class _____

True or False

Read each statement carefully. If the statement is true, write a *T* in the column to the left. If the statement is false, write an *F*. If using a grid sheet, blacken in the appropriate column for each question, making sure to use the correctly numbered line for each question and its answer.

_____ 1. Control of the clubhead comes from the highest hand on the club.

_____ 2. Taking your eye off the ball usually changes your swing.

_____ 3. Tom scored 87 and Sue scored 85. Susan won the round.

_____ 4. You would use the same club to hit a pitch as you would to hit a chip.

_____ 5. The lie is the way the ground slopes.

_____ 6. Courses allow a different number of shots to get to the green plus two putts for par.

_____ 7. If someone shouts "Fore," duck because a ball is headed your way.

_____ 8. A divot adds a penalty stroke to your score.

_____ 9. When you need more distance, swing harder on the downstroke.

_____ 10. Golfers can only tee off on the first shot of a hole.

 From Isobel Kleinman, 2009, *Complete Physical Education Plans for Grades 5 to 12, Second Edition* (Champaign, IL: Human Kinetics).

Beginner Golf Answer Key

True or False

1. F—The upper arm is the power arm, and control comes from the lower hand on the grip.

2. T—Looking up causes the shoulders to lift, thereby changing your swing.

3. T—The lowest score wins.

4. F—A pitch uses a 9-iron or a wedge because the ball travels a longer distance but then should stop with no roll. The chip usually uses a 7-iron and hits the ball so it runs a little.

5. T

6. T—No matter how long the green is, once players arrive on the green, they are given two more strokes for par.

7. T—If a ball is hit toward another golfer, the golfer who hit it should send out the "Fore!" alert so people can protect themselves from being hit by the ball.

8. F—A divot is the result of a good shot. Courtesy mandates that you replace the grass where it came from.

9. F—Altering the swing is the single most destructive thing a golfer can do.

10. T—Golfers can use any club when they tee off, but they cannot tee off once they are on the fairway.

Handball (One Wall)

Chapter Overview

1. Combine some aspect of the game with each lesson.
2. Introduce one skill at a time: the serve, right-hand swing, left-hand swing, clearing shot, and rollout (killer).
3. Teach strategies as students get more involved in the game:
   - Positioning—taking the center of the court
   - Hitting—to the open court, to the weaker side
   - Passing shots—down the line, over the head
4. Teach the rules of the game as the skill is being taught:
   - Serve—long, short, turn of service, order of service
   - Scoring rules when getting students into games
   - Interference and blocking when teaching students to take the center
5. Allow noncompetitive practice time daily so students can improve their skills without performance pressure.
6. Conclude lessons with a contest that emphasizes the point of the lesson.
7. Develop a short tournament.

Handball Study Sheet

Fun Facts

- Handball was played in ancient Rome. The French and Spanish called the game *pelota*.
- One-wall handball has been played in Ireland and Scotland since the 15th century and remains popular there.
- It is believed that the Irish introduced handball to the United States in the late 1800s.
- New York, a city with lots of walls, built hundreds of handball courts in the 1930s and now has 2,052 handball courts in the public parks.

Skills

- Serve—With a cupped hand, use a sidearm or overhead swing to contact the ball with the cupped palm of the hand, letting the ball come off the fingers. Use the fingers for direction.
- Right-hand hit—With the left foot stepping closer to the target, bend at the knee and swing the right hand so that it meets the ball in line with the left foot.
- Left-hand hit—With the right foot stepping closer to the target, bend at the knee and swing the left hand so that it meets the ball while the ball is in line with the right foot.
- Overhead shot—An overarm throwing motion is used to contact the ball when it is above the shoulders.
- Clearing shot—Shot goes high on the wall and deep into the court to force opponents to retreat from the wall.
- Rollout (killer) shot—Low shot rolls back from the wall so that it cannot be hit by opponents.

Strategies

- Positioning—Take the center of the court as soon as possible.
- Hitting—Hit to the open court, to the weaker side, or above opponent's reach.
- Passing shots—Pass down the line, over the opponent's head.

Rules

Serve

- The server may serve from anywhere within the service zone and cannot step out until the ball passes the short line. If playing doubles, the server's partner must stand off the court behind the side boundary line until the ball passes the short line.
- The serve is hit off one bounce inside the server's zone.
- The serve must hit the wall and land behind the short line but in front of the long line.
- If the serve is short of the short line, it is called a *short* and is a fault.
- If the serve lands behind the long line but inbounds, the serve is called a *long* and is a fault.
- Servers continue to serve until they are put out, serve two longs, serve two shorts, serve one long and one short, or hit the serve out of bounds.
- Doubles:
  - Only the first server on the team that serves first can serve for the team's first turn.
  - The first server of a team remains the first server of that team throughout the game.
  - When the first server is put out, the second server's turn begins.
  - The nonserving partner must straddle the service line from behind the sideline during the serve.

»continued

»continued

Playing the Game

- Receiver cannot return a served ball until it passes the short line.
- Only the hand may play the ball.
- A hit ball must reach the wall before touching the floor.
- A hit must take place before the ball hits the ground inbounds a second time.
- It is the duty of the player farther from the wall to move out of the way to allow the opponent a fair shot at playing the ball.
- A hinder that could have been avoided results in either a point or an out (blocking and interfering with a player's ability to play the ball is illegal).

Scoring

Only the serving team can win a point.

From Isobel Kleinman, 2009, *Complete Physical Education Plans for Grades 5 to 12, Second Edition* (Champaign, IL: Human Kinetics).   **693**

Handball Extension Project

Name _____ Date _____

Teacher _____ Class _____

List three classmates with whom you can play handball.

If you want to play handball, what equipment do you need to have?

During what seasons of the year can you play one-wall handball?

Do you have official courts anywhere in your neighborhood?

Where is the closest wall that you can play on?

How does playing one-wall handball benefit you?

 From Isobel Kleinman, 2009, *Complete Physical Education Plans for Grades 5 to 12, Second Edition* (Champaign, IL: Human Kinetics).

Handball Student Portfolio Checklist

Name _____   Date _____

Teacher _____   Class _____

_____ Able to use hand to serve.

_____ Has knowledge of and can follow safety rules.

_____ Can follow game rules for singles or doubles.

_____ Knows how to score.

_____ Has learned how to hit a low ball.

_____ Has learned to hit a rollout (kill shot).

_____ Has learned to hit a ball coming high off the wall.

_____ Has learned to hit high on the wall so the ball drops deep into the court.

_____ Is developing some sense of strategy for handball.

_____ Can play a short game.

From Isobel Kleinman, 2009, *Complete Physical Education Plans for Grades 5 to 12, Second Edition* (Champaign, IL: Human Kinetics).

Handball Learning Experience Outline

Making a Case for Handball

Team handball (a team sport) and handball (an individual or dual sport) are often confused. This unit introduces a one-wall handball game that is popular in urban areas that have more walls than fields. Handball has many advantages. It is the safest wall sport, uses movements that are similar to those used in racket sports, can be played on any flat wall, costs almost nothing, is extremely rigorous, is relatively easy to play at the beginner level, and is a lifetime sport.

Contents and Procedure

1. Combine a game aspect with each lesson.
2. Introduce one skill at a time: serve, right-hand hit, left-hand hit, clearing shot, and rollout (killer) shot.
3. Teach strategies as students get more involved in the game:
   a. Positioning—taking the center of the court
   b. Hitting—hitting to the open court, weaker side
   c. Passing shots—down the line, over the opponent's head
4. Introduce rules applicable to the skill or strategy being taught:
   a. Serve—long, short, turn of service, order of service
   b. Scoring rules when students begin to play games
   c. Interference and blocking when teaching students to take the center
5. Allow daily practice time so students can improve skills without performance pressure.

6. Conclude lessons with a contest that emphasizes the point of the lesson.

7. Develop a short tournament.

Teaching Tips for Special Considerations

Disabilities that prevent students from moving well will prevent them from playing this game. Learning the skills independent of the game might be possible for some. Other assignments such as keeping score, officiating, coaching, developing strategies for classmates, writing class notes for charts or bulletin boards, and documenting the progress of the tournament might be more appropriate. If they cannot be with the class, other appropriate ways to include students in this unit are assigning a report (e.g., studying the history, level of modern participation, who the stars are, if there are professional players and a circuit, where and when they compete, what kind of income a professional player might expect, the cost of building an adequate facility) or having them do an independent study (e.g., monitor the heart rate of handball players during practice, games, and recovery; analyze the most effective shot; study who is most successful at this game, shorter people who have an easier time reaching low or taller people who have a bigger arm spread).

Facilities

- This one-wall game can be accommodated indoors as well as out.
- Courts should be marked with sidelines, short lines, and long lines (see figure 17.1).

Materials

One light ball for each student

Unit Safety

Handball is played in close quarters. Opponents have to learn to run around each other or stop and repeat the play if collisions seem imminent. Clearly, problems decrease when players use only their hands and not a racket, but once students learn to play handball safely, they will be able to safely play racquetball, squash, and four-wall handball. Stretching should be done after the muscles are warm—at the end of class during review.

Unit Timeline

This unit includes 12 lessons for beginners:

- 5 lessons to develop enough skill to enjoy a game
- 7 lessons for a class tournament

Suggested Resources

Be a winner, play handball. 2008. www.youtube.com/watch?v=ASR _YeefPoc.

Handball City. 2008. www.handballcity .com.

Lowy, L. 1991. *Handball handbook: Strategies and techniques.* Boston: American Press.

United States Handball Association. 2008. New and official United States Handball Association one-wall rules. www.ushandball.org/onewall/ handball/rules.html.

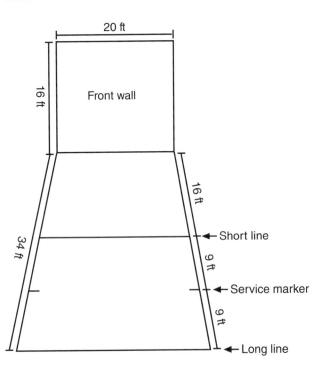

Figure 17.1 Handball court diagram.

Hit and Serve

Facilities

Wall with no obstructions

Materials

One ball per person

Performance Goals

Students will do the following:

- Swing and hit the ball with their right hand.
- Serve the ball.

Cognitive Goals

Students will learn the following:

- Service rules
- That the swing begins from the shoulder
- To step into the ball so weight moves forward in order to improve power

Lesson Safety

Practice wall areas should be separated by a minimum of 15 feet (5 meters) per group with a ball.

Motivation

Handball is a great game. All you need is a wall, an opponent, and a small ball and you can have a game anywhere. Ask if anyone has seen kids hitting a ball against the wall. If they did, they were watching some form of handball. Explain that you will be teaching a one-wall game that uses a lot of the same rules that paddleball and racquetball use. The major difference is since there are no rackets in handball, players do something that might feel strange at first—occasionally hitting a ball with their nondominant hand.

Warm-Up

1. Have students jog around the playing area.
2. Lead the following mimetics, which teach the right- and left-hand swing with footwork.
   - Swing the right arm back and forward (5 times).
   - Swing the left arm back and forward (5 times).
   - Step forward on the left foot so body pivots to the right (5 times).
   - Step forward on the left foot and as body pivots right, bring right arm back (5 times).
   - Step forward on the left foot, pivot, backswing, and forward swing (5 times).
   - Run right three steps, bringing right arm back at the same time. Plant left foot and swing (5 times).
   - Reverse; step forward on right so body pivots left (5 times).
   - Step forward on right and pivot left while taking left arm back and forward swing (5 times).
   - Run three steps to the left, plant right foot, and swing left (5 times).

Lesson Sequence

1. Give every student a ball. Ask them to follow you.
   a. Bounce and catch the ball with the left hand (5 times).
   b. Hit the ball to the ground with the palm of the left hand, catch it, and do it again (5 times).

c. Hit the ball immediately as it comes back from the ground, asking how many times they can do it in a row (aim for 5 times).

d. Use the easier (dominant) hand and repeat what was done previously.

e. Move students 5 feet (1.5 meters) from the wall and have them hit to the wall. If each student doesn't have 5 feet (1.5 meters) on either side, group the students in the smallest groups possible and give each student 30 seconds to practice hitting against the wall.

2. Demonstrate the sidearm serve and teach the service rules (see figure 17.2).

a. The server must come to a stop before bouncing the ball to serve.

b. The server must be in the service zone.

c. The serve must pass over the short line and into the receiving area but in front of the long line.

d. The server cannot leave the service zone until the ball passes the short line.

e. If the serve is a fault (long, short, or a hinder), the server gets a second serve. (A hinder is when someone on the court is in the way of their opponent playing the ball.)

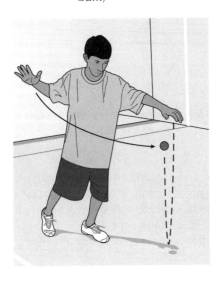

Figure 17.2 Dropping the ball to hit a serve.

3. Have students practice until each has 10 successful serves.

4. Demonstrate how in pairs, one person will serve while the other practices receiving the serve. Be sure to explain that receivers:

- Cannot hit the ball back until it passes the service line.

- Must make their hit after one or no bounces.

5. If there's time or if students look bored, challenge them:

a. Out of five serves, how many can you return?

b. Who can hit the ball on one bounce five times in a row or more?

c. Who can use their left (nondominant) hand to hit the ball three times in a row or more?

Review and Stretching

As students stretch, ask the following:

- Can anyone point to the short line?

- What importance do the short and long lines have for the server?

- What happens if the serve does not land on the ground between the two lines?

Handball (One Wall)
BEGINNER
LESSON 2   Nondominant Hand

Facilities

Wall with no obstructions

Materials

One ball per person

Performance Goals

Students will do the following:

- Swing and hit the ball with the left hand.
- Respond to shots of varying heights.

Cognitive Goals

Students will learn the following:

- Rules that apply to the receiver
- Safety rules applying to blocking and interference

Lesson Safety

- Game areas should be separate.
- Sidelines should be clearly marked.
- Rules emphasizing safety must be understood and practiced daily.

Motivation

Explain that everyone favors one arm but needs to use both when a ball is out of reach of the dominant arm. Explain that they are likely to feel uncomfortable, but they shouldn't give up because with practice they will start to feel fine. Announce that if there is time, they will use the rules they learned for a short game.

Warm-Up

Have balls available for students to pick up and practice with. When they have arrived and had 5 minutes practice, lead them through the following mimetics:

- Imagine balls to the right: Left foot steps so the body pivots right while taking right arm back, run three steps, plant left foot, and swing (5 times).
- Imagine balls to the left: Right foot steps forward as body pivots left and left arm swings back. Run three steps, plant right foot, and swing (5 times).
- Imagine balls above the head: Pivot right (if right-handed) by bringing right foot back first, cross-step back three steps as arm comes back and overhead, and stop and swing.

Lesson Sequence

1. Using the nondominant hand, have students do the following:
   a. Bounce the ball with the weak hand and catch it.
   b. Hit the ball to the ground. Can they hit it five times without losing it?
   c. Move 5 feet (1.5 meters) from the wall and rally off the wall with the nondominant hand. After two turns, move back 5 feet (1.5 meters) and continue. After a few more turns, move back 5 more feet (1.5 meters).
2. React to high balls.
   a. Have students throw the ball high on the wall and as it comes off, hit it (see figure 17.3).
   b. Ask them to throw it to themselves and hit it high on the wall.
3. Emphasize safety. Explain the need for concern and that rules try to eliminate collisions.
   - Players are obligated to get out of the way of an opponent.
   - Hinders (ball is dead and the point is replayed) occur when the following happens:
     - Playing a ball would cause contact (player calls a hinder).
     - An inbound shot hits an opponent.
     - Interference prevents seeing or playing the ball.
   - Avoidable hinders result in a point or a side-out.
     - Player makes no effort to get out of the way.
     - Player moves in the way of opponent or path of the ball.

Figure 17.3 Preparing to take a ball out of the air.

4. Teach the following rules:

   a. When receiving serves, either player on a doubles team can return the serve as long as contact with the ball occurs behind the short line.

   b. The first server of a doubles team always begins a team's turn of service.

   c. Servers continue their turn of service until they or their team (if playing doubles) are put out. In doubles, except on the first turn of service, the second hand (the server's partner) then serves until the team is put out.

   d. The server's partner must stand off the court, straddling the service box outside the side boundary line until the serve passes the short line.

   e. After the serve, teams alternate who must contact the ball.

5. Allow a short 5-point game. If there's time, rotate opponents.

Review and Stretching

As students stretch, ask the following:

- Why is there a blocking rule?
- What is a hinder? What happens after it is called?
- If the receiving team allows the ball to bounce twice, who serves the next point?
- If the serve doesn't cross the short line, what should the server do?

Assessment

Observe to see if students are ready for a game. If they are not, stick to practicing skills. If students are disinterested, make their practice into a contest. If they are ready for the game, be vigilant about the ability of students at each court to play safely and react accordingly.

Handball (One Wall)
BEGINNER
LESSON 3

Hinders

Facilities

Wall with no obstructions

Materials

- Blackboard, magnetic board, or charts that show court positioning and boundaries
- One ball per person

Performance Goal

Students will play a short, modified game.

Cognitive Goal

Students will learn court positioning.

Lesson Safety

Review hinders and who is responsible for calling a stop of play when hinders occur.

Motivation

After a couple of days, the students will appreciate getting in a short game and finding out what it is like to play different opponents.

Warm-Up

1. Encourage students to take a ball and practice as soon as they come in.
2. Lead mimetics for hitting a ball on the right, on the left, and overhead.

Lesson Sequence

1. Diagram and explain court positioning for singles (or doubles if not enough courts).
   a. Taking the middle
   b. Hinders
2. Rotate opponents after each 5-point game. Match winners with winners.

Review and Stretching

As students stretch, ask if they can explain why they want to take the middle.

Killer Rollout Shot

Facilities

Wall with no obstructions

Materials

- Blackboard, magnetic board, or charts that show court positioning and boundaries
- One ball per person

Performance Goals

Students will do the following:

- Hit low shots and killers.
- Play a game.

Cognitive Goals

Students will learn the following:

- The strategy of hitting a rollout or kill shot and when to use it appropriately
- The difference between a rollout and a pinch

Lesson Safety

Emphasize that students must follow all the blocking and interference rules.

Motivation

Explain that there is a kill shot in handball that you want everyone to try. It's a ball that hits the wall so flat and low that it rolls off the wall. It is impossible to return, so if they can do it, it's a point winner. The trick is to learn how to get the ball to roll out.

Figure 17.4 Hitting a low ball.

Warm-Up

Students practice upon entering. Lead the class through the following:

- Hitting with right hand and moving to designated space on the floor
- Hitting with left hand and moving to designated space on the floor
- Bending down and hitting flat to the bottom of the wall
- Bending down and hitting with an upward follow-through (clearing shot) so imaginary ball hits near top of wall
- Dropping back to hit a ball going over the head, using the overhead motion

Lesson Sequence

1. Demonstrate the point of contact and flat arm swing necessary to get a killer (a kill shot) to roll off the wall (see figure 17.4). Let students practice until each has had 5 successful killers.

2. Teach rules that treat a pinch (crouch) shot and a killer differently and explain:

   a. A hit ball must touch the wall before touching the ground. A kill shot hits the wall first and rolls off it so low that it is impossible to return. A kill shot is also called a *killer* or *rollout*.

   b. Shots that hit the ground and wall simultaneously are considered to have touched the ground first. These are pinch or crouch shots and are not legal.

3. Remind students that long serves and short serves are not legal. Remind them that during the rally, balls passing the back line before bouncing are out of bounds.

4. Allow 11-point games. Switch opponents if there's time.

Review and Stretching

As students stretch, ask the following:

- Why is a rollout such a good shot?
- If the ball seems to be pinched, is it playable?
- Is a short serve legal? Is there such a thing as a long serve?

Clearing Shots

Facilities

Wall with no obstructions

Materials

- Blackboard, magnetic board, or charts that show court positioning and boundaries
- One ball per person

Performance Goals

Students will do the following:

- Hit clearing shots.
- Play a game.

Cognitive Goals

Students will learn the following:

- Strategy of clearing the ball
- How the path of their swing affects the direction of the ball

Lesson Safety

Emphasize that students must follow all the blocking and interference rules.

Motivation

Explain that the students know that the best position on the court is the middle, but they don't always come back to the middle. Ask what would be a great strategy when their opponents are clustered near the wall, trying for a "kill." Is there anything they could do to make them get away from the wall? Explain that hitting a high ball that passes high overhead so that it cannot be reached if the player stays by the wall will force the opponents to move away. Moving someone away from the wall is called a *clearing shot*.

Warm-Ups

Make equipment available for practice as students enter. Lead the class through mimetics for the right-hand drive, left-hand drive, right-hand rollout (kill shot), left-hand rollout (kill shot), and hits that follow through high.

Lesson Sequence

1. Demonstrate and explain the mechanics of the clearing shot.
    a. The position of the palm of the hand on the hit
    b. The point of contact to hit a clearing shot
    c. The arch in the swing for a clear
2. Have students practice hitting high clearing shots that come off the wall and land deep in the court.
    a. Have students practice until each has five successes.
    b. Explain that the strategy for moving opponents from the middle of the court is to use the high shot as a clearing shot.
    c. Remind them that the follow-through must go up.
3. Finish the class with games.

Review and Stretching

As students stretch, ask the following:

- What shot brings players to the wall?
- What shot gets them away?
- What must your arm and hand do to hit a high shot?
- If you want to hit a rollout, what things must you do?

Teacher Homework

Prepare the draw so you can run several small round-robin tournaments, basing each of the tournaments on the level of skill displayed to date. Place teams that are competitive in the same draw.

Round 1

Facilities

Game areas with boundary lines, one area for every four students

Materials

- Visual aid that shows court and game schedule
- Round-robin tournament charts for game schedule and standings
- One ball per person

Performance Goals

Students will do the following:

- Improve skills in game situations.
- Play competitive games. (Doubles play is more complex but less rigorous. It is a compromise to be used only when classes are too large to accommodate everyone in singles. If your facilities are adequate and you can run singles, save this doubles lesson for the end of the unit as a special culminating event.)

Cognitive Goals

Students will learn the following:

- The length of game (time or score)
- How to proceed in the class tournament
    - Who and where to play
    - What to do if opponents do not arrive
    - What to do if partners do not arrive
    - How to report scores

Lesson Safety

Emphasize that students must follow all blocking and interference rules.

Motivation

Explain that there are several tournaments. After everyone in a tournament plays each other, there will be one winner. Explain that games are posted and that if they learn how to read the schedule, they can get to their courts and begin without wasting time. First, they have to learn to read the charts. Then they have to learn that the tournament goes on with or without their opponent or partner and what to do if someone isn't there.

Warm-Up

Have balls available for sport-specific practice as students arrive.

Lesson Sequence

1. Post and explain an enlarged round-robin tournament chart. (See appendix A for appropriate tournament charts.)
2. Post and explain how to read the game schedule and how to report scores.
3. Encourage daily attendance and preparation, noting that when a doubles partner is absent, the attending partner has to play alone or can play with a substitute and forfeit the match.
4. Ask if they want to start the tournament and count this day's games.

Review and Stretching

As students stretch, ask the following:

- Are there any questions?
- Did you all report your scores and see them entered?

Teacher Homework

Post and update the round-robin standings each day.

Tournament Conclusion

Facilities

Game areas with boundary lines, one area for every four students

Materials

- Posted tournament schedule
- Updated round-robin standings

Performance Goal

Students will play competitive games.

Cognitive Goals

- Students will compete with emphasis on the following:
  - Maintaining good sportsmanship
  - Playing by the rules
  - Not physically or psychologically hurting their opponents
- Students will assume responsibility for the following:
  - Getting to assigned court for game
  - Returning equipment
  - Reporting scores

Lesson Safety

Emphasize that students must follow all the blocking and interference rules.

Motivation

The tournament will provide the motivation.

Warm-Up

Have balls available for pregame practice as students arrive.

Lesson Sequence

1. Students follow the posted game and court schedules and play their games.
2. Students enter their scores before leaving.
3. Use teachable moments to discuss game strategy or rules. If the whole class will profit, discuss these strategies during the review.

Review and Stretching

As students stretch, review common problems and answer questions.

Assessment

Observe for performance standards as outlined in the beginner handball skills rubric and use the following quiz for objective assessment.

Beginner Handball Skills Rubric

Name _____ Date _____

Teacher _____ Class _____

	0	1	2	3	4	5
Serve	No effort.	• Clears short line occasionally. • Serves from correct position on court.	• Serves underhand. • Sometimes puts ball in play. • Tries to avoid shorts and longs.	• Consistently puts ball in play. • Does not drive ball back into self.	• Serve can be driven. • Does not drive serve into partner. • Controls left or right serves.	• Varies speed, depth, and direction of serve. • Gets into good position immediately after serve.
Hits	No effort.	• Hits ball to wall off self-bounce with both hands.	• Meets slow-moving object with dominant hand. • Redirects ball to wall after it bounces once.	• Meets a slow ball after it bounces with weak hand. • Reacts well to all balls on dominant side.	• Meets the ball on the run on dominant side. • Hits a volley. • Returns low, fast balls on strong side.	• Hits return with purpose. • Chooses correctly between volley and swing. • Controls depth and varies speed.
Play	No effort.	• Tries to return ball hit nearby.	• Covers all play to forehand side. • Remembers to keep score.	• Covers play to backhand side within one step. • Covers half court to forehand side.	• Feet react to shots on all sides. • Avoids a hinder or block. • Moves to center.	• Gets opponents out of center. • Uses strategic placement. • Is developing a killer.

From Isobel Kleinman, 2009, *Complete Physical Education Plans for Grades 5 to 12, Second Edition* (Champaign, IL: Human Kinetics).

Beginner Handball Quiz

Name _____ Date _____

Teacher _____ Class _____

Multiple Choice

Read each question and each answer carefully. Be sure to choose the best answer that fits the preceding statement. When you have made your choice, put the appropriate letter on the line to the left of the numbered question.

_____ 1. Opposing players must return the ball when

    a. the server serves the ball so that it bounces outside the sideline

    b. the server serves the ball so it passes the short line

    c. the server serves the ball so that it hits herself

    d. all of the above

_____ 2. A kill shot is

    a. a shot that hits the opponent

    b. a shot that hits the lowest part of the wall and rolls back

    c. an ace serve

    d. all of the above

_____ 3. All players try to get to the center of the courts because

    a. it enables them to block other players from getting to the ball

    b. they have the best chance of getting more open space in which to play

    c. they can more easily reach the shots their opponents hit

    d. all of the above

_____ 4. When the ball is served behind the long line, the following should occur.

    a. The opponents should take over the serve.

    b. The server should begin taking his second serve.

    c. The server gets a point.

    d. The ball is in play and no one gets a point until the point is played out.

_____ 5. When a ball is sent out of bounds by the serving team, opponents

    a. get a point

    b. take over the serve

    c. give the ball to the server for another try

    d. take over the serve and get a point

_____ 6. The ball is served. Receivers allow the ball to bounce twice before returning it with a killer. The serving team led 8 to 7 before the point was played. The score should now be

    a. 8 to 8

    b. 9 to 7

    c. 8 to 6

    d. 9 to 6

»continued

»continued

_____ 7. The ball is served so that the server blocked the opponent's ability to get to it. The correct thing for the server to do is

    a. claim the point, declaring that the shot was too good for opponents to get

    b. replay the point without anyone getting a point

    c. end the game because it is not right to be told to get out of the way

    d. all of the above

_____ 8. To hit a kill shot,

    a. you should hit the ball just before it bounces the second time

    b. you should hit the ball when it is at the height of the bounce

    c. you should wait for a time when you are near the wall

    d. you should do both a and c

_____ 9. The following is true of handball.

    a. It is expensive to play since so much equipment is necessary.

    b. You need many people to play a game.

    c. You can set up a game on just about any wall you can find.

    d. All of the above.

_____ 10. Sometimes the best strategy is to

    a. aim for a killer on every shot

    b. stay near the long line

    c. hit to the left side of the court if your opponent is right-handed

    d. wait for the ball to bounce twice

Beginner Handball Answer Key

Multiple Choice

1. B—All other examples are illegal.

2. B—The only reason it is called a *killer* is because no one can get it after it bounces—it never does.

3. C—The center of the court is equidistant from every possible shot the opponent can hit.

4. B—The server is allowed one long or one short serve. If he has one, he gets a second chance.

5. B—Sending a ball out of bounds ends the point. Since the server sent it out, she loses her turn of service. No one gets any points on this play.

6. B—The score is 9 to 7. The serving team wins a point in this situation because the receivers let it bounce twice.

7. B—Blocking is not a legal strategy. The ball must be replayed.

8. D—Aiming for a winning shot should be done when you will make the least amount of errors. If you accidently hit a pinch, your opponents will win the point. Wait for the right moment.

9. C—The other statements are the opposite of what they should be; it is the least expensive and requires the fewest people to play.

10. C—All the other statements will make success either difficult or impossible.

18

Pickleball

Chapter Overview

1. Introduce the use of the paddle and its grip and encourage success by teaching beginning skills at a wall, then at close distances with a partner, and then over the net.

2. Teach the forehand, backhand, serve, and volley.

3. Explain that pickleball is called *slowed-down tennis* because some of its rules duplicate tennis and others don't. Teach the rules of pickleball:

   - Players cannot allow the ball to bounce twice before returning it.
   - Players must follow the service rules.
     - The serve must go over the net into the diagonal box.
     - The serve must pass the short line before bouncing.
     - The server must change sides of the court, serving each point to alternate boxes.
     - Each team player serves before the opponents take over the serve, except for the first service of the game.
     - The first server of a team is always the person standing in the right-hand box.
   - Players must follow the receiving rules.
     - The receiver must return all serves directed to her box if they are good serves.
     - The receiver must allow the ball to bounce before returning it.

4. Teach the two-bounce rule (unlike any rule in tennis).
   - The ball must bounce on each side of the court before any player can run to the net to volley.

5. Teach the short-line rule: No player can hit a ball on a fly if he is closer to the net than the short line (again, unlike any rule in tennis).

6. Introduce doubles positioning and have students play doubles games.

Pickleball Study Sheet

Fun Facts

- Pickleball is the 1965 invention of a U.S. congressman, Jack Pritchard, and his friends, William Bell and Barney McCallum, who wanted to create a game their families could play in driveways or on dead-end streets on Bainbridge Island, off the coast of Seattle.
- Pickleball is such a strange name, especially for a game that combines aspects of tennis, badminton, and paddleball. It was named after the dog of one of the founders because the dog used to run away with the ball during the game. The dog's name was Pickles.
- The pickleball court uses the same dimensions as the badminton court.

Rules

Serve

- When a team takes over the serve, the player on the right side serves first.
- Servers must keep one foot behind the back line and contact the ball in the air while their paddle is below their waist.
- The ball cannot be bounced and then hit.
- The ball must pass over the net, clear the no-volley zone, and land on the line or in the diagonal service box.
- If it touches the net on the way to the service box, the serve is repeated.
- If the serve does not land in the proper box, the server loses his turn to serve and his partner begins serving from the box his partner is in. However, if this is the beginning service of the game, the team is allowed only one fault before losing serve. Servers continue serving, alternating the box they serve to after every point, until they cannot return the ball on the court.

Game play

- Once the ball is put in play with a legal serve, the receiving team must allow the serve to bounce and the player on that side of the court must return it.
- If the receiving team makes an error, the serving team wins a point and continues their turn of service.
- The ball must be allowed to bounce on each side of the net before a player may approach the net to volley the ball back.
- The point is over when the ball is not returned, the ball is hit in the air before it bounces on each side of the net, the ball is hit into the net or out-of-bounds, or a player volleys while inside the no-volley zone.

»continued

 From Isobel Kleinman, 2009, *Complete Physical Education Plans for Grades 5 to 12, Second Edition* (Champaign, IL: Human Kinetics).

»continued

Doubles Positioning

This is the best positioning while the team on the right is serving. The receiving team is back in their court so they can allow the ball to bounce. The serving team is back so they can also let the ball bounce (leaving a player at the net would make that player vulnerable for making a volley and breaking the two-bounce rule.) Once the point is in play, it is best that doubles teams move up and back together so they are side by side (see figure 18.1).

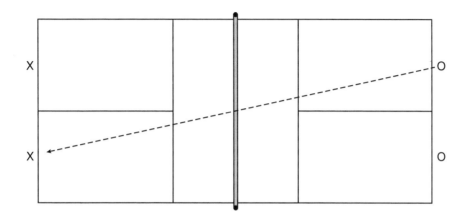

Figure 18.1 Doubles positioning to receive serve.

From Isobel Kleinman, 2009, *Complete Physical Education Plans for Grades 5 to 12, Second Edition* (Champaign, IL: Human Kinetics).

713

Pickleball Extension Project

Name _____ Date _____

Teacher _____ Class _____

List three friends you would play pickleball with outside school.

Name two places where you can play pickleball.

What equipment would you need?

Where can you get pickleball equipment and how much would it cost?

How does playing pickleball benefit you?

Pickleball Student Portfolio Checklist

Name _____ Date _____

Teacher _____ Class _____

_____ Uses proper grip.

_____ Shifts the paddle and footwork to go from forehand to backhand.

_____ Can direct the ball so it passes over the net.

_____ Can direct the ball so that it travels diagonally across the court.

_____ Can meet a bouncing ball on the forehand side.

_____ Can meet a bouncing ball on the backhand side.

_____ Can meet the ball without a bounce (volley).

_____ Has learned the rules of pickleball.

_____ Can play a doubles game.

_____ Maintains good sportsmanship while in competition.

_____ Can follow directions of the tournament schedule.

_____ Assumes responsibility for getting and returning equipment.

_____ Assumes officiating chores when not playing.

From Isobel Kleinman, 2009, *Complete Physical Education Plans for Grades 5 to 12, Second Edition* (Champaign, IL: Human Kinetics).

Pickleball Learning Experience Outline

Contents and Procedure

1. Familiarize students with the paddle and the proper grip.
2. Teach ball control: at a wall, with a partner at close distances, and then over a net.
3. Teach major skills: forehand, backhand, serve, and volley.
4. Teach the rules that duplicate tennis.
   a. The ball must be hit before it bounces twice.
   b. The serve must pass over the net into the diagonal box.
   c. A let serve gives servers a second attempt to hit a legal serve.
   d. Servers serve from the right side of the court first.
   e. Servers must switch sides to serve the next point.
   f. Receivers must return legal serves to their own side of the court.
   g. Balls are good if they hit any part of the line.
   h. The serve must bounce before returning it.

5. Teach exclusive pickleball rules.
   a. Servers must hit underhand with one foot outside the court.
   b. Servers continue their turn of service until they lose a point.
   c. Each partner takes a turn of service, except on the first service of the game.
   d. The two-bounce rule requires that the ball bounce on each side of the net before it can be volleyed.
   e. Players cannot volley when inside the 7-foot (2-meter) no-volley zone.
6. Introduce doubles positioning if the class is playing doubles.
7. Create an intraclass tournament for all levels of play.

Teaching Tips for Special Considerations

- Medically excused students can officiate games, collect game scores as games end and give out court assignments, keep tournament charts up to date, write assignments on a blackboard, and keep the time, making sure game time is equal.
- Absenteeism can ruin a tournament. To keep it flowing and fair and to guarantee that players have a good daily experience, the following accommodations are suggested for doubles tournaments when a partner is absent:
  - Play the whole court alone.
  - Officially lose (forfeit) but play with a substitute in the absent partner's place.

Facilities

- Convert volleyball courts by dropping the net. Lay a 7-foot (2-meter) line for the short line and the no-volley-zone line. Official courts are 20 feet by 44 feet (6 meters by 13.4 meters). The no-volley zone ends 7 feet (2 meters) from the net, with the remaining area split into two service boxes (see figure 18.2).

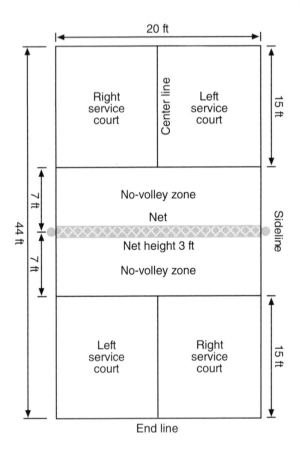

Figure 18.2 Diagram of a pickleball court.

- Convert one tennis court into two pickleball courts. Lines must divide the service box and indicate a short line and no-volley zone.
- Because space may be limited and every student deserves equal court and game time, try this rotation for total involvement.
  - Assign players A, B, and C to court 1.
  - Divide class time into three playing rounds.
  - Round 1—Player A plays B while C officiates.
  - Round 2—Player B plays C while A officiates.
  - Round 3—Player C plays A while B officiates.

Fotelica.com/Wes Paz

Figure 18.3 Pickleball and paddle.

Materials

- One paddle for every student (see figure 18.3)
- One ball for every two students (see figure 18.3)

Unit Timeline

The 13 lessons in this introductory unit include the following:

- an introduction to the equipment,
- opportunities to learn and practice the forehand and backhand swings and the volley,
- the rules of service and play,
- basic doubles positioning strategy, and
- tournament play.

Assessment

The unit concludes with a written quiz and beginner performance rubric.

Suggested Resources

Freidenberg, M. 1999. *The official pickleball handbook.* Seattle, WA: PB Master.

Pickleball.com. 2008. www.pickleball.com.

USA Pickleball Association. 2008. www.usapa.org.

Pickleball
BEGINNER
LESSON 1

Forehand

Facilities

One court or specified area for each group

Materials

- One pickleball per student
- One paddle per student

Performance Goals

Students will do the following:

- Hold the pickleball paddle correctly.
- Meet the ball on one bounce on the forehand side.
- Play safely with implements in a small space.

Cognitive Goals

Students will learn the following:

- How to anticipate where the ball goes after bouncing
- Safety concerns of playing in smaller places with a paddle
- How to improve their focus on the ball

Lesson Safety

Make sure practice areas are separated by a minimum of 10 feet (3 meters).

Motivation

Announce that students are going to love this game, even though it has a funny name. Not only is the game fun, but while they play, they will learn skills that will help them in table tennis, handball, paddleball, racquetball, badminton, and tennis. It's amazing that a game that is easy to learn and fun to play can give every student a head start in all these other sports, but it can because it uses many of the same skills. A few things are different, though, including some rules, the paddle, the ball, and the size of the court.

Warm-Up

1. Have students take a pickleball and bounce it as they jog around the playing area.
2. Teach mimetics for the forehand swing.
   - Open the dominant hand so it faces a target and swing it from the hip across the opposite shoulder so the hand ends up near the ear (5 times).
   - Step forward with the opposite foot and take a forehand swing (5 times).

Lesson Sequence

1. Distribute paddles and check the proper grip.
2. Demonstrate hitting the ball to the floor using the paddle and ask if students can do the same, keeping the ball going five times. What about 10 times?
3. Demonstrate the forehand volley 5 feet (1.5 meters) from the wall. Hit the ball so when it comes off the wall, it can be rallied back.
   a. Set up players 5 feet (1.5 meters) from the wall so they are 10 feet (3 meters) from each other.
   b. Explain safety concerns when using a paddle in shared space.
      - What to do when the ball flies to someone else's area
      - Returning the ball properly to the person asking for it
   c. Ask if students can hit the ball without a bounce five times. What about 10 times?
      - Discourage swings.
      - Have them concentrate on meeting the ball at its height, using a firm wrist on contact, and keeping their eyes on the ball.
   d. Demonstrate hitting off one bounce and following through.
      - Have students try rallying with the ball coming off the wall.
      - Allow multiple turns.
4. If students are ready, try rallying over the net.
   a. Choose a student who can help demonstrate. Try sticking to forehands to rally over the net.
   b. Set students up so they can practice rallying with each other over a net.

Review and Stretching

As students stretch, explain that they practiced the volley and a forehand ground stroke.

- Ask if they knew which was which.
- Explain that in the game they will play next time, sometimes they must let the ball bounce once, and other times they may hit it before it bounces, but they are never to let it bounce twice or they will lose the ball and maybe even the point.

Backhand and Service Rules

Facilities

One court or specified area for each group

Materials

- One pickleball per student
- One paddle per student

Performance Goals

Students will do the following:

- Meet ball on the backhand side.
- Hit a diagonal serve from off the court.
- Use service rules to practice playing points.

Cognitive Goals

Students will learn the following:

- The difference between the forehand and backhand
- Pickleball service rules

Lesson Safety

Encourage students to practice in the same direction to avoid getting in each other's way.

Motivation

Explain that since the class is doing so well hitting the ball, you thought that they'd like to learn how to play a pickleball game. That means learning how to put the ball into play using pickleball rules. But first, you have to teach them how to handle balls coming to their nonpaddle side—their backhand.

Warm-Up

1. Allow students to practice on court with equipment.
2. Lead the class in mimetics for the following:
   - Forehand—Step forward and to the side with the opposite foot as you bring the paddle back. Bend down and swing forward, following through to the opposite shoulder (10 times).
   - Backhand—Using the foot on the same side of the body as the paddle, step forward and to the side, allowing the paddle shoulder to turn away from the target and the paddle to come back. Let the swing open the body so the paddle ends up with the front edge pointing toward the target (10 times).

Lesson Sequence

1. Demonstrate hitting backhand to backhand with a partner who is 5 feet (1.5 meters) from the net.

   a. Have students line up opposite a partner so the backhand sides of their paddles are lined up with each other. Ask that they hit backhand to backhand from a few feet away and try to keep the ball going.

   b. Increase the distance they are from each other when they can rally three times before losing control. Increase the distance as they increase their consecutive contacts.

   c. Ask students to count how many consecutive hits they get.

   d. Tell students the best record of hits to date, challenging them to beat it.

2. Explain that to serve legally, they must do the following:

   a. Keep one foot off the court.

   b. Meet the ball below the waist without it touching the floor first.

   c. Make the ball land on the line of or in the diagonal service box.

   d. Continue serving from alternating boxes until put out.

   e. When a team gains the serve, the person on the right serves first.

3. Demonstrate an underhand serve and how to make the ball go on a diagonal.

4. Have students serve a minimum of 10 serves successfully before going on.

5. If there's time, explain the following:

   a. Receivers must let the serve bounce before returning it and return serves that are in or on any line of their box.

   b. Both partners serve when their team takes over the service except during the first service of the game.

6. Allow a game using whatever rules the students already know.

Review and Stretching

As student stretch, ask the following:

- What is the easiest way to get a ball to travel on a diagonal?
- What happens if you don't get your serve in the diagonal box?
- Why do you need a full stroke to get the serve over the net?

Pickleball
**BEGINNER
LESSON 3**

Playing the Game

Facilities

One court for every four students, or a specified area to go to or job to do if students have to wait for a court

Materials

- One pickleball per student
- One paddle per student

Performance Goals

Students will do the following:

- Improve their paddle skills.
- Follow the rules of the game.
- Understand scoring.
- Play games.

Cognitive Goal

Students will review service and receiver's rules.

Lesson Safety

If you do not have a court for every four students but have outside space that will not interfere with court play, equip everyone to practice and have those who are waiting for a court practice in the other space. If there is no safe place other than on the courts, collect the extra equipment and have the remaining students officiate from the net post while waiting for their turn on the court.

Motivation

Explain to students that they haven't learned all the rules yet, and in order to get into a game, they need to learn what they do when they are the receiving team. Once they understand the receiving rules, they will be ready to play games.

Warm-Up

1. Encourage students to come in, get equipment, and see how long they can sustain a rally. If there is not enough court space, encourage them to use the back court or walls behind the back court to rally with themselves.

2. Lead students through footwork and mimetics.

    a. Use a three-step approach (if right-handed, run left, run right, cross the left in front of the right, plant the foot, and bend the knee) to have students run toward the net. Then take a forehand swing, following through to the opposite shoulder (see figure 18.4) (10 times).

    b. Use a three-step approach to have students run toward the net (right, left, right crosses in front of the left and bends at the knee) to take a backhand swing, following through so the front edge of the paddle faces a target (10 times).

Lesson Sequence

1. Teach the following rules:

    a. Players must return serves that are hit to their box.

    b. The receiver must let the serve bounce before returning it.

    c. The serving team must let the return of serve bounce before hitting it back (two-bounce rule).

    d. Volleying the ball is illegal until the ball bounces on each side.

    e. Only the serving team wins points.

2. Answer questions before sending students to courts to play games.

3. Rotate courts after a set time to enable playing with a variety of players and to reduce the competitive atmosphere.

Fotelica.com/Wes Paz

Figure 18.4 Moving forward to hit with a forehand swing.

Review and Stretching

As students stretch, ask the following:

- What side of the court should the turn of service start from?
- Where should teams put their best player if they win first serve, right or left? Why?
- Can a server run in to hit the returned ball before it bounces? What rule must servers follow?
- If the serve to the right side is served down the middle and it is easier for the receiving team player on the left to hit it back, who must return it?

Volley

Facilities

One court for every four students, or a specified area to go to or job to do if students have to wait for a court

Materials

- One pickleball per student
- One paddle per student

Performance Goals

Students will do the following:

- Continue to improve paddle skills.
- Volley.
- Play games.

Cognitive Goals

Students will learn the following:

- Rules and mechanics of volleying
- What it's like to play with different people

Lesson Safety

If you do not have a court for every four students but have outside space that will not interfere with court play, equip everyone to practice and have those who are waiting for a court practice in the other space. If there is no safe place other than on the courts, collect the extra equipment and have the remaining students officiate from the net post while waiting for their turn on the court.

Motivation

The class must be getting excited since most students are feeling comfortable hitting the ball. Acknowledge how good they are getting and remind them that hitting a ball before it bounces is a volley and that pickleball has special rules for the volley. Volleying should be easy because the class just practiced its mechanics during the warm-up. What they still need to learn is how important it is to meet the ball out in front. Encourage them to try.

Warm-Up

1. Encourage students to pick up equipment as they enter and practice.
2. Lead mimetics in the following:
   a. Waiting position, paddle resting in second hand in front of body (5 times)

    b. Forehand volley (from waiting position)

- Turn the face of the paddle toward the net on the forehand side (5 times).
- Step to net with opposite foot while positioning the paddle (5 times).
- Repeat previous steps, pretend to make contact, and punch the paddle to its target (5 times).

    c. Backhand volley (from waiting position)

- Turn backhand side of paddle to the net so it is out in front (5 times).
- Step to net with paddle foot while getting paddle in position (5 times).
- Repeat previous steps and on contact, punch the paddle forward (5 times).

    d. Three steps right, plant proper foot, bend, and use a full forehand swing (5 times)

    e. Three steps left, plant proper foot, bend, and use a full backhand swing (5 times)

Lesson Sequence

1. Demonstrate the volley. Have students practice with a partner, exchanging who feeds the ball until they each volley successfully (10 times).
2. Teach the rules that involve the volley.
   a. The short line is the end of the no-volley zone.
   b. Review the two-bounce rule, which prevents servers from rushing the net on the serve.
   c. Ask if anyone has questions.
3. Instruct students to play a 5-point game. When they are done, have them report to you so you can send them out to play new opponents. Make an effort to have winners of the minigames play other winners.
4. This is a good time to get a feel for how to develop the class tournament so it is competitive and interesting for all skill levels.

Review and Stretching

As students stretch, ask the following:

- Does anyone have questions about scoring or the game rules?
- Who can explain the two-bounce rule?
- What line can't you cross to volley?
- When is it OK to volley?

Teacher Homework

Start scouting the partnerships for the strongest and weakest teams. This will help when you develop the class tournament.

Side-by-Side Strategy

Facilities

One court for every four students, or a specified area to go to or job to do if students have to wait for a court

Materials

- Blackboard or other visual aid
- Tournament charts
- One pickleball per student
- One paddle per student

Performance Goals

Students will do the following:

- Choose a permanent tournament partner.
- Commit to a doubles partner.
- Play practice games.

Cognitive Goals

Students will learn the following:

- Side-by-side doubles positioning
- How to respond to the timer's horn and follow court assignments
- What to do if a partner is absent once the tournament begins

Lesson Safety

Have students make sure that when they leave the court to report the outcome of their 5-point games and to get reassigned, they walk well behind the courts so as not to interfere with games in progress.

Motivation

Explain that there is an advantage to playing doubles with the same teammate. Players get to know each other's habits. They discover who covers the shots that go down the middle, when to back each other up, when to calm each other down, when to give each other confidence, and when to simply play their position. As in other sports, court responsibility is divvied up. Successful doubles teams know what to expect from each other and have more fun together because they work as a unit. For all those reasons, everyone will commit to a doubles partner and learn the most common positioning in small-court doubles strategy—side by side.

Warm-Up

1. Allow students to get equipment and practice upon entering the gym.
2. Lead mimetics for the backhand, forehand, low volley, and high volley, making sure to include footwork (5 times each).

Lesson Sequence

1. Bring the class to the blackboard to show the side-by-side doubles strategy (see figure 18.5)
   a. Show how partners split responsibilities and discuss the following:
      - How to decide who plays the left and right
      - Balls down the middle
      - Balls going short
      - Balls passing over one person's head
      - How, when, and why to switch sides of the court during play
   b. Diagram the best position to be in during the serve (see figure 18.1 on page 713).
   c. Put court assignments on the board as they would appear in the tournament schedule. Send assigned students out to play using side-by-side doubles strategy.
   d. As students play, have someone go around and write down the names of the doubles teams.
2. End first games with timer's horn and bring the class back to the blackboard.
   a. Show how teams should indicate winners.
   b. Indicate the second game assignments as they would appear on a tournament chart and send students to play with new opponents.

3. At the end of the second game, bring students back to the blackboard to explain the following:

   a. What to do when they aren't scheduled to play

   b. What to do when their teammate is absent

      • Ask a nonplaying person to fill in and don't count the win.

      • Play the doubles match alone.

   c. How to report winners

Review and Stretching

As students stretch, discuss the following:

- Is everyone sure your doubles team is on the list?

- Before scoring, what should all opposing players do? (Get some warm-up hits.)

- What is one way a doubles team can divide court responsibilities?

- If there are three playing rounds and three games must take place during class, what happens if players are late getting to their court? What should the others do while they wait?

- During a tournament, what is a fair way to adjust for someone's absence?

- The next lesson will simulate tournament conditions, but the games won't count.

Teacher Homework

List student teams by skill level. Make a round-robin tournament for each skill level if the skills in the class are vastly different. Make sure you have at least four teams in each tournament. With only 12 teams in a class, a class would need 11 rounds to accommodate the entire round-robin and each day would require two rounds to guarantee that everyone played if there were five courts. See appendix A for the round-robin tournament schedules and scoring forms.

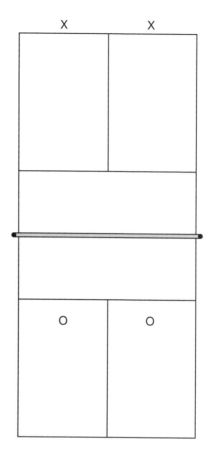

Figure 18.5 Side-by-side doubles positioning from the baseline and up to the no-volley zone after the two-bounce rule is met.

Simulating Tournament Play

Facilities

One court for every four students, or a specified area to go to or job to do if students have to wait for a court

Materials

- Blackboard or other visual aid
- Tournament charts
- One pickleball per student
- One paddle per student

Performance Goals

Students will do the following:

- Simulate responsible tournament play.
- Play practice game.

Cognitive Goal

Students will be self-sufficient in following game, scheduling and reporting winners.

Lesson Safety

Have students make sure that when they leave the court to report the outcome of their 5-point games and to get reassigned, they walk well behind the courts so as not to interfere with games in progress.

Motivation

Explain that to have all the game time possible during the tournament, the class must learn the routine. Teams should get their equipment, go directly to the courts they are assigned to, and warm up by the time game time begins. When the timer's horn blows, those playing in the second round should take the court and take a warm-up rally before beginning the game. The teams coming off the court should report the outcome of their game and go back to their court to officiate. When there are not enough courts for everyone, these procedures help guarantee each team the most playing time possible.

Warm-Up

Have students get equipment and practice upon entering the gym.

Lesson Sequence

1. Bring the class to the blackboard.
    a. Discuss options when a partner is absent during a tournament.
    b. Put court assignments on the board as they appear on the tournament schedule.
    c. Ask students to remember what rounds they play and when they officiate.
    d. Send first players to play.
    e. Ask the teams who have to wait to go to the court to officiate, call lines, keep score, or be ball boys and girls.
    f. Remind students that at the timer's horn, players not playing the second round should get off the court, indicate who won their game, and return to officiate. Players who are up in the new round should take the court immediately, warm up, and then begin their games.
2. End the first round with the timer's horn.
    a. Remind teams coming off the court to come to indicate game winners.
    b. Remind teams waiting to get on the court to get on and start.
3. Use the timer's horn at the end of the second round.

Review and Stretching

As students stretch, ask the following:

- Does anyone have questions about the procedure?
- Which strategy suited your team most?
- Does everyone understand that whether you are playing at the moment or not, you should be at your assigned court?
- Does everyone understand what to do if your partner is absent? For the game to count, the lone teammate must play alone.
- Do you know that when you come in you should check your court assignments and playing round and go to the court to warm up?

Teacher Homework

Make up the tournament charts. (See appendix A for appropriate round-robin tournament forms.) One chart should list all doubles teams with their code number and a place to indicate their wins and losses against the other teams they play. The other chart should indicate court assignments, playing rounds, and which teams play and which officiate in each round. Post the charts.

Round 1

Facilities

One court for every four students, or a specified area to go to or job to do if students have to wait for a court

Materials

- Blackboard or other visual aid
- Tournament charts
- One pickleball per game (with extras available in case of breakage)
- One paddle per student

Performance Goals

Students will do the following:

- Play round 1 of the tournament.
- Exhibit good behavior during competition.
  - Play by the rules.
  - Exhibit good sportsmanship.
  - Follow tournament procedure.

Cognitive Goal

Students will find a strategy that they and their teammate can use to play their best.

Lesson Safety

Send nonplaying students off the court and to work as officials. Collect unneeded equipment. Explain that students leaving the court should walk behind the baseline to avoid interference and getting clobbered with a paddle.

Motivation

The excitement of the tournament will be the motivation.

Warm-Up

Have equipment available for students to warm up with on the court as they arrive.

Lesson Sequence

1. Post schedules on the blackboard and in the entrance to the gym so students can easily see where they belong.
2. Once the warm-up is over, collect any equipment not needed for the games.
3. Follow the tournament procedure taught in the last two classes.

Review and Stretching

As students stretch, ask that they make sure their game results have been submitted.

Assessment

Observe each court and their ability to officiate, start in a timely fashion, and make use of their playing time. If the procedure is too complicated with only tournament charts to guide them, make changes in the next lesson.

Tournament Conclusion

Facilities

One court for every four students, or a specified area to go to or job to do if students have to wait for a court

Materials

- Blackboard or other visual aid
- Tournament charts
- One pickleball per game (with extras available in case of breakage)
- One paddle per student
- Performance rubric for beginners

Performance Goals

Students will do the following:

- Warm up on the courts before games.
- Play a tournament by the rules and with good sportsmanship.

Cognitive Goals

Students will learn the following:

- How to be self-sufficient by reading charts and following their progress by using math skills to figure out who is in the lead
- How to meet the challenge of playing at their highest level

Lesson Safety

Now that students are involved in competition, be vigilant about the psychological welfare of all students. Be prepared to step in if behavior becomes intimidating physically or emotionally.

Motivation

The tournament itself will be the class motivation.

Warm-Up

Have equipment available for students to warm up with on the court as they arrive.

Lesson Sequence

1. Schedules should be clearly posted on the blackboard and available upon entry to the gym. Equipment should be out and available for students' pregame warm-up.
2. Games begin as soon as warm-ups are over.
3. Students must circle their team number if they win so the wins can be entered on the round-robin tournament chart.

Review

During the tournament, if students have to share courts with multiple teams, use most of the class for playing. Limit this section of the lesson to collecting scores and equipment, answering questions, and commenting on events that occurred during class.

If you're giving a quiz at the end of the unit, remind students and review possible questions.

Assessment

During the tournament, post the skills rubric or performance expectations so students are aware of how they will be evaluated. Assess students during the final days of the unit.

Quiz and Culminating Activity

Facilities

One court for every four students, or a specified area to go to or job to do if students have to wait for a court

Materials

- One quiz per student
- Pens or pencils
- One pickleball per game
- One paddle per student
- Blackboard or other visual aid
- Tournament charts

Performance Goals

Students will do the following:

- Take a short quiz.
- Conclude their tournament or participate in another culminating activity.

Cognitive Goal

Students will get a measure of their pickleball understanding.

Lesson Safety

As students finish their quiz, you can allow them to pick up equipment and begin warming up if they are well away from the students still taking the quiz.

Motivation

Tell your students how proud you are of them handling their own tournament, playing so well, improving so much, and having such a wonderful competitive spirit. Explain the plan for the day and the culminating activity: play-offs, winners of one tournament meeting winners of another, switching partners in a systematic arrangement that will make games different but competitive, allowing half the class to play singles while the other half completes the quiz, or whatever you think will keep the class motivated.

Warm-Up

Have equipment available for students to warm up with on the court after the quiz and before games.

Lesson Sequence

1. Allow students to get their equipment and warm up as usual.
2. If your class is too large to be accommodated on the court, ask people who would usually officiate for the first playing round to take a copy of the quiz and something to write with and sit on the bleachers to complete their quiz. Send the players scheduled for the first round to the courts to play it. As each round ends and students come off the courts, have them pick up a quiz and complete it on the bleachers. Make arrangements for students who don't finish the quiz during class.

Review

Leave time for a quick review of the experience, the tournament winners, and the quiz. Offer a hearty congratulations to your class for being so adult!

Beginner Pickleball Skills Rubric

Name _____ Date _____

Teacher _____ Class _____

	0	1	2	3	4	5
Forehand	No effort.	• Uses proper grip. • Uses correct mimetics. • Uses correct side of paddle. • Meets object in center of paddle. • Can make 5 consecutive hits during self-volley.	• Meets object coming from over net. • Able to redirect ball to target 5 ft (1.5 m) away after it bounces. • Pivots before hit. • Can self-volley up and down 10 times.	• Moves to meet ball after the bounce. • Able to rally over net 5 times with partner. • Meets ball with paddle head up. • Controls wall volley 5 times.	• Can run and redirect ball to target area. • Meets ball in center of paddle with firm wrist. • Can return ball with volley. • Uses a full swing.	• Can rally 10 times. • Moves to cover wide shot. • Chooses correctly between volley and full stroke. • Is able to control depth and vary speed.
Backhand	No effort.	• Uses correct mimetics. • Uses correct side of paddle. • Meets object in center of paddle 5 times during self-volley.	• Can meet object coming from over net. • Able to redirect ball to target after it bounces. • Pivots before hit. • Can self-volley up and down 10 times.	• Moves to meet ball after the bounce. • Meets ball with paddle head up. • Controls backhand wall volley 5 times.	• Can run and redirect ball toward target. • Can return ball with volley. • Can rally five times over net.	• Moves to cover backhand side. • Successful whether volley or full stroke. • Controls depth. • Varies speed.
Serve	No effort.	• Uses correct mimetics. • Uses correct grip. • Can get ball over net from self-toss.	• Occasionally able to put the ball in play. • Able to direct ball on diagonal.	• Consistently able to direct ball diagonally. • Serve reaches service box more often than not.	• Serves from off the court. • Performs legal serve. • Able to put the ball in play on a regular basis.	• Consistent serving. • Starting to vary speed or depth. • Shows sign of strategic placement.
Tournament play and officiating	No effort.	• Arrives prepared to play. • Gets equipment immediately. • Warms up without being encouraged.	• Goes directly to proper court. • Handles equipment well. • Makes transitions well.	• Makes good effort. • Avoids repeated behavioral errors. • Uses serving rules properly.	• Exhibits good sportsmanship. • Makes good line calls. • Takes responsibility to report wins and losses.	• Plays by the rules. • Exhibits leadership on and off the court. • Though a tough competitor, can be trusted to do the right thing.

From Isobel Kleinman, 2009, *Complete Physical Education Plans for Grades 5 to 12, Second Edition* (Champaign, IL: Human Kinetics).

Beginner Pickleball Quiz

Name _____ Date _____

Teacher _____ Class _____

True or False

Read each statement carefully. If the statement is true, write a *T* in the column to the left. If the statement is false, write an *F*. If using a grid sheet, blacken in the appropriate column for each question, making sure to use the correctly numbered line for each question and its answer.

_____ 1. A server must serve from off the court.

_____ 2. It is illegal to allow the ball to bounce twice before hitting it over the net.

_____ 3. The no-volley zone is between the net and the short line.

_____ 4. Hitting a ball on the side of the body that holds the paddle is called a *forehand*.

_____ 5. A ball served over the net and into the diagonal box causes the server to lose her turn of service.

_____ 6. The receiving team can win a point if the serving team hits the ball out.

_____ 7. The first server on a team is always the person on the right side of the court.

_____ 8. A server who volleys the return of serve has broken the two-bounce rule.

_____ 9. The volley should not have a backswing.

_____ 10. A player loses the point while serving from the left. His partner begins his turn of service from the left. The receiving team objects and declares the serving team out. The receiving team is correct.

From Isobel Kleinman, 2009, *Complete Physical Education Plans for Grades 5 to 12, Second Edition* (Champaign, IL: Human Kinetics).

Beginner Pickleball Answer Key

True or False

1. T
2. T
3. T
4. T
5. F—That is a legal serve.
6. F—If the serving team puts the ball out, the ball goes to the other team, but no point is awarded.
7. T
8. T
9. T
10. T

From Isobel Kleinman, 2009, *Complete Physical Education Plans for Grades 5 to 12, Second Edition* (Champaign, IL: Human Kinetics).

19

Tennis

Chapter Overview

1. Provide each student with a racket and a ball. Keep everyone engaged in some aspect of playing tennis during each lesson.

2. Follow the lesson plans, which break down the following and focus on one concept per lesson:

   - Racket skill—grip, forehand and backhand ground strokes, serve, and forehand and backhand volley
   - Footwork—waiting position, pivot, knee bend, forward and back, and side-to-side movement
   - Tennis terminology—fault, let, turn of service, love, set, deuce, and advantage in and out (ad-in and ad-out)
   - Rules of service, receiving, and playing out a point
   - Scoring of a point, game, set, and match

3. Teach the economics of tennis:

   - Cost of equipment
   - Public and private courts

Tennis Study Sheet

Fun Facts

- Several Arabic words *(Tinnis* and *rahat)* leave some historians believing that tennis began in ancient Egypt, although despite many Egyptian hieroglyphics and paintings, there are no drawings to support that theory. Others believe that tennis began in an abbey in France when monks stretched a rope across a courtyard and used their hands to strike a ball back and forth. When it became too painful to play, the evolution of striking implements started with a glove with webbing, then a paddle, and then in the 1500s the first strung wooden racket. The game almost died but regained popularity when a bouncy ball was introduced.

- In 1874, Major Walter Wingfield patented tennis equipment and rules. His game was played on an hourglass court, which was changed in 1877 to a rectangular court when the All England Club held its first tennis tournament at Wimbledon. To date, the All England Club at Wimbledon remains a Grand Slam tournament.

- *Love,* a score of zero in tennis, probably came from the French word *oeuf,* which means egg; its oval shape symbolizes the numeral *0.*

Skills

- Forehand—striking the ball on one's dominant side
- Backhand—striking the ball on the nondominant side with the opposite side of the strings
- Volley—striking the ball before it has had a chance to bounce
- Serve—putting the ball in play by sending it to the diagonal service box
- Overhead smash—during play, using a swing similar to the serve to hit the ball overhead
- Lob—hitting the ball high and deep into the opponent's court by using the usual swing but opening the face of the racket

Rules

- Boundaries
  - A ball landing on any part of the line is fair.
  - If the ball touches the ceiling, the walls, a person, or an object outside the court, it is out of play.
- Serving
  - The server must contact the ball from outside the court.
  - Odd points (first, third, fifth) are served from the right.
  - Even points (second, fourth, sixth) are served from the left.
  - The server serves the entire game until it is over.
- Scoring
  - The ball must be returned on the court before it bounces a second time.
  - The team that wins the rally scores a point.
  - Scoring is love (0), 15, 40, and game.
  - Deuce, or 40–40, is when either team needs two consecutive points to win the game.
  - The advantage goes to the team (in for the server, out for the receiver) who won the point after deuce.
  - All games must be won by 2 points.
  - To win a set, one must win six games and be ahead by two games.
  - Sets that reach six games all (6–6) are decided by a game of sudden death.
  - Official matches require winning two or sometimes three sets.

From Isobel Kleinman, 2009, *Complete Physical Education Plans for Grades 5 to 12, Second Edition* (Champaign, IL: Human Kinetics).

Tennis Extension Project

Name _____ Date _____

Teacher _____ Class _____

What equipment do you need to do this activity on your own?

Is there a tennis team at school? Who is the coach?

Is there a tennis intramurals program? Who is in charge?

Where can you participate in tennis outside of school?

Do you have friends who would join you? List their names.

What are the health benefits of participating in tennis?

Tennis Student Portfolio Checklist

Name _____ Date _____

Teacher _____ Class _____

_____ Can hold the racket in a neutral waiting position.

_____ Can come to a forehand grip.

_____ Can shift to a backhand grip.

_____ Can move the racket from forehand to backhand.

_____ Can pivot turn with a crossover forward left step to the forehand side.

_____ Can pivot turn with a crossover forward right step to the backhand side.

_____ Can consecutively self-bounce the ball to the ground, the air, and against a wall.

_____ Can consecutively block a bounced forehand to a target 10 feet (3 meters) away.

_____ Can consecutively block a bounced backhand to a target 10 feet (3 meters) away.

_____ Understands the significance of boundaries and keeping the ball inside.

_____ Understands scoring in tennis games, sets, and matches.

_____ Has a proper service toss and service motion.

_____ Follows tennis service rules.

_____ Is able to block a forehand or backhand volley.

_____ Can take full swings on forehand side without losing control of the ball.

_____ Can take full swings on backhand side without losing control of the ball.

_____ Is able to rally from baseline to baseline.

_____ Understands how to lob and why.

_____ Can begin self-directed match play and use rules of tennis.

Tennis Learning Experience Outline

Contents and Procedure

1. Provide each student with a racket and a ball each class.
2. Keep everyone engaged in an aspect of tennis whether on or off the court.
3. Focus on one concept per lesson.
4. Teach the following racket skills: grip, self-bounce, wall volley, forehand, backhand, serve, and forehand and backhand volley.
5. Include challenges that keep students engaged and improving their skills each day.
6. Use mimetics with footwork to rehearse proper motion during warm-ups.

7. Emphasize racket control, ball control, and keeping the ball in play.

8. Teach terminology: fault, let, turn of service, love, set, deuce, ad-in and ad-out.

   - Fault—A serve that does not land in or on the line of the intended service box.

   - Let—A serve that touches the net before landing in or on the line of the appropriate service box.

   - Turn of service—Serve rotates after each game is complete. In doubles, 1A, 2A, 1B, and 2B serve complete games.

   - Love—A score of zero.

   - Set—Winning at least six games with a two-game advantage or winning a seventh tiebreaker game.

   - Deuce—A score that is 40-40 (or tied), leaving either team with a need to win two consecutive points.

   - Ad-in—When the server wins a point after having reached deuce.

   - Ad-out—When the receiving team wins a point after having reached deuce.

9. Teach service rules and receiving rules when students have to put the ball in play.

10. Teach scoring for a game, set, and match.

11. Game play will begin when students master skills that allow them to play out a point rather than spending their time searching for errant balls.

12. While giving students lots of repetition, change their practice partners, change their opponents, and encourage them to keep the ball in play.

13. Fun and 100% participation are priorities. Raise expectations after 90% of students are ready.

14. If there's time, create a short tournament involving all students as a culminating event.

Teaching Tips

- Encourage students to practice with different classmates. If the least skilled stay together during their learning experience, it is likely to be quite frustrating. If you rotate practice partners in a systematic way, you will avoid that problem.

- If advanced students are bored, have them fill in as teacher assistants, helping their classmates develop by feeding the ball to them and helping them keep the ball in play. Class activities should challenge them too, but it is a worthwhile challenge to their skills (and their citizenship) to be able to control the ball enough to help the students who need near-perfect feeds of the ball to be able to hit it. Advanced players should be encouraged to improve their consistency and accuracy.

- Make every effort to reassure students that improvement is what is valued, not a predisposition to be a great athlete.

- After a book is published, rules, skills, and strategies may change. Check Internet sites listed in suggested resources to keep up with the changes.

Teaching Tips for Special Considerations

Students who have disabilities or are medically unable to play should be given alternative assignments that involve them with the class and the unit. When possible, they should take part in the lesson. Depending on their disability, they may be able to engage in the competition if their opponent is asked to operate with a similar handicap. For example, if students cannot run,

- have opponents hop or jump to ball,

- make boundaries small so students can get to the ball, and

- allow two bounces.

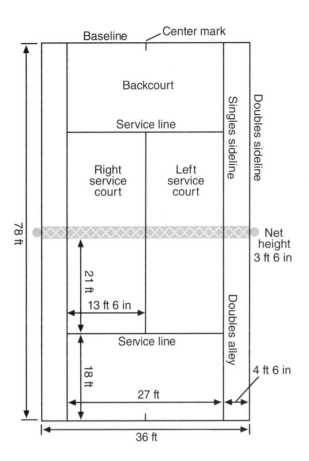

Figure 19.1 Tennis court dimensions.

Facilities

- Instructional groups should be no larger than facilities can accommodate. Optimally, there should be no more than four students per tennis court (see figure 19.1). Early lessons accommodate twice that number safely and allow students to work on tennis skills the entire class. Once games start, more than four students per court is counterproductive. Students should have 20 to 30 minutes to work without having to get off the court so they can get involved in what they are doing, learn to focus, and score. It is best to plan something else for the additional students and have them rotate on the courts for games on alternating days.

- Courts should be surrounded by fences that are a minimum of 20 feet (6 meters) high and go to the ground so retrieving errant balls does not require a great deal of time.

Materials

- One racket for each student
- Three balls for each group of two playing over a net

Unit Safety

Equip all students with rackets and balls so they can perform at the same time. To do that safely, students must adhere to the following court courtesies:

- Run only within their assigned practice area or court.
- Use equipment only for contacting tennis balls.
- Pick up balls so no one trips. If a ball is from elsewhere, find out where and throw it back so it reaches the person on one bounce.
- Stretching should be done after the muscles are warm—at the end of class during review.

Unit Timeline

There are two units of tennis in this chapter (beginner and intermediate), each including the following:

- 4 to 10 lessons to develop skills and learn tennis scoring and terminology
- 7 to 8 lessons for a small class tournament

Assessment

Each unit concludes with a short quiz to assess knowledge and a skills rubric to measure performance.

Suggested Resources

About.com. 2008. Tennis. http://tennis.about.com.

American Sport Education Program (ASEP). 1998. *Coaching youth tennis.* Champaign, IL: Human Kinetics.

BBC. 2008. Mastering the one-handed backhand. http://news.bbc.co.uk/sportacademy/hi/sa/tennis/skills/newsid_2061000/2061499.stm.

Braden, V., and B. Burns. 1998. *Tennis 2000: Strokes, strategy and psychology for a lifetime.* New York: Little, Brown & Co.

Hoctor, H., and R. Desmond. 1995. *Coaching tennis successfully.* Champaign, IL: Human Kinetics.

Thetenniscoach.com. 2008. Lobbing. www.thetenniscoach.com.au/tips_lobbing.html.

Verdieck, J., and D. Van der Meer. 1984. *USPTR manual for coaches.* Houston, TX: United States Tennis Association. (This book and all others by Dennis Van der Meer are out of print, but if you can find a copy, it is worth it. His approach to teaching is used by the United States Professional Tennis Registry [USPTR] and is the one that is used in this chapter.)

Videojug.com. 2008. Mastering the basic forehand. www.videojug.com/film/how-to-master-the-basic-forehand.

Xsports.com. 2008. Tennis diagram. www.xsports.com/recmnd.gif.

Tennis
BEGINNER
LESSON 1

Using a Racket

Facilities

Clear area large enough to safely accommodate the group

Materials

- One tennis ball per student
- One racket per student

Performance Goals

Students will do the following:

- Grip a tennis racket.
- Meet the ball on the center of the strings.
- Develop a firm wrist and forearm.
- Get and return their own equipment.

Cognitive Goals

Students will learn the following:

- How to develop focus and concentration
- What an error is in tennis
- To be responsible for their own equipment

Lesson Safety

- Partners should have a minimum of 20 feet (6 meters) between them.
- Students must learn court courtesies and follow them.
- During the wall volley, make sure students are double-racket distance from the wall and that they have 5 to 6 feet (1.5-2 meters) of space on either side of them.

Motivation

Tennis is a great leisure activity, and most students will have free and easy access to community courts at a nominal cost. Tell students that tennis has advantages over other sports since they don't need a bunch of players if they want to play a game. All they need is one, and if they can't find one, they can practice at a wall, take a lesson, hire a ball machine, or hit with a pro for a workout. The USTA runs leagues at every skill level so there are many opportunities for people at all levels to compete. If they haven't watched Wimbledon, the U.S. Open, the French Open, or any other tennis tournament, they might not already know that the greats in this game, just like in any other game, make a lot of money.

Warm-Up

1. As students arrive, ask them to jog the playing area with one racket in both hands.

2. When they assemble, teach them the waiting position.

   a. Dominant hand is at bottom of grip and nondominant hand is near the throat of the racket. Face the net.

   b. On signal, pivot right by moving the hips over the right foot (pivot on right foot, step forward on left), then return to waiting position. Turning left, pivot hips over the left foot, then step forward on the right.

Lesson Sequence

1. Before beginning to teach use of the racket, teach court courtesy and safety rules.

   a. Never run on anyone's court, even if you need to get a ball.

   b. Pick up the balls on your court, check to see if they are yours, and return those that are not to the people asking for them on one bounce.

2. Teach, demonstrate, and check the forehand tennis grip (shaking hands with the racket achieves the basic forehand grip).

3. Teach and demonstrate bouncing the ball to the ground with the racket. Give students a few minutes to try it and then see who can control it 10 times.

4. Demonstrate bouncing the ball to the ground and then, without changing grips, use the other side of the strings to bounce the ball off the strings and into the air.

   a. Give students a few minutes to try it before asking who can control the ball on the upper side of the strings 10 times.

   b. Bounce the ball off the racket, 10 times down and 10 times up in the air.

5. Demonstrate the volley (no bounce) against the wall.

   a. Demonstrate the same controlled bounces directed at the wall.

   b. From the forehand side, double-racket distance from the wall, give students 5 seconds to volley to the wall. (This will be difficult at first; give them short trials and switch who is at the wall.)

   c. Encourage moderation, just meeting and blocking the ball with no swing at all. Aim to control 10 times but don't stay on this more than a few minutes.

      • Too difficult if not close to the wall using a simple block.

      • If they swing, there will be lots of wild balls and frustration.

6. Demonstrate with a student who is 10 feet (3 meters) away.

   a. Rally the ball back and forth (on one bounce and explain why) so when the ball hits the racket, it comes off slightly up and is able to drop 5 feet (1.5 meters) away on or near the target placed on the ground between you. (Put a ball on the ground between you as the target).

   b. Contact should be similar to the contact made when students bounced the ball down and then up and when they volleyed against the wall.

   c. During the demonstration, point out how to meet the ball on the rise, block it, and send it back so it has a bit of an arch. Show how the racket head stays up, how there is a slight follow-through upward, and how to reach with the racket, get the strings behind the ball, and block it back after it bounces off the ground.

d. Demonstrate consecutive hits, counting each tap.

e. Use a volley to block the ball when partner hits it farther than the target on the ground.

f. Have students partner up, set up in the same line of direction 10 feet (3 meters) apart from each other, put a ball on the ground in the middle, and begin trying to control a rally.

g. Encourage consecutive contacts with a slight upward follow-through.

h. Encourage students to use the volley if their partner loses control and hits the ball a bit long so they can keep the ball in play.

i. Increase focus and concentration by asking:

- Who can rally for 10 hits or more without an error?
- What is the highest number of consecutive taps you can get without an error? (If a class preceded them, you might share how well that class did and see how this class compares.)

Review and Stretching

As students stretch, ask:

- What part of the racket should meet the ball? Should your eyes see it meet?
- Which is better: a limp, dangling wrist that lets the racket head drop, or a firm wrist and forearm that keep the racket head up?
- If you are right-handed, does the forehand meet the ball on your right or left side? What about for a backhand?
- Is it legal to allow the ball to bounce twice before you hit it?

Assessment

Observe the ball control of each group. When 90% of the class can control the ball in this close drill for 10 consecutive taps, the group is ready to move to the next lesson. If not, repeat all aspects of this lesson, leaving the most time for the partner work and rotating partners regularly.

Short Forehand and Backhand Rally

Facilities

Clear area large enough to safely accommodate the group

Materials

- One tennis ball per student
- One racket per student

Performance Goals

Students will do the following:

- Exercise proper footwork and waiting position.
- Address the ball for backhand and forehand.

Cognitive Goals

Students will learn the following:

- What a waiting position is and why to use it
- To adjust to balls on the left and right
- Terminology for forehand and backhand
- The value of being physically consistent when meeting the ball

Lesson Safety

- Partners should have a minimum of 20 feet (6 meters) between them

- Students must learn court courtesies and follow them.

- During the wall volley, make sure students are double-racket distance from the wall and that they have 5 to 6 feet (1.5-2 meters) of space on either side.

Motivation

Tennis is one of the few games where one good shot is not enough. It can take a lot of great shots to finally win a point, and because of that, most players don't win points, they lose them. Why? They never get in the right position to hit it the same way over and over again so the ball stays inbounds. Explain that although some people might think working on consistency at a close range is child's play, most developing pros start their practice at close distances and back up as they get a rhythm and feel for the ball. That is what the students will do in class, but since most of them are just starting, they have to go slowly and do it right so that everyone develops the building blocks to become a fine, steady tennis player. One of those building blocks is good footwork and preparation. Ask everyone not to get lazy because this might come easy in practice, but in games it is the tool that makes Rafael Nadal and Roger Federer the champions that they are.

Warm-Up

1. As students arrive, have them get a ball and racket.

   - Bounce up 10 times and down 10 times.

   - Go to the wall and volley off the wall as taught in lesson 1.

   - Go to the court with a partner and practice rallying at a distance of 10 feet (3 meters) with a ball as the target between partners.

2. Lead mimetics for the forehand and backhand swings.

   a. From a waiting position, pivot to the forehand side and step forward and in with the left foot, planting the foot and bending at the knee (5 times) (see figure 19.2).

   b. Repeat, but let go of second hand on the racket while pivoting and then reach the racket head behind an imaginary ball (5 times).

   c. Repeat, following through so the racket frame goes forward and up with the strings facing the target over the net (5 times).

   d. On backhand side, pivot left and rotate the grip a quarter turn back (see figure 19.3). Step forward and plant the right foot with a bent knee (5 times).

   e. Repeat, letting the racket follow the pivot-turn (5 times).

   f. With firm wrist and forearm, swing to open up, bringing racket forward and completing the follow-through so the heel of the grip faces the person swinging (5 times).

Figure 19.2 Forehand preparation.

Figure 19.3 Back-hand racket position and grips.

Lesson Sequence

1. Begin with a demonstration of the control drill from the last lesson, this time focusing on the following:

    a. Footwork—stepping forward and across on opposite foot

    b. Waiting position—bringing racket and body back to neutral position after each contact

2. Have students practice in pairs, coaching them to

    a. move their feet to the ball and pivot to meet it on either side,

    b. bend from the knee to get under the ball before contacting it, and

    c. return to waiting position after each contact.

3. Stop to demonstrate how to volley from the waiting position and how a volley can cut off a shot to keep the rally going when their partner misses the target on the ground and hits the ball too high or hard.

4. Reinforce goals, reminding students to keep a firm wrist on forehand and backhand side. Have them practice returning to waiting position after every contact and controlling the ball 10 taps or more.

5. Rotate partners every 2 to 3 minutes. Ask who got 10 hits with no errors. Did anyone get more? Get them to work on a school record for the most taps in a rally with no errors.

Review and Stretching

As students stretch, ask:

- Is it legal to allow the ball to bounce twice before you hit it?
- Is it legal to hit it without a bounce? What is that called?

Clearing the Net

Facilities

Minimum of one tennis court for every six students

Materials

- Three balls per pair of students
- One racket for each student

Performance Goals

Students will do the following:

- Hit so the ball clears the net.
- Become more comfortable on both forehand and backhand sides.
- Start from a waiting position and end with a follow-through.

Cognitive Goals

Students will learn the following:

- That the net is an obstacle
- How to improve concentration and focus

Lesson Safety

For this drill, three pairs (a maximum of six students per court) can work over the net at a time. It is only possible to do safely because the target is 5 feet (1.5 meters) from the net and each partner is hitting straight ahead. For students who show no control, let them continue with the first drill until they can gain control (10 taps or more) before hitting over the net since the crowded conditions require control for safety.

Motivation

Explain that while the students were having fun, they were also building the fundation of solid tennis playing, and they are going to add a few skills to those building blocks at a time. Today, they will not only continue mastering control of the racket and ball, but learn to deal with the fact that the net is in the way.

Warm-Up

1. As students arrive, they should equip themselves, go to the wall for a few minutes of wall volleying, bounce the ball up and down off their racket on the way out to the courts, and find a partner to begin practicing a controlled rally.

2. Lead mimetics (10 times each):
   - Forehand—From waiting position, pivot on left foot to the right, stepping toward the net. Keeping wrist and arm firm, reach for the ball. Follow through and return to waiting position.
   - Backhand—From waiting position, pivot left while stepping on right foot toward the left and toward the net. Keep wrist and arm firm. Reach for the ball and follow through. Return to waiting position.

Lesson Sequence

1. Begin with the control drill, challenging the partners to reach 10 or more taps.
   a. Last time they were aiming for 10. Can they do better than that?
   b. Announce the highest score in another class and ask if they can beat it.

2. Demonstrate a drill where the target for the rally is 5 feet (1.5 meters) away from the other side of the net and marked by a ball that has been put 5 feet (1.5 meters) from each side of the net.

   a. Place a ball 5 feet (1.5 meters) from the net on each side (need two balls).

   b. Stand 5 feet (1.5 meters) from the target so forehands are lined up with each other, and begin rallying over the net (see figure 19.4), demonstrating how to block the ball as it rises from the bounce, hitting it with little or no swing but an upward follow-through so it lands near the ball on the other side. When it bounces, the partner meets the ball on the forehand side. Rally forehand to forehand over the net, using the same controlled and steady approach to meeting the ball and following through (no major backswing, no speed) as before.

3. Have students practice, allowing up to three pairs to share a net.

   a. After 5 minutes, ask if anyone got five hits or more before an error. Ten? More?

   b. Rotate partners, allowing more time and encouraging counting on every hit.

   c. Rotate partners again, emphasizing going to waiting position after each contact.

4. Repeat the same procedure for the backhand side.

   a. Who got 10 contacts? More?

   b. Rotate partners again.

Review and Stretching

As students stretch, ask:

- Why is it important to return to the waiting position after each contact?
- Why should the follow-through go up?
- What direction should the strings face when hitting through the ball?
- What happens if the strings face the sky? If they face the ground?

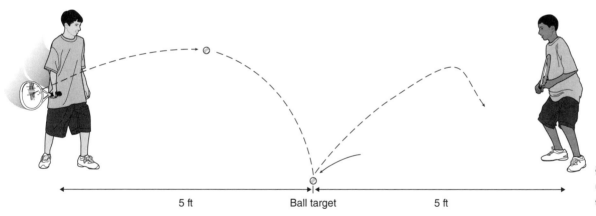

| 5 ft | Ball target | 5 ft |

Figure 19.4 Lining up rackets to practice the forehand volley.

Scoring

Facilities

- Service box area for every two students
- If not enough courts, no more than two pairs to a court

Materials

- One racket for each student
- Three balls per pair of students

Performance Goals

Students will do the following:

- Play a modified game using real tennis scoring.
- Play the game within the defined boundary of the service box.

Cognitive Goals

Students will learn the following:

- How turn of service is determined
- That a full game is served by one person until it is over
- Scoring: love, 15, 30, 40, game; deuce, ad-in and ad-out
- To be concerned for boundaries
- That hitting the ball out turns into a point for their opponent

Lesson Safety

If students are waiting their turn for a court, let them practice a control drill in the back of the court. If errant balls interfere with the games being played, have them go outside the fence and practice volleying the ball back and forth to each other. If there is a wall around, they can practice hitting against it.

Motivation

Scoring in tennis is similar to a foreign language, probably because the game developed in France. If you heard someone call out "40–love," it would make no sense until you knew what it meant. In tennis, "40–love" means the server is about to win and the receiver needs 3 points in a row just to tie the game. Today they're going to learn what scores mean and use this special language during games.

Warm-Up

1. After students pick up equipment, they should take a few minutes to practice the wall volley at a distance of double their racket's length from the wall, bounce it off their strings on their way out to the tennis courts, and when there, find a partner to practice the rally control drill.

2. Lead mimetics, alternating between these and repeating for a minimum of 10 times:

   - Forehand—Run a few steps right, plant left foot, take a forehand swing, and come back to waiting position and their original place on the court.

   - Backhand—Run a few steps left, plant right foot, take a backhand swing, and return to waiting position and place on the court.

   - High forehand volley—Pivot right, step forward on left foot, raise racket in front of the face behind an imaginary ball, and punch the racket forward.

Lesson Sequence

1. Explain scoring:
    a. Love (0), 15 (first point), 30 (second), 40 (third), game (winning fourth point and being ahead by 2).
    b. How a tie (deuce) is handled and what happens if you win the next point after deuce (advantage)
        *   A point is won by someone, no matter who the server is.
        *   The server's score is always called out first.
        *   One person serves until the game is over.
        *   A ball landing on any part of the line is good.
2. Assign each pair to play a control game where the bounce of the ball is confined to the service box.
    a. The same person puts the ball into play until the game is over.
    b. Rally continues until a miss or a hit outside the service box.
    c. After one game is complete, switch servers.
    d. Allow as many games as there is time for, changing servers each game.
3. If students are waiting, have them wait by the box, helping to keep score and taking over the court the minute one game is over.
4. Circulate, answering any questions that arise.

Review and Stretching

As students stretch, ask:

*   If the score is deuce, who is winning?
*   The score is 15–40. Is it the receiver or the server who is about to win?
*   Is love a winning score in tennis?
*   Your opponent hits the ball. It lands half on and half off the line. Is it good?

Playing a Set

Facilities

*   A service box area for every two students.
*   If not enough tennis courts:
    -   Create a space for those waiting.
    -   Use volleyball standards with dropped nets to set up alternative courts on a handball court or basketball court.
    -   Define space behind the baseline for students to practice.

Materials

*   One racket for each student
*   Three balls per pair of students

Performance Goals

Students will do the following:

*   Play a modified game using tennis scoring and try to complete a set.
*   Change sides of the court after every odd game.

Cognitive Goals

Students will learn the following:

- That a game is like a word in a sentence
- What a set (a sentence in a story) and a match (the whole story) are
- Why players change sides of the court and when they do it

Lesson Safety

If students are waiting their turn for a court, let them practice a control drill in the back of the court. If errant balls interfere with the games being played, have them go outside the fence and practice volleying the ball back and forth to each other. If there is a wall nearby, they can practice hitting against it.

Motivation

Ask if it is fair for players to serve a single game, which can be a minimum of 4 points, and walk away declaring victory. Tennis is made of many games. One game is like a word in a sentence. The sentence is only complete when a player wins six games and leads by two games. When that happens, the player has won a set. In some circumstances a player can win six games and lose a set. A set is not over if the game score is 6–6 or 5–6, because no one leads by two games. The solution if the score is tied at six games is a game of sudden death. For now, try to play enough games to complete a set.

Warm-Up

1. Allow students to follow their typical warm-up routine.
2. Lead mimetics:
   - Three running steps to the forehand with recovery
   - Three running steps to the backhand with recovery
   - Low volleys on the forehand and backhand sides
   - High volleys on the forehand and backhand sides

Lesson Sequence

1. Explain switching sides of the court:
   - Why—Sun and wind are huge factors, especially on the serve.
   - When—Players switch on every odd game.
2. Explain rules for the day (play within the service-box boundaries).
3. Review scoring and turn-of-service rules.
4. Assign courts.
5. Students start a set, using the service box and all the rules learned to date. If there are not enough courts, either set up a modified game plan, having students with no court play games to win a set on another practice area, or have students rotate off the court after two games (each player served), encouraging them to remember their game score and continue when they get back on the court.

Review and Stretching

As students stretch, find out if anyone has questions. Then ask:

- Why is it important to change sides after every odd game?
- How many games must you win to win a set?
- Who was in the lead when we stopped? Were you ahead by two games?

Ground Strokes

Facilities

- A service box area for every two students
- If not enough tennis courts:
  - Create a space for those waiting.
  - Use volleyball standards with dropped nets to set up alternative courts on a handball court or basketball court.
  - Define space behind the baseline for students to practice.

Materials

- One racket for each student
- Three balls per pair of students

Performance Goals

Students will do the following:

- Take a proper backswing.
- Work on strokes from baseline to baseline.
- Cover a larger portion of the court.

Cognitive Goals

Students will learn the following:

- The value of a backswing.
- How to adjust to different power and timing from baseline to baseline
- How to safely keep three balls though using only one at a time

Lesson Safety

No more than two pairs should be rallying with their own ball on a court at a time.

Motivation

Ask students not to underestimate how well they are doing and explain that that's why you are asking them to start something that is not too easy—play the whole length of the court while keeping the ball on their own side. Tell them you are confident that they will be able to do it, though lots of more experienced players sometimes have difficulty. Explain what makes you confident: You know that lots of folks who have played for years cannot hit a ball over and over again straight ahead, but that's just what the students were doing on a short court, so now you think they are ready.

Warm-Up

1. Students use equipment to practice as the class gathers.
2. Lead mimetics:
   a. Forehand—Pivot and step forward with the left foot so shoulders and right hip come back. As they do, drop the hand on the racket's throat and let the racket come back behind the right hip. Swing and follow through so the racket comes around to the left ear. Practice until stroke is smooth and fluid (10 times).
   b. Backhand—Pivot left and while stepping forward with the right foot, drop the extra hand and let the racket come back behind the left hip. Swing forward and follow through so the butt of the handle end looks at your face. Practice until stroke is smooth and fluid (10 times).
   c. Add footwork—Take backswing while moving right or left (10 times).

Lesson Sequence

1. Teach students to gather the balls and how to hold them so they aren't in the way.
2. Assign them to courts to practice full strokes down the line.
3. Rotate who they are hitting with every 5 minutes.
4. If there are too few courts, rotate players and reduce the rotation time.

Review and Stretching

As students stretch, ask:

- If you want more depth to your shot, what are some things you can do to get it?
- When is it best to take the backswing—when the ball bounces, when you start running for it, or before the opponent hits it?
- Should your swing be low to high or high to low?
- Why is follow-through important?

Singles Half-Court Game

Facilities

- Half the width of a court for every two players
- Wall or volleying on the field for extra students

Materials

- One racket for each student
- Three balls per pair of students

Performance Goals

Students will play the length of the court using most tennis rules but with the following modifications:

- Allow a drop-and-hit method of putting the ball in play.
- The serve must be to the box straight ahead.
- The play must stay in one's own width of the court.

Cognitive Goals

Students will learn the following:

- Boundaries for whole court
- Service rules:
    - The ball must be put into play from off the court.
    - The serve must land in the service box or on its lines without touching the net.
    - The server is allowed a second serve if the first does not go in.
    - A serve that touches the net is called a *let*.
    - A double fault results in a point for the opponent.

Lesson Safety

This lesson depends on the ability to control the ball. If students are not in control, stay on lesson 5 or 6. Playing a game in half the width of the court can be rewarding. It allows players more hits and a better opportunity to improve their skills, focus, and concentration, but if students are not up to it, don't do it.

Motivation

One frustrating part of tennis is that opponents win games without doing anything simply because servers cannot serve in the service box. Explain that the games they will play today require getting the ball in the service box from off the court. If it doesn't go in on the first try, they get a second time to try. If they fault on both tries, they lose the point.

Warm-Up

1. Students start practicing as they wish while the class assembles.
2. Lead mimetics:
   a. Forehand and backhand ground strokes with footwork, having students return to neutral after finishing each pattern
   b. Volleys, making sure students keep racket out in front, imagine contact, and punch through it

Lesson Sequence

1. Teach the following:
   a. Service rules to be used
      - Server must serve from off the court, behind the baseline.
      - The ball must land in the service box or on the line or it is a fault.
      - A ball touching the net is either a let (done over if it lands in the service box) or a fault if it doesn't.
      - Double faults lead to opponent's point.
      - Servers get two turns to serve on each point.
      - Servers serve the entire game until it is over.
   b. Serving courtesies and expectations
      - Return balls to the server.
      - Server should have two balls when beginning each point.
      - Server should be given an uninterrupted turn of service.
2. Plan equitable court time for all players. If you have more players than courts, substitutes must be given some job: calling the faults, keeping score, or practicing against a nearby wall. (All court space is now being used because games are full court.)

Review and Stretching

As students stretch, congratulate everyone and tell them they have done great work to play a game in half the space used during normal singles play! Then ask questions:

- If a person cannot get the ball in the service box once, what is the score? Twice?
- What if the serve touches the net and goes in the box? What if it doesn't go in the box?
- Why do you want at least two balls in your pockets before you serve?

Serve

Facilities

Tennis courts

Materials

- Buckets of balls
- One racket for each student

Performance Goal

Students will learn and practice an overhead serve, getting a minimum of 30 repetitions.

Cognitive Goals

Students will learn the following:

- Service toss, point of contact, and follow-through for overhead serve
- That the server must serve on a diagonal
- The concept of a second serve
- That servers must alternate service boxes
- Receiving rules for singles and doubles

Lesson Safety

Student must remain on same side of the courts until all the practice balls have been used. When the whole group is finished hitting serves, they should collect the balls and begin all over.

Motivation

Explain that major tennis players get a huge advantage from their serve and name of few of the current big servers in the men's and women's game (e.g., Andy Roddick, 140 miles per hour [225 kilometers per hour]; Serena Williams, 112 miles per hour [180 kilometers per hour]). A big serve is exciting to accomplish—if it makes it to the service box. Today students will get the tools to develop a big serve. It will just be the beginning, though; serving takes lots of repetition, and more important, it also takes learning a reliable second serve so games are not lost by double faulting. Explain that the swing practiced during mimetics will give them a big serve once they learn to get the toss in the right place so the racket can meet it at the height of the swing and out in front of their body. The toss is the critical element, so that's what they're going to start with.

Figure 19.5 Service toss and backswing.

Warm-Up

1. As students arrive, they practice.

2. Lead mimetics for the tennis serve (see figure 19.5):

   - Toss with weight shift—Palm is up, fingers are open, and knees bend (5 times).

   - Backswing—Racket head drops down to begin a semicircle swing that brings the racket between the shoulder blades with the hand near the back of the head and swinging arm bent at the elbow (5 times).

   - Backswing with toss—Combining swing and ball-toss motion, racket arm starts downward as tossing arm goes upward. Finish with tossing arm in the air with fingers open, palm facing the sky, and the hand of the racket arm near the head with the elbow and knees bent (10 times).

   - Swing up to and through the ball (see figure 19.6)—From the racket hand near the back of the head, swing up so swing replaces the hand in the air, swinging fast enough that the follow-through is natural and comes down across the body (10 times).

- Toss with backswing, upswing, and follow-through so that there is no hesitation between the backswing and forward swing. Emphasize extending up to meet the imaginary ball at the height of the toss (10 times).

Lesson Sequence

1. Demonstrate the toss with no racket.
   a. Stand 3 feet (1 meter) from the fence with body perpendicular to it.
   b. Extend the racket arm up and in front of the body as a target.
   c. Toss the ball higher than the extended arm, letting it drop about 6 inches (15 centimeters) in front.
2. Have students practice the toss at least 10 times.
3. Combine the toss (no racket) with the backswing. Combat a loss of control.
   a. Let go of the ball at the height of arm extension.
   b. Keep eyes on where they want the ball to go on the toss while tossing it.
4. Still with no racket, do toss and backswing, and at the height of the toss, swing up to catch the ball (5 times).
   a. Ask them to swing up and hit the ball with their hand so the ball hits the fence (10 times).
   b. As they practice, check their follow-through, encouraging them to really swing at the ball (which will create the follow-through).
5. Repeat steps 2 and 3 with the racket. Take the full practice motion.
6. Try hitting the ball against the fence, as in step 4.
   a. Show where the racket face should be on contact.
   b. Show how a sagging wrist can change the position of the racket face, and encourage them to make the racket and wrist an extension of the arm on contact.
7. Demonstrate the full serve.
   a. The serve must go in or on the line of the diagonal service box.
   b. A serve hitting the net and landing in the proper box is a let, not a fault, and is done over.
8. Divide the balls and, using one at a time, serve over the net to the diagonal box. After all balls have been hit, change sides, collect balls, and try again.

Figure 19.6 Service is a swing up to the ball.

Review and Stretching

As students stretch, ask:

- If the swing is the same, what makes the serve different each time?
- Where should the toss be in relation to your front toe?
- What is the optimum height for the toss?
- Should you swing down to meet the ball or swing up to meet it?
- Where must your serve go in order to force opponents to play out the point?

Doubles Games

Facilities

- One tennis court for each four students
- If class is too large, a separate area for other students
  - Wall for rallying
  - Areas for volleying with a partner
  - Marked zone with net and target area for practicing tennis serves
  - Area for playing another sport (last resort)

Materials

- Can of balls or set with the same markings for each court
- Practice balls for students not in doubles games (if not enough courts)
- Visual aid such as a blackboard, chart, or magnetic board
- Tennis rackets

Performance Goal

Students will play doubles games.

Cognitive Goals

Students will learn the following:

- Rules for doubles
  - Order of service
  - Order of return of service
  - Different boundaries
  - How wider court affects ground strokes and serves
- Team concept in tennis doubles
- Court courtesy in relationship to balls
  - How to identify their balls
  - To clear the court and return the balls from other courts

Lesson Safety

If there are not enough courts to accommodate everyone, players should not be left to simply watch their classmates. Whatever practice and exercise they do must be done off the tennis court. A second space is necessary so that students do not endanger themselves or the people playing on the tennis court.

Motivation

Until now, the class has played some variety of singles, but today, they will not only use the whole court, they will cover it as a team in doubles.

Warm-Up

1. Students pick up equipment and come out to practice.
2. Lead mimetics:
   - Serve
   - Moving wide to hit forehand and recovering
   - Moving to hit backhand and recovering
   - Volleying high and low left
   - Volleying high and low right

Lesson Sequence

1. Explain rules and basic strategies for doubles positioning.
   a. Service:
      - Best server usually serves first, serving the entire game.
      - Servers begin from the right side of the court.
      - Teams either serve games 1, 3, and 5 or games 2, 4, and 6.
      - Servers serve from the same side of the net until the set is over.
   b. Receiving: Receivers receive from the same side of the court throughout a set.
   c. Boundaries:
      - The service box stays the same size.
      - The outside line is the doubles boundary line. The inside line is the singles boundary line.
   d. Court positioning: Server and receiver play deep; their partners play net.
2. Assign evenly matched opponents to a court.
3. Explain how doubles games usually start.
   a. Everyone takes practice serves before scoring.
   b. Take a 5-minute warm-up to practice ground strokes and volleys.

Review and Stretching

As students stretch, ask:

- Is it possible for one receiver to return service attempts to either box? Is it legal?
- Does the return of serve have to land in any specific area on the court?
- After the serve is received and returned, can the person closest to the ball hit it legally?
- Can the player closest to the incoming serve legally return it?

Doubles Positioning

Facilities

- One tennis court for every four students
- Second area for students not scheduled for a game

Materials

- Visual aid such as a blackboard, chart, or magnetic board
- Can of tennis balls with the same identification markings for each court
- Practice balls
- Tennis rackets

Performance Goal

Students will play doubles games.

Cognitive Goals

Students will learn general doubles positioning:

- Up and back
- Right and left

Lesson Safety

Attend to the students who are not on the court, assigning and reinforcing their activity.

Motivation

Announce that you will review the doubles service rules and boundaries and explain how to divide court responsibilities so everyone can enjoy playing with a teammate.

Warm-Up

Lead mimetics:

1. Volley
   - Step into the volley.
   - Keep wrist firm on contact with the ball.
2. Serve

Lesson Sequence

1. Diagram position and transitions:
   a. Covering a wide shot (one gets the ball, the other covers the middle)
   b. Covering a short ball
2. Have students pick partners for a 5-day competition.
3. If there are not enough courts, have remaining students play something elsewhere for the day, allowing scheduled games to go on uninterrupted. (I used to have a softball diamond and basketball courts near the tennis court, and I allowed games there when it was clear that students had lost interest in control games or practicing against the wall.)

Review and Stretching

1. As students stretch, ask:
   - If a ball goes over your partner's head, what should you do?
   - If your partner goes out wide, should you stay or move with your partner so you can cover the middle?
2. Make sure students have given you the names of their tournament partners.

Teacher Homework

Set up a tournament that allows players to compete on their own ability level (see table 19.1), setting up a round-robin among advanced players on one set of courts, intermediate players

Table 19.1 Sample Tennis Tournament for Students of Different Skill Levels

Day	Group A Use service box rules. Teams 8, 9, and 11 cannot maintain a full court rally.	Group B Teams 2, 4, 5, and 10 control the ball but have no pace.	Group C Teams 1, 3, 6, and 7 have good court coverage and hit the ball with pace.
1	Team 8 plays team 9. Team 11 practices (at the wall or with each other).	2 plays 5. 4 plays 10.	1 plays 7. 3 plays 6.
2	11 plays 8. 9 practices.	2 plays 10. 5 plays 4.	1 plays 6. 3 plays 7.
3	11 plays 9. 8 practices.	2 plays 4. 10 plays 5.	6 plays 7. 1 plays 3.
4	Repeat day 1.	Repeat day 1.	Repeat day 1.
5	Repeat day 2.	Repeat day 2.	Repeat day 2.
6	Repeat day 3.	Repeat day 3.	Repeat day 3.
Special final event	Winner plays 4th-place group B. 2nd-place team plays 3rd-place group A.	Winner plays winner of group C. 2nd-place team plays 2nd-place group C. 3rd-place team plays 3rd-place group C. 4th-place team plays 1st-place group A.	Winner plays winner of group B. 2nd-place team plays 2nd-place in group B. 3rd-place team plays 3rd-place group B. 4th-place team plays singles.

on a second set of courts, and beginners on a third set of courts. Everyone should experience the game and have equal court time during the course of the tournament. If court space does not accommodate all players at once, repeat the following lessons, rotating who plays and who practices.

Round-Robin Doubles Tournament

Facilities

- One tennis court for every four students
- Second area for students not scheduled for a game

Materials

- Doubles team roster, tournament schedule, and team standings
- One racket for each student
- Three balls for each game

Performance Goal

Students will play doubles games.

Cognitive Goal

Students will use the team concept and follow applicable rules.

Lesson Safety

If all students cannot be accommodated on the courts, assign an activity to those who have no court and reinforce their productive activity.

Motivation

Explain that the class is starting a doubles competition that is a bit different than match play because class time is too short to do a whole match or even a whole set. Each team will play different people over the course of the next few lessons. The winner will be the team who has won the highest total of games in a division.

Warm-Up

1. As students assemble, they go to the courts to warm up, starting with short control drills and graduating to full-court strokes. Before games begin, each player takes some practice serves.
2. If some students have no court, lead them through tennis mimetics and have them play whatever activity they have been assigned for the day.

Lesson Sequence

1. Answer any questions and explain:
   a. Typical warm-up procedure before matches start
      - Take 5 minutes to warm up.
      - From baseline, hit ground strokes and take practice serves.
   b. Using their own can of balls and returning them at the end
   c. Court assignments
2. Begin the tournament.
3. Students without a court should be given a challenging alternative activity that is related to tennis if possible.

Review and Stretching

1. As students stretch, remind them to be prepared for a quiz on the next rainy day.
2. Answer any questions.
3. Share a situation that came up in class that was a teachable moment.
4. Collect scores.

Beginner Tennis Skills Rubric

Name _____ Date _____

Teacher _____ Class _____

	0	1	2	3	4	5
Forehand	No effort.	• Uses proper grip. • Performs mimetics correctly. • Uses correct side of racket. • Able to meet object in center of racket three consecutive times during self-volley.	• Can meet object coming from over net. • Able to redirect ball to target 5 ft (1.5 m) away after it bounces. • Has proper body pivot. • Can self-volley down 10 times.	• Moves to meet ball after the bounce. • Able to rally over net five times with partner at 30 ft (9 m). • Meets ball with racket head up. • Controls forehand wall volley 3 times.	• Can run four steps or more and still redirect ball to target area. • Meets ball in front. • Can return ball with volley. • Can rally 10 times over net inside service box.	• Moves to cover forehand shots. • Chooses correctly between volley and full stroke. • Able to control depth and vary speed. • Backswing and follow-through are complete.
Backhand	No effort.	• Changes grip. • Performs correct mimetics. • Uses correct side of racket. • Able to meet object in center of racket three consecutive times during self-volley.	• Can meet object coming over net. • Able to redirect ball to target 5 ft (1.5 m) away after it bounces. • Has proper body pivot. • Can self-volley up 10 times.	• Moves to meet ball after the bounce. • Able to rally over net 5 times with partner at 30 ft (9 m). • Meets ball with racket head up. • Controls backhand wall volley 3 times.	• Can run four steps or more and still redirect ball toward target. • Meets ball in front. • Can return ball with volley. • Can rally 10 times over net inside service box.	• Moves easily to cover backhand side. • Equally proficient with volley and full stroke. • Able to control depth and vary speed. • Backswing and follow-through are complete.
Serve	No effort.	• Performs correct mimetics. • Uses correct grip. • Can get ball over net from self-toss.	• Occasionally puts ball in play with an overhead serve. • Can put ball in play underhand. • Able to direct ball on diagonal.	• Consistently able to direct ball diagonally. • Serve reaches service box more often than not.	• Serves from off the court. • Puts ball in play legally more often than not.	• Consistent. • Starting to vary speed or depth. • Shows sign of strategic placement.

From Isobel Kleinman, 2009, *Complete Physical Education Plans for Grades 5 to 12, Second Edition* (Champaign, IL: Human Kinetics).

Beginner Tennis Quiz

Name _____ Date _____

Teacher _____ Class _____

True or False

Read each statement carefully. If the statement is true, write a *T* in the column to the left. If the statement is false, write an *F*. If using a grid sheet, blacken in the appropriate column for each question, making sure to use the correctly numbered line for each question and its answer.

_____ 1. A ball allowed to bounce twice before it is returned is returned legally.

_____ 2. A ball landing on the line is out.

_____ 3. When meeting the ball, the racket should be held firmly and should contact the ball on the center of the strings.

_____ 4. The server begins each new game from the right side of the court.

_____ 5. It is a fault when the ball is served over the net and lands inside the diagonal service box.

_____ 6. If the score is 30 to 40, the server leads the game.

_____ 7. *Deuce* means that no one is leading and both sides need 2 more points to win.

_____ 8. Having love in tennis is like having nothing at all.

_____ 9. A correctly executed volley requires a backswing.

_____ 10. During the serve, the toss and backswing should be done at the same time.

_____ 11. You are preparing to meet a ball on your right side when you pivot by stepping forward with your left foot.

_____ 12. If the face of your racket faces the ground, the ball will go up in the air.

_____ 13. The server serves an entire game until it is over.

_____ 14. A tennis game can be over in 4 points if one team wins all the points.

_____ 15. If the set score is 4 games to 2, the set is over because six games were played and one player is ahead by two games.

Beginner Tennis Answer Key

True or False

1. F—Rules require that ball be returned on one bounce or less.
2. F—The line or any part of it is considered good.
3. T—Although the ball can be hit without a firm wrist and off center, this is the best way to meet the ball.
4. T—All games start from the right side of the center mark.
5. F—The serve must pass over the net and land inside or on the lines of the diagonal service box.
6. F—Because the server's score is always said first, a score of 30 to 40 means the receiving team leads.
7. T—*Deuce* is another word for tied score.
8. T—Love is a score of zero in tennis.
9. F—The volley will be ruined if a backswing is taken.
10. T—Backswing and toss should occur at the same time.
11. T—The left foot should be the forward foot when hitting a ball on the right side.
12. F—Hitting the ball with strings that face the ground causes the ball to go down to the ground.
13. T—The server must complete the service game.
14. T—Scoring would be 15, 30, 40, game.
15. F—A set requires that one team win at least six games and be ahead by two.

 From Isobel Kleinman, 2009, *Complete Physical Education Plans for Grades 5 to 12, Second Edition* (Champaign, IL: Human Kinetics).

Stroke Review

Facilities

One tennis court for every four students

Materials

One tennis ball and racket per student

Performance Goals

Students will do the following:

- Review grip, meeting the center of strings, firm wrist, and forearm.
- Progressive strokes production, starting inside the service box and gradually backing up to the baseline.

Cognitive Goals

Students will review rules and basic tennis concepts:

- Reason for low-to-high swings (reduce errors and get topspin)
- Out-of-bounds ball as point for the other team
- Importance of reducing errors and getting steady
- Taking responsibility for getting and returning equipment

Lesson Safety

Partners will practice on half the width of a full court and should be rallying from the same general position in relation to the net.

Motivation

Announce that you want everyone to make these practice sessions count and that if they focus and follow your lead, they will be ready for some exciting games in a few days. Remind them that there is nothing more boring than hit-and-miss tennis.

Warm-Up

1. Students jog the perimeter of playing area, holding racket in waiting position.
2. Lead mimetics for backhand, forehand serve, and volley; see the beginner unit warm-ups for the breakdown of each (10 times each).
   a. Use full stroke pattern with opposite foot leading the pivot.
   b. Add footwork—Pivot, run three to five steps, plant opposite foot, bend knee, and swing.
   c. On each, emphasize
      - a low racket head on backswing, strings face net at contact point, follow-through forward and up;
      - a smooth unforced motion; and
      - concluding each stroke by returning to a waiting, neutral position.

Lesson Sequence

1. Review grip change for forehand and backhand.
2. Demonstrate a control drill over the net (see beginner unit).
   a. Encourage consecutive hits.
   b. Meet shots that haven't bounced with a volley.
   c. Keep the ball in play.

3. Create a contest out of the control drill:
   a. Who can get to 10 first?
   b. Who can get the highest number of consecutive taps without an error?
4. Move students back progressively until they reach the baseline.

Review and Stretching

As students stretch, ask:

- If your ball goes into the net, what adjustment should you make? (Bend down under the ball when hitting it and hit the ball higher so it clears the net. The safest way to add more topspin is by swinging low to high.)
- Why is it important to be able to keep the ball on the court?
- At what time should you take your backswing?
- Is it better to drop the racket head for a low ball or bend your knees so you can get under the ball?

Assessment

It is important to gauge the progress of the class. When students as a whole are having little or no trouble controlling a short rally and can maintain that rally for 10 strokes, they are ready to move back. If the class progress is slow, spend more time on this lesson. If a good number of students are ready to move on after one lesson while others are not, group the unprepared students on their own court and permit them to gradually move back to the baseline.

Tennis
INTERMEDIATE
LESSON 2

Serve and Volley

Facilities

One tennis court for every four students

Materials

One tennis ball and racket per student

Performance Goals

Students will do the following:

- Practice the serve (at least 30 serves per student).
- Practice volleying at the net.

Cognitive Goals

Students will learn the following:

- Service rules
- To meet the ball out in front with firm wrist for volleys
- The ability to be steady

Lesson Safety

Partners will practice on half the width of a full court and should be rallying from the same general position in relation to the net.

Motivation

Explain that everyone has learned all the necessary skills for tennis—putting the ball into play with a serve, returning the serve, rallying, and volleying at the net. Remind everyone that there is a big difference between knowing how to do something and being able to do it over and over again. Still, by the end of the day, students will have practiced every skill necessary to enjoy a game, so they will start doubles game play next time.

Warm-Up

1. Students pick up equipment and start a control drill on the courts.
2. Lead mimetics for forehand and backhand.
   a. Volley with racket out in front, wrist firm (10 times)
   b. High forehand (10 times)
   c. High backhand (10 times)
   d. Serve (use racket but no ball)
      - Use smooth motion.
      - Toss imaginary ball and use weight shift and racket backswing (5 times).
      - Swing to extend to the height of the imaginary ball (5 times).
      - Practice whole motion, including follow-through.

Lesson Sequence

1. Review the essentials of the serve:
   a. Toss slightly higher than the height of an extended racket arm.
   b. Toss out slightly so the ball is in front of the body as it drops.
   c. Swing up to meet the ball at its height.
   d. Visualize contact at one o'clock on the ball's face.
2. Divide the balls and serve from one side of the tennis courts.
   a. Serve all the balls to the closest diagonal service box.
   b. When all balls have been served, have the group retrieve them.
   c. On the other side of the net, set up and serve all the balls again.
   d. Do this until everyone has had 30 or more serves.
3. Review and demonstrate the essential features of a good volley. (Wait with racket head up and in front of body, meet the ball in front of body, keep wrist firm, and keep eye on the ball. Take no backswing!)
   a. Have students practice volleying to each other's forehand.
   b. Then practice backhand.
   c. See if they can rotate forehand to backhand.

Review and Stretching

As students stretch, ask:
- If your big first serve misses, what should you do on the second serve? Why?
- From what side of the court must you serve first?
- If the ball touches the line dividing the service boxes, is it good?
- Can servers continue to serve from their favorite side of the court?
- Do you feel ready for games, or do you want more practice?

Organizing for Doubles

Doubles is a compromise because of limited court space. If there are enough courts, do singles.

Facilities

One tennis court for every four students

Materials

- One can of balls for each court
- Blank round-robin roster sheet
- Clipboard and pen or pencil
- One racket per student

Performance Goal

Students will play a doubles game with their teammate.

Cognitive Goals

Students will do the following:

- Review:
  - Scoring for game, set, and match
  - Rules for receiving serve
  - Court courtesy
  - How to identify their balls from those of other courts
  - To clear their court of balls before each point and to return balls that are not theirs properly
- Choose their doubles teammate and sign up for tournament play.

Lesson Safety

Partners will practice on half the width of a full court and should be rallying from the same general position in relation to the net.

Motivation

Playing with a teammate leads to concerns beyond how to hit a ball, including how to divide court responsibilities, who should serve first, who should receive in the deuce box or the ad box, and what to do with all the balls on your court that aren't yours. Remind students that they will play today, so they should listen well.

Warm-Up

1. Students do progressive rally—short control drill for volley and short game, then from baseline.
2. Practice serves (5 times).
3. If students are using poor mechanics, lead mimetics for all strokes.

Lesson Sequence

1. Explain about cans of balls.
   a. Each court uses a can of balls with an identifying mark (e.g., Penn 3, Wilson 2, Penn 7).
   b. It is proper court courtesy to
      - clear the court of balls lying around for safety reasons, and
      - return balls that aren't yours by sending them back on one bounce.
2. Review the receiving rules for doubles.
   a. Player on deuce side (right side) must receive all odd points (first, third, fifth).
   b. Player on ad side must receive all even points (second, fourth, sixth).
3. Ask students to pick a partner and send them to courts to begin doubles play.
4. As students play out their games, circulate.
   - Emphasize ball control.
   - Watch for common group problems that should be discussed with the class.
   - Give hints to individuals that should be shared privately.

Review and Stretching

As students stretch, share some common problems you saw.

Doubles Strategy

Facilities

One tennis court for every four students

Materials

- Visual aid such as a blackboard, magnetic board, or chart
- One can of balls for each court
- Round-robin roster sheet
- Clipboard and pen or pencil
- One racket per student

Performance Goal

Students will play doubles.

Cognitive Goals

Students will learn the following:

- Doubles strategies and their rationale:
  - Hit the ball down the middle unless there is an opening.
  - Doubles is a game of angles.
  - Avoid hitting to the other team's net person.
- Poaching (the net person moves to volley a returned shot intended for partner)
- Responses to a shot down the middle that splits both players
  - The forehand takes the shot.
  - The last person to hit is the most natural to take the shot down the middle.

Lesson Safety

Partners will practice on half the width of a full court and should be rallying from the same general position in relation to the net.

Motivation

Confusion is the best friend of tennis opponents, and they create it by hitting between players. Let's get unconfused.

Warm-Up

1. Do a progressive rally—short drill for volley and half volley, and then rally from baseline.
2. Practice serves.
3. If students are still using poor mechanics, lead them in mimetics for all strokes.

Lesson Sequence

1. Explain winning strategies:
   - Being steady and letting opponents make the errors
   - Placing opponents at a disadvantage
     - Poaching
     - Using wide angles
     - Hitting ball to the open spaces

- Creating confusion for partners
  - Hitting the ball down middle and not putting the team at a disadvantage
  - Not hitting the ball to their net person
2. Assign students to courts and begin doubles play.

Review and Stretching

As students stretch, ask:

- How many people hit a shot down the middle?
- How many anticipated that you would and prevented it from becoming a winner?
- Did anyone poach?

Teacher Homework

List all the doubles teams in each category on a round-robin tournament form (see appendix A for forms). Create a master game schedule for each day the class meets and post it.

Round-Robin Doubles Tournament

Facilities

One tennis court for every four students

Materials

- One set of three balls per court
- One racket per student
- Round-robin team roster and game schedule
- Pen or pencil
- Visual aid that enlarges the round-robin tournament charts

Performance Goals

Students will do the following:

- Play doubles games.
- Rotate sides after every odd game is over.

Cognitive Goals

Students will learn the following:

- To focus when playing games that count
- To plan basic strategies before beginning a match:
  - Who serves first
  - What side of the court they should take

Lesson Safety

Partners will practice on half the width of a full court and should be rallying from the same general position in relation to the net.

Motivation

When students are ready for games to count and think they can stay focused, it is time to start a tournament. Suggest that if they run into problems, they should call you because you will be nearby. Explain that in real tennis tournaments, except for the Davis Cup competition, no coaching is allowed. For the most part, tennis players have to learn to solve their problems themselves.

Warm-Up

1. Do a progressive control drill that ends at the baseline.
2. Practice serves.

Lesson Sequence

1. Teach pregame procedure.
   a. Determining who serves first
   b. Other team deciding which side to take based on sun and wind
   c. Warming up with opponents
2. Go over scoring.
   a. Since time is short, teams will play as many games as they can. Each game they win will count as a point.
   b. Teach how to read the round-robin chart and how to enter their points.
3. Assign courts and let the games begin.

Review and Stretching

As students stretch, ask:

- Who had points where both partners went for the same ball?
- Who had points where no one thought the ball was theirs?
- Who won?

Lob and Round 2

Facilities

One tennis court for every four students

Materials

- One set of three balls per court
- One racket per student
- Round-robin team roster and game schedule
- Pen or pencil
- Visual aid that enlarges the round-robin tournament charts

Performance Goal

Students will play doubles in a competitive tournament.

Cognitive Goals

Students will learn more match strategy:

- When to consider hitting the ball up
- Who goes for a ball too deep for the net person to reach

Lesson Safety

Partners will practice on half the width of a full court and should be rallying from the same general position in relation to the net.

Motivation

Explain that going down the middle takes away opponents' angles and makes it harder for them to win a point, but doing it all the time allows them to anticipate it and be ready to make their own good shot. Changing it up is a great idea, but it requires skill. Before playing, they're going to take a minute to learn another shot that opens up the court.

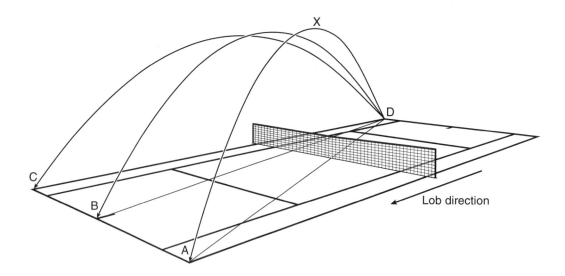

Figure 19.7 Placing lobs.

Warm-Up

For the rest of the unit, students warm up with opponents on scheduled courts. Allow time for progressive rallying and practice serves (5-10 minutes).

Lesson Sequence

1. Demonstrate the lob. Using the same ground strokes, open the face of the racket so strings meet the bottom of the ball and follow through as usual.

   a. Explain when it is best to use a lob (see figure 19.7).
      - When both players are close to the net
      - When it is windy out
      - When opponents are looking into the sun

   b. Ask students to practice a couple of lobs from baseline to baseline while warming up.

2. Announce standings.

3. Assign courts and opponents.

4. As students play, make suggestions.

Review and Stretching

1. As students stretch, ask:
   - Did anyone try to hit a ball over the net person's head?
   - Who had points where no one thought the ball was theirs?

2. Make sure students enter their scores before leaving.

Tennis
INTERMEDIATE
LESSON 7

Doubles Games and Round 3

Facilities

One tennis court for every four students

Materials

- One set of three balls per court
- One racket per student
- Round-robin team roster and game schedule
- Pen or pencil
- Visual aid that enlarges the round-robin tournament charts

Performance Goal

Students will play doubles games.

Cognitive Goal

Students will learn to handle disagreements about the score and line calls.

Lesson Safety

Partners will practice on half the width of a full court and should be rallying from the same general position in relation to the net.

Motivation

Announce standings after two rounds of the tournament. Explain that before the tournament progresses further, you want to deal with problems that can lead to bad feelings and poor sportsmanship.

Warm-Up

Students warm-up on assigned courts with their opponents.

Lesson Sequence

1. Discuss calling the lines. If there is space between the line and the spot the ball made, the ball is out. Balls that land even fractionally on the line are good.
   a. Calls are the responsibility of the person on whose side the ball lands.
   b. When there is a question, look for a mark on the surface.
   c. If they think the calls are consistently wrong, call for a line judge.
2. Assign courts and opponents.
3. As students play, coach.

Review and Stretching

1. As students stretch, answer questions. Ask if disagreements were resolved by finding the mark on the court surface.
2. Share a situation that cropped up with strategy or line calls.
3. Remind students to enter their scores.

Round-Robin Doubles Tournament Conclusion

Facilities

One tennis court for every four students

Materials

- One set of three balls per court
- One racket per student
- Round-robin team roster and game schedule
- Pen or pencil
- Visual aid that enlarges the round-robin tournament charts

Performance Goal

Students will continue their doubles round-robin tournament.

Cognitive Goals

Students will understand and value the following:

- Warming up before beginning competition
- Good sportsmanship during play
- Court courtesy

Lesson Safety

Partners will practice on half the width of a full court and should be rallying from the same general position in relation to the net.

Motivation

Announce standings.

Warm-Up

Students follow the progressive rally routine and take practice serves with their opponents before starting games.

Lesson Sequence

After warm-ups and announcements, students go to assigned courts and play their doubles matches.

Review and Stretching

As students stretch, answer questions and remind them to enter their scores. Remind them to be prepared for a quiz on the next rainy day.

Tennis
INTERMEDIATE
LESSONS
11-12

Match Play

Facilities

One tennis court for every four students

Materials

- One set of three balls per court
- One racket per student
- Round-robin team roster and game schedule
- Pen or pencil
- Visual aid that enlarges the round-robin tournament charts

Performance Goals

Students will do the following:

- Compete against teams that have a similar ranking.
- Complete a real match, two out of three sets.

Cognitive Goals

Students will learn the following:

- What a tennis match consists of
- To enjoy equal and challenging competition

Lesson Safety

Partners will practice on half the width of a full court and should be rallying from the same general position in relation to the net.

Motivation

Announce standings of the round-robin. Explain how match play differs. Explain that each team will play the team that had similar success in the round-robin, which should be fun because they will be evenly matched. Tell them all to go out and have a good time.

Warm-Up

Students meet their opponents on the court and warm up with them.

Lesson Sequence

Assign courts and opponents whose round-robin score totals were closest.

Review and Stretching

1. As students stretch, collect their match scores and remind them that the match will continue from where it left off during the following class.

2. Ask which type of play they enjoyed most, what was their easy win, and what was their tough skills battle where they had to work for every point.

3. On the last day, tell all students that the USTA sponsors local tournaments for players at their own playing level. Teams that are successful, whether beginners or advanced, have play-offs and go to sectional, regional, and national tournaments.

Intermediate Tennis Skills Rubric

Name _____ Date _____

Teacher _____ Class _____

	0	1	2	3	4	5
Forehand	No effort.	• Has proper body pivot. • Uses proper grip and mechanics. • Able to rally inside service box 10 times.	• Can return ground strokes. • Able to volley during game if ball is not hit too hard.	• Moves up to four steps away for ball. • Can control baseline rally up to three times. • Able to return service.	• Volleys are directed. • Ground strokes are directed.	• Able to control depth and vary speed. • Has complete backswing and follow-through when hitting the ball.
Serve	No effort.	• Has correct mechanics. • Toss is above head. • Able to direct ball on diagonal.	• Toss is correct height. • Swings up to meet the ball. • Occasionally able to put the ball in play. • Serves from the correct place on the court.	• Usually puts ball in play. • First serve reaches service box one of four tries.	• Makes sure second serve goes in. • Can serve deep into service box occasionally. • Consistent.	• Serve is a weapon. • Serves with power and depth. • Shows sign of strategic placement.
Court position	No effort.	• On the court promptly. • Goes to correct position for serve.	• Shifts in direction of the ball. • Covers most shots on own side of court if shots are in front.	• Covers own alley. • Volleys shots down the middle if close. • Backs up balls over partner's head.	• Moves to poach. • Takes the ball in the air when overhead. • Switches sides to keep court covered.	• Puts ball away when shifting to poach. • Comes to net at every opportunity. • Recovers quickly if drawn off court.

From Isobel Kleinman, 2009, *Complete Physical Education Plans for Grades 5 to 12, Second Edition* (Champaign, IL: Human Kinetics).

Intermediate Tennis Quiz

Name _____ Date _____

Teacher _____ Class _____

True or False

Read each statement carefully. If the statement is true, write a *T* in the column to the left. If the statement is false, write an *F*. If using a grid sheet, blacken in the appropriate column for each question, making sure to use the correctly numbered line for each question and its answer.

_____ 1. The server of the first game of a doubles match does not serve again until the fourth game of the match is completed.

_____ 2. All games start with the server serving from the left side of the court.

_____ 3. The game score is 40 to 30 and the serving team has five games to one game. The serving team can win the set if they win 1 point more.

_____ 4. A receiver who begins play in the deuce box must receive all serves directed to the box on the right side of the court.

_____ 5. The most confusing shot in doubles play is the shot that splits teammates by going down the middle.

_____ 6. A volley does not allow the ball to bounce and requires the person to meet the ball with no backswing.

_____ 7. *Deuce* means that no one is leading and both teams need 2 more points to win.

_____ 8. A shot that lands 1/16 on and 15/16 off the line is still good.

_____ 9. If you want to hit hard but keep the ball on the court, swing so the racket brushes the ball from low to high as you swing.

_____ 10. The service toss should be over and behind your head instead of over and in front of your head.

_____ 11. Poaching finds the net person cutting off a ball meant for her partner.

_____ 12. To hit a lob, take a normal ground stroke with an open racket face.

_____ 13. Any player can hit any ball in tennis as long as the serve has been returned by the proper receiver.

_____ 14. "Ad in" means that the server is probably about to win the game.

_____ 15. It is discourteous to run onto someone's court to get your ball.

From Isobel Kleinman, 2009, *Complete Physical Education Plans for Grades 5 to 12, Second Edition* (Champaign, IL: Human Kinetics).

Intermediate Tennis Answer Key

True or False

1. T—All four players must serve a complete game before anyone can serve again.
2. F—Each game starts from the right.
3. T—If the serving team wins, they will have six games.
4. T—Players cannot switch sides for return of serve once the game begins. The deuce box is the even (0, 2, 4, 6) box on the right side of the court.
5. T—Partners hesitate to take a shot they think their teammate is going after.
6. T
7. T—When the score is tied, either team needs 2 points to win.
8. T—Any fraction of the ball touching a line means that the ball is good.
9. T—The topspin imparted on the ball will help it drop into the court.
10. F—The toss should be out in front.
11. T
12. T—The ball will go in the direction the strings face: up.
13. T—Court coverage is only predetermined on the service return. After that players can play the ball wherever they want.
14. T—To win, the receiving team needs to gain 1 point to reach deuce and 2 more to win the game.
15. T—It interrupts their game.

20

Wrestling

Chapter Overview

1. Teach a short history of wrestling.
2. Teach the importance of conditioning while building strength, stamina, and endurance.
3. Teach a healthy approach to wrestling and to life.
   - Relay the importance of good nutrition, rest, and hydration.
   - Warn of the dangers of improper eating and dieting.
   - Discuss the dangers of substance abuse.
4. Combine the concepts of basic strategy with specific moves and counters, introducing one move at a time:
   - The proper alignment of varying positions: neutral, referee
   - The proper footwork to initiate or respond to motion:
     - For speed
     - To maintain a base of support, moving the foot closest to the line of direction
   - How to change levels
   - How to penetrate with good posture:
     - When advancing on the upper body or legs
     - When attempting a double leg, single leg, or fireman's carry with center steps
     - When going for the high crotch, high single snatch with outside steps
5. When teaching lifts, teach the cognitive aspects as well as the mechanics of execution:
   - Valuing the fact that counters are impossible against a solid support base
   - The rules of safety
   - The importance of using the legs and hips and not the back

»continued

»continued

6. Teach the basic moves and holds from the neutral position:
   - Takedowns—a double-leg attack
   - Counters to the double-leg attack
   - Escapes from the bottom
   - Counters of bottom escapes
7. Teach pinning and back arching.
8. Teach finishes and scoring:
   - Takedown = 2 points.
   - Reversal = 2 points.
   - Escape = 1 point.
   - Near fall with shoulders 4 inches (10 centimeters) from the mat = 2 or 3 points.

Wrestling Study Sheet

Fun Facts

- Images of wrestling appear in 15,000-year-old cave drawings in France.
- With the exception of track and field, wrestling is the most ancient sport to have survived in the modern world. Ancient Egyptian and Babylonian reliefs depict most of the wrestling holds used today.
- Wrestling was prominent in legend and literature in Greece and became an Olympic sport in 708 BC.
- The first U.S. national wrestling tournament took place in New York in 1888.

Skills

- From neutral position: Maintain a good stance (square, staggered) with bent knees, hips under rolled shoulders, elbows in, and one hand at knee height, the other at chest height.
  - Head: Keep head up in most situations.
    a. Penetration—Move feet to get head in middle of opponent's chest.
    b. Defending—Keep forehead the same height as opponent's.
  - Hips:
    a. On attack—Drive hips forward into opponent's hips.
    b. Hip pop—Make explosive effort to get hips up and forward into opponent.
    c. On defense—Keep hips over bent knees and aligned with shoulders.
  - Changing levels—Lower the head and hips at the same time.
    a. Drop step, one back-step, planting instep in the mat at a 45° angle, then one long forward step (12-18 inches [30-46 centimeters]) into opponent, reaching for the legs with both hands, elbows in.
  - Hand control—Grab opponent's hands and then wrists for control.
  - Work for inside position—Drive thumbs in opponent's armpit, elbows in.
  - Most common takedowns are from single-leg attacks.
  - Counters—The best counter is a proper stance and a solid stable base of support while trying to extend the opponent or force his head to the mat.
- Referee position—With head up and hips under shoulders, form a triangle with legs and feet.
  - Wrestler on bottom
    a. Keep the head up.
    b. Separate the knees to widen the base of support and create a triangle with the legs and body.
  - Wrestler on top.
    a. Keep one knee on the mat.
    b. Place one foot behind the opponent's feet and wrap an arm over and around the bottom wrestler until it reaches his or her navel.

»continued

From Isobel Kleinman, 2009, *Complete Physical Education Plans for Grades 5 to 12, Second Edition* (Champaign, IL: Human Kinetics).

»continued

Rules

Scoring

- Pin—Get opponent's back and part of shoulders on the mat for 2 seconds (wins).
- Takedown—Take opponent down to the mat and control him (2 points).
- Escape—Get away or get to a neutral position when opponent has you down on the mat (1 point).
- Reversal—Come from underneath and gain control when opponent has you down on the mat (2 points).
- Near fall (near pin)—When you almost but not quite get the opponent pinned (2 points if the near fall lasts 2 seconds, 3 points if 5 seconds):
  - Both shoulders are held for 2 seconds within 4 inches (10 centimeters) of the mat.
  - One shoulder touches, the other shoulder is at a 45° angle to the mat (wrestler is held in a high bridge or back on both elbows).

Penalty points—awarded points for infractions (1 or 2 points)

- Illegal holds
- Technical violations
  - Going off the mat to avoid wrestling (fleeing the mat).
  - Grabbing clothing, mat, or headgear.
  - Incorrect starting position or false start (two cautions before points are awarded).
  - Locked or overlapped hands: If down on the mat and in control, you cannot lock or overlap your hands, fingers, or arms around your opponent's body or both legs unless you have the opponent in a near pin, or the opponent stands up and has all weight on both feet.
  - Leaving mat during the match without the referee's permission.
- Unnecessary roughness
- Poor sporting behavior
- Flagrant misconduct (ejection; match is over)
- Stalling (one warning before points are awarded)

Wrestling Extension Project

Name _____ Date _____

Teacher _____ Class _____

What equipment do you need to wrestle on your own?

Is there a wrestling team at school? Who is the coach?

Is wrestling an intramural activity? Who is in charge?

Where can you wrestle outside of school?

Do you have friends who would join you? List their names.

What are the health benefits of participating in a wrestling program?

Where can you watch amateur wrestling?

From Isobel Kleinman, 2009, *Complete Physical Education Plans for Grades 5 to 12, Second Edition* (Champaign, IL: Human Kinetics).

Wrestling Student Portfolio Checklist

Name _____ Date _____

Teacher _____ Class _____

_____ Knows brief history of wrestling.

_____ Appreciates the need for proper conditioning.

_____ Understands how to properly gain conditioning.

_____ Understands the need for proper nutrition and hydration.

_____ Understands the need for muscles to rest.

_____ Understands what proper alignment is.

_____ Can adjust body to get into proper alignment from a variety of positions.

_____ Has learned how to score a wrestling match.

_____ Knows and follows safety rules.

_____ Has learned how to create motion.

_____ Has learned how to change levels.

_____ Has learned how to penetrate in order to begin an attack.

_____ Has learned to lift an opponent in the same weight classification.

_____ Has learned to return opponents to the mat safely.

_____ Has learned to counter a double-leg attack from neutral position.

_____ Has learned to escape from referee's position.

Wrestling Learning Experience Outline

Contents and Procedure

1. Teach a short history of wrestling, its evolution to the present, and why it is considered the most democratic sport (rules make certain competitors start on equal footing so they must overtake someone of equal size and weight).

2. Teach the importance of conditioning while building strength, stamina, and endurance.

3. Teach a healthy approach to wrestling and to life.
   a. Relay the importance of good nutrition, rest, and hydration.
   b. Warn of the dangers in improper eating and dieting.
   c. Discuss the dangers of substance abuse.

4. Combine basic strategic concepts with specific moves and countermoves, introducing one move at a time.
   - Proper alignment of varying positions—neutral, referee
   - Proper footwork for initiating, responding to speed, maintaining a base of support, and changing levels
   - Penetrating while maintaining good posture in the upper body and legs

5. Teach lifts, both cognitive as well as mechanical aspects.
   a. Counters are impossible against a solid support base.
   b. Use the legs and hips to lift, not the back.
   c. Go over safety rules.

6. Teach basic moves and holds.
   a. From neutral position
   b. Takedowns—how to set up, penetrate, and finish
      - Double-leg attack
      - Post and drive in the back trip
      - Upper-body lock
      - Single-leg action
   c. Counters to double-leg attack
      - How and why to increase the base of support
      - Moves—turn the corner, sprawl and cross-face, snap-down, lateral drop
   d. Moves from referee's position
   e. Strategies for escapes from bottom
      - Be aggressive quickly.
      - Fight to get good position.
      - Try for hand control.
   f. The stand-up and the cut-and-roll
   g. Counters of bottom escape: follow-and-lift, cover and suck-back

7. Teach pinning and back arching.

8. Teach finishes and scoring.
   a. Takedown = 2 points.
   b. Reversal = 2 points.
   c. Escape = 1 point.

9. Teach near fall (wrestler is pinned for up to 2 seconds but manages to escape before the 3-second pin) with shoulders 4 inches (10 centimeters) from the mat (length of time shoulders down, 2-3 points).

10. Allow noncompetitive practice, or time to learn and improve without pressure.

11. Each lesson includes some kind of contest that emphasizes the point of the lesson.

12. Conclude with a tournament and objective assessment.
    - Written quizzes for each unit
    - Performance rubrics for each unit

Teaching Tips for Special Considerations
- Students need their own location to work in 100% of class time.
- Students with problems that exclude them from regular play can usually do conditioning exercise. By remaining in the class structure, they can learn about healthy

living, develop proper movement fundamentals, move so they have no physical contact with opponents, and officiate and score matches.

- Students who must temporarily sit out can learn to cite movement problems, provide feedback to classmates, and reinforce their understanding of basic concepts such as positioning, footwork, and initiative while they watch and coach. They can assume responsibilities during the matches; for example, they can time, score, and officiate. They can also write reports related to the history, development, benefits, and dangers of wrestling.

- Although this unit may not appeal to many girls, things are changing. Numerous organizations promote competition for girls and women, often posting their photos and results on the Internet. Wrestling is becoming an activity for both genders, so girls might want the opportunity to learn what it is about. Certainly, the emphasis on conditioning is a win–win situation for all participants. If your school is considering making wrestling part of the physical education program, you might hold a short introductory course and then offer an in-depth unit as an optional course.

- Teachers will need to augment their professional library with a resource that fully explains specific wrestling attacks, counters to attacks, holds, escapes, reversals, and finishes so that everyone has a common terminology and so that you are aware of the proper body mechanics. The attacks, holds, counters to the attacks, escapes from holds, reversals, and finishes are complex and not completely explained in this text.

- After a book is published, rules, skills, and strategies may change. Check Internet sites listed in suggested resources to keep up with the changes.

Facilities

- Clean floor surface
- Mat large enough to conduct a match (see figure 20.1) or multiple modified matches

Materials

- Clock
- Headgear

Unit Safety

Wrestling competitions require headgear. Good practice would require that students wear headgear for class matches.

Unit Timeline

There are three units in this chapter, each including the following:

- 2 to 4 lessons to work on conditioning and develop basic skills to enjoy a low-level match
- 2 to 4 lessons to teach more specific wrestling holds, attacks, and responses in a cooperative learning environment, participating in limited matches
- 1 lesson to learn scoring and organize a class tournament
- 6 lessons for a class tournament
- 1 lesson for a quiz and culminating activity

Assessment

A short quiz and skills rubric for objective assessment are available at the end of each unit.

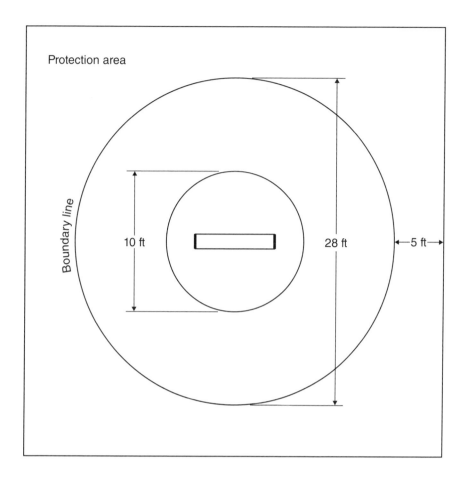

Protection area

Boundary line

10 ft

28 ft

5 ft

Figure 20.1 Official wrestling mat dimensions.

Suggested Resources

Amateurwrestlingphotos.com. 2008. Wrestling technique illustration. www.amateurwrestlingphotos .com/technique.html.

American Coaching Effectiveness Program. 1991. *Rookie coaches wrestling guide: American Coaching Effectiveness Program in cooperation with USA Wrestling.* Champaign, IL: Human Kinetics.

BYC Slammers. 2008. Wrestling moves. http://byc-wrestling.tripod.com/moves/frame.html.

Fortunato, T. 2008. Wrestling clip art gallery. www.wrestlingsbest.com/gifs/wrespictclips03.html.

Fortunato, T. 2008. Wrestling links for amateur wrestling. www.wrestlingsbest.com/wreslink2 .html.

Gable, D. 2005. *Dan Gable's wrestling essentials.* DVD. Champaign, IL: Human Kinetics.

Hickok Sports. 2008. Wrestling glossary. www.hickoksports.com/glossary/gwrestling.shtml.

Jarman T., and R. Hanley. 1983. *Wrestling for beginners.* Lincolnwood, IL: NTC Contemporary.

Keith, A. 1990. *Successful wrestling: Coaches' guide for teaching basic to advanced skills.* Champaign, IL: Human Kinetics.

Mysnyk, M., B. Davis, and B. Simpson. 1999. *Winning wrestling moves.* Champaign, IL: Human Kinetics.

Wongkk.com. 2008. Wrestling counters. http://wongkk.com/video-clips/wrestling/overview.html.

Wrestling fundamentals. 2008. http://homepage.mac.com/gdemarco1/WA/BasicFundamental.doc.

Wrestling instruction. 2008. www.youtube.com/watch?v=ossAI6tX9MM.

Neutral Stance

Facilities

Clean floor with mats

Materials

Clock

Performance Goals

Students will do the following:

- Take and maintain a neutral stance when changing levels and location.
- Build their strength, stamina, and endurance.

Cognitive Goals

Students will learn the following:

- What democracy in sport means
- What constitutes a good base of support
- The value of conditioning, nutrition, and rest

Lesson Safety

To prevent twisted ankles, avoid having students work near the edge of a mat, and during the setup do not allow the mats to overlap. Pairs should have their own space to work in.

Motivation

Explain that longer warm-ups will make everyone fit for the most democratic sport on earth, wrestling. Each matchup starts with an even playing field because wrestlers compete in their own weight category so no one has an obvious physical advantage. With an equal playing field, it is incumbent on the athletes to develop themselves. Some of the most important fundamentals start with the individual wrestler's physical well-being and ability to prevail over someone who is the same size.

Warm-Up

1. Jog around the playing area for 3 minutes.
2. Do 20 push-ups and 30 sit-ups.

Lesson Sequence

1. Discuss strategies:
   a. Conditioning for strength, stamina, and endurance
   b. Proper eating habits despite wanting to be in lowest weight category
   c. Need for rest
2. Demonstrate a proper neutral stance (opponents face each other with bent knees for the best base of support from a square or staggered stance; see figure 20.2).
   a. Practice bouncing off someone who is trying to push or pull them so each student can avoid being held and can get back into a proper stance.
   b. Practice initiating upper-arm movement while maintaining a proper stance.
   c. Practice penetrating (step in) to a hold, maintaining a proper stance.
   d. Try changing levels while maintaining a proper stance.
3. If there is time, find a way to make the practice challenging.
   a. Have students get a partner of equal height.
   b. At the start signal, see who can get out of the neutral position first.

Figure 20.2 Two boys in the neutral stance.

Review and Stretching

By this unit, your class should have a routine for stretching at the end of each lesson. If not, develop one now. Stretch the hamstrings, quadriceps, gastrocnemius muscles, hips, heels, shoulders, neck, and back. While students stretch, discuss:

- Describe a proper stance in neutral position.
- What can you expect if you let you feet get too close together?
- What can you expect if you let your head drop?
- Should you keep your arms in or allow them to take up lots of space?

Assessment

Observe students' response to warm-ups and ability to work independently in pairs. Your observation of their ability to keep up with your instructions and with each other will guide how fast you move ahead in lessons and how and when to introduce competitive elements into the lesson.

Double-Leg Kick Attack

Facilities

Clean floor with mats

Materials

Clock

Performance Goals

Students will do the following:

- Perform a double-leg attack from the neutral position (see figure 20.3).
- Build up strength, stamina, and endurance.
- Practice maintaining good levels of hydration.

Cognitive Goals

Students will learn the following:

- How to respond to changing levels with a good base of support
- What constitutes being an aggressor and its advantages
- What weight group they belong in
- The importance of water to the body

Lesson Safety

Have students work with partners who are the same size.

Motivation

Explain that you bet everyone is tired, and you want to discuss how conditioning, which they have started, is often dehydrating. Everyone should get in the habit of drinking water during and after a workout. Suggest that they might have lost water already. Ask how they would know if they did. Is it possible to have water loss without visibly sweating? Can they think of a reason why some people want water loss? Do they know the result of not replacing body fluids? Do they know where the closest water fountain is?

Explain that they are going to learn an attack from a neutral stance, the double-leg attack. They will learn how to set up for it, how to decide whether to be the attacker, and how to penetrate once the decision is made. If there is time, they will also learn how to finish this attack for a score.

Warm-Up

1. Develop a 6-minute routine of aerobic movement, including the following:
   a. Sprinting for 5 seconds followed by jogging for 1 minute (3 times)
   b. Changing directions
   c. Changing levels
      - Squatting
      - Jumping
      - Rolling
2. Do isometrics.
3. Do sit-ups.
4. Do push-ups.

Figure 20.3 Double-leg attack from neutral position.

Lesson Sequence

1. Before doing attacks, students have to find their weight classification.
2. Discuss the strategy of being the aggressor who attacks first.
3. Demonstrate the double-leg attack (a wrestler moves in to take down an opponent by grasping and pulling on both legs). For a pictorial explanation of the attack (and defense), go to www.budoseek.net/articles/double_leg.htm or see figure 20.3.
   a. Have students practice without stating who the aggressor is.
   b. Instruct the other partner to become the aggressor.

4. Demonstrate the finishes, instructing the class to choose one to practice today.

   a. Back trip—Hook outside hand around opponent's nearest knee, inside hand on the mat, and outside knee off the mat and head in front of opponent's nearest hip. Step outside foot behind opponent's ankle, hooking his foot so he can't go back. Drive your chest and shoulders into the hip over the foot that was trapped. Finish with both hands on the mat, 45° from your body. Keep elbow in and place inside hand between opponent's legs, hook the leg, and pressure his chest with yours to make the fall.

   b. Upper-body lock—Lock arms around opponent's upper body to take her down to the mat.

   c. Single-leg action—Lift one leg to take opponent's balance away.

5. Allow partners to practice the finish they have chosen.

6. Change partners in the same division and continue practice.

Review and Stretching

As students stretch, ask questions:

- What was the name of this attack?
- What stance do you have to be in to begin this move?
- What did you notice that was different between your original partner and the new one?
- Could you tell the advantage of making the first move? Were there disadvantages?
- What fundamentals should you concentrate on when you want to penetrate?

Assessment

Observe whether the pace of the lesson is too fast or slow. Adjust to student needs so the learning experience is exciting and successful for 90% of the students before moving on.

Wrestling
BEGINNER
LESSON 3

Countering a Double-Leg Attack

Facilities

Clean floor with mats

Materials

Clock

Performance Goals

Students will do the following:

- Perform counters to the double-leg attack from the neutral position.
- Continue building strength, stamina, and endurance.

Cognitive Goals

Students will learn the following:

- The purpose of an attack and a counter
- The difference in responding to and initiating an attack
- How to score a takedown and a reversal
- To practice good hydration habits

Lesson Safety

Have students work with partners who are the same size.

Motivation

Last time students learned how to start an attack from the neutral position and practiced the double-leg attack. They saw three ways to finish the attack but not how to stop it and get the advantage. This lesson will focus on reacting to several finishes in an effort to prevent an opponent from scoring and to create scoring opportunities for oneself.

Warm-Up

Perform the 6-minute warm-up routine started in the previous lesson, building cardiorespiratory strength while improving footwork fundamentals, balance, upper-arm strength, and abdominal strength.

Lesson Sequence

1. Review. Discuss countering the double-leg attack by increasing the base of support (see figure 20.4).

    a. Have students get some water if they are thirsty.

    b. Demonstrate the three finishes used and have students practice each once.

2. Discuss the strategy of turning the tables on the aggressor and scoring results.

    a. Reversal—Player on the bottom reverses position and comes to take control on the top (1 point).

    b. Takedown—Bring an opponent down to the mat from a neutral position (1 point).

3. Demonstrate how to turn the corner with the necessary circular motion and have students practice with partners.

4. Teach the following one at a time and practice.

    a. Crawl (turn under the hold of the opponent) and cross-face (drive opponent's face away with the biceps of the upper arm into the side of his face).

    b. Snap-down—Drive opponent back to create a head and shoulder lead, move right hand behind opponent's head, and with right leg move back and down, pulling opponent with you.

    c. Lateral drop—Bring opponent down to the mat on her side.

5. Change partners in the same general weight classification with each new counter.

Figure 20.4 Countering the double-leg attack by increasing base of support.

Review and Stretching

1. As students stretch, ask questions:
   - Who can tell us why water is important? Is it okay to wait to drink until you are thirsty?
   - What is a counter?
   - What is its purpose?
   - If you want to score, what must you do first?
   - What fundamentals should you concentrate on?
2. Tell students that tomorrow they will get a chance to practice everything they learned for the neutral position and have a few practice matches in this position.

Counter and Finish

Facilities

Clean floor with mats

Materials

Clock

Performance Goals

Students will do the following:
- Perform the double-leg attack from the neutral position with counters.
- Continue to build strength, stamina, and endurance.
- Practice successful counters and penetrations.

Cognitive Goals

Students will learn the following:
- Concerns about creatine and natural substances
- Fundamentals that lead to successful penetrations and counters
- What it is like to work against time and waning energy

Lesson Safety

Have students work with partners who are the same size.

Motivation

As students become more interested in wrestling, express your concern about good health habits. Discuss the use of creatine, a supplement made popular by the success of home-run hitting greats of the late 1990s, Mark McGwire and Sammy Sosa, and the use of other natural substances that are sold as performance enhancers to help athletes break records in their sports. Discuss whether such substances should be recommended to give everyone an equal advantage and if the lack of information on negative effects means that there aren't any negatives. Then discuss the downside of creatine: It increases a user's weight, and it is dehydrating; a few wrestlers who used it while dieting suffered sudden deaths. Wrestlers tend to diet. They get into rubber suits and sweat water weight away. Dehydration lowers weight and changes the wrestler's classification, but it is also dangerous. Tell students that when they compete, you hope they will not do the same.

Warm-Up

1. Perform the 6-minute warm-up routine started in previous lessons, building cardiorespiratory strength while improving footwork fundamentals, balance, upper-arm strength, and abdominal strength. Emphasize moving and increasing the base of support.

2. Students partner up and take turns moving against partner's weight. Emphasize increasing the base of support.

Lesson Sequence

1. Review how to complete the three attacks and counters.

2. Discuss the strategy of time.

3. Set up a minimatch, having noninvolved students in the class keep score.

4. Change partners with each new counter.

Review and Stretching

As students stretch, ask questions:

- What effect did time have on your performance?
- What did you do differently with the threat of scores and people watching?
- What is the ultimate goal in wrestling?
- Did anyone score a reversal? A takedown?

Wrestling
BEGINNER
LESSON 5

Back-Trip Escape

Facilities

Clean floor with mats

Materials

Clock

Performance Goals

Students will do the following:

- Review the following, then learn their counters and escapes.
    - Back trip—Hook outside hand around opponent's nearest knee, inside hand on the mat, outside knee off the mat, and head in front of opponent's nearest hip. Step outside foot behind opponent's ankle, hooking his foot so he can't go back. Drive your chest and shoulders into the hip over the foot that was trapped. Finish with both hands on the mat, 45° from your body. Keep elbow in and place inside hand between opponent's legs, hook the leg, and pressure his chest with yours to make the fall.
    - Upper-body lock—Lock arms around opponent's upper body to take her down to the mat.
    - Single-leg action—Lift one leg to take opponent's balance away.
- Continue building strength, stamina, and endurance.
- Have minimatches in neutral position.

Cognitive Goals

Students will learn the following:

- Counter for each move learned to date
- That counters are impossible without a good base of support
- How to compete when starting from neutral position

Lesson Safety

Have students work with partners who are the same size.

Motivation

Since part of the ability to overtake opponents is the element of surprise, and surprise is increased by the opponent not knowing which move the aggressor will make, today students are going to review the specific counters and escapes to the back trip, upper-body lock, and single-leg takedown (see figure 20.5). Then they will break into minimatches and try the moves on opponents.

Warm-Up

1. Perform the 6-minute warm-up routine started in previous lessons, building cardiorespiratory strength while improving footwork fundamentals, balance, upper-arm strength, and abdominal strength. Emphasize moving and increasing the base of support.
2. Students partner up and for 1 minute take turns moving against each other's push. Emphasize increasing the base of support.

Lesson Sequence

1. Review the back trip and then learn its counter, having students practice once each.
2. Review the upper-body lock and learn its counter, having students practice once each.

Figure 20.5 The single-leg attack.

3. Review the single-leg action and learn its counter, having students practice once each.

4. Set up multiple minimatches and let the games begin.

Review and Stretching

As students stretch, ask questions:

- How many of you think you could improve your performance by widening your base of support?
- By knowing more locks and responses?
- By getting quicker?
- By being the aggressor?

Referee's Position

Facilities

Clean floor with mats

Materials

Clock

Performance Goals

Students will do the following:

- Take the referee's position and respond to being on the bottom.
- Continue building strength, stamina, and endurance.

Cognitive Goals

Students will learn the referee's position (see figure 20.6).

- Strategy of being on the bottom in referee's position
- Ways of reversing position when on the bottom

Lesson Safety

Have students work with partners who are the same size.

Motivation

If students watch wrestling matches, they will see that attacks don't always start from the neutral position. The second starting position is the referee's position, and today they're going to learn it.

Warm-Up

1. Perform the 6-minute warm-up routine started in previous lessons, building cardiorespiratory strength while improving footwork fundamentals, balance, upper-arm strength, and abdominal strength. Emphasize moving and increasing the base of support.

2. Rotate to move against partner's push. Emphasize increasing the base of support. Spend 1 minute on this move, alternating pushing.

Lesson Sequence

1. Demonstrate the referee's position (on mat on hands and knees with one opponent kneeling behind the other with one arm around the waist). Have everyone try it, experimenting with getting out.

   a. Weight is equally distributed.

   b. Aim for large base of support.

Figure 20.6 Referee's position.

2. Teach the strategy for the person on the bottom, allowing students to experiment again with getting out.
   a. Be aggressive quickly.
   b. Fight to keep good position with head up and hips under shoulders.
3. Direct experimentation.
   a. Get hand control.
   b. Try to stand up.
   c. Cut and roll (see figure 20.7).

Review and Stretching

As students stretch, ask:

- What are the most important things to remember about preventing a score when in referee's position?
- What about scoring yourself from the bottom?

Figure 20.7 Beginning the cut and roll.

Referee's Position: Responses

Facilities

Clean floor with mats

Materials

Clock

Performance Goals

Students will do the following:

- Practice responses from the referee's position.
- Continue building strength, stamina, and endurance.

Cognitive Goal

Students will review everything they learned in the previous lesson.

Lesson Safety

Have students work with partners who are the same size.

Motivation

Last class the agenda was so full that most students didn't have enough time to practice. Today they're going to set aside a little time to practice the possibilities of coming out of the referee's position, and if there is time, perhaps there will be some minimatches.

Warm-Up

1. Perform the 6-minute warm-up routine started in previous lessons, building cardio-respiratory strength while improving footwork fundamentals, balance, upper-arm strength, and abdominal strength. Emphasize moving and increasing the base of support.

2. Give 1 minute to practice rotating against a partner's push. Emphasize increasing the base of support.

Lesson Sequence

1. Review the basics about the referee's position and maintaining it.
2. Review the strategy for the person on bottom.
3. Direct experimentation for escapes.
   a. Get hand control.
   b. Try to stand up.
   c. Cut and roll.
4. Set up minimatches if time allows.

Review and Stretching

While students stretch, call their attention to three issues that cropped up during their practice and make sure students understand what they should try to do in those situations.

Step-Back and Lift

Facilities

Clean floor with mats

Materials

Clock

Performance Goals

Students will do the following:

- Practice being the top person in the referee's position and responses.
- Practice the back-step and prepare for lifts.
- Build strength, stamina, and endurance.

Cognitive Goals

Students will learn the following:

- Problems inherent in being on top in referee's position
- The preparation, body mechanics, and rules for a lift
- The cover and suck-back

Lesson Safety

Have students work with partners who are the same size.

Motivation

After two lessons of worrying about the person on the bottom, it's time to think about what to do and how to do it when on the top. Tell students to imagine lifting. That's the way to gain control and go for a pin.

Warm-Up

1. Perform the 6-minute warm-up routine started in previous lessons, building up cardio-respiratory strength while improving footwork fundamentals, balance, upper-arm strength, and abdominal strength. Emphasize moving and increasing the base of support.

2. Try 1 minute of rotating to move against partner's push. Emphasize increasing the base of support.

Lesson Sequence

1. Review the basics of the back-step and the need to keep legs and hips aligned and to never take more than two steps back (see figure 20.8).

2. Teach the rules and body mechanics for lifting
   a. Lift with legs and hips, not the back.
   b. It is the responsibility of the lifter to return the opponent to the mat safely.

3. Demonstrate and teach the fireman's carry. Place one arm between the opponent's legs and the other around the opponent's arm. Roll your opponent over your shoulder.

Review and Stretching

As students stretch, ask questions:

- Which would you prefer, the top or the bottom?
- Which is harder and why?

Figure 20.8 Step-back and lift.

Scoring

Facilities

Clean floor with mats

Materials

Clock

Performance Goal

Students will improve previously learned skills.

Cognitive Goals

Students will learn the following:

- How to react to a variety of situations at the moment
- How to score

Lesson Safety

Have students work with partners who are the same size.

Motivation

Explain that it's time to stop learning new things and work on using what they've learned in a fun and challenging way.

Warm-Up

1. Perform the 6-minute warm-up routine started in previous lessons, building cardio-respiratory strength while improving footwork fundamentals, balance, upper-arm strength, and abdominal strength. Emphasize moving and increasing the base of support.

2. Try 1 minute of rotating to different partners to practice moving against partner's push. Emphasize increasing the base of support.

Lesson Sequence

1. Review the basics of the back-step and rules for lifting.

2. Set up a procedure for matches.

   a. Teach scoring.

      - Takedowns, escapes, and correct holds that don't get opponent's shoulders to the mat = 1 point.

      - Near fall and reversals = 2 points.

      - Taking a person from standing to a point of danger (wrestler's back is less than 90° angle from the mat) = 3 points.

      - Grand amplitude throw to immediate point of danger = 5 points.

      - Pin = wins the match.

   b. Teach how and when to change positions.

3. Play matches.

Review and Stretching

As students stretch, ask questions:

- Who was more successful from the neutral position?
- The referee's position?
- The top?
- The bottom?
- Why?

Teacher Homework

Set up tournament chart and post it.

Matches: Round 1

Facilities

Tournament wrestling mat

Materials

- Tournament schedules by classification
- Individual standings sheets
- Clock

Performance Goal

Students will compete in first round of matches.

Cognitive Goals

Students will learn the following:

- To assume responsibility for their own matches
- To score classmates' matches

Lesson Safety

- Follow standard operating procedure with attention to lifting rules.
- Have students work with partners who are the same size.

Motivation

This is round 1. Review students' responsibilities as athletes, officials, and scorers.

Warm-Up

1. Perform the 6-minute warm-up routine started in previous lessons, building cardio-respiratory strength while improving footwork fundamentals, balance, upper-arm strength, and abdominal strength. Emphasize moving and increasing the base of support.
2. Allow 1 minute of rotating to move against partner's push. Emphasize increasing the base of support.

Lesson Sequence

1. Review expectations for the scorer, the official, and the athlete.
2. Divide remaining time so that everyone gets to participate in each role.
3. Play matches.

Review and Stretching

As students stretch, ask questions:

- Have you entered the scores of the matches you officiated? If not, do so now.
- Did anyone score 3 points?

Assessment

Begin assessment based on performance standards. Announce the standards and teach the class to observe for them.

Teacher Homework

Update charts.

Round 2

Facilities

Clean floor with mats

Materials

- Beginner wrestling skills rubric
- Clock

Performance Goal

Students will compete in the second round of matches.

Cognitive Goals

Students will continue to assume responsibility for the following:

- Getting to their own match
- Scoring other matches
- Using strategy
    a. You cannot lose if you do not allow the opponent to score.
    b. The best defense is maintaining a large base of support.

Lesson Safety

Have students work with partners who are the same size.

Motivation

Compliment everyone on their efforts. Address a few issues like finding yourself on the mat during a match or feeling your opponent trying to gain advantage by grabbing your clothes before starting. Announce standings. Suggest concentrating first on defense and preventing the opponent from scoring any points.

Warm-Up

1. Perform the 6-minute warm-up routine started in previous lessons, building cardiorespiratory strength while improving footwork fundamentals, balance, upper-arm strength, and abdominal strength. Emphasize moving and increasing the base of support.

2. Allow 1 minute to move against partner's push. Alternate who is doing the pushing. Emphasize increasing the base of support.

Lesson Sequence

1. Review the importance of keeping a large base of support.
2. Assign places and matches, making sure everyone gets to participate.
3. Play matches.

Review and Stretching

As students stretch, ask if they have any questions, and make sure they entered the scores of the matches they officiated.

Assessment

Teach students to evaluate their own improvement, using the standards in the performance rubric as a guide.

Teacher Homework

Update charts.

Round 3: Headlock

Facilities

Clean floor with mats

Materials

Clock

Performance Goal

Students will compete in the third round of the tournament.

Cognitive Goals

Students will learn the following:

- To recognize several locks
- To assume responsibility during matches

Lesson Safety

Have students work with partners who are the same size.

Motivation

Suggest that during competition, as in most sports, students should concentrate first on defense. If they think about it, they will realize that they cannot lose if their opponent doesn't score. They must also recognize that in order to win, they must take control. What does that mean?

Warm-Up

1. Perform the 6-minute warm-up routine started in previous lessons, building cardio-respiratory strength while improving footwork fundamentals, balance, upper-arm strength, and abdominal strength. Emphasize moving and increasing the base of support.

2. Allow 1 minute of practice moving against partner's push. Emphasize increasing the base of support. Alternate who is pushing.

Lesson Sequence

1. Have three pairs demonstrate the headlock (keep your head and shoulders on opponent's back, grab his chin and pull it back and with other hand, and grab his elbow on the other side, pulling it off the mat to your rib cage).

2. Assign places and matches, making sure everyone gets to participate.

3. Play matches.

Review and Stretching

As students stretch, ask if they have any questions, and remind them to enter the scores of the matches they officiated.

Assessment

Continue observing and training students to observe as well.

Round 4: Back-Step

Facilities

Clean floor with mats

Materials

Clock

Performance Goal

Students will compete in the fourth round of the tournament.

Cognitive Goals

Students will learn the following:

- The back-step and how it helps gain success with several locks
- To assume responsibilities during matches

Lesson Safety

Have students work with partners who are the same size.

Motivation

Announce standings.

Warm-Up

During the warm-up routine, work on taking proper back-steps and changing direction while increasing the base of support.

Lesson Sequence

1. Have three pairs of students demonstrate the back-step followed by the hip lock (step into opponent's hip, pivot, and step back so both feet are next to each other and you have turned your back so that you both face the same direction).
2. Assign places and matches, making sure everyone gets to participate.
3. Play matches.

Review and Stretching

1. As students stretch, ask questions:
   - Did anyone use any locks during your match today?
   - Did you take a back-step first? Was it easier?
2. Make sure students have entered the scores of the matches they officiated.

Round 5

Facilities

Clean floor with mats

Materials

Clock

Performance Goal

Students will compete in the fifth round of the tournament.

Cognitive Goals

Students will learn the following:

- The basis for the skills grade, observing others' accomplishments
- To take responsibility during matches

Lesson Safety

Have students work with partners who are the same size.

Motivation

Compliment the conduct of the tournament and announce standings.

Warm-Up

Perform the usual warm-up routine, but add footwork for taking proper back-steps and changing direction while increasing the base of support.

Lesson Sequence

1. Demonstrate the arm throw (throwing the opponent over your shoulder by holding her arm).
2. Review performance standards.
3. Assign places and matches, making sure everyone gets to participate.
4. Play matches.

Review and Stretching

1. As students stretch, ask how many thought they met specific items in the performance standards.
2. Make sure students have entered the scores of the matches they officiated.
3. Tell students to be prepared for a short quiz and then ask if they have questions.

Assessment

- Continue observation, having students discuss strengths they observed.
- Consider documenting student conclusions by having them assess themselves or each other.

Round 6

Facilities

Clean floor with mats

Materials

Clock

Performance Goal

Students will complete their tournament.

Cognitive Goals

Students will learn the following:

- The basis for a skills grade
- To take responsibility during the tournament

Lesson Safety

Have students work with partners who are the same size.

Motivation

Announce the final round of the tournament and the standings after five rounds, as well as what people have to accomplish to change rankings in their weight category.

Warm-Up

Perform the warm-up routine, working on taking proper back-steps and changing direction while increasing the base of support.

Lesson Sequence

1. Post and explain standards in the performance rubric.
2. Assign places and matches, making sure everyone gets to participate.
3. Play matches.

Review and Stretching

As students stretch, make sure they have entered the scores of the matches they officiated and remind them that next time, there will be a short quiz.

Assessment

- Assessment proceeds.
- Consider putting students in charge of the final assessment, using the performance rubric as their guide.

Assessment and Final Matches

Facilities

Clean floor with mats

Materials

- Quizzes for everyone
- Pens and pencils
- Clock

Performance Goals

Students will do the following:

- Demonstrate their knowledge during a short quiz.
- Get a measure of learned skills.
- Conclude matches.

Cognitive Goals

Students will assume responsibility for the following:

- Recognizing performance levels on the assessment rubric
- Scoring other people's matches

Lesson Safety

Have students work with partners who are the same size.

Motivation

Once the quiz is over, it's time to enjoy the conclusion of this activity. Announce the rankings of the top three people in each weight category.

Warm-Up

1. Do a quick jog.
2. Stretch.

Lesson Sequence

1. Hand out quizzes as students enter and allow them to begin right away.
2. After quizzes are collected, wrap up any loose ends, do a quick warm-up, and assign places and matches so everyone participates. Make arrangements for students who haven't finished when the time is up.
3. Play matches and finish the assessment process.

Review and Stretching

1. As students stretch, ask questions:
   - How many of you enjoyed wrestling?
   - Did you expect to when we began?
2. Congratulate students on their achievements.

Assessment

- Written quiz
- Performance rubric

Beginner Wrestling Skills Rubric

Name _____ Date _____

Teacher _____ Class _____

	0	1	2	3	4	5
Stamina and conditioning	No effort.	Tries most exercises.	Completes class exercises in slower rhythm.	• Keeps pace with exercise regime. • Shows 5% gain in stamina and strength.	• Shows 10% gain in strength, stamina, and speed. • Enters match with energy.	• Energetic throughout the lesson. • Shows 15% gain in stamina, speed, and strength. • Shows no fatigue during matches.
Balance	No effort.	Attempts to maintain a good base of support in referee's position.	Attempts to maintain a good base of support when in both the neutral stance and the referee's position.	• Keeps head up in both positions. • Makes effort to keep center of gravity over base.	• Adjusts base of support when there is outside force. • Keeps head up when moving. • Uses level change to keep more stable.	• Strives to adjust base to maintain center of gravity. • Enlarges base during attacks.
Matches	No effort.	Can counter one learned attack.	Can initiate a double-leg attack.	Demonstrates one finish for an attack.	• Uses several attacks and finishes. • Can escape.	• Frequently scores. • Able to reverse. • Has variety of moves.

From Isobel Kleinman, 2009, *Complete Physical Education Plans for Grades 5 to 12, Second Edition* (Champaign, IL: Human Kinetics).

Beginner Wrestling Quiz

Name _____ Date _____

Teacher _____ Class _____

True or False

Read each statement carefully. If the statement is true, write a *T* in the column to the left. If the statement is false, write an *F*. If using a grid sheet, blacken in the appropriate column for each question, making sure to use the correctly numbered line for each question and its answer.

_____ 1. Weight classification makes competitive wrestling truly democratic.

_____ 2. To create a winning imbalance between two wrestlers, one must develop more strength, speed, and stamina than the opponent.

_____ 3. Winning in the lowest weight category is easier, so a good strategy for wrestlers is to limit their calories and keep their weight down.

_____ 4. Water weighs a lot, so wrestlers should avoid drinking to avoid going up a weight category.

_____ 5. Taking the most weight you can lift and lifting it once daily improves strength.

_____ 6. Keeping your center of gravity above your strong leg leads to a good support base.

_____ 7. You are more vulnerable to a takedown when you change levels.

_____ 8. If you lift your opponent from the mat, you are responsible for returning him safely.

_____ 9. To escape a hold, it is more important to be aggressive and quick than to know specific responses to holds.

_____ 10. The ultimate finish in a match is a pin.

Beginner Wrestling Answer Key

True or False

1. T
2. T
3. F—Reducing caloric intake for inappropriate reasons, such as to compete at a lower category, is a dangerous habit that at its extreme can become an eating disorder.
4. F—Dehydration is a risk of avoiding drinking. Water intake is extremely important to maintain health.
5. F—Strength is more than a function of one quick lift; it requires the ability to sustain power and repeat it.
6. F—To get a good base of support, the center of gravity should be aligned with the center of the base of support. Leaning over one leg moves the center of gravity away from the center of the base of support and can result in an easy loss of balance.
7. F—The lower the center of gravity, the greater the stability. Lowering levels can be a good strategy.
8. T
9. T
10. T

From Isobel Kleinman, 2009, *Complete Physical Education Plans for Grades 5 to 12, Second Edition* (Champaign, IL: Human Kinetics).

Lifts From Neutral Stance

Facilities

Clean mats covering the working area

Materials

Clock

Performance Goals

Students will do the following:

- Perform lifts from a neutral stance.
- Build their strength, stamina, and endurance.

Cognitive Goals

Students will learn the following:

- The neutral stance and importance of a good base of support
- How to use the double-leg attack to create lifts
- How to safely lift and return an opponent to the mat

Lesson Safety

- Make sure rules about lifts are firm and well understood and that students who have no respect for the safety of their opponents are promptly removed from practice. After being cautioned, students who do not take heed should be given time out to reflect, apologize, and give assurances that they will mind the rules.
- Make certain that students don't twist an ankle by working near the edge of a mat.
- Groups need their own space in which to work.

Motivation

Last year was spent on fundamentals. This year students will concentrate on actual moves. Having done little with lifts, start with them, reminding students that if they learned anything, they must realize that they can counter attacks with good footwork that maintains a base of support and keeps the center of gravity balanced over it. The advantage of a lift is that once you get an opponent in the air, they have no base of support, no balance, and no opportunity to create power of their own. Their attack is prevented and their ability to escape is neutralized.

Warm-Up

Develop a 6-minute routine of aerobic movement including the following:

1. Sprinting for 5 seconds followed by jogging for 1 minute (3 times)
2. Change of direction
3. Change of levels
    a. Squatting
    b. Jumping
    c. Rolling
4. Isometrics
5. Sit-ups
6. Push-ups

Lesson Sequence

1. Discuss the rules.
    a. Dangers inherent in incorrectly returning a partner to the mat
    b. Rules requiring wrestlers to protect opponent

2. Demonstrate footwork for lifts. Practice lift choreography alone.
   a. Stepping in
   b. Lowering level
   c. Popping hips
   d. Extending
3. Discuss weight classes and the biggest weight difference allowed for their age (8 pounds [3.5 kilograms]). Have students find a partner within their range.
4. Teach and practice the lift from the double-leg attack.
5. Teach and practice the counter for the lift from the double-leg attack.
   a. Push hips in.
   b. Spread legs wide.
6. Verbally review general strategy for the lift and its counter.
7. If time remains, allow a minimatch, awarding points to those who lift first.

Review and Stretching

As students stretch, ask questions:

- What is the biggest weight difference allowed wrestlers of your age?
- What is the value of a lift?
- What parts of the body do the action—the hips and legs or the arms?
- What do the arms have to do to help the legs and hips?
- Who is the one who ultimately lifts her opponent, the aggressor or the responder?

Assessment

Observe the students' response to warm-ups and their ability to work independently in pairs. As always, if the lesson content is not covered so that 90% of the class is comfortable with it, do not move on.

Wrestling
INTERMEDIATE
LESSON 2

Reverse Lift

Facilities

- Clean floor
- Clean mats covering the working area

Materials

Clock

Performance Goals

Students will do the following:

- Lift from the single-leg attack.
- Practice the reverse lift and the tuck.
- Build their strength, stamina, and endurance.

Cognitive Goals

Students will learn the following:

- The single-leg attack

- What successful lifts require
  - Good footwork
  - Change of level
  - Strength from the legs and hips, not the upper body
- How to use the opponent's motion and change as momentum for their lifts

Lesson Safety

- Make sure rules about lifts are firm and well understood and that students who have no respect for the safety of their opponents are promptly removed from practice. After being cautioned, students who do not take heed should be given time out to reflect, apologize, and give assurances that they will mind the rules.
- Make certain that students don't twist an ankle by working near the edge of a mat.
- Groups need their own space in which to work.

Motivation

Explain that students will work in the neutral position, learning how to finish a takedown from a lift, and that they will explore the finish from a single-leg attack, doing a reverse lift and the tuck.

Warm-Up

1. Use the 6-minute routine developed previously, making sure the footwork requires quick changes of direction, turning, pivoting, and changes of levels. Add footwork and body mechanics that would yield a lift—penetrate, drop hips, pop, and extend.
2. Follow the footwork drills with a required number of sit-ups (30 or more) and push-ups (15 or more).

Lesson Sequence

1. Review and demonstrate the single-leg attack (see figure 20.9).
2. Explain and demonstrate the lift from the single-leg attack.
   a. Break it down in parts and practice mimetics.
   b. Practice the single-leg attack with lift so everyone gets several chances.
3. Demonstrate, teach, and practice the reverse lift.
4. Practice the tuck and its conclusion, dropping the opponent's back to the mat.
5. If time remains, allow a mini-match. Have the class keep cumulative score.

Review and Stretching

As students stretch, ask questions:

- How many lifts have you learned from the neutral position?
- How do they differ?

Figure 20.9 Single-leg attack with head penetration.

Back-Step

Facilities

- Clean floor
- Clean mats covering the working area

Materials

Clock

Performance Goals

Students will do the following:

- Perform the back-step to promote upper-body throws from neutral position.
- Build their strength, stamina, and endurance.

Cognitive Goals

Students will learn the following:

- The value of the back-step
  - The ability to unbalance opponents
  - Enabling the back to be the fulcrum
- How to throw their opponent

Motivation

Quote from *Wrestling for Beginners* by Jarman and Hanley (1983): "Back stepping takes hours and hours to perfect, but the wrestler who spends the time and effort will be rewarded with spectacular throws and quick falls" (p. 82). With the word *spectacular* in mind, it is worth beginning to learn the back-step right now.

Warm-Up

1. Use the 6-minute routine developed in previous classes, making sure the footwork requires quick changes of direction, turning, pivoting, and changes of levels. Add footwork and body mechanics that would yield a lift—penetrate, drop hips, pop, and extend.
2. Make sure the routine includes sit-ups and push-ups.

Lesson Sequence

1. Review footwork.
   a. Show good penetration.
   b. Show how foot placement assists the hips and legs in creating the throw.
   c. Show how footwork helps turn back to opponent.
   d. Emphasize close feet.
2. Practice the whole sequence in parts and without a partner.
   a. Practice pivot to a 180° turn.
   b. Teach lowering level while pivoting.
   c. Practice the pivot in the preparation for the throw.
   d. Practice the pivot with extension.
   e. Add the shoulders and arms to the partnerless movement.
3. Review rules for returning a partner safely to the mat, because throws will result.
4. Students partner up and practice the back-step as a double-leg attack.
5. If time remains, allow a minimatch. Have the class keep cumulative score.

Review and Stretching

As students stretch, ask questions:

- Why do you think the back-step will aid you in getting "spectacular throws and quick falls"?

- Should feet be spread wide to help the pivot, or should they be close together?

- Is stability more important than motion, or is motion what makes the back-step sequence worthwhile?

Fall From Neutral

Facilities

Clean floor and mats covering the working area

Materials

Clock

Performance Goals

Students will do the following:

- Use the back-step to initiate a near fall from neutral position.

- Continue to build their strength, stamina, and endurance.

Cognitive Goal

Students will review the back-step and scoring.

Lesson Safety

- Students who have no respect for the safety of opponents should be promptly removed.

- Make certain that students don't twist an ankle by working near the edge of a mat.

- Groups need their own space in which to work.

Motivation

Explain that a lot has been thrown their way already, and considering the quote from before ("Back stepping takes hours and hours to perfect, but the wrestler who spends the time and effort will be rewarded with spectacular throws and quick falls"), it makes sense to continue what they learned in the last class to get the spectacular throws promised. After practice, they will have a minimatch from the neutral position.

Warm-Up

1. Use the 6-minute routine developed previously, making sure the footwork requires quick changes of direction, turning, pivoting, and changing levels.

   a. Add footwork and mechanics to yield a lift—penetrate, drop hips, pop, and extend.

   b. Add mechanics for the back arch from a variety of positions.

2. Make sure the routine includes sit-ups and push-ups.

Lesson Sequence

1. Review and practice the sequence, using different starting points.

   a. Alone

   b. With a passive partner

2. Allow a minimatch.

Review and Stretching

As students stretch, ask questions:

- Who used the back-step during your match?
- Was it successful?
- Why?

Standout Escape

Facilities

Clean floor with mats covering the working area

Materials

Clock

Performance Goals

Students will do the following:

- Escape from the referee's position (standout or stand-back).
- Continue to build their strength, stamina, and endurance.

Cognitive Goals

Students will learn the following:

- Strategy for making the first move to escape referee's position
- The three most important aspects for successful escapes

Lesson Safety

- Students who have no respect for the safety of opponents should be removed promptly.
- Make certain that students don't twist an ankle by working near the edge of a mat.
- Groups need their own space in which to work.

Motivation

Explain that in this lesson, the class will devote attention to the problems that the person on the bottom of the referee's position might have. Being on the bottom can be demoralizing. Think about it—carrying the opponent's weight is exhausting, to say nothing about the danger of being turned onto their back for a fall or near fall. Clearly, escape would be a good idea, and today they're going to learn how.

Warm-Up

1. Use the 6-minute routine developed previously, making sure the footwork requires quick direction changes, turning, pivoting, and level changes.
   a. Add footwork and mechanics to yield a lift—penetrate, drop hips, pop, and extend.
   b. Add mechanics for the back arch from a variety of positions.
2. Make sure the routine includes sit-ups and push-ups.

Lesson Sequence

1. Teach the theory behind the strategy.
   a. Explain good position and fighting for it.
   b. Keep back squared to opponent.
   c. Take control of opponent's hands.

2. Teach and practice the standout. Students accelerate their weight back against their opponent, gaining balance as they do so, enabling them to stand, all the while keeping control of their opponent's hands.

Review and Stretching

1. As students stretch, explain why the standout might be called the *stand-back*.
2. Review position, when to pop and how, what hand position to attempt, and how to finish.

Sit-Out Escape

Facilities

Clean floor with mats covering the working area

Materials

Clock

Performance Goals

Students will do the following:

- Practice a new escape from the referee's position—the short sit-out or sit-back.
- Build their strength, stamina, and endurance.
- Compete in the referee's position.

Cognitive Goal

Students will learn the fundamentals of a successful sit-out.

Lesson Safety

- Students who have no respect for the safety of opponents should be removed promptly.
- Make certain that students don't twist an ankle by working near the edge of a mat.
- Groups need their own space in which to work.

Motivation

Explain that you want to help students add to their escaping repertoire before going into competition. Today they're going to learn an escape that does not push to stand but rather to sit (see figure 20.10).

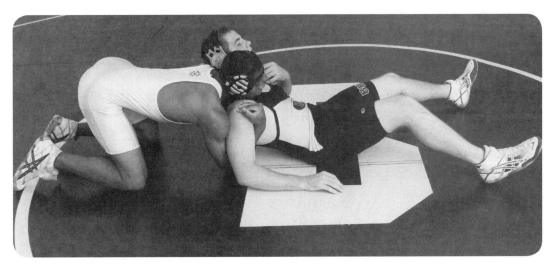

Figure 20.10 Sit-out.

813

Warm-Up

1. Use the 6-minute routine developed previously, making sure the footwork requires quick changes of direction, turning, pivoting, and changes of levels.

   a. Add footwork and mechanics to yield a lift—penetrate, drop hips, pop, and extend.

   b. Add mechanics for the back-arch from a variety of positions.

2. Make sure the routine includes sit-ups and push-ups.

Lesson Sequence

1. Demonstrate, teach, and practice the sit-out.

   a. The position

   b. The objective—quick way of clearing feet and squaring back to opponent

   c. How to take control of opponent's hands

   d. One finish (underarm spin)

      - Take left arm and rotate hips.

      - Main idea is to do it quickly.

2. Have a competition only from referee's position.

Review and Stretching

As students stretch, review the position, when to pop, how to pop, what hand position to take, and how to finish.

Finishes

Facilities

Clean floor with mats covering the working area

Materials

Clock

Performance Goals

Students will do the following:

- Perform new finishes (underarm spin and hip switch).
- Continue to build strength, stamina, and endurance.

Cognitive Goals

Students will learn the following:

- What a finish is
- The fundamentals that allow them to finish their escapes
- How to finish a reversal

Lesson Safety

- Students who have no respect for the safety of opponents should be removed promptly.
- Make certain that students don't twist an ankle by working near the edge of a mat.
- Groups need their own space in which to work.

Motivation

This lesson works on finishing escapes. One is called the *underarm spin,* and it gets you facing your opponent. Depending on how much time is left, the class might cover a finish called the *hip switch,* which can create a reversal.

Warm-Up

1. Use the 6-minute routine developed previously, making sure the footwork requires quick changes of direction, turning, pivoting, and changes of levels.

    a. Add footwork and mechanics to yield a lift—penetrate, drop hips, pop, and extend.

    b. Add mechanics for the back arch from a variety of positions.

2. Make sure the routine includes sit-ups and push-ups.

Lesson Sequence

1. Demonstrate, teach, and practice the underarm spin.

2. Explain how the sit-out can result in facing the opponent.

3. Have students practice the sit-out followed immediately by the underarm spin.

4. Teach the hip switch.

    a. Show the cut back.

    b. Show that the arm is taken instead of the hand.

    c. Show how to lift the hip and turn.

5. Practice the hip switch.

6. Demonstrate again, emphasizing completion of the hip switch for a reversal.

7. Have students practice the hip switch for a reversal.

Review and Stretching

As students stretch, ask questions:

- What two finishes did we learn?

- What advantage is gained with a successful hip switch over the underarm spin?

Wrestling
INTERMEDIATE
LESSON 8

Cut Roll

Facilities

Clean floor with mats covering the working area

Materials

- Scale
- Clock

Performance Goals

Students will do the following:

- Perform the cut roll.
- Continue to build strength, stamina, and endurance.

Cognitive Goals

Students will learn the following:

- A finish that works out of both escapes taught
- More about weight categories and what category they belong in

Lesson Safety

- Students who have no respect for the safety of opponents should be removed promptly.
- Make certain that students don't twist an ankle by working near the edge of a mat.
- Groups need their own space in which to work.

Motivation

Today the class will finish learning the finishes for the season. Some would say they've saved the best for last because the cut roll is fun and safe, can result in a score, and can be done from both the standout and sit-out. While practicing it with partners, they will do an official weigh-in to set up classifications and organize a tournament.

Warm-Up

1. Use the 6-minute routine developed previously, making sure the footwork requires quick changes of direction, turning, pivoting, and changes of levels.
    a. Add footwork and mechanics to yield a lift—penetrate, drop hips, pop, and extend.
    b. Add mechanics for the back arch from a variety of positions.
2. Make sure the routine includes sit-ups and push-ups.

Lesson Sequence

1. Teach the cut roll.
    a. Show how instead of using wrist control to escape, it pulls in the wrist to start the opponent's rolling action.
    b. Show how to roll your own hip under the opponent until the hip heist, where lifting the hip unweights the opponent making it possible to drop or spin him to the bottom.
    c. Show how the hip heist reverses the person who is on bottom.
2. Practice the cut roll.
3. Hold weigh-in while allowing students to practice on their own.

Review and Stretching

As students stretch, ask questions:

- What finish did we learn?
- What position can the finish be used from?
- What is the scoring value of a reversal?

Wrestling
INTERMEDIATE
LESSON 9

Countering an Escape

Facilities

Clean floor with mats

Materials

- Clock
- Scale
- Blackboard or chart with tournament schedules and standings

Performance Goals

Students will do the following:

- Counter escapes.
- Build their strength, stamina, and endurance.
- Meet in competition.

Cognitive Goals

Students will learn the following:

- Match procedure
- How fundamentals can avoid bad scores

Lesson Safety

- Students who have no respect for the safety of opponents should be removed promptly.
- Make certain that students don't twist an ankle by working near the edge of a mat.
- Groups need their own space in which to work.

Motivation

After spending time on escapes, students will want to learn how to stop an escape, so explain that it is time to review concepts and particulars that will prevent escapes. Today the class will spend time learning a counter for an escape from the standout and then begin competition in the neutral position.

Warm-Up

1. Use the 6-minute routine developed previously, making sure the footwork requires quick changes of direction, turning, pivoting, and changes of levels.
   a. Add footwork and mechanics to yield a lift—penetrate, drop hips, pop, and extend.
   b. Add mechanics for the back arch from a variety of positions.
2. Make sure the routine includes sit-ups and push-ups.

Lesson Sequence

1. Discuss the overall strategy of avoiding an escape.
   a. Be aggressive.
   b. Maintain base of support and good position.
2. Teach the follow-and-lift.
   a. Show locking arms around body and bringing hips under opponent.
   b. Show footwork to get a better lifting angle and block of opponent's leg.
   c. Show the lift.
3. Allow practice while getting students into their weight categories.
   a. Announce where each category is to meet.
   b. Take turns practicing the follow-and-lift from the standout.
4. Review match procedure
   a. How to read the schedule
   b. Set a class rule for what to do if an opponent is absent and how it will be scored. Decide whether to reschedule the match or default the opponent and have the person present practice or assist with officiating.
   c. Preparation so that all matches begin on time
   d. What nonparticipants are to do
      - Medically excused students
      - Students waiting for space
      - Students who are unprepared
5. Review scoring.
6. Begin matches between one pair in each weight category, starting from neutral position.

Review and Stretching

As students stretch, ask: If you did not know any particular move with which to respond to an opponent's efforts, what are the two things you should try to do to maintain position?

Teacher Homework

- Develop tournament schedule.
- Chart names in their categories so that results of matches can be posted.
- Post all charts.

Wrestling
INTERMEDIATE
LESSON 10

Scoring a Match

Facilities

Areas that are clean, padded, and marked with boundaries

Materials

- Clock
- Scale
- Tournament charts

Performance Goal

Students will compete in their weight category.

Cognitive Goal

Students will assume personal responsibilities before the match.

Lesson Safety

- Students who have no respect for the safety of opponents should be removed promptly.
- Make certain that students don't twist an ankle by working near the edge of a mat.
- Groups need their own space in which to work.

Motivation

Today everyone will have the opportunity to score from the neutral start. As of this moment, no one has a score. Tell students that if they score, they should make certain to record the entry after the match. If they win by default, record their entry with a *D* next to it and use their match time to practice with someone else whose match is later in the class.

Warm-Up

1. Use the 6-minute routine developed previously, making sure the footwork requires quick changes of direction, turning, pivoting, and changes of levels.
   a. Add footwork and mechanics to yield a lift—penetrate, drop hips, pop, and extend.
   b. Add mechanics for the back arch from a variety of positions.
2. Make sure the routine includes sit-ups and push-ups.

Lesson Sequence

1. Send groups to their areas.
2. Begin the clock when everyone is ready.
3. At the end of the class, allow time for scores to be recorded, next opponents to get ready, and students to find someone to practice with if their opponent is out.

Review

1. Congratulate the group for their effort.
2. Ask if they have any questions.
3. Make sure all scores are collected.

Teacher Homework

Update charts.

Class Tournament

Facilities

Areas that are clean, padded, and marked with boundaries

Materials

- Clock
- Scale
- Tournament charts

Performance Goal

Students will compete in class tournament for their weight category.

Cognitive Goals

Students will discuss the following:

- Proper diet
  - Discuss the wrestler's habit of dehydrating to lose weight.
  - Discuss the dangers of dehydration.
  - Discuss the importance of a proper diet.
- Dietary supplements, steroids, and strength enhancers
- Taking responsibility for following match procedure

Lesson Safety

- Students who have no respect for the safety of opponents should be removed promptly.
- Make certain that students don't twist an ankle by working near the edge of a mat.
- Groups need their own space in which to work.

Motivation

Announce standings and some general coaching hints. Wish everyone a good match.

Warm-Up

1. Use the 6-minute routine developed previously, making sure the footwork requires quick changes of direction, turning, pivoting, and changes of levels.
   a. Add footwork and mechanics to yield a lift—penetrate, drop hips, pop, and extend.
   b. Add mechanics for the back arch from a variety of positions.
2. Make sure the routine includes sit-ups and push-ups.

Lesson Sequence

1. Discuss diet, hydration, dietary supplements, and steroids.
2. Review the position that the competition will start from and send groups to their areas.
3. Begin the clock when stated.
4. At the end of the class, allow time for scores to be recorded, next opponents to get ready, and students to find someone with whom to practice if their opponent is out.

Review and Stretching

1. Congratulate the group for their efforts.
2. Make sure all scores are collected.
3. Announce skills grading standards.
4. Announce the upcoming quiz and ask if there are any questions.

Assessment

Observe and grade for technique in initiating attack, effort to maintain base of support, responses to attack, and ability to score as outlined in the intermediate skills rubric.

Teacher Homework

Update charts, post skills standards, and get quiz ready.

Assessment and Final Matches

Facilities

Mats prepared for matches

Materials

- Intermediate skills rubric
- Quizzes for everyone in class
- Pens or pencils
- Clock

Performance Goals

Students will do the following:

- Take a wrestling quiz.
- Decide whether to have final matches or begin the next unit.

Cognitive Goal

Students will find out how much they know about wrestling.

Lesson Safety

- Students who have no respect for the safety of opponents should be removed promptly.
- Make certain that students don't twist an ankle by working near the edge of a mat.
- Groups need their own space in which to work.

Motivation

Explain that after the quiz, students will decide whether they want to have a last challenge match or begin the next unit.

Warm-Up

1. Use the 6-minute routine developed previously, making sure the footwork requires quick changes of direction, turning, pivoting, and changes of levels.
   a. Add footwork and mechanics to yield a lift—penetrate, drop hips, pop, and extend.
   b. Add mechanics for the back arch from a variety of positions.
2. Make sure the routine includes sit-ups and push-ups.

Lesson Sequence

1. Answer student questions before distributing the quiz.
2. Give everyone 10 minutes to complete the quiz. If students need extra time, allow them to complete it after school or during lunch.
3. Vote on whether students want to have some last challenge matches or begin the next unit.

Review and Stretching

Conclude with a review of questions, last announcements of the unit, and comments to prepare everyone for the next unit.

Assessment

- Grade quiz
- Grade skills based on performance rubric

Intermediate Wrestling Skills Rubric

Name _____ Date _____

Teacher _____ Class _____

	0	1	2	3
Conditioning and balance	No effort.	• Works to increase strength, speed, and stamina. • Has good stance.	• Keeps head up. • Makes constant effort to maintain good base while moving.	• Shows no signs of fatiguing. • Has good base of support while changing levels.
Attacking	No effort.	• Initiates one attack from a neutral position. • Mimetics have proper body mechanics.	• Can initiate attacks from referee's position. • Uses various attacks. • Gets good penetration.	Can initiate attacks from either position.
Countering	No effort.	Performs good rehearsal of standout and sit-out.	Gains control of opponent's hands.	• Controls opponent's arms. • Finishes facing opponent.
Lifts	No effort.	• Pops hips in practice. • Can lift own center of gravity.	Can lower center of gravity during a hold.	Lifts center of gravity during hold.
Safety and sportsmanship	No effort.	Works in own weight classification.	Safely returns opponent to the mat after a lift.	Competitive within the rules.

From Isobel Kleinman, 2009, *Complete Physical Education Plans for Grades 5 to 12, Second Edition* (Champaign, IL: Human Kinetics).

Intermediate Wrestling Quiz

Name _____ Date _____

Teacher _____ Class _____

True or False

Read each statement carefully. If the statement is true, write a *T* in the column to the left. If the statement is false, write an *F*. If using a grid sheet, blacken in the appropriate column for each question, making sure to use the correctly numbered line for each question and its answer.

_____ 1. The best way to increase your base of support when someone is pulling from behind is take the foot closest to him and move it back.

_____ 2. Lifting an opponent will result in a score.

_____ 3. Avoid bringing your hips under an opponent you intend to lift.

_____ 4. The best strategy is to engage your opponent slowly and methodically.

_____ 5. Many escapes finish with a turn so the two opponents face each other.

_____ 6. Pushing your back into your opponent is a good method of getting out from under her.

_____ 7. The person on the bottom scores 2 points if he ends on top of the opponent.

_____ 8. Back-stepping, arching, and then popping your hips can lead to a throw.

_____ 9. The cut roll pulls the opponent forward rather than pushing the opponent back.

_____ 10. An advantage of the cut roll is that it can be done from the standout and sit-out.

From Isobel Kleinman, 2009, *Complete Physical Education Plans for Grades 5 to 12, Second Edition* (Champaign, IL: Human Kinetics).

Intermediate Wrestling Answer Key

True or False

1. T—The most important lesson in footwork is to increase the base of support by using the foot closest to the pressure to widen the base.

2. F—Being able to lift only results in neutralizing an opponent and preventing scoring.

3. F—Using the hips and legs to lift is of primary importance; therefore, it is necessary to get the hips under the opponent's center of gravity. One must move in and under in order to do that.

4. F—Quick movement and explosive force is most effective.

5. T

6. T—That is why the standout and sit-out are humorously called the *stand-back* and *sit-back*.

7. T—Reversal results in 2 points.

8. T

9. T

10. T

From Isobel Kleinman, 2009, *Complete Physical Education Plans for Grades 5 to 12, Second Edition* (Champaign, IL: Human Kinetics).

Reviewing Basics

Facilities

Clean floor with mats marked with boundaries and set up for competition

Materials

- Weight-Room Workout Chart (see page 70)
- Clock

Performance Goals

Students will do the following:

- Perform a review of elementary positions and moves on your cue.
- Review the short sit-out and its counters—cover and suck-back.
- Improve strength, stamina, and endurance.

Cognitive Goals

Students will learn the following:

- The importance of good nutrition, hydration, and conditioning
- How to gear thinking to scoring strategies—escapes, reversals, and pins

Lesson Safety

- Set up mats so they do not overlap.
- Keep students from working near the edges so they don't twist an ankle.
- Provide every pair with their own space to practice in.

Motivation

The majority of this wrestling unit will allow students to compete. Tell students that you will spend a few minutes of each lesson teaching combination moves and let them practice, but this year, they will have more opportunity to get their opponent's shoulders to the mat.

Warm-Up

1. Emphasize footwork to improve cardiorespiratory fitness and wrestling mobility.
2. Target strengthening exercises to the upper body and abdominal muscles.

Lesson Sequence

1. Discuss proper nutrition, hydration, and conditioning.
2. Use verbal cues to have students physically review stances and moves that were second nature from units taught over the previous years.
3. Demonstrate and allow practice of the sit-out with the counter.
   a. Cover and its finish
   b. Suck-back
4. Have students fill out the headings of their chart.
   a. Conditioning progress
   b. Body weight and wrestling category

Review and Stretching

As students stretch, ask them what the dangers are of improper food and water intake.

Assessment

Observe to determine proper pacing of each lesson so you can decide if the class is ready to learn more or if it would be better to stay with a short wrestling vocabulary, using the variety learned in previous years to have more matches.

Half Nelson

Facilities

Clean floor with mats

Materials

- Free weights and bars
- Workout chart for each student
- Pens and pencils
- Scale
- Clock

Performance Goals

Students will do the following:

- Review the cut roll.
- Learn the half nelson.
- Independently work on their conditioning and stamina.

Cognitive Goals

Students will learn the following

- How to assume personal responsibility for their conditioning program
- Their weight and what category they are in

Lesson Safety

- The use of the weights should be restricted to a defined area of the gym.
- Students must be taught that hands must not go on the neck when executing a half nelson.
- Students must demonstrate the ability to safely return lifted opponents to the mat.

Motivation

Announce that this year, students will be expected to work out to get into condition when they have no mat space and are between matches, but you expect everyone to stay together while you teach. Tell them that they need to pick up and fill out their chart each day. Before the class breaks up, announce that you will review the cut roll and teach the half nelson. Then, if pairs have no mat space to practice on, they should go to the weights, work out, and wait for the signal to switch stations.

Warm-Up

Emphasize footwork to improve cardiorespiratory fitness and meet wrestling needs.

Lesson Sequence

1. Demonstrate and have class move through the mechanics of the following:
   a. Cut roll
   b. Half nelson (see figure 20.11)
2. Have students pair off.
   a. Let them practice both.
   b. Coach when necessary; encourage and praise where possible.
   c. As they work, send pairs to weigh in and record their weight.
   d. Use half the time for conditioning and half for practicing wrestling moves.

Figure 20.11 Half nelson.

Review and Stretching

As students stretch, ask questions:

- What parts of the body does the half nelson control?
- Should you pop your hips to control your opponent, or should you sag them?

Wrestling
ADVANCED
LESSON 3

Outside and Inside Ankle Breakdowns

Facilities

Clean floor with mats

Materials

- Free weights
- Workout chart for each student
- Pens and pencils
- Scale
- Clock

Performance Goals

Students will do the following:

- Take control when on top in the referee's position.
- Perform specific breaks—outside ankle and inside ankle.
- Improve strength, stamina, and endurance.

Cognitive Goals

Students will learn the following:

- To break down the bottom person, minimizing the distance between hips
- To bring their weight forward to break down opponents

Lesson Safety

- Use of the weights should be restricted to a defined area of the gym.
- Students must be taught that hands must not go on the neck when executing a half nelson.
- Students must demonstrate the ability to safely return lifted opponents to the mat.

Motivation

Last year students focused on the referee's position and being on bottom. Now it is time to be on top and get the bottom person down to the mat—which is more fun than trying to stop the person beneath from escaping and then reversing. Today they're going to look at some of the alternatives.

Warm-Up

Emphasize footwork to improve cardiorespiratory fitness and mobility.

Lesson Sequence

1. Review the outside ankle breakdown. Allow students to practice, coaching and encouraging them.
2. Students without mats start conditioning and making entries on their charts while waiting for the wrestlers to switch from wrestling to conditioning.
3. Demonstrate the inside ankle, and provide time and space for practice.

Review and Stretching

As students stretch, ask questions:

- In the outside ankle, which arm grabs the ankle?
- What should be done once the ankle is grabbed?
- In which direction do the hips move?
- What is the difference between the inside ankle and the outside?

Teacher Homework

Make and post the weight categories with the register of who falls into each category.

Rotary and Spiral Breakdowns

Facilities

Clean floor with mats

Materials

- List of each category and the students in it
- Free weights
- Workout chart for each student
- Pens and pencils
- Scale
- Clock

Performance Goals

Students will do the following:

- Perform the rotary and spiral breakdowns.
- Perform one pinning combination—half nelson.
- Perform their conditioning workout.

Cognitive Goals

Students will learn the following:

- Dangerous practices wrestlers use to drop their weight classification
- The ramifications of taking on dangerous habits
- Who is in their division
- How scoring works

Lesson Safety

- Use of the weights should be restricted to a defined area of the gym.
- Students must be taught that hands must not go on the neck when executing a half nelson.
- Students must demonstrate the ability to safely return lifted opponents to the mat.

Motivation

Today they're going to try a few new breakdowns—the rotary and spiral—and review the half nelson. It's a lot to do, so they need to get started right away.

Warm-Up

Do footwork to improve cardiorespiratory fitness and specific wrestling needs.

Lesson Sequence

1. Demonstrate the rotary and the spiral breakdowns. Allow students to try them, coaching and encouraging.
2. Students without mats should start conditioning, making entries on their charts.
3. Demonstrate the half nelson, re-emphasizing points made during lesson 2. Provide time and space for practice.

Review and Stretching

1. As students stretch, ask questions:
   - What parts of the body are in control in the half nelson?
   - Both the rotary and spiral move the bottom person to which part of the body?
2. Survey students to learn if they want more pinning combinations and counters to them or if they want to use what they have and go into competition.

Teacher Homework

Prepare tournaments. Draw up a list of each weight category. Draw up a round robin for each list of weight categories. Schedule matches so each student has equal time to compete.

Wrestling
ADVANCED
LESSON 5

Match Procedure and Cradle

Facilities

- Clean floor area
- Wrestling mat with official boundaries

Materials

- Tournament schedule and individual standings
- Free weights
- Workout chart for each student
- Pens and pencils
- Scale
- Clock

Performance Goals

Students will do the following:

- Begin matches.
- See the cradle.
- Continue improving strength, stamina, and endurance.

Cognitive Goals

Students will learn the following:

- Match procedure
- How to score matches

Lesson Safety

- Use of the weights should be restricted to a defined area of the gym.
- Students must be taught that hands must not go on the neck when executing a half nelson.
- Students must demonstrate the ability to safely return lifted opponents to the mat.

Motivation

Tell students they can begin their matches as soon as they answer questions about procedure and learn what to do when they do not have a match.

Warm-Up

1. Lead footwork drills to improve fitness and mobility.
2. Work on level changes.

Lesson Sequence

1. Demonstrate the cradle (see figure 20.12).
2. Review the expected routine that will keep competition fair and keep students active even when not in competition.
3. Start matches.

Review and Stretching

1. As students stretch, ask if anyone was able to score a pin, a reversal, a takedown, or an escape.
2. Make sure everyone has entered scores.

Figure 20.12 The cradle.

Match 1 and Look-Away

Facilities

- Clean floor area
- Wrestling mat with official boundaries

Materials

- Tournament schedule and individual standings
- Free weights
- Workout chart for each student
- Pens and pencils
- Scale
- Clock

Performance Goals

Students will do the following:

- Compete.
- See one counter to a pinning combination—the look-away.
- Work on their strength and endurance.

Cognitive Goals

Students will learn the following:

- How to compete within the rules
- That they always have class responsibility and must be dependable

Lesson Safety

- Use of the weights should be restricted to a defined area of the gym.
- Students must be taught that hands must not go on the neck when executing a half nelson.
- Students must demonstrate the ability to safely return lifted opponents to the mat.

Motivation

Announce standings. Explain that before the match, you'd like the class to see the look-away, which counters the pin or hold.

Warm-Up

Lead the class in footwork, level changes, and balance drills.

Lesson Sequence

1. Demonstrate the look-away.
2. Students compete, officiate, and work on conditioning. Each lesson, they have a minimum of two responsibilities.

Review and Stretching

1. As students stretch, ask questions:
   - Did anyone use a half nelson today?
   - Did anyone use the look-away?
   - Anyone score a pin?
   - What did you use?
2. Make sure students have submitted the scores.

Match 2 and Chicken Wing

Facilities

- Clean floor area
- Wrestling mat with official boundaries

Materials

- Tournament schedule and individual standings
- Free weights
- Workout chart for each student
- Pens and pencils
- Scale
- Clock

Performance Goals

Students will do the following:

- Compete, demonstrating good sportsmanship.
- See another pinning combination—the chicken wing.
- Improve strength and endurance.

Cognitive Goals

Students will learn what characteristics make them a good class citizen:

- Responsibility
- Dependability
- Good sportsmanship

Lesson Safety

- Use of the weights should be restricted to a defined area of the gym.
- Students must be taught that hands must not go on the neck when executing a half nelson.
- Students must demonstrate the ability to safely return lifted opponents to the mat.

Motivation

Compliment the citizenship that has developed in class, praising students' ability to work on their own, assume responsibility for smooth running of matches, and exhibit exemplary behavior during competition, win or lose. Tell them how proud you are of them.

Announce standings and continue the competition after a brief demonstration of the chicken wing.

Warm-Up

Lead footwork, level changes, and balance drills.

Lesson Sequence

1. Demonstrate the chicken wing. (From behind the defender, the attacker hooks one arm, bringing elbows of the defender together so the arms are wrapped around each other and hands are linking at the defender's shoulder. An escape would use the free arm and legs to twist or turn, attempting to throw the attacker off balance.)
2. Students compete, officiate, or work out. During the class, they will have a minimum of two responsibilities.

Review and Stretching

1. As students stretch, ask if anyone scored a pin, and if so, what did they use?
2. Make sure students have submitted the scores.

Match 3 and Wing Roll

Facilities

- Clean floor area
- Wrestling mat with official boundaries

Materials

- Tournament schedule and individual standings
- Free weights
- Workout chart for each student
- Pens and pencils
- Scale
- Clock

Performance Goals

Students will do the following:

- Compete.
- Observe a counter to pinning combinations—the wing roll.
- Improve their strength and endurance.

Cognitive Goals

Students will learn the following:

- That there is a system and physical response for a hold
- That picking up when the attack is early, before losing control, makes getting out of it easier

Lesson Safety

- Use of the weights should be restricted to a defined area of the gym.
- Students must be taught that hands must not go on the neck when executing a half nelson.
- Students must demonstrate the ability to safely return lifted opponents to the mat.

Motivation

Show the wing roll, explaining that it is a counter to the chicken wing seen the last time the class met. Announce the standings and send students off to their scheduled match or scheduled responsibilities.

Warm-Up

Lead drills in footwork, change of levels, and broadening the base of support to increase aerobic endurance as well as teach essential skills for wrestling.

Lesson Sequence

1. Demonstrate the wing roll.
2. Students compete, officiate, and work out.

Review and Stretching

1. As students stretch, ask if anyone scored a pin. What did they use?
2. Make sure students have submitted the scores.

Match 4

Facilities

- Clean floor area
- Wrestling mat with official boundaries

Materials

- Advanced skills rubric
- Tournament schedule and individual standings
- Free weights
- Workout chart for each student
- Pens and pencils
- Scale
- Clock

Performance Goals

Students will do the following:

- Compete.
- Improve strength and endurance.
- Continue assuming responsibilities for helping to run matches.

Cognitive Goal

Students will appreciate the value of responsibility and sportsmanship.

Lesson Safety

- Use of the weights should be restricted to a defined area of the gym.
- Students must be taught that hands must not go on the neck when executing a half nelson.
- Students must demonstrate the ability to safely return lifted opponents to the mat.

Motivation

After complimenting whatever you found noteworthy in performance and class citizenship, let students know that the standards they will be graded on are posted. Announce standings and send them off to their matches and responsibilities.

Warm-Up

Lead drills in footwork that will improve cardiorespiratory fitness, balance during level changes, and having center of gravity changed by an outside force.

Lesson Sequence

1. Discuss minimal performance standards, answering any questions.
2. Students compete, officiate, or work out.

Review and Stretching

As students stretch, ask if they have any questions, and make sure they have submitted scores.

Assessment

Observe for demonstration of performance standards.

Matches 5 and 6

Facilities

- Clean floor area
- Wrestling mat with official boundaries

Materials

- Tournament schedule and individual standings
- Free weights
- Workout chart for each student
- Pens and pencils
- Scale
- Clock

Performance Goal

Students will continue the tournament and assume responsibilities assigned to them.

Cognitive Goal

Students will understand the relationship between freedom and responsibility as they continue operating in a class that mixes self-directed workouts and a tournament.

Lesson Safety

- Use of the weights should be restricted to a defined area of the gym.
- Students must be taught that hands must not go on the neck when executing a half nelson.
- Students must demonstrate the ability to safely return lifted opponents to the mat.

Motivation

Announce standings each day.

Warm-Up

Lead warm-up that builds cardiorespiratory endurance and enhances each student's ability to change levels while maintaining balance.

Lesson Sequence

Students either compete, officiate, or work out.

Review

Announce a quiz if you are going to give it and entertain questions. Tell students that the quiz will take a short time and that they should be prepared so they can complete their matches.

Assessment

Performance grades can be based on the standards posted in the advanced skills rubric.

Assessment and Final Matches

Facilities

- Clean floor area
- Wrestling mat with official boundaries

Materials

- Quiz for each student
- Tournament schedule and individual standings
- Free weights
- Workout chart for each student
- Pens and pencils
- Scale
- Clock

Performance Goal

Students will take a quiz and complete the wrestling unit or go on to the next unit.

Cognitive Goal

Students will exhibit knowledge of the rules and strategies of wrestling in a quiz.

Lesson Safety

- Use of the weights should be restricted to a defined area of the gym.
- Students must be taught that hands must not go on the neck when executing a half nelson.
- Students must demonstrate the ability to safely return lifted opponents to the mat.

Motivation

Announce standings and what results would change the rankings.

Warm-Up

Go through a quick footwork warm-up after quizzes.

Lesson Sequence

1. Distribute quizzes and allow students to begin immediately.
2. After a quick footwork warm-up and discussion of standings, start posted matches.

Review

1. Announce the winners.
2. Compliment your students' citizenship in this unit. Tell them the activity was fun, the tournament was exciting, the classes ran smoothly, and they developed both physically and emotionally. They were great in using time wisely, doing the things they needed to do for themselves, and helping when it was their turn. If all the people in the school, the country, and the world behaved in a similar fashion when it came to doing everyday things for themselves and their families, it would be wonderful. Thank them for proving that they could do it.

Assessment

Finish grading performance standards and grade the quiz.

Advanced Wrestling Skills Rubric

Name _____ Date _____

Teacher _____ Class _____

	0	1	2	3
Competitive success	No effort.	Scores on escapes.	Scores on reversals.	Can score on pins.
Countering	No effort.	Counters attacks from neutral.	Counters attacks from above.	• Reverses attacks. • Avoids having shoulders squared to mat.
Mechanics	No effort.	• Has good balance. • Keeps head up.	Lifts center of gravity from hips and legs.	Generates spiral pivot movement from hips.
Safety and sportsmanship	No effort.	Works in own weight classification.	Competitive within the rules.	Performs safe throws.

From Isobel Kleinman, 2009, *Complete Physical Education Plans for Grades 5 to 12, Second Edition* (Champaign, IL: Human Kinetics).

Advanced Wrestling Quiz

Name _____ Date _____

Teacher _____ Class _____

True or False

Read each statement carefully. If the statement is true, write a *T* in the column to the left. If the statement is false, write an *F*. If using a grid sheet, blacken in the appropriate column for each question, making sure to use the correctly numbered line for each question and its answer.

_____ 1. If a wrestler can never get his opponent's shoulders to the mat, he can never score.

_____ 2. Because being in a lower weight category yields great advantage, a good strategy for dropping weight is to avoid drinking fluids for 2 to 3 days before a match.

_____ 3. The sit-out can counter the cover.

_____ 4. If you control someone's head, the body will follow.

_____ 5. There are successful escapes that use the hips to pop.

_____ 6. The hip space between two wrestlers is enjoyed by the person on the bottom, but for a breakdown it should be minimized by the person on the top.

_____ 7. The initiator in a match has the least advantage.

_____ 8. Breakdowns are actions taken by the person on top in the referee's position.

_____ 9. The rotary and spiral move a person on the bottom from her feet and seat to her hips.

_____ 10. There are 3 points waiting for the wrestler who achieves a reversal.

Advanced Wrestling Answer Key

True or False

1. F—Points are also awarded for reversals (2 points) and escapes (1 point).
2. F—Attempting to lose water weight will result in dehydration; it is very important to stay properly hydrated.
3. T
4. T
5. T
6. T
7. F—Being the initiator gives you the element of surprise which is part of the ability to overtake opponents.
8. T
9. T
10. F—A reversal scores 2 points.

From Isobel Kleinman, 2009, *Complete Physical Education Plans for Grades 5 to 12, Second Edition* (Champaign, IL: Human Kinetics).

Tournament Charts

Table A.1   Round Robin Schedule: Three Courts, Three Days, Six Teams

	Court 1	Court 2	Court 3
Day 1			
Round 1	5 v. 6	1 v. 3	4 v. 2
Round 2	1 v. 6	2 v. 5	3 v. 4
Day 2			
Round 1	6 v. 4	1 v. 5	2 v. 3
Round 2	1 v. 2	3 v. 6	4 v. 5
Day 3			
Round 1	5 v. 3	6 v. 2	1 v. 4
Play-off schedule			

From Isobel Kleinman, 2009, *Complete Physical Education Plans for Grades 5 to 12, Second Edition* (Champaign, IL: Human Kinetics).

Table A.2   Sample Round-Robin Tournament Chart After Two Rounds

	1	2	3	4	5	6	7	8
1	X	2						
2	0	X	0					
3		2	X	2				
4			0	X	2			
5				0	X	1		
6					1	X		
7							X	
8								X

Win = 2 points
Tie = 1 point
Loss or default = 0

From Isobel Kleinman, 2009, *Complete Physical Education Plans for Grades 5 to 12, Second Edition* (Champaign, IL: Human Kinetics).

Table A.3   Team Tournament Record by Game and Class

Class	Team number	Captains and cocaptains	Tournament points for each match	Total points	Class place
	1				
	2				
	3				
	4				
	5				
	6				

From Isobel Kleinman, 2009, *Complete Physical Education Plans for Grades 5 to 12, Second Edition* (Champaign, IL: Human Kinetics).

Table A.4   Twelve-Team Round-Robin Tournament Schedule

	Court 1	Court 2	Court 3	Court 4	Court 5	Court 6
Round 1	1 v. 12	2 v. 11	3 v. 10	4 v. 9	5 v. 8	6 v. 7
Round 2	5 v. 6	1 v. 11	12 v. 10	2 v. 9	3 v. 8	4 v. 7
Round 3	2 v. 7	3 v. 6	4 v. 5	1 v. 10	11 v. 9	12 v. 8
Round 4	3 v. 4	2 v. 5	12 v. 6	11 v. 7	10 v. 8	1 v. 9
Round 5	1 v. 8	9 v. 7	10 v. 6	11 v. 5	12 v. 4	2 v. 3
Round 6	8 v. 6	1 v. 7	9 v. 5	10 v. 4	11 v. 3	12 v. 2
Round 7	11 v. 12	10 v. 2	9 v. 3	8 v. 4	7 v. 5	1 v. 6
Round 8	1 v. 5	9 v. 12	7 v. 3	6 v. 4	8 v. 2	10 v. 11
Round 9	5 v. 3	1 v. 4	6 v. 2	7 v. 12	9 v. 10	8 v. 11
Round 10	4 v. 2	8 v. 9	1 v. 3	6 v. 11	5 v. 12	7 v. 10
Round 11	6 v. 9	7 v. 8	5 v. 10	4 v. 11	3 v. 12	1 v. 2

From Isobel Kleinman, 2009, *Complete Physical Education Plans for Grades 5 to 12, Second Edition* (Champaign, IL: Human Kinetics).

Table A.5   Round-Robin Tournament Chart

Name _____

	1	2	3	4	5	6	7	8	9	10	11	12	13	14
1	X													
2		X												
3			X											
4				X										
5					X									
6						X								
7							X							
8								X						
9									X					
10										X				
11											X			
12												X		
13													X	
14														X

From Isobel Kleinman, 2009, *Complete Physical Education Plans for Grades 5 to 12, Second Edition* (Champaign, IL: Human Kinetics).

Table A.6   Racket Sports: Scheduling a Large Class

	Court 1	Court 2	Court 3	Court 4	Court 5
Round 1	1 v. 2 3 officiates	4 v. 5 6 officiates	7 v. 8 9 officiates	10 v. 11 12 officiates	13 v. 14 15 officiates
Round 2	2 v. 3 1 officiate	5 v. 6 4 officiates	8 v. 9 7 officiates	11 v. 12 10 officiates	14 v. 15 13 officiates
Round 3	1 v. 3 2 officiates	4 v. 6 5 officiates	7 v. 9 8 officiates	10 v. 12 11 officiates	13 v. 15 14 officiates

From Isobel Kleinman, 2009, *Complete Physical Education Plans for Grades 5 to 12, Second Edition* (Champaign, IL: Human Kinetics).

General Performance Rubrics

Table B.1   Personality Attributes Assessment

Name _____

Marking period	0	1	2	3	4	5
	• Does not work with others • Does not participate	• Blames others • Does not assume responsibility for assignments • Needs outside supervision to stay on task • Interferes with others	• Is challenged • Is self-directed	• Is self-motivated to participate with others respectfully	• Cooperates with others and shows concern for others	• Helps others achieve success • Has leadership skills • Shows initiative • Has generosity of spirit
1						
2						
3						
4						

From Isobel Kleinman, 2009, *Complete Physical Education Plans for Grades 5 to 12, Second Edition* (Champaign, IL: Human Kinetics).

Table B.2   General Skills Assessment

Name _____

Skill	0	1	2	3	4	5
	• No effort	• Is awkward • Is unsuccessful • Is haphazard • Is unfocused	• Is intentional • Is focused • Is occasionally successful	• Is successful • Is automatic • Is consistent	• Combines skills • Reacts properly in predictable situations • Is accurate and controlled	• Performs in many changing conditions • Is able to modify approach if situation demands it • Has complex performance
Catch						
Throw						
Body mechanics						
Footwork						
Defensive use of hands						
Defensive position						
Offensive position						

From Isobel Kleinman, 2009, *Complete Physical Education Plans for Grades 5 to 12, Second Edition* (Champaign, IL: Human Kinetics).

Table B.3   Team Play Assessment

Name _____

Game	0	1	2	3	4	5
	• No effort	• Generally directs or controls an object	• Maintains possession in different ways and speeds • Is able to assist team • Combines two skills	• Plays the game within the context of the rules • Implements team strategies	• Successfully focuses on skills for an offensive or defensive game plan • Maintains team possession or effectively works to regain possession • Understands one's own space and responsibility and how they relate to the team	• Rarely violates rules while playing the game • Plays a flowing game • Uses specialized skills that integrate responsibilities with team members • Uses a variety of skills that can meet team objectives of maintaining possession or scoring
Football						
Basketball						
Volleyball						
Softball						
Soccer						
Badminton						
Tennis						

From Isobel Kleinman, 2009, *Complete Physical Education Plans for Grades 5 to 12, Second Edition* (Champaign, IL: Human Kinetics).

Appendix C

Fitness Testing Standards and Norms

Table C.1 Fitnessgram Standards for Healthy Fitness Zone

			BOYS										
Age	\$\dot{V}O_2\$max (ml · kg⁻¹ · min⁻¹)		20-m PACER (Enter # laps in software)		15-m PACER (Enter in software)†		1-mi (1.5-km) run (min:sec)		Walk test (\$\dot{V}O_2\$max)		Percent fat		Body mass index
5			Participation in run. Lap count standards not recommended.				Completion of distance. Time standards not recommended.				25	10	20	14.7
6											25	10	20	14.7
7											25	10	20	14.9
8											25	10	20	15.1
9											25	7	20	13.7
10	42	52	23	60	30	80	11:30	9:00			25	7	21	14.0
11	42	52	23	72	30	94	11:00	8:30			25	7	21	14.3
12	42	52	32	72	42	94	10:30	8:00			25	7	22	14.6
13	42	52	41	83	54	108	10:00	7:30	42	52	25	7	23	15.1
14	42	52	41	83	54	108	9:30	7:00	42	52	25	7	24.5	15.6
15	42	52	51	94	67	123	9:00	7:00	42	52	25	7	25	16.2
16	42	52	61	94	80	123	8:30	7:00	42	52	25	7	26.5	16.6
17	42	52	61	106	80	138	8:30	7:00	42	52	25	7	27	17.3
17+	42	52	72	106	94	138	8:30	7:00	42	52	25	7	27.8	17.8

Age	Curl-up (# completed)		Trunk lift (in.)		90° push-up (# completed)		Modified pull-up (# completed)		Flexed arm hang (s)		Back-saver sit and reach* (in.)	Shoulder stretch
5	2	10	6	12	3	8	2	7	2	8	8	Healthy fitness zone = touching fingertips together behind the back on both the right and left sides.
6	2	10	6	12	3	8	2	7	2	8	8	
7	4	14	6	12	4	10	3	9	3	8	8	
8	6	20	6	12	5	13	4	11	3	10	8	
9	9	24	6	12	6	15	5	11	4	10	8	
10	12	24	9	12	7	20	5	15	4	10	8	
11	15	28	9	12	8	20	6	17	6	13	8	
12	18	36	9	12	10	20	7	20	10	15	8	
13	21	40	9	12	12	25	8	22	12	17	8	
14	24	45	9	12	14	30	9	25	15	20	8	
15	24	47	9	12	16	35	10	27	15	20	8	
16	24	47	9	12	18	35	12	30	15	20	8	
17	24	47	9	12	18	35	14	30	15	20	8	
17+	24	47	9	12	18	35	14	30	15	20	8	

Number on left is lower end of HEALTHY FITNESS ZONE; number on right is upper end.

*Test scored pass or fail; must reach this distance to pass.

†Conversion chart for PACER on page 94 of *FITNESSGRAM/ACTIVITYGRAM Test Administration Manual, Fourth Edition*.

© 1992, 1999, 2004, The Cooper Institute, Dallas, Texas.

From Isobel Kleinman, 2009, *Complete Physical Education Plans for Grades 5 to 12, Second Edition* (Champaign, IL: Human Kinetics). Reprinted, by permission, from The Cooper Institute, 2006, *FITNESSGRAM/ACTIVITYGRAM test administration manual, 4th ed.* (Champaign, IL: Human Kinetics), 61.

Table C.2 Fitnessgram Standards for Healthy Fitness Zone

			GIRLS										
Age	$\dot{V}O_2$max (ml · kg^{-1} · min^{-1})	20-m PACER (Enter # laps in software)		15-m PACER (Enter in software)†		1-mi (1.5-km) run (min:sec)		Walk test ($\dot{V}O_2$max)		Percent fat		Body mass index	
5		Participation in run. Lap count standards not recommended.				Completion of distance. Time standards not recommended.				32	17	21	16.2
6										32	17	21	16.2
7										32	17	22	16.2
8										32	17	22	16.2
9										32	13	23	13.5
10	39	47	7	41	9	54	12:30	9:30			32	13	23.5	13.7
11	38	46	15	41	19	54	12:00	9:00			32	13	24	14.0
12	37	45	15	41	19	54	12:00	9:00			32	13	24.5	14.5
13	36	44	23	51	30	67	11:30	9:00	36	44	32	13	24.5	14.9
14	35	43	23	51	30	67	11:00	8:30	35	43	32	13	25	15.4
15	35	43	32	51	42	67	10:30	8:00	35	43	32	13	25	16.0
16	35	43	32	61	42	80	10:00	8:00	35	43	32	13	25	16.4
17	35	43	41	61	54	80	10:00	8:00	35	43	32	13	26	16.8
17+	35	43	41	72	54	94	10:00	8:00	35	43	32	13	27.3	17.2

Age	Curl-up (# completed)		Trunk lift (in.)		90° push-up (# completed)		Modified pull-up (# completed)		Flexed arm hang (s)		Back-saver sit and reach* (in.)	Shoulder stretch
5	2	10	6	12	3	8	2	7	2	8	9	Healthy fitness zone = touching fingertips together behind the back on both the right and left sides.
6	2	10	6	12	3	8	2	7	2	8	9	
7	4	14	6	12	4	10	3	9	3	8	9	
8	6	20	6	12	5	13	4	11	3	10	9	
9	9	22	6	12	6	15	4	11	4	10	9	
10	12	26	9	12	7	15	4	13	4	10	9	
11	15	29	9	12	7	15	4	13	6	12	10	
12	18	32	9	12	7	15	4	13	7	12	10	
13	18	32	9	12	7	15	4	13	8	12	10	
14	18	32	9	12	7	15	4	13	8	12	10	
15	18	35	9	12	7	15	4	13	8	12	12	
16	18	35	9	12	7	15	4	13	8	12	12	
17	18	35	9	12	7	15	4	13	8	12	12	
17+	18	35	9	12	7	15	4	13	8	12	12	

Number on left is lower end of HEALTHY FITNESS ZONE; number on right is upper end.

*Test scored pass or fail; must reach this distance to pass.

†Conversion chart for PACER on page 94 of *FITNESSGRAM/ACTIVITYGRAM Test Administration Manual, Fourth Edition*.

© 1992, 1999, 2004, The Cooper Institute, Dallas, Texas.

Table C.3 New York State Physical Fitness Norms
Seventh Grade Fitness Conversion Table

BOYS								
Fitness level	Percentile rank	Agility (side step)	Strength (sit-ups)	Speed (shuttle run)	Endurance (mile)		Achieve-ment total	Fitness level
					11 yrs	12 yrs		
10	99	25+	60+	18.5 or less	6.04	5.4	33+	10
9	98	22-24	55-59	19	6.5	6.27	30-32	9
8	93	21	50-54	19.5-20.0	7.19	6.44	28-29	8
7	84	19-20	44-49	20.5-21	7.3	6.57	25-27	7
6	69	17-18	40-43	21.5-22	8.21	7.48	22-24	6
5	50	16	34-39	22.5	9.06	8.2	20-21	5
4	31	14-15	30-33	23	10.4	9.3	16-19	4
3	16	12-13	25-29	24-25	12.4	11.2	13-15	3
2	7	9-11	20-24	25.5-26.5	13.37	12.07	11-12	2
1	2	7-8	14-19	27-28	15.25	13.41	8-10	1
0	1	0-6	0-13	28.5			0-7	0

GIRLS								
Fitness level	Percentile rank	Agility (side step)	Strength (sit-ups)	Speed (shuttle run)	Endurance (mile)		Achieve-ment total	Fitness level
					11 yrs	12 yrs		
10	99	23+	52+	16.5 or less	7.07	6.27	32+	10
9	98	21-22	46-51	17-18	7.46	7.26	30-31	9
8	93	19-20	41-45	18.5-20.5	8.1	7.44	27-29	8
7	84	18	36-40	21-22	8.36	8.05	25-26	7
6	69	16-17	32-35	22.5-23	9.44	9.08	22-24	6
5	50	15	28-31	23.5-24	10.27	9.47	19-21	5
4	31	13-14	23-37	24.5-25	11.51	11	16-18	4
3	16	11-12	18-22	25.5-26.5	13.16	12.35	13-15	3
2	7	9-10	15-17	27-29.5	14.41	13.34	10-12	2
1	2	7-8	11-14	30-31.5	16.56	14.46	8-9	1
0	1	0-6	0-10	32+			0-7	0

From Isobel Kleinman, 2009, *Complete Physical Education Plans for Grades 5 to 12, Second Edition* (Champaign, IL: Human Kinetics). Reprinted, by permission, from the New York State Education Department.

Table C.4 New York State Physical Fitness Norms

Eighth Grade Fitness Conversion Table

BOYS								
Fitness level	Percentile rank	Agility (side step)	Strength (sit-ups)	Speed (shuttle run)	Endurance (mile)		Achievement total	Fitness level
					13 yrs	14 yrs		
10	99	26+	61+	18.5 or less	5.44	5.36	32+	10
9	98	24-25	56-60	19	6.11	5.51	30-31	9
8	93	22-23	51-55	19.5	6.22	6.05	28-29	8
7	84	20-21	46-50	20	6.33	6.13	25-27	7
6	69	18-19	42-45	20.5-21	7.06	6.48	22-24	6
5	50	17	37-41	21.5-22	7.27	7.1	19-21	5
4	31	15-16	32-36	22.5-23	8.24	7.54	16-18	4
3	16	13-14	27-31	23.5-24	9.09	8.43	13-15	3
2	7	10-12	21-26	24.5-25.5	9.39	9.3	10-12	2
1	2	7-9	15-20	26-27.5	10.23	10.32	7-9	1
0	1	0-6	0-14	28 or more			0-6	0

GIRLS								
Fitness level	Percentile rank	Agility (side step)	Strength (sit-ups)	Speed (shuttle run)	Endurance (mile)		Achievement total	Fitness level
					13 yrs	14 yrs		
10	99	23+	56+	16 or less	6.2	6.44	32+	10
9	98	21-22	50-55	16.5-18	7.1	7.18	30-31	9
8	93	20	43-49	18.5-20.5	7.45	7.39	27-29	8
7	84	18-19	39-42	21-21.5	8.01	7.54	25-26	7
6	69	17	35-38	22-22.5	8.41	8.37	22-24	6
5	50	16	31-34	23-23.5	9.27	9.35	19-21	5
4	31	14-15	26-30	24-25	10.31	11.11	16-18	4
3	16	11-13	21-25	25.5-26.5	12.20	13.56	14-15	3
2	7	9-10	16-20	27-28	13.09	15.20	11-13	2
1	2	7-8	12-15	28.5-29.5	14.55	16.59	8-10	1
0	1	0-6	0-11	30 or longer			0-7	0

From Isobel Kleinman, 2009, *Complete Physical Education Plans for Grades 5 to 12, Second Edition* (Champaign, IL: Human Kinetics). Reprinted, by permission, from the New York State Education Department.

Table C.5 New York State Physical Fitness Norms

Ninth Grade Fitness Conversion Table

Fitness level	Percentile rank	Agility (side step)	Strength (sit-ups)	Speed (shuttle run)	Endurance (mile)		Achievement total	Fitness level
BOYS								
					14 yrs	15 yrs		
10	99	27+	62+	18.5	5.36	5.44	33+	10
9	98	26	58-61	19	5.51	6.01	31-32	9
8	93	22-25	53-57	19.5	6.05	6.08	28-30	8
7	84	21	48-52	20	6.13	6.18	25-27	7
6	69	19-20	44-47	20.5	6.48	6.56	22-24	6
5	50	18	40-43	21-21.5	7.1	7.14	19-21	5
4	31	16-17	35-39	22-23	7.54	7.52	16-18	4
3	16	14-15	31-34	23.5-24	8.43	8.48	13-15	3
2	7	10-13	24-30	24.5-25.5	9.3	9.25	11-12	2
1	2	8-9	20-23	26-27.5	10.32	10.37	8-10	1
0	1	0-7	0-19	28 or longer			0-7	0

Fitness level	Percentile rank	Agility (side step)	Strength (sit-ups)	Speed (shuttle run)	Endurance (mile)		Achievement total	Fitness level
GIRLS								
					14 yrs	15 yrs		
10	99	24+	54+	16 or shorter	6.44	6.36	32	10
9	98	23	48-53	16.5-18	7.18	7.39	30-31	9
8	93	21-22	43-47	18.5-20.5	7.39	8.01	28-29	8
7	84	19-20	39-42	21-21.5	7.54	8.1	25-27	7
6	69	18	34-38	22-22.5	8.37	9.1	22-24	6
5	50	16-17	29-33	23-23.5	9.35	10.05	19-21	5
4	31	14-15	24-28	24-25	11.11	12.05	16-18	4
3	16	12-13	20-23	25.5-26.5	13.56	14.07	13-15	3
2	7	10-11	14-19	27-28	15.20	15.25	10-12	2
1	2	8-9	10-13	28.5-29.5	16.59	16.22	8-9	1
0	1	0-7	0-9	30 or longer			0-7	0

Table C.6   New York State Physical Fitness Norms

Tenth Grade Fitness Conversion Table

					BOYS			
Fitness level	Percentile rank	Agility (side step)	Strength (sit-ups)	Speed (shuttle run)	Endurance (mile)		Achievement total	Fitness level
					15 yrs	16 yrs		
10	99	27+	63+	18.5 or less	5.44	5.4	33+	10
9	98	25-26	59-62	19	6.01	5.48	31-32	9
8	93	24	53-58	19.5	6.08	6.02	29-30	8
7	84	22-23	50-52	20	6.18	6.12	26-27	7
6	69	20-21	44-49	20.5	6.56	6.47	22-25	6
5	50	18-19	40-43	21	7.14	7.11	19-21	5
4	31	16-17	35-39	21.5-22	7.52	7.51	16-18	4
3	16	14-15	31-34	22.5-23.5	8.48	9.1	13-15	3
2	7	11-13	26-30	24-25.5	9.25	9.52	10-12	2
1	2	9-10	22-25	26-27	10.37	10.40	7-9	1
0	1	0-8	0-21	27.5			0-6	0

					GIRLS			
Fitness level	Percentile rank	Agility (side step)	Strength (sit-ups)	Speed (shuttle run)	Endurance (mile)		Achievement total	Fitness level
					15 yrs	16 yrs		
10	99	25+	53+	20.5 or less	6.36	6.33	34+	10
9	98	24	47-52	21	7.39	7.07	31-33	9
8	93	21-23	42-46	21.5	8.01	7.47	28-30	8
7	84	19-20	38-41	22	8.1	8.13	25-27	7
6	69	18	33-37	22.5-23.5	9.1	9.52	22-24	6
5	50	16-17	30-32	24-24.5	10.05	10.45	19-21	5
4	31	14-15	25-29	25-26	12.05	12.32	16-18	4
3	16	12-13	21-24	26.5-28	14.07	14.49	13-15	3
2	7	10-11	15-20	28.5-29.5	15.25	15.02	11-12	2
1	2	8-9	11-14	30-31.5	16.22	15.3	9-10	1
0	1	0-7	0-10	32			0-8	0

From Isobel Kleinman, 2009, *Complete Physical Education Plans for Grades 5 to 12, Second Edition* (Champaign, IL: Human Kinetics). Reprinted, by permission, from the New York State Education Department.

Table C.7 New York State Physical Fitness Norms

Eleventh Grade Fitness Conversion Table

				BOYS			
Fitness level	Percentile rank	Agility (side step)	Strength (sit-ups)	Speed (shuttle run)	Endurance (mile)	Achievement total	Fitness level
				16 yrs			
10	99	29+	66+	18 or less	5.4	33+	10
9	98	26-28	60-65	18.5	5.48	30-32	9
8	93	24-25	55-59	19	6.02	28-29	8
7	84	22-23	50-54	19.5	6.12	25-27	7
6	69	21	46-49	20	6.47	22-24	6
5	50	19-20	41-45	20.5-21	7.11	19-21	5
4	31	17-18	36-40	21.5-22	7.51	16-18	4
3	16	15-16	32-35	22.5-23	9.1	13-15	3
2	7	12-14	27-31	23.5-24.5	9.52	10-12	2
1	2	9-11	23-26	25-26.5	10.4	7-9	1
0	1	0-8	0-22	27+		0-6	0

				GIRLS			
Fitness level	Percentile rank	Agility (side step)	Strength (sit-ups)	Speed (shuttle run)	Endurance (mile)	Achievement total	Fitness level
				16 yrs			
10	99	25+	53+	19.5 or faster	6.33	34+	10
9	98	24	47-52	20-20.5	7.07	31-33	9
8	93	21-23	42-46	21-21.5	7.47	28-30	8
7	84	20	38-41	22	8.13	25-27	7
6	69	18-19	33-37	22.5-23	9.52	22-24	6
5	50	16-17	30-32	24-24.5	10.45	19-21	5
4	31	15	25-29	25-26	12.32	16-18	4
3	16	12-14	21-24	26.5-27.5	14.49	13-15	3
2	7	10-11	15-20	28-29.5	15.02	11-12	2
1	2	8-9	11-14	30-31	15.3	8-10	1
0	1	0-7	0-10	31.5+		0-7	0

From Isobel Kleinman, 2009, *Complete Physical Education Plans for Grades 5 to 12, Second Edition* (Champaign, IL: Human Kinetics). Reprinted, by permission, from the New York State Education Department.

Table C.8 New York State Physical Fitness Norms

Twelfth Grade Fitness Conversion Table

				BOYS			
Fitness level	Percentile rank	Agility (side step)	Strength (sit-ups)	Speed (shuttle run)	Endurance (mile)	Achievement total	Fitness level
				17 yrs			
10	99	29+	70+	17.5 or less	5.42	35+	10
9	98	27-28	63-69	18	5.48	31-34	9
8	93	25-26	57-62	18.5	6.02	28-30	8
7	84	23-24	51-56	19-19.5	6.12	25-27	7
6	69	21-22	47-50	20	6.47	22-24	6
5	50	20	42-46	20.5	7.11	19-21	5
4	31	18-19	38-41	21-21.5	7.51	16-18	4
3	16	15-17	33-37	22-22.5	9.1	13-15	3
2	7	13-14	29-32	23-24	9.52	10-12	2
1	2	10-12	23-28	24.5-25.5	10.4	7-9	1
0	1	0-9	0-22	26 or longer		0-6	0

				GIRLS			
Fitness level	Percentile rank	Agility (side step)	Strength (sit-ups)	Speed (shuttle run)	Endurance (mile)	Achievement total	Fitness level
				17 yrs			
10	99	26+	54+	19.0 or less	6.54	35+	10
9	98	24-25	49-53	19.5-20	7.26	32-34	9
8	93	22-23	44-48	20.5-21.5	8.08	28-31	8
7	84	20-21	39-43	22	8.28	25-27	7
6	69	18-19	34-38	22.5-23.5	9.41	22-24	6
5	50	16-17	30-33	24-24.5	9.47	19-21	5
4	31	15	25-29	25-26	10.5	16-18	4
3	16	13-14	21-24	26.5-27.5	12.5	13-15	3
2	7	10-12	16-20	28-29.5	13.05	10-12	2
1	2	8-9	12-15	30-31	15.24	8-9	1
0	1	0-7	0-11	31.5 or more		0-7	0

About the Author

Isobel Kleinman, MSE, taught physical education for 31 years at the junior and senior high levels in the New York metropolitan area and coached 10 sports in that period. Since then, she has supervised student teachers for St. Francis College in Brooklyn and presented at the AAHPERD National and Eastern District Conventions and at staff development programs in New York City and Naperville, Illinois.

In addition to authoring the first edition of this book, Ms. Kleinman is the author of the novel *Too Dangerous to Teach.* She also has written articles related to teaching and served as a contributing editor for www.pelinks4u .org.

In her leisure time, she enjoys the performing arts, traveling the world, playing tennis and golf, dancing, and biking.

How to Use the CD-ROM

System Requirements

You can use this CD-ROM on either a Windows®-based PC or a Macintosh computer.

Windows

- IBM PC compatible with Pentium® processor
- Windows® 98/2000/XP/Vista
- Adobe Reader® 8.0
- Microsoft® Office PowerPoint 2003 or higher
- 4x CD-ROM drive

Macintosh

- Power Mac® recommended
- System 10.4 or higher
- Adobe Reader®
- Microsoft® Office PowerPoint 2004 for Mac or higher
- 4x CD-ROM drive

User Instructions

Windows

1. Insert the *Complete Physical Education Plans for Grades 5 to 12, Second Edition* CD-ROM. (Note: The CD-ROM must be present in the drive at all times.)
2. Select the "My Computer" icon from the desktop.
3. Select the CD-ROM drive.
4. Open the file you wish to view. See the "00Start.pdf" file for a list of the contents.

Macintosh

1. Insert the *Complete Physical Education Plans for Grades 5 to 12, Second Edition* CD-ROM. (Note: The CD-ROM must be present in the drive at all times.)
2. Double-click the CD icon located on the desktop.
3. Open the file you wish to view. See the "00Start" file for a list of the contents.

For customer support, contact Technical Support:

Phone: 217-351-5076 Monday through Friday (excluding holidays) between 7:00 a.m. and 7:00 p.m. (CST).

Fax: 217-351-2674

E-mail: support@hkusa.com